Dialectic and Gospel
in the
Development
of
Hegel's Thinking

Stephen Crites

Dialectic and Gospel in the Development of Hegel's Thinking

The Pennsylvania State University Press
University Park, Pennsylvania

Library of Congress Cataloging-in-Publication Data

Crites, Stephen.
    Dialectic and gospel in the development of Hegel's thinking /
Stephen Crites.
        p.   cm.
    Includes bibliographical references and index.
    ISBN 0-271-01759-7 (alk. paper)
    1. Hegel, Georg Wilhelm Friedrich, 1770–1831—Religion.   2. Hegel,
Georg Wilhelm Friedrich, 1770–1831—Views on Christianity.
3. Hegel, Georg Wilhelm Friedrich, 1770–1831—Contributions in
dialectic.   4. theology, Doctrinal—Germany—History—19th century.
5. Philosophy and religion—History—19th century.   6. Dialectic
—History—19th century.   7. Hegel, Georg Wilhelm Friedrich,
1770–1831. Phänomenologie des Geistes. I. Title.
B2949.R3C73   1998
193—dc21   97-39499
                                                                              CIP

It is the policy of The Pennsylvania State University Press to use acid-free
paper for the first printing of all clothbound books. Publications on uncoated
stock satisfy the minimum requirements of American National Standard for
Information Sciences—Permanence of Paper for Printed Library Materials,
ANSI Z39.48-1992.

Dedicated to the Memory of Louis O. Mink
a True Philosopher and my Dearest Friend

Contents

Preface

When a reader is presented with a very long book by a thinker of genius its length requires no justification. I am sure it never occurred to Hegel to apologize for the great length of his *Phenomenology of Spirit* or *Science of Logic*. But if a book of inordinate length is written by an author who really has nothing to commend him but earnest toil, some justification is needed, and only one justification is possible: that he has been toiling earnestly on it for a very long time. So it is with this book. I hesitate to admit just how long I have been at it, but when I began my beard was red, and now, at the finish, it is entirely white.

I worked on this project for several extended periods, each time reading obsessively in Hegel and in the secondary literature, and writing at least a hundred pages. Then other projects beckoned or teaching duties intervened, and I didn't get back to it for many months and sometimes several years. Meanwhile I have had a life. But each time I took the project up again my mind had changed or further reading required revision of what I had written before, and I had a different conception of its design as a whole. I am sure I discarded at least twice as many pages as I kept. In recent years I have wondered whether I would outlive the project. It is not the way I would recommend writing a book, but I have not found it frustrating. I actually enjoyed it, for every time I returned to serious engagement with Hegel I greeted him as an old friend whom I knew would teach me things I could not learn elsewhere. I had discovered in him a thinker of rare originality and penetration, bearing no resemblance at all to popular caricatures. These intermittent studies in his thinking, conducted more for my own sake than for eventual publication, have nourished several other seemingly unrelated projects. So there has been a fruitful rhythm between this study and other work.

Early reading in Kierkegaard and Marx and the Young Hegelians had led me to intensive study of Hegel in the first place, just to understand how he could have had such influence and could have excited so much scorn. But nothing could have prepared me for what I found when I began studying his mature work in earnest. Early in my professional career I aspired to composing a work that would illuminate the major crisis in Christian belief that grew out of Hegel's thought among the Young Hegelians and Marx and Kierkegaard in the 1830s and 1840s, and later culminated in Nietzsche. I had already begun such a study in my doctoral dissertation, which gave central attention to Hegel's mature writings and lectures ("The Problem of the 'Positivity' of the Gospel in the Hegelian Dialectic of Alienation and Reconciliation," Yale, 1961). But alas for overweening ambitions! For I decided, fatefully, to begin the new project by tracing Hegel's own development through his earlier writings, focusing on his youthful critique and transformation of central Christian themes, and that turned out to be as far as I would get. Once again, as when I turned from the post-Hegelians to Hegel's later work, I found in his earlier work far more than I had expected: something both significantly different than the later work, and also a way into Hegel's thinking that forced me to read the later works in a different way.

An intriguing difference between the early works and the later is in the relation of the thinker to his writings. In the writings and lectures of his maturity Hegel was a philosopher lucidly presenting ideas he had already carefully considered and systematically ordered. The earlier works, including the *Phenomenology,* are far rougher and denser in style. Here we find a young man *thinking* on paper, with pen in hand. To trace the silent progress in the thinking of a highly original mind may not seem very exciting, but it is arguably one of the most dramatic of human phenomena. There are tremendous struggles, not to communicate what he thinks, but to *discover,* with the written word as the medium of his discoveries. The *Phenomenology,* rightly called Hegel's "voyage of discovery," still exhibits this immediacy of thought-in-progress, with many false starts and dead ends, entangled syntax, and passages of stupefying obscurity, complexity, and freshness. It is often noted that his writing style later improved somewhat, particularly after he had begun teaching young Gymnasium students in Nuremberg

(1808–16), who seem to have forced him to give more attention to the arts of communication. He never became a master of limpid prose, but this more lucid style is already evident in his *Science of Logic* (1812–16), which is mercifully more accessible than the *Phenomenology* and the writings that preceded it. But there was also some loss: somewhat less in evidence were the vitality and intensity of the young man thinking new thoughts in the very process of writing. This lively availability of the thinking of a philosopher-in-formation is what has attracted me to the earlier writings as my particular object of study. The task also engaged an odd and unenviable talent of mine: when I went fishing with friends as a boy, I was the one who could untangle hopelessly snarled fishing lines.

That commitment to the early writings had certain consequences in the way this study has been conducted. In the first place it called for a developmental format designed to discover and exhibit the way Hegel's thinking progressed from his early twenties through his mid-thirties; that is, during the 1790s and when with enormous energy he found his philosophical vocation from 1800 to 1807. Mostly I have focused on his texts relevant to my theme, published and unpublished, in the order in which they were written, giving them as close a reading as I could. For these texts actually exhibit the unfolding of his thinking. I have also written about his early life and times, and have framed each significant body of writing by biographical sketches, not because I have supposed that the course of his personal biography or his social background explains his thinking, but because it does after all provide its context. Knowing a little about the man and his situation spares us some of the false impressions of his thinking that have cluttered the literature. He was not, for instance, a desiccated thinking machine. His circumstances, his temperament, his circle of acquaintances, do situate, but do not provide the magic key to his thinking. We do not gain any advantage over him by knowing something about him, but we do gain some advantage over interpreters who know much less about him. I was fortunate to have conducted these studies when the order of Hegel's writings and their correlation with his biography had been clarified by German scholarship in the 1960s and early 1970s, after a great deal of confusion earlier.

So my study is developmental. Furthermore, since it addresses the progress of Hegel's thinking through the large body of his early writings, I have wanted to let Hegel speak as much as possible in his own voice, through copious translations of passages from these writings. This commitment entangled me in all the notorious difficulties of Hegel translation—especially acute in these earlier writings, which are particularly dense and entangled after 1800 when he turned decisively to philosophy. Resisting the temptation to make the style of these extracts smoother than they are in the original, I have been as literal as possible. But in every case I have tried to interpret the translated passage in terms less baffling than the passage itself, though without simplifying its meaning. That seems to me the obligation of a commentator, and it is heavy labor, since he has to stick with passages that sometimes seem almost incoherent until he himself has made sense of them.

There is a third commitment reflected in this study, one that sets it apart from many other treatments of Hegel's development. Since I have been concerned with the dynamics of Hegel's *thinking,* I have paid less attention to his changing opinions than to the deeper changes in the issues he addressed and in the way these issues came to be thematized. I think, in general, that the originality of major philosophers is exhibited primarily in the penetration of the questions they ask. The great thinkers of the past remain of unsurpassed importance to serious students of philosophy because they lead us into depths of inquiry that remain vital long after their particular doctrines seem antiquated and culture-bound. That is especially true in the early phases of their thinking, when it is still restless and fluid. The young Hegel is a case in point. The questions he asked, and the ways he framed the problems he addressed, were ground-breaking even when he himself was still dissatisfied with the conclusions on which he came to rest for a while. We shall therefore follow him into this matrix of questioning, interested in possible roads not taken for the ways they contextualize the paths he eventually did take and also for paths we might wish to take that he did not. Hence the orientation to Hegel's "thinking," rather than to any distillation of his "thought."

Of course Hegel's mature writings and lectures are of greater intrinsic importance than these early works. But I believe this reading of the earlier writings does illuminate the later in two complementary ways. Certainly I have had the later work in mind in what I have emphasized in the earlier writings. Whenever we have come upon a moment in Hegel's thinking that crystallizes a theme that continued to be significant in the later system, it has been given special attention. But the original process by which he formulated such a theme always illuminates its meaning in its later systematic context. Nor is that the case only with particular ideas in their fresh-minted appearance. The entire character of the mature philosophy of Hegel, with its admittedly superior systematic integration, is more compelling when it is read in light of its origins and development, less cut-and-dried, more vital and incisive and risk-taking, with the prodigious struggles of his youth still visibly informing it. That reading is not only more engaging, but truer to the spirit of the mature system itself, for really the struggles never ceased behind the systematic facade.

Perhaps no philosopher has ever been so ill-served by standard summary interpretations as Hegel has, because there is no simple upshot of his thinking. The familiar mechanical three-step, for instance (thesis-antithesis-synthesis, a formula he never used), is a dead caricature of everything Hegel ever meant by dialectic. Furthermore, the standard ideological readings, of either the left or the right, entirely conceal the philosopher who, as a thinker, is the enemy of all ideology. It is my fond hope that the present study will provide a modest antidote to the subphilosophical readings of this philosopher.

This, to be sure, is far from the first developmental reading of Hegel's thinking, and I am indebted to the others, from Wilhelm Dilthey (*Die Jugendgeschichte Hegels* [1905]) to Laurence Dickey (*Hegel: Religion, Economics, and the Politics of Spirit, 1770–1807* [1987]) and H. S. Harris. Harris, in particular, has most recently covered the same ground I have, even much more compendiously, in four magisterial volumes, *Hegel's Development: Towards the Sunlight (1770–1801)* (1972); *Hegel's Development: Night Thoughts (Jena, 1801–1806)*, (1983); and the two volumes of *Hegel's Ladder* (1997), on the *Phenomenology of Spirit*. Certainly Harris's portrait of the philosopher is not among the superficial caricatures! But the single-minded Harris has always finished his large volume on a particular phase of Hegel's career a little after I had finished my mere chapter on that phase. Still I read his hefty tomes on the early and the Jena writings after having written my chapters on those texts, and though I have been full of admiration for his thoroughness, his scholarly care and his ingenuity as a commentator, I have seldom agreed with him about the larger issues of Hegel interpretation, and never wanted to change a single sentence I had written as a result of reading him. I added a few notes detailing my disagreements with his earlier volumes. But now that I have finished this book, I have not yet had the opportunity to read his two-volume commentary on the *Phenomenology*. So in the lengthy concluding chapter of this study, also devoted to the *Phenomenology*, I have had simply to let the chips fall where they may, leaving it to others to ferret out whatever differences there may be between our two readings and to decide which of us may be nearer to the truth. Other important works relevant to my first three chapters have appeared since the mid-1980s, when these chapters were substantially finished. I have sometimes discussed them in the notes.

This study differs from that of Harris and other students of the earlier Hegel in its thematic focus on Hegel's engagement with the peculiar claims and narrative structure of the Christian gospel. With this focus I have entered a hornet's nest of controversy among right- and left-wing interpreters of Hegel, for here the ideological battle over the upshot of Hegel's thought has been particularly frenzied. Hegel, it is said, both by pious interpreters and by their most virulent opponents, was a theist, an apologist for traditional Christian beliefs, thinly disguised by his dialectical apparatus. That, according to James Stirling, in the first extensive study of Hegel's philosophy in English, *The Secret of Hegel* (1865), was the secret. The aim of Hegel's works was "to restore our faith, faith in God, faith in Christianity as the revealed religion" (1:78). Hegel's numerous atheistic debunkers have said the same, and have deplored it. On the other hand, a host of interpreters, beginning with Bruno Bauer's satirical exposé of the "real" Hegel (*Die Posaune des jüngsten Gerichts über Hegel den Atheisten und Antichristen* [1841]) have claimed that he was an atheist. Robert C. Solomon, in his lively but rather slapdash reading of the *Phenomenology* (*In the Spirit of Hegel* [1983]), declares that the *real* secret of Hegel "is that Hegel was essentially an atheist" (582), though for prudential reasons he never admitted it in so many words. From such an axiom one can prove anything, including the reductionistic conclusion of the left Hegelians of the 1830s and 1840s, to which Solomon subscribes, that "humanity is everything, in the guise of *Geist* or 'Spirit'" (1b:7). Others have opted for a pantheistic Hegel, or a panentheistic or a mystical Hegel. But none of the traditional options catch the subtlety and distinctiveness of Hegel's various ways of posing the question about God.

His treatments of that question, furthermore, are inseparable from his thinking about religious ideas and practices generally, and about the Christian gospel in particular. "The gospel," to be sure, can mean different things. Most narrowly it signifies the central message of traditional Christian preaching: that salvation is offered through the death of Jesus Christ. Four New Testament texts, however, are called gospels in a sense that seems to include the entire story of the savior's life, mission, passion, and resurrection. But traditionally this story, in turn, has entailed a sweeping narrative encompassing all time, begun, climaxed, and ending with divine works. It is a drama in several acts, the creation, the fall of the human race, God's covenant with Israel, the incarnation of the divine Word, the death and resurrection of the incarnate Lord, the dispensation of the Holy Spirit, the mission of the church, and the last judgment. When we speak here of the gospel we refer to this entire narrative pattern that constitutes the Christian mythos.

Now Hegel's thinking, early and late, critically engaged the claims of this mythos and the social practices associated with it. He questioned these claims (indeed, he rejected their literal sense), and yet he kept coming back to them, interpreting and even appropriating them at different points in his career, sometimes by brief allusion, sometimes by sustained reflection. Not only did these claims preoccupy him, but their narrative configuration formed a kind of template in his thinking that affected the way he framed other topics in the ever-widening range of his philosophical inquiry. This particular channel in the development of Hegel's thinking is the subject of the present study, in counterpoint with his emerging dialectical method which, with its roots in classical philosophy, became in his work a highly original means of rationally comprehending the material realization of spirit in nature and history, particularly in dramatic historical change. This counterpoint of dialectic and gospel produces some dissonance, as we will see. But my thematic focus does not imply that Hegel's preoccupation with the gospel is "the secret" at the core of his philosophy. Many other channels flowed into the turbulent fluidity of his thinking, and the passion for system was inspired by the need to exhibit the precise relation among the many subjects that gave him no rest. The gospel was one of them, and it led him on some paths few philosophers have trod; with respect to its claims, however, Hegel was, first and last, neither an apologist nor a debunker, but the golden mean between those two leaden gestures: a critical thinker. Better still, he was a philosopher of great range and penetration, whose thinking cannot be cut to the Procrustean bed of any conventional labels. He was not even a "Hegelian."

What he *did* think, I have attempted to expound in this study. It has no grand thesis. But the thinking of a philosopher, like God, is in the details. Here are the details.

I

Prelude: The Intellectual and Religious Climate of Hegel's Youth

Twentieth-century Hegel scholarship has devoted an extraordinary amount of attention to the philosopher's earlier years. This attention to the young Hegel has permitted us to read the works of his middle and later years quite differently than they were read during the nineteenth century and, particularly in English-speaking countries, for some decades thereafter. We have a keener sense of the trajectory of his thinking. That is one of the factors that separates modern Hegel studies from those of earlier generations. It is hardly too much to say that we hear a new voice when we turn, say, to the *Philosophy of Right* or the Berlin lectures, because we are attentive to accents we have heard in the youthful productions that seem otherwise so far removed.

The increased interest in the young Hegel received its impetus from Dilthey's monograph of 1905[1] and from the publication in 1907 of Hegel's early writings, previously unpublished, edited by Dilthey's associate, Herman Nohl.[2] Virtually all available materials of importance for the study of Hegel's early development have by now been published in German, and a fair sampling has been translated into English: besides the Kroner-Knox translation of the most important texts from the Nohl volume, we have Walter Kaufmann's translation of letters and documents in his intellectual biography of the philosopher[3] and the translation of several important fragments by H. S. Harris as an appendix to his meticulous study tracing Hegel's development through 1801.[4] There are in fact monographic studies in several languages devoted exclusively to the early Hegel, of which Harris's work is an outstanding example.

The early Hegel has indeed proved so absorbing that he seems to arouse more enthusiasm in some quarters than the later Hegel. Certainly he is less formidable and forbidding. Certainly, too, there is an intrinsic interest in the life and development of a young thinker who reflected so many of the cultural currents of a fascinating age, and at the same time began to show original powers of his own in the way he reflected them. It was an age of transition, and in following Hegel's development we see profound aspects of that transition taking place before our eyes: the transition from the Enlightenment to idealism, Romanticism, and the new historical understanding of human activity; from supernaturalistic orthodoxy to liberalism in Protestant theology; from quiescence under absolute monarchy to powerful stirrings toward republican forms of government; from an aristocratic to a bourgeois organization of society and its economy.[5]

Still, there would be no point in singling out this particular young man for our attention were it not for the fact that he was later to become the author of the *Phenomenology* and the *Logic* and the lecturer of unparalleled influence at the University of Berlin. The early life is important above all because it sheds light on the philosopher gestating in it, the early writings because in them one finds him gathering his thoughts, meeting some of his long-range problems, working his way slowly and patiently through to a new philosophical comprehension of things. There are many strokes in his early writings that clearly bear the marks of his peculiar genius, together with a youthful stylistic élan that often lights up the page. But he did not regard them as publishable at the time, and later could not have regarded them as belonging to the real body of his work. Hegel used to remark ironically that Schelling had carried on his education in public (Rosenkranz, *Leben,* 45), and he prided himself in his own reserve in the matter. No doubt he was hoping to write something publishable in these early efforts, but he showed good judgment, a self-critical discretion rare in young writers, in concluding that none of them finally met the standard he wanted to set for himself.

I am concerned in this study with shedding light on the interpretation of Christianity in the works of the mature Hegel. But Hegel himself has taught us the importance of early stages in comprehending the outcome of a process. He has also taught us that the significance of the initial stages is revealed only in the outcome. I propose to apply this dual canon in treating his own life and work. I shall not be offering anything like an adequate biography, nor do I intend to offer a total interpretation of the early writings as such. In these introductory chapters I shall try to indicate, through biographical references, the character of his early exposure to Christianity, to trace the course of his own reaction to this exposure, and to discuss his early treatments of those themes that were to be of importance in his mature consideration of the subject at hand. Since our subject is the interpretation of Christianity, that task is quite enough to require two lengthy chapters. For nothing bulks so large in his first decade of adult life as his attempt to come to terms with Christianity, as a religious teaching and a historical phenomenon.

1. The Model Pupil of Stuttgart

It is difficult to imagine Hegel as a child. The difficulty is not primarily that the documents extant are so scanty. Even if his childhood were much more fully documented it would be difficult to picture the child. When he was not yet twenty years old his friends in the university dubbed him "the old man." "He was one of those people," says Dilthey, commenting on this nickname, "who were never young and yet in whom even in old age a hidden fire still glows."[6] Rosenkranz, his first and best biographer, who had known him personally, characterizes Hegel as an "autumn nature."[7] As a boy he was precocious, but no prodigy. There was no brilliant flowering in his youth, as in the case of Hölderlin and Schelling, his university comrades. He quietly put down roots, was nourished, grew steadily but unnoticed, and meanwhile patiently bided his time until he was fully ripe. When his time came one could only compare him with a few other great figures in the whole history of

Western philosophy. He saw himself, indeed, as the philosopher of autumn in a special sense, not essentially an originator but a consummator, a philosopher in whose thought a historic course begun in ancient Athens and Jerusalem received its intellectual summation and fulfillment. Our metaphor can happily accommodate the fact that he became at the same time a seminal influence in the modern world. He was at once the last of the classical philosophers and the first of the moderns. But of such destiny one could have detected scarcely a trace in the first thirty years of his life. His early years were a prolonged period of gestation.

Hegel was born in 1770, in the Swabian city of Stuttgart, the eldest of three children born to Georg Ludwig Hegel, a public official, and his wife Maria Magdalena, a cultivated lady for her time who died when Hegel was eleven years old. Hegel seems to have been especially close to her, as he was not to his father; children in proper bourgeois households were not normally close to their fathers. He marked the date of his mother's death for the rest of his life. Aside from this terrible shock and bouts of severe illness Hegel's childhood was stable and secure. His parents detected his facility for learning at an early age and bent every effort to provide him with an excellent education. He was sent to the German school at the age of three, then to the Latin school in his fifth year, having already been taught his first declensions by his mother. Hegel is sometimes described by his German biographers as a "model pupil *(Musterschüler),*" though it is not clear that the expression bears the same ambivalence to them as to us. He won prizes every year, and was first in his class in the Gymnasium from his tenth to his eighteenth year.[8] In two respects he did not excel: He seems to have been heavy of foot and of tongue. Rosenkranz, who tries to make the boy appear as well-rounded as possible, manages to discover a fondness for jumping in his background, but has to admit that the dancing master found him clumsy and that his later ventures into riding and fencing at the university were not a success.[9] As an elocutionist he was the despair of his teachers in Stuttgart as he was to be of his students in Berlin to the end of his days. But he was a favorite of his teachers. He not only learned quickly and willingly, but was the sort of child who is candid and at ease in adult company. He took walks with favorite teachers and enjoyed private conversations with them on scholarly matters. His most beloved teacher, Löffler, gave him a twelve-volume set of Shakespeare, in German translation, when he was eight years old, with the comment, "You will not understand it right now, but you will soon learn to understand it."[10] A few years later the boy inscribed in his journal a lament on the death of his teacher, which reveals as much about the fifteen-year-old boy as about the teacher. It is dated July 1785:

> Herr Preceptor Löffler was one of my most venerable teachers. . . . He was the most upright and impartial man. His chief concern was to be useful to his pupils and to the world. He did not think so basely as others, who suppose that now they have their bread and dare not study further, since they can only carry on with their eternal class routine, repeated every year. No! the blessed man did not think this way. He knew the worth of the sciences and the consolation they provide in the varied turns of fortune. How often and how contently and cheerfully he sat with me in that dear little room, and I with him. —Few knew his worth. It was a great misfortune for the man that he had to work so far below his sphere. And now he has passed away! But I will bear his memory eternally, immovably in my heart.[11]

Hegel grew up with the Greek and Roman classics, and also with the Bible. He was also intensely interested in mathematics and the sciences, and continued studying them on his own into his maturity, but classical literature was the heart of his education, and he took to it personally with so much zeal that it became the foundation of his intellectual life. Many comments in his private journal and school essays express a heartfelt enthusiasm for the Greek and Latin poets. But his devotion to them is also given expression in a way that was especially characteristic of Hegel. He began already as a young schoolboy a procedure that he pursued throughout his life, and that reveals a great deal about his temperament and method: He made extended verbatim excerpts from his readings, in German or in Latin, sometimes translating them.[12] These excerpts were generally made, in his earlier years, entirely without comment. Such comments as there are are merely pedantic notations that reveal no counterposition taken by the schoolboy, indeed no point of view at all. If there was in him any boyish pugnacity, leaping to break an impetuous lance with the masters, or even an exuberant imagination driven to reconstruction and further development of what he had read, there is no trace in his notebooks. They reveal so little of the personality of the boy that the reticence, the almost ascetic pedantry, is itself revealing. It is as though he were concerned simply with dissolving his mind and imagination in the texts, to appropriate them whole. On the basis of Hegel's journals and notebooks, Haym says flatly: "The life of the boy consisted in the fact that he learned; his sole interest consisted in repeating, calling to mind, impressing upon himself what he had experienced and learned."[13] There is nothing in the record to contradict this judgment, but the record, after all, is one-sided. Schoolboys do not commonly reveal all their interests in their notebooks!

At any rate, we find Hegel excerpting during his Gymnasium years not only from the classics but from leading authors of the German Enlightenment, mostly literary but also scientific. For while Hegel's education was dominated by the study of the classics, its principles and methods were those of the Enlightenment. His journals reflect his sense of belonging to an age of reason that was being purged of the errors and superstitions of the past. On the other hand the past was treated as essentially like the present, in the sense that all ages reflect a simple conflict between reason and the ignorance, emotionalism, superstition of unreason. One therefore could judge the past in terms of the enlightened moral and intellectual standards of the present, and on the other hand could assume that one's own standards were essentially present in reason's ancient standard-bearers. Hegel himself, at age fifteen, relates an egregious example of this procedure in his journal: One of his teachers had attempted to explain away the detail in the *Phaedo*'s account of the death of Socrates in which Socrates requests that a cock be sacrificed to Asclepius. The teacher explained that this classical hero of the Enlightenment must have already had his mind beclouded by the poison when he made this request. Hegel was not satisfied. As he reconstructed the scene in his journal, Socrates had thought, "because it is the custom, I do not wish entirely to offend the rabble through neglect of this slight gift."[14] The journals also reflect Hegel's sense that the age-old tension between reason and unreason was still very much alive in his own enlightened age. As we shall see, he still found all too many unenlightened elements in the religion of the masses. The journals also contain unexceptionably "enlightened" reflections on morals, and upon the woeful failure of drunken peasants and the like to reflect their elevated age. This moral fastidiousness was particularly offended by the lively survival of folk superstition. Horror, indignation, and mirth intermingle in his account of the revival of the old Stuttgarter superstition of the Valiant Horde *(mutige Heer)*. Like an eighteenth-century U.F.O., the Horde was slighted in various forms by perfectly respectable people, as a fiery wagon or wagons filled with people, or in some variations containing the devil himself, with an angel flying in front and crying, "Out of the way! the Valiant Horde is coming!" Furthermore, Hegel reports,

> Whoever would not heed this warning would be dragged by the Herr Devil to his residence.
> . . . I have been given the names of various characters who have seen or heard it (for it makes a hideous clatter). A few days ago it became clear that it (O disgrace! disgrace!) was [really made by] coaches. For Herr von Türkheim gave a concert that was very well attended; it lasted until two; now in order not to let the guests grope home in the dark he had them all be taken home with coaches and torches. And that was the Valiant Horde. Ha! Ha! Ha! O tempora! o mores! Occurred Anno 1785. O! O![15]

Hegel's family and milieu were Protestant-Pietist in religion, but tempered by the Enlightenment. His family was of old Lutheran stock, having settled in Swabia in the sixteenth century in order to live in a Protestant land. His ancestors included a number of pastors, as well as craftsmen, scholars, and public officials. Swabia, which proudly points to an extraordinary number of her sons among Germany's greatest artists and thinkers,[16] has, so we are assured on all sides, its own peculiar character and spirituality, though it is very difficult for an *Ausländer* to grasp this peculiarity very precisely. There is a strong mystical hue to its characteristic spirituality, dating back at least to the Middle Ages and given expression in Eckhart and Tauler. Hegel still liked to quote Eckhart even during his later years. He seems to have been true to his Swabian background in the peculiar and, so to speak, Gothic combination of introversion and self-abnegation with a heaven-storming eros for the sublime and the universal. But let us permit Haym to tell us something about this Swabian *Gemüt*:

> For not only does the wine which grows by the Neckar have a different taste and play different pranks than Rhine wine: the people from that region are also of a different breed and a different disposition, and even in the element of the universal, in the "aether of thought and of philosophy," Hegel's Swabian temperament was never fully evaporated.

Who has never encountered the general difference of the North German from the South German character? It is easier to become aware of it and to sense it than to designate it in words. We are speaking of the harmlessness, the good nature, the naive and easy character of the South German, and claim for ourselves [Northerners] lucidity, awareness, and the discipline of reflection. There appears to us to be more nature and sensuousness there, here more culture and deliberation, there an abandonment to feeling and fantasy, here a self-control in will and thought. In order to get to the truth one must bring together the expressions of this contrast and modulate them in many different ways. The Swabian character would still at least fit into the schema of this characterization. Yet the naturally determined differences are criss-crossed and modified through historical influences! It was the Reformation in particular which partially reinforced this contrast, partially entangled and obscured it. Luther brought to the nation a Lower-Saxon peasant's nature with a new spiritual principle, before which the Catholicism and the poetry of the Middle Ages, the life element of the South, broke asunder. But Protestantism also was no more a religion of the understanding, of criticism and of reflection than the religion of inwardness and depth of emotion. The North attached itself predominantly to the side of the understanding. The new Brandenburgian-Prussian state in the north-east corner of Germany founded itself on Protestantism, on the understanding, and on a serious, ethically disciplined vigor. But Württemberg also cast its lot with Protestantism and clung to it tenaciously. So Württemberg came more nearly to approximate the cultural motifs of the North, and in this way showed that it had had from the beginning an inner affinity to the character of the North. It was and it meant to be a mediating link between the two sections of Germany. Its inhabitants are altogether constituted by the poetic propensity of the South: yet this propensity is altogether encased in a prosaic shell. The basis of the Swabian temperament is a shy and reserved naïveté, which, however, conceals in its depths, stirring in its quietude, an active drive toward brooding and reflection. There is little of the luxuriant and lax capacity for enjoyment, of the worldly, careless and unconcerned gaiety, of the utopian and carefree life of, say, the people of Vienna. And again there is nothing of that urgent and quick, of that prying and super-clever calculation, of that biting, heartless wit, that frivolous parading with insight and craftiness, that propensity for sport and irony, all of which characterize the esprit of the Prussian capital. Here the critical drive is much more under the reign of the most sensitive inwardness, the sensuousness again under the discipline of the most reflective seriousness. Hence—to say with Vischer, whom I have been following all the while in this description of his countrymen—hence that peculiar "wooden-headedness" and the "simple-mindedness," the practical clumsiness and doltishness of the Swabians, in short the world-reknowned "Swabianfoolery [*Schwabenstreiche*]." Hence, in the same way, that completely different species of wit than the caustic sort that flourishes among us in the North—that amiable humor which prevails there in place of irony and sarcasm. Hence finally the heavy tongue of the Württemberger, this depth and judiciousness of speech along with poverty and embarrassment in speaking, this ponderous and laborious breaking forth of the word, but at the same time this often amazing facility for the choice image, this curious mixture of abstract helplessness and then again of sensuous and striking vividness, which above all lends such a peculiar coloration to the Hegelian style.[17]

It is difficult for an *Ausländer* to know how much weight to give such testimony. It is not only impressionistic but suspiciously Hegelian in its characterization of Hegel's own background as a kind of higher synthesis of the North and South German. The neat self-reflexiveness, accounting for Hegel in a Hegelian way, is of course one of the things that makes the account attractive. What gives it a coloring of plausibility as well, at least as much plausibility as such a nebulous matter permits, is the fact that it does evoke a type of character that corresponds roughly to what the internal evidence of Hegel's own work reveals about the temperament of the philosopher. Certainly Hegel was always very self-consciously Swabian, and liked during the height of his fame in Berlin to refer to his Swabian roots. He may also have been a little self-conscious about it in the more awkward sense of the term, even as a child. Rosenkranz tells us that when the boy employed the Swabian dialect in writing he regularly added, "as we Swabians are wont to say."[18]

The Enlightenment, in the form in which the young Hegel encountered it, tended to support rather than basically to undercut this

Swabian-Protestant piety. The Enlightenment in Germany, while critical of rigid and dogmatic religious sectarianism and scornful of anything
smacking of superstition, did not have the same anti-religious flavor
as in England and France. The models Hegel had before him as a
schoolboy were writers like Lessing and Garve and Wieland and Klopstock rather than Diderot or Holbach or Voltaire or Hume. The German
Enlightenment was a humanistic revival, which exhibited a reverence
for the classics, a degree of religious tolerance, a keen interest in science,
a sturdy moralism, and a passion for the universal that easily became
tinged with pantheism, but turned aside from materialism or atheism.
Certainly this German Enlightenment was reformist in religion, but
as such was able to regard itself as a genuine continuation of the
Reformation itself. In politics it was still less radical. Friedrich the
Great of Prussia, after all, was a well-known patron of the Enlightenment, which he was able comfortably to yoke with the absolute state.
The Swabian despot, Duke Carl Eugen, against whose tyranny Hegel
and his university friends were later to inveigh so vehemently,[19] was
also able to consider himself not only an "enlightened" monarch but a
purveyor of the spirit of the Enlightenment in his duchy.[20] So the currents of the Enlightenment did not disturb either the aristocratic politics or the Protestant piety that reigned in the house of Hegel's father,
reflecting there the union of Church and State existing unshakably in
the duchy at large. Evidently it had always been a foregone conclusion
in that house that Hegel would become a student of theology. But it is
most unlikely that it could ever have occurred to him in those days
that there should be any serious conflict between Christianity and the
classical learning in which he had been schooled, or between Christianity and leading cultural currents of his own age. Theological critics of
his later philosophy have always complained about the accommodation
of Christianity to modern culture that seems to have been embodied
in it. Such a complaint would have puzzled Hegel. He had only given
philosophical form to the cultural accommodation of Christianity which
he had experienced from his earliest days. But Protestant Swabia could
consider itself still close to the wellsprings of Lutheranism without
supposing that any drastic cultural renunciations were involved. What
Rosenkranz says of young Hegel's attitude toward Greek culture applies
equally to his attitude toward the German Enlightenment: "Permeated
at an early age by the nobility and the beauty of Hellenism, Hegel was
never able to recognize true Christianity in a form which excluded from
itself the seriousness of antique serenity."[21]

Lessing's *Nathan the Wise* was surely Hegel's favorite modern work. We find him quoting from it with special fondness already as schoolboy, and for several years thereafter. His attraction to this play tells us something about his early religious attitudes, for the play is a primary document of the German Enlightenment on the subject of religious truth. The central character, Nathan, a wealthy Jew living in Jerusalem during the third Crusade, is a mine of eighteenth-century religious wisdom. Despite this anachronism and also the heavy didacticism of the play, the wise Nathan is an appealing theatrical creation. Jerusalem, at the time in which the play is set, is a meeting-place of Moslem, Christian, and Jew, and this setting provides the occasion for some warm lessons in religious tolerance. Without attempting to summarize the play, it may be worthwhile to call attention to a few scenes which convey the spirit that Hegel seems in particular to have appreciated in it.

Nathan's daughter, Recha, has been rescued from fire by a young man who left the scene immediately thereafter. She and her enthusiastically Christian maid jump to the conclusion that her rescuer must have been an angel. Nathan is displeased by this interpretation. It is a piece of impious pride, he thinks, for Recha to suppose that the supernatural would intervene directly on her behalf. Certainly it is a miracle; the daughter herself in her individuality is indeed already a miracle, and that someone should have risked his life for her is miraculous enough, for which God as well as the rescuer should be thanked, but not a miracle in the sense of a direct divine intervention.[22] The rescuer turns out to have been a young Knight Templar, who at first receives Nathan's expressions of gratitude ungraciously. He wants no thanks from a Jew. He had only done his duty, as specified by his order.

TEMPLAR: You know how Templars are supposed to think.
NATHAN: Only Templars? merely *supposed* to? and merely
         Since the Order's rules so specify?
         I know how men think, and know
         That such good men are born in every land.

But surely it makes some difference what people we belong to?

NATHAN: Are
         We our people? What does "people" mean, then?
         Are Christian and Jew rather Christian and Jew
         Than men?
                                                    (2.5)

As it turns out, Recha is not Nathan's daughter. His own family had been murdered in a Christian pogrom. But after three days of prayer in dust and ashes, he had been reconciled to his fate, had even turned aside his hatred of the Christians. So when a Christian infant, Recha, had been secretly brought him shortly afterward he took her in his arms and raised her as his own child. He tells this story to a lay brother, who is moved to exclaim:

> Nathan! Nathan!
> You are a Christian!—By God, you are a Christian!
> A better Christian never was!

Nathan replies:

> Happy for us! For what
> Makes me a Christian in your eyes makes you in mine
> A Jew![23]

There is a basic piety and a warmth and uprightness of character that lies at the heart of all three religions. A good deal of what is peculiar to each is custom on the one hand and fanatical excess on the other. More essentially, the three are differentiated by their history. Nathan is a faithful Jew because he has been nourished in that faith by the tradition and example of his fathers (3.5). This theme of differentiation within basic unity of purpose is beautifully expressed in Nathan's parable of the three rings, surely a high point in the play.

The parable is introduced, however, by a comment that has an independent interest and to which Hegel often alluded. It is a hint about the nature of truth, or at any rate about what truth is not. Nathan has been summoned by Saladin, he supposes for the purpose of demanding money. This does not disturb him. His money bag seems to be open to anyone who wishes to dip into it. But no. The Sultan has been troubled by the diversity of religions, and having heard that Nathan is wise asks him where the truth really lies. He leaves him for a few moments to ruminate. Hegel took particular notice of this comment in his rumination:

> I am
> Prepared with money; and he wants—truth. Truth!
> And wants it such—so bare, so stark—as if
> The truth itself were coins.[24]

Pedantic as his methods were, Hegel understood at an early age that the truth was not something that one could simply hand over, like money over the counter. In this connection let us quote another passage from the play which young Hegel often cited: Recha is explaining to Saladin's sister why she has never learned to read books.

RECHA: My father cares
          For cold book-learning, that only
          Presses itself with dead signs into the brain,
          Too little.
SITTAH: Ei, what are you saying!—Still,
          He's not so very far from being right!—And all the wisdom
          That you show . . . ?
RECHA: I have received from his mouth alone.
          And for most of it I could still tell you
          How? where? why? he taught me it.

                                                        (5.6)

Book-learning seems to have constituted so much of Hegel's early life that it is worth mentioning that he particularly liked to quote from this passage in connection with his beloved classic poets. He praises the "simplicity" of the ancients: Unlike most modern poets, who are preoccupied with form rather than content, the ancients were so constituted by training and culture

          that each had wrought his ideas out of experience itself, and
          knew nothing of
                   cold book-learning, that only
                   presses itself with dead signs into the brain
          but in all that they knew could still say:
                   How? Where? Why? they learned it.[25]

Even as a schoolboy, Hegel was already anxious to get more from books than book-learning. He wanted wisdom, with some concrete relationship to experience.

   Now Nathan's parable of the rings. Refusing to treat the truth like cash on the barrelhead, Nathan spins a lovely tale for Saladin. A ring of great value had been in the possession of a family for many generations, the father always passing it on to his most beloved son. At last a father had three sons, all equally worthy and equally beloved. So the father had a skilled craftsman make two copies of the ring that were indistinguishable from the original. Upon his deathbed he gave each of the sons a ring. Now the bearer of the ring was also to be sole heir. In the confusion that followed the three sons betook themselves to a judge. The judge could not distinguish the true ring, and it was clear to him that the father had loved each son equally. So the judge perpetrated a pious fraud. He has heard, he said, that

> the true ring
> Possesses the miraculous power to make its owner beloved;
> Pleasing before God and man. That must
> Decide.
>
> (3.7)

Only the character of the three sons and of their descendants can determine which is the true ring, and which should receive the father's inheritance. It is hardly necessary for Nathan to add that the three rings are Judaism, Christianity, and Islam. The ingenuity of the parable is that it affirms the essential unity of religion, a single ultimate purpose that is to make men human; yet the importance of the historical differentiation receives its due.[26] The unity is further underlined in the conclusion, where the old theatrical device of newly discovered parents and siblings is employed to demonstrate the common humanity of the three religions. Indeed, the didactic point prevails to the ruin of the sole romantic interest in the drama: Recha and the Templar, who are by now madly in love and anxious to marry, turn out to be brother and sister! Their father turns out to be Saladin's brother. The curtain falls with ecumenical embraces all around.

There is extant a school essay by Hegel, dating from 1787, that already reflects a good deal of the spirit of the wise Nathan. Entitled "On the Religion of the Greeks and Romans," its observations are expressly applied both to biblical and to modern religion as well. "The conception of a divinity," says young Hegel, "is so natural to man that it has developed among all peoples."[27] Already he sees a simple sort of development taking place on the basis of this fundamental conception. In the childhood of a people they conceive the deity as a Lord over life and death whose good will is necessary to any undertaking, and who must therefore be expiated by gifts and his commands blindly obeyed. Furthermore, he adds, "the notions of the greater part of the people of our so highly praised enlightened times are constituted no differently."

They may not offer sacrifices in the primitive manner, for example, but they still do not realize that the "highest Being" cannot be won over through gifts and offerings (44).

In fact the schoolboy is not altogether contemptuous or unsympathetic toward the more primitive forms of religion. He offers rather sophisticated interpretations of some of these forms. Burnt offerings are a common phenomenon among most diverse peoples, because of the fact that the smoke ascends beyond sight to the heavens where the immortals dwell. Again, there were so many gods in the Greek and Roman pantheon because "these nations were a mixture of such diverse peoples." Temples were built on the mountains, near the heavens and with a sublime view over "a great piece of the beautiful creation" (44–45). Such elemental religious conceptions, furthermore, were susceptible to profounder interpretations supplied by poets and priests as a people became more sophisticated, giving imagination freer range and the beliefs a more genuinely holy meaning. Most people, to be sure, stuck to their anthropomorphic beliefs because "the grounds of reason and a purer religion are in their eyes not efficacious enough," but still "many enlightened and sublime concepts of the divine" developed among the wise (46–47). The result is a complex mixture of truth and error, even in the great civilizations of antiquity: "This ought to make us give some attention to our own inherited and transmitted opinions, especially to examine those concerning which neither doubt nor conjecture have ever come into our minds, to see whether they could perhaps be quite false or only half true." Such considerations, he concludes, should also help us to see that there may be some truth in the notions of other peoples that are so foreign to us, "so that we will not hate them, nor judge them unkindly. We know how easy it is to fall into errors, and therefore will not so often attribute evil and ignorance to them, and so will always show more justice and good will toward others" (47–48).

Such sentiments are certainly safely within the canons of the Enlightenment. Yet in hindsight one can recognize in them the first traces of a kind of sympathetic historical imagination that made his later achievements possible. The intensive classical studies of the schoolboy, for all their pedantry, were serving him well.

2. Hegel As a Theological Student in Tübingen

> I, Georg Wilhelm Friedrich Hegel, legitimate son of Georg Lud-
> wig Hegel, Secretary of the Chamber of Revenue, and Maria
> Magdalena née Fromm, do acknowledge and make known
> through the efficacy of this letter, to his most Serene
> Highness Duke and Lord, Herr CARL, Duke of Würtemberg and
> Teck, Count of Mömpelgard, Lord of Heydenheim etc., Knight of
> the Golden Fleece; and the Praiseworthy General-Field-Mar-
> shal-Lieutenant of the District of Swabia, my most humble plea
> and proposal that I might be most graciously accepted for Your
> Ducal Serene Highness' Theological Scholarship to Tübingen,
> that I might bring to fruitful completion the studies which I have
> begun (to direct myself exclusively, with the dispensation of
> divine grace, to theology alone, in order in time to be employed
> as a servant in the Churches of God or in the schools, according
> to His divine Will, and also in accordance with the calling decreed
> by Your Ducal Serene Highness).[28]

So begins a long letter, dated October 21, 1788, requesting a scholarship
for Hegel to study theology in Tübingen. The letter resounds to the
end with the sonorities of official address and solemn pledges, written
according to a stipulated form but also no doubt owing some debts in
point of style to his father's experience as a public official. This letter
to the despotic Duke Carl is of some independent interest for what it
conveys about the character of the united church-state establishment.
At any rate the eighteen-year-old applicant goes on to promise compliance with the conditions of the scholarship and obedience to the administration and faculty of the institution, naturally along with fealty to
his Serene Highness. He promises "to study with all seriousness and
diligence, but in particular to apply myself to no other profession than
theology," and agrees to stringent penalties, involving financial forfeiture, "in case I should defect or be found apostate in the continuation
of my study, in service of Church or school, from the true Augsburg
Confession and religion according to the Formulae of Concord (which
may indeed the most high GOD graciously will to prevent), or otherwise
be seized by flagrant excess, misbehavior, and disobedience."[29] Hegel's
father also pledges himself to take whatever measures necessary to

ensure his son's seriousness and industry. The letter is signed by both father and son.

Hegel received the scholarship and entered the university at Tübingen the following month. The university was small in those days, numbering two or three hundred students, most of whom were studying to be pastors or Gymnasium teachers. Students studying medicine or law went instead to the Karlsschule in Stuttgart. The university in Tübingen was in fact commonly called the Tübinger Stift (seminary), and a student there was called a Stiftler. The Stift had been an Augustinian cloister until it was converted in the sixteenth century; indeed a good deal of the cloistered atmosphere was preserved there, students in black robes faced in white, strict daily schedule, premises austere enough for the most ascetic taste. An inspector in 1788 compared the student bedrooms to "miserable prison cells." Students suffered especially in the winter when they had to be crammed together because of scarcity of heat; those by the stove roasted while the others froze, and none had privacy. Another inspection in 1789 resulted in the report that the rooms were woefully unprotected against wind, rain, and snow.[30] New construction during Hegel's time made life a bit more comfortable, but only to place students more closely under the supervision of the repetents (graduate assistants or preceptors) whose rooms were judiciously spaced among those of the students. The setting and surrounding countryside, to be sure, were idyllic: the Stift lay along the Neckar surrounded by beautifully wooded hills. Hegel often hiked during his free time with friends, but the beauty outside would have been likely to make the austerity inside all the more bitter.

Let us outline a day in the life of a Stifler of Hegel's time:[31] Up at 5:00 A.M. in summer, 6:30 in winter, the Stifler first went to prayers in the common room. Attendance was taken, as it was for all meetings and classes during the day, and absence was punishable by forfeiture of the delinquent's portion of wine at dinner! After prayers the Stiftler went back to his room, where he read and expounded a chapter of the Greek New Testament, under the direction of repetents and seniors. Then breakfast, and off to the morning lectures. Dinner was at 11:00 A.M., and was a rather solemn affair for which, again, attendance had to be taken. It began with prayer, and during the meal there was a public reading from the Bible and the *Konkordienbuch,* followed by a sermon by a Stiftler (each had to take his turn preaching, but got better food that day), then hymn singing. There was free time for shopping and hiking from 12:00 to 2:00 P.M., and the Stiftler spent the rest of the afternoon in his room studying. Supper was at 6:00, after which students could go out until the closing of the gates, generally at 9:00. The repetents counted the students under their charge at 10:00, and anyone not back was declared *abnoctant* and sent next day to the student jail. Thursdays and Sundays were free, generally with music after dinner, except of course that church attendance was mandatory on Sunday morning (until 1790 the students marched from Stift to church in procession).

There were numerous rules, many dating from centuries past and clearly antiquated. Minor infractions were usually punished by forfeiture of the dinner wine, though it is questionable how effective this punishment was, since the wine seems not to have been terribly good and was avoided by most of the students anyway. There was incarceration in the student jail for more serious offenses, such as smoking. Going to dance-halls or to "open taverns, beer-halls or other drinking places," dancing, or participation in Mardi Gras festivities, were all *streng verboten*. All infractions were solemnly inscribed in the student's records. Hegel's tended to multiply with each passing year; he became especially negligent about attending lectures, and was once incarcerated in the student jail for a few hours for having arrived late from a vacation. His semester reports regularly gave him good marks *(ingenium bonum, diligens)* for aptitude and diligence, but in *mores* he slid from his early mark of *boni* to a mere *probi* or *recti,* and once was reported *languidi*.[32] In practice the rules were often broken and despite such odious practices as the employment of student spies they seem not always to have been very stringently enforced by the authorities. A good many students, for example, smoked—to keep warm in the winter!—and there was really no way to keep them away from public houses in the locality. A recent student wrote an article in 1785 describing this scene in a tavern in Tübingen (perhaps exaggerated by a touch of braggadocio):

> One finds students here by the fifties and sixties dressed in the habit of their order, in one hand a beer glass and in the other a pipe. One party plays ninepins: one party plays tarok, one party curses: one party is wrestling. —Actually there is a stiff punishment for visiting taverns, but it is not possible to enforce it. What's funny is to see the eyes made by strangers or inlanders from distant parts when they observe the future shepherds of their souls in these attitudes.[33]

Hegel seems to have been no stranger to such Auerbach's-cellar scenes, though in this regard as in more significant aspects of Hegel's student life such a fog of legend has descended that it is very difficult to get an accurate impression of our seminarian. One Magister Lautwein, a fellow student who later claimed to have been a close friend of Hegel's, attributes to him "a certain joviality" that endeared him to his peers, and remarks that his "morality was better than his legality," and that "he had also not disdained occasional attendance at social revels at which offerings were made to Bacchus."[34] There is also a story about the gatekeeper who upon Hegel's late return one evening is supposed to have cried out, "O Hegel, you'll surely souse away the little bit of sense you have!"[35] However there is evidence that the Stift's cloister-statutes were no less onerous for being so often winked at. They were a present and annoying embodiment of what the more rebellious students found most objectionable in traditional Christianity.

Certainly it was from Hegel's time onward the peculiar fate of the Stift, which had for centuries been "the training ground of Württembergian theologians and . . . a mighty fortress of Württembergian Protestantism,"[36] to be a remarkable breeding ground of religious dissent and theological innovation. To the triumvirate of Hegel, Schelling, and Hölderlin were added in the nineteenth century such alumni as F. C. Baur, D. F. Strauss, F. T. Vischer, Eduard Zeller, and Albert Schwegler. And certain it is that Hegel himself underwent a quiet transformation in the Stift, in quite another direction than that for which the Stift's authorities might have hoped. He entered as a relatively docile "model pupil" from Stuttgart, bent on a theological career and so thoroughly reflecting his enlightened-conservative background that he was critical of it only on a basis thoroughly understandable from the point of view of his background itself. By the time he left he had, probably long since, renounced a career in theology, and had planted some unmistakably revolutionary seeds in his thinking, as we shall see. It is not so clear just when this change took place or why. Surely his mild rebellion against the authority of the Stift was a surface manifestation of the deeper transformation, and not its cause.[37] In any case the caricature of Hegel's student years as an Auerbach's-cellar existence has even less basis than the caricature of the schoolboy as a learning machine. He enjoyed beer and conversation. He had at least one passionate love affair. He did not take the cloister-statutes very seriously. Such facts hardly add up to a philistine existence. His academic record, on the other hand, while not brilliant, was quite good. If he was nevertheless what in current jargon would be called an "underachiever" the reason was probably in good part the classic one: he did not find his studies stimulating. In particular, as his letters shortly after leaving the Stift suggest, he was dissatisfied with the kind of theological fare that made up the bulk of his last three years (the first two years in the Stift were devoted to philosophical and humanistic studies, the last three to theology). He remained in the Stift, perhaps at the insistence of his father,[38] worked in a rather "desultory" and "eclectic" way—he even studied anatomy on the side—but began developing the interests we find dealt with in the early writings: there is an intense concern for the phenomenon of Christianity, but not approached in the mode of Stift theology. In general, one finds no love for the Stift expressed by Hegel or by his closest friends. Hölderlin, while still a student, complained fiercely about the bad air and unappetizing food, the limitation of freedom, the "annoyances," "chicanery," "injustices," "pressure and contempt," "ill-treatment" he suffered there, and was afraid that his university years would turn out to have embittered his life forever.[39] The early Hegel-Hölderlin-Schelling letters have nothing good to say about Alma Mater. On the other hand a visit to the Stift by Duke Carl in January 1790, issued in a report that complained of the students' belittling of theology and distaste for the pastoral calling, their tendency to frivolity and "good living," their insubordination and "false sense of freedom."[40]

The university faculty was considered good for its time. Even Hölderlin has warm words for Conz, a poet and repetent in classics who shared the three friends' enthusiasm not only for the Greeks but for the French Revolution as well. Although the theology was staunchly orthodox and was supernaturalistic in worldview, there seems to have been an earnest effort made, as the saying goes, to relate the faith to the times. The spirit of the Enlightenment reigned in the theological as in the other faculties. Kant was seriously studied, expounded, and expanded upon. One of the theologians, Schnurrer, was a man of European fame whom Rousseau went out of his way to visit. Gottlob Christian Storr (1746–1805) was the theologian under whom Hegel chiefly studied, and was the guiding spirit of the Stift. He was an energetic apologist, devoted to reconciling revealed truth and modern learning. His *Doctrina christiana e sacris litteris repetita* was the official *Lehrbuch* in dogmatics in Württemberg. He was an enthusiastic Kantian, and his *Annotationes theologicae ad philosophicam Kantii de religione doctrinam* (1793) is said to have been highly regarded by Kant himself. He was a biblicist, for whom dogmatics and New Testament theology were identical. He saw the Bible as a dogmatic textbook, a unity containing apparent contradictions that he took pains to reconcile. He offered historical proofs for the integrity of the biblical text, together with appeals to the "character" of its teachers as the attestation of its essential truth. Jesus, for example, claimed to be sent from God, and his "character" attests to the truthfulness of the claim: "One may take him at his word, because he was a man of this sort of thought and behavior." Furthermore, "probative above all for the truth of the sayings of Jesus regarding the divinity of his mission are those works of Jesus which one calls *miracles*."[41] Hölderlin was for a time attracted to Storr's apologetic use of the miracles and of the sublimity of Christ's teaching.[42]

Hegel's specific views on such questions at that time are not recorded. There are extant some markedly uninspired sermons by Hegel, who after all had to take his turn preaching during the dinner hour.[43] In light of Hegel's notorious reputation as a speaker, one suspects that their delivery must have been something of an ordeal for both preacher and listeners. In any case, Rosenkranz is probably right in suggesting that these sermons "appear to have been only *opera operata*."[44] Certainly they are a dubious source for reconstructing Hegel's views at the time. They bear Storr's Kantian-orthodox mark. In one sermon, for instance, on divine justice (January 10, 1792), he undertakes to show how this justice rewards and punishes. We have two bulwarks against the reign of sensuousness *(Sinnlichkeit):* conscience, that is, the "inner voice of reason" which is in all men; and the divine commandments. The man who offends against this twofold counsel "destroys his own machine." The result is pain and remorse, and fear of future punishment.

But the righteous will find a reward in their own virtue and its consequences, and through the death of Christ will be free from fear of punishment; their death will be "only a passage to a wider arena for the perfection of creation and the greatness of the Creator."[45] The young preacher does indeed quote the consoling word that "God repays us not according to our sins, but according to his great mercy," but the doctrine of salvation through grace alone is given only formal obiesance. The moralistic view predominates in all the sermons, though it is a morality of inward motivation and not mere legalism. Another sermon (Saint Philip and Saint James's Day, 1793), on true faith, establishes two theses: That true faith "is based on the conviction that Christ was the true Son of God," and that it is established "through the works which he calls forth."[46] The theme of "reconcilability *(Versöhnlichkeit),*" to which he was later to give such a rich interpretation, receives a similarly moralistic treatment in another sermon. Various obstacles, such as self-love, are discussed, and the preacher concludes that reconciliation and the forgiveness of sins requires our fulfillment of the "virtue" of love. Only that faith is true which is fulfilled through love.[47]

These sermons are by and large fairly pedestrian, as required exercises tend to be. There is neither internal nor external evidence to suggest that the young dinner-table preacher does not believe what he is saying. Rather there is a certain slackness about the sermons, a lack of the tension that is present when speakers are expressing ideas that have vitality for them, certainly a lack of that tension which we find very early in Hegel's own work when he is wrestling with conceptions that fully engage him. Only occasionally in these sermons does he rouse himself a bit, but he does so invariably when he touches upon the motif of inwardness. Righteousness, faith, love, are not simply outward observances or forms of behavior; they are movements that involve a person's most basic motivations, the wellsprings of character. The love that reconciles is to be sure a virtue, but this virtue is a form of selfhood in which reconciliation and forgiveness are present by its very possession. It is not simply assent to the facticity of certain historic events or supernatural beings but a contemporaneous state of character. When this theme of inwardness is touched the preacher actually reaches for something like eloquence. Such a quickening of pace beyond the required exercise certainly seems to occur at points in his sermon on the kingdom of God. The kingdom of God, as we shall see, had by this time become a potent symbol among Hegel's circle of friends. It was not simply a term in Stift dogmatic theology. In the sermon (second after Trinity, 1793) his first main point is that the kingdom "is not outward but something inward." It not only is not a worldly state, but is also not the visible church, nor is it manifested in outward ceremonies of the church:

> We are all called Christians—the Christian religion extended over the earth—today in all the pulpits of half the world—the teaching of Christ proclaimed. . . . —Is this the kingdom of God—through communion with this church [are we] citizens of the kingdom of God? That we profess outwardly, are baptized in his name, say Lord! Lord!?[48]

Closely identified with the kingdom of God, beyond any outward religious forms, is the "invisible church," again a kind of talisman in Hegel's circle of friends, here identified with the company united in inward virtue; and "to this Christ has opened the way for us,"[49] the other main point developed in the sermon. But the theme of grace through Christ is again left in pious generalities, while the young preacher hastens to add that only insofar as a person becomes active in combatting lusts and self-love "can the true faith arise which is fruitful in good works."[50]

The friendship of Hegel, Schelling, and Hölderlin as fellow students in Tübingen is clearly the sort of happy accident out of which legends are made. Enthusiasts for German culture may surely be forgiven a propensity to exercise romantic imagination in contemplating such an association at a romantically youthful age of three men who were to be among the giants of that culture. Significant documentary data stemming from the student years of the three friends is scanty, however, though such data is supplemented by their exchange of letters dating from the next few years, which doubtless reflects something of the spirit of their association in the university. It is no mere legend that the three were bound by a really close friendship. And despite great differences in temperament each had a keen sense that they were engaged in a common enterprise, a spiritual-cultural movement pointing toward the future, a common revolutionary enthusiasm.

Some months after both had left Tübingen, Hölderlin sent Hegel a letter that begins as follows:

Dear Brother!

I am certain that you have thought of me occasionally since we parted from one another with the watch-word "kingdom of God." By this watch-word we would, I believe, recognize each other again after every metamorphosis. I am sure that no matter what happens to you, time will never expunge that impulse in you. I think that will also be the case with me. It is that impulse above all which we love in one another. And so our friendship is certain to eternity. Still I have often wished that you were near me. You were so often my genius. I thank you very much. I feel the full force of that especially since our separation. I would like to learn much more from you, also occasionally to share something of mine.[51]

Hegel, writing Schelling six months later, closes his letter with equal warmth, and still more eschatological overtones:

> Let the kingdom of God come, and let our hands not lie idle in our laps! . . .
> . . . Let reason and freedom remain our watch-word, and our point of union the invisible church.[52]

One sweeping sentence of Schelling's reply from Tübingen reflects the tone of his contribution to this extraordinary trio:

> We both want to go further, we both want to prevent the greatness which our age has brought forth from getting mixed up again with the spoiled leaven of past times; —it must remain pure among us, just as it came from the spirit of its originator, and if possible it must pass from us to posterity, not defaced and depressed into the old ready-made form but in its complete perfection; in its most sublime form and with the loud proclamation that it challenges the entire previous constitution of the world and of the sciences to a conflict unto triumph or destruction.[53]

The precise substance of these expressions and these hopes is more difficult to establish than their tone. In the next sections we shall discover some of the ideas around which the three friends rallied with such enthusiasm, particularly as these ideas affect the course of Hegel's development. But the exuberant tone is already part of the substance. The three young friends felt themselves to be men of destiny, on the threshold of a great new age which they were to have a part in establishing. They lived in expectation, and this expectation bound them closely together despite great differences in personality and interest.

Hegel and Hölderlin, who had entered the Stift at the same time, seem not to have been on particularly intimate terms until after Schelling's arrival two years later, when the three became roommates. Only then do we read, in Hölderlin's correspondence, of long walks in the woods with Hegel. Hegel and Hölderlin were certainly poles apart in temperament. The internal evidence of literary style confirms the reports on their personalities. There is a mercurial lyricism in Hölderlin, a rhetoric that is passionate, magical, earnest, and too openhearted for much irony or wit. Hegel also reaches sometimes for lyricism, but his boiling point is very much higher. There is passion in him but it is controlled. He is good-humored, methodical, and cool; he views his own enthusiasms with a slightly skeptical eye. Hölderlin soars. Hegel sometimes marches smartly enough, sometimes picks his way carefully, but always with at least one foot on the ground. It is easy to guess why they did not readily come into close contact, but it is also easy to see why, once the barriers were broken, each felt so perfectly complemented by the other. Hegel certainly came to regard Hölderlin as his dearest friend, whom he not only loved but admired so much that he actually tried his own hand at writing verse in a transparently Hölderlinian mode, notably the long poem "Eleusis" which he dedicated and sent to Hölderlin in August 1796. The attempt was no great success poetically; having one foot anchored to the ground is a bit awkward when one is trying to soar. But there is something touching in the fact that he made the attempt. Hölderlin, for his part, shortly after the poem was written succeeded in his strenuous attempts to secure a post for Hegel in Frankfurt, where he himself was living at the time. He wrote a friend about his joy in being restored to companionship with Hegel: "Hegel's company is very wholesome for me. I love the easy-going people of good sense [*die ruhigen Verstandesmenschen*], because one can orient oneself so well by them, when one doesn't quite know how things stand with oneself and the world."[54]

But it was Schelling's arrival in Tübingen that had originally brought all three together. He seems to have been the catalyst of the friendship. Five years younger than Hegel and Hölderlin, he was not yet fifteen years old when he entered the Stift in the fall of 1790, and was already recognized on all sides as a genuine *Wunderkind*. Schelling was from the first a polemical and revolutionary spirit. One can detect in him a character common among prodigies whose brilliance necessarily so far outruns their experience: his boundless self-confidence, his joy in his own sheer intellectual agility, his impatience with what struck him as the hoary stupidities of the older generation, an aggressive intelligence that dared to sprint where graybeards feared to tread. Whatever may have been their relationship in the beginning, by the time their exchange of letters began Hegel seems to have stood in a kind of awe of the young genius, whose thinking always seemed to be a few steps ahead of his own. Mingled with the admiration, though, is a clear determination not to be shaken out of his own more cautious pace.

The association of the three, along with their wider circle of friends, seems first and foremost to have grown out of common political enthusiasm. The initial stages of the French Revolution, before the outbreak of terror caused some sober second thoughts, was greeted with great excitement among young German intellectuals, who saw in it the enactment into political and social reality of the ideals of the Enlightenment. Rosenkranz, evoking the perspective of that time, speaks of "this genuinely philosophical drama" of the birth of "a state out of the idea of the state," which "the noblest Germans" found so irresistible.

> A Klopstock and a Schiller, a Kant and a Forster, a Baggesen and a Schlabrendorf, a Merk and a Jacobi, all joined with one another in the glowing expectation of an *ethical rebirth of Europe,* after the rights of mankind were decreed. Is it any wonder that young men, from the neighborhood of the Rhine, from Strassburg, were addicted to the most decided enthusiasm for the French Revolution, that through what was occurring in France they were also aroused to a critique of conditions at home, to indefinite hope that these conditions would progress to higher forms?[55]

A political club formed in the Stift, in which Hegel and Schelling played leading roles. French newspapers were shared, revolutionary songs sung, there were speeches and heated discussions. Hegel (according to Lautwein's recollections) zealously lent such oratorical powers as he possessed to the cause of liberty and equality. Members of the club fought duels with the defenders of reaction, and Rosenkranz reports that at least once a republican emigrant was concealed in the Stift for several days and then spirited over the Rhine under cover of a concert organized by the head of the club.[56] There is also a legend according to which Hegel and Schelling joined some friends one fine spring morning in planting a Liberty Tree *(Freiheitsbaum)* on a nearby meadow and presumably danced around it in honor of liberty, equality, fraternity.[57] The activities of the club seem not to have been entirely harmless. Duke Carl was sufficiently alarmed by the reports at one point to make a personal visit to the Stift in order to condemn such activities; he is said to have singled Schelling out for public reprimand for having translated the "Marseillaise" into German.[58]

The French Revolution, and the wider movement that Hegel and his friends hoped it represented, was not regarded simply as a political movement in a narrow sense, with the limited purpose of changing the form of government and redressing specific injustices of long standing. When one is young, if one's self-concern is interwoven with concern about the world, if one combines high expectations about human life with a low estimate of the present human condition, one may want very much to be persuaded that a promising new movement—social, political, religious—will so basically alter conditions that all one's happiest dreams will become realities. Certainly these young men during their university years infused concepts and ideals drawn from diverse cultural sources into their zeal for the Revolution. However much their enthusiasm for the French Revolution abated in the next few years in the face of some of its grimmer consequences, they continued to believe that the hopes that they had invested in it would be brought to fruition, that they stood on the brink of a radical change in the condition of human life and that the ideas they were now absorbing foreshadowed the shape of things to come.[59]

3. Hegel, Schelling, Hölderlin, and the Winds of Doctrine

It is possible to list some of the sources of the ideas that influenced the three comrades, though virtually impossible, and perhaps not so important anyway, to know exactly what they made of these ideas during their university years. There are records of some of the books they studied, and we are able to find in his university and postuniversity studies some sources of Hegel's later thinking.

It is safe to say that the most important direct influences were not those derived from the theological studies that dominated his curriculum during the last three years at the Stift. Still, it is worth reminding ourselves that Hegel and his friends did after all receive a decent theological education, perhaps in spite of themselves. There was intensive work in the Bible, pursued in the Hebrew and Greek original, there were studies in church history and in historical and contemporary theology. Our three seminarians had at least to be competent enough in these studies to pass examinations, and all three did so creditably.

Anyone who has passed some examinations himself will recognize that this feat does not necessarily testify to any very deep and lasting impression made by such studies. But Hegel's later work, at least, does exhibit signs that his biblical and theological studies left their imprint,

however languidly they may have been pursued at the time. His manuscripts dating from the first seven years after leaving the Stift in 1793
reflect his continued preoccupation with the Christian tradition, and
even when he is sharply critical of it he shows an exact knowledge of
what he is attacking that is by no means to be taken for granted among
philosophical critics of Christianity. His mature writings and lectures
continue to reflect, from a more friendly standpoint, this knowledgeable
relationship to the Bible and to Christian doctrine. Mention should
also be made of an indirect and perhaps unconscious influence of
biblical and theological patterns of thought, not so obviously identifiable
and appearing even when the subject seems most remote from explicitly
Christian ideas. This indirect influence, archetypal and, from some
points of view, insidious, surely affects his view of the alienated condition of man and his view of history, at once so tragic and so optimistic.

   But nontheological studies, curricular and extracurricular, had the
greatest immediate impact on the thinking of the three friends. In the
first place, Hegel and Hölderlin in particular continue during their
university years to deepen their studies in classical antiquity, finding
there an integration of politics, religion, and art in the culture in which
every citizen could find his or her identity reflected. This view of the
ancients, particularly in the great age of Athens, was the reverse of
the fragmentation they experienced in their own institutions, where it
seemed to them that politics was brute force in support of social privilege, art an irrelevant ornament, and religion an escape into the otherworldly or an empty ceremonial charade, each at odds with the others,
and none reflecting the best aspirations of individuals. Individuals, in
fact, were debased by their culture, and reflected its fragmentation in
their own divided souls. With this sense of their own situation, it is no
wonder that the three friends turned to the classics as relics of a golden
age, where the culture was of one piece, in which the ideals of the
citizenry found free expression. Nostalgia for such a golden age was a
deep strand in their own emotional bond, which particularly found
utterance in Hölderlin's early poetry. But what they insisted on finding
in the ancients was also a model for their vision of the future: not a
restoration of classical Greek culture as such, but the establishment
in a new form of the beauty and integrity of life that they believed had
existed in antiquity. What they hoped for was not an empty ideal. They
believed it had once seen the light of day, and that its achievement
under new conditions was a realistic possibility.

Of course the friends also read modern authors.[60] They read a good deal in the French, especially Montesquieu, Voltaire, and Rousseau. They found in the French authors not only support for their sense that they were living in a stale and corrupt civilization, but also, in Montesquieu and Rousseau, the notion of a collective cultural consciousness (e.g., Rousseau's *volonté générale* seems an important source for Hegel's conception of *Volksgeist*).[61] The friends also read Shaftesbury with special interest, and such German writers as Goethe, Schiller, Hippel, Lessing, Herder, Winckelmann, Mendelssohn, and Jacobi. These writers certainly represented the Enlightenment, but in a form that resisted its more rigidly rationalistic side. They helped make the young friends sensitive to the affective life, spurred them to think of freedom as extending to the bodily, emotional, social existence. They were much impressed, for example, by Mendelssohn's view that the love of virtue is aroused by the sharpening of feeling and sensation. Such influences helped keep Hegel from ever fully agreeing with Kant's rigorously nonsensuous view of freedom. Still, when the friends intoned the revolutionary slogans of liberty, the word certainly took on some Kantian overtones, as well as some derived from Schiller's *Don Carlos* and *Die Räuber*.

The mention of Kant calls to mind a curious fact about the early development of Hegel. Considering that Hegel was to become one of the most technically complex of philosophers it is extraordinary how small a part technical philosophy played in his education. He certainly did not think of himself at that time as destined for a career in philosophy. Philosophical writings were of course included in his education, but there is no sign of serious engagement with the more formidable metaphysical or epistemological texts. He did read Leibniz, for example, but apparently in the *Theodicy* rather than in the more technical works. It is likely that he read Spinoza also (Rosenkranz [*Leben*, 48] mentions Spinoza's *Tractatus theologico-politicus* among the texts Hegel read in Bern, shortly after leaving the university), though the comments that pass in the correspondence among the three friends reflect more of a popular Spinozism than intensive engagement with Spinoza's *Ethics*. Hegel's preoccupation with the Greeks extended to Greek philosophers, Plato in particular; lengthy translations of Plato are included in his excerpts from this period (the method of excerpting continues during his university career). So far as his early reading of Kant himself is concerned there is a good deal of disagreement and uncertainty. There is evidence that the study of Kant flourished in the Stift at that time, at least in some circles; we have already noticed the Kantian influence on the faculty, particularly Storr, who was Hegel's chief theological mentor. Yet Hegel seems not to have been among the real Kant scholars at the Stift. My own impression is that he did conduct fairly serious studies in Kant's ethical writings—the *Critique of Practical Reason* and the *Foundations of the Metaphysics of Morals*—but left the more theoretical writings, notably the *Critique of Pure Reason,* virtually untouched at that time and for some years to come.[62] The Kantianism with which we find him engaged during this period is in fact of a fairly loose and popular sort, ideas that could as readily be inhaled from the intellectual atmosphere of the times. It was Kant's view of freedom in particular that engaged him the most, and in a form he could have encountered through Schiller and other Kantians almost as readily as through the work of the master himself. He was interested in philosophy in general primarily from this humanistic side, in the interpretation of the ethical, social, religious concerns. It is surely of the first importance in approaching Hegel as a philosopher to recognize this primarily humanistic origin of his philosophical interest, this primary interest in the concerns that philosophy shares with literature, social theory, religious thought, and the arts. Hegel was to become a philosopher of enormous technical complexity. But he was not drawn to philosophy through a preoccupation with epistemological or metaphysical problems. He was rather driven to such problems in the attempt to construct an intellectual resolution of broad questions about the ethical, historical existence of human beings. Remote as the *Logik* may seem from such concerns, the remoteness is only apparent, a function of his determination to drive to the roots of his problems.

Hegel and his university friends were influenced on the religious side by works of a mystical and pantheistic tendency. They read the medieval mystics, particularly Eckhart and Tauler; they warmly greeted the revival of Spinozism; and Neoplatonic authors were one important focus of their interest in classical thought. It is doubtful that they were impressed by strict metaphysical monism as such. But they found in these writers a religious extension of the substantial identity between individual and culture that so filled their dreams of Greek culture, and also of a similar identity of human life with the natural world. That human beings need not be divided against one another, that the fragmentation they experienced in their own culture was at odds with the essential nature of things, that human life belonged to a common natural soil and shared a common spirit, that individuals need not be naked in the pride and misery of their isolation—such convictions were reinforced by the vision of the essential unity of all things in a divine life. This vision lent profound support to the current political strivings for human solidarity. Love, the experienced realization in social existence of the essential unity of humankind, was another of the friends' watchwords. This realized unity, beyond hostility or greed or social stratification, is surely what the friends have in mind above all when they speak so ecstatically of the kingdom of God. Beyond every possible fragmentation of experience is that vision of the unity of reality which is the Spinozistic "intellectual love of God."

But this cosmic endorsement of their social longings is not all that the friends found in the mystical and Neoplatonic writings. There was also the vividness of experienced participation in the divine life of the world. The unity of the individual with a social or cosmic whole is not simply an ideal teaching, a doctrine to set alongside alternative views of the nature of things. What the three friends long for, and these writings seem to offer, is an experienceable reality, not a theory to be entertained by the mind. One can actually participate in the divine life that is the unity of things. The divine is not a remote personage, the absent subject of abstract theories and oft told tales. The divine is a contemporaneous presence in whose vitalities one may actually share, a divine life drawn upon for one's own life and for that common life of humanity which is love. Freedom, life, love, the kingdom of God, the invisible church—such expressions have a way of passing over into one another, and important as they are in the rhetoric of the early Hegel one looks in vain for very precise definitions. Such terms do not receive exact formulation because they represent something too fundamental in his thinking, something against which to measure the validity of those ideas that are precisely defined. His early thought revolves around these obscure expressions, and systematic terms are employed in order finally to illuminate what is obscurely signified in them.

It may seem paradoxical that such ideas were given such revolutionary significance in the minds of Hegel and his university comrades. It is common to view mystical and monistic ideas as culminating in an ultimately static vision of things: the unity is a placid pool in which the vitalities of existence are entirely absorbed, if not drowned. Yet clearly Hegel, Hölderlin, and Schelling found in such ideas the very opposite of deathlike placidity. The stasis, the deadness, was in the old accepted condition of society with its unending divisiveness and injustice. It was the stagnation of the old order that needed stirring, and the call to the unity beyond division was one with the call to the kingdom of God and the call to liberty, equality, fraternity; the restoration to a wholeness in which "life" could flourish. Difficult as it is to grasp clearly this turn that the young men gave to their attraction to the mystical tradition, it is of great importance in understanding the origins of German Idealism and of Hegelian thought in particular. One may even find here the seeds of what is perhaps the central paradox of Hegel's philosophy, that a philosophy of process through conflict should be informed ultimately by a vision of harmony, even identity. But the young Hegel was able to begin recognizing and diagnosing the conflict because he had at least some notions about what a harmony of life would be. One recognizes the sickness because one knows what health is. Surely it was an important and perhaps fateful stroke that in the first beginnings of his thought Hegel came to identify health with participation in essential unity. In light of this conviction the experienced state of affairs loses the acceptability bred of mere familiarity, loses its apparent harmlessness, its appearance of being more or less the way things ought to be. Its apparent fixity and stability is in fact its evil, a suspension in a state of sickness. It *must* be broken up, revolution must be set in motion, and it *can* be broken up and set in motion because it does not correspond to the natural or essential order of things at all. What is simply in the nature of things could presumably not be changed in any fundamental way, but a condition that is itself a painful distortion of the natural condition is inherently unstable and subject to the most radical change. Its apparent formidable stability is simply the rigidity of desperation, or the inertness of sickness unto death. But in order to see it as such, in order to be delivered from the blindness bred of familiarity, one must have been confronted with the alternative, given insight into "life" as it naturally or essentially would be. That the mystical outlook should function in this way, and bear such revolutionary implications, is in fact by no means unusual. There is ample precedent in the tradition of Western mysticism for this significance given it by Hegel and his comrades. If it seems a strange use of mystical ideas, that is only because of the widespread modern tendency to dismiss all mysticism as mere otherworldliness. It is much rather an extraordinary vision of the truth about this world.[63]

Lessing continued to be one of Hegel's heroes, especially since he also had moved toward a type of mysticism. The three students seemed especially impressed with some comments of Lessing to Jacobi that Jacobi recorded in his brief work, *On the Doctrine of Spinoza in Letters to Herrn Moses Mendelssohn.* According to Jacobi, Lessing had become a Spinozist. Jacobi, for example, quotes Lessing as having said not long before his death:

> The orthodox concepts of the divine exist no longer for me; I cannot appreciate them any more. ἐν και παν! I know nothing else.[64]

This motto, ἐν και παν, "one and all," is appended to Hölderlin's entry of February 12, 1791 in Hegel's album, under an inscription from Goethe which runs:

> Joy and Love are
> the wings to great deeds.[65]

It is not clear whether the added ἐν και παν is written in Hölderlin's own hand or in Hegel's, but it is easy to understand why the All-One may have been a potent symbol for both. Still, Hegel was probably not a pantheist in any strict metaphysical sense, if only because he did not yet insist on working out his ideas in any very systematic way. Hölderlin moved only very slowly toward a more pantheistic point of view,[66] in part under the influence of the persuasive Schelling, who came early to systematic philosophical rigor, and was powerfully drawn to pantheistic views. By 1795, in a letter to Hegel which we will discuss presently, Schelling was able to state flatly with Lessing: "For us also the orthodox concepts of God do not exist any longer."[67] But Hegel does not express himself quite so unconditionally. And when Schelling goes on to proclaim that he has become a Spinozist he clearly expects Hegel to be a bit shocked, adding, "Do not be astonished."

Kantian moralism probably functioned for a time to counterbalance these pantheistic tendencies in some measure. But when followers of Kant, notably Fichte, began to develop Kantianism itself into a philosophy of Absolute Idealism, the three comrades were prepared to respond enthusiastically. In fact, as we shall see, the "Spinozism" of which Schelling speaks in the letter mentioned above sounds much more Fichtean than Spinozistic; it is revealing that he is able to regard this Fichtean development of Kant as belonging generally under the banner of Spinozism. Hölderlin made the same identification at this time, in a letter to Hegel, but had more reservations about this Fichtean "Spinozism" than Schelling had.[68] At any rate, by the time the three

friends, separated by Hegel's and Hölderlin's graduation from the Stift, begin communicating their concerns through correspondence, the idealistic developments of Kantian philosophy are the primary focus of their enthusiasms. Hegel, at first, has to confess that he has not yet made much headway with these developments, and in his case Kantian moral philosophy is clearly more in the center of his thinking than is the case with his friends. But the later development of Kantian thought by Fichte and by Schelling himself soon begins to exert a dominating influence on his thinking as well. On the other hand there is a contrary development of Kantian thought against which Hegel and Schelling inveigh unsparingly: the attempt by apologists in the Stift, notably Storr, to reconstitute traditional Christian doctrines on a Kantian basis. It will be worthwhile to look more closely at these diverse uses being made of Kant.

4. The Emergence of German Idealism from Kantianism in the Early Intellectual Association of Hegel, Schelling, and Hölderlin

At the time of the three friends' separation, Hegel went to Bern where he suffered in a position as a private tutor in a wealthy Swiss household. He complained often of his onerous position and of his isolation from the intellectual currents that were moving his friends. Hölderlin soon became the envy of the trio, hearing lectures by Fichte in Jena and receiving the personal encouragement of Goethe and Schiller in his poetic productivity. Schelling had to stay in Tübingen, where he was impatiently completing his student career and already embarking upon ambitious projects of philosophical writing. But the three friends, Hegel and Schelling in particular, kept in touch by mail, and their letters reflect not only their disaffections with the theological tradition in which they had been schooled, but the enthusiastic beginnings of a major transition in German intellectual history. As I have indicated, both of these developments revolve around their appropriation of Kant and his successors. A major point of departure for their thinking was provided by Kant's procedure in devising the postulates of practical reason. Let us briefly review this procedure:

Kant had shown, in the first critique, that theoretical reason could neither conclusively prove nor disprove doctrines regarding alleged matters of fact that transcend the limits of possible sensory experience. Reason, for example, could provide equally plausible grounds for both believing and disbelieving in the existence of God or in the freedom of the will, but cannot finally settle such issues. For the sphere of knowledge is confined to those objects that can be established on the basis of possible experience, and the legitimate exercise of theoretical reason is therefore also confined to those limits. This means that the most fundamental doctrines of traditional metaphysical and religious thought cannot be the objects of any possible knowledge in the strict sense. Yet for Kant this conclusion was not negative. The implication he drew was that theoretical reason must not meddle speculatively in ideas of the transcendent. The limits of proper knowledge leave an "empty place" at the speculative summit that speculation itself cannot legitimately fill: "I had therefore to transcend *(aufheben) knowledge,* in order to have a place for *faith,* for the dogmatism of metaphysics, i.e., the prejudice prevailing in it without a critique of pure reason, is the true source of all the unfaith which contends against morality."[69]

The "faith" of which Kant speaks in this famous remark in the preface to the second edition of the first critique is the faith that morality has a transcendent basis, a basis that is nonsubjective and substantial even though it transcends the limits of possible experience and therefore of knowledge. Kant certainly does not intend that this "empty place" should be filled by the dogmas of traditional theology any more than by metaphysical speculation. It is to be filled by reason, but by reason in its practical rather than its theoretical employment, a function of reason not to establish knowledge but to establish the presuppositions of genuine morality. As he already suggested in that preface and tried to show in detail in the second critique, Kant held that three transcendent ideas in particular could be so presupposed as postulates of reason in its practical or moral employment: the existence of God, the freedom of the will, and the immortality of the soul. (This procedure is often misleadingly labeled a "moral proof.") The validity of such ideas could not be proven because they lay beyond the limits of proper knowledge, beyond confirmation or denial by appeal to possible experience, yet Kant thought that they could properly be postulated in the "empty place" at the summit of thought, beyond the limits of proper knowledge.

Not that such postulates of practical reason were required in order for men to do their duty; the moral imperative, established by practical reason, was unconditional. Duty was to be performed for its own sake. Yet if the will were not free no one could in fact do his duty for its own sake; human motivation would be entirely reduced to the causal order that is the subject of empirical psychology; that is, reduced finally to sensuous grounds. And if there is no God and no immortality the man who does his duty for its own sake has no assurance of ultimate happiness. He is not to do his duty merely for the sake of ultimate happiness, yet Kant argues that if there were no such reward there would be no moral world order corresponding to and endorsing the unconditional commands of the categorical imperative. "By a postulate of pure practical reason, I understand a theoretical proposition which is not as such demonstrable, but which is an inseparable corollary of an a priori unconditionally valid practical law."[70] God, freedom, and immortality seem to him to be three such postulates.

Now it was a very great temptation for theologians wishing to reconstitute Christian dogmatics on the basis of the latest and most advanced philosophy to extend this list of postulates of practical reason until it included virtually the whole range of traditional dogma. It appears that Storr and his associates in the Tübinger Stift were not the least interested in resisting this temptation. Stift apologetics by 1790 seem to have consisted in large part in more or less ingenious demonstrations that first one and then another church doctrine were required as corollaries of unconditionally valid moral laws, or were projected by the presupposition of a moral world order. Hegel, and especially Schelling, found the procedure execrable. Not that they criticized Kant himself for supplying as postulates of practical reason what could not be established by theoretical reason. Far from finding Kant's own program strange, they seized on it eagerly and were soon—Schelling very soon—ready with their own ideas about expanding the scope of the postulates of practical reason. In fact German Idealism received its charter at precisely this point: bypassing the restrictions that Kant had placed around theoretical knowledge, it was born in the attempt to construct a new mode of speculation based on a more broadly conceived practical reason. Thought was not to proceed primarily from the empirical object-knowledge of theoretical subjects, but from the activities of persons as agents of moral, social, religious, aesthetic life. The new speculation was not to be confined by Kantian moralism. For Schelling and Hölderlin, the creative artist rather than the performer of duty was the primary model of the person as agent. But it was in general the enactments of agents rather than the empirical knowledge of subjects in a subject-object scheme from which the new speculation was to proceed. In fact this orientation to the active agent rather than to the empirical knower is what so sharply distinguishes the important continental philosophies of the past two centuries from the dominant Anglo-American schools. At any rate, Hegel and his comrades were far from rejecting the heady possibilities opened up by postulations from practical reason. But that was all the more reason for them to shower their scorn on the Stift apologetes for attempting to pour such stale old wine into these fine new wineskins. The apologetic procedure seems to them not merely to rest on a superficial understanding, but to be retrograde and perverse because it inhibits the development of the revolutionary implications of the new ideas; it merely accommodates them to old purposes as though everything were left essentially as it had been. But for these young men the sources and purposes had changed with the advent of the new philosophy. Kant had established a new beginning, and Fichte was showing the way to carry the cause further.

The matter receives a spirited discussion in the exchange of letters between Hegel and Schelling. Hegel, in Bern, does not pretend to understand the new developments perfectly, particularly those which proceed from Kant's theoretical philosophy. But he initiates the discussion by asking Schelling how things are going in Tübingen and then anticipating the answer: "Until someone like Reinhold or Fichte takes the rostrum there nothing real will result. Nowhere can the old system be so faithfully propagated as there; —and while this has no influence on the few good heads, still the thing is maintained among the greater part, in the mechanical heads."[71]

Schelling replies in mixed metaphors but in no uncertain terms:

> Do you want to know how things stand with us? —Dear God, an *auxmos* [drought] has descended that will help the old weeds to grow again. Who will do the weeding? —We expected everything from philosophy and believed that the push that it had given even to the Tübinger spirits would not so quickly give way to fatigue again. Unfortunately it has happened! The philosophical spirit has already reached its meridian here, —perhaps to circle for a while in the heights in order then to go under with an accelerated fall. There are indeed droves of Kantians now—philosophy has called forth praise from the mouths of chil-

dren and sucklings, —but after great pains our philosophers have now finally found the point beyond which one . . . may not go with this discipline. On this point they have found a foothold, settled down and built shacks which are good to live in and for which they praise God Almighty! . . . Properly speaking, they have taken a few ingredients from the Kantian system (from its superficialities, of course), out of which now *tamquam ex machina* such potent philosophical broth can be produced over *quemcunque locum theologicum* that theology, which had already begun to get consumptive, will now soon be moving about healthier and stronger than before. All possible dogmas are now already stamped as postulates of practical reason, and where theoretical-historical proofs never suffice, there the practical (Tübingish) reason cuts the knot. . . .

. . . Fichte, when he was here last time, said that one needs to have the genius of Socrates in order to penetrate into Kant. I find that truer every day. —We must carry philosophy still further! —Kant has cleared *everything* away, —but how are they to notice it? One must smash it in pieces before their eyes so that it will be palpable to them! O the great Kantians that are everywhere now! They stop at the literal, and bless themselves because so much is still left. I am firmly convinced that the old superstition, not only of positive but also of so-called natural religion, is already combined in the heads of most of them with their literalistic Kantianism. It is joy to see how well they know how to pull the string on the moral proof. Before you can blink an eye out springs the deus ex machina, —the personal, individual Being that sits in heaven above![72]

Schelling goes on to mention a new work by Fichte that he is reading and expresses his boundless enthusiasm for this bright new light. He also speaks with characteristic self-confidence of his own plans:

Now I am working on an ethic *à la* Spinoza; it will set forth the highest principles of all philosophy, in which the theoretical and practical reason will be united. If I have courage and time it will be done by the next meeting or by next summer at the latest. —I'll be happy just to be one of the first to greet the new hero, Fichte, in the land of truth! —Blessed be the great man! He will complete the work![73]

In his reply, after warm personal greetings and modest disclaimers about his own competence to deal with some of the newer issues raised, Hegel undertakes to respond to Schelling's report. Typically, his reaction is a little calmer, without trying to match the outbursts of his ebullient friend. It is also typical of him to point out, with a certain worldly wisdom, that the issue does not have to do altogether with the correct interpretation of the implications of Kantian philosophy, or any other purely philosophical issue. He is not so purely caught up in the world of ideas as his friend. He sees that where certain matters of social position and privilege are at stake, ideas, Kantian or other, can always be rigged as a defense. The fact that scholars manipulate ideas so energetically does not mean that they actually take the ideas seriously. Still, Hegel endorses a serious critique of ideas frivolously and defensively conceived, if only in order to expose the true state of affairs.

What you tell me about the theological-Kantian *(si diis placet)* course of philosophy in Tübingen is not surprising. Orthodoxy is not to be shaken so long as its profession is interwoven into the whole of a state, with worldly advantages attached. This interest is too strong to be so quickly given up, and has its effect if one is not clearly conscious of it as a whole. So long as that is so it will have the whole troop, always most numerous, of thoughtless parrots and scribblers without higher interests on its side. If a member of this troop reads something that challenges his conviction (assuming one wished to do his word-traffic the honor of calling it that) and the truth of which he is able somewhat to feel, he says "Yes, that is surely true," and then he lays himself on his ear and next morning drinks his coffee and pours some for his friends as though nothing had happened. . . . But I think it would be interesting to disturb as much as possible these theologians in their antlike zeal, as they procure Critical building material to fortify their Gothic temple—to make everything difficult for them, to whip them out of every corner of refuge and evasion until they cannot find any more and are compelled to expose their nakedness to the light of day. Among the building material which they carry off from the Kantian pyre in order to prevent the incineration of dogmatics, they always carry home some burning coals as well; —they bring the general dissemination of philosophical ideas.[74]

But Hegel is not so unreserved in his admiration for Fichte as is Schelling. It seems to him that Fichte's recent *Critique of all Revelation* contains all too much of the very kind of speculation so dear to Stift theology; what he has done judiciously will encourage others who are less cautious or scrupulous: "He reasons from the holiness of God to what God must do in virtue of his purely moral nature etc., and in this way has again introduced the old manner of offering proofs in dogmatics."[75]

Hegel would like to determine more precisely the relationship of moral faith to a legitimate idea of God and to the "physico-theological" concept of cosmic purpose, in order to illuminate the idea of providence with which he was concerning himself a good deal at this time. But he complains of lack of time and of books, though he promises to do what he can to join hands with his friend in a common literary enterprise: "I am convinced that only through continuous jarring and jolting from all sides can any effect of importance finally be hoped for." This is the letter that ends with Hegel's two bursts of eschatological rhetoric, already cited, but in the original the rhetorical flight is grounded by the interposition of a searching question to his friend:

> Let the Kingdom of God come, and let our hands not lie idle in our laps!
>
> I don't quite understand one expression in your letter, about the moral proof: "which they know how to manipulate in such a way that the individual, personal Being springs forth." Do you believe we really cannot reach that far? Farewell!
>
> Let reason and freedom remain our watch-word, and our point of union the invisible church.[76]

The query so gingerly interposed between these two bold declamations is revealing. Hegel defers somewhat to his brilliant younger friend, does not feel quite secure about his own thinking, yet he resists being stampeded. He is not quite prepared to dismiss the God of traditional theism with a jibe. He stands in a kind of admiration of his friend's bold, clean strokes, and wants to be considered his comrade-at-arms. He says in the same letter, "Let us repeat your motto often: 'We shall not hang back!'" Yet he clearly does hang back a bit on this issue. There is a different kind of mentality at work here, not so ready to dismiss traditional ideas as so many Errors of the Past, not so ready to wipe the slate clean with one sweep of the eraser, determined not to let his convictions outrun what he had actually understood.

Schelling could not have failed to recognize this difference in intellectual style, and in his reply seems anxious to rally his friend to the cause in a way that would forestall any lagging. This is the letter from which we have already quoted Schelling's call to arms, assuring his friend that "we both want to go further," to create a clean break between "the greatness which our age has brought forth" and "the entire previous constitution of the world and of the sciences," and to challenge the latter to a struggle to the death. He tries to brush aside Hegel's reservations. He admits that there is rather too much of accomodation in Fichte's *Critique of all Revelation,* and advances the unlikely suggestion that Fichte may have partly composed it with tongue in cheek. He himself—Schelling—has been tempted to satire, to deducing the whole body of dogma "with all the accretions of the darkest centuries" from the grounds of practical reason.

> But I haven't the time, and if the satire would be *carried out,* God knows whether it wouldn't be taken seriously by most of them, and already in my early years I would have the fun, at least secretly, of shining as a philosophical light of the church. —The matter must be taken hold of seriously, and from your hand, friend, I would like to expect a beginning. —Now for an answer to your question, whether I believe we cannot extend the moral proof to a personal Being. I must admit that the question surprised me; I wouldn't have expected it from a devotee of Lessing; but you have probably only posed it in order to find out whether I have *entirely* decided it for *myself;* for you it is certainly long since decided. For us also the orthodox concepts of God do not exist any longer. —My answer is: we reach still *further* than to a personal Being. I have meanwhile become a Spinozist! —Do not be astonished. You will soon hear how. —According to Spinoza the world (the object absolute, in opposition to the subject) was—*everything;* to me the *ego* is everything. The real difference between the Critical [Kantian] and the dogmatic philosophy appears to me to lie in the fact that the former proceeds from the absolute ego (not yet conditioned by any object) while the latter proceeds from the absolute object or nonego. The latter leads in its ultimate consequence to Spinoza's system, the former to the Kantian. Philosophy must proceed from the *unconditional.* Now

the question is simply wherein this unconditional lies, in the ego or in the nonego. Once this question is decided *everything* is decided. —To me the highest principle of all philosophy is the pure, absolute ego, i.e. the ego insofar as it is ego alone, not yet conditioned by objects at all, but posited through *freedom*. The alpha and omega of all philosophy is freedom. —The absolute ego has to do with an infinite sphere of absolute being, and in this the *finite* spheres form, which subsist in virtue of the *confinement* of the absolute sphere through an object (spheres of existence—theoretical philosophy). These spheres are obviously conditioned, and the unconditional leads to contradictions. —But we *ought* to break through these limits, i.e. we ought to proceed from the finite spheres into the infinite (*practical* philosophy). This therefore *requires* the destruction of finitude and leads us thereby into the supersensible world. . . . There is no supersensible world for us except the absolute ego. —God is nothing but the absolute ego, the ego insofar as it has abolished everything theoretical, and hence in the *theoretical* philosophy=0. Personality subsists through the identity of consciousness. But consciousness without an object is not possible; but for God, i.e. for the absolute ego there is *no* object *at all,* for if there were it would cease being absolute, consequently there is no personal God, and our highest striving is for the destruction of our personality, the passing over into the absolute sphere of being, which however in eternity is not *possible;* —therefore only a *practical* approaching of the absolute, and therefore—*immortality*. I must close. Farewell. Answer soon

your
Sch.[77]

While there is much here that is unclear, it is clear enough that Schelling's Spinozism is of an altogether Fichtean order. Not only is the Absolute conceived as pure ego, but Spinoza's distinction between *natura naturans* and *natura naturata*[78] has been replaced by the distinction between the world as conceived by theoretical reason and the pure ego as postulated by practical reason. Still, the personal God of theism is plainly as impossible on these terms as on Spinoza's: such an individual Being could only be conceivable as an object of theoretical reason, but no such object is apparent in the empirical world or demonstrable on the basis of the empirical world. The supersensible can only be postulated by practical reason, but personal, individual beings do not exist as such for practical reason, since practical reason has nothing to do with the empirical world.

Schelling enclosed with this letter a highly speculative work of his that had recently been published.[79] Hegel, in reply, can only express his admiration for the brilliance of his friend and his pride that he should be able to claim such a friendship to a man "who will make his great contribution to the most important revolution in the system of ideas for all Germany."[80] He does not claim more than a rough grasp of his friend's main ideas, and does not make bold to address himself to the questions in the same terms, much less try to criticize any of the arguments. He is plainly exercised by more directly political problems, and opens his letter with some caustic comments about the aristocratic constitution and oligarchical social structure of Bern. His response to Schelling's ideas soon turns as well in the direction of such down-to-earth social issues. Of the idea of God as absolute ego he remarks only that it will belong to the "esoteric philosophy" that "will of course always remain," alongside the working-out of those implications of Kantian philosophy from which he expects "a revolution in Germany." But there is no sign that such esoteric verities engage him much. What he evidently hopes for is a new humanism.

> From a new study of the postulates of practical reason I had gotten some notions about the things which you explained so clearly to me in your last letter and which I found in your essay, and which Fichte's *Grundlage der Wissenschaftslehre* will doubtless fully open up to me. Many men will be thrown into astonishment by the consequences which these ideas will yield. Their heads will swim before this highest pinnacle of all philosophy, through which humanity will be so greatly exalted. But why have people come so late to the point of fixing the dignity of the human at a higher level, of acknowledging its capacity for freedom that places it in the same order as all the spirits [*in die gleiche Ordnung aller Geister*]? I believe there is no better sign of the time than this, that humanity in itself has been presented as worthy of so much regard; it is a proof that the nimbus is disappearing from around the heads of the oppressors and idols of the earth. The philosophers prove this dignity, the peoples will learn to feel it, and will not only demand those rights of theirs which have been flattened into the dust, but will themselves take

them up again, —will appropriate them [*sich aneignen*]. Religion and politics have played under *one* blanket, the former has taught what despotism desired, contempt for the human race, its incapacity to be anything good at all through itself. With the propagation of ideas about how things *ought* to be, that indolence of sedate people forever to accept everything as it is will disappear.[81]

Hegel looks for "this revivifying power of ideas" to raise people's spirits from lethargy and lead them to sacrifice unjust and irrational states of affairs even though they have always been taken for granted, such as the use of political constitutions to serve privileged interests.

This correspondence continues for some years,[82] revolving largely around the motifs exhibited in the above selections, as they develop in the thought of the two young men. For some time to come, in strictly philosophical matters Schelling leads and Hegel follows, encouraging his friend, offering very tentative comments of his own but generally claiming little competence in such matters. Schelling is in fact already publishing philosophical works, such as his *Philosophical Letters on Dogmatism and Criticism*[83] which echoes many passages in his correspondence with Hegel. There is, on the other hand, little reflection in this correspondence of the interests that Hegel is at the time developing in his so-called early theological writings, and indeed he disparages his own current efforts: "Of my work it is not worth the trouble to speak; perhaps before long I will send you the plan of something which I am considering working out, so that in time I will be able to appeal to you especially for some friendly help, also in subjects in church history where I am very weak and where I can best profit from your advice."[84] Hegel was feeling discouraged and isolated, missing the intellectual stimulation of direct contact with his friends. In the same letter, written from Switzerland in August 1795, he remarks concerning a meeting between Schelling and Hölderlin a few months earlier, "How much I wish I could have been the third man!" in their conversation.[85]

However, there is one further document that we must consider, because more than any other it reveals the new possibilities that were opening up in the intellectual association of these three young friends. It was only discovered shortly before its publication in 1917 by Franz Rosenzweig, but Rosenzweig did not exaggerate its importance in giving it the title, "The Earliest Programme for a System of German Idealism."[86] One might even call it a kind of manifesto.

Not the least of its fascination has been the mystery surrounding its authorship. The only surviving copy is in Hegel's handwriting, written probably in 1796 but perhaps as late as early 1797, after Hegel had ended his Swiss exile and joined Hölderlin in Frankfurt. But Rosenzweig argued that Hegel was not its author; Hegel had copied out a document originally written by Schelling. Hölderlin's influence has been widely acknowledged (particularly in the exalted position assigned to poetry and to the Idea of beauty), and we do know that he and Schelling had spent some time together again in late autumn of 1795. Indeed, Hölderlin's primary authorship of the piece has been proposed, but most recently strong arguments have been advanced for attributing it to Hegel himself.[87] While these arguments make it difficult to rule Hegel out as the possible author, it appears to me that they fall short of establishing very strong probability, and on grounds of both content and style[88] I am inclined to think that Rosenzweig's hypothesis is still the most likely. Even those who claim the piece for Hegel freely admit that the influence of his friends is transparent in it;[89] I should have to say that if Hegel did write it he did so in a markedly Schellingian mood and spirit. At any rate, the very difficulty of determining which of the three was the author is itself a considerable testimony to their deep mutual influence, and it is safest to say simply that the document provides a revealing view into the new complex of ideas in which all three were absorbed.

In rough, free strokes the Programme sketches the philosophy of the future. From beginning to end it is to be a philosophy that proceeds from human freedom. Here the new charter offered by Kant's postulates of practical reason is proclaimed and expanded, and its most radical implications are boldly set forth. The postulates are taken up into a new doctrine of Ideas, from which a new mode of speculative philosophy is to proceed, and the Idea of Freedom in particular is to underlie the whole.[90] Further on in the document the basis seems to shift to aesthetic grounds, but the Programme begins, on Kantian grounds, with

> an Ethic. Since in the future the whole of metaphysics will fall to *moral doctrine*—Kant with his two practical postulates has only given an *example* of this, without *exhausting* it—hence this ethic will be none other than a complete system of all Ideas, or what is the same thing, of all practical postulates. The first Idea is naturally the representation *of my self* as an absolutely free being [*Wesen*]. With the free, self-conscious being there comes

forth at the same time an entire *world*—comes forth out of nothing—the single true and intelligible *creation out of nothing.*—Here I would descend into the fields of physics; the question is this: How must a world be constituted for a moral being? I should like to give wings once more to our slowly progressing physics, wearily toiling on experiments.

So, if philosophy provides the Ideas and experience the data, we can eventually get a physics of grand dimension [*die Physik im Großen*], which I expect from ages to come. It does not seem that the present physics could satisfy such a creative spirit as ours is, or should be.

From nature I come to the *work of humans* [*Menschenwerk*]. Given the Idea of humanity—I want to show that there is no Idea of the *state,* any more than there is an Idea of a *machine,* since the state is something *mechanical.* Only what is the object of freedom is called *Idea.* We must therefore go beyond the state! —For every state must treat free human beings as mechanical cogs; and that it ought not to do; therefore it ought to *cease.* You can see for yourself that here all the Ideas of perpetual peace and the like are only *subordinate* Ideas under a higher Idea. I wish at the same time to lay down here the principles for a *history of humanity* and expose the whole miserable human work of state, constitution, government, legislation—stripped clear to the skin. Finally come the Ideas of a moral world, divinity, immortality—the overthrow of all superstition, the ferreting out of the priesthood which nowadays makes pretense of reason, through reason itself. —Absolute freedom of all spirits, which bear the intellectual world in themselves and may not seek either God or immortality *outside themselves.*

Last of all the Idea which unifies them all, the Idea of *beauty,* taking the word in its higher Platonic sense. I am now convinced that the highest act of reason, that in which it embraces all Ideas, is an aesthetic act, and that *truth and goodness only in beauty* are akin. The philosopher must possess as much aesthetic power as the poet. The people without aesthetic sense are our philosophers-of-the-letter [*Buchstabenphilosophen*]. The philosophy of the Spirit is an aesthetic philosophy. One cannot be spirited [*geistreich*] in anything, not even about history can one reflect in a spirited way—without aesthetic sense. Here it ought to become evident just what people really lack who do not understand any ideas, —and confess guilelessly enough that everything becomes obscure to them as soon as it gets beyond tables and index.

Poesy attains thereby a higher dignity; she will again become at the end what she was in the beginning—*educator of humanity.* For there will be no philosophy, no history any more, the poetic art alone will outlive all other sciences and arts.

At the same time we hear so often that the great rabble must have a *sensuous religion.* Not only the great rabble, but the philosopher needs it as well. Monotheism of reason and the heart, polytheism of the imagination and of art, this is what we need.

I would speak here first of an idea which, so far as I know, has never before come into anyone's mind—we must have a new mythology, but this mythology must stand in the service of the Ideas, it must be a mythology of *reason.*

Until we make the Ideas aesthetic, i.e. mythological, they have no interest for the *people;* and conversely, until the mythology is rational the philosopher must be ashamed of it. So the enlightened and the unenlightened must finally join hands, the mythology must become philosophical and the people rational, and the philosophy must become mythological in order to make the philosophers sensuous. Then eternal unity will reign among us. Never again the contemptuous glance, never again the blind quaking of the people before their wise men and priests. Only then can we expect the *same* cultivation of *all* powers, of those belonging to each person as well as those common to all individuals. No power will be supressed any more. Then universal freedom and equality of spirits will reign! —A higher Spirit sent from heaven must found this new religion among us, it will be the last greatest work of humanity.[91]

As I hope the meaning of the document is generally clear enough in light of material that has been presented earlier, I do not want to take the edge off its exuberance by subjecting it to detailed analysis. But a few observations may be in order, just to underline motifs that particularly reveal the heady new world of ideas into which Hegel was moving.

Implicit in the Programme is an understanding of "the Idea" that was characteristic of early German idealism. An Idea is of course not an empirical concept. Beauty, for example, is not a datum; it is not a quality of sensory objects in the same sense that their shape, color, and hardness are. One may judge a particular shape to be beautiful, but this judgment is not part of the empirical description of the object, though the shape itself is. A pure judgment with respect to beauty is an exercise of freedom, as Kant had pointed out in the *Critique of Judgment:* This judgment is pure only when it is made independently of the sensuous pleasure one may take in the object and also independently of whether the object is functionally suited to intrinsic or extrinsic purposes; for there is no exercise of freedom involved in finding something pleasant or in the discovery that a shoot seems healthy enough to become a tree. In this respect an aesthetic judgment is like an ethical act: it can only be realized in freedom. The beauty of an object, Kant argued, is determined by a judgment of taste. It is determined, not by deduction from a concept or from a descriptive definition, but by a free exercise of imagination.[92] It does not follow that beauty is a matter of subjective whimsy for Kant, and still less for the author of the Programme, who means to take the term "in its higher Platonic sense." Kant appeals to a common aesthetic sense, so that when I say that something is beautiful I mean that all rational beings ought to find it so.[93] But the Programme appeals to the Idea of beauty itself, as the supreme Idea that unites all others. The Idea informs the thought, action, and imagination of a human being precisely in his exercise of freedom. For freedom is the opposite of arbitrariness; the Idea is its logical and metaphysical ground. The person who judges an object beautiful, like the one who obeys the categorical imperative, is acting in freedom just because the act is informed by reason without ulterior motive. Only that which provides the rationale for such a free and disinterested act counts as "the Idea." It is the rationale embodied in an activity, not a concept abstracted from experience. The self is related to the Idea, not as a subject to its object, but in the way that matter is related to its form, the form into which it is conforming itself, and only in freedom can such a self-transformation occur. One is reminded of the medieval conception of contemplation, in which the soul seeks actively to re-form itself into the image of that which it contemplates: an *itinerarium mentis in Deum* (Bonaventura). The Idea in-forms the life and thought of a person insofar as that person thinks and acts in freedom.

This way of employing the postulates of practical reason doubtless goes much further than Kant himself had intended. For these young "Kantians" the postulates are not simply doctrines correlative to a moral world order, but introduce us into an indubitable world order of highest actuality, under the sovereignty of Idea. So certain is this world order in which persons participate through the exercise of freedom, that one can actually dream of giving wings to the science of physics on this basis—a dream that surely ran afoul of Kant's sharp distinction between the theoretical and the practical employment of reason. Physics above all, on his terms, belonged entirely within the former sphere. But even though the "data" of the new idealistic physics is still to be drawn from "experience" it is not clear that the purely theoretical employment of reason is, as such, to have any role in the establishment of this new *Weltanschauung*. Physics and metaphysics are to be established on a purely ethical basis; "the world" is to be understood as coming forth ex nihilo, the ideal environment projected by the existence of the free human being.

The model of the free person is at the outset drawn from Kantian moral philosophy, but as we proceed it becomes clear that this model was only the point of departure. It soon fades into the model of the creative artist and poet informed by beauty as the Idea supreme. Indeed, philosophy and history are to pass over into poetry, into the free play of imagination presumably unconfined by gross empirical matter. Again, of course, the poetic imagination is not arbitrary. The "aesthetic act" is in fact "the highest act of reason," an exercise of synthetic vision that brings all Ideas, including truth and goodness, into unity. The aesthetic act does not displace the ethical act, but embraces it. On this basis our author finds no contradiction in speaking of a rational mythology, a mythology that is fully sensuous and indeed polytheistic, yet fully rational, moral, monotheistic.

But the Programme does not merely proceed beyond Kant, for good or ill, in including the affective and sensuous in the exercise of freedom itself, and in its idealistic projection of a natural world cut to dimensions of the free person. More than the manifesto of a new philosophy, it presents a vision of the religious reform of society. Freedom is not merely a matter of an individual doing his or her duty or creating a work of art. It is a *social* possibility, a transformation of the communal consciousness through its permeation by the Ideas in a form that can be described, mutatis mutandis, as both aesthetic and mythological. The mythology is to be constituted and consummated in aesthetic act, but the Idea of beauty is to be socially shared, as mythology. It is to bind society together into liberated community. This possibility is expressed in the quasi-apocalyptic note on which the Programme concludes, with the messianic expectation of a "higher Spirit" incarnate in culture that will make the society and every individual whole: beyond fragmentation into the dualities of reason and sense, philosophy and myth, science and art, priesthood and people. This messianic Spirit is of course not an individual Messiah as such. What is intended is doubtless another expression for the Idea, but the Idea incorporated, embodied in the common life of a people.

It is just at this point, where it holds out the possibility of a kind of religious revolution that will sweep away the religiously reinforced oppressions and divisions of the past and will bring about a religiously constituted social liberation, that the Programme makes its most direct contact with the themes we will find Hegel pursuing in Bern and Frankfurt. His language, to be sure, will differ in important respects from the idealistic language employed here; we will not yet find him speaking much in terms of "the Idea" or "Spirit," nor does he characteristically speak of the living content of religion as "mythology." And when he wishes to find a term for that which will unify opposites he is more likely to speak of "life" or "love" than the Idea of beauty or the aesthetic act. But it would not be difficult to find passages in his writings that express a very similar vision in other terms.[94]

It is much more difficult to imagine Hegel approving, much less writing himself, what the Programme says about the state. The state is attacked as something merely "mechanical," having no reflection to the Idea except opposition; that is, as the ineluctable enemy of freedom. "For every state must treat free human beings as mechanical cogs." Since it ought not to do so, the state ought to cease—presumably, to cease existing at all. The state is simply one of the oppressive features under which humanity groans so long as the Idea remains unrealized and people remain unfree. There were recent precedents for such an attitude toward the state (e.g., in Rousseau and even Fichte), and it is not at all farfetched to see the Marxist doctrine of the withering away of the state as a lineal descendent of this idealistic view that the state will cease with the full realization of freedom. But any such denigration of political life as such seems very far from Hegel's thinking, certainly in his maturity, but even in his youth. He always regarded the state as an essential structure of a free social existence, and was far from excluding it from the domain of the Idea. We have already seen, on the other hand, how critical he could be of current political conditions. His writings of the 1790s testify that he considered the modern state as he knew it to be a debased and repressive form of political life. If the Programme had simply reported that the state had almost always in fact treated free people as mechanical cogs, it would have expressed his own known views very well.[95] But Hegel attacked existing states for thwarting the human development they ought to be supporting; that is, for failing to realize the true Idea of the state. That is very different from regarding the state as such as though it were essentially at odds with the Idea. Even when he became more comfortable with this idealistic language than he seems to have been at this time, Hegel's conception of the Idea was rooted in what he regarded as actual and necessary social structures.

There are other portions of this buoyant manifesto that must have caused the more cautious Hegel to frown a bit; even if he did in fact write it himself in an enthusiastic hour, reading it in a more sober frame of mind would have made him shake his head here and there. But with some reservations he could have accepted its basic intentions as his own. It was his center of interest rather than philosophical point of view that separated him from his two friends. On the one hand he was occupied with practical political and economic problems as they related to his humanistic interests. And on the other hand he was preoccupied with the Christian religion as a crucial phenomenon shaping the Western cultural spirit. Unlike the other disenchanted seminarians of his circle, his writing during the seven years after he departed from the Stift was in largest part devoted to a strenuous attempt to come to terms in his own mind with the Christian tradition. To this attempt, in the manuscripts known as his "early theological writings," we now turn.

Notes

1. Wilhelm Dilthey, *Die Jugendgeschichte Hegels* (Berlin: Königlichen Akademie der Wissenschaften, 1905). Reissued in Dilthey's *Gesammelte Schriften* (Stuttgart: B. G. Teubner, 1962–65), vol. 4.

Hegel's early life and work were also, to be sure, treated in some outstanding nineteenth-century biographies of the philosopher, notably that of his student, Karl Rosenkranz, *Georg Wilhelm Friedrich Hegel's Leben* (Berlin: Duncker und Humbolt, 1844; reprinted by photomechanical process, Darmstadt: Wissenschaftliche Buchgesellschaft, 1963). Also Rudolf Haym, *Hegel und seine Zeit* (Berlin: R. Gaertner, 1857; reprinted, Hildesheim: Georg Olms, 1962).

2. *Hegels theologische Jugendschriften,* nach den Handschriften der Kgl. Bibliothek in Berlin, ed. Dr. Herman Nohl (Tübingen: J. C. B. Mohr, 1907), hereafter cited as *HtJ.*

The most important essays and fragments from *HtJ* have been translated into English in Hegel, *Early Theological Writings,* trans. T. M. Knox, with an introduction and fragments, trans. Richard Kroner (Chicago: University of Chicago Press, 1948; reprint, Philadelphia: University of Pennsylvania Press, 1971). Other writings, mostly fragmentary, from *HtJ,* are translated in G. W. F. Hegel, *Three Essays, 1793–1795,* ed. and trans. with introduction and notes by Peter Fuss and John Dobbins (Notre Dame: University of Notre Dame Press, 1984).

3. Walter Kaufmann, *Hegel: Reinterpretation, Texts, and Commentary* (Garden City, N.Y.: Doubleday, 1965). Chapter 7 contains Kaufmann's translation of a generous selection of letters and documents. Subsequent chapters contain his translations of the Preface to the *Phenomenology* and of Hegel's lively little essay, "Who Thinks Abstractly?"

4. H. S. Harris, *Hegel's Development: Towards the Sunlight (1770–1801)* (Oxford: Clarendon Press, 1972). Included among the translations are several selections from *HtJ* not included in the Kroner-Knox translation, and also the so-called earliest system-programme of German idealism, which will be discussed at the end of this present chapter.

Harris's massive book not only details Hegel's early biography, but traces the record of his writings fragment by fragment, from school essays to the turn-of-century political essays. It can claim a place among the most rigorous works of basic Hegel scholarship in any language, and adds by a full two inches to the slender shelf of important Hegel studies in English. It had not been published when I wrote the first two chapters of the present study, which treat the same period, and since a careful subsequent reading of *Hegel's Development* has not seemed to me to call for a basic revision of my text, a little *Auseinandersetzung* may be in order here.

While Harris's work draws on the whole literature on the early Hegel in German, French, and Italian, he makes important contributions of his own, particularly to the philology and chronology of Hegel's early writings, plausibly challenging some of the recent scholarship in this area. Fortunately, the interpretation contained in my two much less detailed chapters is only marginally affected by such refined questions of dating and textual reconstruction.

Harris's overall interpretation of the early Hegel is another matter. It is in important respects in conflict with my own, and I remain unpersuaded by it. I have added a few footnotes calling attention to some of the conflicts. In general, I think Harris exaggerates the continuity, the consistency over several years, in Hegel's youthful thinking. The young man who appears in Harris's pages is purposeful indeed! Very early on he stakes out a vocation for himself as a quasi-public figure, a *Volkserzieher* who will reform if not revolutionize his society. The early writings are intended to serve this ambitious aim. Harris perceives them collectively as the working out—admittedly in unfinished form—of a single vast project conceived as early as 1793, when Hegel ended his student years. Without any evidence, internal or external, that Hegel ever thought of his fragmentary writings during the next seven years as belonging to any such single grand design, Harris devotes an excess of ingenuity to constructing this design out of these unlikely materials, and tries at every point to show that Hegel never basically changed his thinking during this period but only refined it, developing and adding to what was already implicit. Against the view, for instance, of scholars as different as Lukács and T. M. Knox that Hegel underwent both a psychological crisis and a revolution in his thinking during the Frankfurt period (1797–1800), Harris retorts that "there was in fact no 'revolution' in Hegel's thought, which develops with such steady and organic continuity that we might never have suspected a crisis of self-doubt if it were not externally documented" (259). Again, Harris speaks of "the almost astounding consistency of Hegel's development" up to 1800 (331), and declares that "one of the most remarkable things about the development of Hegel's philosophy is that ideas mature in a sort of steady procession and, once matured, remain fairly stable even while other ideas are developing around and above them" (390). But after fending off every evidence of upheaval in Hegel's thinking during this period, Harris then hypothesizes a most drastic upheaval when Hegel moved to Jena: that Hegel altogether threw over his grand literary design and his reformist ambitions as well. He became a philosopher instead. But such discontinuity also seems to be an exaggeration. In fact, I think Harris is only able to put together that extraordinary continuity among the earlier writings by reading back into young Hegel's meaning a great deal too much of the thought of his later works (with the important exception of his later valuations of Christianity).

It will be obvious from the interpretation that follows how much I disagree with Harris's reconstruction of Hegel's early career. Still, he carefully and helpfully explains many points in Hegel's early writings, and I commend his work to any reader who wishes to delve further into the puzzles of interpreting them. He will find much in Harris's study that is not badly bent by the larger designs, and will be initiated into the scholarly refinements of these puzzles.

5. The way in which Hegel reflected this transition and came to comprehend it in his thought provides an important Leitmotiv in Georg Lukács, *Der junge Hegel: Über die Beziehungen von Dialektik und Ökonomie* (Zurich: Europa, 1948; Berlin: Aufbau, 1954). From his Marxist standpoint, Lukács regards the economic transition as the clue to the whole, and credits Hegel with having understood this transition to the bourgeois order in a way that prepared the ground for Marx's viewpoint. "Hegel has not only the highest and most correct insight in Germany into the essence of the French Revolution and the Napoleonic period, but is at the same time the sole German thinker who seriously came to terms with the problems of the *industrial revolution* in England; the only one who brought the problems of classical English economics into relation with the problems of philosophy, with those of dialectics. . . . He strove to grasp the actual inner structure, the actual driving forces of his age, of capitalism, in thought, to establish the dialectic of its movement" (21). The one-sidedness of Lukács's often brilliant study of the young Hegel consists in his attempt to reduce Hegel's developing dialectical insight to this allegedly fundamental economic basis. "It would be false," he continues, "to limit this tendency of the Hegelian philosophy to those remarks in which he expressly and directly concerns himself with the problems of capitalistic society. This concern determines rather the whole construction of his system, the peculiarity and the greatness of his dialectic. Just here lies one of the most important sources of his philosophical, his dialectical superiority over his contemporaries" (ibid.). The purpose of Lukács's study, he adds, is to establish this thesis, over against other interpretations of Hegel's fundamental intent. He is at his best in criticizing other such reductions, for example, to a metaphysical, or an aesthetic, or a religious, or a historical basis. But in establishing his own thesis he must either interpret "problems of capitalistic society" so broadly that the thesis becomes trivial—after all, anything that happens to take place in a capitalistic society, from mystical visions to card games (on which Hegel wrote a short essay in 1798), can be regarded as among its problems—or, if he attempts to restrict himself to more directly socioeconomic problems, he must ignore or explain away huge portions of the total corpus.

6. Dilthey, *Die Jugendgeschichte Hegels*, 9.

7. Rosenkranz, *Leben*, 25.

8. See the letter from Hegel's sister Christiane to his widow, written shortly after his death, describing his early schooling and other details of his childhood, in Johannes Hoffmeister, *Dokumente zu Hegel's Entwicklung* (Stuttgart: Fr. Frommanns, 1936), 392f. (hereafter cited as *Dokumente*). See also Friedhelm Nicolin, *Der junge Hegel in Stuttgart:*

Aufsätze und Tagebuchaufzeichnungen, 1785–1788, Marbacher Schriften 3 (Marbach: Bernhard Zeller, 1970), which quotes Christiane's letter, 83–84, as well as publishing a good deal of interesting material Hegel wrote as a student in the Gymnasium.

9. Rosenkranz, *Leben,* 5, 30.

10. *Dokumente,* 13. Rosenkranz, *Leben,* 7, tells the story but mentions the wrong edition of Shakespeare. Cf. Harris, *Hegel's Development,* 3n.

11. *Dokumente,* 11–13. Also Rosenkranz, *Leben,* 9–10.

12. *Dokumente* contains generous selections from these excerpts, and Rosenkranz, *Leben,* lists the authors most frequently excerpted (10–15).

13. Haym, *Hegel und seine Zeit,* 21.

14. *Dokumente,* 10. Citation for July 2, 1785. See also Rosenkranz, *Leben,* 8–9. Harris (*Hegel's Development,* 14–16, 134) discusses Hegel's further reflections on this episode.

15. *Dokumente,* 13–14. Citation from the journal for July 9 and 10, 1785. Hegel tells another anecdote about the Horde in the citation for July 11. Also Rosenkranz, *Leben,* 8.

16. The following jingle, popular in Swabia, can remind an American of nothing so much as a football cheer:

> Der Schelling und der Hegel,
> der Schiller und der Hauff,
> das ist bei uns die Regel
> und fällt uns gar nicht auf.

(Roughly translated: Schelling and Hegel, Schiller and Hauff, that's so much the rule with us, they hardly stand out at all.) In Franz Wiedmann, *G. W. F. Hegel in Selbstzeugnissen und Bilddokumenten* (Hamburg: Rowohlts Monographien, 1965), 12.

17. Haym, *Hegel und seine Zeit,* 16–18. Haym goes on, in a similarly impressionistic vein, to discuss the way the Swabian temper continued to affect Hegel's mature life and thought. In the above passage he acknowledges his debt to Friedrich Theodor Vischer, and cites in particular Vischer's "Dr. Strauss und die Wirtemberger," *Hallische Jahrbücher* (1838), 476.

18. Rosenkranz, *Leben,* 6. Laurence Dickey's impressive historical study *Hegel: Religion, Economics, and the Politics of Spirit, 1770–1807* (Cambridge: Cambridge University Press, 1987) lays heavy stress on the way Hegel's Old-Württembergian roots furnish the tacit ground-tone of his early thought and writing. He argues that this social and religious background is far more formative than such factors as Hegel's Hellenic enthusiasm. He points out the admittedly scanty documentary sources for reconstructing Hegel's boyhood and university years biographically, and proposes instead to treat his early thinking as an outgrowth of this background, presenting a Geertzean "'thick description' of the world in which he lived" (ix) in three substantial chapters on the religious and political "culture of Old-Württemberg" from the sixteenth through the eighteenth century (33–138). Hegel was "as it were, a member of the 'last generation' of Old-Württemberg Protestants—which is to say that his writings of the early 1790s may be approached, at least initially, from the vantage point suggested by the Württemberger preoccupation with civil piety as a Protestant ideal" (140). Dickey suggests (3) that Hegel's schoolmates gave him the nickname "the old man" to make fun of his stodgy Old-Württembergian values and behavior.

19. See *Briefe von und an Hegel,* ed. Johannes Hoffmeister (Hamburg: Felix Meiner, 1952–60), 1:31.

20. See Haym, *Hegel und seine Zeit,* 27.

21. Rosenkranz, *Leben,* 12.

22. Lessing, *Nathan der Weise* (first published in 1779), act 1, scene 2. Citations in text are to act and scene.

23. Ibid., 4.7. Cf. *HtJ,* 10, 170.

24. Ibid., 3.6. Cf. *HtJ*, 15; also *Phänomenologie des Geistes*, ed. Johannes Hoffmeister (Hamburg: Felix Meiner, 1952), 33; *Phenomenology of Spirit*, trans. A. V. Miller (Oxford: Clarendon Press, 1977), 22; *Phenomenology of Mind*, trans. J. B. Baillie (London: George Allen & Unwin; New York: Macmillan, 1955), 98.

25. "Über einige charakteristische Unterschiede der alten Dichter [von der neueren]," August 7, 1788, *Dokumente*, cited in Rosenkranz, *Leben*, 18. See also a similar essay employing this quotation, written by Hegel as a university student: "Über einige Vorteile, welche uns die Lektüre der alten klassischen griechischen und römischen Schriftsteller gewahrt," December 1788, *Dokumente*, 169, 172. See also *HtJ*, 17.

26. Ibid. This was not Lessing's only work on the problem of faith and history. See his *Über den Beweis des Geistes und der Kraft* (1777), which provided Kierkegaard with the formulation of the central problem of *Philosophical Fragments* and *Concluding Unscientific Postscript:* "Is a historical point of departure possible for an eternal consciousness?" But Hegel had already taken up Lessing's problem of the historical point of departure in the 1790s, under the category of "positivity." See my monograph, *In the Twilight of Christendom: Hegel vs. Kierkegaard on Faith and History* (Chambersburg, Pa.: American Academy of Religion, 1972), 33–34 and passim.

27. "Über die Religion der Griechen und Römer," *Dokumente*, 43.

28. *Briefe,* ed. Rolf Flechsig, 4:74.

29. Ibid., 4:74–76.

30. See Walter Betzendörfer, *Hölderlins Studienjahre im Tübinger Stift* (Heilbronn: Salzer, 1922), 13. Also Julius Klaiber, *Hölderlin, Hegel und Schelling in ihren schwäbischen Jugendjahren: Eine Festschrift zur Jubelfeier der Universität Tübingen* (Stuttgart, 1877), 179–206, quoted at length in *Briefe*, 4:160–66.

31. Following Betzendörfer, *Hölderlins Studienjahre*, 27–31.

32. Klaiber, quoted in *Briefe*, 165.

33. Betzendörfer, *Hölderlins Studienjahre*, 32, quoting from an article by C. Fr. Reinhard in *Schwäbischen Museum*, 1785.

34. Lautwein's letter on Hegel as a student in Tübingen, written a few years after Hegel's death, has been given a good deal of prominence in the scholarship on Hegel's biography. Albert Schwegler, while a student in the Stift and only nineteen years old, first published an article in the *Zeitung für die elegante Welt* in 1839 (Nos. 35–37) in which he paraphrased portions of the letter under the pretense of reporting on a word-of-mouth conversation with a "dissipated genius" who had been Hegel's fellow student. This report was already quoted at length in Rosenkranz, *Leben*, 28–29. Then Schwegler published a version of Lautwein's letter in 1844 in his own journal, *Jahrbücher der Gegenwart*, 675–78 (reprinted in *Dokumente*, 428–30). It has since been widely used as a primary source of information on Hegel's student life—understandably enough, in view of the paucity of other documents on this period. (Kaufmann's *Hegel* includes portions of these standard versions of Lautwein's memoir, 36–37.) To be sure, Hegel scholars have generally resented the rather philistine picture it paints of the philosopher, and have turned a suspicious eye on Lautwein himself. Hoffmeister, for example, has commented on Lautwein's "vanity and narrowness of outlook" (*Dokumente*, 428), and Haering has remarked indignantly that what is really "recht philiströs" is Lautwein's own letter (*Hegel: Sein Wollen und sein Werk*, 2 vols. [Leipzig 1929, 1938], 1:37). It is therefore surely a blot on the legendary thoroughness of German scholarship that until recently no one had bothered to consult the original manuscript of the letter itself. Dieter Henrich has removed this blot and reported exhaustively on the letter in his "Lautwein über Hegel. Ein Dokument zu Hegels Biographie," in *Hegel-Studien*, ed. Nicolin and Pöggeler (Bonn: Bouvier, a continuing series beginning in 1961), vol. 3 (1965): 39–77. Since we

will wish to make a discriminating use of the letter in what follows, it may be worthwhile to summarize some of Henrich's discoveries: First, Lautwein had had a stormy career after graduating first in his class from Tübingen. Finally removed from a pastorate for excess drinking, he devoted himself to the study of the Book of Revelation, publishing two works on the Apocalypse in 1821 and 1825 in which he inveighed against the institutional church and its theology, which had been corrupted by the Enlightenment and by German idealism. Himself a fervent apocalyptist, he took a dim view of Hegel's mature work and influence. Hegel had "dreamed" that man could come "to moral perfection through the help of reason" (quoted by Henrich, 51). Second, the letter was written, not to Schwegler, but to one of Schwegler's fellow students whom Lautwein may have suspected of having some tendencies toward Hegelianism. Third, Schwegler had been equally imaginative in his treatment of facts in the way in which he first reported on Lautwein's alleged remarks and then edited the letter. Henrich offers the first complete publication of Lautwein's letter and puts Schwegler's version in a parallel column (he also includes Schwegler's first article), so that the many liberties Schwegler took become transparently clear. There are significant additions and deletions, and Schwegler sometimes twists Lautwein's words so as to give them quite a different intent. A number of the oft-repeated legends about Hegel's student days can in fact be traced back to Schwegler's own additions; it is difficult to tell whether he invented them or based them more or less on independent oral sources. I shall call attention to some of these dubious legends in what follows.

35. "O Hegel, du saufscht dir gewiss no dei bissle Verstand vollends ab!" *Dokumente*, 433. In another version, the irate gatekeeper says, "Hegel, now you've soused yourself to death! [Hegel, Du saufscht di no zum Tod!]" to which Hegel replies that he has only refreshed himself a bit. *Briefe*, 4:165–66.

36. Betzendörfer, *Hölderlins Studienjahre*, 9. It is not clear what source Betzendörfer is quoting in this allusion to "Ein feste Burg," but it is probably some official document of the Stift. Luther, it will be recalled, thought that "our God" is the "mighty fortress."

37. As Lautwein, it now seems clear, wanted to suggest in his letter. As Henrich points out ("Lautwein," 66–67), Lautwein repeatedly points to a dramatic "Umschwung" (reaction) which he claims took place during Hegel's student years, a reaction against theology and by extension against the Christian faith. After pointing out that Hegel did not always find himself in accord with the cloister statutes and that his morality was better than his legality, Lautwein adds, "which had as a consequence his subsequent reaction. [Schwegler interposes here: Otherwise he was regarded in the Stift as a *lumen obscurum*.] It is also here, as so often the case, that if one traces to its origin something that is brilliant in the world's eyes, one's admiration will be cooled off a bit." But Lautwein does not simply attribute Hegel's *Umschwung* to his rebellion against the cloister statutes. Still more incredibly, he introduces at this point the suggestion that Hegel's transformation resulted from a blow to his pride when he dropped from third in his class to fourth, behind his fellow Stuttgarter Märklin. As Lautwein sees it, this blow, along with his rather lighthearted and "desultory" and "eclectic" attitude toward his studies and his rendezvous with Bacchus,

> was quite certainly the secret source of the transformation which occurred in him after passing through his academic years, for earlier his father's resistance stood in the way. —Philosophical insights it certainly was not as yet. Had he been third in the promotion he would certainly not have seen Berlin, nor would he have given the German fatherland and the encyclopedia anything to say and to write about the absolutist Hegel and about Strauss. At least Märklin, that arch-Kantian and

metaphysician at a time when Hegel had little taste for Kant and metaphysics, did not strive for any such reaction at all.

This bit of tittle-tattle would be scarcely worth recording were it not for the kernels of probable fact it contains and were it not for the confusion that, compounded by Schwegler's editing, it has introduced into Hegel scholarship. Lautwein's position is at least fairly clear: Hegel's academic disappointment helped turn him against theology, which he could not drop immediately because of the objections of his father (that Hegel's father insisted on his remaining in theology even though his interest in it had waned is probably true). In Lautwein's eyes this was the beginning of Hegel's apostasy, but it did not yet take any other definite direction. He simply drifted in an eclectic and desultory way through his university years, and only later became the absolutistic perverter of the faith and the intellectual father of Strauss, the enemy of the faith. Again there is a kernel of probable truth, in the suggestion that Hegel, having no burning theological interest, worked rather aimlessly during his years in the theological Stift. In editing Lautwein's letter, however, and even more in his own earlier paraphrase, Schwegler gave the impression that Hegel was spurred by his disappointment to work with renewed energy, and it was this that directly gave birth to his "new reshaping of philosophy"; he attributes to Hegel's student experience a new goal and the devotion to a new undertaking that Lautwein did not intend.

38. In addition to Lautwein's testimony (see previous note), there is a letter from Hegel's sister Christiane which suggests that after the first two years in the Stift he wanted to transfer to the study of law (*Dokumente,* 394). In a curriculum vitae that Hegel prepared in 1804 (published in Nohl's preface to *HtJ,* vii–ix) he writes that he studied for the pastorate "in accordance with the wish of my parents," though he adds that he "was faithful to the study of theology out of enjoyment, because of its connection with classical literature and philosophy." He also significantly mentions that only after the death of his father, in 1799, did he devote himself fully to philosophy.

39. Betzendörfer, *Hölderlins Studienjahre,* 34.

40. Ibid., 32–33.

41. Quoted in ibid., 54–55.

42. Ibid., 108.

43. *Dokumente,* 175–92.

44. Rosenkranz, *Leben,* 26.

45. *Dokumente,* 175–79.

46. Ibid., 182–84.

47. Ibid., 184–92.

48. Ibid., 180.

49. Ibid., 179.

50. Ibid., 181.

51. *Briefe,* 1:9, written by Hölderlin, July 10, 1794. Most of this letter is translated in *Hegel: The Letters,* trans. Clark Butler and Christiane Seiler, with commentary by Clark Butler (Bloomington: Indiana University Press, 1984), 24, hereafter cited as *Letters.* Not all the letters, particularly those written to Hegel, are included in this single thick volume. But Clark Butler's running commentary makes a valuable contribution to the biography of both the early and the mature Hegel.

52. *Briefe,* 1:18, written by Hegel at the end of January 1795 (*Letters,* 32).

53. *Briefe,* 1:20–21, written by Schelling, February 4, 1795. The "originator" mentioned is Kant. Schelling considers that "the dawn broke with Kant" (21).

54. Letter from Hölderlin to Neuffer, written from Frankfurt, February 16, 1787. Hölderlin, *Sämtliche Werke,* ed. F. Beissner (Stuttgart: W. Kohlhammer, 1954), 1:236.

55. Rosenkranz, *Leben,* 32–33.

56. Ibid., 33.

57. Unhappily, Henrich has cast doubt upon the truth of this appealing and oft-repeated legend ("Lautwein," 74). He shows that it has its sole origin in Schwegler's original article in the *Zeitung für die elegante Welt,* where it is made to appear as one of the recollections of the "dissipated genius" who was an old comrade of Hegel's (Lautwein), and whom Schwegler pretends to have personally interviewed. But there is no mention of any such story in Lautwein's letter, which is the source for other parts of the "interview." Henrich hesitates to regard the story as completely fabricated by Schwegler. It could have stemmed from a report independent of Lautwein's. The planting of a *Freiheitsbaum* was a common enough expression of revolutionary zeal that it would be surprising if there had not been some such goings-on in Tübingen at the time. But the story, as Schwegler tells it, shows such clear signs of poetic license as to cast doubt on it from start to finish. My own suspicion is that the youthful Schwegler, who revered the two giants of German idealism as philosophical oracles of freedom, found the very possibility of their disporting themselves with a *Freiheitsbaum* too irresistible to be omitted, whatever the evidence, a plausible fiction justified as poetic truth. Here is Schwegler's report: "One morning, on a Sunday, it was a beautiful, clear spring morning, Hegel and Schelling are said to have gone with a few friends to a meadow not far from Tübingen and there erected a Liberty Tree. A Liberty Tree! Was that not a prophetic word? In the East, where at that time the founder of Critical Philosophy had wiped dogmatism out, the word liberty was spoken; in the West it was dipped up out of the streams of blood which were poured out in its cause—and now the two founders of the absolute philosophy erect a Liberty Tree." (For the full text of Schwegler's article, see "Lautwein," 57–61; quoted at length, including this passage, in Rosenkranz, *Leben,* 29.)

58. Betzendörfer, *Hölderlins Studienjahre,* 113.

59. Important works on Hegel as a *Stiftler* in Tübingen are: Gunner Aspelin, *Hegels Tübingen Fragment* (Lund, 1933) and Carmelo Lacorde, *Il primo Hegel* (Florence: Sansoni, 1959).

60. In this account we follow, in part, Haering, *Hegel: Sein Wollen und sein Werk,* 1:40–42, 54, and Rosenkranz, *Leben,* 40–41.

61. Lautwein writes of Hegel as a student reading in Rousseau in particular, "and others dominated by similar sentiments, and wherein one rid himself of certain general regulations of the understanding or, as H. said, fetters." Unfortunately, Schwegler omitted the reference to the other writers dominated by similar sentiments and added the word "beständig" regarding Hegel's reading in Rousseau, so that in his version Hegel is said to have read "constantly" in Rousseau. This misrepresentation has led to an exaggeration of the influence of Rousseau on Hegel in Hegel scholarship, as though Rousseau had been the young Hegel's *Organon* rather than one among a number of influences. See Henrich, "Lautwein," 68–69.

62. This view is consonant not only with the internal evidence extant, but with Lautwein's testimony as well. Lautwein makes a special point of reporting that Hegel had not joined Lautwein himself and other students whom he names in an intensive study of Kant. Lautwein says that Hegel, "was never really acquainted with Father Kant in Tübingen" and adds that in private conversation Hegel never had much to say when the discussion turned to Kant or Reinhold or Fichte. Henrich ("Lautwein," 69–70), who wishes to claim for Hegel an early acquaintance with Kant, points out that Lautwein's testimony does not altogether exclude any reading in Kant. Lautwein prides himself upon having been a serious student of Kant at that time, and wants to make it clear that Hegel was not in the same league with him in that respect. Henrich shows further

that the case is again muddied by Schwegler's tampering with Lautwein's testimony. In his original article in the *Zeitung für die elegante Welt,* quoted by Rosenkranz (*Leben,* 28–29) and thus introduced into the Hegel literature, Schwegler gives the impression that Hegel was an altogether indifferent student. He "did little work, did nothing at all in theology, barely read his Kant at best [*höchstens seinen Kant gelesen*], but most of the time played taroc. Although a society of young Kantians was organized in the Stift at that time, Hegel read Rousseau and in the realm of knowledge only conducted aimless excursions." Now Lautwein did not precisely say any of these things. For example Lautwein does mention a number of students who devoted themselves seriously to Kant, and out of this list Schwegler has fabricated a mythical society of young Kantians, though, as Henrich points out, a number of the men on this list did not even overlap as students in the Stift. Had there been such a society, Hegel's refusal or incapacity to join it might indicate something about the state of his Kant scholarship at that time, but there is in fact no evidence that any such society existed.

Still, leaving Schwegler's mischief aside, the burden of proof is still on the side of those who claim that Hegel had an extensive early acquaintance with Kant. Lautwein clearly was unimpressed with Hegel's knowledge of Kant, which on my theory would be a perfectly reasonable attitude for one who prided himself on being a real *Kantkenner* to take toward someone only acquainted with Kant's ethical writings. Henrich points out that Hegel, writing Schelling from Bern in January 1795, speaks of taking up the study of Kant again, thus implying that he had studied Kant earlier. But reading further in the passage in question simply confirms the impression of virtually no acquaintance with and indeed little interest in the theoretical, as opposed to the practical, philosophy of Kant and the Kantians: "For some time I have again devoted myself to the study of the Kantian philosophy. . . . I am just as little acquainted with the newer efforts to penetrate into the deeper depths as I am with the Reinholdian, since these speculations seem to me to be of more direct significance only for the theoretical reason, rather than being of great applicability to more generally useful concepts. I therefore understand these efforts no better so far as their purpose is concerned, I only guess at it more obscurely" (*Briefe,* 1:16). Here Hegel, unlike Schelling, seems both ignorant and a bit unconcerned about issues arising out of Kant's treatment of theoretical reason. One may not wish to take this statement at face value. Hegel was a personally modest man, and may in part be deferring to Schelling in this matter. Certainly it does not follow that he knows nothing at all about the theoretical philosophy of Kant and his followers. But it does seem safe to say that he was not yet deeply enough into it for it to make much impression on him.

As Henrich points out, Rosenkranz reports "extensive" excerpts from "Kant's works" (as well as Locke's and Hume's) among Hegel's papers from his student days ("Lautwein," 14). Many of Hegel's notebooks which were available to Rosenkranz in the 1840s have unfortunately meanwhile been lost; most of them were reportedly thrown in a stove (*Dokumente,* vii), and there are no Kant excerpts included in what is left. So we cannot be sure just how extensive these excerpts were, or out of which works they were taken. Rosenkranz does immediately add: "The study of Kant's *critique of reason* [*Vernunftkritik*] definitely begins at least in the year 1789." The impression is given that the "extensive" excerpts are from the first critique, though Rosenkranz does not expressly say so, and one must be cautious on the point. Rosenkranz was convinced of the essential unity of classical German philosophy, and bent every effort to establish as much continuity as possible between Kant and Hegel. In a later passage he is more explicit. He says that shortly after ending his student days Hegel excerpted from the *Critique of Practical Reason,* with comments, "as he had also done earlier in the Stift from the *Critique of*

Pure Reason" (*Leben,* 86–87). But even if we infer that Hegel conducted studies in the first critique as early as 1789, it does not follow that he penetrated very far into it. It is not uncommon, after all, for students to give up on *The Critique of Pure Reason.* On the other hand Kant's philosophy was already widely discussed in other works—Adikes' Kant Bibliography (*Philosophical Review,* 1893–95) already numbers more than one thousand titles on Kant by 1793! (Henrich, "Lautwein," 69–70). One must no doubt reckon with some indirect influence of Kant's theoretical philosophy on the young Hegel. There are, for example, two excerpts from Hegel's notebooks dating from 1788 that refer to the teachings of the first critique, one by J. A. Ulrich on freedom and necessity, one by A. W. Rehberg on the relation of metaphysics to religion (*Dokumente,* 149–66).

What seems decisive, however, so far as substantial influence is concerned, is the fact that Hegel's own early writings through the 1790s, which allude repeatedly to Kant, do not contain a single reference that cannot be derived from Kant's works on ethics and the late work on religion (*Die Religion innerhalb der Grenzen der blossen Vernunft,* 1793). So I believe we must conclude with Haering (*Hegel: Sein Wollen und sein Werk,* 1:55) that it is impossible to establish any substantial, direct influence of Kant's theoretical philosophy on Hegel during this period. Haering even suggests that the influence of Kant's practical philosophy on the young Hegel was more indirect (e.g., through Schiller) than direct. But in *Glauben und Wissen,* published in 1802 in his and Schelling's *Kritisches Journal der Philosophie,* Hegel directly cites Kant's first and third critiques.

63. This mystical dimension in Hegel's thinking gets major attention in Cyril O'Regan, *The Heterodox Hegel* (Albany: State University of New York Press, 1994). O'Regan's rhetorically dazzling and occasionally bewildering work is a major engagement, in the mode of speculative theology, with virtually the entire body of Hegel's writings, from the 1790s through the 1820s. In the interpretive tradition of Iwan Iljin's *Die Philosophie Hegels als kontemplative Gotteslehre* (Bern: Francke, 1946), O'Regan places Hegel in lifelong conversation, direct or subliminal, with the most esoteric spiritual writers within or at the margins of Christian speculation about the divine over the entire course of Christian history, addressing issues on the very frontiers of their thinking. Perhaps he exaggerates the centrality of this conversation in Hegel's own thinking. But at the very least he shows that Hegel's early attraction to mystical ideas was no ephemeral moment in his development.

64. Fr. H. Jacobi, *Über die Lehre des Spinoza in Briefen an Herrn Moses Mendelssohn* (Breslau, 1785), 12.

65. *Briefe,* 4:48.

66. According to Betzendörfer (*Hölderlins Studienjahre,* 107–11), Hölderlin was an orthodox Christian during his earlier period in the Stift, and was for a time very impressed with Storr's apologetics. But by the time he wrote his first fragmentary version of *Hyperion,* published in Schiller's *Neuer Thalia* in 1794 (volume 4, dated 1793) but begun already while he was still a student in Tübingen, inclinations toward a kind of nature-pantheism are clear. Near the end of the fragment, Hyperion hears Nature calling to him on a soundless autumn evening: "From inside the grove it seemed to admonish me, out of the depths of the earth and the sea to call to me, Why do you love me not? From now on I was no longer able to think anything that I had thought before, the world had become holier to me but more mysterious." In a later version (though not yet the final version), written in 1795, the poet declares: "I know that there, where the beautiful form of Nature proclaims the present Divinity to us, we ourselves ensoul the world with our souls." Yet Hölderlin never simply rejected theism, and continued to honor Christianity as the religion of human love; he still considered the possibility of becoming a pastor, in order to cultivate not so much faith but love in his flock.

67. *Briefe,* 1:22.

68. *Briefe,* 1:19–20. Kaufmann's *Hegel* translates the relevant passage, 302.

69. *Kritik der reinen Vernunft,* B XXX.

70. *Critique of Practical Reason,* trans. Lewis White Beck (New York: Liberal Arts Press, 1956), 127. See *Kritik der reinen Vernunft,* B XXIV–XXXV; *Kritik der praktischen Vernunft,* Part 1, Book 2, chap. 2, §§III–IX; *Kritik der Urteilskraft,* appendix, §§86–91.

71. *Briefe,* 1:12. Written by Hegel in Bern, Christmas Eve, 1794 (*Letters,* 28).

72. *Briefe,* 1:13–14. Written by Schelling, Epiphany, 1795 (*Letters,* 29).

73. *Briefe,* 1:15.

74. Ibid., 1:16–17 (*Letters,* 31).

75. *Briefe,* 17 (*Letters,* 31).

For a much more detailed treatment of Kant's moral recuperation of the idea of God, the Fichtean development of it, the efforts of the Tübingen theologians to exploit it, and the way Hegel came to terms with it, see the first chapter of Walter Jaeschke, *Die Vernunft in der Religion: Studien zur Grundlegung der Religionsphilosophie Hegels* (Stuttgart: Friedrich Frommann, 1986); translated as *Reason in Religion: The Foundations of Hegel's Philosophy of Religion,* by J. Michael Stewart and Peter C. Hodgson (Berkeley and Los Angeles: University of California Press, 1990). This magnum opus by one of the most thorough and astute contemporary interpreters of Hegel's philosophy of religion is a critical history of the speculative idea of God in four connected chapters, each a monograph on its subject: the formulation, diffusion, and rejection of Kant's moral postulation of the idea; the foundation of Hegel's speculative philosophy of religion in Jena; its full development in Hegel's Berlin lectures; and the post-Hegelian controversy over its viability. This is critical philosophical history of a high order.

76. *Briefe,* 1:18 (*Letters,* 32).

77. *Briefe,* 1:21–22. Written by Schelling, February 4, 1795 (*Letters,* 32–33). What Schelling seems to have in mind in the last few hopelessly contracted phrases is the following argument: Insofar as human beings are confined in the finite world of empirical objects in space and time (the parameters of theoretical philosophy), they cannot be transported to the sphere of the unconditional. They can only be related to the unconditional morally, by unconditional obedience to the moral law (the sphere of practical reason). But assuming that reality ultimately contains a moral order corresponding to their unconditional obedience, and that empirical existence contains no guarantee that such obedience will bring happiness, immortality must be postulated by practical reason if there are to be any grounds for thinking that happiness is the necessary consequence of obedience.

78. See Spinoza's *Ethics,* proposition 29.

79. Schelling, *Über die Möglichkeit einer Form der Philosophie überhaupt* (Tübingen, 1793).

80. *Briefe,* 1:23. Written by Hegel, April 16, 1795 (*Letters,* 35).

81. *Briefe,* 1:24 (*Letters,* 35–36).

82. For an admirably lucid and concise treatment of the mutual intellectual influence of the three friends, against the background of Fichte, Kant, and Schiller, see Franz Nauen, "Revolution, Idealism, and Human Freedom: Schelling, Hölderlin and Hegel and the Crisis of Early German Idealism" (Ph.D. diss., Harvard, 1969).

83. *Philosophische Briefe über Dogmatismus und Kritizismus,* in *Philosophical Journal,* ed. Fr. I. Niethammer (Neustrelitz, 1795), 2d Band., 3 Heft, and 3d Band., 3 Heft.

84. *Briefe,* 1:33. Written by Hegel, August 30, 1795 (*Letters,* 43).

85. *Briefe,* 1:33 (*Letters,* 43).

86. "Das älteste Systemprogramm des deutschen Idealismus. Ein handschriftlicher Fund, mitgeteilt von Franz Rosenzweig." *Sitzungsberichte der Heidelberger Akademie der Wissenschaften,* Philos. hist. Klasse, Jahrgang 1917, 5. Abh. Reprinted in *Dokumente,* 219–21 (with a note regarding the document, 455), and also in the collected works of both Hölderlin and Schelling.

87. Rosenzweig identified the handwriting as Hegel's, identifying it as a copy of a lost original by Schelling, who had written it under the considerable influence of Hölderlin. W. Böhm attributed the authorship to Hölderlin (*Dt. Vierteljahresschrift für Literaturwissenschaft und Geistesgeschichte,* 1926, 339ff.), but this attribution was attacked and Rosenzweig's view defended by Ludwig Strauss (ibid., 1927, 679ff.).

The claim that Hegel was the author of the Programme was categorically staked out by Otto Pöggeler, one of the most meticulous modern Hegel scholars, in "Hegel, der Verfasser des ältesten Systemprogramms des deutschen Idealismus," *Hegel-Studien* (Bonn, 1969), 4:17–32. Pöggeler argues not only that there are ideas in the *Systemprogramm* that are reminiscent of Hegel's writings in Bern, but also that there are some ideas in it that are at variance with works Schelling had published in 1796. He concludes that Hegel must have written it, probably in Frankfurt early in 1797, under the influence of Hölderlin.

Harris had completed his reconstruction of Hegel's early development without thinking "of reclaiming the fragment for Hegel." But Pöggeler's article convinced him, and it seemed to him that the Programme indeed confirmed the lines of his own reconstruction. "The fact that the fragment . . . fits neatly into its place in my account is—I hope—an argument for the essential soundness both of my views and of Pöggeler's thesis. But if the missing letter or rough draft were to turn up and the sceptics were to be vindicated, nothing in my general account of Hegel's development would be affected in the slightest" (*Hegel's Development,* 249 n). Thus covering all bets, Harris inserted an appendix (249–57) advancing additional arguments for Hegel's authorship.

88. Pöggeler and Harris sift some of the distinctive ideas of the Programme with some care, but pay remarkably little attention to the no less distinctive style in which these ideas are expressed. Not merely the assertive use of the first-person singular and the exuberant claim to be revealing ideas never before imagined, but also the whole declamatory ring of the piece reminds one of Schelling and is very foreign to Hegel's characteristic ways of expressing himself. During this time, to be sure, Hegel did write a mystical poem in Hölderlinian style ("Eleusis"), so it is conceivable that he might have assumed a Schellingian rhetorical persona for this piece; but only barely conceivable. On the sheer content of ideas alone, furthermore, the situation is perhaps more uncertain than it is with respect to style. The ideas of all three young men, and particularly Hegel, were so fluid at that time that it is not possible to say with any certainty just what any one of them might or might not have written, say, on some particular moonlit night. The debate over authorship assumes far too much crystallization in the thought of all three. Still, the *kind* of project being launched in this Programme, as well as its prominent motifs, are much more akin to Schelling's interests at this time than to those of either Hegel or Hölderlin.

89. Pöggeler acknowledges ("Hegel, der Verfasser," 28) that Hegel is speaking for his friends as much as for himself, and has to appeal again and again to the influence of one or the other to make the attribution of the Programme to Hegel plausible. Harris, on the other hand (*Hegel's Development,* 253), does point out that the influence generally ascribed to Hölderlin need not be assumed, since the central position given the Idea of beauty could as well have been derived from Kant's third *Critique* or Schiller's *Aesthetic Letters.*

90. One can see how far "beyond" Kant the Programme has moved from the fact that the postulate of freedom, which for Kant was a derivative of morality and an outermost possibility of the speculative employment of practical reason, is here made the axiomatic foundation of the new philosophy. See Pöggeler ("Hegel, der Verfasser," 21). As he points out, "In accordance with the Fichtean rootage of the whole of philosophy in practical philosophy, now all ideas are postulates." Pöggeler goes on to suggest that the attempt to establish a metaphysics on the moral grounds of Kant's *Postulatenlehre* is the basis on which these young men appropriated Spinoza's project: "Was not philosophy for Spinoza an ethics? Schelling, in his publications as well as in his correspondence with Hegel, had committed himself to Spinoza's concept of philosophy as ethics, and tried to show why philosophy was ethics for Spinoza: philosophy was ethics and was to be so again, because philosophy proceeded from a practical purpose" (22). This move surely stands Spinoza on his head, as it does Kant, since for Spinoza ethical conclusions proceeded from his metaphysics rather than the reverse. Perhaps it is true, as Pöggeler adds, that "only such philosophizing was interesting for the young Hegel." But still it was Schelling and not Hegel who early in 1795 announced his intention to work out "an ethic *à la* Spinoza" (51 above). And while it may be true that "this engagement with Kant *and his agreement with Schelling* is in Hegel's Bern period the genuine 'esoteric' center of his thinking" (Pöggeler, "Hegel, der Verfasser," 22; my emphasis), still it was already the exoteric center of Schelling's own thought. Strange grounds for claiming that Hegel and not Schelling was the author of the Programme!

Pöggeler's bold stroke of claiming the Programme for Hegel was the occasion for devoting a conference to the document (the Hegel-Tage of 1969 in Villigst) issuing in Beiheft 9 of *Hegel-Studien: Das älteste Systemprogramm: Studien zur Frühgeschichte des deutschen Idealismus*, ed. Rüdiger Bubner (Bonn: Bouvier, 1973). This fine volume of essays shows that the question of authorship was as much in dispute as ever, while most of the essays deftly skirt this issue to discuss questions regarding the early development of German idealism that are rightly regarded as of greater philosophical and historical interest. Taken together, the essays do supply the Programme its context, if not its author.

91. Translated from *Dokumente*, 219–21. Harris has also translated the Programme (*Hegel's Development*, 510–12), rendering some passages differently than I have.

Regarding the clause in the final paragraph, "die Mythologie muss philosophisch werden, und das Volk vernünftig," Ludwig Strauss plausibly suggests that the "und" in the surviving manuscript is a miscopying of "um." In that case the sentence would read: "The mythology must become philosophical in order [to make] the people rational, and the philosophy must become mythological in order to make the philosopher sensuous." The nice grammatical parallelism does improve the sense. It is surprising that Harris (*Hegel's Development*, 511 n) accepts this reading, however, since Hegel would not have been likely to make such an error unless he were copying a draft written by someone else.

92. *Kritik der Urteilskraft* (1790), Book 1, "Analytic of the Beautiful," especially §§12–16.

93. Ibid., §§18–22.

94. In Pöggeler's discussion of this motif—the new mythology that will unite the corporate consciousness of the masses with the wisdom of the wise—he presents his strongest arguments for claiming the Programme for Hegel. ("Hegel, der Verfasser," 26–27). Not only does he point out the affinity of the Programme with Hegel's thinking in this matter, but he also argues that Schelling's preoccupation with mythology, both in his earliest writings and in those he published as part of the Romantic circle in Jena, has quite a different orientation. That is certainly true of the "historical" view of mythology that appears in Schelling's works before the Programme. But in such a rest-

lessly energetic thinker as the young Schelling we would expect a programmatic sketch to anticipate work soon to come rather than what has already appeared, and in his *System des transzendentalen Idealismus* (1800), written in Jena, there are many passages that remind us of the Programme. For example, in the conclusion to Part 6, §3 (Hamburg: Meiner 1957, 298), the point is made that philosophy and the other arts and sciences were born of poetry (in the same broad sense of the term as in the Programme) and to poetry shall return, with mythology as the mediating form that both attended the birth and can be expected to bring about the return. But for the latter a new mythology will be needed.

95. That is more or less the way Pöggeler seems to construe the Programme's remarks concerning the state, though I cannot imagine that he would have so interpreted them if he were not trying to make the case for Hegel's authorship. Both he and Harris, recognize, of course, that this section of the Programme is the one most difficult to ascribe to Hegel. But they undertake to solve the problem in quite different ways. Pöggeler argues that the "mechanical" state condemned by the Programme is the autocratic "modern state" that atomizes its citizens, not the republic of classical antiquity. Therefore it is not the state as such that is being condemned. That distinction is certainly true to Hegel's own thinking, but the Programme denounces the state categorically, and not simply the debased modern state. There is "keine Idee" of the state, "*jeder* Staat *muss* freie Menschen als mechanisches Räderwerk behandeln" (my emphasis). The distinction Hegel made, early and late, between an authentic state and the debased machine state that reduces its citizenry to an atomized aggregate is precisely what is lacking in the Programme.

Harris recognizes that the Programme is speaking of the state as such. He states the problem clearly, showing in some detail that this view is at odds with what Hegel wrote about the state both immediately before and immediately after the writing of the Programme (251). So how can Hegel have written the Programme? "All that we have to do is to find a plausible reason why Hegel should momentarily and for his present purpose have accepted the 'machine State' as the State *sic et simpliciter*. And such a reason is not far to seek. For we know that the 'machine State' which he attacks in the German constitution manuscripts is the State of Fichte in theory and of Prussia in practice." The appearance of Fichte's *Grundlage des Naturrechts* at Easter, 1796, may have led Hegel, in reaction, to have set out "to show that the whole structure of contemporary political thought must be discarded." This, in turn, may have led to the new theoretical constructions that we find in the Programme. "It is no wonder, therefore, if the excitement of his new discovery combined with his critical reaction to Fichte and his jaundiced observation of the political scene to upset his intellectual balance a little, and cause him to say things that were valid only within a conceptual scheme which he could not finally accept." Harris immediately attempts to soften this conclusion: "It is clear that he does not really accept it even here. For he says that the treatment of free men as cogs must cease; and some kind of political life will exist even when we have 'gone beyond the State'" (citations from Harris, *Hegel's Development*, 251–52). But it is the *state* that is to cease, and not simply its mistreatment of free human beings: "das soll er nicht; also soll er *aufhören*"; the pronoun in each clause clearly has the same referent, "jeder Staat." And there is no hint in the Programme that *any* political order will survive as such. So we are left with the hypothesis that the Programme represents, in its view of the state, what Harris is otherwise so reluctant to attribute to the young Hegel: a momentary aberration that radically breaks the continuity of his intellectual development.

II

The Problem of the Positivity of the Gospel in Hegel's Early Writings

It was a common practice in Hegel's time for young German university graduates to spend some time in the post of private tutor to the children of wealthy families. They lived comfortably enough in the homes of their patrons, generally taking their meals with the family, but young men of high spirit commonly found this position of genteel servitude uncongenial. The advantage of the arrangement from their point of view was that it gave them the opportunity to continue their studies on their own, until they were ready to accept a more demanding and elevated position, for example, in church, school, university, or government service. Hegel suffered this indenture for a biblical seven years, with a family in Bern from autumn 1793 to autumn 1796, and with another family in Frankfurt, from the beginning of 1797 to the end of 1800, complaining to his friends all the while, particularly while he was in Switzerland. He was liberated through a modest inheritance from his father, who died in 1799; only then did he have enough financial independence to begin casting about for an academic post.

But the years in Bern and Frankfurt were productive. Despite his complaints about lack of time he read and excerpted diligently and began seriously plying his pen to working over some of his own ideas. He did not write voluminously, certainly did not come close to matching Schelling's output during this period, and he did not publish what he had written. But he wrote fairly steadily, and while his writing clearly reflects his reading he was no longer passive, no longer content with absorbing. He was beginning to think his own thoughts. He may have hoped that some of the results would turn out to be publishable; we have seen in his correspondence with Schelling from Bern that he hoped to join his friend publicly in the cause, but we have also seen that he did not think highly of his earlier efforts, and the primary purpose of his writing was undoubtedly self-clarification. Yet these early works are of great importance to us, in understanding the sources of Hegel's philosophy. The issues with which he was wrestling in them pose many of the most important questions that he sought to answer in his mature work. Nohl collected the early works that are of most importance for our particular purposes in his 1907 edition of *Hegels theologische Jugendschriften*. He did not include everything that Hegel wrote during this period,[1] but he collected those works that deal at all directly with religion: A set of five fragments to which Nohl gave the title, *Folk-Religion and Christianity*; three extended essays, on *The Life of Jesus, The Positivity of the Christian Religion,* and *The Spirit of Christianity and Its Fate*; a *Fragment of a System* composed in 1800; and thirteen miscellaneous fragments.[2] The earliest of these miscellaneous fragments and the first fragment on Folk Religion actually date from Hegel's student days in Tübingen, as is evident from a rather dramatic change in Hegel's handwriting when he moved from there to Bern. There are also constant changes in Hegel's point of view, some subtle and some dramatic, during the period of seven or eight years in which these writings were composed. If our purpose were to trace Hegel's intellectual biography in detail, it would be necessary to discuss these texts fragment by fragment.[3] But since we have no such purpose in view it will be sufficient for us to notice only the more important developments, treating the earlier fragments in particular as a unit and thus ignoring the shifts in purpose and point of view that take place in them. For throughout this period Hegel is getting his bearings, conducting thought experiments, crystallizing and reformulating his ideas. What is of primary importance for our purposes in this material are not so much the convolutions of his thinking as certain seminal concepts and issues that begin to emerge with varying degrees of clarity from these convolutions and deeply affect his later religious thought. Some facets of his ideas appear more clearly here, where they still created vexatious problems for Hegel, than after he considered that he had solved these problems.

1. Toward a "Living" Folk Religion: Some Polarities

We begin by exploring some of the fundamental terms employed in the earliest of these writings, in the five fragments on "Folk Religion and Christianity," and in the four miscellaneous fragments that date from the same period (1792–94).[4] In these earliest and most fragmentary reflections we find Hegel's thinking revolving around several pairs of contrasting concepts, experimenting with them and trying by means of each pair to clarify some basic religious problems and to deal critically with an otherwise indigestible mass of material. We will be concerned less with his particular opinions during this time than with the concepts associated with these paired terms, since these concepts, in revised forms, continue to guide his thinking long after he has outgrown the youthful opinions expressed through them. In formulating each of them he makes use of ideas already current among established writers of the period. But the tracing of precise influences need not detain us in most cases, because what he borrows is always adapted quite freely and eclectically, as a point of departure for pursuing his own ends. Each pair of terms in fact flows through the others, is in some cases even absorbed, as though the dialectical method were already unconsciously stirring in him as a kind of reflex. In any case we will sort out some of the polarities that emerge in these brief private reflections, without puzzling very much about obscurities or inconsistencies of detail.

Living versus Dead Religion

The first of these polarities we may mention briefly, by way of introducing the others. Though Hegel only touches explicitly on this distinction in a few passages (e.g., *HtJ,* 6, 36ff., 61), it is implicit in all his early thinking: Religions are born, they have periods of vitality, and they can die—usually a lingering death, their vitality ebbing away. For already in the earliest fragments Hegel treats religion as a historical phenomenon, intrinsically related to the cultural life of a people. He sometimes draws rough analogies between the life of a people (a *Volk*) and the maturation of an individual. A religion that was appropriate to the naive childhood of a culture, upon which its spontaneous piety and imagination may have been nurtured, may simply be outgrown as it becomes more sophisticated and faces more complicated problems. In that case the religion may die. There is loss in its death, which may be regarded with sadness, but may on the other hand be a liberation. There is also the possibility, by no means merely hypothetical, that it may hang on in its death like the albatross, as an oppressive burden. At the same time, a religion that is itself capable of maturation may remain alive, and not merely in the sense that it persists. The meaning of religious vitality is disclosed in some of the other concepts we will explore, and indeed this motif issues finally in the exalted life-mysticism that we shall find Hegel developing a few years later. For the contrast between living and dead religion is both an instrument of historical analysis and a critical perspective on the religion that dominates a society, including Hegel's own.

"Religion" versus "Theology"

This second distinction, again, never appears in isolation from other, more carefully drawn distinctions. Yet one has a keen sense that it plays a primary role, at least in Hegel's attitude toward his material, from the beginning. After three years of Storr's theological lectures, he hasn't a favorable word to say about theology. Yet he is never simply antireligious, nor even anti-Christian, sharply critical though he is toward many facets of historic Christianity. He is, for example, impatient with any highly elaborated system of dogmatics, since it is necessarily so remote, in virtue of its very complexity, from concrete experiences or problems of living. "It flatters the human understanding," he says, "to contemplate its own work: a great, high edifice containing the knowledge of God and the knowledge of human duties and of nature." People delight in adding to it and ornamenting it over the years. But the more imposing it becomes, the less possible it is for anyone to claim that it actually belongs to him.

> A person who merely copies this construction, who merely assembles it for himself, who has not built a cottage of his own to live in, by himself and out of his own resources, . . . where he is completely at home, each stone of which he has turned over in his hands and set in place, even if he has not mined it himself—such a copier is a bookish literalist [*Buchstabenmensch*] who has not himself lived and moved. (*HtJ*, 16–17)

A man who builds himself a palace after the plan of the great edifice "lives in it like Louis XIV in Versailles, he hardly knows all the chambers of his estate, and occupies only a very small closet."[5] The man in the cottage is better off, who knows the story of every nook and cranny—who respecting all that he knows or thinks or believes can refer to his own experience and can declare, with Nathan's Recha, "How! where? why I learned it" (*HtJ*, 17; see also Chapter 1). "Religion" can help people build the cottage that is their own to live in, while "theology" builds only its remote and grandiose monuments. However, as Hegel acknowledges in another fragment, if people concerned with the immediacies of existence undertake to explore Christianity they are immediately challenged by the theologian: How can you know what Christianity is unless you have read my Compendium? But the Compendia do not agree among themselves, and each seems bent on solving problems that it itself has raised—Hegel wishes to steer clear of "the error of those who give people the itch in order to be able to scratch them"—so Compendium theology is of little use to those who seriously want to know what Christianity has to say to them. They must turn to the New Testament and to those generally accepted teachings that are "more than the doctrines of a system" (*HtJ*, 60–61). Real religious concern has its own criteria, drawn from the interests and entanglements of common life; it does not need any criteria that are tailored to meet the specialized interests of theologians.

Just what these religious criteria are, indeed, Hegel's meaning when he talks about "religion," remains a bit nebulous during this period. There is to be sure a deceptive appearance of clarity in some of his attempts to define genuine religion, since he commonly linked it with the cultivation of morality and expressed this link in generally Kantian terminology. The influence of Kant's moralizing view of religion is at least vaguely present throughout these fragments, becoming, as we shall see, very pronounced in the passages written last. For example, in connection with the above-mentioned critique of Compendium theology, which came from one of these later passages, he speaks this way of what "religion" should do: "The effect of religion is the strengthening of ethical motivations through the idea of God as moral lawgiver—and the satisfaction of the concerns of our practical reason with respect to the ultimate purpose which it establishes for us, the highest good."[6]

Even in earlier passages, in which the language is not so obviously Kantian, we often find him giving "religion" this fundamentally moral meaning. Yet his Kantianism is never quite rigorous. Religion does not so much lead people to consider abstract moral laws, but rather forms their experience of life. It engages the passions and imagination by means that a strict Kantian would consider a dubious basis for upright conduct. We will examine this infusion of practical reason with "heart" in more detail below. But it should be said at once that young Hegel had as little use for casuistical calculations of our ethical duty as he had for compendious theology. It is too rarified, too distant from the urgencies and from the pathos of life as it is experienced. On the same grounds, he had even less use for the concocted consolations that clever theologians sometimes offer the stricken and the bereaved. A living religion, and that part of any of the historic religions which remains vital, will indeed have its "teachings" or "maxims," but these will be simple and few and will touch experience closely. Their profundity will consist in the fact that they must be lived to be fully understood, and not in the scope they furnish for theoretical elaboration. The most sublime teachings

> seem indeed only to be the property of a few tried and proven people who through long experience have worked their way through to wisdom, and in these they have become not a shaky conviction but a firm faith, precisely in the situations in which it ought to support them. Of this sort is especially the faith in a wise and benevolent providence, with which, when it is living and appropriate, the entire devotion to God is bound up. (*HtJ*, 21–22)

Hegel's remarks about faith in providence in this context are worth pursuing further, not only because they best illustrate his sense of a genuinely religious faith, but also because this confidence in providence is perhaps the deepest "religious" strain in Hegel's life and thought from his early days to the end of his career. Neither later nor at this time, however, does this confidence imply supernaturalistic doctrines. He did later seem to think that the meaning of providence could be philosophically elaborated, and even that the course of history itself, despite all appearances to the contrary, provided a kind of indirect proof of its essential truth. But here he stresses its elemental simplicity as an unconditional personal faith, and insists that only this, in the "wise," can prevail in the face of all impatience, disappointed hopes, and calamities. He even suggests that the effort to buttress this faith in providence by appeal to reason or evidence or divine revelation, can only have the effect of weakening it. Experience shows, he says, how quickly this faith can evaporate in the heat of calamity among the very people who have been taught it as a chief doctrine of Christianity with every assurance that theological ingenuity could devise. Indeed, the sufferer is showered with such a torrent of consolations and blessings in adversity "that in the end one may feel sorry that one does not have to lose a mother or father or be stricken with blindness every eight days."[7] But the sufferer is not really convinced by such contrivances, nor is faith in providence served.

> As soon as we do not content ourselves in this matter with laying the finger on the mouth and falling silent, full of holy reverence, then nothing is more common than that a presumptuous inquisitiveness is given leave to attempt mastering its ways also, a tendency which is becoming strengthened, though to be sure not among common people, through the many idealistic ideas now prevailing. All of which has little to do with furthering any devotion to the will of God or any contentment. (*HtJ*, 22–23)

Hegel adds for comparison a discussion of the way in which religious faith functioned among the Greeks, who are described as attributing what is good to the gods and the evil to Nemesis. This faith, he says, was

> built upon the deep moral requirement [*Bedürfnis*] of reason, gently moved through the warm breath of the sentiments, not upon the cold conviction, deduced from isolated cases, that everything will turn out for the best—a view that can never be brought into true life. On the other hand misfortune was misfortune among them; pain was pain. They could not brood about the

purpose in what had happened and could not be changed, for their μοιρα, their ἀναγκαια τυχη was blind. But they then also willingly subjected themselves to this necessity with all possible resignation. . . . This faith, since it includes a regard for the current of natural necessity and at the same time the conviction that people are ruled by the gods according to moral laws, seems humanly appropriate to the sublimity of deity, and to the weakness, the dependence of people's nature, and to their limited perspective. (*HtJ*, 23)

Despite the admiration that always warms his references to the Greeks, what Hegel seems to be commending here is not so much the details of Greek belief as such, but rather the immediacy with which life was brought to bear on the form of their faith and with which faith in turn was brought to bear upon the realities of life. This immediacy of bearing is what he found lacking in so much traditional Christian theology, and particularly in the rationalistic theologizing of the Enlightenment.

As soon as there is a partition between life and teachings, or merely a separation and wide distance between the two, the suspicion arises that the form of the religion contains an error. Either it is concerned too much with trafficking in words or it makes exaggerated, sanctimonious demands on people, opposing their natural needs, the drives of a well-ordered sensuous life [*Sinnlichkeit*], τη σωφροσυνη; or it does both at once. (*HtJ*, 26; see also 14–15)

Subjective versus Objective Religion

This distinction is the first that we find Hegel developing in these writings in any systematic way. The distinction between theology and religion was first formulated in terms of this more carefully drawn distinction. Hegel sometimes seems to speak of subjective and objective religion as though they were two different kinds of religion altogether, but this way of treating the distinction is secondary. According to the primary meaning of the distinction the subjective and the objective are rather dimensions or poles that are generally present in any living religion. Often, especially at first, Hegel identified objective religion with a body of doctrines and moral teachings, treated it, that is, as the virtual equivalent of "theology" (*HtJ,* 6, 8, 48, 355). Its objectivity in this case consists in the fact that it can be formulated in propositions, discursively treated, taught as a body of presumptive knowledge in church and school. It will be obvious from the foregoing discussion that Hegel was suspicious of objective religion in this sense. But implicit in his various discussions of objective religion is a wider reference. It includes, in fact, all of the outwardly definable or observable forms of a religion: its doctrines, but also its traditions, its ceremonies and festivals, its institutions and its formal relationships to the state and other institutions, its organization and priesthood. Any public religion clearly has this "objective" side (*HtJ,* 20ff., 62ff.). As such, it is always in danger of degenerating into "fetishism" [*Fetischglauben, Fetisch-dienst*], in which "merely the works, the mechanism remains, and the spirit evaporates" (*HtJ,* 20–21, 26). But Hegel does not seem finally to imagine that a socially animating religion, a folk religion, could dispense with such objective forms altogether. What is crucial is that the objective religion directly express and kindle the vital center of faith, the "subjective" religion that is alive in the experience and motivations of the believers. The question then arises whether subjective religion is necessarily good. But let us suspend this question until we have penetrated further into the meaning of subjective religion.

Certainly it is not directly specifiable in the way objective religion is, just because Hegel is attempting in this notion to express what is essential and alive in a religious faith. Objective forms can be "observed," in both senses of the word, without the observer being in any serious way devout. But people who make this point are generally hard put to identify exactly the all-important factor that is missing in objective descriptions. Hegel himself follows the usual practice of resorting finally to the familiar rhetoric of piety, the language of the heart.

> Subjective religion manifests itself only in sentiments and actions. If I say of a person that he has religion that does not mean that he has a wide knowledge of the subject, but that his heart feels the deeds, the wonders, the nearness of deity, that it discerns, it sees God in his natural world and in the destinies of human beings. He prostrates himself before God, thanks him and praises him in his deeds; he does not regard his action merely according to whether it is good or clever, but its motive, often

> the strongest, is to him also the thought that it is well pleasing
> to God. When some pleasure comes, or a happy event, he immedi-
> ately directs a glance to God and thanks him for it. Subjective
> religion is alive, an efficacy in the inner core of the being and
> an activity outwardly. (*HtJ*, 6–7)

Since subjective religion is such an intensely personal matter, the objective religion to which a group of people give formal allegiance will
always be modified in one way or another as it is internalized in the
life of each individual in the group. Indeed, the most fundamental
religious motivations are modulated according to the propensities and
limitations of each individual. So, on the one hand, subjective religion
is an individualizing and sometimes limiting factor (*HtJ*, 7). Yet on the
other hand when it is properly developed Hegel finds in it that universal
basis, so earnestly sought and so variously proclaimed by religious
thinkers of the Enlightenment, underlying all the (objective) diversities
of historic religions.

> Subjective religion is among good people pretty much the same,
> regardless of what coloring the objective may have—"What
> makes me a Christian in your eyes makes you in mine a Jew,"
> says Nathan—because religion is an affair of the heart, which
> often behaves inconsistently with the dogmas that its under-
> standing or memory accept. (*HtJ*, 10; see also Chapter 1)

Deeper than the diversity of dogma and custom that divides people
is a community of the heart, at least among the good. But this qualification of goodness does not essentially dissipate the universal humanity
of the bond. At this point we find Hegel appealing to something like
the doctrine of "moral sense" developed by Shaftesbury and his followers, an original, instinctual propensity that to be sure is not in itself
sufficient to make people good, but which gives them a natural suscepti-
bility to virtuous influences. Moral teaching has an ally, as well as
various antagonists, in human nature itself.

> Nature has implanted in everyone a seed of the more refined
> sentiments [*Empfindungen*] proceeding from morality, it has
> placed in them a sense for what is moral, for a further purpose
> than mere sensuousness; that these beautiful seeds may not be
> choked, that from them an actual receptivity for moral ideas and

sentiments may arise, that is a matter of training and upbringing. Religion is not the first thing that can fasten roots in the
disposition; it must meet with a cultivated soil in which it can
first flourish.[8]

Here the seeds of morality are given a primacy, more elemental than
religion in human nature. But it is clear that subjective religion re-
sponds directly to these instinctual moral propensities, nurturing them
and being nourished by them. Hegel goes on:

> Everything depends on subjective religion. This has a genuinely
> true worth. The theologians like to argue over dogmas, over
> that which belongs to objective religion, over the more precise
> definitions of these principles. But every religion has as its basis
> just a few fundamental principles which in the various religions
> are merely more or less modified, distorted, or exhibited more
> or less pure, and these produce the basis for all the faith, all the
> hopes, which religion offers us for our aid. When I speak of
> religion I abstract altogether from all the scientific or rather
> metaphysical knowledge of God, of our relation and that of the
> whole world to him, etc. Such a knowledge, with which merely
> the calculating [räsonierende] understanding is preoccupied, is
> theology, no longer religion. I include the knowledge of God and
> immortality in religion here only insofar as the requirement of
> practical reason demands, and whatever stands in an easily
> perceivable connection with it. More precise elucidations of the
> special provisions of God in the best interests of human beings
> are not thereby excluded.
>   But of objective religion I speak only insofar as it constitutes
> an ingredient in the subjective. (HtJ, 8)

One of the things worthy of note in this passage is the apparently
casual eclecticism with which practical reason is made to stand alongside moral sense as the basis of subjective religion. The connection
between practical reason and moral sense is certainly not precisely
established, yet it is not a matter of mere carelessness. We have already
observed that Hegel often speaks of practical reason in a way that
displays a very un-Kantian infusion of passion and emotion. He is
scrupulous enough about distinguishing practical reason, the distinctively moral capacity of persons in their freedom, from their "empirical"

character as corporeal, sensuous beings, but this distinction implies
no sharp separation between the two. Reason, in principle, is universal,
since it is able to grasp universally valid principles and laws; as such,
our reason "recognizes itself again in every rational being, as a fellow-
citizen of an intelligible world." But reinforcing this kinship among men
in the intelligible world is a kinship of sentiment in the empirical world:

> On this earth it is not probable that mankind or even a single
> person should be able to dispense with the . . . motivations—and
> such sentiments are woven into our nature itself—which, al-
> though they are not moral, since they do not stem from the
> regard for law, . . . are still amiable, hindering evil impulses and
> promoting the best in people. Of this sort are all the benign
> impulses, sympathy, good will, friendship, etc. . . . The basic prin-
> ciple of the empirical character is love, which has some analogy
> to reason inasmuch as love finds itself in others. (*HtJ,* 18)

Hegel goes on to argue that love is not simply a refined form of self-
regard, but is basically unselfish in its regard for others, so that even
though it is a passion it corresponds to the universal, disinterested will
to goodness in reason itself. There is therefore no necessary conflict
between practical reason and sentiment. Practical reason provides the
formal criteria for the adequacy of religion, yet religion is not simply
a matter of dutiful obedience to moral law. "Religion is an affair of the
heart, engaging our interest for the sake of a requirement of practical
reason" (*HtJ,* 9). Religion at its best is a kind of mediator between
reason and heart. For in order to be alive in human existence morality
must touch the total affective life, and this it is able to do through
religion, at least insofar as religion nourishes the instinctual seeds of
morality already implanted in human nature. For religion "interests
the heart" and "has an influence on our sentiments and on the determination of our will":

> Our duties and the laws possess a strong reinforcement through
> the fact that they are represented to us as the laws of God; . . .
> the representation of the sublimity and the goodness of God
> toward us fills our hearts with veneration and with sentiments
> of humility and thankfulness.
>   Thus religion gives morality and its motivations a new, sublime
> impetus, and it provides a new, strong dike against the force of

sensuous drives. For sensuous people religion is sensuous also; the religious impulses to good conduct must be sensuous in order to be able to have effect on the sensuous life. Of course they commonly lose thereby something of their dignity as moral motivations. But they have gained such a human influence thereby, have been adapted so much to our sentiments, that, drawn by our hearts and enticed through beautiful fantasy, we often find it easy to forget that a cold rationality disapproves of such picture-representations or even forbids the bare mention of them. (*HtJ*, 5)

Hegel understands perfectly well that the inclinations of the heart can lead in quite other directions than morality, and as a child of the Enlightenment and a student of Kant he certainly endorses the view that reason must prevail over wayward impulses. Yet he has begun to cast a critical eye on the assured verities of the Enlightenment and has come to view pure rationalism as one-sided and something less than rational in its sovereign disregard or moralistic suspicion of the sensuous side of life as such. He is concerned about the achievement of the good life in a total sense, for the individual and for society. If one is serious about achieving a real reform in people's lives, "then one must take them as they are, and seek out all the good impulses and sentiments." For a folk religion, for a religion through which the whole life of a society is to be revitalized, "it is of the greatest importance that fantasy and heart should not be left unsatisfied."[9] Indeed the rationalistic "understanding," as an instrument of analysis and prudential calculation, is from a moral point of view as corruptible as the sentiments. In one passage he stops just short of Luther's strong language on the harlotry of reason:

> The understanding is a courtier who accommodates himself to the moods of his master; it knows how to come up with justifications for every passion and every undertaking. It is primarily a servant of self-love, which is always very cunning. . . .
> The enlightenment of the understanding does to be sure make one more clever, but not better.[10]

The understanding may not be simply an instrument of amoral cunning. But on the other hand, if it is devoted to the most high-minded purposes it may then try to exercise a subtle moralistic tyranny, deducing endless codes of rules and principles until people take every step in a state of acute moral anxiety that is the opposite of free moral resolution. So far as religion is concerned, "the understanding serves only objective religion," which can never in itself make people's thought and action their own. "One ought to act for himself, produce himself, decide for himself, not let others act for him—then he is nothing but a mere machine" (*HtJ*, 15).

Here Hegel strikes the chord that integrates his otherwise diffuse rhapsodizing on subjective religion. Religion must be subjective in the sense that people are able to make it their own, so that, to recur to the image mentioned earlier, it shall be the house they live in and not simply an alien monument. The heart must be touched, satisfied, moved to respond, and not left cold while the arms and legs go through the motions of moral obedience or ceremonial observance. And of course, despite the hard things he has to say about the understanding, Hegel is no enemy of reason. The mind, elevated to wisdom, "practical wisdom,"[11] out of one's own experience of life, must be able to grasp the truth of its beliefs and the rightness of its moral principles. This is the sense in which he appeals to practical reason as the touchstone of religious truth. It is the universal humanness of practical reason that commends it to Hegel. He recognizes that this reason, universal in principle, may in fact be present in various cultures or even in various individuals in different stages of development; the light of reason shines more brightly and steadily in some than in others. This difference will inevitably affect the kind of religious truth that is alive for a people or an individual. In no case will reason be able to contrive a religion simply out of its own resources; "it is impossible that a religion for a people in general can consist of universal truths, to which only extraordinary persons arrive in any age" (*HtJ*, 14). A religion will always contain "positive" elements drawn from its tradition, originating not in reason but in the history of a people. Yet nothing can be finally or for long acceptable to a people that cannot be penetrated by the light of reason, in the degree to which reason has developed among that people. It is not that reason sits imperiously on its judgment seat, passing sentence upon the mysteries of religion after a brief analytic examination. But if a religious teaching finally makes no sense to the practical wisdom of a humane and experienced person, if it comes to seem simply arbitrary or morally fruitless or harmful, it can play no vital role in that person's life. One may be driven to a conscious rejection or condemnation of it, or may unconsciously allow it to atrophy, disregarding it in practice even though it may still have a place in the objective religion to which one gives formal allegiance:

> [Religious] teachings must necessarily, even if their authority rests on a divine revelation, be so constituted that they are really authorized through the universal reason of human beings, that every person realizes and feels the obligation they impose when he becomes attentive to them.

If this condition is not met, if religious doctrines are insisted upon purely as a matter of esoteric knowledge or of arbitrary divine command,

> sooner or later they become an object of attack by thinking people and an object of conflict, whereby the practical interest is always lost, or just because of the conflict they are set up as intolerant symbols. Besides that, since their connection with the true requirements and demands of reason always remain unnatural they can never achieve in the feelings the importance of a pure, genuine, practical factor related directly to morality. (*HtJ*, 21; see also 50–54)

Only that which can be appropriated and internalized so that it shapes the total character in a vital way belongs to subjective religion. Necessarily excluded from such a role are religious teachings that are unconvincing to practical reason, as well as the more remote conclusions of speculative thought.

It now becomes possible to answer the query we introduced earlier, whether subjective religion as so conceived is necessarily good. According to Hegel's optimism about human nature it can never be entirely bad. Yet it can assume unwholesome or pathological or socially destructive forms. But sharing as it does in the dynamism of human life as a whole it is subject to a constant pressure to correct itself. As people's experience of life deepens, as the light of reason becomes more steady, as moral sensitivity becomes more acute, the subjective religion necessarily assumes more productive forms. Objective religion is not, as such, subject to the same processes of self-correction. It can be subject to these processes to the extent that it remains responsive to the deepest currents in the subjective religion of an age, and can in turn mediate these deeper currents, through its teachings and institutions, to the living spirit of a culture at large. Yet inherent in these objective forms is a certain inertia, a tendency to self-perpetuation independently of the spirit of an age or its subjective religious currents.

Folk Religion versus Private Religion

The revolutionary dreams of a transformed social existence that we found Hegel sharing with his friends during this period are expressed in these writings in terms of his notion of folk religion. While a Volksreligion necessarily assumes objective forms, what is important to Hegel is its subjective efficacy as a medium for social reform from the inside out, a reform in inner attitudes and goals. As such there is an inherent link between it and the social heritage and political structures within which a people lives.

> The spirit of the folk [*Geist des Volks*], history, religion, degree of political freedom, cannot be regarded separately in terms either of their influence on one another or of their condition. They are interlaced together into one cord. Like a triumvirate, none of them can do anything without the others, yet each also receives something from the others. To cultivate the morality of individual persons is the affair of a private religion, of parents, of their own efforts and circumstances. To cultivate the spirit of the folk is also partly an affair of the folk religion, partly of political conditions. (*HtJ*, 27)

While Hegel does find a role for "private religion," he is clearly more interested in the public, the folk religion, a notion in which we find one of the most important early sources of his mature thought. It is already linked in the most intimate way with a conception that was to find its place among the most characteristic ideas of his later philosophy: the Volksgeist. This conception of the folk spirit does not receive clear definition in the early writings, but it already has an important function in his thinking. Here he speaks of it as being constituted by the common history, religion, and political order through which a particular people identifies itself as a cultural entity. Despite the aethereal-sounding name he gives it, it is therefore a fairly sober, if problematic, concept of social theory. The Volksgeist refers to the corporate way of life that identifies a people sharing a common language and history: a characteristic way of thinking, a sense of justice and of acceptable behavior, a coherent artistic culture and order of values, a sense of being at home with one another that is not shared by even the most sympathetic alien. Hegel never thought that a "folk" was created merely by the accident of political boundaries; rather being molded into unity by its common cultural life, it demands political expression and recognition, and to that extent is the social source of nationalism. While the Volksgeist has to do particularly with the public sphere, it is obvious that it powerfully influences the formation of personal life as well. Yet diversity and even conflict may flourish within the shared atmosphere of the common spirit. Such, at least, is the case when a people is in happy rapport with its own spirit.

In fact, whenever young Hegel wrote about Volksreligion or the Volksgeist, he had in mind a shining model of a folk that had enjoyed just such a happy rapport: After making the general, sketchy comments on the folk spirit quoted above he gives himself over to a rhapsody on the Greek spirit.

> O, from the distant days of the past an image shines on the soul which has a feeling for human beauty and for greatness in the great, the image of a genius among peoples, a son of fortune and of freedom, schooled in beautiful fantasy. The unbreakable cord of natural needs fettered even him to the mother earth, but through his sentiment, through his fantasy he has so worked upon it, refined and beautified it, with the help of the graces has so garlanded it with roses, that he delighted in these fetters as in his own work, as a part of himself. His servants were joy, gaiety, charm; his soul filled with the consciousness of its power and its freedom, his more serious playmates were friendship and love—not the satyr, but the sensitive, soulful Amor, adorned with all the allure of the heart and with sweet dreams. (*HtJ*, 28)

As the rhapsody modulates into allegory, Hegel goes on to describe the upbringing of this young genius, this dancing spirit of the Greek Volk: His father and mother—namely the historical process that engendered this people, and its political order[12]—had been permissive parents, encouraging his freedom and self-confidence. But the longest passage is reserved for his wet nurse, which is the role assigned to the Volksreligion!

In harmony with such parents, the nurse could not bring up this child of nature with fear for the rod or for a ghost of the darkness, nor with the sour-sweet sugar-bread of mysticism, which wears out the stomach; nor did she wish to raise him to young manhood tied by the apron-strings of words that would have kept him a dependent minor forever. Instead, she fed him with the unadulterated, healthy milk of pure sentiments, and with the aid of beautiful, free fantasy she adorned with her flowers the impenetrable veil by means of which the divine withdraws from our sight; this space behind the veil she populated with lively images and conjured with them, so that upon these images he could transfer the great ideas of his own heart with the entire fullness of higher and more beautiful sentiments. —Just as among the Greeks the nurse was a friend of the family and remained the friend of her charge through her whole lifetime, so she always remained his friend, to whom the unspoiled youth brought his free thanks and free love and with whom, as his friendly companion, he shared his joys and his play, without having his joys troubled by her. Thereby she kept her dignity upright, and his own conscience punished him for any neglect of her. She preserved her dominion forever, for it was built upon the love, upon the gratitude, upon the most noble feelings of her pupil. She flattered with her ornaments and obeyed the moods of his fantasy, but she taught him to honor iron necessity, she taught him to follow this unalterable fate without grumbling.[13]

Implicit in this wistful effusion is the unhappy contrast presented by the role of religion as Hegel experienced it in his own age and society, in which he found so much inhibition and artificiality and fear, such a generally unwholesome relationship to the common life. The spirit of a people can certainly be ill-born and badly nurtured by its religion as we shall see. But in the idealized relationship between the Olympian religions and the Greek spirit of which he dreams, Hegel finds his model for the proper function of folk religion. It is to shape, but not create, the character of a people; it "begets and nourishes" the propensities already stirring in its common life, disciplines and encourages these propensities and provides ideals and images for their expression and celebration. As such it is no authoritarian system, imposing an alien mold, but it "goes hand in hand with freedom" (*HtJ*, 27).

Folk religion is furthermore a mediating structure in the social existence of a people, reconciling conflicting claims and purposes, and binding its otherwise fragmented experience into a coherent life. The burden of providing for physical subsistence, for example, cannot be avoided, but the folk religion provides images and ceremonies through which the fulfillment of natural needs is elevated beyond sheer animal necessity into an act laden with personal, human meaning, part and parcel of the free human expression of a people. Hegel has in mind observances such as harvest festivals and sacrifices of thanksgiving and of repentance.[14] Such natural rhythms of animal life as birth, mating, death are also given communal ceremony, are socialized, humanized, given meaning in the projection on them of symbolic forms that unite them with the aspirations of the spiritual life.

Folk religion also mediates between the claims of reason and the affective life of people. We have already noted the way in which Hegel at this time modified the ideal of rational religion, as it was current in the Enlightenment and particularly in Kantian circles. He means for folk religion to be "rational" but not in a sense that sets it against appetite and emotion and natural necessity. Furthermore, he is much more attentive to the historical situatedness of religion than many of his contemporaries were (though, to be sure, such writers as Herder and Mendelssohn called precisely this factor to his attention). Folk religion is indeed a rational religion, but reason in it is given a social sense, universal in principle yet situated in a particular social context. Asking "How must folk religion be constituted?" Hegel outlines three equally essential factors, which he then goes on to expound:

1. Its teachings must be founded on universal reason.
2. Fantasy, heart and sensuousness must not thereby be sent away empty.
3. It must be so constituted that it attaches to itself all the needs of life and the public affairs of the state.

(HtJ, 20)

From this summary it is evident that Hegel's treatment of tension between reason and "heart" is directed particularly toward the constitution of folk religion. Its teachings are to be few and simple, and such as to stand the test of developing rationality, but also adjustable to "the stage of morality . . . at which a people stands" (*HtJ*, 21). It is essentially the sociocultural context of folk religion, its basic role as the educator (*paedogogos*) of a people, that makes it the mediator between reason and life. It is this inherence in the common life that makes folk religion the mediator between subjective and objective religion. Folk religion must necessarily, as a social form, have institutional structures and teachings, and "no folk religion is thinkable" that does not express itself in ceremonies; but "nothing is more difficult than to keep the ceremonies from being taken by the masses for the essence of religion itself" (*HtJ*, 24)—and similarly with the other objective forms; hence the danger of fetishism, that is by no means avoided "in our verbose age" "through tirades over enlightenment and such" (*HtJ*, 20–21). But in a folk religion the developing experience of a whole civilization is brought to bear upon the forms of religious expression, and despite the ever-present dangers of fetishism Hegel seems to think that this thorough immersion of religion in developing culture will keep the objective forms of religion in touch with the actual life of people and hence with the subjective heart of religion itself, at least in the long run.

Yet Hegel does not believe that folk religion, this cultural, public religion, exhaustively fulfills the religious needs of individuals. He also speaks, though without very clear definition, of private religion. The distinction between private and folk religion cuts across, rather than coinciding with, the other distinctions we have noted; for example, private as well as folk religion has both subjective and objective poles.[15] We recall that Hegel assigns to private religion, along with parental guidance and the particular circumstances and efforts of individuals themselves, the function of cultivating the morality of individual persons as such. There are other passages in which he distinguishes private from folk religion in the same loose way: "The formation of the individual, appropriate to his character, the instruction concerning cases of the collision of duties, the special means of promoting virtue, consolation and comfort in particular cases of suffering and misfortune, must be left to the cultivation of private religion" (*HtJ*, 19).

Hegel goes on to argue that such functions are beyond the province of folk religion in the sense that they extend too far into the personal temperament and special circumstances of individuals. Folk religion, for example, can encourage and celebrate virtue. But aside from a few simple, general principles, it cannot prescribe the concrete form that virtue should take in every decision of every individual's life. It would become tyrannical and also hopelessly complex if it tried. So some scope is afforded for the kind of religious commitment that individuals may voluntarily assume to nourish their personal lives in accordance with their particular experiences and needs. That is what Hegel seems to be groping for when he speaks of private religion: the basis of voluntary, self-selective religious groups, but inappropriate as the public religion that must nurture a civilization.[16]

Thus far in our consideration of Hegel's early fragmentary writings, we have identified four overlapping pairs of concepts that he employed as instruments of analysis in the study of religions: living/dead, "religion"/"theology," subjective/objective, folk/private. These polarities form a kind of conceptual grid that continues, variously deployed, to shape his thinking about religion in the 1790s, surviving rather dramatic changes in his point of view in which other concepts become more dominant.

But in these same earliest fragments a polemical theme begins to gather energy. For the notion of private religion was more developed than Hegel's vague general comments might suggest. He had a specific case in mind when he spoke of it, just as he had the model of Greek antiquity before him in his remarks on Volksreligion. To this countermodel we now turn.

2. Hegel's Early Critique of Christianity

Young Hegel argued at length that Christianity was essentially and incorrigibly a private religion. Yet for centuries it had functioned as the established, public religion of European civilization, a role which it was singularly ill-equipped to play. Hegel attributed many of the oppressive woes of his own culture to that contradiction: a private religion assuming the position of a dominant Volksreligion. That contradiction had incidentally ruined whatever was of value in genuine Christianity as well. As a consequence of confounding folk religion with private religion, the church was also confounding subjective with objective religion, religion with theology, and even the living with the dead. This contradiction and its fatal consequences formed the burden of the critique that Hegel directed against Christianity in the early fragments we have been discussing, and with some new dimensions for some time thereafter. No summary of this critique can quite adequately convey the vehemence and sarcasm with which our liberated theological student conducts it, but we shall attempt to grasp the essential argument that is sometimes overlooked in all the thunder.

Of the factors that seemed to the young Hegel to stamp Christianity as a private religion, we may mention the four most important.[17] First is the observation that teachings such as those in the Sermon on the Mount are exclusively directed to unusual persons able to interpret the spirit of these teachings and freely desiring to adopt them as a personal style of life. Hegel argues that there is no way to derive the moral constitution of a whole society from them. Made a public norm of behavior and taken literally—as they must be in order to function as a public law—they would obviously lead to chaos. "Many of the commandments of Christ are opposed to the basic foundations of legislation in civil society, the principles of the right of property, self-defense, etc." (HtJ, 41). Not even a small organization, or village, could long exist if, for example, it were the public norm for people to sell their goods and distribute the money to the poor. "From all this it is clear that the teachings of Jesus . . . were appropriate only for the cultivation of individual persons, and were directed to such" (HtJ, 41; see also 360). The incorporation of such teachings into a public religious establishment, however, has necessarily led on the one hand to hypocrisy and to strained efforts to expound them or explain them away, and on the other hand to oppressive attempts to force such teachings on society as a whole, to religious tyranny and all the perversions attending a constant state of guilt and bad conscience. It is not the social establishment of religious norms that leads to a vicious legalism, but the incorporation in such laws of teachings that go against the natural grain of the people and indeed that contradict the very social character of the establishment. And in the process the original intent of the teachings themselves is distorted beyond recognition. They pass over into the purely objective side of the religion, elaborated into complex codes and inculcated through wearisome and unwelcome disciplines; it is impossible for such teachings to express the subjective spirituality of the people as a whole.[18] Whatever effect they may have on those individuals disposed to follow them and on the small fellowships of the early church, as principles of a public religion they necessarily turn oppressive for all.

> This church discipline for Christians is not something which had been brought for the first time into the statutes of the Christian society only some time after its founding, but as we have seen it was already present in its first unsophisticated outline—and then was made use of and extended by lust for power and hypoc-

risy. Even though it has begun to lose the traces of its crudest misuse, yet there is still infinitely much of its spirit left behind, and it adds one more example to the many showing that institutions and laws of a small society, where each citizen has the freedom to be a member or not, are never suitable if they become extended to a large civil society, and cannot exist together with civil liberty.[19]

But there is a second still more basic level at which Christianity shows itself to be a private religion, unable to assume the function of folk religion: The drama that dominates the Christian gospel, of fallen man redeemed by grace, gives it a quite different fundamental interest than a folk religion must have. For the purpose of a folk religion is essentially ethical. In this context, Kantian language is employed in putting Christianity to this test. "Practical reason establishes for humanity as the highest purpose of its striving . . . the bringing forth of the highest good in the world, morality and the happiness appropriate to it." But "the rather general teaching of Christianity" seems to be "that the hope of an eternal blessedness is what has the greatest interest for the Christian, in comparison with which everything else has a subordinate worth." This interest in itself does not directly contradict the dictate of practical reason. However,

> according to the Christian religion the chief condition of eternal blessedness is faith in Christ and in the power of his reconciling death—and indeed not because this faith can lead in the end to morality, which in that case would be the real condition and this faith only the medium, but the faith in itself is the basis for God's good pleasure, and this good pleasure therefore confers eternal blessedness on those who believe in Christ, though they could never really deserve it. (*HtJ*, 62)

Faith, not works: that is the basis of the Christian religion. Its end is blessedness, not morality! In fact, according to the doctrine of original sin we are incapable of the sort of goodness that would fit us for blessedness. If a folk religion is to speak of blessedness at all, it must present it as a direct consequence of virtue; Kant had followed many venerable religious traditions in insisting upon this direct link between virtue and blessedness. Without this direct link, the idea of blessedness would subvert the edifying mission of folk religion, its mission to upbuild the ethical organization of social life. But the doctrine of original sin reduces this link to a merely abstract and irrelevant possibility. Christianity certainly teaches that "the good person deserves blessedness, can demand it as a right, is worthy of it—only with the presupposition that it is impossible to become a good person" (*HtJ*, 63). In fact Augustine, identified only as "an empty-hearted church father," had articulated the dominant Christian position in declaring that the virtues of "so many virtuous heathen," even a Socrates, were merely "splendid vices"—a view that "for a person full of feeling, who believes in virtue, is outrageous," an offense against healthy common sense and against "the universal moral nature of humanity."

The proposition so deeply grounded in this universal moral nature, "that the good is worthy of blessedness," is effectively sustained by Christianity only in its negative corollary, that evil deserves damnation. But the depravity "not only of persons, but of human nature" makes every person finally dependent upon "the undeserved, free grace of God, from whose justice that person would have to expect nothing but misery and punishment."[20] The result is that the nerve of human courage and moral aspiration is cut. One is counseled to trust, but in this trust there lies an ennervating passivity, waiting patiently upon the Lord, not the spur to active virtue on a heroic scale: "The Christian religion has many martyrs—heroes in endurance are produced, but not heroes in action" (*HtJ*, 357; see also 33–34, 58).

There are, of course, Christian virtues, but they are of the personal, individual sort exhibited in the perseverance of the martyr. They lack social efficacy. True Christians know themselves to be sinners redeemed by grace; the political, social virtues have no direct bearing at all on the redemption toward which their faith is directed, yet in their private behavior they seek at all costs to be worthy servants of Christ. There is nothing to criticize in this, so long as they follow this arduous path as members by choice of a private religious community. But again, the issue is the anomaly created when a religion dominated by such an ideal becomes the spiritual guide of an entire civilization. It cannot nourish a healthy body politic. Furthermore, the Christian mission itself becomes hopelessly confused, the language of visible and invisible church simply covering over a basic contradiction. The visible, worldly church must try to function as a Volksreligion, at cross-purposes with the distinctively Christian ideals that are relegated to a phantom church without worldly visibility.

A Christian is supposed to be a perfect man. If he sins, he ceases to be a Christian, *quoad ecclesiam invisibilem,* but still professes the folk religion, is still a member of the Christian church. What is the Christian church: a multitude of individual persons (not a collective multitude of persons) who have attained a certain perfection of morality? or is it the Christian folk-religion, the learning of dogmas by rote, that even a Christian scoundrel has in common with the true Christian?

Good behavior in little things, no great common spirit that sets aside petty passions and knows how to act for a whole, the many petty things add up to one great effect which is very petty, very meager. Is this a combined effect of religion and of despotism together?

Why are women more religious than men? (*HtJ*, 357)

We have mentioned two basic factors that disqualify Christianity as a folk religion: that the teachings of Jesus are not suitable as the foundation of a public ethos, and that the whole cast of traditional Christian anthropology molds people into a human image inimical to the indispensable virtues of social life, particularly those of a heroic sort. Closely connected with this second factor is a third, on which we may touch briefly here: Again in contrast to the sense of life affirmation, generous spaciousness, sensuous abundance, light, which he finds in the cultural expressions of Greek religion, Hegel finds in Christianity's cultural expressions an introverted and gloomy spirit. He has in mind particularly the medieval heritage in Germany. "Our cities," for example, "have narrow, stinking streets. The rooms are narrow, dark panelled, with dark windows." But the Greeks! The Greek genius

lived free, in wide streets, in their houses were open, unroofed courts; in their cities were numerous large plazas; their temples were built in a beautiful, noble style, simple as the Greek spirit, sublime as the god to which they were dedicated. The images of the gods were the highest ideal of the beautiful. The most beautiful human form, as it might have gone forth in the dawning of the resurrection, everything presented in the highest power of its existence and life, no images of decay. The hideous mask of death was for them the tender genius, the brother of slumber.

But the Judeo-Christian tradition bans all images of God—and puts the crucifix in their place. The faces of human joy and pain alike are "grinning caricatures" with the muscles of the body contorted. "The brush which made most of the old pictures appears to be dipped in night. No bright, happy fantasy animated it." Hegel of course knows that there have been some great monuments of Christian art, that indeed "the Christian religion affords fantasy a wide scope" that has been exploited by artists in all media. But its greatest artistic achievements have not been in harmony with the religious forms in which the common people have been indoctrinated, they have not really inspired the imagination of the folk culture. Even Catholic worship, which has borrowed its beautiful features from the Greeks and Romans—the Madonna, the fragrant incense—has been enclosed in "gothic masses" and has "buried" its artistic masterworks "in a corner." Christians do not even drink well. The German's compulsive drunkenness, either boisterous or brooding, has nothing in common with "a Socratic, carefree goblet" (*HtJ,* 358–59). All of these cramped cultural expressions result from the contradiction: Christianity functioning as a folk religion.

Finally, we may mention here a fourth factor that limits the proper functioning of Christianity to the confines of private religion: that its teachings appeal to alleged historical events and divinely inspired persons, now remote in time and place. The dimensions of this theme were to develop in Hegel's mind into his critique of the "positivity" of the gospel, about which we shall have more to say. But already in the fragments on Volksreligion we find him echoing a critique common among deists, Spinozists, and other Enlightenment thinkers, and luminously expressed by Lessing in particular: Miraculous events, fulfillments of prophecy, special divine revelations and interventions in history, could only be believed on the basis of questionable testimony. Even if such events had actually occurred, their historical facticity could not support a morally elevating and rational religious belief.[21] Now Hegel points out that, so long as a religion built upon such alleged "historical truths"[22] remains a private religion, "each one is free to believe it or not, but as an official religion there must always be unbelievers" (*HtJ,* 49). That is, not everyone could reasonably be expected to believe "truths" of this sort, which are particularistic by their very nature. But in an authentic Volksreligion there would presumably be no unbelievers worth mentioning.

For at the heart of a sound folk religion must be teachings, experiences, virtues, practices, that are directly ingredient in the life of a people. The religion will seem reasonable and fitting to people on the basis of their own current experience, without the need of elaborate theological acrobatics to demonstrate its relevance. It may indeed include exemplary stories from history and a lively sense of the folk history of its own people, because such historical references can be a living part of the contemporary memory and imagination. This is the sort of historical memory that can be passed from parent to child. But Christianity, like Judaism, is a religion of the book, of a historical book. It appeals to revelation in historic events. Above all, it finds God revealed in the person of a man who actually lived, many centuries ago.

> The grounds of faith in Christ rest on history. —So long as simplicity of ethos is preserved in a people, before there is great inequality of classes, and the history has been enacted on the people's own soil, then the sagas are propagated from parents to children, they are in the same measure everyone's property. But as soon as special classes are formed in a nation, the father of the family is no longer at the same time high priest, and so a special class will soon come to the fore as the depository of the sagas, from which knowledge of these sagas is thereupon transmitted among the people. This will particularly be the case if the sagas originate from a foreign land, with foreign customs, in a foreign language. Then the basis, the content of the saga in its original form can no longer be the property of all, since a great deal of time and a manifold apparatus of information will be required in order to learn to understand that form. In this manner that special class attains to a dominance over the official faith which can be broadened into a very extensive power, or at least with respect to the teaching of the folk religion keeps the book in its hands. (*HtJ*, 65–66)

So Hegel finds, in the first place, that a faith which takes an essentially historical form leads to religious authoritarianism. With respect to alleged historical revelations, people must believe what they are told by the authorities. In virtue of the very form of such a faith, particularly when the history is foreign and remote, their own moral judgment, their own experience and reflection, are irrelevant. Hegel admits that it is possible to investigate a historical faith rationally, "but it does not lie immediately in its nature to awaken the spirit of reflection." The very facticity of the historical faith tends to reduce people to passive receivers of it (*HtJ*, 66).

If reason does awaken in such a situation, and does achieve enough self-confidence to subject the alleged sacred history to investigation, it can count on the determined opposition of the priestly class. It is not the priests, but the philosophers who have purged our inherited religion of its grossest barbarities. Indeed, in this situation reason can only be destructively critical of the received religion, exposing the absurdities in the historical tradition on which it rests. Reason, allowed no real basis in the faith itself, necessarily assumes a skeptical role, and if the folk religion has this historical, irrational form, reason simply becomes the enemy of faith, attacking the very religious foundation of the culture and possessing for its own part no foundation except a shallow secularity (*HtJ*, 66–67, 359–60). If, on the other hand, the public religion of a people is so constituted "that sense and fantasy and the heart are stirred, without reason thereby going away empty," no authoritarian priestly class will be necessary. Religious celebration and ceremony will arise out of its own common life: "and if through indigenous institutions its sense is engaged, its imagination aroused, its heart stirred and its reason satisfied, then its spirit will feel no need of—or rather would take no satisfaction in—lending an ear every seven days to phrases and images which were only understandable and in place a few thousand years ago in Syria."[23]

The trouble with a folk religion that is constituted on a historical basis is that it soon becomes locked in a purely objective religious form, in the sense in which "objective religion" was discussed in the preceding section: With the passing of years it loses touch with the subjective religion which gave it birth, and its own forms become so alien that it is no longer productive of subjective religious life in the later ages. However vital a religion may have been in its childhood origins, the survival of its forms many centuries later condemn it to a "childish" old age, toward which reason can only occupy a polemical position (*HtJ*, 36ff.). Indeed, the enmity of reason is a sign that a religious tradition is moribund. This enmity is intensified to the extent that a religious tradition, bereft of any real purpose of its own, lends itself to reactionary and inhuman policies. When critics of Christianity, for example, consider such affairs as the Crusades, the Inquisition, the conquest of America, the slave trade, which have been carried on under Christian auspices, in face of the high and holy claims made on its behalf, then these critics "must become filled with a bitterness, with a hatred toward the Christian religion, which its defenders often attribute to a devilish wickedness of the heart" (*HtJ, 39*). Reason is not directed against the mysteries of religion as such, but against the arbitrariness and decadence and the consequent hypocrisy and authoritarian oppression to which a historical faith is particularly susceptible.

Most of Hegel's early criticism of Christianity is based on these four factors we have surveyed. It is not directed against the private religion that Christianity essentially is, but against its unavoidable malfunction when it occupies the position of an official, public religion. But the details of this critique recall fairly common lines of attack against official Christianity during the Enlightenment. There is a short fragment, however, one of the last passages written in this series on Volksreligion,[24] which brings the critique of Christianity into a sharpened social focus that anticipates Feuerbach and Marx more than it recalls the Enlightenment. This remarkable fragment presses the notion of private religion much more critically than Hegel previously had, regarding it as a sign of a collapse into a generally asocial privatism. In this context Hegel sees a sinister inner connection between a fragmented cultural individualism and the authoritarian susceptibilities of a historically oriented religion. A civilization that founds its religion on historical signs and wonders, for which "the inner certainty of faith in God and immortality must be established through external assurances," shows by that very fact that it is an oppressed and decadent civilization in which an authentic social life is already dead. There had been a vital folk religion among the "free republicans" of Greece and the ancient Germanic peoples, but it had no such artificial basis. On the other hand, "only a people of the greatest corruption, of the deepest moral impotence," to which it could be brought only through "the utter forgetfulness of a better condition," is capable of "blind obedience under the bad moods of depraved men." Religious authoritarianism has a social basis.

> Such a people, forsaken by itself and by all the gods, leads a private life—needs signs and wonders, needs assurances from the divinity that it has a future life, since it can no longer have this faith in itself. But that still does not bring it far enough to grasp the idea of morality and to build its faith on this; the ideas are dried up, are now chimeras, so that its faith can only depend on an individual [Christ], can only prop itself upon a person, who is an example to it, the object of its veneration. Hence the

open, welcome reception of the Christian religion at the time
when public virtue was vanishing among the Romans, and their
external greatness declining.[25]

When a society has lost its collective spirit, when its community life
has been crushed (as Hegel thought had happened to European peoples
under late Roman despotism) and its own folk religion and shared
public life are lost, the individual must unavoidably retreat into a
purely private existence. No longer nourished by a rich culture, the
inner lives of such individuals are pitifully impoverished. They have
spiritual needs, but no spiritual or ethical resources of their own. Hegel
is suggesting that it is precisely these private individuals, in this asocial, dehumanized state, who are susceptible to the appeal of a religion
based on far-off revelatory events, miracles, a divine person. Having no
inner affinity of their own to anything spiritual, they fix upon particular
alien events and figures to which they can relate in a purely external
way. They have no ideas, since ideas are interactive, self-transformative,
arising out of a shared common life. Since belief in quasi-external things
that can be imaginatively pictured is necessarily based on outside authority, their only recourse is authoritarian religion. Such, Hegel now
thinks, is the fatal symbiosis between the atomized subjects of the
empire and the claims of the Christian gospel. The veneration for a
divine individual, for whom they can have no inner affinity, is symptom-
atic of the self-contempt into which asocial individuals fall.

But Hegel goes on to express the hope that has clearly been stirring
in him as he has composed these fragments on folk religion: for the
formation of a common life in which the spirit will again be engendered.
In that case even the figure of Christ will acquire a new meaning. Hegel
speaks this hope in a single sentence that he can scarcely bring himself
to end:

> Therefore, if after centuries humanity will again become capable
> of ideas, the interest in what is individual [about the Christ-
> figure] will disappear, the experience of human corruption indeed
> remaining but the doctrine of human depravity declining, and
> that which interests us in that individual [Christ], simply as
> idea in its beauty, will come by and by to the fore . . . [and]
> become our own property, the beauty of human nature, which
> we ourselves invested in an alien individual . . . we shall joyfully
> recognize as our own work, shall again appropriate it to our-

selves, and thereby learn to feel respect for ourselves, since previously we considered as our own only what can only be an object of contempt. (*HtJ*, 71)

How the gospel is received, it seems, depends on the condition of those who receive it, and ultimately on the health of their social matrix. With the revival of an ethical and cultural life of their own, people will find in the Christ-figure a mirror of their own spiritual fullness rather than a disclosure of their emptiness. But this is only one aspect of an entire network of interacting factors. This remarkable fragment ends by again drawing the moral, political, and religious life of a people together as aspects of a single predicament and a single possibility. For if Hegel's hope for the revival of a social humanity can be realized, the impasse of merely private life will dissolve in all its parts.

> In the private life the love for the comforts and embellishments of life must be our highest interest (which in a system founded on prudence then constituted our morality). Now if moral ideas can find a place among human beings, these values will sink in worth, and constitutions which only guarantee life and property will never be regarded as the best. The whole anxious apparatus, the artificial system of motivations and consolations in which so many thousand weaklings find their comfort will become more dispensable. The system of religion, which always took on the color of the age and of the political constitutions, the highest virtue of which was humility, the consciousness of its incapacity, and which expected everything from somewhere else . . . will now receive its own, true independent dignity. (*HtJ*, 71)

In finally setting his early critique of Christianity into the context of this incipient social theory, Hegel had arrived at a kind of resolution, one feels, of the concerns with which he had been struggling throughout these fragmentary reflections on Volksreligion. He had been trying to discover how the Christian West had been brought to an oppressive, asocial spiritual condition, and what a rebirth might mean. A phase in the development of his thinking was complete. But he was not through with the problem of Christianity and its fragmented society. Even while he was completing that first phase, a new phase in his thinking was already beginning, in which his old ideas were being brought into a new light.

3. A Young Kantian Attacks the "Positivity" of the Gospel

In the writings that date from 1795, indeed already in the latest of the fragments on folk religion written in 1794, young Hegel's thinking took a new course in two important respects: He turned intensively to the exploration of the origins of Christianity, and he did so from a predominantly Kantian point of view. In both cases, to be sure, it was a matter of something that had been recessive in his earlier thinking becoming dominant. But the concern with Christian origins as well as the Kantianism were given such powerful impetus at this time that the motifs that had earlier been central now became subordinate to them, though without by any means disappearing from his writings.

The ascendancy of Kant's moral and religious philosophy in Hegel's thinking during this time was precipitated by the powerful impression of Kant's *Religion Within the Limits of Reason Alone,* which had been published in 1793.[26] Hegel's fragments and the writings that followed suddenly not only become studded with allusions to this work, but show its influence in the way he formulates his problems. Above all, obedience to the moral law becomes the unequivocal criterion and purpose of religion.

Kant had declared this same proposition in a dozen different ways in his late and—compared with his other works in point of style—amazingly prickly and spirited book on religion. It is only by "good life conduct," disinterested obedience to the rational law of free moral action, that a person can be well-pleasing to God. Everything else that goes under the name of religion is "mere religious illusion and pseudoservice of God."[27] This principle is taken to be virtually self-evident, requiring no proof because it is rooted in our rational nature itself. Without attempting to review Kant's whole performance, it is to our purpose to note that this principle results in a distinction between two types of religion. The first he calls natural religion, though of course not in the seventeenth- and eighteenth-century sense of the term that he and Hume had discredited. This natural religion is grounded in our own practical reason, religion that is obedience to duty regardless of consequence or reward. Natural religion involves a moral faith in the objective moral order and its eventual triumph, a faith that the universe is ordered on principles in accord with the unconditional command, a faith that a good act is not an arrow shot into the darkness. This faith is at the heart of Kant's so-called moral argument for God's existence, as the sovereign presiding over a universal moral kingdom. The true worship of this God is our unconditional reverence for our duty, regardless of immediate or ultimate results. But opposed to this natural religion there is revealed, or clerical, or ecclesiastical, or historical religion, the grounds of which are largely arbitrary. Kant acknowledges some validity in this latter form as a temporary concession to human frailty, preliminary to the ethico-religious commonwealth. But this revealed religion is based on commandments and supposed divine disclosures that do not pretend to be rational, are not accessible to all people in virtue of their rationality but are accessible only through events that are contingent at best and of doubtful authenticity at worst. Further, this religion is developed and codified in a particularistic human movement, a church in the sectarian sense, where special priestly interests prevail. Suffering as it does from such arbitrariness, many of its features are not only irrelevant but pernicious, because it obscures true moral faith, robs it of its ultimacy. Its cultus, its prayers, become efforts to win favors from God quite apart from moral excellence; it therefore mocks God's moral purpose in the world. Kant has traditional Christianity especially in mind, of course, with its doctrines of grace and atonement, its employment of special rites and sacraments as means of grace. All this means to Kant that a select group of people can be blessed without being good, a doctrine utterly subversive of God's true intent, which is that humanity should form an ethical commonwealth based on universal practical reason. The very basis of this ecclesiastical faith is merely contingent; it is founded on certain books accounted sacred, a historical record of contingent events, certain authorities. It cannot claim that its principles or even its ultimate object *must* be so and cannot be otherwise, but can only assert that what it says somehow *is* so. But "pure" faith, obedience to the categorical imperative, is grounded "wholly upon reason, can be accepted as necessary and therefore as the only one which signifies the true church."[28]

This Kantian distinction, in particular, is what young Hegel brought to his examination of Christian origins. His own earlier distinctions, which we surveyed in the first section of this chapter, were not abandoned; I shall argue, in fact, that what attracted him in this Kantian "natural" religion was that it could provide the basis for a proper Volksreligion. Yet for almost two years his own characteristic ideas were molded into a Kantian form, and his reflection on the original Christian gospel was conducted in Kantian terms. This new historical preoccupation itself, however, grew directly out of his critique of Christianity qua folk religion. In the last fragment on folk religion, after describing the true purpose of religion in strictly Kantian, moral terms, he goes on to consider the enormous effect the official religion has on the life of a people, even if it is not fulfilling its true purpose. So two searching questions must be asked about a dominant religion:

> Is the religion which for this people was once adequate to its purpose . . . still just as adequate in the same form, under completely altered circumstances? Was the religion in its original source so constituted that it was capable, with every change in the form of government and in enlightenment, of preserving its dignity and its adequacy to its purpose, of exercising its effectiveness, not only as a private religion but also as a universal religion?[29]

The second question is obviously the more basic, since it has to do with the very essence of a particular religious tradition. At this time Hegel thought that one could discover this essential character of a religion, apart from accidental accretions, by examining its origins. That is why, for the next few years, he was so constantly preoccupied with the beginnings of the Christian religion.

We have seen that the problem of historicity, the appeal to particular revelatory events, already belonged to Hegel's earlier critique of Christianity: Christianity is a historical religion, not only in the sense that it is oriented to a remote history and sustained through a historical tradition, but also in the sense that it makes divine disclosure itself a matter of historical contingency. The critical perspective that Hegel brought to his consideration of Christian origins grew directly out of this line of reflection, as its implications developed in Hegel's mind under the prompting of Kant. Is Christianity not essentially a purely historical religion, in the sense that Kant had so sharply differentiated from the rational, moral type of religion?

In the fragments we have been discussing the problem of the historicity of Christian revelation is most clearly recognized in connection with the peculiar veneration demanded for the "name," that is, the person, of Christ. A person becomes a Christian, not through virtue, but through belief in Christ: a belief in Christ, not so much as a moral examplar, but primarily as a particular historical individual who was the incarnate God and who died for our sins. It is a belief that does not arise out of our own rational nature and experience, but is directed to an alleged fact reported by others.

> Faith in Christ as a historical person is not a faith grounded in a requirement of practical reason, but a faith which rests on the testimonies of others. . . . Historical faith . . . is in its very nature limited, its extension depends upon accidental circumstances, it is a spring from which not everyone can draw, and yet it is supposed to be the condition for God's good pleasure toward us, our eternal destiny is supposed to depend on it. (*HtJ*, 64)

Indeed, the uninformed are left to damnation. The problem, furthermore, is not simply a late accretion in Christianity. Hegel had noted earlier that Christ was understood by his own disciples to demand faith in himself. Indeed, to become a disciple one had to leave family and social responsibilities behind and follow him. Anyone "not receptive to becoming a kind of adventurer" (*HtJ*, 32) could not be a true disciple. Christ is compared in this respect with Socrates, who had no disciples in this sense, who did not lead or preach, but helped any persons who came into conversation with him to cultivate the virtue inherent in themselves (*HtJ*, 32–35).

Of course, Christ was also a teacher of moral virtue, and like other eighteenth-century critics of Christian doctrines, Hegel had regarded Christian moral teaching as deserving the highest respect. In a passage that already shows the influence of Kant's *Religion,* Hegel even suggested that Christ offers a kind of moral inspiration for mankind that is impossible for a Socrates: Christ was not only a teacher and example, but a personified ideal of virtue for the believing imagination. It might seem that Socrates could be a more convincing example of virtue for us, just because he was a purely human teacher.

> But fantasy pays no attention to this calculation of the cold understanding, and precisely the mixture, the addition of the divine, qualifies the virtuous man Jesus to be an ideal of virtue. Without the divinity of his person we should have had only the human, but here we have a true superhuman ideal, to which the human soul is still not alien, however distant from it it must think itself. Besides, this ideal has the further advantage of being no cold abstraction—its individualization, that we hear it

speaking and see it acting, brings this ideal, that is already akin
to our spirits, still nearer for our sentiment. Here for the believer
is therefore no longer a virtuous man, but rather virtue itself
has appeared.[30]

But Hegel goes on to observe that at the center of the Christian religion
this personified ideal is eclipsed by the figure of Christ as the sacrificial
offering for our sin, and that the Christian mission in the world is not
so much the teaching of the ideal as the preaching of the redeemer's
name.[31] A mission so defined is necessarily a proselytizing endeavor,
since there is not much to be done with Christ's name but to win
adherents to a sect celebrating it.

Furthermore, in the later revision of the fragment under discussion,[32]
Hegel has second thoughts about the efficacy of the personified ideal
itself. For if such an ideal resides only in an incarnate God, people are
not able to appropriate it as a possibility of their own human nature.
It is a possibility for us only insofar as we share in the indwelling of
the divine in a kind of *unio mystica*. "This derogation of human nature
therefore does not permit us to recognize our own selves in virtuous
persons—for such an ideal to be an image of virtue for us a God-man
is needed" (*HtJ*, 67). In spite of itself, as it were, such an ideal becomes
entangled in the web of revealed theology, and people view themselves
as fallen creatures whose only hope rests on a historical drama of
salvation performed long ago and far away. Faith in the "name" of
Jesus divides the believer's own self from the basis of his spiritual life.
Therein, as we shall see, lay the self-alienating consequence of what
Hegel was soon to call the "positivity" of the gospel.

But within a few months after bringing his critique of received Christianity to a climax in the final fragments on Volksreligion, Hegel's
private writing took a bizarre turn. In a lengthy manuscript dated May
9 to July 24, 1795, written while he was still in Bern, Hegel undertook
to retell the gospel story. Nohl, following earlier scholars, entitled this
manuscript "The Life of Jesus," though it exhibits very little interest
in the events of Jesus' life as such, and in fact takes pains to subordinate
the person and works of Jesus (i.e., his "name") to his teachings—or
rather to an extraordinary rendering of his teachings. For the teacher
who appears in these pages is a convinced Kantian, even to the point
of uttering paraphrases of the categorical imperative that only narrowly
escape plagiarism![33] This Gospel according to young Hegel, in fact,
begins with a reconstruction of the prologue to the Gospel according

to John, in which Kantianism is carried well beyond Kant. For the divine logos in John's Gospel, Hegel reads Reason, which in the context of this essay is to be construed as the systematic principle of a moral world order, unknown to theoretical understanding but embodied in pure practical reason. Not only is Reason in this sense divine: Hegel opens his Gospel by declaring that

> Pure Reason beyond all limits is the divinity itself. According to Reason, therefore, is the plan of the world in general ordered; it is Reason which teaches the human being to know his destiny [Bestimmung], an unconditional purpose of his life; it is to be sure often obscured, but yet is never entirely extinguished, even in the darkness a feeble glimmer of it is preserved.[34]

Practical reason inheres in the moral order of the world; it is not merely a subjective human possession. Yet it is our own, inherent in our moral nature. This uniting of the subjective and the objective, the universal and the individual in reason is what has attracted Hegel to Kant's idea of practical reason. He continues his reconstruction of John's Prologue by suggesting that it was the mission of the Baptist to nurture this "divine spark" among the Jews, among whom it was clouded by their sensuality and their pride of descent from Abraham. In this mission the Baptist was superseded by Christ.

Some details of the Gospel account of Jesus' life are recorded, but carefully purged of all references to the miraculous and the supernatural. His parents were simply Joseph and Mary (HtJ, 75). In place of the temptations of Satan we are told of a period of solitary reflection in which he renounced the folly of attempting to overcome nature in any sense other than the cultivation of moral dignity, and in which he became convinced of the vanity of mere earthly power (HtJ, 77). He gathered a few "friends" to accompany him, "and he sought through his example and his teaching to expel from them the narrow spirit of Jewish prejudice and Jewish national pride, and to fill them with his own spirit which placed a value on virtue alone" (HtJ, 78). At the Last Supper he tells them that if they should again eat together in a circle of friendship, "then remember also your old friend and teacher," let the bread recall his sacrificed body and the wine his shed blood, that "my example may be a powerful means for the strengthening of virtue among you."[35] He meets his death like a stoic sage, and the account ends with his burial.[36]

But the pages of this document are mainly filled with Hegel's reconstructions of the teachings of Jesus, of which the earnest intent is clear, but in which the awkward insertion of the language of Kantian moral philosophy into the language of the Gospels produces a rather comic blend. The Lord's Prayer, for example, comes out this way:

> Father of humankind, to whom all heaven is subjugated, you who are alone holy are the ideal image that is held before us, to which we aim to approach, that your kingdom may come at last, in which all rational beings make the law alone the rule of their action. This idea will little by little subjugate all inclinations, even the cries of nature! In the feeling of our imperfection before your holy will, how shall we raise ourselves to be strict or even vengeful judges of our brothers? We wish rather to work only on ourselves, that we may improve our hearts, ennoble the motives of our actions, and purge our dispositions more and more of evil, in order to become more like you, whose holiness and blessedness is alone infinite. (*HtJ*, 85)

While this Jesus does sometimes commend brother love, the Gospel teaching that it is insufficient to love one's friends and hate one's enemies is recast in a way that sheds a stern Kantian doubt on the value of love itself, as a mere natural emotion without distinctively moral worth.

> For if you love those who love you, doing or loaning your benefactors some good in order to receive back the same value, of what merit have you thereby? This is a sentiment of nature, which is not renounced by evil people either; you have still done nothing for the sake of duty thereby. May holiness be your aim, as the divinity is holy. (*HtJ*, 84)

Again, the seed scattered by the sower in the parable is identified as "knowledge of the ethical law."[37] And so it goes.

But a motif to which this Kantian Gospel returns again and again, so persistently as to be its major theme, is the renunciation of all appeal to special or historical revelation, of what we may as well begin to call the *positivity* of Christianity. We have seen this theme emerging as a problem in the fragments on folk religion. Now it is set forth as the great religious obstacle to the moral virtue that this Kantian Jesus comes to awaken. He declares repeatedly that this virtue, which is the only true piety, is implicit in the rational nature of every person, is in no wise dependent on special revelations or extraordinary discoveries. He merely awakens what is already in people; he does not bring it to them or establish it on his own authority (*HtJ,* 78–79, 98, 111–12, and passim). So we find him inveighing repeatedly against signs and wonders (e.g., *HtJ,* 103), against the Jewish claim to be a chosen nation and against special commandments and ordinances,[38] and even against the very notion of messiahship:

> This waiting for a messiah will yet plunge my countrymen into great danger, and combined with their other prejudices and their blind stubbornness, will dig their complete ruin. They will make this chimerical hope into a game for cunning deceivers or brainless fanatics. Be very careful that you do not also let yourselves be led thereby into error.[39]

Not only does this Kantian Jesus thus render any suggestion of his own messiahship out of the question; he also explicitly forbids any special veneration for his own person at all, denies that he himself is in any way essential to the faith of those whom he teaches.

> But do I then demand respect for my person? or faith in me? or do I wish to inculcate in you a standard of my invention by which to measure the worth of persons and to judge them? No, respect for yourself, faith in the holy law of your reason, and attentiveness to the inner judge in your bosom, to conscience, a standard that is also the standard of divinity: this is what I wished to awaken in you.[40]

Scholars have puzzled over Hegel's intentions in writing this strange document. He certainly cannot have thought he had reconstructed the Jesus of history, nor was he so blindly Kantian that he could not read the gospel story any other way. The anachronism of this Kantian Jesus was as obvious to him as to us. There was, to be sure, a lively interest in the life of Jesus during this period; it was common for critics of church dogma during the Enlightenment to appeal to the life and teachings of Jesus himself to justify their attacks on the dogma that had grown up around him.[41] Furthermore, the historical accuracy of traditional characterizations of Jesus' actual life and teachings had become a matter of lively dispute, particularly since Lessing's publication of Reimarus's *Wolfenbüttel Fragments* during the 1770s, which called into question the reliability of the evangelists and other biblical writers. Meanwhile a number of imaginative renderings of the life of Jesus had appeared, of which Klopstock's *Messias* (1773) had made the greatest impression.[42] It certainly was not uncommon to see in Jesus the exemplar of that Religion of Reason espoused by those of rational piety in the eighteenth century, and generously imputed by them to good folk universally. Hegel's writings before and after his so-called *Life of Jesus* suggest that he shared this attitude to some degree, but not to the extent that could account for his Kantian portrait of Jesus. Those same writings reveal that his historical sense was already too highly developed to make it plausible that he could naively have submitted this portrait as a serious entry in the "quest for the historical Jesus" already under way.

Dilthey points us in a more promising direction in suggesting that Hegel may have been following a hermeneutical principle proposed by Kant himself in his *Religion*. Every biblical text is to be interpreted according to the principle that its purpose is moral improvement.[43] But Dilthey's suggestion simply pushes our question back a step: Why did Hegel accept this hermeneutical principle with such apparent whole-heartedness in composing his Life of Jesus? Even during this period, when the influence of Kant on the young Hegel reached its maximum, Hegel was by no means a slavish or uncritical disciple.[44] But one would be hard put to detect any reservations about Kant's moral and religious philosophy if attention were confined to this document alone. It appears to me that the key to Hegel's intentions is not to be found in the document itself, but in the writings that precede and follow it. Hegel is still pursuing the question posed in the earlier fragments, whether Christianity can be construed, at its very foundation, in such a way as to constitute a salutary public religion for a whole civilization. Kantian moral religion commends itself to Hegel, not purely for its own sake, but because it seems to offer a way in which the founding of Christianity could be so construed. The basis of this morality is, in principle, universal, appealing to the light of reason in every person. On such a basis, purged of positive, historical elements or at any rate interpreting them in its light, a religion could fulfill the wholesome, public function in the life of a modern society that Christianity, as traditionally construed, had so woefully failed to fulfill. So, with the example of other updated lives of Jesus before him, young Hegel had set out to conduct an experiment: to see how far he could go in reconstructing the career and message of Jesus on this Kantian, but really universally human basis.

But even if this interpretation of Hegel's intentions is correct, it must immediately be added that Hegel had no sooner completed the experiment than he recognized its failure. For the burden of his next extended writing, *The Positivity of the Christian Religion*,[45] is that Christianity is intractably "positive" at its very roots. While he returns in this work, therefore, to the critical position of his earlier fragments toward Christianity, and indeed intensifies and clarifies his point of attack, the new basis of the attack is essentially that from which he had attempted to reconstitute the founding of Christianity in his *Life of Jesus*. Only now the Kantian, moral view of religion, directly conjoined with the vision of a sound Volksreligion, furnishes the ground from which to attack the Christian religion at its foundations. Different as these two works appear to be on the surface, so that one could hardly suspect that the same author could write both within the same year, at root they are in fact very similar, and the two works together represent, as we have suggested, the high-water mark of Kant's influence on the moral and religious thought of the young Hegel.[46] Hegel declares his fundamental norm near the beginning of his essay, *The Positivity of the Christian Religion*:

> The basic principle to be laid down as the foundation for all judgments on the varying forms, modifications, and spirit of the Christian religion is this—that the purpose and essence of all true religion, our religion included, is human morality, and that all the special teachings of the Christian religion, all means of propagating them, and all its obligations to believe and to observe practices otherwise arbitrary in themselves, have their worth and their sanctity appraised according to their closer or more distant connection with that aim.[47]

The hands are young Hegel's, but the voice is clearly that of the aged sage from the north. Kant's distinction between the two types of religion appear in Hegel's essay as the distinction between a rational "virtue religion" and a "positive sect," and provides the basic perspective for Hegel's analysis. In this essay we do meet, to be sure, many of the important motifs of Hegel's earlier fragments,[48] but we meet them on these new terms.

On the other hand, in turning to the notion of "virtue religion" it is important to note at once that this Kantian religious ideal receives at Hegel's hands a heavy infusion of what he had earlier called Volksreligion. This infusion is most evident in his conviction that a form of the rational religion of virtue had once actually seen the light of day: For Hegel's old wistfulness toward classical antiquity is assimilated to his new Kantianism. The Greek citizens, and the Roman republicans before the days of empire, were free people for whom the objective forms of religion and government were outward social expressions of their own moral subjectivity—and their moral subjectivity was illuminated by that light of practical reason that shines in every rational being!

> As free people they obeyed laws that they gave to themselves, obeyed persons whom they themselves had appointed to office, waged wars on which they had themselves decided, spent their property and their passions, sacrificed their lives by the thousands for an end that was their own. They did not teach and learn but practiced in their actions the maxims of virtue which they could call entirely their own; in public as in private and domestic life each was a free person, each lived according to his own laws. (HtJ, 221–22)

Though these free persons reverenced the gods and considered that the gods held power over their fortunes, gods did not control them, could not constrain them by arbitrary moral decrees. Reason, ingredient in their own nature and as such their own proper possession, could alone legislate for their will. Even then they were free to disobey; but as Kant had shown, they were never more free and unconstrained than in their obedience. As for the gods:

> If a person clashed with these lords of nature and their power, he could set over against them his freedom and his own self. His will was free and obeyed its own laws; he knew no divine commands, or if he called the moral law a divine command, the command was nowhere given in words but ruled him invisibly (Antigone). (HtJ, 222)

This emphasis on the individual's freedom did not imply that each simply went his own way. Each person "lived according to his own laws," but these laws were also inherent in the "idea" of the state.

People could immerse themselves in the political, cultural, religious institutions of the Volk without losing their freedom, for these institutions were concrete expressions of their own will. The "idea" of their state was the very purpose of their "world," a purpose to which they could give themselves because it was their own. Freedom was not merely subjective, powerless, wistful, but potent to effect its own purposes in the institutions of social life. "Confronted by this idea," says Hegel of the noble Hellene or Latin, "his own individuality vanished." That is to say, people became immersed in this idea in such wise that they were not concerned about their private existence as such, were not for example interested in immortality as a prolonging of their lives in their mere particularity. Their lives and their freedom were given an objective and continuing embodiment in the culture that expressed their own purposes (*HtJ*, 222–23).

This effectual view of freedom remained with Hegel, to be developed in his mature work. At this time it was Kantian in its view that human freedom is fulfilled, not frustrated, by moral obedience in compliance with the demands of reason; it preserves the unity of the individual and the universal in practical reason. But even in this most "Kantian" period, young Hegel interjects a mediating term between universal reason and the moral freedom of the rational individual, namely the specific social and cultural matrix of the individual's life. People's freedom is realized only if their state, their property, and so forth, are really their own, extensions of their own moral intention. When these are made into objects that restrict and inhibit their rational will, they lose their freedom and the institutions and materials become alien, spiritless, forbidding. They have become so many dead weights. This view is an important source of Hegel's idea of alienation. It also opens up a small crack, soon to become an open breach, between the disciple and his master. The break is not yet apparent to Hegel himself, because in *The Positivity of the Christian Religion* the theme of alienation emerges primarily as the religious problem of positivity, which is dealt with in largely Kantian terms.

For to this Kantian religion of virtue, which Hegel had infused with his "Hellenic ideal,"[49] he juxtaposes the notion of a positive sect. The "positivity" of such a sect consists in the fact that its basis is "posited" for believers altogether independently of their own capacities, that its doctrines consist in information that they must be taught to believe and its ethical principles consist in commands that they must be taught to obey. Both the belief and the obedience are enjoined as unquestionable duties, that is, as commands to be obeyed.

A positive faith is a system of religious tenets of the sort that supposedly ought to have truth for us because it is commanded us by an authority to which we cannot refuse to subject our belief. First and foremost in this concept there appears a system of religious tenets or truths which, independent of our convictions [*von unserm Fürwahrhalten*], ought to be regarded as truths; even if they had never been known by anyone, had never been held as convictions by anyone at all, they would still remain truths, and in that sense are frequently called objective truths. Now these truths supposedly ought to be truths for us, to become subjective truths. If the understanding or reason encounter truths of this kind, they *ought* to be accepted by them as such; if they contain commands for our will, they *ought* to be accepted by it as maxims, and that is indeed the first command, the basis for all the rest. . . . It belongs essentially to the concept of a positive faith that it is a duty for us to believe it. For historical beliefs and the belief in what parents, teachers, friends tell us, are similarly forms of belief in authority, except that these beliefs have their basis in our voluntary trust in these persons, which for the most part rests on the credibility for us of what they tell us. But belief in the authority of the positive teaching, on the contrary, is nothing that lies within our volition, and the trust in it must be established prior to all acquaintance with or evaluation of the content of the given teaching. God's claim on us and the duty of our obedience to him now rests on the fact that he is our mighty Lord and Master and we are his creatures and servants, on his good deeds to us and our duty of gratitude, and further on the fact that he is the fount of truth and we are ignorant and blind.[50]

This definition of positivity explores its authoritarian character in particular. Elsewhere the accent falls on its historicity or its supernaturalism. But these are all aspects of a single problem. Authoritarianism is already, as such, super- or contranatural, in the sense of demanding that people exhibit beliefs and actions and attitudes that do not arise out of their own nature. Positive faith claims their highest allegiance without being theirs at all. It is external, coercive, deriving its authority from special revelatory events, miracles, and venerated personalities. Its devotee has cast his life at the feet of alien powers, and since his religious life has no rational grounding in his own human nature, his religion is essentially sectarian.

It is clear that Christianity is now such a positive sect, which, however, in alliance with an autocratic state and contrary to its essentially sectarian character, dominates the spiritual life of a whole civilization. It is true that Hegel is revolting, as Kant had before him, against this autocratic unity of church and state and all that went with it, the censorship, the power of state-appointed churchmen over the life of the university, and so forth. But striking at the root of the matter he attacks the positivity of the church's faith as such.

"The fundamental error at the bottom of the church's entire system," young Hegel roundly declares, "is that it ignores the rights pertaining to every capacity of the human spirit, in particular to the chief of them, reason." Kant has tried to restore by philosophical analysis the "sound intuition" of the Greeks, that the "moral commands of reason" are not to be treated as merely "objective rules with which the understanding deals." Hegel is phrasing this important statement of the problem of positivity in terms of the Kantian distinction between reason *(Vernunft) and understanding (Verstand)*: The understanding grasps, in its own categories, the given, contingent facts that are, for example, the concern of natural science; these are legitimate "objects" (not, of course, "things in themselves," but objects formed by the understanding from the sensuous manifold), are indeed the only proper objects of knowledge. However, when moral and spiritual truths are regarded in the same way, as externally given facts grasped objectively by the understanding, then the delegation of powers that had been Kant's great achievement has been subverted and moral freedom has been destroyed. Just as reason alone cannot determine matters of fact, the understanding that is directed to given "objects" cannot be the medium of moral insight. Here "necessary and universally valid laws" are needed, which practical reason alone can legislate. These laws are not "objective" in the sense of being externally given to the moral subject, as are the arbitrary customs, conventions, and so forth, that are within the province of the understanding. The genuinely moral laws belong to the individual's own rational subjectivity (i.e., they are "objective" only in the entirely different sense that they are implicit in universal reason itself). But even when the church acknowledges moral laws that are rational in themselves, it establishes the motivation for obedience to such laws, not in pure respect for "law itself," but in ulterior considerations of their divine source and the sanctions that God holds in his hand. Appealing to the external objectivity of divine acts and commands, the church has reduced the moral law to a positive system of objectified rules, "a system which despises humanity."[51]

In fact the church had gone still further in this respect than Judaism, which is assumed throughout the essay to be an altogether positive, legalistic sect. If Christians boast that they have discarded the Jewish insistence on external ceremonies and laws in favor of a morality of inner motivation, the truth is that they have only internalized the Jewish legalism. So the real difference is that "still in Judaism only actions were commanded," while the church took the "self-contradictory" further step of "commanding sentiments" (*HtJ*, 209). That means that even a person's inner life is not fully that person's own, but contains "sentiments produced in a spiritual hothouse." Between a man's own natural attitudes and these forced sentiments there is excruciating conflict, with consequent self-deception, moral anxiety, and bad faith. Hegel treats with a certain sympathy the frequently noted and despised phenomenon of the Sunday Christian, whose piety is put away with his prayerbook while he conducts his weekday affairs. The man is a genuinely divided self:

> Along with all the riches of spiritual sentiments, on the whole he retains his own character, and the ordinary man lives along-side the spiritual. . . . It is often too harsh to charge such a character with real hypocrisy, since that entails the conscious-ness of the contradiction between the real motive of an action and the label which is applied to it; in this case, on the contrary, this consciousness is altogether lacking, and the man simply has no unity at all. (*HtJ*, 209–10)

Here, then, in his treatment of the idea of positive religion, we find the early source of the Hegelian concept of self-alienation.

Much of the essay is devoted to investigating just how Christianity has come to have this positive character. It is axiomatic for young Hegel, as it was for Kant, that Jesus was a virtuous man who could not have intended things to turn out that way. He did not believe that Jesus was a fool, a knave, or a fanatic. It was equally axiomatic that Jesus could not have been the Son of God in any unique sense.[52] He only wished to reveal what was already accessible to the practical

Reason of every person. He was the teacher of a pure "virtue religion," still a Kantian, who sought to overthrow Jewish positivity in favor of a truly moral religion. Jesus "undertook to raise religion and virtue to morality and to restore to morality the freedom which is its essence" (*HtJ*, 154). He is in fact still recognizable as the figure we met in Hegel's *Life of Jesus,* except that now Hegel has to concede to the original Gospel records the fact that Jesus did weaken and submit to certain fatal compromises. For the sake of expediency he had tried to combine the commands of true virtue with certain positive principles and practices. He recognized of course that the former were the essential, but since an appeal to the Jews on the basis of reason alone "would have been the same as preaching to fish," Jesus accommodated himself somewhat to the preconceptions of his hearers. He tried to buttress the sheer rationality of his teaching by appeal to his own authority as a teacher; he was forced to speak about himself, "to demand faith in his person, a faith which his virtue religion required only for its opposition to the positive doctrines of Judaism" (*HtJ*, 158–59). He made use of the already existent Messiah concept, and did not contradict when people tried to apply it to his own person, because he hoped by this means to hold their attention so that he could "lead their Messianic expectations more into the moral realm" (*HtJ*, 160). Furthermore, many of his acts were construed by his unsophisticated observers as miracles, and this reputation as a miracle worker served further to muddy the waters by concentrating attention upon the man rather than upon his message. The result was fatal:

> This detoured route to morality via miracles and the authority of a person, together with the many stations at which one has to stop along the way, has the defect of any detour because it makes the destination further away than it really is, and it may readily induce the traveler to lose sight of the road altogether in the course of his deviations and the distracting way-stations. [Furthermore] it violates the dignity of morality which, being independent, disdains any foundation outside itself, and insists on being self-sufficient and self-grounded. (*HtJ*, 161)

The hero's flaw led to consequences that were the tragic reversal of his intentions. The seeds of positivity that Jesus' compromises had planted were eagerly cultivated by his disciples, since these compromises made it possible to assimilate his message to the positivistic religious mentality with which they had been infected from their earliest years. They made Christianity into a thoroughly positive sect, centered in the divine authority of Jesus himself. They misconstrued Jesus' final discourse, taking it not as a call to virtue, but as a command to believe in him and to proselytize for his sect, conferring the external mark of baptism in his name as a way of separating believer from unbeliever (*HtJ*, 164). Salvation came to depend on obedience to the teaching of Jesus as such, or of his vicars; that is, reason became "a purely receptive faculty, instead of a legislative one," responding purely to positive authority.

> Even the doctrines of virtue, now made obligatory in a positive sense, i.e. not on their own account, but as commanded by Jesus, lost the inner criterion whereby their necessity is established, and were placed on the same level with every other positive, special command, and with every external ordinance grounded in circumstances or on mere prudence. And though this is otherwise a contradictory conception, the religion of Jesus became a positive doctrine of virtue. (*HtJ*, 165–66)

Again Jesus is compared with Socrates, who had the good fortune to teach among free people. His disciples "loved Socrates because of his virtue and his philosophy, not virtue and philosophy because of him." So his teaching was spared the fate of degeneration into positivity. On the other hand it did not grow into a public religion either, and in this connection Hegel suggests that it was ironically the positivity of the gospel that, in the cultural milieu in which it was received, made it possible for Christianity to become a public religion (*HtJ*, 163). Otherwise it would have made no headway among the Jews, or later among the Romans; for

> the despotism of the Roman emperors had chased the human spirit from the earth and spread a misery which compelled people to seek and expect happiness in heaven. Robbed of freedom, their spirit, their eternal and absolute element, was forced to take flight to the deity. The objectivity of deity is a counterpart to the corruption and slavery of the human, and it really is only a revelation, only a manifestation of the spirit of the age.[53]

A correlative of the objectification of spiritual life, which is the defining character of positive religion, is the reduction of the divine spirit itself to pure object. And again, in a way that anticipates Feuerbachian and Marxist critiques of religion, our young Kantian takes a step beyond Kant in arguing that this positive religion and its object-God are the products of a degenerated form of social existence. Only by an occasional hint does he reveal the active, reformist motivation behind all this historical speculation on the origins and development of Christianity: "Apart from some earlier attempts, it has been reserved in the main for our epoch to vindicate at least in theory the human ownership of the treasures formerly squandered on heaven; but what age will have the strength to make good this right and take possession of them?" (*HtJ*, 225).

Here we clearly recognize the young man we met in our first chapter, corresponding with his friends in revolutionary and almost conspiratorial accents.

4. The Life-Mysticism of a Young Anti-Kantian

Turning from *The Positivity of the Christian Religion* to Hegel's next extended treatise, written two years later, one meets a startlingly different outlook. The earlier work could have been written by any bright young man at the peak of the Enlightenment and in the full flush of the Kantian revolution. But in *The Spirit of Christianity and Its Fate* (1798–1800) we are in a different intellectual world. Many of the same themes and problems appear, but the originality of the writer who treats them is much more obvious. He shows clear signs of becoming what we can only call a Hegelian—or better still, he shows signs of being Hegel!

The change in fact begins to appear soon after Hegel had completed the essay on *Positivity* in early summer 1796. Dilthey describes as the "turning point" his long romantic-mystic poem, "Eleusis," composed already that August.[54] Clearly modeled on the style of Hölderlin, to whom it is dedicated, the poem celebrates the paradoxical union of brilliant clarity and deep darkness in the Eleusinian mysteries. But there is also an undercurrent of Hölderlin's lyric melancholia in the poem: the living truth of the mysteries has withdrawn, glimpsed only in dreamful yearnings, and leaving men to their own arid sophistries.

> Flown is the circle of gods back to Olympus
> from the desecrated altars . . .

Hegel was soon to begin pursuing them again, but no longer through the ratiocinations of the Enlightenment and Kant. It is no accident, one suspects, that the new pursuits coincided with a welcome change of scenery: That fall he returned from his Swiss exile, and January 1797 found him in Frankfurt, again indentured as a private tutor, but reunited with Hölderlin and other old friends in a cultural atmosphere he found vastly more stimulating. Hegel's serious philosophical studies really date from this period, he wrote political pieces, he absorbed himself in music and poetry, even rousing his own ungainly muse on occasion, and Rosenkranz tells us that "like a genuine Faust he acquired a poodle at that time."[55]

Of particular significance for our purposes is the fact that he immersed himself afresh in close exegetical studies in the Greek New Testament, especially in the Gospels. In this new frame of mind he soon begins exploring his religious themes again, in a series of fragments that culminate in *The Spirit of Christianity and Its fate*. Besides the inherent interest of Hegel's romantic mysticism during this period, there is in these pages the high drama of a powerful thinker restlessly sifting his material and trying to find a new way to grasp it whole.

The idea of alienation has broadened and deepened, but religious positivity is still its paradigm. Now, however, Judaism and not Christianity is made to bear the full brunt of this line of criticism.[56] The Hebrew God is a particular, an "infinite Object," jealously demanding all glory for himself, set radically over against the human world. All life is deposited in this Object. Therefore the Jews know themselves, as well as the rest of humankind and the natural world of which they are the antithesis, as lifeless objects, spiritless, dead, "only a something, insofar as the infinite Object makes them into something, not being but a thing made, which has no life, no rights, no love of its own" (*HtJ*, 250). All the venerated figures of the Old Testament seem to Hegel to reflect this nullity: Noah, Moses, the prophets, especially father Abraham himself, in whose spirit Hegel professes to find the entire "fate" of the Hebrew people down to his own day. Following the call of his alien Lord alone, Abraham tore himself loose from all his own social and family ties; in his rootless wanderings he regarded the goods of the natural world purely as something provided for his use and recognized no kindred humanity in the peoples whose hospitality he abused; and he passed the ultimate test of obedience to his unworldly Object by his willingness to slay his son.[57] This spirit of estrangement was the "fate" Abraham bequeathed his posterity. By its sectarian devotion to this God, for example, and its consequent contempt for the mere "idols" of other peoples, Israel is bitterly estranged from its neighbors. This estrangement leads to continual warfare, yet Israel knows no heroic deeds of its own (in the style of the epic Greeks), but knows only that God has smitten the enemy and in this knowledge takes a mean pleasure (*HtJ*, 249). There is neither bravery nor compassion, neither beauty and nobility nor tragedy. The Jews are simply slaves, having nothing to call their own and devoting only servility, not loyalty, to that which is above them. Being soulless, they have no truth. Even the existence of God can be said to be true for them only in a sardonic sense:

> What deeper truth is there for slaves than that they have a master? But . . . what we find as truth among the Jews did not appear to them under the form of truths and matters of faith. For the truth is something free which we neither master nor are mastered by; that is why the existence of God appears not as a truth but as a command. On God the Jews are dependent throughout, and that on which one depends cannot have the form of truth. For truth is beauty intellectually represented, the negative character of truth is freedom. But how could they have an inkling of beauty who saw in everything only matter?[58]

In this savage interpretation of Judaism Hegel has at any rate sharpened his concept of positivity. But now he can no longer commend, in opposition to this religious positivity, the moral universality of Kantian reason. In an important step toward his mature dialectic, Hegel now argues that universality, even universal reason, when set over against the particular, becomes particular itself. It is what he will later call an "abstract" universal: It is not the "one" in which the "many" are overcome, embraced, reconciled; rather, the universal one is left to stand outside the many; that is, becomes one of the many, estranged from the others as they are estranged from one another. Specifically, Hegel sees the Kantian categorical imperative as but another form of alien-

ation. The universal command is scarcely less positive than the Jews'
divine "laws," for all its rationality, because it still stands in harsh
opposition to our own free nature and inclination. Reason, after all, is
not the only element in human nature; it can simply be a constraint
on our will, a burden that oppresses us. Kant had made the point that
there is no difference in principle between the Shaman of the Tungus,
the Voguls, and the European prelates and Connecticut Puritans, since
they are all obeying external commands that do not make them "better
men"; that is, that have nothing to do with universal moral reason.[59]
But now Hegel thinks that Kant did not carry this fine impartiality
far enough. The real difference between all these religious positivists
"and the man who listens to his own command of duty" is not

> that the former make themselves slaves, while the latter is free,
> but that the former have their master outside themselves, while
> the latter carries his master in himself, yet at the same time is
> his own slave. For the particular—impulses, inclinations, patho-
> logical love, sensuousness, or whatever else it is called—the uni-
> versal is necessarily and always something alien and objective.[60]

The Kantian ethic simply internalizes the opposition between human
nature and an alien God into an opposition within human nature itself.
The alienation within positive religion is not reconciled, but simply
made a form of self-alienation.

In all the writings of the Frankfurt years we find Hegel trying to
find a way to unify the opposites. The irrational and the particular are
not evil as such; the evil is in the dualism: rational/irrational, universal/
particular. Similarly with the Fichtean dualism between pure Ego and
nature. Hegel comes to see no difference whether consciousness is situated as in positive religion, in fear of a God above all nature, or whether
it identifies its true self "as pure Ego, above the wreckage of the body
and the shining suns."[61] Such a dualism elevates to an absolute, metaphysical standing the dualism between subject and object that in the
end stands behind many of these oppositions that Hegel now finds so
troublesome. As subject of experience a person is self-enclosed: the
divine, the natural world, the institutions of culture, and other persons
become so many dead objects of the understanding, separated from the
subject. Even one's own body, one's own actions and emotions, become
objectivized, so that the separation reaches even into the life of the
self. Hegel wants to find an inclusive reality, in which the infinite, the

rational, the immutable, can find itself in its apparent opposite; the quest is of no merely theoretical interest, but bears directly on the reconciliation of the self. So one finds him restlessly experimenting with various concepts, life, love, being, spirit, in quest not merely of an all-embracing concept, an abstraction, but a substantial inter-penetration of things, uniting even individual subjects—but without again establishing a new dualism between their unity and their indi-viduality. That is the way in which the mystical motifs that had played such a prominent part in the correspondence among Hegel and his friends began to be powerfully expressed in his own private writing.

Thus in a fragment on love, love is said to be the unity that overcomes all separateness as such; that is, love unites life with life in such a way that although the lovers remain distinct from one another they are no longer foreign to one another, no longer in opposition to one another, no longer mutually limiting, as mere objects are. Lovers are no longer "objects" to one another, and so neither is, as such, a subject; in their unity "the living senses the living."[62] The lover does not annihilate the beloved, but is fulfilled in the beloved. Since love overcomes all oppositions, it is no longer merely a finite relationship (finitude implies mutual limitation, opposition). Such infinitude cannot be claimed for the understanding, nor even for reason, since the understanding relates its terms as a manifold and reason opposes itself to that which it determines. But when love is complete there are no more hostile powers within it. If one of the lovers persists in possessing something exclu-sively his or her own, as a "private property" of which the beloved cannot partake, then their love is not complete, because this dead thing, not brought into the unity of their love, threatens the living. But in love's consummation, even the most elemental possessions of the two individuals, their mortal bodies, lose their "character of separability" (as Hegel delicately puts it). Even when the lovers part, "what is united is not again separated," for a new creature, a child is begotten, the unity of both and the property of neither: "a seed of immortality, a seed of the eternally self-developing and begetting, a living being has come into existence." In fact, in this statement of the relation of the lovers with their child one hears the first faint premonition of the Hegelian dialectic: "the united, the separated, and the reunited."[63] Furthermore, in this mysterious unity of opposites Hegel now finds the meaning of religion, a meaning that reflection cannot comprehend, for it is a paradoxical unity embracing even divinity: "Religion is one with love. The beloved is not opposed to us, he is one with our essence; we see ourselves only in him—and then again he is not we after all—a miracle which we are not able to grasp."[64]

Now when Hegel returns, with such ideas in mind, to his consideration of Christian origins, he looks at the Christian religion with new eyes. He discovers that Christianity is, after all, the religion of love. Jesus is now seen as a teacher and an embodiment of reconciling love. Divine and human, and humans among themselves, are to be united in love. Therefore, for example, Hegel interprets much more sympathetically Jesus' hard sayings about riches and private property that had so scandalized him earlier. Property is a "fate," a dead objectivity resisting the fulfillment of love; it does not preclude duties and virtues, but among those who lay up treasures on earth even the virtues become exclusive and limiting, one person's right opposing another's.[65] Jesus elevates life above this whole sphere.

Even more sharply than in Hegel's earlier treatments, the new religion of Jesus is wholly antithetical to Judaism, is in fact in Hegel's hands torn out of its Old Testament foundations in a way that can only remind the student of church history of some of the ancient heresies. As always in such cases, the "Christianity" to which Hegel now is so sympathetic is of a very peculiar sort. Yet its peculiarity is no longer Kantian. This Jesus radically opposes Jewish positivity, but wisely rejects the abstract universality of the moral law as an alternative. He still teaches virtue, but now virtues are only modalities of love, each fulfilled in love in such wise that its one-sided rigidity is removed. Love creates "a living bond of virtues," a unity quite unlike the unity of a concept from which rules and discrete duties could be deduced. Every virtue overflows its own restricted form, expressing in each actual situation the unity of love (*HtJ*, 293–95). There is no longer the opposition between inclination and moral obligation that is implicit in the idea of duty; love does not, like duty, overcome its opposite, but overcomes the very opposition. That is why it is nonsense to say that one "ought" to love.

> Love itself pronounces no "ought" [*Sollen*]; it is no universal opposed to a particular, no unity of the concept, but a unity of spirit, divinity. To love God is to feel one's self in the All of life, limitless in the infinite. In this feeling of harmony there is no universality, since in the harmony the particular is not dissonant but consonant. . . . Only through love is the might of objectivity broken, for love upsets its whole sphere.[66]

The "spirit of Jesus," exhibited in the Sermon on the Mount, is said to be "elevated above morality," both Jewish and Kantian. Jesus' teachings are not commands in the sense of setting an "ought" over against what "is." Rather, they evoke a new "is," "a *to be* [Sein] a modification of life" that reconciles the opposition of duty against inclination implicit in the "ought [*Sollen*]." This new "is" fulfills the law in the sense that it is no longer a universal object of thought, like duty, but a reality that is "the synthesis of subject and object" (*HtJ*, 266–67, 268). The subject is no longer a particular, the object no longer an abstract universal, in their unification in love. "The concept is displaced by life" (*HtJ*, 269), by the common life in which individuals, too, become a human community.

Love renders the law "wholly superfluous," by reconciling people to one another rather than condemning, by evoking their common life rather than putting to death (*HtJ*, 269ff.). Love does not treat the transgressor as though he were defined essentially by his transgression; the transgression, far from being his whole, is a violation of himself because it is a violation of the encompassing "life" he shares. But love recalls him to himself again, love does not try to fix him in the posture of this nonself; being the unity of life itself, love appeals to the life in him, treats him as a human being. Now, this is the sense in which Jesus presumed to forgive sins. Within this plenitude of life and "not outside of nature"

> Jesus found the cohesion between sin and the forgiveness of sin, between alienation [*Entfremdung*] from God and reconciliation [*Versöhnung*] with him . . . he posited reconciliation in love and the fullness of life. . . . Where he found faith, he used the bold expression: Your sins are forgiven you. This expression is no objective cancellation of punishment, no destruction of the still subsisting fate, but the confidence which recognized itself in the faith of the woman who touched him, a heart [*Gemüt*] like his own, read in it her heart's elevation above law and fate, and declared to her the forgiveness of sins. (*HtJ*, 289)

Jesus' act of forgiveness was not merely a "positive" act committed on the basis of his own divine authority alone upon an existence essentially severed from the divine life. The woman can be forgiven by Jesus because of a capacity in her own nature; she has "a heart like his own." Hegel continues, making his point more explicit:

Faith in Jesus means more than knowing his real personality, feeling one's own reality as inferior to his in might and strength, and being his servant. Faith is knowledge of spirit through spirit [*Geistes durch Geist*], and only like spirits can know and understand one another. (*HtJ*, 289)

The mysticism of Hegel's love ethic has begun to come clearly into view. Love is a recognition of likeness of spirit, which is therefore able to call life into unity with itself. Faith accepts the recognition, knows itself as one in spirit with its object. In this sense and in this sense alone is to be understood the church's witness to the divinity of Christ. Jesus is indeed divine, the Son of the Father. But matter cannot recognize spirit, the dead cannot recognize the living. If Jesus is known as divine, he is known as such only in virtue of the likeness of spirit between himself and the believer. Thus Hegel paraphrases Jesus' reply to Peter's confession in Matthew 16: Peter says "You are the Christ" and Jesus replies,

"My Father in heaven has revealed this to you," i.e. the divine that is in you has recognized me as divine; you have understood my essence, it has echoed in your own. (*HtJ*, 313–14)

This is no isolated passage. On the same page Hegel has explained that "faith in the divine is only possible if in the believer himself there is a divine element which rediscovers itself, its own nature, in that which it believes."[67] The believer is not illuminated by an alien fire; rather "his own tinder catches fire and is a flame of his own." Nevertheless a distinction is still posited in faith between fire and tinder, God and the self, even though the essential unity is at least implicit. Faith is thus a "middle state between darkness . . . and a wholly, divine life of one's own" (*HtJ*, 313). So faith is only a stage preliminary to mystical participation in the divine; but the participation is implicitly presupposed in it already as the condition for any relation to the divine at all. This means that there is no difference in essence between Jesus and those who believe in him; what they see in him they are themselves (*HtJ*, 315).

Yet so long as believers are limited to faith (that is, see divinity only in Jesus and not in themselves as well), they have not grasped the full plenitude of life. Jesus knew that his followers must progress beyond faith in him to identity of being with him. Hence the prophecies of his own death and of the subsequent coming of the Holy Spirit. Jesus had brought his disciples to the point from which they could move on to blessedness, to that one true religion which is the divine life itself. But having brought them to this point of departure—to the stage of faith—Jesus' personal presence had now become a barrier to their further progress. So long as he was on the scene they would continue to be dependent on him, remain fixed on his individual self as the center of their spiritual life and therefore be prevented from claiming the fullness of the divine life in themselves. For the disciples "could not separate his essence from his person; they were still only believers." His person, that is to say, is a positive element that blinds them to the true nature of his essence: the universal divinity, the spiritual life in which they must participate as well. Therefore Jesus tries to convince them of the necessity for his death, his removal as an individual. And he prophesies the coming of the Comforter when he is gone:

> When you behold the divine no longer merely in me and outside yourselves, but have life in yourselves as such, then it will also come into your consciousness (John 15:27) that you have been with me from the beginning, that our natures are one in love, and in God. —The Spirit will lead you into all truth (John 16:13), and will bring everything into remembrance that I have said to you; he is the Comforter . . . for everything you believe yourselves to have lost in me, you will discover in yourselves.[68]

The kingdom of God is to be the fulfillment of this prophecy, the kingdom of love in which people are united with one another and with God in one spirit (*HtJ*, 321).

Jesus had attempted to overcome Jewish positivity in this divine-human harmony of life. He taught that God is related to us as a father to his children: a teaching that Hegel takes to mean that we actually are of the stuff and lineage of our Father; that is, are divine. Hegel opposes the Fatherhood of God in this sense to the Jewish consciousness of God as estranged from men, their absolute "Lord and Governor." Jesus had attempted to overcome the dead positivity of the Jews by denying the otherness of God: "Jesus was opposed to the Jews on the question of their Most High" (*HtJ*, 302). An existence in which men feel themselves separated absolutely from God, in which their morality consists in mechanical obedience to an external legislation, in which there is only the community of a sect and not a universal kingdom embracing all humankind in love: such an existence is dead, estranged. Jesus' religion was the religion of life as a concrete unity in which all things are embraced and all oppositions are overcome. Now, life in this sense is the divine itself![69] God is not alien to anything "living."

We will return in the next section to this important essay, to consider the "fate" suffered by this new Christian "spirit." Just now let us look a little further into the implications of the life-mysticism Hegel embraced so warmly at this point in his career. It was an extremely critical juncture in his thinking. Despite the intensive philosophical studies of these years, he was not yet committed to philosophy. In fact no form of philosophical reason then known to him seemed capable of grasping the sort of unity he found in this life-mysticism. "Life," "love," "spirit" and so forth—the terms that held such fascination for him—were characterized precisely by their opacity to thought. He was later to see this opacity as another form of alienation, and was to develop his own view of dialectical reason as a unity of "life" and thought. But his tireless philosophical quest for such a new view of reason grew out of a conclusion reached at this critical juncture, that the traditional forms of thought were alienated, incapable of grasping "life." At this point, therefore, he is not able to define the divine-human unity of his life-mysticism, any more than any other fundamentally mystical outlook can define this unity. Concepts can be defined, since it is de-finition, limitation, that creates distinct concepts. They can be "understood," and so can "objects" in their opposition to one another, because the opposition is abstract. But the concrete unity of opposites in life, love, being, spirit, eludes by its very comprehensiveness the grasp of thought, and therefore frustrates thought's demand for a definition. One might of course develop an idea of the harmony of things, but even this idea would oppose itself to the things in their disharmony. As Hegel points out in the "Fragment of a System," reflection posits new oppositions in its very effort to unify.

> If I say that life is the union of opposition and relation, this union itself can again be isolated, and it can be argued that union is opposed to non-union. So I would have to put it that life is the union of union and non-union, i.e. every way of putting it is a product of reflection, and so it can be shown of anything posited that just because it is posited there is at the same time another something that is not posited, that is excluded. Reflection is thus driven on and on without rest; but this process must

be checked once and for all by keeping in mind that, for example, what has been called a union of synthesis and antithesis is not something posited, understood, reflected upon, but has for reflection the unique character that it is a being [*Sein*] outside reflection. (*HtJ*, 348)

Here the *problem* of the Hegelian dialectic is already enunciated; indeed, the problem is already highly dialectical: how a reality can contain its own opposite, how, as Hegel goes on to discuss, even death and opposition itself can be contained "in the living whole."

But Hegel does not now think that this dialectical problem has a philosophical solution. Its solution exists "outside reflection," in a "to be"—*Sein*—that is, a reality that is essentially religious: "This partitioning of the living is transcended in religion, the confined life elevates itself to the infinite; and only because the finite is itself life does it bear in itself the possibility of elevating itself to infinite life." Philosophy has an important function, since Hegel's mysticism is not mindless. However,

> philosophy must stop short of religion [*Die Philosophie muss . . . mit der Religion aufhören*], just because it is a process of thinking, and therefore involves an opposition with the nonthinking as well as an opposition between the thinker and what is thought. It must disclose the finitude in all that is finite, and through reason must demand its completion. In particular, it must acknowledge the illusions arising through its own infinite, and so posit the true infinite outside its circumference.[70]

Philosophy can illuminate the problem, can establish the need for the unification of the opposites, and hence turns out to be, in a new sense, a handmaid of religion. But "religion," as Hegel repeatedly insists in this "Fragment of a System," is not merely the unification of finite objects in the concept of the infinite, but is the actual elevation of finite *life* to the infinite life with which it is encompassed in the unity of life itself. Philo-sophia is, for its part, a wistful "love of wisdom" after all, a love that, as Hegel had declared in oracular tones in "Eleusis," the "scholar's curiosity" seeks in vain to consummate.

> In vain! at best he clutches only dust and ashes
> in which thy Life shall nevermore return to him.

Hegel is not yet ready to propose, as he will in the Preface to the *Phenomenology,* that thought may surpass mere philo-sophia to embrace sophia itself, a living wisdom or "actual knowledge" encompassing even the vitality of spirit.[71] The mysticism of the Frankfurt years, while not mindless, is not yet at heart intellectual.

In fact, Hegelian wisdom never became intellectual in the sense of being accessible to traditional kinds of philosophical reflection, or to the understanding, or to the practical reason that merely grasps what ought to be. That is why this mystical moment in Hegel's development was so important to his future course. It was a point of no return. What he here rejects, he never again affirms. He continues to assign "the abstract understanding" of traditional rationalism and of the Enlightenment the merely subsidiary, analytical role to which it is relegated here: it can clarify the oppositions but cannot resolve them, and therefore remains as such an alienated form of thought. Furthermore, Hegel continues to pursue the unity of what he here calls "life" as the fulfillment of his philosophical vision. For what he here sees as a religious possibility alone, he later regards as the achievement of a new form of reason.

5. "Positivity" Reconsidered: A Transition to Historical Dialectic

As the turn of the century approached, Hegel took some important steps toward another major motif in his mature thought. These steps were taken in connection with his old problem of positivity. We have seen that his concern with this problem survived his repudiation of the Kantian terms in which he had originally posed it. His view of the problem in fact deepened, both metaphysically and historically, in ways well worth noticing.

Already in the fragment on "Love and Religion" (summer 1797), Hegel had cryptically suggested that positivity appears "when the ununifiable"—a divine Object over against the human subject—spuriously "becomes unified" (*HtJ,* 377). True religion, which is "one with love," on the contrary proceeds from a paradoxical unity of the two, without distinction of subject and object. This hint Hegel developed at length the following winter in a dense fragment that Nohl entitled "Faith and Being."[72] Authentic faith is an *activity,* that, like love in the earlier fragment, proceeds from an ontological unity with what is believed. The unity of *being* [Sein] here is what Hegel elsewhere calls the unity of "life."

> Unification and being mean the same thing; in every proposition the copulative "is" expresses the unification of subject and predicate—a being. Being can only be believed [*geglaubt*]; faith [*Glauben*] presupposes a being; it is therefore contradictory to say that in order to believe one must first be convinced of the being [of what is believed].[73]

Now the "being" of which Hegel speaks here is not that of a divine Object, as if that would have to be presupposed somehow by a believing subject. The very distinction between subject and object arises in reflection, and genuine faith is not primarily a form of reflection. Rather, faith is an activity within a unity of being. The fact that he *is* unites the believer with what is believed, precisely in his activity of faith. Only in a secondary sense is the activity reflective, and in this reflection an object is posed for the reflecting subject: that is, a "representation" appears to him, abstracted from his activity. That is the sense in which "faith" is defined at the outset:

> Faith is the way in which the unified, through which an antinomy is unified, is available in our representation [*Vorstellung*]. The unification is the activity; this activity reflected as object is what is believed. In order to unify them, the members of the antinomy must be felt or recognized as opposed, their relation to one another as antinomy; but what are opposed can only be recognized as opposed insofar as they are already united. (*HtJ,* 382)

The unity is primary; within the unity of being the activity occurs, the activity of believing and even of thinking. The opposition between subject and object arises when that which is believed or thought is abstracted from the activity: "That which is thought, as something separated, must now be unified, and only then can it be believed; thought is a unification, and becomes believed; but that which is thought is not yet so" (*HtJ,* 383).

Now positivity is a reification of the abstract object, as if it had a separate being of its own. But that abstracted being is no longer the being which the activity of faith shares. "In place of the sole possible being"—that in which thinking and authentic faith live with their realities—"a positive faith . . . places another being" with which it can only artificially appear to be united (*HtJ*, 383). Positive religion remains constituted by the subject-object dualism, which therefore thwarts even its attempt to unify the believer with the divine Object. "All unification is in positive religion to be something given; what is given is something that one does not have until one is given it." The very attempt to unite with the abstract being is contradictory, since the attempt could succeed only if the "being" in question were the genuine, encompassing being in which the believer already shares. Hegel in fact suggests that the object of a positive faith is essentially contingent, however it is defined. Even if it is defined as absolute, the fact of being defined (i.e., objectified) contradicts the absoluteness claimed. "The positive faith demands belief in something that is not; what is not can merely either become or not become at all; that which is defined is to that extent no real being." The believing subject, correlative to this self-contradictory object, is passive. The positive faith, unlike the authentic faith, is not essentially an activity. Its subject, like its object, is something limited, defined. Within this limitation it may engage in certain activities, also defined, such as seeing, hearing, moving, but its mode of uniting with its object cannot transcend the inherent limitations of these activities.

> In every unification there is a defining and a becoming-defined, that are one. But in the positive religion the one defining, even insofar as he defines, is himself defined. His action is not to be an activity, but a suffering. The one defining, through which he suffers, is to be sure something unified as well, and in this unification the one acting could have been active. But this is a lower kind of unification; for in the action that occurs out of positive faith, what is unified is again itself something set in opposition, defined by its opposite.[74]

There is no way to overcome the essential passivity of the positive believer, once his allegiance has been given to an abstract object. So positivity is now understood, not over against rational religion, but over against an encompassing self-activity within the living unity of being. Positivity is an obstruction of this self-activity, its faith fixed in a dualism between the mutually defining subject and object. Its subject as well as its object is a reified abstraction. In positive religion the self actually *becomes* that abstract subject; that is its bondage.

We have seen in the previous section how Hegel, in *The Spirit of Christianity and Its Fate,* soon came to regard Christ's religion of love as a deliverance from that bondage. For love is, again, an activity, in the unity of which individuals are freed from their own fixated subjecthood. We have even heard Hegel speaking of love's unity as concrete *being,* an "is" subjected neither to an abstract "ought" nor to the equally abstract being of a divine Object.

But now we must notice that even this exalted "spirit" of Christianity, of which Hegel speaks with so much more warmth than he had earlier, was subject to certain fateful limitations. If "religion" signifies the elevation of finite to infinite "life," then even this sublime love falls short of it, as Hegel suggests more than once.

> This love is a divine spirit, but it is not yet religion. To become religion, it must at the same time manifest itself in an objective form. Love, a sentiment, something subjective, would have to be fused with something represented [*Vorgestellten*], with the universal, and thereby achieve the form of an essential being [*Wesens*] both susceptible and worthy of prayer. This need to unify the subjective and objective, sentiment and its demand for objects, and the understanding, through fantasy, in something beautiful, in a god—this need, the highest of the human spirit, is the impulse toward religion.[75]

This insistence on the need for an objective form, indeed for a definite form of deity, sounds strange in light of our discussion of the fragment on "Faith and Being," in which the objectification of deity is the mark of positivity. But it appears to me that this position taken in *The Spirit of Christianity* represents only a change of emphasis and a further development, not an essential departure from the viewpoint of "Faith and Being." Even there, he had argued that faith must represent (*stelle vor*) its unity of being objectively, though without reifying its object as an abstract being, that is, without suspending or fixating its active process. Here he is not retracting those qualifications: while the sort of unifying process represented by love is not a sufficient condition for authentic religion, it is clearly a necessary condition. And here he explains why, in addition, it must find an objective expression: because

love, insofar as it is a purely subjective sentiment, is able to overcome
the reified, positive objectivity only by assuming another form of fixation, the subjective bond of an intimate community. We do speak of the
bond of love, and Hegel is pointing out that it does indeed imply bondage, a limitation and an exclusion, however rich the affective relationships may be within it. Though Hegel has given up the abstract
universality of Kantian reason, he still insists that a true religion must
find objective expressions that are like being itself, or life, universal
in principle, that it cannot be confined within a purely subjective bond.
However, he goes on in the passage quoted above to argue that Christianity does not meet that condition:

> The Christian community could not satisfy this impulse toward
> religion in its belief in God, for in its God could be found only
> its communal sentiment. In the God of the world all creatures
> are unified; in him are no members of a community as such.
> Their harmony is not the harmony of the whole; otherwise they
> would not form a particular community, would not be bound
> together through love. The Godhead of the world is not the mani-
> festation of their love, of their divinity. (HtJ, 332)

"A circle of love," Hegel says, "is a *little* Kingdom of God," however rich
the common associations and hopes may be within it (HtJ, 333; my
emphasis). Even divinity is scaled down to parochial stature, because
the unity of its members is so inward that it never achieves visible
form of universal scope. Here we find amplified Hegel's old observation
that Christianity is, after all, a private religion.

Hegel develops this point in detail in connection with a searching
interpretation of the original Eucharist, as a love feast. In the bread
and wine he finds a significant gesture toward an objective image, yet
in the end it seems to him that the host remains separate from the
bond of love, rather than being the image in which that bond becomes
visible to itself (HtJ, 297–301). The little brotherhood is too spiritual,
in every sense of the term too inward-looking, to incorporate itself
visibly and so to embrace the world. We sense Hegel's old ideal of folk
religion in the background of this sympathetic critique. A true religion
must express its own spirit in living but tangible forms that can be
grasped by society at large. But Christ's Kingdom can embrace human
beings only on the terms of its own ideal inwardness.

> Outside this communal pleasure, prayer, eating, joy, faith, and
> hope, outside the sole activity of spreading the faith, of enlarging
> the community of worship, there still lies a prodigious field of
> objectivity which establishes a fate, many sided in scope and of
> powerful might, and which claims many kinds of activity. In the
> task of love the community scorns any unification save the most
> inward, any spirit save the highest. . . . [The community] must
> stop with love itself—apart from the kinship of the common faith
> and its expression in religious actions related to it, every other
> bond in anything objective, for a purpose or a development of
> another side of life, is . . . alien to the congregation, . . . would
> be a desertion of the love which is its sole spirit and an infidelity
> to its God. (*HtJ*, 323)

The problem of Christianity seems on this account to be the opposite
of positivity: not the investment of faith in an alien objectivity, but in
a bond so inward as to exclude all objectivity as alien to its spirit. Yet,
in this dialectical consideration of the matter, the very exclusiveness
of this love is positive in a subtler sense. Over against itself it sets
"this world," the "prodigious field of objectivity" that Christ's kingdom
cannot embrace. That kingdom becomes one pole of an opposition, to
which the irreconcilable worldly objectivity looms as a menacing fate.
The problem is created in part by the very soullessness of the Jewish
and Roman worlds, against which the little community is obliged to
define itself. These it cannot approach without its spirit being devoured
by them. But the problem is also inherent in the limitations of its own
spirit of love, which dialectically constitutes a new fate in its very
repulsion of the fateful objectivity.

> This restriction of love to itself, its flight from all forms even if
> its spirit already breathes in them or if they sprang from it, this
> removal from all fate is just its greatest fate, and here is the
> point where Jesus converges with fate, in the most sublime way,
> to be sure, but where he suffers from it. [76]

Jesus could not preserve the beautiful common "life" to which he called
his followers without excluding the world of death and bondage, an
opposition that soon became an active hostility.

Yet even within his own circle there remained a positive element:
his own individuality, or rather the veneration in which his disciples

held him, much as he tried to wean them from it. Hence his attempt to convince them of the necessity that he should perish, should no longer be interposed as an obstacle to their realization of the divine life in themselves; and hence also his promise of the Holy Spirit in which they should be united in the divine life when he was gone (*HtJ*, 314–18; see Chapter 1). And indeed in the drama of crucifixion and resurrection Christianity might yet have overcome its "fate." The "positive" element of Christ's individuality was effaced, and from its death arose precisely what had been lacking in the little circle of love: an "image and form" at once objective, ideal, and living, for "the divine in the community of love."

> . . . in him who was resurrected and then exalted to heaven the image again found life, and love found the manifestation of its oneness. In this remarriage of spirit and body the opposition between the living and the dead has disappeared and been unified in a God. The longing of love has found itself as living essence and can now enjoy itself, the worship of it is now the religion of the congregation. The need of religion finds its satisfaction in this resurrected Jesus, in love thus given form. (*HtJ*, 334)

With this consummation of its drama, the earlier scenes in which deity condescends to assume the form of a servant, a limited individuality, would not necessarily have infected the community's faith with positivity. There would have been no fateful positivity if Christ's "actuality" as a historical personage could have existed "to be a husk and to pass away." But in the faith of the church this husk, "this blemish of humanity," refused to fall away: "the husk of actuality stripped off in the grave has ascended again out of the grave and attached itself to the one who is risen as God" (*HtJ*, 335).

The earthly image of Jesus continues to dominate the church's worship and its mission, becomes in fact the very face of its God. Rather, therefore, than being the quintessential expression of all religious truth, that finite life is transformed into the infinite life, Christianity obtruded the finite form of an individual into the infinite itself. The Chalcedonian Christological formula, "truly God and truly man," accurately represented Christian belief and practice—and also, in young Hegel's terms, the static paradox in which Christian belief and practice were fixated. Jesus' essential tragedy was his failure to wean the church.

In this context Hegel can proceed to touch on the forms of positivity that he treated in detail in his earlier essays. The preoccupation with miracles, historical revelations, proselytizing in Jesus' "name," authoritarian governance, and so forth—all follow from the church's veneration of the husk. The Christians could not share in the divine life, because they could recognize it only in its fixation in the image of Jesus. They were united only in having "a common master and teacher." Divinity was something "given."

> This is a remarkable side of the spirit of the community, that the divine which united them had for them the form of something given. To spirit, to life, nothing is given; what it has received it has itself become, has so passed over into it that it is now a modification of itself, is its own life.[77]

But with the extension of the Christian community to a great mass of people, even the intimate love that had been its treasure became an empty ideal, something not its own, for which it could only long. Having failed to grasp a "living" form of objectivity—that is, one expressive of its own common life—the love itself became an alien object for the community. Love was something commanded by Jesus and yet embodied in him alone. For the community "the unfulfilled ideal of love was something positive," that the community "recognized as set over against itself" (*HtJ*, 336).

So even in this very rich interpretation of Christianity Hegel in the end concludes that alienation is, if not its "spirit," at any rate its "fate." The problem of alienation is still expressed in terms of positivity, but the term is understood much more dialectically than in Hegel's earlier explorations of Christian origins. Not only authentic religion, but also its perversions, must be grasped in the dynamics of a community's developing belief and practice. Positivity is not a static attribute of its faith, abstractly considered, but is precisely the stasis, the fixation, reached when an impasse develops that it cannot overcome. At this stage in his thinking, Hegel still believes that such an impasse may be a "fate" implicit in the original development of a religious group. He is later to abandon that belief, and with it his preoccupation with Christian origins as such. He will later argue that the meaning of Christianity, and of any other historical movement, is revealed only in its whole course of development, in particular in its outcome rather than in its origins. In *The Spirit of Christianity and Its Fate* he carries the question about as far as he can on the basis of Christian origins, and in the process takes some important steps toward the historical dialectic that will underlie his mature view.

Hegel himself saw the importance of these steps, though of course without at that time realizing where they would lead. Within a few months after completing this culminating essay of his youth, he explicitly argued that positivity was a historically relative phenomenon. He did so, oddly enough, in a revised introduction (dated September 24, 1800) to his old essay on *The Positivity of the Christian Religion*. It is remarkable that he thought the old essay could be patched up, when his outlook had changed so thoroughly; evidently he did soon abandon the attempt. But in the revision he opened with a definition of positivity in the old terms[78] only in order at once to criticize that definition. For to oppose positive religion to natural religion—that is, to religion that accords with universal human nature and is therefore single as opposed to the plurality of positive religions—is to assume that there is such a thing as "pure human nature." If you could assume that, then the "manifold variety of manners, customs, and beliefs among peoples or individuals," insofar as they deviate from pure human nature, could be regarded as "accidents, prejudices, and errors." A positive religion, then, insofar it belongs to the mere historical life of a people, could also be relegated to that sorry rubbish heap (*HtJ*, 140).

But this ahistorical, indeed antihistorical way of posing the problem, so common in the century that had just ended, must itself be subjected to criticism. "Pure human nature" is a general concept, what Hegel will later call an abstract universal. Hegel does not dismiss the notion of human nature, but he gives it the social resonances that had been expressed even in his earliest writings, and therefore insists that it must embrace the concrete forms of actual cultural life. A bare concept cannot express the essentially human: "the living nature is always other than its concept, and therefore what for the concept is a bare modification, a pure accident, a superfluity, becomes a necessity, something living, perhaps the only thing that is natural and beautiful" (*HtJ*, 141).

The validity of any form of religious life must be assessed according to the way it answers to the real human needs expressed in the situation of a particular time and place. One might deplore the sort of religion that a particular age requires, but the fact that a religion is superstitious and barbaric by other standards does not make it positive. It becomes positive only when it continues to be imposed upon a people whose living human needs and conditions are no longer met by it, when it goes against the grain of their real life. Positivity does not refer to the content of a religion, abstractly considered in relation to universal norms, but to the form in which it inheres in life. The issue is whether it is imposed as "something altogether given" or whether it "is to be given as something free and freely received" (*HtJ*, 144). If we are to deal with the way religion actually functions in life, we must recognize that even what is most beautiful and imperishable must be linked in every case to *something* accidental which belongs to an age.

With respect to Christianity, Hegel makes it clear that he intends no mere apology for everything that has been done in its name. But the inquiry into its alleged "positive commands and doctrines" as measured by "universal concepts of human nature and God's attributes is too empty" to be pursued any more:

> The frightful chatter in this vein has, through its endless extension and inner vacuity, become too boring, has so utterly lost all interest, that the prior need of the age is perhaps to hear proven the very opposite of this enlightening application of universal concepts; with the understanding that the proof of this opposite would not proceed on the principles and methods that the old dogmatics were provided by the culture of their age, but would derive that now discarded dogmatics from what we now recognize as a need of human nature, thus exhibiting its naturalness and necessity. Such an attempt presupposes the belief that the conviction of many centuries, that for which millions in these centuries lived and died and regarded as duty and holy truth, has not been utter nonsense and immorality, at least according to their intentions. (*HtJ*, 143)

This program, which the old *Positivity* essay could hardly be reshaped enough to fulfill, does point quite prophetically to his own future treatment of Christianity. The aim is not so much to defend it as to understand it, sympathetically and in the deepest sense historically, as a form in which human life shaped itself for compelling reasons.

To achieve that kind of understanding it was necessary to renounce the abstract "reason" that could not grasp such "reasons" and therefore treated with contempt the historical (i.e., human) shapes of life that did not meet its own criteria. But Hegel would not be satisfied until he had found a form of reason capable of grasping the historically concrete forms of life in their inner development. The life of reason capable of comprehending its movement he would call *dialectic*.

Notes

1. Among his writings not included by Nohl, some of them indeed no longer extant, are the following: material on history and on politics, of which only fragments published in Rosenkranz's *Leben* (cited in Chapter 1, note 1) are extant (85ff., 515ff.; reprinted in *Dokumente* [cited in Chapter 1, note 8] 247ff., 278ff.); a translation from the French, which Hegel published anonymously, of an exposé of the oligarchy of Bern, entitled *Vertraulichen Briefen über das vormalige Staatsrechtliche Verhältnis des Wadtlandes (Pays de Vaud) zur Stadt Bern* (Frankfurt, 1798; Hegel's role as translator of this work was only discovered in 1909 [*Dokumente*, 247ff., 457ff.]); a regrettably lost commentary on Stewart's *Inquiry into the Principles of Political Oeconomy* (London, 1767) described by Rosenkranz (*Leben*, 86); a first draft of the essay, later revised and expanded in Jena, on the German constitution (*Dokumente*, 282ff., 468ff.); and a number of poems, collected in *Dokumente*, 377ff.

2. The Kroner-Knox translation of the *Early Theological Writings* includes only the essays *The Positivity of the Christian Religion, The Spirit of Christianity and Its Fate,* the *Fragment of a System,* and one of the miscellaneous fragments, on "Love." Since the editors followed the useful practice of providing the corresponding page numbers from the Nohl edition (as cited in Chapter 1, note 2; cited throughout text as *HtJ*) in brackets, it will not be necessary here to cite the English translation. But I have made use of it when I could, sometimes adopting or revising the translations of Knox.

3. Haering, in his monumental *Hegel: Sein Wollen und sein Werk* (as cited in Chapter 1, note 34) does carefully trace the philosopher's development in this way, "step by step," as he likes to say. His two large volumes bring the reader up to the composition of Hegel's *Phenomenology,* with pages 59–582 devoted to the "step by step" exposition of the Nohl essays and fragments.

4. These fragments have been translated in the first two of *Three Essays, 1793–1795* by Peter Fuss and John Dobbins (as cited in Chapter 1, note 2) the so-called "Tübingen Essay" of 1793 and the "Berne Fragments" of 1793–94. Only by courtesy can either of these fragmentary documents be considered essays, but Fuss and Dobbins followed Harris and others in calling the first five fragments, written in Tübingen, an essay. Harris also translated it (*Hegel's Development* [as cited in Chapter 1, note 4], 481–507), directly from the rough Nohl edition, but Fuss and Dobbins translated it from a smoother, less literal Suhrkamp edition that made it read more like a proper essay. But their translation of that and the "Berne Fragments" is quite good, and happily follows the practice of Kroner and Knox in indicating the Nohl pagination for all three of their "essays." So it will not be necessary to cite their translation here in addition to Nohl. My translations are from the "rougher" but more literal Nohl edition. I shall treat the first two, more fragmentary pieces in some detail, because the notion of folk religion and other conceptions associated with it presage important themes in Hegel's later thinking on religion.

5. *HtJ*, 17. There is, ironically, an echo of this metaphor in a well-known gibe that Kierkegaard directed primarily against Hegel himself, first in his *Journals* (trans. Alexander Dru [London: Oxford University Press, 1938], no. 583), and then in *The Sickness Unto Death* (ed. and trans. with introduction and notes by Howard V. Hong and Edna H. Hong [Princeton: Princeton University Press, 1980], 43–44): "A thinker erects a huge building, a system, a system embracing the whole of existence, world history, etc., and if his personal life is considered, to our amazement the appalling and ludicrous discovery is made that he himself does not personally live in this huge, domed palace but in a shed alongside it, or in a doghouse, or at best in the janitor's quarters." There are often these uncanny anticipations in Hegel's early writings of ideas and images developed among his radical young successors in the 1840s, not least among the left Hegelian critics of Christianity, who were of course unacquainted with these writings and were reacting in various ways against the mature Hegel. In some respects Hegel anticipated the *Zeitgeist* of the 1840s by fifty years.

6. *HtJ*,61. Cf. an earlier passage of similar purport, but expressed in less Kantian language, 51–52.

7. *HtJ*, 22. Cf. 20: "The single true consolation in suffering . . . is trust in the providence of God, everything else is empty prattle, that leads away from the heart."

8. *HtJ*, 8. Cf. Shaftesbury's *Inquiry Concerning Virtue and Merit*.

9. *HtJ*, 19; see also 23–26. This direct social-reformist motive in the young Hegel is perhaps the main factor that separates him from Kant and Fichte, on whom he is otherwise so dependent. Fichte's *Kritik aller Offenbarung* had just been published in 1792, and Hegel adopted the very distinction between subjective and objective religion from that work (*HtJ*, 355). Further, while Fichte does not go so far as Hegel in making religion an affair of the "heart," he is clear that if religion is to become subjective it must go beyond theology and not appeal simply to the head. Yet Fichte's basic purpose in this work is to produce a "critique" on the Kantian model: to determine the extent to which the possibility and necessity of divine revelation can be postulated by the requirements of practical reason. Hegel's interest in these early fragments is at the farthest remove from this quasi-theoretical problem; there is no hint of it here, and as we have seen, in his correspondence with Schelling (see Chapter 1) he takes a dim view of Fichte's procedure. His concern with practical reason is far more "practical" in the common meaning of the term. See Haering, *Hegel: Sein Wollen*, 1:72ff.

10. *HtJ*,12. The understanding may, on the other hand, try to show that virtue makes a person happier in the long run, but Hegel finds this calculation "too subtle and too cold to have any effect in the moment of action." It is remarkable that Hegel's polemic attitude toward "the abstract understanding," which was to become one of his trademarks as a philosopher, should have begun so early.

11. *HtJ*, 15. But he sharply distinguishes such wisdom from "enlightenment," "calculation" (*Räsonnement)*, "science."

12. Hegel had identified the characters of the allegory in a passage which he later struck out, apparently forgetting that it was a necessary key to the present passage. Not only is Chronos identified as the father and the *politeia* as the mother, but appropriate roles were found for music and the fine arts. That is the passage in which religion is directly identified as the midwife and wet nurse of the young genius. Nohl preserves the passage in a footnote (*HtJ*, 27 n–28 n).

13. *HtJ*, 28–29. See also 26–27, 54, and 357–59 for similar passages, particularly contrasting classical Greek with Christian religion in its function as a Volksreligion, nurturing culture and public ethical values.

Laurence Dickey (*Hegel: Religion, Economics;* cited in Chapter 1, note 18) consistently downplays the importance of Hegel's Hellenic ideal as the source of his notion of Volksreligion, arguing that it stems, instead, from a long-standing Old-Württembergian Protestant commitment to civil piety. As we have seen, Dickey recounts the history of this tradition in detail, and he argues, less convincingly, that Hegel in his student years was a quintessential Old-Württemberger in lifestyle and values. He says, for instance, that "Hegel did not have to read the Greeks to develop enthusiasm for Volksreligion. Württembergers had already admitted that kind of ethic to their conception of what public life should consist in among Protestant people. And, as we saw, they ethicized piety and made it public as a prelude to sanctioning politics as a vehicle of religious recollectivization and collective salvation" (144). He also ascribes Hegel's closely related concept of *Sittlichkeit,* which continues to play a central role in the Jena writings, including the *Phenomenology,* to this same background. We can only be grateful to Dickey for exhuming Hegel's Old-Württembergian roots, that have been generally ignored, but we may also suspect that he exaggerates their importance in comparison to sources of Hegel's thinking that are well documented in his early writings. Dickey also has to explain away young Hegel's sharp criticisms of the Christian tradition generally. Not just any Old-Württemberger might have written the fragments on Volksreligion, not to speak of the *Phenomenology!* Perhaps Hegel did not *have* to read the Greeks to construct his idea of Volksreligion, but in point of fact he did read them and referred to them repeatedly. In chapter 4, to be sure, Dickey acknowledges that "the young Hegel" does not simply continue to be the Old-Württembergian "old man" of the earliest fragments, and undertakes to show how the "old man" became "the young Hegel."

14. *HtJ,* 24–26, in which Hegel gives a sympathetic interpretation of the practice of sacrifice, particularly as an act of thanksgiving to the generous powers upon which mortals are dependent. But he also defends with some qualifications the sin-offering, not as an easy means of dissipating moral responsibility for one's own acts, but as a means of restoring a person who precisely in this act acknowledges guilt.

15. Haering strenuously attempts to sort out this complex of distinctions, though without succeeding in making quite clear what after all was probably not very clear in Hegel's own mind at this time; see *Hegel: Sein Wollen,* 1:84ff.

16. Those are the lines along which Hegel developed the idea of the private religion or small religious society when it had become clearer in his mind, in his later essay *The Positivity of the Christian Religion.* Cf. *HtJ,* 166ff., 187, 194. Charity, for example, is an admirable ideal that might be properly pursued in a voluntary religious society, but it could not be enjoined by an institution of society at large, as though people had a *right* to one another's charity. *HtJ,* 173–74.

17. See *HtJ,* 49–50, where Hegel summarizes his case against public Christianity in outline form.

18. *HtJ,* 41–45. Hegel particularly takes the Protestant reformers to task for wedding the Christian religion so intimately to the state and allegedly making New Testament teachings into social principles, enforced by the police.

19. *HtJ,* 44. Hegel developed this theme at length in *The Positivity of the Christian Religion; HtJ,* 166–205.

20. *HtJ,* 63. A modern reader is reminded of Bonhoeffer's polemic against "cheap grace" in the opening pages of *The Cost of Discipleship* (Macmillan and SCM Press, 2d ed., 1959). Bonhoeffer's paradoxical alternative, "costly grace," of course lies outside the young Hegel's purview, but his polemic has the same target: the use of the orthodox Protestant doctrine of justification by grace alone to "justify" an insipid ethical mediocrity. "Grace alone does everything, they say, and so everything can remain as it was before" (35).

21. Henry Chadwick has selected and translated the most important articles in which Lessing develops this theme, under the title, *Lessing's Theological Writings* (Library of Modern Religious Thought, London: A. & C. Black, 1956; Stanford: Stanford University Press, 1967). See especially the article, "On the Proof of the Spirit and of Power." Chadwick's introduction provides an admirable summary of the problem and traces its background from Spinoza to Lessing.

22. I borrow the term *Geschichtswahrheiten* from the key proposition of Lessing's article mentioned in the preceding note, "Über den Beweis des Geistes und der Kraft": "accidental truths of history [*Geschichtswahrheiten*] can never become the proof of necessary truths of reason." *Lessings Philosophie*, ed. Paul Lorentz (Philosophische Bibliothek, Leipzig: Verlag der Dürr'schen Buchhandlung, 1909), 94. Chadwick translation, 53.

23. Ibid., 39. The theme of home-grown versus foreign traditions is further developed in *The Positivity of the Christian Religion; HtJ,* 214–19.

24. Nohl, in fact, sets this brief fragment apart (*HtJ,* 70–71) as the last of the five on *Volksreligion und Christentum*. But Gisela Schüler, in an essay "Zur Chronologie von Hegels Jugendschriften" (*Hegel-Studien* [Bonn: Bouvier, 1963], 2:129, 140–41), has argued, on the basis of a close examination of Hegel's handwriting in the original manuscripts, that this fragment in fact was written between the original section of the fourth fragment (*HtJ,* 50–60) and Hegel's slightly later revision and development of it, which Nohl edited as a continuation of the fourth fragment (*HtJ,* 60–69). Schüler's reconstruction of this chronology confirms Haering's (*Hegel: Sein Wollen,* 1:178ff.), who regards the fifth fragment and pages 60–69 of the fourth as very close in time. (I have generally followed Schüler's chronology in this interpretation of the early writings.)

25. *HtJ,* 70–71. Hegel expands upon this theme of Roman decadence as the preparation for authoritarian Christianity in *The Positivity of the Christian Religion; HtJ,* 222ff.

26. It is not certain just when Hegel first read this book. Nohl (*HtJ,* 404) and others profess to find evidence of its influence even while Hegel was still in Tübingen, shortly after its appearance. But only late in 1794 does it noticeably dominate his thinking.

27. Kant, *Die Religion innerhalb der Grenzen der blossen Vernunft,* 260–61 in the original pagination. (The pagination of the edition of 1793 is conveniently provided in the margins of the modern edition edited by Karl Vorländer [Hamburg: Felix Meiner, 1956]. Translated as *Religion Within the Limits of Reason Alone* by Theodore M. Greene and Hoyt H. Hudson, with a new essay by John R. Silber [New York: Harper and Row, Torchbooks series, 1960], 158.)

28. Ibid., 167. See the whole of this section, 167ff. (Greene and Hudson trans., 105ff.). Moral faith in this sense, not the "ecclesiastical" faith of traditional religion, is what Kant had in mind in his famous remark in the preface to the second edition of *Kritik der reinen Vernunft* (B XXX): "Ich musste also das Wissen aufheben, um zum Glauben Platz zu bekommen"; see Chapter 1.

29. *HtJ,* 61. This passage is from the revision and development of the fourth fragment, which Nohl edited as part of that fragment. But according to Haering and Schüler, this section, 60–69, was the last one belonging to the fragments on *Volksreligion*. See note 24.

30. *HtJ,* 57. Cf. Kant's *Die Religion,* 73ff. (in the original pagination; Greene and Hudson trans., 54ff.), for his discussion of Christ as "personifizierte Idee des guten Prinzips," which directly inspired this passage. But even Kant is here articulating a view widely held among eighteenth-century writers. As Chadwick points out in his introduction to *Lessing's Theological Writings* (35), "In the Age of Reason if Christianity is accepted it is on account of its ethical teaching. To say Christ is Son of God is to say that he is the incarnation of man's highest aspirations and ideals."

31. *HtJ,* 58–60. Hegel alludes in this connection to a remark by Sittah in Lessing's *Nathan* (act 2, scene 1):

> Not his virtue; his name
> is to be broadcast everywhere.

32. The fourth fragment on Volksreligion. See note 24 above.

33. See especially the improved version of the Sermon on the Mount that Hegel puts into Jesus' mouth (*Das Leben Jesu,* in *HtJ,* 82–88); e.g., in place of the Golden Rule, which is identified as a mere "general rule of prudence" (cf. the discussion of "maxims of prudence" in Kant's *Grundlegung zur Metaphysik der Sitten,* 402–3, contrasted to the "principle of duty"), Hegel's Jesus proposes the following "rule of morality [*Sittlichkeit*]": "What you could will that it be binding as a universal law among human beings, it is also binding among you to act according to such a maxim—this is the fundamental law of morality, the content of all legislation and of the sacred books of all peoples" (*HtJ,* 87). This *Life of Jesus* is translated by Fuss and Dobbins as the third of the *Three Essays,* with Nohl's pagination in the margins. See *HtJ,* 154 n, where a similar critique of the Golden Rule appears in *The Positivity of the Christian Religion.*

34. *HtJ,* 75. Cf. the much richer, and much more Johannine exposition of this prologue in *The Spirit of Christianity and Its Fate*; *HtJ,* 306ff.

35. *HtJ,* 126. Cf. 168ff. for a similar treatment of the Supper in *The Positivity of the Christian Religion,* and also some remarks on its later degeneration.

36. *HtJ,* 134–36. The date of composition follows in Hegel's own hand, dispelling any doubt whether he intended to end there, without hint of any sort of resurrection.

37. *HtJ,* 92. Cf. 125, where Jesus tells his disciples that he has aroused, and "the spirit of truth and virtue" will cultivate, "the seed of the good, which reason emplanted in you."

38. *HtJ,* 89: "If you regard your churchly statutes and positive commands as the highest law that is given to man, then you ignore the dignity of man, and the capacity in him to create out of himself the concept of divinity and the knowledge of his will"; cf. 123.

39. *HtJ,* 121. The warning continues for two more pages, in which all the evils of sectarianism and fanatical religious conflict are said to be implicit in this belief.

40. *HtJ,* 119 and passim. Cf. Kierkegaard's *Philosophical Fragments*—also, in a way, a peculiar philosophical retelling of the gospel story—which makes precisely the opposite point about the relation of Christ to his true disciple.

41. See, for example, Lessing's little essay on "The Religion of Christ" in which Christ's religion is set in stark contradiction to the Christian religion; *Lessing's Theological Writings,* 106. See also part one of Chadwick's introduction for a discussion of others in Lessing's background who had posed the reasonable religion of Jesus in opposition to the irrationalities of church dogma.

42. See Rosenkranz, *Leben,* 50ff., for a discussion of Hegel's *Leben Jesu* in the context of other contemporary reconstructions. Also see the first four chapters of Albert Schweitzer's famous *Von Reimarus zu Wrede* (1906), translated under the title *The Quest of the Historical Jesus.*

43. "Therefore if a writing be accepted at the same time as a divine revelation, its highest criterion as such a revelation is: 'All scripture given by God is useful for teaching, for punishment, and for improvement' etc. and since the latter, namely the moral improvement of human beings, constitutes the authentic purpose of all rational religion, so this will also be held to be the highest principle of all scriptural interpretation" (Kant, *Die Religion,* 161; see 157ff., 199 [Greene and Hudson trans., 102, 100ff., 123]). Kant points out that there is ample precedent for such determined moralizing of mythopoeic texts among the Greek and Roman moral philosophers, as well as among "the more enlightened

segment" of believers in all the major religions; ibid., 159f. (Greene and Hudson trans. 100f.). See Dilthey, *Jugendgeschichte* (cited in Chapter 1, note 1), 21f.

44. Dilthey himself points out that Hegel was at the same time expressing doubts, in letters, whether Jesus could adequately be construed in terms of a Kantian moral *Vernunftglauben* (*Jugendgeschichte*, 21, 30). Haering argues at length, in his interpretation of *Das Leben Jesu* (*Hegel: Sein Wollen*, 1:183–96), that Hegel did not in fact accept the simple moralistic reduction of the religion of Jesus that this document seems so clearly to imply. Haering insists that Hegel meant to make a distinction between the purely moral teaching of Jesus and Jesus' full religious meaning, and that *Das Leben Jesu* confines itself, as a limited experiment, to the former. Unfortunately, however, Haering's distinction begs the question, and requires him to minimize the influence of Kant during this period.

45. Also not Hegel's own title, but one given by Nohl to an untitled essay, loosely connected at some points, to which Hegel turned from time to time over the course of almost a year (summer 1795–summer 1796).

46. Cf. Herbert Wacker, *Das Verhältnis des jungen Hegel zu Kant* (Berlin: Junker und Dünnhaupt, 1932), which essentially confirms my reading of Hegel's relation to Kant during the 1790s. Wacker considers the period up to the middle of 1794 as "pre-Kantian," sees "Hegel as Kantian" from then until mid-1796, and "Hegel as opponent of Kant" from then on. Haering, on the other hand, minimizes as far as he can the influence of Kant even during this middle period. For instance, he points out (*Hegel: Sein Wollen*, 1:193) that Hegel never mentions "the struggle of the evil principle with the good," which is certainly a major motif in Kant's *Religion*, and he repeatedly stresses the fact that morality has a social nuance for Hegel that it lacks for Kant, even when he uses Kantian language. Such considerations are a justified reminder that Hegel never followed any rigorously consistent philosophical path during the 1790s. Just how Kantian Hegel ever was is still a disputed question. The Kantian language of both the *Life of Jesus* and the *Positivity* essay is obvious, but for instance Fuss and Dobbins, in their introduction to *Three Essays*, 14–15, deny that the real intent of Hegel's pieces is Kantian (though they do not mention Kant's *Religion*), and Dickey (*Hegel: Religion, Economics,* 175) reaches the same conclusion (though he does discuss the *Religion* at length). But the Kantian language is not merely a facade: I think it evident that Hegel was indeed broadly and not very critically under the influence of Kant during this period, that he was indeed so intent on pursuing some of the implications of Kant's *Religion* for his reflections on early Christianity that he expressed even his own ideas in a fundamentally Kantian sense.

47. *HtJ*, 153. See also 166 and 175. We treat at this point only Hegel's original essay (*HtJ*, 152–231), composed in 1795–96. Much later, in 1800, and from a very different point of view, he undertook a revision of the first several sections, which Nohl misleadingly placed before the original essay in his text (*HtJ*, 139–51). Knox placed his translation of the revision after that of the original.

48. I have called attention to the reappearance in this essay of important motifs of earlier pieces when these motifs were under discussion. I shall largely ignore these motifs in the present discussion, partly to avoid repetition, partly because the *Positivity* essay is available in T. M. Knox's excellent translation.

49. See J. Glenn Gray, *Hegel's Hellenic Ideal* (New York: King's Crown, 1941), reissued under the title *Hegel and Greek Thought* (New York: Harper and Row, Torchbooks series, 1968), for a brief and lucid survey of the way Hegel's dream of Greek culture affected his thought from the early writings to the mature works.

50. *HtJ*, 233–34. This attempt to define positivity opens a separate fragment, written between the writing of the two main parts of the original essay (152–213, mostly written

during 1795, and 214–31, written during the spring or summer of 1796; see Schüler, "Zur Chronologies," 130, 143–44) on *The Positivity of the Christian Religion*. Its pages are not numbered, in the manuscript, in continuity with the essay, and Knox left it untranslated. But the theme of this highly interesting fragment is integrally related to the subject of the essay, and it seems more than possible that Hegel intended to incorporate it into the essay somewhere. For another, less carefully drawn attempt to define positivity early in the essay itself, see 157–58. Positivity is also defined in roughly these terms at the beginning of the revision of 1800 (*HtJ*, 139; Kroner-Knox trans., 167).

The aspect of positivity highlighted in this quotation is what Kant called "heteronomy" in his moral writings, the acceptance of moral principles on alien authority rather than on the basis of the self-legislation of one's own practical reason.

51. *HtJ*, 211–12. Within a year after completing this essay, in a fragment entitled "Moralität, Liebe, Religion," Hegel offered the following succinct definition of positivity as a confounding of this Kantian distinction between theoretical "objects" and practical laws: "A faith will be called positive, in which the practical is theoretically present—what is originally subjective is stated only as something objective, a religion that treats the representations of something objective, that cannot become subjective, as the principle of life and conduct" (*HtJ*, 374).

52. Kant doubtless spoke for the young Hegel during this period in applying the traditional Christological predicates to "*Humanity* (the rational world-essence in general) *in its entire moral perfection*": it is this which proceeds from the substance of the Father, is the only-begotten Son, the Word in which all things are created, and so forth; Kant, *Die Religion*, 73 (Greene and Hudson trans., 54). Hegel was later to deny that Humanity or universal Reason in this "abstract" sense is the content of Christology; but the idea was revived by his left-Hegelian follower, D. F. Strauss, in his famous *Life of Jesus* of 1835.

53. *HtJ*, 227–28. Also 224–25. Here Hegel strikes again the note we have heard in the fifth fragment on Volksreligion, a note that, with some new overtones, was to be incorporated into his mature philosophy of history: that social decadence was the condition for the reception of positive religion, with its objectivized God.

54. Dilthey, *Jugendgeschichte*, 41–43 (trans. in *Letters*, 46–47). Haering testified to the importance he gave this poem by publishing a fold-out facsimile of the manuscript, together with a transcription, as the frontispiece to his *Hegel*. (It is also printed in Rosenkranz, *Leben*, 78–80.) See Chapter 1.

Hegel wrote this ecstatic poem during a long vacation in the Alps, the other memento of which is a singularly boring travel-diary (published in *Dokumente*, 221–44). It is of some small biographical and perhaps even philosophical interest to note, however, that while he seemed generally unimpressed with the great static masses of the mountains and glaciers, he was deeply fascinated by the waterfalls, in which one sees "eternally the same form, and at the same time sees that it is never the same," sees in fact in the essential vitality of the falls "the eternal life, the powerful nimbleness within itself" (231, 232).

55. Rosenkranz, *Leben*, 83. On the same page appears a poem in which the master, sounding not at all Faustian, recounts his trials in training the poodle.

Hegel's thinking undergoes such a transformation after his move to Frankfurt that a good deal of the secondary literature suggests he underwent an "identity crisis" there (discussed and dismissed by Harris, *Hegel's Development*, 258–65). Dickey suggests that the crisis is less psychological than theoretical, induced by the challenge of immersing himself in the writings of Scottish economists (*Hegel: Religion, Economics*, 150, 192ff.). Dickey's discussion of this influence is a major contribution of his work, but it can hardly explain the romantic-mystical turn I shall highlight in this section. It is tempting in that regard to suspect that Hölderlin's influence was decisive, but that would be guessing. We lack evidence to support any single factor that may have precipitated this transformation.

56. Shortly after arriving in Frankfurt Hegel began sketching his critique of Hebraic religion, several fragments and revisions appearing in *HtJ*, 368–74. This material, further revised and extended, was incorporated as a first long section in *Der Geist des Christentums und sein Schicksal* (*HtJ*, 243–60).

It is remarkable that Hegel never fundamentally revised this view of Hebraic religion as such. It was somewhat tempered and developed in later work, and he does seem to show more appreciation for this form of spirituality when he treats it in his lectures on the philosophy of religion twenty-five to thirty years later under the rubric of "The Religion of Sublimity." But even then his critical line shows a remarkable similarity to the analysis in this early work. He continued to read the Old Testament itself with a jaundiced eye, and he never did justice to the independent development of historical Judaism beyond its biblical sources and alongside Christianity. There is a similar continuity through Hegel's career in his treatment of the Greeks, to whom the Hebrews were always juxtaposed. But the juxtaposition took significantly different forms in the later work: Tempering his enthusiasm for the Greeks as he tempered his contempt for the Hebrews, he later came to treat both more dialectically, finding in Athens and Jerusalem the two great sources of the cultural destiny of the West. But he continued to see Athens as its joyous and beautiful source, Jerusalem as its unhappy if equally necessary source.

I suppose it still needs to be added that this harshly critical view of Hebraic religion and culture has nothing to do with any racist anti-Semitism, either personal or ideological. Hegel's philosophical interpretation of historico-cultural ways of life was, whatever its limitations, at the furthest remove from a racist ideology of *Blut und Boden*.

57. *HtJ*, 243–48. These pages bear fascinating comparison with Kierkegaard's famous interpretation of Abraham in *Fear and Trembling*. The attitudes of the two authors toward their subject are entirely different, but there are some points in the analysis itself that have an uncanny similarity.

58. *HtJ*, 253–54. See Knox's footnote on Mendelssohn's *Jerusalem*, to which Hegel ironically refers in connection with this passage.

59. Kant, *Die Religion*, 270 (Greene and Hudson trans., 164).

60. *HtJ*, 265–66; see also 268. Here and later, my citing of some of Hegel's complaints against Kant without comment does not necessarily imply that I consider the complaint decisive, or even fair to Kant. But our interest here is in Hegel's own developing ideas.

61. The so-called "Fragment of a System" of 1800; *HtJ*, 351.

62. "Die Liebe" (1797); *HtJ*, 397. This fragment is translated in the Kroner-Knox edition.

63. Ibid., 380–82.

64. "Liebe und Religion" (also 1797, untranslated); *HtJ*, 377.

65. *Der Geist des Christentums und sein Schicksal*; *HtJ*, 273ff. See also 349–50 in the "Systemfragment" for a discussion of property. Rosenkranz quotes a passage dating from this time in which Hegel criticizes the Kantian view that church and state should be entirely separate, each functioning independently without interfering with the other. That seems to Hegel to be impossible, because of a fundamental conflict over the status of private property. "If the state has the principle of *property*, its law is contrary to the law of the church." So long as property rights lie at the basis of the state—and Hegel here anticipates Marx's view that such is the case—the state must reduce the citizen to an owner, contradicting the church's view of the human status. "Either the citizen is not serious in his relation to the state, or not serious in relation to the church." One of the two

must in reality give way to the other, whatever appearances of autonomy are preserved. Rosenkranz, *Leben,* 87f., quoting from extended comments Hegel wrote, beginning in August 1798, in the course of an intensive study of Kant's *Rechtlehre, Tugundlehre,* and *Metaphysik der Sitten.*

66. *HtJ,* 296. Such passages recall the language of Schleiermacher's *Reden über die Religion,* particularly the second Speech. Since the *Reden* appeared in 1799, and according to Schüler ("Zur Chronologie," 133) the composition of this part of Hegel's *Geist des Christentums* extended into 1800, some direct influence is more than possible. Oddly, Nohl (*HtJ,* 405) uses the publication of the *Reden* to establish the terminus ante quem of Hegel's piece—arguing that it must therefore have been completed before summer 1799—on the assumption that Hegel could not have been acquainted with Schleiermacher's work when he wrote *Geist des Christentums.* (Even on that assumption his reasoning is faulty, as Schüler points out, 153 n, since one need not assume that Hegel read Schleiermacher's work as soon as it appeared.) But passages like the one quoted make that assumption insecure. At the same time I should not venture so far as to argue that they presuppose Hegel's acquaintance with the *Reden,* for the similarities in idea and language could be accounted for in terms of the romantic-mystical milieu common to the two young thinkers. Certainly Hegel does not directly cite the *Reden* in this work, as he does later.

67. *HtJ,* 313. Again, "faith in the divine grows out of the divinity of the believer's own nature; only a mode *(Modifikation)* of the deity can recognize it."

68. *HtJ,* 317. These Johannine passages conceding the coming of the Comforter continued to be decisive for Hegel's interpretation of Christianity; and he steadily held to the fundamental line of exegesis of these passages laid down here.

69. *HtJ,* 302ff. See also the so-called "Systemfragment von 1800": "out of that which is mortal, transitory, infinitely opposed to itself (and) at war with itself, this thinking life raises that which is living, imperishable, the relationship within the multiplicity (of objects) which is neither dead nor killing, not a (conceptual) unity, a relationship in thought, but all-living, all-powerful, infinite life; and it calls this God (*HtJ,* 347). Walter Jaeschke argues (*Vernunft in die Religion* [cited in Chapter 1, note 75]; Stewart and Hodgson trans. 119–20) that therefore "the concept of love is inferior to that of life. Love and unification presuppose something separate, whereas life involves both opposition and unification, association and nonassociation. The loftiest definition of the concepts of God and religion is therefore based on the concept of life."

70. *HtJ,* 348. See 346–47, on the dialectical plurality-in-unity of "life."

71. *Phänomenologie des Geistes,* ed. Hoffmeister, 12; Miller trans., 3–4; Baillie trans., 2d ed., 1949, 70. See Chapter 1, note 24.

72. "Glauben und Sein" (*HtJ,* 382–85). Haering devotes one of his most illuminating chapters to this fragment (*Hegel: Sein Wollen,* 1:391–413), to which he appends an excursus on the relation to Schelling during this period (413–30).

73. *HtJ,* 383. It is unfortunate that in English, unlike German, we have no verb form for "faith" and must resort to the ambiguous verb "believe."

74. *HtJ,* 384. Hegel already suggests (385) that Kantian philosophy, as well as positive religion, exhibits this dualistic impasse.

75. *Der Geist des Christentums und sein Schicksal,* in *HtJ,* 332.

76. *HtJ,* 324. Cf. 321–22, 327–29. One is reminded of the discussion, with quite different examples in view, of the "beautiful soul" of romantic piety that ends chapter 6 of *Phänomenologie des Geistes.*

77. *HtJ,* 336. See 336–42 for the development of the earlier themes of positivity in this context.

78. *HtJ,* 139. This revision, which Nohl placed at the beginning of the old essay, was undertaken ten days after the completion of the *Systemfragment von 1800.*

III

The Formation of Hegel's Philosophy in Jena: Religious Configurations

1. Hegel's Philosophical Debut

On November 2, 1800, Hegel wrote Schelling that he was ready to leave Frankfurt and wanted his friend's advice in choosing a town that might be suitable for settling down temporarily and pursuing his own studies. Schelling had been in Jena since 1798, when he was appointed *ausseror-dentlicher* professor of philosophy at the most extraordinary age of twenty-three. Hegel, now thirty years old, and relieved of the necessity of earning his bread for a while by a modest inheritance from his father, is clearly buoyed by his new independence and looking forward to some major changes in his life. Eventually he will join his friend in Jena. However, "before I dare to commit myself to the literary whirl of Jena I want first to fortify myself through a stay in some third place." Perhaps Bamberg or Erfurt or somewhere else not too far from Jena, someplace where Schelling has some contacts. Enjoying the luxury of being able to choose, he is looking for a town that offers "cheap food, a good beer for the sake of my bodily dispositions, a few acquaintances; other things being equal I should prefer a Catholic city to a Protestant; I want to observe that religion once at close hand."

But Hegel also wants to tell his old friend, with whom he had lost contact for a few years, about the turn his intellectual interests had taken. He has been following Schelling's great philosophical strides "with admiration and joy" and wants to renew their friendship. As for himself:

> In my intellectual development [wissenschaftlichen Bildung], which set out from the more subordinate needs of men, I had to be driven on to science [Wissenschaft], and the ideal of my youth had at the same time to be transmuted into the form of reflection, in a system; I ask myself now, while I am still busy with that, what sort of return is to be found to the engagement in the life of men.[1]

Besides the ethical, historical, religious ideas that we have seen Hegel working out in Bern and Frankfurt, he had also been intensely involved in political questions; he had been somewhat active politically in Frankfurt, and had recently begun writing his essay "The German Constitution," closely related both in content and style to the "theological" writings, and also left unpublished. These concerns had always arisen out of broad humanistic interests and had been pursued with a view toward some practical effect on the life of society. But now he has been "driven on" from his preoccupation with "the more subordinate needs of men," that are given religious and political expression, to the kinds of theoretical concerns that require systematic philosophical treatment: to what may be called the "need" of reason itself for some more comprehensive insight. Though he is already launched upon this new undertaking, he does not imply that he already has a system of his own in hand.[2] But already he is worried about how to integrate speculative pursuits, of the sort he had earlier kept at arm's length, with that practical "engagement in the life of men" that had always been much closer to the heart of his studies. And he goes on to say that Schelling alone seems to him to have shown the way! Schelling, who had published his *System of Transcendental Idealism* earlier that year, had also, according to Hegel, had an effect on the world, had "grasped human beings purely, i.e. whole-heartedly and without vanity," in a way that had inspired Hegel to join hands with him in common cause. Furthermore, he fully trusts that Schelling, for his part, will appreciate "my unselfish endeavor, even if its sphere be lower," and that his friend "can find a value in it."[3]

Though Schelling's reply has not survived, it seems to have been all Hegel could have wished for. Hegel in fact came directly to Jena, doubtless at Schelling's urging, and plunged with great energy into a philosophical career. By the end of the following July (1801) he had written his first philosophical work for publication, *The Difference between the Fichtean and Schellingian Systems of Philosophy*—a "difference" that seemed to the author to be altogether to the advantage of the latter. By August 23 he had completed his *Habilitation* thesis for the university at Jena, *De orbitis Planetarum,* and on the twenty-seventh his *Habilitationdisputation* was held, in which he orally defended a series of paradoxical propositions that ranged over the whole field of philosophy; between August 23 and 27 he somehow found time to write the first of a series of substantial book reviews for the *Litteratur-Zeitung* of Erlangen! Hegel was appointed docent and began lecturing at the university during the winter semester on logic and metaphysics. Meanwhile his literary activity continued unabated. He and Schelling, who were rooming together, decided to launch a new *Critical Journal of Philosophy,*[4] and by autumn 1801, Hegel was already busy writing essays for it. He continued to write quite voluminously for the *Journal* during the two years (1802–3) in which it appeared.

Hegel had found his metier. It was now clear that he was a philosopher. If one simply attends to his writings before and after the turn of the century, this blossoming forth as a philosopher seems astonishingly sudden. But he had been quietly devoting himself to philosophical studies in Frankfurt, patiently working through the writings of Kant and his followers, especially Fichte, and was deepening his knowledge of, and also his distaste for, the philosophers of the Enlightenment. He read each of Schelling's works as they appeared, with a sympathy that soon became apparent in Jena. But he particularly immersed himself in the ancients, in Plato above all; Hegel's first philosophical writings were so directly addressed to contemporary philosophical issues, and the influence of Schelling is so obvious, that it is easy to overlook the less obvious but probably more profound influence of classical Greek thought on his philosophical development. At any rate, one could easily trace Hegel's increasing philosophical sophistication through the "unphilosophical" writings of his Frankfurt years. Though it found only indirect expression in these writings, we recall, for example, his deep-going critique of Kant's philosophy of religion, and the influence of the *Phaedrus* is evident in his reflections on the theme of love. Not even the venture into speculative astronomy in his *Habilitation* thesis was a sheer bolt from the philosophical aether. Not only was Hegel clearly within the "orbit" of the Schellingian philosophy of nature when he wrote his thesis, but he had been carrying on intensive studies in the natural sciences since his school days. His excerpts had shown a close acquaintance with the works of Kepler, Newton, and more recent as-tronomers, as well as Kant's writings on astronomy and mechanics.[5]

Still, nothing in Hegel's past quite prepares us for that extraordinary eruption of philosophical vitality that began as soon as he arrived in Jena. To be in Jena was to be at stage center in Germany's cultural life. It was, in particular, a philosophical hothouse, in which philosophi-cal talent was brought quickly into full bloom. Rosenkranz speaks of it as a "philosophical Eldorado"[6] where the most gifted philosophers had gathered. Reinhold had launched the post-Kantian philosophical movement there, Fichte had arrived in 1794 and soon required the largest hall in the university to hold the crowds of students who came to his lectures. Four years later he was joined by Schelling, whose elan as a lecturer was as brilliant as the originality of his ideas. The faculty in philosophy boasted a number of other, only slightly lesser lights who illuminated every field in the broad range of philosophical sciences, psychology, natural law, ethics, philosophy of nature, mathematics, and so forth, with a special concentration in logic. Around the professors swarmed a large and constantly shifting company of docents, and stu-dents who wished to share in the excitement generated by the latest philosophical movements came in great numbers from every part of Germany. Jena had been a center of literary activity as well. Schiller had been a professor of history and aesthetics. Goethe maintained a second residence there; Hegel was to strike up a friendly association with Goethe that lasted for the rest of their lives. The Romantic move-ment, drawn by the presence of Novalis, Tieck, and August Schlegel, also found its center in Jena. It is not surprising that Hegel had felt the need for some fortification before plunging into Jena's literary whirl.

When Hegel arrived, however, Jena's greatest days were just past. In 1800 Novalis had died, Tieck had moved away, and Schlegel's *Athe-naum,* the Romantic literary journal, had ceased publication. As a result of the so-called atheism controversy Fichte had been forced to resign in 1799, and the *Atheismusstreit* still left a sour taste. But even the afterglow of Jena's recent brilliance was bright enough to inspire extraordinary energies in Hegel. He remained until the university collapsed before Napoleon's advancing army in 1806. During those years the Hegelian philosophy was born and brought rapidly to maturity. If seven years had been spent toiling in Bern and Frankfurt for Leah, Hegel was to crown his seven years in Jena by winning Rachel.

Schelling had been generous in seeing to it that the unknown Hegel was soon introduced into Jena's intellectual circles. The collaboration with Schelling in producing the *Critical Journal* also gave him a wider reputation among scholars and students with philosophical interests. He became known, in fact, as Schelling's disciple. An associate of Jacobi's, replying to a critique of Jacobi that Hegel had written for the *Journal,* remarked with some wit that it really made no difference who the author of the essay had been. "Assuming that it was Herr Hegel, then we have a certain *name,* and with the name a person," but this information has little importance since, whoever the author was, "according to the principles of the Schellingian philosophy he *had* to write as he wrote." Rubbing the point in a bit, a footnote asks the reader "to understand by the name *Hegel* in the following discussion merely an individuality adhering to the Schellingian System."[7] Schleiermacher also seems to have seen Hegel in that light. In a letter to a friend, written in November 1803, he mentions the Schelling-Hegel collaboration as an instance, among others, of the "frightful evil" of "disciplemania," a form of "slavery" that "seems to me to be equally bad from both sides."[8] Actually there is a good deal that is original in Hegel's contributions to the *Critical Journal.* It was not quite fair even at that time to regard him simply as a disciple of Schelling, but in the loose game of labels and reputations it was no gross injustice either. The very fact that each essay published in the *Critical Journal* was unsigned, as if it were a matter of indifference which of the two editors had written it, certainly gave the impression that they spoke with one voice and that the journal was a kind of organ of Schellingian philosophy.

But in his lectures, more than in his early published work, Hegel soon began to develop a distinctive voice of his own. When Schelling left Jena in 1803 to accept an appointment in Wurzburg, the *Critical Journal* ceased publication and the close association between Schelling and Hegel soon ceased also, never to be resumed. By then Hegel was already writing drafts of systematic essays, related to his lectures, in which his own philosophy was beginning to take shape. It is doubtful that he and Schelling could for much longer have continued working together so harmoniously in any case. But warm letters continued to pass between them both before and for a while after Schelling had decided to accept the Wurzburg appointment. Correspondence between them during the summer of 1803, when Schelling was traveling and Hegel remained in Jena, reflects a general exodus from Jena; not only Schelling but a good many other remaining luminaries including the distinguished theologian Paulus and Hegel's friend Niethammer were considering or actively seeking academic posts elsewhere.[9] Schelling also mentions his recent marriage to Caroline Schlegel, who had divorced his friend, August Schlegel, a couple of months earlier; though the Schellings and Schlegel remained on friendly terms, in the spirit of Romantic high-mindedness, the scandal this domestic realignment caused in Jena doubtless made Schelling the more eager to leave. Expressing warm good wishes to his friend, Hegel jokingly adds that he might at least have composed a sonnet for the occasion, had Schelling not always expressed a preference for his prose.[10] This particular exchange of letters also contains a poignant note out of Hegel and Schelling's common past: "The saddest sight I have had during my stay here," Schelling wrote from Stuttgart, "was that of—Holderlin." Schelling is shaken by the very sight of their old friend, who, he reports, is neglecting his external appearance "to the point of being disgusting" and has fallen fully into the manner of the insane. Schelling sees no hope for Holderlin in his present circumstances, and wonders whether Hegel might be willing to look after him in Jena, warning at the same time that his care would be fearfully demanding. Hegel's reply, expressing shock and concern, indicates that he is open to such an undertaking. "I hope that he still places a certain trust in me that he used to have, and perhaps this will be able to accomplish something for him if he comes here."[11] But nothing ever came of these overtures.

So by the end of 1803 Hegel's visible ties to his youth had mostly been broken by circumstances beyond his control. He was on his own, and indeed was left behind in the mass exodus from Jena of his most distinguished colleagues and their student following. But he made of Jena's rather desolated circumstances an opportunity to establish unmistakably his intellectual independence and his own modest sphere of intellectual influence. Writing Goethe of the conditions in Jena in the autumn after the departure of Schelling and the others, Schiller reports that "philosophy has not fallen entirely silent, and our Dr. Hegel is said to have received many hearers, who are not unsatisfied even with his delivery."[12] Hegel's obvious philosophical seriousness and intellectual gifts were appreciated in what was left of Jena's cultural circles, and his good-humored, rather unassuming ways won him a good deal of affection as well; he was a frequent guest at the teas that were then the fashion in those circles. Goethe and Schiller expressed more than once in their correspondence their solid respect for his philosophical capacities, even while lamenting his laborious manner of expressing himself in his lectures and writings. In an exchange that followed Schiller's little report on Hegel, Goethe and he seriously discussed a plan to bring Hegel together as frequently as possible with Fernow, in the hope that some of Fernow's facility in speech might rub off on Hegel and that Hegel, in turn, might help remedy Fernow's intellectual shallowness. The names of Hegel and Fernow accordingly appeared rather frequently on Goethe's guest list for teas and other social occasions that winter.[13] It is not reported whether the scheme had the desired effects on either side. Certainly Hegel did not create the sensation in Jena that Fichte and Schelling had before him. Between twenty and thirty students generally signed up for his lectures. But the first small band of Hegelians, a new philosophical breed, began to form among them. There was no longer any question of Hegel's being anyone else's disciple. When he first lectured on the history of philosophy, in 1805, some students were shocked to find not only the great systems of the past but also the most recent philosophies passed in review and found wanting. Once after Hegel had left the room one of his older auditors cried out, "That's the very death, and so must everything pass away!" In the heated discussion that followed, one of Hegel's disciples earnestly declared that by such a death life is purified and unfolds the more brilliantly. To the disciples it was clear that the unfolding had already begun, in Hegel's systematic lectures. It still seems to have been a surprise to many, however, when even the Schellingian system was discussed in the lectures on the history of philosophy, and was found to have fallen short like the others.[14] But by that time at least the disciples were prepared to accept the refutation of Schelling as definitive, along with whatever else Hegel uttered. They so idolized him that they made careful investigations into the details of his personal habits—they knew he took snuff, but did he or did he not smoke? (he did)—and read deep meanings into his most casual remarks. They eagerly recruited other students for his lectures with promises of highest enlightenment. The enlightenment did not always result, however; one "raw nature" who had been buttonholed in this way declared after the lecture that he couldn't even tell whether the subject was ducks or geese.[15] But the disciples were not to be shaken, and by 1805 their master had begun writing a masterpiece indeed: his *Phenomenology of Spirit*. According to a famous story, he completed its final pages with Napoleon's army thundering at the gates of Jena, in autumn 1806.

2. "Philosophy" versus "Un-Philosophy" in the Critical Writings, 1801–1803

Hegel's first philosophical writings were largely critical in character. Besides reviews of current philosophical books there were long essays and monographs interpreting and criticizing a variety of contemporary points of view: Modern skepticism, for instance, is compared (unfavorably) to the ancient, and the positive contribution of skepticism to authentic philosophy is assessed; common sense philosophy, represented by W. T. Krug, is lampooned and taken to task for its failure to understand the new idealism; Kant, Reinhold, Fichte, Jacobi, and many lesser figures are expounded, their errors exposed, and their work sifted for the kernels of truth they may contain. To put it mildly, these critical writings express a general displeasure with the current state of philosophy. There is also something of the novice's mischievous pleasure in attacking thinkers of established reputations.

In a letter at the end of December 1801, to an old friend of his Frankfurt days, the theologian and schoolmaster W. F. Hufnagel, Hegel describes the aims of the newly launched *Critical Journal of Philosophy* in humorous but pugnacious terms:

> The tendency of the new venture is partly to increase the number of journals and partly to lend goal and measure to the unphilosophical confusion; the weapons the journal will employ are very manifold; one might call them cudgel, whips and rods;—it is all for the sake of the good cause and the gloriae Dei; people here and there may well have some grievance about it; but cauterization has in fact become necessary.[16]

The cudgeling and cautertization had already begun with the recent publication of Hegel's *Differenzschrift* (as it is customary to call *The*

*Difference between the Fichtean and Schellingian Systems of Philoso-
phy).* In a mocking "Letter from Zettel to Squenz" that appeared in the
first issue of the *Critical Journal,* Schelling writing in the person of
Zettel (i.e., Reinhold, who had received some very rough treatment in
the *Differenzschrift*) has him complain to Squenz that this Hegel "is a
pretty categorical person altogether, who can't put up with a good many
conditions in philosophy and even so has all the more appetite."[17] Fichte
himself, who received more respectful treatment in the *Differenzschrift*
but was still dealt some rather hard knocks, expressed in a rather stiff
letter to Schelling the hope that he and Hegel would not pursue the
controversy further until they had seen his forthcoming work (a new
Darstellung der Wissenschaftslehre), so as "not to make the misunder-
standings more numerous."[18]

  After the first issue of the *Critical Journal* had appeared, Jacobi
wrote to Friedrich Bouterwek, who had already been subjected to a
sharp critique in it, that a "powerful wrath" seemed to dominate this
new journal edited by Schelling and "a Herr Hegel who is completely
unknown to me."[19] Jacobi would encounter Hegel soon enough, from
the end of his cudgel. J. J. Wagner, however, upon reading the Schelling-
Hegel journal, wrote a friend: "I find indeed that the gentlemen delight
in a strident tone, but there is, by Jupiter, no injustice done thereby."
Wagner also passes on a report that Fichte is declaring in Berlin "that
Schelling has never understood him and that he need not read Hegel's
Differenz."[20] Of course it was a great age of philosophical polemic, and
Fichte, Jacobi, and other targets of the *Critical Journal* did not take
its attacks lying down. The *Journal* was repaid in kind, being subjected
to both serious criticism and lampoon. Both the rather murky "philosophy of identity" it espoused and the style of at least Hegel's contributions to it were inevitable subjects for satire.

  There are some luminous passages in Hegel's essays, particularly
where he is developing some of his own new insights. But a good deal
of the critical analysis is tortuous, repetitious, and heavy-handed. We
now find Hegel expressing himself in the quasi-Scholastic manner that
Kant had made the standard for serious *Wissenschaft,* with only an
occasional breath of that pungency with which the writings in Bern
and Frankfurt were suffused. We can generally detect the hand of
Schelling in the *Critical Journal* when the analysis becomes less thorough but more incisive, and vivid and *geistreich* in style. In Hegel's
writings there is something of the peculiar heaviness and dogmatism
of the epigone, "more Schellingian than Schelling," as Haym says of

the *Differenzschrift*,[21] lacking Schelling's originality but beating down all challengers from the fortified heights of the true philosophy; one can recognize some of the same accents in the work of Hegel's own faithful disciples thirty years later. Where Schelling himself was inclined to be conciliatory (e.g., toward Fichte, with whom he still liked to consider himself essentially bound in common cause), we find Hegel, indeed perhaps more accurately, insisting that the similarities between their systems are superficial and the differences fundamental.[22] We also find in Hegel's essays the tendency he later criticized in Schelling, to defend his position by forceful and repeated assertion rather than by careful argument.

At any rate, these early Jena writings make up a distinct, transitional stage in Hegel's development. If he launches his critiques of other philosophers primarily from the standpoint of the Schellingian system, it should be remembered that that system was itself still evolving, and there is evidence that Hegel played a role in shaping its development during that period in which the two old friends were in such close, daily association. Hegel is not simply defending someone else's finished system, and though Schelling was undoubtedly the senior partner in the team, at least for a while, the influence between them was not altogether one-sided.[23] Furthermore, for Hegel himself these writings served quite a different function than mere defense of the Schellingian system. Still a relative beginner in technical philosophy, Hegel uses these critiques of established thinkers to clarify his own aims and methods, to identify pitfalls and to establish the standards by which he expects to measure his own work. Meanwhile, he is preparing himself to meet those standards. In his first Jena essays he wrestles with the nature of philosophical thinking. As in the "pre-philosophical" writings of Bern and Frankfurt, we find here certain issues posed with a kind of naked clarity, just because they are not yet clothed in their systematic resolutions. For that very reason they offer us an illuminating entry into Hegel's mature thought: like the earlier writings they enable us to understand some of the questions out of which his mature system will evolve, and that aim will again guide our interest in the writings at hand. So we will not rehearse his detailed criticisms of this philosopher and that, nor attempt to assess their adequacy, though they sometimes seem to me to be wide of the mark; for that would involve us in the endless task of offering independent interpretations of the philosophers in question. We shall have our hands quite full just trying to understand this one philosopher in his first rigorous venture into philosophy, and we will be interested in what he says about the others only for the sake of what he thereby reveals about himself.

So in the remainder of this section and in the next, we shall concentrate on two of the most substantial of these critical writings: the monograph on *The Difference between the Fichtean and Schellingian Systems of Philosophy* (1801) and the essay, also really a monograph, taking up one full issue of the *Critical Journal* (vol. 2, no. 1), entitled *Faith and Knowledge: or the Reflection-Philosophy of Subjectivity in the Completeness of Its Forms as Kantian, Jacobian and Fichtean Philosophy* (1802). With an occasional glance at other essays in the *Critical Journal*, we shall find in these two monographs Hegel's most ambitious attempts to establish his own directions in taking the measure of other systems.

In an introduction he wrote for the first issue of the *Journal* Hegel undertook to explain what was implied in the founding of a *critical* journal. There he distinguished between "philosophy" and "unphilosophy."[24] This distinction is implicit in all these works and is made explicit in a variety of terms. However it is expressed, the distinction is a little like that Tolstoy draws between happy and unhappy families: "philosophy is only one, and can be only one," Hegel says, because "reason is only one,"[25] while each of the many forms of unphilosophy is unphilosophical in its own way.

Of course, the one perennial philosophy has also been expressed in a variety of systematic forms. But in the Introduction to the *Differenzschrift* Hegel had launched a lively polemic against the treatment of the history of philosophy as a mere succession of opinions or "peculiar viewpoints" held by the philosophers of the past, each influencing his successors and being superseded and improved upon in a kind of linear progress. Any genuine philosophical expression is essentially true, but its truth is only recognized by genuine philosophers.

> The living spirit which dwells in a philosophy requires, in order to disclose itself, that it be born through a kindred spirit. When it meets up with the historical manner, interested somehow in information about opinions, it brushes past it as an alien phenomenon and does not reveal its innermost. It is quite indifferent to the insistence that it serve to enlarge the collection of mummies and the general heap of curiosities; for it has itself slipped through the fingers of the inquisitive information-collector.[26]

The collector of philosophical curiosities "has not recognized that there is such a thing as truth." That is why he imagines that the procession of philosophies can be historically cumulative, on the model of technological progress.

> But if the Absolute like its manifestation, reason, is eternally one and the same, as indeed it is, then every reason which is directed toward itself and has recognized itself has produced a true philosophy and has solved the problem which, like its solution, is the same in every age. Since in philosophy the reason which recognizes itself has only with itself to do, its entire work as well as its activity thus inheres in itself, and with regard to the inner essence of philosophy there are neither predecessors nor successors.
>
> Talk about *peculiar viewpoints* in philosophy is no more appropriate than the talk about steady improvement. How can the rational be peculiar? What is peculiar to a philosophy can belong, just because it is peculiar, only to the form of the system, not to the essence of the philosophy.[27]

It is worth mentioning that Hegel never abandoned this view that a single, perennial, self-reflexive truth had been expressed in every authentic philosophy, despite his own later historicizing of philosophical systems. The special qualities of a philosophy may have reflected the age in which it was conceived,[28] but what makes it a philosophy is what it has in common with all genuine philosophy. From this time on, indeed, we find Hegel claiming to speak for "philosophy" itself, and when he does so he does not refer simply to his own system but to the perennial vision he shares with all true philosophers, of reason participating in the very truth which it expresses, as against all merely subjective opinions.

Philosophy in this sense is what Hegel declares, in his introductory essay to the *Critical Journal,* to be the "measuring-stick" of all would-be philosophical ventures. Philosophical criticism (and also art criticism) requires such a measuring-stick, "which is just as independent of the one who is judging as it is of the one who is judged" and which proceeds "not from the single appearance nor from the particularity of the subject, but from the eternal and unalterable prototype of the matter itself."[29] For only with such a measuring-stick in hand will it be possible to show how the manifold forms of unphilosophy fall short: for example, by their resort to unexamined common sense, or by their coming to rest in one or another form of irreducible dualism, or by their imposition of arbitrary limits on reason's power to know what is in fact most akin to itself, or by their frivolous trafficking in opinions and *geistreich* popular philosophizing, without the discipline of rigorous method. In some cases, indeed, such unphilosophy seems to have full sway; a Reinhold, a Jacobi, a Krug is analyzed with scarcely concealed impatience and then consigned with scorn to the outer darkness. Others (e.g., Kant and Fichte), though subjected to occasional sarcasm and indignation, are treated seriously. They are genuine philosophers. In such cases the task is to separate the philosophical wheat from the unphilosophical chaff, a process that we will examine presently.

However, the error of unphilosophy may be characterized very generally as subjectivism: "since philosophy is defined as a knowledge of the Absolute, whether as God or in some other aspect as nature, it would be thought in immovable and absolute opposition to knowledge as subjective."[30] That, indeed, is the way philosophy transcends its own apparent diversity, in becoming "altogether passive" and by rigorous discipline expunging from its thought the individual circumstances and opinions of the philosopher himself. By such strict abnegation the thinker "who is to be capable of this reception of deity or the pure, objective intuition of nature" must "restrain all of his own activity, since through it the purity of receiving is obscured."[31]

Upon that requirement most would-be philosophers come to grief. It is not only that they do in fact interpose their own idiosyncratic opinions, methods, and aims into their thinking, perhaps to make a name for themselves as the inventors of the latest philosophies—Hegel is suspicious of a good deal of what passes for originality in philosophy[32]—but, more serious, they elevate such interposition to an epistemological principle, assuming in one way or another that knowing is essentially and necessarily an activity of the human subject as such. They are not only subjectivists in fact but subjectivistic in principle. They proceed as if the knowing subject, separated by an unbridgeable gulf from its proper object, must fabricate such knowledge as it can from its own sense data, feelings, and/or mental activity. Such subjectivism is, in particular, the modern legacy of Cartesian dualism that has penetrated every branch of knowledge and represents the abandonment of reason by the "understanding."[33] For reason itself is essentially speculative: Hegel has already begun to use the term "speculation" with something like the etymological force it carried in medieval thought, reason as a mirror *(speculum)* that directly reflects its proper object. Indeed, to speak of "object" in this case is misleading, if unavoidable; since reason mirrors the same light it receives there is in genuine speculation precisely not the radical dualism between subject and object that is postulated by post-Cartesian philosophy. Reason and Absolute are one, an identity in difference, to be sure, but not as if they were two self-enclosed "things" simply external to one another. For "the Absolute itself . . . is . . . the identity of identity and non-identity; opposition and unity is simultaneous in it."[34]

Upon the basis of this "philosophy of identity" the editors of the *Critical Journal of Philosophy* bravely set forth to do battle with the Cartesian-infected philosophies and unphilosophies of the Enlightenment. But before we look more closely at the general lines of this critique, we must pause for a while to notice what a prodigious issue has already been joined. By now Hegel had been thoroughly immersed in Kant's *Critique of Pure Reason,* and understood clearly that that work had raised the most massive obstacle to precisely the sort of speculative philosophy that Hegel intended to employ as the basis of his own critique of post-Cartesian thought. In fact, Kant had denied the validity in principle of the very kind of speculative system that Hegel was already energetically setting out to construct. Since Hegel had this Kantian objection to his enterprise clearly before him from the outset, and had to struggle with it in order even to embark on his own task, it may be useful for us briefly to review the Kantian critique of speculative philosophy.

The empiricists, particularly Hume, had already objected to the speculative extension of reason to metaphysical questions that could not be settled by induction from any possible sensory data: "Our line is too short to fathom such immense abysses."[35] Kant's objection is not so simple. He did hold, with the empiricists, that there can be no proper knowledge apart from experience, but he also held, with the rationalists, that knowledge has an a priori basis. For the principles of science must have a basis that is necessary, and not merely subjective and pragmatic. Kant found this a priori basis by establishing the necessary conditions for any possible experience, within the understanding *(Verstand)* of the empirical subject himself. The so-called metaphysical and transcendental deductions in the first two chapters of the Transcendental Analytic show how the categorial principles of all knowledge can be deduced, first from the logical forms of thought, and then from the requirements for the possibility of experience in general. These formal, rational conditions necessary for any experience obviously cannot be derived from the sense impressions themselves, but according to Kant are present in the understanding of any experiencing subject. Thus the categories are necessary, a priori. Yet, even though sensuous "intuitions without concepts are blind," it is equally true that "thoughts without content are empty."[36] The a priori categories can advance knowledge—that is, yield synthetic judgments—only insofar as they are applied to the givenness of the sensible material. With Hume and against the rationalists, then, Kant had argued that knowledge of reality is not deducible from concepts. The only proper knowledge we have is empirical, and empirical knowledge is "a synthesis of sense perceptions," but the synthesis "is not itself contained in the sense perceptions."[37] We derive knowledge from the sensory material as it is synthesized in relation to the categories of the understanding. The objects of knowledge are not things-in-themselves, existing outside this synthesized experience, but they are the only objects we can have, and nature as we know it is composed of such objects. But that is the only "nature" we need; science, dealing with "nature" in this sense, can build complete systems of knowledge, founded on principles of which there is a priori certainty. Kant insists that this knowledge is not merely "subjective," since it deals with objects that are accessible to the experience of any human subject and its categories are the universal bases of experience. The distinction between subjective and objective is a distinction within experience.[38]

A result of this analysis is that speculative knowledge becomes, as such, a contradiction in terms. Kant's Transcendental Logic has a priori categories, but because these are empty in the absence of sensible material, the Transcendental Logic can be a logic of truth only when it deals with the concepts and principles of the pure understanding, as in Kant's own treatment in the Transcendental Analytic. Its employment beyond these limits, treating concepts that are not related to objects of possible experience, would convert it into a "logic of illusion"; significantly, in relation to Hegel, the discussion of this "logic of illusion" comes under the heading of "*die transzendentale Dialektik.*"[39] Nor, of course is the traditional logic of any use in expanding knowledge beyond empirical limits, since its propositions are entirely analytic, and can provide a mere *Kanon,* a mere negative criterion for knowledge; when treated as an *Organon* for the production of knowledge itself it falls into obvious illusion.[40] When concepts are applied beyond the limits of proper (empirical) knowledge, reason falls into irresolvable antinomies, mutually contradictory conclusions each of which is equally possible from the standpoint of proper knowledge and therefore equally doubtful.[41] Reason that is not bound at every step to objects of possible experience can yield only illusion; any claim to advance on its own basis beyond these limits can be only a "pseudorational" *(vernunftelnde)* pretension.[42]

However, as Stace says,

> the effect of this solemn warning upon the philosophic world was truly astonishing. No sooner had Kant thus cried "Halt!" to philosophy than philosophy, forming its adherents into a sort of triumphal procession, proceeding, so to speak, with bands playing and flags waving, marched victoriously onward to the final assault, confident of its power to attain omniscience at a stroke, to occupy the very citadel of reality itself. And, strangest of all, this was to be done with the very weapons which Kant himself had forged.[43]

In fact, the position that philosophy sought to win against Kant was not its old one, which Kant had left in ruins; it had to advance to quite a new domain with these Kantian "weapons." Hegel's program must not be confused with a rationalism of the pre-Kantian type. Kant's critique of rational knowledge defined for Hegel a point of no return. Indeed, despite his polemics against Kant, he built on substantially Kantian foundations, at least to the extent that he accepted Kant's formulation of the basic problem of metaphysical knowledge as definitive.[44] "Philosophy" advanced through Kant, not over him.

Hegel accepted Kant's "Copernican revolution," but considered that Kant had not carried it far enough. Kant had correctly seen that thought, and not raw sense-perception, is what is objective in knowledge, in virtue of its universality and necessity. But Kant had limited thought, insofar as it pertained to knowledge, to the understanding, the categories of which are finite, abstract, falling into irresolvable abstract antitheses: the understanding contains a fixed structure of thought forms standing in rigid opposition. That is why Kant cannot complete his "Copernican revolution" in philosophy. To do so would require that thought find its essential truth fully reflected in reason itself. But the categories of the understanding impose themselves on whatever is grasped through them, parceling it out according to their own abstract oppositions. Kant's "object of knowledge" as a composite of sensory material and antithetical thought forms, cannot in principle be the ontologically real object. Indeed, the principle of opposition *(Entgegensetzung)*, which the understanding can never get beyond, is extended in its most irreducible form in the way it conceives the relation between the understanding itself and the ontologically real: the latter is a sheer "beyond" *(ein Jenseits)*, an impenetrable thing-in-itself that the understanding can never grasp. Therefore, charges Hegel, both "subjective" and "objective" in Kant's language are ultimately subjective abstractions cut off from what is objectively true.

Actually the thinking of Kant's predecessors had been vitiated by this same alienation of thought from its true object. It was assumed that the true object was in an "outside world" that thought must somehow penetrate; indeed, it is of the very nature of the understanding that the knowing subject is confronted by an alien object. Kant had taken the important step of making this alienation explicit, by showing that in this case thought cannot in principle penetrate the thing-in-itself. But he had therefore had to deny the true objectivity of thought. Hegel was to state the issue succinctly many years later, in the following comment on a section of his *Encyclopedia*: "Thoughts, according to Kant, although universal and necessary categories, are *only our* thoughts—separated by an impassable gulf from the thing as it exists apart from our knowledge. But the true objectivity of thinking means that the thoughts, far from being merely ours, must at the same time be the real essence of the things, and of whatever is an object to us."[45] This step would complete the Copernican revolution that Kant began.

Already in the Jena critical essays, Hegel again and again pointed out what seemed to him to be genuinely speculative motifs in Kant and Fichte, concepts plastic enough to have grasped the whole had their implications been fully developed and applied without artificial restrictions. But Kant and Fichte had in the end let these fruitful possibilities break apart into restrictive oppositions. The deduction of the categories is a case in point.

> The Kantian philosophy needed to have its spirit separated from the letter, and the pure speculative principle lifted out from the rest, which belonged to quibbling [*raisonnirenden*] reflection or could be used for it. In its principle of the deduction of the categories this philosophy is genuine idealism, and this principle is what Fichte has singled out in purer and stricter form and called the spirit of Kantian philosophy. But that the things-in-

themselves—a formulation through which nothing is expressed objectively except the empty form of opposition [*Entgegensetzung*]—have again been hypostasized and posited as absolute objectivity, like the "things" of the dogmatic thinkers; or that the categories themselves have been made partly into static, dead compartments of the intellect and partly into the highest principles, by means of which any term in which the Absolute itself is expressed, such as Spinoza's Substance, could be demolished, and negative quibbling could thereby be put in the place of philosophizing as before, only with more presention, under the name of "critical philosophy"—these circumstances stem, at most, from the form of the Kantian deduction of the categories, not from its principle or spirit.[46]

What Hegel sees as the true principle of the deduction of the categories is the identity Kant had discovered within the very difference between subject and object, thought and experience. The identity does not obliterate the difference, but by showing that the form of the object is fundamentally determined by the subject, experience by thought, the predicate of a judgment by its subject, it establishes a synthetic unity in which the stark opposition is overcome. The synthetic unity is possible because identity, the identity of the ego in its pure act of consciousness, in fact precedes and conditions the very otherness of the empirical object or of the predicate. That is why Kant could triumphantly conclude that a priori synthetic judgments are indeed possible: because "the original absolute identity of what is diverse" can produce the "separate appearing subject and predicate, particular and universal in the form of a judgment" only through the self-differentiation of the "unconditional" identity itself.[47] But Kant drew back from the radical implications of his own discovery because he clung to the assumption that opposition must take priority after all, and reduced the identity to the sort of formal synthesis that is constituted by the copula, "is," in a judgment or proposition.

Dualism is in fact what Hegel finds to be the great perennial problem of philosophy. The traditional dualisms of "spirit and matter, soul and body, faith and understanding, freedom and necessity" have now, however, been taken up into the Kantian and post-Kantian dualisms of "reason and sensuousness, intelligence and nature" and more generally into that "of absolute subjectivity and absolute objectivity." Hegel's critical writings therefore carry on an unremitting attack against these modern forms of dualism.

> To transcend [*aufzuheben*] such firmly fixed opposites is the single interest of reason. This interest should not be construed to mean that it sets itself against opposition and limitation altogether, for the necessary passing into duality [*Entzweyung*] is one factor of life, which is eternally fashioning itself through opposition, and totality is possible in its highest vitality only through the restoration out of the most profound separation. But reason sets itself against the absolute fixation of duality through the understanding, and all the more if the things placed in absolute opposition have in fact sprung from reason itself.[48]

It is remarkable that this statement from Hegel's very first philosophical work should contain such a clear adumbration of the aim to which Hegel was to devote himself in developing his dialectical method. In these earlier Jena writings dialectic is still only an aim, but the "philosophy of identity" as Hegel understands it already implies no mere denial of duality or reduction of the many to some species of illusion, but the comprehension of finite, differentiated forms as a process retaining its vital connection with a unitary source. Confronted with duality that the thought of an age has hardened into rigid dualism, the philosophical task is

> to transcend [*aufzuheben*] the opposition of fixated subjectivity and objectivity, and to conceive the having-become [*Gewordensein*] of the intellectual and real world as a becoming, its being qua product as a producing. In the infinite activity of becoming and producing, reason has unified what was separated and has reduced the absolute duality to a relative one, which is conditioned by the original unity.[49]

The totality that philosophy must grasp is not static; it is to be grasped precisely in this fluidity, and what Hegel now calls reason is precisely this grasp.

That is why we find him complaining constantly that Kant and Fichte at so many points introduce the standpoint of reason in this sense, but in every case end by subjecting it to the standpoint of the understanding, with its static dualisms. His complaint is particularly bitter when he speaks of their treatment of nature. Fichte relegates it to the lifeless objectivity of the nonego, to be overcome or shaped as so much inert matter by the strenuous moral efforts of the ego.[50] Kant, in the first *Critique,* finds it sufficient for strict theoretical purposes—that is, for the purposes of proper knowledge—to regard nature as the system of those objects synthesized by the understanding.

Of course "nature" in this sense is merely phenomenal; beyond it lies the "realm" of things-in-themselves, which "insofar as it is abandoned by the categories cannot be anything but a formless lump." But in the third Critique this realm receives its due as the sphere of beauty.[51] In the aesthetic judgment, indeed, Hegel finds another of those points at which Kant seems to be reaching for a genuinely speculative synthesis. We recall the excitement with which Hegel, Schelling, and Holderlin had earlier laid hold of the idea of beauty in the *Critique of Judgment,* and Hegel still speaks of the treatment of the aesthetic imagination as "the most interesting point in the Kantian system." Here at last the empirical manifold seems to be synthesized with a rational identity in the principle of beauty, and the concept of nature with the concept of freedom. Nature is grasped as an organic unity, and not merely as a mechanical system of atomistic objects; beauty, no mere sensuous intuition, is recognized as the thoroughly rational, intelligible "substratum of nature."[52] But not within the sphere of proper knowledge!

> An aesthetic idea cannot, according to Kant, become knowledge, because it is an intuition of the imagination, for which an adequate concept can never be found; an idea of reason can never become knowledge, because it contains a concept of the supersensuous, for which an intuition can never properly be found—the former is an unexplainable representation of the imagination, the latter an indemonstrable concept of reason. As if the aesthetic idea did not have its explanation in the idea of reason, the idea of reason did not have in beauty what Kant calls demonstration, namely the presentation of concept in intuition![53]

Again, the "truly speculative side of the Kantian philosophy" comes to grief by being subjected in the end to the rule of the understanding, the organic view of nature being replaced in the sphere of proper knowledge by the purely mechanical model of an object-world of "things."

The case is similar with respect to the postulates of practical reason. We recall (see Chapter 1, §4 above) how Hegel and his friends, following Fichte's lead, had earlier seized upon the doctrine of the postulates as a way of establishing a new basis for speculative philosophy. Proceeding

from the postulate of moral freedom, the conceptions both of world order
and of religious truth were to be founded anew, beyond the confines of
the new empiricism and the old dogmatic rationalism alike. It still
seems to Hegel that in the postulated "practical faith" in God

> nothing less is expressed than the idea that reason has at the
> same time absolute reality, that in this idea all contradiction
> between freedom and necessity is transcended [aufgehoben], that
> infinite thought is at the same time absolute reality, or the abso-
> lute identity of thought and being. Now this idea is none other
> than that which the ontological proof and all true philosophy
> recognizes as the first and only idea, which is alone true and
> philosophical.[54]

But of course for Kant this postulate merely expresses a practical faith;
far from finding in it any legitimate basis for philosophical speculation,
Kant scrupulously excludes it from the sphere of genuine knowledge
altogether. Hegel now takes Fichte to task for not having respected the
proper limits within which Kant confined his postulates. For "according
to Kant the postulates and their faith are something subjective," in the
sense that "postulating the absolute reality of the highest idea" or
believing in it is not rooted in knowledge of what is, but in moral
requirements concerning what ought to be.

The content of this faith, God or the reality of the idea, is not merely
subjective but ultimate; the form, the postulating or believing, however,
is subjective, reducing the putative reality of the idea to something
that merely ought to be.[55] In other words, Kant's sharp distinction
between the theoretical employment and the practical employment
of reason introduces another fundamental dualism into the heart of
Kantian philosophy, and signals that the whole is dominated by the
bifurcating propensities of the understanding. What is, is one thing; it
can be known, and made the basis of sound theory. What ought to be
is something else, and the postulations of practical reason are projections of what ought to be into a "beyond" (ein Jenseits): literally a "that-
side" or other side beyond what is, beyond what can be known, beyond
any human, social condition that human beings can recognize as their
own. The Absolute, God, nature as the manifestation of beauty, is an
infinite "beyond," beyond the finite sphere of what can be known to be.

But for Hegel the Idea in its reality is the infinite. The infinite is not
separated from the finite, but embraces the process in which all that

is finite, the many, proceeds from identity and retains its identity even in its self-differentiation: "in the Idea the finite and the infinite are one, and therefore finitude disappears as such insofar as it is to have truth and reality in and for itself; but only what is negation in it is negated, and thus the true affirmation constituted."[56]

The Idea, in which finite and infinite are both differentiated and unified, is the proper object of reason. That is why reason cannot be confined to the bifurcated products of the understanding. Its truth is the fluid whole, not a mere ought *(Sollen)* nor the object of longing to which human beings mired in the finite lift their wistful eyes. That is Hegel's fundamental bone of contention with Kant, and with Jacobi and Fichte as well, all of whom seem to him to represent variations on "the reflection-philosophy of subjectivity." For "reflection" is thinking within the limits of the understanding, which, however, from its position on "this side" of those limits projects something else on "that side," beyond the limits: something that ought to be or is believed to be or for which one may yearn. Kantian thought itself is a paradigm of "reflection."

> This character of the Kantian philosophy, that knowledge is something formal, and that reason as a pure negativity is an absolute beyond [*Jenseits*], which as "that-side" and negativity is conditioned by a this-side [*Diesseits*] and positivity, infinitude and finitude, both in their opposition equally absolute: this is the general character of the reflection-philosophy of which we speak.[57]

"Reflection" in this sense falls short of philosophy. It is confined by the understanding, with its abstract antitheses; it is analytical in its methods and dualistic in its assumptions. Since it can grasp objects and concepts only in their opposition to others, everything that falls within the purview of reflection is necessarily finite. Reflection is also reifying, capable of grasping what it acknowledges to be real only as finite "things"—a soul-thing versus a body-thing, nature as a total thing made up of lesser things, and so forth. Reification *(Verdinglichung),* reduction to fixed "thingness" *(Dingheit),* is in fact another constant target of Hegel's critiques, generally linked to his attack on reflection.[58] Not that reflection has no philosophical function at all; reflective analysis is a necessary preparation for proper speculation. In the announcement of Hegel's lectures for summer 1802, logic is designated as "systema reflexionis," metaphysics as "systema rationis." In Hegel's earliest systematic ventures, philosophical thinking must proceed through reflection, in logic, to the standpoint of reason, in speculative metaphysics. But when thinking stopped short of reason, remaining fixed and suspended in abstract oppositions, the result was mere "reflection-philosophy," or the "unphilosophy" against which Hegel's critical writings were directed.

There is still another term that Hegel added to his catalogue of philosophical horrors in these writings: *Raisonnieren,* a term often joined to *Reflexion,* is a French verb that Hegel employs in German form as a kind of enemy alien. While he never bothers defining it precisely, one suspects that it generally connotes a manner of thinking he associates with the French Enlightenment in particular. *Raisonnieren* is argumentative reasoning, attempting to establish a point by marshaling as many "arguments" for it as possible, as if arguments were quantitatively cumulative, like bricks in a wall. The formal criterion of such arguments is that they may not be contradictory. No doubt it was against the assumptions of such *raisonnierenden Reflexion* that he directed the first thesis of his *Habilitation* disputation: "Contradictio est regula veri, non contradictio falsi."[59] The point of this deliberately paradoxical proposition was not that traditional logic could be transgressed in ordinary reasoning. The law of noncontradiction is a perfectly adequate rule in relating the terms of an argument or syllogism. But it is not an adequate rule of truth, and when it is treated as though it were it becomes much rather the rule of falsehood. Speculative reason grasps the truth only in what Hegel already calls "Idea," and "Idea" cannot be expressed in straightforward propositions at all. For a proposition is ordinarily defined by what it excludes, but the Idea is an encompassing, fluid totality that synthesizes apparent opposites in their essential unity. If the Idea is given propositional expression, the propositions are paradoxical, like these theses of Hegel's or many of the propositions of Spinoza, the systematic terms being used in ways that contradict their ordinary meanings. Speculative reason has a skeptical side, undermining the apparently unambiguous certainties of experience and logical deduction in order to achieve some more capacious insight.[60] The simple rule of noncontradiction defines the limit of reflection, understanding, thingness, *raisonnieren*—all of which Hegel continued in later years to employ as terms of opprobrium. *Raisonnierenden Reflexion* is serviceable enough, for that matter, in analysis of what appears on a finite, quantifiable plane; but the task of reason is synthesis. As Hegel expressed it in his sixth thesis: "Idea est synthesis infiniti et finiti et philosophia omnis est in ideis."[61]

3. Speculative Good Friday: Negation and Transfiguration in the Critical Writings

We certainly find in Hegel's Jena writings a good deal of what Stace referred to when he spoke of "philosophy" rolling over Kant's objections with bands playing and flags waving. He already understood Kant's epistemological problems as derived from subject-object dualism, but a rigorous attempt to show how that was so and how this dualism could be resolved—his only satisfactory answer to Kant—had to await the *Phenomenology of Spirit.* In the writings of 1801–3 he can only confront Kant and the others with a very different view of philosophy, really with not much more than the program for a nondualistic philosophy, defended more by suggestive assertion than by argument.

This is not surprising, considering what a new recruit he was to the philosophical wars. What is surprising is what a rich program it is, partly because Hegel succeeded in gathering up so many of his "pre-philosophical" insights of the Frankfurt years into the new philosophical venture. We will attend in this section to some of the central motifs of this incipient philosophy because the religious issues are still very much alive in it, and his treatment of them is all the more promising for being indirect. Because the exploration of these new motifs will require a good many pages, I shall divide this section by the use of subheadings. But in the texts themselves they are intertwined, tangled together in fact, because the meaning of each is complete only in relation to the others. While I have tried to disentangle them a bit here, they cannot be made to fit too neatly under the subheadings without losing the sense of interconnection.

From the "Religion" of Frankfurt to the Jena "Philosophy"

The continuity in Hegel's thinking between Frankfurt and Jena is not obvious on the rhetorical surface. The critical writings of 1801–3, jousting with current philosophers and addressed to rather technical philosophical problems, seem hardly to be by the same author as the Frankfurt essays and fragments. But the issues are substantially the same, transported from the directly political and religious terms in which he had so recently addressed them to a conceptual frame in which he hoped to get closer to the root of the matter. The assumption of some manner of ultimate dualism is attacked in Jena, with Hegel's new philosophical weapons, as vigorously as it was in Frankfurt, where he struggled with it primarily in its religious forms. Nature, the divine, the Absolute, are not to be located in a "beyond," outside the living source of human action and the possibilities of human knowledge. At the same time, Hegel is not satisfied with any subjectivistic solution to that problem, as if what human beings recognize as ultimate were merely the projection or creation of the human imagination itself.

In fact, Hegel has long been clear that the solution to the problem of abstract dualism cannot be an equally abstract monism that merely reduces one pole of the dualism to the other. One might try, for instance, to resolve the spirit-matter dualism by reducing what has been defined (in the dualistic terms!) as spirit or mind to the complex motions of matter, in the manner of the French materialists; or by reducing matter to a projection of mind, as in subjective idealism. Either reduction is sterile and unconvincing, because neither this idealism nor that materialism challenges the fundamentally dualistic terms in which the problem was posed. When Hegel attacks dualism he wants to dig it out at the roots. He will not be satisfied until he has transformed the very terms of the problem.

But dualism takes many forms. The fact that it has ruined modern metaphysics by relegating it to arid squabbles among contending schools is the least of its baleful consequences in Hegel's eyes. He had been "driven on to science," after all, from concrete problems affecting "the life of men."[62] He had come to the philosophical problem of dualism from a long period of wrestling with religious, social, moral dualities: the self morally divided against itself, a puritanical or a Kantian conscience set against the sensuous, bodily life; the individual as such set against the claims on his allegiance made by social or political authority; a religious life that was supposed to be rooted in the events of a distant and alien past; people joining together in a little community of love only at the cost of separating themselves from the larger life of society, inwardness turned hectic and indulgent by being unable to find external expression; relations among human beings reduced to a quasi-commercial basis of external exchange, without being grounded in a common participation in the organic unity of a *Volk*, without a common language of the imagination, of commitment, of the spirit. When Hegel declared that "the ideal of my youth" had to be "transmuted into the form of reflection, in a system," he imported into his "scientific" constructions all of these problems against which the ideal of his youth had been formed. When Kant and Fichte treat nature as a mechanical complex of inert "things" separate from the spirit except insofar as it can be morally subjugated, they repeat in sophisticated form the error Hegel had attributed to Abraham and Moses, with their God for whom nature was a mere artifact. When Fichte treats the state as an authoritarian moral agency to regulate the unruly lives of individuals, he merely reflects the abject condition of contemporary political life, and in turn interiorizes this pattern of domination in a theory of natural law that teaches "the complete dominion of the understanding and servitude of what is alive, a construction in which reason has no part." Hegel again sets "life" as an organic interplay of the many in the one against the mechanical model of the human condition, as he had in Frankfurt. For this *"Verstandes-Staat"* is a mere "machine," in which the Volk is "not the organic body of a common and rich life, but an atomistic life—impoverished aggregation."[63] Hegel's old political and religious problems are never far from the surface of his new "scientific" writings. Nor is the problem he had expressed in his letter to Schelling ever far from his mind: given his technical philosophical preoccupations, "what sort of return is to be found to the engagement in the life of men."

But as was the case with many other problems, he soon came to think that this one could be addressed only by being recast. He no longer accepts any fixed distinction between *theoria* and *praxis*—either in theory or in practice! That is, he not only attacks the philosophical assumptions behind the distinction, as we shall see, but is also becoming convinced that philosophical reconstruction is already an important way of engaging in the life of men. *Reflexionsphilosophie,* after all, is a sign of the times, inseparable from the odious political, social, religious situation Hegel had uncovered in his earlier writings. In exposing the poverty of bifurcated reflection in the critical essays, he is also exposing the ultimate presuppositions of a whole culture. Moreover, he remains convinced that this culture is already on the defensive, struggling for its wretched life against inchoate forces that are groping for richer possibilities. Authentic philosophy will not only destroy the questionable intellectual underpinnings of the old order but will answer to the deepest needs of the new. But Hegel's view of this philosophical role in culture is not simple, even in the earlier Jena years. He does not believe that philosophers are going to be kings, or make any spectacular, direct public impact. His rather Olympian view of authentic philosophy certainly does not call for any compromising popularizations, and he is disdainful of the popularizing efforts of others. "Philosophy is by its nature rather esoteric," not for the masses. Far from accommodating itself to the common sense understanding of an age, "the world of philosophy is in and for itself an inverted world" from the common sense point of view. Philosophy fulfills its function by adhering rigorously to its own task—and thereby precisely turning the commonly accepted assumptions of the age upside down. In order to fulfill this function, "philosophy must, to be sure, acknowledge the possibility that the people may be elevated to it, but it must not lower itself to the people."[64] Nor can philosophy permit itself to be drawn into the strident contentions of an age of unrest and confusion. Yet Hegel suggests that this unrest can be regarded as the "ferment through which the spirit struggles up out of the decay of a dead culture to a new life," and in this struggle philosophy can play a decisive role, offering "remedy" for the social and intellectual dismemberment the world has suffered,[65] simply by seeing its own work through to the end. Indeed, Hegel had devoted a section of the Introduction to the *Differenzschrift* to the "Need of Philosophy" *(Bedurfniss der Philosophie),* an ambiguous expression that can mean either philosophy's need or the need for philosophy: in fact, it seems to mean both. For this "need" arises from the vast patchwork of fundamental dualisms into which the whole life of the age has been fractured.[66] To the extent that recent philosophy has simply given intellectual expression to this fractured life, philosophy is itself in most desperate need. But that is its need for a genuine philosophy. This need seems to parallel what Hegel had come to recognize in his own life, when he wrote Schelling of being "driven on to science" from "the more subordinate needs of men." The ideal of his youth had to be transmuted into systematic speculation, encompassing and unifying all the fragmented human sciences into an integral vision. Nothing less could answer the need of philosophy, and supply the culture with a sense of wholeness at its intellectual core. Precisely by pursuing its austere purpose without concessions to popular understanding, speculation would itself become the "highest praxis."[67]

It is clear, in fact, that Hegel now looks to philosophy for the point of union between thought and being, nature and spirit, the particular and the universal. We recall that in the so-called "Fragment of a System" of 1800, he had concluded that "philosophy must stop short of religion,"[68] precisely because the unification of opposites could occur only in "life" or "being," "outside reflection"—reflection at that time referring to any possible activity of thought as such. For being could embrace thought, but thought by its very nature could not embrace nonthought. "Religion," however, was an activity in being itself, the elevation of the finite to the infinite.

Now, however, Hegel has taken the step so decisive in the formation of a distinctively Hegelian philosophy: he has denied the legitimacy of the opposition between thought and being. That opposition seems to him simply a form of the subject-object dualism that it is the vocation of philosophical reason to overcome.[69] Reason is not merely subjective reflection, but is itself the movement of the actual; thought can comprehend the actual to the extent that it becomes fully rational, and that is the philosophical task. That is why philosophers need not be kings or counsellors in order to contribute significantly to human life. Whatever else they may do, their primary objective is to let thinking move beyond the constraints of mere reflection to become rational. Philosophy is itself, no less than religion, a movement in being that unites human consciousness with infinite truth, the truth that is infinite because it is all-encompassing, fully rational. Philosophical thinking is no longer regarded as a preliminary activity on the way to religious consummation. But then what Hegel had earlier considered to be the limited nature of philosophical thinking he now considers to be merely the limit of "reflection"; that is, of that form of thinking which philosophers of the Enlightenment had supposed was the very standard of rational inquiry. Hegel has not changed his mind about that. In light of his radically different conception of reason, however, he no longer equates such reflection with philosophical thought as such. It still has its function, as a preliminary stage on the way to the rational consummation of thought. But as Hegel had earlier regarded philosophical thinking as an activity to be transcended and taken up into the comprehensive totality of religious life, its finite opposition to being as overcome in the religious elevation to the infinite: so now reflection, with its finite opposition of subject and object, thought and being, is transcended in reason. Reason is the elevation of the finite to the infinite.

Yet it is not as if philosophy had simply displaced religion in this absolute movement. Certainly there is nothing in principle *beyond* what thought can unite with itself, or from which philosophy is excluded. That is the important change in Hegel's position between the Frankfurt and the Jena periods. But the religious movement does not stop short of the infinite either. Hegel has not changed his mind about that. If anything, the new conception of reason, by means of which Hegel intends to free philosophy from the confines of mere reflection, is modeled on that mystical religious movement he had articulated in Frankfurt. For now he considers the relationship between philosophy and religion to be much closer than he had earlier supposed. *Reflexionsphilosophie,* for that matter, has its affinities with Protestant Christianity; and speculation can recognize a higher religious life akin to itself.

But to get clearer about the relationship between philosophy and religion in the critical writings, we must first get clearer about the new philosophical perspective on which it is based. For while the new view of reason owes a great deal to the religious position Hegel had developed in Frankfurt, it was given its direct philosophical basis in the Fichtean and Schellingian notion of transcendental intuition.

Transcendental Intuition: The Identity of Identity and Difference

The transcendental or intellectual intuition is the very center of the philosophical position to which Hegel appeals throughout the critical writings. It was, in the strongest sense, what held the Schellingian-Hegelian Philosophy of Identity together. A version of it had already been developed by Fichte, and despite all his criticism of Fichte, Hegel declares in the *Differenzschrift* that in his doctrine of transcendental intuition "Fichte's philosophy is . . . a genuine product of speculation."[70] It is "transcendental" in the Kantian sense that what is intuited is the subject itself, prior to or apart from any of its experience. For Kant, of course, an intuition could not be transcendental or a priori in this sense; intuition, at least for human beings, must be empirical, and only the conditions of experience can be located a priori in the subject. Kant did entertain the possibility of a nonsensuous, purely intellectual intuition, but concluded that it was conceivable only for God.[71] Indeed, the notion of intellectual intuition is sometimes traced to that motif in medieval contemplative theology according to which direct knowledge of God is possible only if God is its subject as well as its object; that is, for human beings, is possible only in mystical union.[72] Fichte, at any rate, went beyond Kant for good or ill in suggesting that the ego has an immediate intuition of its own activity, and indeed that the true subject and sole object of this intuition is the absolute ego, abstracted from the individuated empirical consciousness altogether. The mere empirical manifold becomes elevated into genuine knowledge only to the extent that the ego comes to recognize its own activity in this apparently "external" brute facticity. The ego ultimately grasps itself in its freedom, I=I, in every act of genuine knowledge.

Now Hegel's only complaint about that extraordinary claim for the transcendental intuition is that it does not go far enough! For the intuition is still that of a self-conscious subject, and therefore its union of subject and object is subjectivistic. The object is subjectivized, but not the reverse. But "in order to grasp the transcendental intuition purely" we must "abstract" from this "subjective" orientation, must comprehend the intuition to be "neither self-consciousness opposed to material nor material opposed to self-consciousness, but absolute identity, neither subjective nor objective."[73] The transcendental intuition can be approached objectively, from nature, as well as from the ego, for it is precisely the point of their convergence. Perhaps because the word "intuition" (Anschauung) inevitably carries subjectivistic connotations, Hegel more commonly employed the curious term, Indifferenzpunkt: for the transcendental intuition, rightly understood, is the point of identity or of "nondifference" between intelligence and nature, the conscious and the nonconscious, subject and object, ideal and real. In fact, to speak of the Indifferenzpunkt in terms of the disjuncts that are united in it is a concession to mere "reflection." By a similar concession, one might say that the transcendental intuition is the immediate recognition of their indifferenz, but that language seems to imply that there is a subject of the intuition distinct from the intuited Indifferenzpunkt. Strictly speaking the transcendental intuition is the Indifferenzpunkt, and this identity is the metaphysical ground of all the disjuncts. From this ultimate identity all the distinctions recognized by reflection proceed, even the distinction between the thinking consciousness and the actuality its thought attempts to grasp. And to this identity all distinctions finally converge; only so do they achieve genuine synthesis. Such a synthesis is not arbitrary, because it reintegrates its elements into the original identity.

A genuinely speculative philosophy must grasp all its concepts and categories, its ideal and real objects, in their unfolding from this *Indifferenzpunkt* and their reintegration in it. Of course there is not an actual process of unfolding and folding as such, nor is the moment of differentiation a mere illusion. The differentiated has its relative truth precisely because the identity subsists in it. The speculative insight is that the one and the many are one, identity and difference are identical; though the point is variously expressed in the critical writings, it is always clear that one cannot deal speculatively with any question apart from that insight. Still, as Hegel remarks in the *Differenzschrift,* philosophy does indeed have its theoretical and its practical side: its "science of nature" and its "science of intelligence."[74] The one is concerned with the real, the other with the ideal; at least they begin that way, and the starting-point is important. If one begins with the ideal, with freedom, then the real or being will appear to be no more than "schematized intelligence." If, on the other hand, one takes up the standpoint of being or necessity, "then thinking is only a schema of absolute being." If one remains fixed in either of these standpoints, the result will be either dogmatic idealism, in which intelligence is somehow the cause of the sensible object, or dogmatic realism or materialism in which the object is the cause of the subject. But in transcendental knowledge or transcendental intuition being and intelligence are united.

> In philosophical knowledge the intuited is an activity of intelligence and of nature, of consciousness and the nonconscious at the same time; it belongs to both worlds, the ideal and the real: to the ideal, since it is posited in intelligence and thereby in freedom, to the real, since it has its position in the objective totality, deduced as a ring in the chain of necessity. . . . In transcendental intuition all opposition is transcended [*aufgehoben*], the entire difference between the construction of the universe through and for intelligence, and as an objectively intuited, independently appearing organization, is eliminated. Producing the consciousness of this identity is speculation, and because ideality and reality is one in it, it is intuition.[75]

Only if the science of nature and the science of intelligence are set in rigid opposition can each seem to be complete, independent of the other.

> Insofar as they are opposed they are to be sure internally enclosed in themselves, and totalities; but at the same time only relative totalities, and as such they strive toward the *Indifferenzpunkt*.[76]

The "absolute totality" extends beyond either science because it embraces both.

The *Indifferenzpunkt* is the *"Mittelpunkt"* (center-point) that defines this absolute totality, within which the theoretical science of nature and the practical science of intelligence constitute the two poles. Since they each "strive" toward that center in which the differentiation of the two breaks down, that *Indifferenzpunkt* is also the "point of passing over" *(Punkt des Ubergangs)* between the two, and the "turning point" *(Wendepunkt)* of each from a mere reflective science to a speculative science of the Absolute.

> The *Indifferenzpunkt,* toward which both sciences . . . strive, is the whole represented as a self-construction of the Absolute, its last and highest. The center, the point of passing over from the identity that construes itself as nature to its construction as intelligence, is the internalization [*Innerlichwerden*] of the light of nature, what Schelling calls the lightning of the ideal striking in the real, and its constituting itself as a point. This point, which as reason is the turning point of both sciences, is the highest peak of the pyramid of nature, its final product to which, in perfecting itself, it arrives; but as a point it must at the same time expand itself to a nature.[77]

Conscious intelligence, after all, appears as a product of the unconscious processes of nature, and is thus teleologically immanent in them, while "the entire self-construction of nature" is consciously appropriated by intelligence as "a real factor" in its own scientific development.[78] In neither case, however, is the relation a causal one, but an identity in difference: each factor is immanent in the other, the "product" in the "producing," and neither finally has an independent subsistence.[79]

The notion of transcendental intuition was obviously attractive to people trying to recover a sense of wholeness that would unite the expressive life of the psyche with the natural universe. The Romantics, particularly Novalis, appealed to this notion, following the lead of Fichte and Schelling, and Holderlin, too, had found in it the basis for a poetic that would unite the objectivity of the classics with the subjective expressionism of the moderns.[80] And if for Hegel the overcoming of dualism was the "need of philosophy," the notion of transcendental intuition or *Indifferenz* was designed for that very purpose! For it *stipulated* that there was an identity prior to every division and subsisting in them all. As the stipulative nature of this solution became obvious to Hegel he abandoned it, and in the famous chapter on the beginning of science in the *Logik* of 1812 he mentions intellectual intuition along with inner revelation and faith as the sorts of spurious starting-points for philosophizing that are produced "as if out of a pistol."[81] One could not simply assert such an inarticulable presupposition as a fixed, dimensionless "point" and proceed to argue from that. The *way* the apparent diversity of things and the categorial dualities were bound in essential unity had to be articulated in detail. Yet Hegel never deviated from the guiding insight that they *are* so bound, and the transcendental intuition and associated terms at least gave him a way of expressing that and provided a kind of holding action while he was getting his philosophical bearings. It not only gave him a critical standpoint against all forms of *Reflexionsphilosophie,* but also got him started in the development of a system that differentiated nature and spirit while denying that they were ultimately separable.

Rehabilitation of the Conception of Nature

Under Schelling's influence, Hegel was particularly concerned that nature should be grasped in its productive vitality as an authentic mode of the Absolute, and not as a mechanical system of dead material "things" determined by causal necessity. That lifeless view of nature seemed to him perhaps the most baleful consequence of the dualistic reflection that had gained the ascendancy in earlier German idealism. We noted in the previous section his disappointment that Kant had in the end refused to admit into the sphere of proper knowledge the promising treatment of nature he had introduced under the rubric of the aesthetic imagination. Again and again in these critical writings Hegel takes Kant and Jacobi and particularly Fichte to task for asserting the subjective freedom and dignity of the individual at the expense of nature, treated as a wasteland of dead objectivity. He writes indignantly, for instance, of the "monstrous arrogance, this conceited madness" of the Fichtean Ego that is so horrified at the prospect that it might be "at one with the universe," subject "to the eternal laws of nature and to their holy and strict necessity." For this Ego would "fall into despair if it were not free, free from the eternal laws." The freedom of the will is of course precisely the issue for Kant and Fichte. If the Ego were subject to those laws of nature, it could not be free. But for Hegel that proposition is based on false assumptions.

> It presupposes a most generalized view of nature and of the relationship of the individual to it that is altogether devoid of all reason, a view that is entirely alien to the absolute identity of subject and object; indeed its principle is their absolute non-identity, and therefore it can comprehend nature . . . only under the form of absolute opposition, thus as pure object on which it is only possible to be dependent, or else to make it dependent on oneself, considered entirely in a causal connection, a view of nature as a thing, in which "differences of green, sweet, red, smooth, bitter, fragrance, rough, violin sound, bad smell, trumpet tone" are to be found.[82]

If nature were indeed an objectified "thing" merely exhibiting such external qualities and determined by the sort of causal necessity by which the parts of a machine coordinate their operations, then the conscious subject would have to transcend or to conquer nature in order to realize its own free self-determination. But already in the *Differenzschrift* Hegel argued that "freedom and necessity are ideal factors, therefore not in real opposition."[83] So it is with all the dualities: to the extent that they are brought into relation with the *Indifferenz-punkt* they form a system of overlapping but not entirely coinciding polarities, subject and object, ideal and real, knowledge and being, the inner and the outer, freedom and necessity, intelligence and nature, and so forth. The first term in each polarity predominates and finds its fullest expression in systematic relation to the first terms in the other polarities, and similarly with the systematic relation among the second terms. But precisely because the *Indifferenzpunkt* mediates between the poles of each polarity, the first term of each also manifests itself in a diminished way in relation to the second terms of all the other polarities. Only in abstraction do they appear as opposites; for example, freedom as the formal property of the interior capacity of conscious intelligence, necessity as the formal property of the external relations within nature. But grasped in relation to the *Indifferenzpunkt,* freedom and necessity form a polarity within the absolute totality, coordinating poles each of which requires the other to achieve its own truth and indeed partially passes over into the other in order to fulfill its own truth. Freedom as a "character of the Absolute" still may express itself inwardly, but precisely as freedom cannot be *confined* to sheer interiority. Even when it expresses itself within those confines, it "remains what it is, something not confined," and therefore may pass beyond the confinements of mere inner expression to manifest itself objectively, externally, and thus subject to the necessary structures of the real world. If either pole is isolated from the other, the pole of freedom appears as arbitrary caprice *(Willkuhr),* the pole of necessity as mere chance *(Zufall);* that is, as determination by purely external, irrational causes. But precisely as modes of the Absolute, freedom and necessity appear without contradiction both inwardly and outwardly, in intelligence and in nature alike.

> Caprice and chance, which have their place only from subordinate standpoints, are banished from the concept of sciences of the Absolute. Necessity, however, belongs to intelligence as well as to nature. For since intelligence is posited in the Absolute, it likewise approaches the form of being: it must divide and manifest itself; it is a completed organization of knowledge and intuition. . . . Nature, on the other hand, has freedom, for it is not a static being but also a becoming, a being that is not divided and synthesized from the outside but separates and unites itself within itself, and in none of its forms does it posit itself as merely something confined, but freely, as the whole. Its unconscious development is a reflection of the vital power that endlessly divides itself, but in each confined form posits itself and retains its identity; and to that extent no form of nature is confined, but free.[84]

Here Hegel struggles to give rational form to that sense of nature so dear to the Romantics, as a living organism to whose embrace human beings must return, as to a nourishing mother, in order to find psychic health and wholeness. Without sharing their suspicion of civilization as such, Hegel is deeply sympathetic with the Romantic protest against the estrangement from nature that modern civilization has suffered, of which the denigration of nature in earlier German idealism seems to him a symptom.

It must immediately be added, however, that Hegel never considered nature as such to be the ultimate expression of the Absolute, nor was he for very long, if ever, content to set it on the same niveau as spirit. If in the *Differenzschrift* he does appear to balance the spheres of nature and "intelligence" on the *Indifferenzpunkt* in a kind of equilibrium, by the time he composed his *Treatise on Natural Law,* his final major contribution to the *Critical Journal* (1802–3), he had clearly come to subordinate nature to spirit. By that time, when the practical sphere had already come to be identified as spirit (*Geist*), he had begun to develop his philosophy of spirit through a rich systematic treatment of the ethical life *(Sittlichkeit)* of the Volk and its religious and cultural expressions, assimilating many of the motifs surrounding the conception of Volksgeist he had worked out during the 1790s. Spirit could still not exist without nature or in abstraction from it, but by then it was clear, on the other hand, that nature required spirit to complete the actualization of the Absolute that could achieve only rudimentary form in nature as such.[85] While nature as well as spirit is an "attribute" of the Absolute, in which the Absolute was present, the absolute could only come to self-conscious recognition of itself in spirit: "so . . . spirit is higher than nature."[86] That is the position Hegel struggled to articulate during the next few years in his attempts to write a complete system of philosophy, with Part 2 assigned to the philosophy of nature and the third and culminating part to philosophy of spirit.

Yet Hegel never abandoned the effort to give systematic rigor to a recognizably Romantic appreciation for nature, and he could not tolerate any point of view, either philosophical or religious, that did not recognize in nature an immanent, absolute life. By the same token, he responded with evident enthusiasm, at least in that respect, to Schleiermacher's *Speeches on Religion to Its Cultural Despisers,* which had been published anonymously in 1799. Despite the anonymity, it was obvious that the *Speeches* had originated in the same Romantic circle, in Berlin and Jena, to which they were directly addressed.

Schleiermacher's *Speeches* and Protestant Subjectivity

Hegel cannot have read the *Speeches on Religion* long before embarking on his own *Differenzschrift,* and he concludes the Preface by singling the *Speeches* out as a healthy sign of the times, particularly in their celebration of the sacredness of the natural universe and their wedding of religious feeling with the sense of reunion with nature. Hegel acknowledges that the *Speeches* do not themselves meet the "need" for speculative treatment of their central concerns, but they do manifest a striving "among the better spirits, particularly in the more uninhibited and still youthful world," for a point of view that will answer to the inchoate stirrings of the age in a more satisfying way than recent philosophy had. In particular, the *Speeches* and the "reception" they have enjoyed are among those signs of the times that manifest the need for a philosophy reconciled to nature (to compensate for "the mistreatment it suffers in the Kantian and Fichtean systems"), a philosophy in which "reason itself will be placed in harmony with nature—not of the sort in which reason renounces itself or must become an insipid imitation of nature, but a consonance arising when reason moulds itself to nature out of its own inner power."[87]

In *Glauben und Wissen* Hegel again praised the *Speeches* for their piety toward nature, but he was sharply critical of them on other grounds. Both the praise and the blame reflect not only some of Hegel's own central religious concerns, but also his sense at that time of the meaning and limits of a characteristically Protestant spirituality, of which he regards the *Speeches* as an advanced expression. In the Introduction he had already suggested that there is an intrinsic affinity between Protestantism and *Reflexionsphilosophie*. For all the errors with which he belabors the latter in this work, he does not think its emergence is accidental. A "mighty *Geistesform*" has come to full expression in *Reflexionsphilosophie*, preeminently in the thought of Kant, Fichte, Jacobi.

> But the great form of the world-spirit that has recognized itself in those philosophies is the principle of the North and, in regard to religion, of Protestantism: the subjectivity in which beauty and truth are expressed in feelings and convictions, in love and understanding; religion builds its temple and altars in the heart of the individual, and with signs and prayers seeks the God it dares not behold, because of the danger that the understanding will regard what is beheld as a thing. . . . To be sure, . . . the immediate religious sentiment must be expressed in external movement, and the faith that flees the objectivity of knowledge must become objective in thoughts, concepts and words; but the

understanding precisely separates the objective from the subjective, and it becomes something that has no worth.[88]

The *Speeches* press heavily against the limits of this particular manifestation of the *Weltgeist,* but still fall within its range.

On the one hand, by placing the relation to nature so at the heart of the religious life, the *Speeches* advanced well beyond the position of Jacobi, to which they are otherwise akin. According to Hegel, Jacobi had considered nature only in its temporal, empirical aspects, not as the "universe" encompassing in its fullness all that is. As a religious thinker, then, Jacobi understands faith as the turning away from this impoverished nature, in longing for something "beyond" the merely natural that would fulfill the human yearning for spiritual reconciliation. Here the dualism that Hegel had found both in Protestantism and in recent philosophy, between a *Diesseits* and a *Jenseits,* is given particularly poignant expression: between an accessible but unfulfilling "this-side" and a "that-side" or a "beyond" that is the object of all spiritual yearning but not within the reach of any natural or rational capacities. But in the *Speeches on Religion* this particular impasse is overcome, precisely because religious feeling is redirected toward the natural universe as the all-embracing *Diesseits* in which the individual subject of those feelings is himself encompassed. No longer regarded as a mere aggregate of finite entities, nature is "acknowledged as the universe," embracing the whole. As a result, faith's yearning "is brought back from its flight beyond actuality toward an eternal Yonder *(Jenseits),* the barrier between the subject or his knowledge and the absolute unattainable object is torn down, the pain is reconciled in enjoyment while the endless striving is satisfied in vision."[89] This position achieved by the *Speeches* seems to Hegel to be as far as one could go without abandoning "the Jacobian principle" of religious feeling, and indeed Protestant subjectivism, altogether.

But Hegel goes on to criticize the *Speeches* very sharply for remaining within the confines of this subjective religiosity, the great defect of which, even at its best, is that it cannot find its way out of the toils of a purely internal, personal, individuated experience into objective, publicly accessible and socially significant manifestations of the spirit. The reunion with nature as universe, for instance, is not itself universal in its conditions. It is essentially limited by the particular gifts and circumstances of individuals possessing special talents and sensibilities. The "virtuosity of the religious artist" with his personal idiosyncrasies gets mixed into "the tragic seriousness of religion." Hegel's old ideal of a Volksreligion clearly lies behind this line of criticism. He finds something frivolous in a religious movement that does not find its way into the ordeals and predicaments of social life. In terms, furthermore, that remind us of his analysis in the Frankfurt essays of the tragic fate of Christianity, Hegel points out that the religious virtuoso of the inner life is unable to give his intuitions concrete, objective expression in culturally available forms, such as epic or tragedy, or a body of legislation. This curious religious "artist" produces no "works of art" even in the broadest sense. Even if he gathers a band of followers around him, each virtuoso makes the peculiarity of his private intuition the principle of their movement, with the resultant splintering into cells and sects, abandoning both the objectivity of truth and the catholicity of religious life. So the "intuition of the universe is again reduced to subjectivity," without "receiving its objectivity and reality in the corporate life of a people and a universal church."[90]

The terms of this criticism remind us again of the practical social and religious issues that still lie just below the surface of Hegel's discussions of such speculative concepts as the transcendental intuition. What he finds resolved in Schleiermacher's *Speeches on Religion,* as well as the great problem he still finds there, are both instances of dualism, the overarching formal problem for which he seeks solution in the transcendental intuition. The transcendental intuition grasps (indeed *is*) that *Indifferenzpunkt* at which nature and consciousness, inner and outer, subject and object meet and interpenetrate. Furthermore, any form of rigid separation between a sacred reality and a mundane natural or social reality is also disclosed in the transcendental intuition to be a product of mere reflection. "Reflection," in fact, typically supplements its self-limited grasp by appealing to "faith" in a God that exists beyond both the subject of reflection and its possible objects of knowledge or experience. "Faith" in this restricted sense of the term is a state of consciousness that acknowledges an Absolute that is totally and permanently "beyond" anything with which that consciousness can in any manner unite itself. Such a "faith" is indeed the recourse of a "reflection" that has confined itself within a horizon of finite empirical objects and dualistic concepts. Its dualism between faith and knowledge represents a defensive posture that is designed precisely to prevent faith from being interfered with by any sober knowledge, and also to prevent the intrusion of any higher truth into the restricted range of its modest cognitive certainties. Hegel freely acknowledges that faith may exist among ordinary folk in a sense that is entirely free of this calculated defensiveness.

> The faith of people who have not elevated themselves to abstract reflection possesses the unaffectedness that is not opposed to reflection; it is also free of the reflection that the relation to the eternal in the form of faith as an immediate certainty . . . stands over against rational knowledge without necessarily contradicting it. It bears no relation to opposition generally—it is an uncalculated position, not a negation, either of another faith in something else or of another form for the content of this faith.[91]

It is quite a different matter when "faith" is assigned precisely that defensive function, and is invoked in order to negate any rational knowledge that might grasp a truth higher than subjectivity and finitude: and "faith arises in this negating, conscious form among Kant, Jacobi, and Fichte." Faith that is introjected into philosophy for such purposes

> entirely loses that pure unaffectedness; for now it is reason that flees to it out of reflection, in order to annihilate finitude and to transcend subjectivity—but faith is itself affected by this predetermined opposition to reflection and subjectivity. The opposition remains in it, because it here possesses the meaning of this negation at the same time, the reflection on the annihilation of reflection and the subjectivity of the consciousness of the annihilation of subjectivity, so that subjectivity has saved itself in its very annihilation.[92]

In rejecting "faith" in this self-contradictory, calculatedly defensive sense, Hegel does not suppose that he is attacking faith as it actually exists among "unaffected" believers. He rejects this pseudo-philosophical resort to faith because it seems to him to be a subterfuge, the real purpose of which is to place rigid limits on speculative reason and so to sustain the dualism between reflection and subjective religiosity, maintaining each as supreme in its respective sphere. In Hegel's eyes it is an unphilosophical device to serve both antiphilosophical and antireligious purposes.

The Eternal Incarnation

It is to philosophy itself, on the other hand, that Hegel turns to resolve this all too convenient antinomy between faith and knowledge. Jacobi, for instance, had insisted on the antinomy in order to sustain what he perceived as the religious truth of God's objective existence, which was recognized by faith though it lay beyond the capacity of reason. But philosophical reason, according to Hegel, has disclosed precisely what is so religiously questionable in the idea of God as a supreme Object. It has also shown the way to an understanding of the relation between the divine and the human that is more religiously profound than any conceived by pseudo-philosophical reflection.

> Jacobi says; "God is, and is *outside* me, a living being existing for himself, *or* I am God. *There is no third position.*" *There is a third position,* says philosophy on the contrary, and it is through philosophy that a third position exists. For it predicates of God not merely a being but also thought; that is, an ego, and recognizes him as the absolute identity of both. It recognizes no *outside* for God, and thus still less does it regard him as any such being existing *for himself,* which is defined through something outside him, that is, outside which there might be still other existence; but outside God it acknowledges no existence, nothing at all, and therefore the *either-or,* which is a principle of all formal logic and of the understanding that renounces reason, is simply eradicated in the absolute middle term.[93]

Here God, understood as the Absolute, is precisely the middle term, the *Indifferenzpunkt,* that mediates between thought and being, and renders finally impossible any simple separation between the divine and the human, the sacred and the mundane.

But they are not a simple identity either. A few pages later Hegel speaks of evil as a "necessity of the finite nature, as at one with its very concept." This, he says, is the essential view held by "religion" as against that of the "absolute subjectivity" he attributes to Fichte, according to which evil is an accidental feature of the world that can be mitigated and overcome through moral effort in society and the taming of nature. "Religion," however, finding evil necessarily inherent in finitude as such, also understands that this finitude is eternally transfigured and redeemed, a redemption "not displaced off into an infinite progress and never to be realized, but a truly real and present redemption." For the transfiguration of its finitude as such is also a necessity of the finite nature. There is an "eternal necessity," not to be sure the mere "empirical necessity that is the same as chance," but "an eternal necessity which is one with freedom, the necessity of wisdom existing as the course of the world [*Weltlauf*]," just as "Plato says of the world, that God's reason has given birth to it as a blessed god."[94]

Now this divine wisdom that has given birth to the world and is immanent in its course of events is reminiscent of the logos of the Johannine prologue: this logos that was with God in the beginning, and was God, is not only that through which all things were made but is also the "life" which is the light of men. Hegel often refers to this logos doctrine, and at least alludes to it in the present passage. To him it meant that the rational logos in nature and in mind is one and the same, and the redemption of nature and of humankind, despite the tragic necessity of evil, consists precisely in the immanence of this divine wisdom in them. In the present passage he speaks of this immanence of the divine wisdom as God's "eternal incarnation" *(ewigen Menschwerdung)*, not the logos become flesh in Christ but the generalized presence of the logos in creation and in humankind of which the Johannine prologue speaks in its opening verses.

Indeed, the notion of a special incarnation in time was pointless in the context of Hegel's thinking in the early 1800s. The evil built into the nature of things, as finitude, was simultaneously overcome through the immanence in this finitude of the divine wisdom, that is, through the "eternal" incarnation. Hegel had already spoken of the "eternal incarnation" in the *Differenzschrift*—directly identified there with the Johannine "witness of the Word from the beginning." In that context Hegel was explaining that the *Indifferenzpunkt* is expressed in the relative polarity of nature and intelligence: "The original identity" expands into the "objective totality" of spatial extension and temporal succession, which in turn contracts "into the self-recognition point of (subjective) reason" that is the "subjective totality." The objective totality, in short, is nature; the subjective totality is self-conscious intelligence. These two relative totalities coincide in what I take to be a simultaneous expansion and contraction, and the absolute totality must be the unity of both: which is achieved "in the intuition of the Absolute becoming itself objective in completed totality—in the intuition of the eternal incarnation of God, the witness of the Word from the beginning."[95]

Here the intuition of the eternal incarnation and the witness of the Johannine logos are alternative expressions for the transcendental intuition. The ideal one and the real many, intelligence and nature, not only stand in "indifferent" equilibrium, but the former inheres timelessly in the latter as the logos eternally incarnate. That is the basic conception Hegel still has in mind when he refers to the eternal incarnation in *Glauben und Wissen*. Against the Fichtean notion of accidental evil being gradually overcome, Hegel sets his coincidence of opposites: necessary evil qua finitude transfigured by the immanent presence of an infinite rationality. Only now an additional term is introduced: *Geist* (spirit), and this term implies a more dynamic conception of the relation of ideal and real than the simple *Indifferenz* of the earlier passage. There is still no need for a historical incarnation, much less a Fichtean program of moral progress, but still something must *happen* in order for the transfiguration of the finite to be complete: the finite consciousness must *comprehend* the eternal incarnation of divine wisdom in the world of finitude, and in particular must recognize its *own* unity with this incarnate wisdom; that is, its recognition of this wisdom must also be self-recognition. And Geist is that self-conscious recognition, the eternally incarnate logos become consciously aware of itself. Hegel suggests that the potential capacity of the finite human consciousness to achieve this reconciliation is what is meant by its being made in the image of God. But only as spirit is this capacity activated: The finite nature,

> insofar as it is considered in its finitude and particularity, exhibits [only] a possible reconciliation, the original *possibility* of which, the *subjective,* is in the original image of God, but its *objective* [manifestation] is its *actuality* in his eternal incarnation; but the identity of that possibility and this actuality is achieved through the spirit as the unification of the subjective with the God-become-man, and thus the world as *in itself* reconstrued, redeemed, . . . sanctified.[96]

The view of spirit to which this exalted function is assigned still seems purely stipulative; spirit can be so defined, but it is utterly unclear how it is realized, and that is why this brave talk about a world already redeemed and sanctified has such a hollow ring. Later Hegel will articulate the view of spirit realizing the unity of finite and infinite through a conception of historical development; then he will also find some significance in the notion of historical incarnation. But one cannot read such conceptions into the early Jena writings. In the pattern we have found variously expressed in these writings, of diremption from original identity and timeless return to it, Geist signifies the return, while "eternal incarnation" expresses the crucial point that the identity is present, as rational logos, even in the movement into externality and plurality and time.

Art/Religion and Speculation

This speculative use of religious language was no mere concession to the theologians, however. Hegel had argued in the *Differenzschrift* that it is precisely at the breathtaking height of the transcendental intuition that speculation, religion, and art meet, and find their proper relation. Each in its own way manifests the *Indifferenzpunkt* in which thought and being are one. But although in each case the intuition transcends the opposition between subjectivity and objectivity, each does so primarily under a subjective or an objective aspect, in which, furthermore, either the conscious or the nonconscious predominates. "Religion," in fact, is here treated as one of the modes of "art," the other mode being the production of objectified works of art as such. In "art"—embracing both artistic work in the narrower sense and religion—the transcendental intuition appears in a form in which the nonconscious *(bewusstlos)* predominates over consciousness. The work of art, indeed, is objective and enduring, while the intuition appears in religion "as a living movement, which as subjective is only momentary." To the reflective understanding, in fact, the work of art can seem a dead externality, religion merely something inner. But that is because the understanding reifies into fixed opposition what is in truth a polarity within a dynamic unity, in which each side must manifest something of the other in order to fulfill its own function. The work of art, however, is "a product of the individual, of genius, though it belongs to humanity," while religion is "the product of a multitude, of a universal ingenuity, though it also belongs to each individual." The nice symmetry of this formulation expresses the polarity and at the same time the overlapping, the interpenetration of the two, that makes it possible to speak of both as modes of "art."

But "art" itself, with its balancing of religious inwardness and universality with aesthetic objectivity and individuality, again makes up one pole, tending toward the nonconscious, balanced within a polarity against "speculation" that moves toward the fully conscious and deliberate. The transcendental intuition, however, is manifest in both.

> In *speculation* that intuition appears more as consciousness and as something expanded in consciousness, as an act of subjective reason which transcends [*aufhebt*] the objectivity and the nonconscious. If in art within its true scope the Absolute appears more in the form of absolute being, so in speculation it appears more as something self-engendered in its infinite intuition. But since indeed it grasps this as a becoming, it posits at the same time the identity of becoming and being, and what appears to it as self-engendered will at the same time be posited as the original absolute being, that can only become insofar as it is. In this manner it knows how to take even the predominance which consciousness has in it, a predominance that is in any case a nonessential. Both, art and speculation, are in their essence worship, both are a vital intuition of absolute life and thus a being at one with it.[97]

In speaking of art and speculation as essentially forms of worship *(Gottesdienst),* Hegel is of course not reverting to the position he had held in Frankfurt, in which aesthetic and philosophical movements are fulfilled in religion. But the basic meaning he had assigned to "religion" at that time appears to be precisely what he now means by worship: the elevation of the finite to the infinite.

Now, however, this elevation connotes a movement that passes beyond any limited definition of that movement. Worship is no more religious than it is aesthetic or philosophical, and even as a religious mode it is not defined in terms of Christian doctrine as such; in this "worship" art and speculation approach that *Indifferenzpunkt* at which no such distinctions can any longer express the fullness of either. It is the movement that begins with an apparently limited form of activity, artistic and solitary, religious and communal, or intellectual, and passes by its own internal necessity, in order to complete itself, into an Absolute that is in an austere sense divine, the totality, itself internally expansive, that contains them all. Thus speculation is a human activity, a pursuit of knowledge that people deliberately set out to engage themselves in, but precisely as worship it remains no longer within the limits of subjective thoughts and intentions, but becomes incorporated in the very substance it has sought to grasp: only so is it genuine speculation.

Negation: The Darkness of Identity

As a movement transpiring between the human and the divine, this "worship" in all its forms implies negation. The metamorphosis of the worshiper in this movement carries him beyond the particular subjective consciousness with which he began, thus negating the finite limits of that consciousness and its objects. Not of course that the worshiper ceases to exist as a human being, but his awareness and his self-awareness are no longer bound up within that narrow existence. The divine also, for that matter, is negated in its objective givenness. Worship is a journey in which both the traveler and his destination are progressively annihilated as such. For if the transcendental intuition expresses itself, in art, religion, and speculation alike, as a kind of worship, then worship as the transfiguration of the finite must contain this moment of negation.

We have emphasized the synthesizing aspect of transcendental intuition, that it comprehends the differences in their *Indifferenz*. But every synthesis is also the negation of the factors that had entered the synthesis, and this negativity is the seminal insight in the development of a dialectical method. Hegel was already at work, as we will note in the next section, on a logic in which all the concepts are self-negating. But it may already be clear that this emerging view of negation as the other side of synthesis is powerfully reinforced by Hegel's metaphysical commitments during this period. We recall that the transcendental intuition grasps the entire manifold of being and all the ideal objects of consciousness in their return to the identity from which they proceeded, which is to say that the many is negated by the one. In Hegel's essay on skepticism in the *Critical Journal,* this negation of the many by the one is the central insight of that skepticism that is said to be an implicit moment in every true philosophy; the great exponent of this genuine skepticism "in its pure explicit form" is the Parmenides of Plato's dialogue.[98]

Sometimes Hegel expresses the absolute identity in language derived from the Rhineland mystics and from Jakob Bohme, as a night of total darkness, an abyss of nothingness, from which differentiated thoughts and realities break forth first as light and then in the full splendor of their variegated manifold, only to return in their negation to the darkness of simple identity. For Hegel, of course, this movement is not an actual process with a beginning and an end, but is at once the abiding, dynamic condition of anything actual and the course of speculative reason in grasping it. Nor is his monism of the sort that in fact creates a dualism between the one and the many. It is one of the deepest errors of the reflective understanding to set the one and the many in opposition, so that any return to identity must be perceived as lying "beyond" the present, actual condition of things. The identity or *Indifferenz* given in the transcendental intuition is not the simple negation of the many, but the negation of the one and the many in their abstract opposition. For that opposition is simply one of the forms of *Entzweiung* (division, bifurcation), along with subject/object, ideal/ real, practical/theoretical reason, and so forth, that *Reflexions philosophie* has erected into absolute presuppositions of philosophical thinking.

But *Entzweiung*, Hegel argues in the Introduction to the *Differenzschrift*, is in fact the problem, the "need" that it is the task of philosophy to overcome. Within the bifurcated consciousness, the Absolute and its finite manifestations are themselves necessarily split asunder: "The Absolute is the night and the light is younger than it, and the distinction between the two, as well as the proceeding of the light out of the night, constitutes an absolute difference: the nothingness is the first, out of which comes forth all being, the whole manifold of finitude."

Correctly understood, this theosophic vision is not simply false, but its significance needs to be comprehended rationally. The passage continues: "But the task of philosophy consists . . . in positing being in the non-being, as becoming; estrangement [*Entzweiung*] in the Absolute, as its appearance; the finite in the infinite, as life."[99] That is what it means for philosophy to become rational, speculative. Yet Hegel still finds the mystical language appropriate to the extent that the real manifold of nature and the ideal objects of thought are alike grasped in their diremption from absolute identity and in that self-negation which is their return to it.

For philosophy has its visionary side which, as worship, it shares with art and religion: The ego and its every object, perceivable or conceivable, from the meanest to the most sublime, are so many sparks flying up in the night and flickering out in utter darkness again. Hegel soon came to criticize very sharply those who attempted to build a philosophy on any such visionary foundation, and even in the early Jena years he was clear that such a vision is not yet a philosophy, though it may be incorporated into the metaphors in which a philosophy is expressed. But the transcendental intuition is itself a kind of pure, nonsensuous vision that can be expressed in such metaphors, since on its negative side it is precisely an intuition of the vanity, the impermanence and insubstantiality of every possible object of human preoccupation, including the human mind itself. And having the intellectual courage to accept such a self-abnegating sense of the truth of things is for Hegel a fundamental condition of speculative insight, apart from which no amount of diligence or logical acuity could suffice to admit a thinker to the ranks of philosophers. Unless one is prepared for a resignation so severe that he can suspend with equanimity his sense of self and its sentimental certainties, he can scarcely view even the most trivial objects rationally. His thinking will take the form of apologetic special pleading and self-justification. That was the fate of *Reflexionsphilosophie,* which precisely by means of its apparently modest denial of the possibility of ultimate knowledge had tried to render invulnerable the self-certain egoism of the human subject and his fondest fancies and conceits. In Hegel's eyes it was a matter not simply of errors but of a failure in intellectual courage. Speculative philosophy, on the contrary, is a kind of ascetic discipline, certainly not renouncing beer and sausage, but purging thought of all concessions to sentimental self-indulgence. For it must reflect in itself the negation of all finitude in the night of absolute identity. In this spirit Hegel is said to have introduced his lectures of 1801–2 on logic and metaphysics by admonishing his students in the words of the inscription over Dante's hell: Abandon all hope, ye that enter here![100]

A Dark Passage Illuminated: Commentary on the Conclusion of *Glauben und Wissen*

In the same spirit, and in terms still reminiscent of Böhme and the mystics, *Glauben und Wissen* concludes with a brooding meditation on total negation and the death of God. The body of the treatise has consisted in a fairly sober critique of Kant, Jacobi, and Fichte, each of whom in his own way was said to have introduced a dualism between "faith and knowledge" or "believing and knowing," confining knowledge to a *Diesseits* while directing faith toward an inaccessible *Jenseits*. In the variations among these three systems, the possibilities open to *Reflexionsphilosophie* seem to Hegel to have run their course; and since *Reflexionsphilosophie,* as we have seen, is not just an accidental phenomenon but a manifestation of the *Weltgeist* in its northern, Protestant phase, it would seem that the exposure of its errors may be a sign that the *Weltgeist* is bestirring itself for new adventures. And indeed in the conclusion Hegel does suggest that the changes that have been rung in Kantian and post-Kantian philosophy may in a historical sense have prepared the way for a true philosophy, one that has profited from their discipline and appropriated what is genuinely speculative in them, but profited from the disclosure of their errors as well. These systems have recognized that the Absolute is infinite in form, but by creating a dualism between this infinitude and the manifold appearances of the finite they have stopped short of the radical implications of their own insight. It is left for the true philosophy to realize those implications, recognizing

> thought as infinitude and the negative side of the Absolute—which is the pure annihilation of the opposition or of finitude, but is also at the same time the source of the eternal movement, or of the finitude that is infinite, i.e. that eternally annihilates itself: out of this nothingness and pure night of infinitude the truth rises up as out of the secret abyss that is its birthplace.[101]

This extraordinary vision of rebirth through conceptual annihilation is to be the basis of the new philosophy, for which the speculative side of *Reflexionsphilosophie* has already prepared. Not recognizing "the positive Idea, that being is not outside the infinite, ego, thought, but both are one," *Reflexionsphilosophie* has come closest to "the philosophy of the Absolute" in this insight into the negative infinitude of pure thought. For the Absolute itself has this negative side; it is not simply a perverse, skeptical passion among philosophers, but their participation, through thinking, in the life of the Absolute. The Absolute as nothingness and pure night into which all finitude passes in perpetual self-annihilation, is also the darkness into which thought has got to pass in order to discover the truth: The truth is not incremental, putting together facts and bits of insight until they form a pattern. The truth is a self-defined totality that takes its rise from the already total negation of finitude and partial insight.

Hegel expresses this visionary sense of death and transfiguration, life through death, in the closing sentence of the treatise, an extraordinary statement that merits our close inspection. Unfortunately this sentence is also of untranslatable and almost unendurable length and complexity. I shall try to unravel it bit by bit:

> But the pure Concept or the infinitude as the abyss of nothingness into which all being sinks must designate the infinite pain [*muss den unendlichen Schmerz . . . bezeichnen*] . . . purely as a moment, but also as no more than a moment of the highest Idea . . .

This first part of the sentence, broken by a long interpolation to which we will return, is already confusing enough. It is crucial to register, however, that "the pure Concept [*der reine Begriff*] or the infinitude" is the subject of the whole sentence. Hegel's understanding of the Concept during this period, furthermore, must not be confused with the consummating sense he will give the term in the later *Logik* and in his mature philosophy generally. Here it signifies precisely that infinitude of thought which he has just called "the negative side of the Absolute." The Idea is what contains both sides: positively it is transcendental intuition, negatively it is Concept.[102] The "infinite pain" suffered in the dissolution of "all being" is exacted by the Concept itself, through its own internal necessity. The Concept is an infinitude in the sense that it is not only the limitless negation of all that is (Hegel uses the Bohmian expression, *Abgrund des Nichts*), but also establishes the boundless pain of that negation as a moment of the Idea. The same necessity by which, as the nihilating side of the Absolute, the Concept negates all being and all thought, is also its necessary limitation, that it cannot be the whole.

It is easier to parody such a statement than to understand it. The dissolution of all being as a moment (but no more!) in the internal life of the Idea would seem to produce a pain of an uncommonly abstract sort. Hegel does not yet clearly invoke historical development and historical negation to give actual content to the Concept. But the interpolation takes an important step in that direction, associating the pain with something rather more identifiable than its infinity:

> ... the infinite pain, —that earlier was only historically in the culture [*in der Bildung geschichtlich*], and as the feeling on which the religion of modern times is based, the feeling: God himself is dead (the same feeling that was, as it were, only empirically articulated in Pascal's expression: la nature est telle qu'elle *marque* partout un *Dieu perdu* et dans l'homme et hors de l'homme), —purely as a moment, but also as no more ...

The feeling that God is dead has made its appearance as a cultural event (which long antedated Nietzsche). Here, however, we are not dealing directly with a crisis of civilization and its tradition, neither with the sense of abandonment to the Pascalian silences of the universe nor with the outrage against an authoritarian image that Hegel himself had so eloquently expressed in Bern and Frankfurt, but with the logically necessary negation of even the highest being by the pure Concept. For the Concept is the infinite totality grasped in its negativity. No particular object, whether of experience or of thought or of belief, can be considered a substantial entity, subsisting in itself, once it is recognized as an aspect of that totality. Even the most sublime being, whatever its relative truth may be, must in an absolute sense also sink into the abyss of nothingness. For the Concept is that abyss precisely in the sense that it is the negation of every particular existence as such. In the tradition of Western philosophical theology, after all, God as absolute fullness of being is understood in like manner to negate all merely contingent beings, which in their coming to be and passing away reveal their radical dependence on God to sustain their merely provisional hold on existence. But the Concept is not only being itself and ideality itself but the negation of both as such, not in the sense that they are merely temporal and contingent, but in the sense that they are revealed as finite after all, by their very opposition to one another and to temporal, contingent entities.

Very well. The point is metaphysical, not cultural. Yet this particular manifestation of the infinite pain is not chosen at random. The Concept confirms in an absolute sense the feeling that had developed historically, in culture, that God is dead. The Concept, furthermore, designates that infinite pain, of which the death of God is the instance par excellence,

> ... purely as a moment, but also as no more than a moment of the highest Idea, and so must give a philosophical existence to

what was perhaps either a moral prescription for a sacrificing
of empirical being [*Wesens*] or the concept of formal abstraction,
and therefore must restore to philosophy the idea of absolute
freedom . . .

Formal *(formell)* abstraction is the logical reduction of the particular
to the generic; morally one must sometimes be prepared to sacrifice
one's own empirical being in a higher cause. Both are limited forms of
negation relevant to this absolute negation, to its theoretical and its
practical side respectively, but the pure Concept makes negation an
all-embracing speculative principle. Unconfined by any fixed objects
or inviolable logical constraints, the otherwise unrealizable and even
unimaginable idea of an absolute freedom thus becomes philosophically
coherent, as a self-existence that is both unrestricted and fully complete—but only as another expression for the infinite pain: The Concept

> . . . therefore must restore to philosophy the idea of absolute
> freedom and with it the absolute suffering or the speculative
> Good Friday, that was otherwise historical, and must restore it
> even in the full truth and hardness of its Godlessness . . .

The death of God, after all, has another aspect: not merely the aggressive atheism or the reluctant bereavement that have characterized the
modern age, but also the central image of traditional Christianity, of
the incarnate God crucified. The horrendous notion that God himself
has died on the cross, which has been obscured by harmless conventional renderings of the story, is here restored not merely as a historical
event but as a supreme speculative insight, and restored in all its
original force of truth and pitiless severity: we are left without God,
Godless or Godforsaken like Christ on the cross. Philosophy become
speculative has suffered the loss of everything, and precisely in its
disillusionment and austerity enjoys an absolute freedom.

The Concept, however, prepares the way for a surprising inversion,
that reminds us that the infinite pain of its negativity was after all
"no more than a moment" of the Idea: The Concept gives philosophy
its Good Friday, a speculative one to be sure, but suffered

> in the full truth and hardness of its Godlessness, out of which
> hardness alone,—for the more serene, superficial and idiosyn-
> cratic of the dogmatic philosophies must disappear along with

the nature-religions—the highest totality can and must be resurrected in its utter seriousness and out of its deepest ground, encompassing everything at once, and in the most serene freedom of its form.[103]

Well, after Good Friday comes Easter. That is the gospel, and its crucifixion-resurrection pattern is not infrequently subjected to rhetorical exploitation to provide upbeat endings to otherwise rather cheerless stories. Here too, the introduction of the resurrection motif in the closing words of the treatise is rather too cryptic to be entirely convincing. Hegel owes us a fuller explanation of its meaning. Still, its appearance is not entirely arbitrary either; some pointers have been left along the way that anticipate it. We have, after all, been told a story of a most uncommon sort, a timeless narrative enacted altogether within the Idea, its "moments" not episodes in a drama nor events in an unfolding process, but a logico-dialectical sequence within an unchanging but internally complex whole. It purports to tell us, not what has been nor what shall be, but what eternally subsists as a totality. It must account, among other things, for the world as it is. The moment of negativity is pivotal, dissolving the mere appearance of things in its abyss, but that obviously cannot be the final moment. Everything must reappear in its truth.

Yet the "most serene freedom" in which this totality is resurrected is not merely the outcome of one of those serenely cheerful philosophies referred to a few lines earlier. It is in fact the "absolute freedom" that we have already been told is the obverse side of "the absolute suffering or the speculative Good Friday." The movement from this Good Friday to Easter is neither that of philosophical optimism, showing how the universe turns out fortunately despite its drawbacks, nor that of the nature religions, with their springtime rebirth following the winter desolation; they must disappear because the logical and empirical premises of both have already disappeared into the abyss of nothingness. The Spinozistic model, that Hegel still took very seriously, is more illuminating: we have a single totality in two modes, in the mode of appearance and in the mode of truth. But here the Concept actively negates the appearances, both empirical and ideal; relative to them it is the abyss of nothingness and the rack of unmitigated pain. Only out of the "hardness" of this severe and Godless truth can the totality, the same totality purged of its illusory appearances and all-embracing, stand forth "in its utter seriousness" and in its "most serene freedom."

"Faith and Knowledge," then, are not synthesized by leaving a few mysteries beyond knowledge to which faith can still cling, nor by reinterpreting the objects of faith in the flickering light of our supposed knowledge. Any such apologetic procedure is cut off by the moment of negativity, into which the objects of our cognitive certainties disappear along with those of the religious imagination. Faith and knowledge are synthesized in the very negation of both, in the return to an identity the intuitive grasp of which is at once the transcendence of mere "knowledge" by speculative comprehension and the transcendence of mere "faith" by that "religion" that shares with speculation its austere worship.

In no sense does Hegel appear in these critical writings as a defender of Christianity. His misgivings about it, about current Protestantism in particular, are fairly muted in these essays, but he is more outspoken in his Jena lectures and manuscripts, in which it is also clearer that when he speaks of religion in a positive way he is not identifying it with Christianity as such, any more than he did in Frankfurt. In fact, as we have observed, many of his criticisms of *Reflexionsphilosophie* tax it with having repeated in sophisticated form some of the same basic errors he had found in the Christian tradition—an ironical charge to make against Fichte, who had been more or less drummed out of Jena because of the imputation of atheism. The "religion" Hegel defends, on the other hand, owes at least as much to ancient Greece as it does to Christianity, and is so fundamentally informed by speculative principles that it does indeed approach a point of "nondifference" with speculation itself.[104]

What is therefore surprising is how ready Hegel already is at this time to employ Christian categories in expressing his most fundamental speculative insights. We need only recall those already mentioned in this section. There is his employment of Johannine logos theology in his view of nature and at the same time his argument that evil is a necessary feature of finitude, reflecting an old Christian paradox: that we live in a fallen world, despite the immanence in creation of the divine logos from which it issued. Then there is Hegel's talk of an eternal incarnation, a speculative Good Friday, and an equally speculative resurrection. This language is all carefully scrubbed clean of the specific content it has in the gospel itself; none of these expressions refers, as they all do in Christian teaching, to the figure of Jesus himself. Still, Hegel does not introduce this language casually, or merely for rhetorical effect, or because he had no alternative expressions available. Not only the language but the sequence seems in a singular manner to force itself on him. For there is a pattern here: creation constituted through the logos, a view of evil reminiscent of original sin, incarnation within conscious human being of the logos immanent in nature, crucifixion or total negation, and resurrection. The pattern is essentially that of the gospel itself, a drama in several acts, recognizable even when it is carefully abstracted from the personalities and details of the gospel story. It is apparent particularly in what is beginning to emerge as the dialectical character of this new speculative philosophy, for instance, in the insistence that negation is an essential moment in the absolute Concept: that the all-encompassing reality neither subsists eternally nor develops progressively, but arises out of total negation, death and resurrection. The theological terminology Hegel occasionally adopts suggests that he himself was well aware of the extent to which this pattern had impressed itself on his thinking, not in its peripheral observations but precisely at its speculative core. The adoption of this pattern became even more pronounced in the years that followed, though Hegel's intent always remained remote from any sort of Christian apologetics. It is altogether misleading, in fact, to see Christian apologetic as the issue for Hegel. It is obvious how far he is from being a Christian apologist in the Jena writings, and yet the pattern of the gospel drama is already clear enough.

4. Toward a System: The Jena Manuscripts

After the demise of the *Critical Journal* Hegel did not publish anything until his *Phenomenology of Spirit* appeared in 1807. There were always ambitious plans for major systematic works, but no finished manuscripts were ever turned over to the publishers. As early as summer 1802, the announcement for Hegel's lecture course on logic and metaphysics implied that he would be following his own published book on those subjects. It was a legacy of the medieval university that lecturers would generally expound recognized textbooks, and some would write their own. That was what Hegel wanted to do, and to present his system to a wider public as well. The Cotta publishing house in Tubingen confidently ordered a thousand copies of "Hegel's Logic" from the printer, expecting it to be ready by autumn 1802; then the order was pushed back to Easter 1803, but still no completed work was forthcoming. Hegel also intended that his announced lectures on natural law would be based on his own text, but that did not appear either. In 1805 he announced a work that would treat "the entire science of philosophy." At that time he still intended that the "Science of the Experience of Consciousness" would serve as an introductory section of this compendious work. But that introduction grew into the monumental *Phenomenology of Spirit,* and the publication of the system itself had to wait for many years.[105]

These premature announcements of projected works were not merely a matter of wishful thinking on Hegel's part. The considerable mass of manuscript material dating from the Jena period that was found in his files testifies to his strenuous efforts to make good on these promises. Most of these manuscripts were not published until this century; critical editions only appeared in the 1970s, and their context and chronology have become clear through the work of Heinz Kimmerle and the other editors of the critical editions. They were known in the nineteenth century only through the extracts and paraphrases that appeared in the Hegel biographies by Rosenkranz and Haym (to whom, indeed, we are indebted for preserving some important fragments of and references to manuscripts that have subsequently disappeared). Yet they shed important light on Hegel's development, particularly during the period in which he set about developing a rigorous systematic *Wissenschaft.* Many of these manuscripts, furthermore, show careful revision and some are fair copies that seem to have been through several drafts. Most of them are directly related to the subjects of his Jena lectures and were obviously being prepared for publication. Yet all of them remain fragments, some of large book length but still unfinished. Some problems bearing on the very form of the system remain unresolved, and that is no doubt the most important reason they were never completed for publication.

The Jena manuscripts fall roughly into four periods. In this section I shall survey the manuscript material belonging to each of these periods in turn, pausing occasionally for some remarks about the development of Hegel's thinking from one period to another and the problems that arose for him, particularly in his early efforts at systematic construction. In the next section I shall treat some themes directly relevant to the special interests of this study, as they take shape in these Jena manuscripts. Again, of course, I shall not be attempting to trace Hegel's development in detail. That is an arduous task of specialized scholarship in itself, and it is already well under way, particularly among the scholars whose editorial work has made the materials for such a reconstruction of the Jena period possible. My survey in this section may serve some readers as an introduction to this thorny project in intellectual biography, but it will also supply the context for the themes I shall be examining in the next section, and also for the chapter on the *Phenomenology* that follows.

Manuscripts of 1801–1803

The first period (1801 to mid-1803) includes the manuscripts written more or less at the same time as the *Differenzschrift* and the essays in the *Critical Journal*. Some preliminary drafts of *The German Constitution* date from the Frankfurt period, but the work as we have it was composed in part between February and April 1801, and then revised and expanded during the last two months of 1802 and later. In between these two periods of work on *The German Constitution* Hegel wrote the thematically related essay on *Natural Law (Über die wissenschaftlichen Behandlungsarten des Naturrechts)* which was published in the *Critical Journal*. Even more directly related to the essay on *Natural Law* is a manuscript composed in systematic form during the winter of 1802–3 or later, to which Rosenkranz gave the title, *System der Sittlichkeit.* Rosenkranz also reported and quoted lengthy extracts from a lecture manuscript on natural law that may belong to the same period, but has unfortunately been lost.[106] Taken together, these unfinished manuscripts and the text on *Natural Law* represent Hegel's efforts to develop a practical philosophy sharply opposed to the Kantian/Fichtean conception of it as a system of normative moral obligations. Here practical "intelligence" issues in *Sittlichkeit,* an ethos as well as an ethic, not a system of "oughts" for rational individuals but a subsistent fabric of law and custom in the public, social existence of the Volk. These essays develop more rigorously some of the themes adumbrated in Bern and Frankfurt, and again they assign a problematic role to religion that must be considered in the next section. In hindsight this group of writings can be seen as preparing for the mature *Philosophy of Right.*

But Hegel was developing other sides of his thinking during that same period, in his first treatments of logic and metaphysics in lecture manuscripts that have all been lost. According to fragments preserved by Rosenkranz, apparently from an introduction to early lectures on logic and metaphysics, Hegel at that time treated logic as an introduction to philosophy, beginning with forms of "reflexion" and issuing in the properly speculative science of metaphysics. In the manner familiar to us from his essays in the *Critical Journal,* he distinguished between "reflexion" as the sphere of finite knowledge governed by the forms of the understanding, and "speculation" as "science of truth," which has "infinite knowledge or the knowledge of the Absolute as its object" and is governed by reason. At that time he still used the traditional term, metaphysics, to designate the latter, the grasp of that "absolute identity" from which the "finite knowledge" with which logic begins is the fragmented abstraction—"and there is a finite knowledge through this abstraction alone." The task of "a true logic," then, will be

> to position the *forms of finitude,* not to be sure as they are put together empirically, but rather as they come forth out of reason, yet appear only in their finitude through the plundering of reason by the understanding. —Then the strivings of the understanding must be presented, how it *imitates* reason by producing an identity, but can only bring forth a *formal [formelle] identity.* In order to recognize the understanding as imitative, we must at the same time always hold up the original that it copies, the expression of reason itself. —Finally we must transcend [*aufheben*] the forms of understanding themselves through *reason,* showing what significance and what content these finite forms of knowing have for reason. The knowledge of reason, insofar as it belongs to logic, will thus only be a *negative* knowing of them.[107]

As a propaedeutic in this sense to philosophy itself, logic must systematically fulfill the function performed in a different way by the criticism of "unphilosophy" carried on in the *Critical Journal.*[108] Hegel continued to feel the need for such a propaedeutic path of negation. A few years later, when he had begun to develop a logic that was itself speculative through and through, he designed a new science to perform that task: different as it is, the *Phenomenology* would also begin with finite forms in their opposition, determined by subject-object dualisms, and in the movement to "absolute knowledge" would negate these forms step by step. The concluding, third part of this early logic, too, must demonstrate "the Aufheben of this finite knowing through *reason*," to prepare the way for speculative science.

> From this third part of logic, namely the negative or annihilating side of reason, the transition will be made to genuine philosophy or to *metaphysics*. Here above all we must completely construct the *principle* of all philosophy. From the true knowledge of that the conviction will arise that there has been in all ages only one and the same philosophy. Not only do I promise thereby nothing new, but I devote my philosophical endeavors to rehabilitating actually the oldest of the old and to freeing it from the misunderstanding in which the more recent times of unphilosophy have buried it.[109]

Manuscripts of 1803–1804

During Hegel's second period in Jena, from summer 1803 to summer 1804, the manuscript material seems to suggest that he was less occupied with his battle against "unphilosophy." More than two years of writing for the *Critical Journal* had perhaps sated his appetite for polemics for the time being, and with Schelling's departure we find him preoccupied with ordering and systematizing his thought, struggling to bring the many sides of his thinking into a single coherent structure. For the winter semester, 1803–4, Hegel announced a course of lectures devoted to *"philosophiae speculativae systema,* complectens (a) Logicam et Metaphysicam sive *Idealismum transscendentalem* (b) philosophiam naturae et (c) *mentis."* All the extant manuscript materials from this second period seem to be devoted to this ambitious project. They do not include manuscripts for the lectures on logic and metaphysics, which have either been lost or were not written; Hegel may have used older manuscripts for that part of the course. What we do have are copious materials on the philosophy of nature and the philosophy of spirit, which clearly presuppose and refer back to a logic and metaphysics. Even these manuscripts are extremely fragmentary, and the philosophy of spirit breaks off unfinished, but the general structure of the whole is fairly clear.[110] The philosophy of nature develops from mechanics through chemism and physics to the organic, which culminates in sensitive life. The discussion of sensitive life prepares for the transition to the philosophy of spirit, which begins with the foundations of social life and of consciousness and develops into the cultural forms and media of civilization. The conscious, social, cultural life of human beings is rooted in the natural world: that proposition is not so much stated as exhibited, in detail, in the very structure of the system. This development of human life within nature is of course not to be understood in an evolutionary sense, as a process in time (though Hegel's scheme would have no difficulty accommodating an evolutionary process), but as an organic structure of internal relatedness, which the systematic pattern serves well to explicate.

The systematic form of Hegel's thinking also makes it possible to articulate his sense that nature and spirit are themselves permeated by an ideal rational structure; that is why these second and third parts of the system must presuppose a logic and metaphysics as their speculative groundwork. Spirit or mind (*Geist*, which Hegel renders in Latin as *mens*) is in fact inherent in all three parts, and not only in the third. Recapitulating the earlier parts in introducing the third, Hegel says that "the first part of philosophy"—logic and metaphysics—"construed spirit as Idea. . . . This Idea fell absolutely apart in the philosophy of nature; absolute being, aether, separated itself from its becoming or infinity." Even then, the essential unity of indeterminate being and the manifold becoming was the inner secret, "the concealed" in nature, and in organic life moved out of this concealment. However, "in the philosophy of spirit it exists as the recovery of itself in absolute universality," the absolute unity made "real" as "absolute becoming."[111]

Hegel has begun to understand this real becoming of spirit in human culture as the actualization of the Idea that had been rendered in logic/metaphysics and as its recovery from dispersion and concealment in nature. While the systematic ordering renders fairly transparent the way in which nature provides the conditions for the existence of conscious beings and "real" spirit, there is no question of any reductive, causal analysis. "Nature exists in spirit, as that which is its [nature's] essence."[112] It must be said, furthermore, that this philosophy of nature is still not very scientific. Written at a time when Hegel was not only still under the influence of Schellingian philosophy of nature, but still impressed by the theosophical speculations of Jakob Bohme, the view of nature presented here—for instance, the treatment of light and sound—is suffused with notions of a Romantic, alchemical, magical sort. The notion of "aether"—which Hegel continued to employ even after he had deliberately turned away from Schelling and Bohme to develop a more "scientific" concept of nature—has an important mediating role not only between Idea and material but also between nature and spirit. Aether as the undifferentiated nonmaterial *Indifferenz* of being, differentiated in nature, returns from its endless dispersion to recover itself in its infinite unity as spirit.[113] Again, "the essence of consciousness" consists in an "absolute unity of opposites" that subsists "immediately in an aethereal identity."[114] Yet the actual treatment of consciousness and spirit, in its details, is not all that aethereal, but proceeds on recognizable social, cultural grounds. The primary themes that Hegel had developed in his "practical" philosophy during the first period, in the *System der Sittlichkeit* in particular, dominate the philosophy of spirit here, transmuted into the total systematic framework: speech, memory, tools, work, property, family, Volk.[115] In the *System der Sittlichkeit* there was already an effort to develop these "potencies" of the ethical life in continuity with vegetable and animal life, but here, within the context of a system, such continuities become more transparent despite the significant gaps that remain.

Manuscripts of 1804–1805

The manuscript materials from the third period, dating from summer 1804 through the winter semester, 1804–5, are devoted to another massive reconstruction of the system. Hegel announced lectures for that semester on *"totam philosophiae scientiam,* i.e., philosophiam *speculativam,* (logicam et metaphysicam) *naturae et mentis"* and as a relic of his heroic attempt to write a book on that all-encompassing subject left behind another manuscript in several hundred pages of fair copy devoted to logic, metaphysics, and philosophy of nature. Yet the philosophy of nature breaks off unfinished, and there is no manuscript for a philosophy of spirit.[116]

It is not known how Hegel went about completing, in the lecture hall, all of these courses for which we have only unfinished manuscripts. The great thing about a semester, after all, is that it ends whether the lecturer has completed his announced subject or not.

Opening pages of the Logic are also missing, but later references to its first section suggest it was entitled "Simple Connection" *(Einfache Beziehung).*[117] The second section treats "Relation," and the third "Proportion," which in turn is divided into subsections entitled "Definition,"

"Classification," and "Knowing" *(Erkennen)*. Now "knowing" is in fact the fundamental rubric of the Metaphysics, so that concluding subsection of the Logic is transitional. Hegel still employs his old categories of *Differenz* and *Indifferenz* to distinguish this knowing in which the Logic culminates from the metaphysical knowing: The differentiated categories of logic, still determined by oppositions, are aufgehoben at the stage of knowledge, but so long as this knowing remains within the confines of logic it is still differentiated from its contents, while true metaphysical knowing determines the moments of the Ideas as "indifferent"; that is, its ideal moments are themselves self-reflexive totalities that are not different from the Idea itself. The knowing and the known no longer stand in opposition. "Knowing" is the irreducible unit, containing both knower and known. The knowing that completes the Logic, on the other hand, culminates in the recognition that its differentiated categories are diremptions from that indifferent, self-identical ideal knowing.[118] "Knowing, as it passes over into metaphysics, as dialectic or idealism, is the Aufheben of logic itself."[119] In this sense Hegel still retained his earlier distinction between logic as a science of reflective "understanding" and metaphysics as the properly speculative science.

But the distinction between logic and metaphysics was becoming tenuous, a formalistic construction that was beginning to get in the way of the new conception of the first, ideal moment of the system as it was beginning to form in Hegel's thinking. As we shall see, Hegel was already coming to view the moments of the Idea in a circular formation, each internally related to the others and leading to a culmination that would coincide with the beginning. But this emerging circular conception was still being superimposed on the earlier two-level construction of a differentiated logic on the ground floor giving way to the speculative *Indifferenz* of the upper story. It was more than a clash of images. The circular construction really could not accommodate the relegation of logic to a pre-speculative position, outside the system proper. Indeed, Hegel's announcement of lectures for winter 1804–5, for which he prepared this manuscript, implies that logic as well as metaphysics is speculative: the "whole science of philosophy" is comprised of the three italicized moments of philosophy, "philosophiam *speculativam,* (logicam et metaphysicam) *naturae et mentis.*" Furthermore, it was already clear that the whole speculative circle had to receive full systematic articulation; it could not culminate in an ineffable *Indifferenz.* Hegel was very soon to move beyond the orbit of the

Schellingian "philosophy of identity" altogether, and in the Preface to the *Phenomenology* would lampoon the notion of an undifferentiated Absolute as "the night" in which "all the cows are black."[120] Once he abandoned such notions, and developed a conception of the Idea that called for a very different sort of unity among its moments, there was no longer any reason to retain the distinction between logic and metaphysics. But developing logic itself as the metaphysical or speculative basis of the system did not solve the problem for which the earlier logic was originally designed. In order to be a speculative science the new logic would have to presuppose that the forms of reflective understanding, with their subject-object dualism, had already been negated. But that could be presupposed in logic only if it had been demonstrated elsewhere, and for that task the new propaedeutic science of phenomenology was needed.

At any rate, the Metaphysics composed during this third period was completed shortly before metaphysics as a distinct science dropped out of Hegel's system altogether. Still, it is the only version of the Jena metaphysics for which we have a substantially complete manuscript, and it is worth pausing over it a bit because it contains perhaps the heart of Hegel's systematic conception at that time. A brief summary will help us point up some problems he was wrestling with in these persistent efforts to build a system. The outline of the Metaphysics is as follows:

1. Knowing (*Erkennen*) as System of Ground Principles (*Grundsatzen*)
   A. Principle of Identity or of Contradiction
   B. Ground Principle of Excluded Middle
   C. Principle of Ground

2. Metaphysic of Objectivity
   A. The Soul
   B. The World
   C. The Highest Being (*Das hochste Wesen*)

3. Metaphysic of Subjectivity
   A. Theoretical Ego, or Consciousness
   B. Practical Ego
   C. The Absolute Spirit

The first part completes the Aufhebung of logic by offering a dialectical, speculative interpretation of the fundamental principles of all knowing. The Ground of these Ground Principles is the self-identical or "indifferent" totality that is both (A) the identity of identity and contradiction and (B) the unity of the one and the many.[121]

This Ground, in fact, "is the same as what knowing is insofar as it has a content," and indeed "this ground or knowing is what is called the soul," which is the *Indifferenz* that unifies all reflection within itself.[122] But with the triad soul–world–highest being, the identity of knower and known in the knowing comes more clearly into view: The soul is itself a substance of a peculiar sort, a particular content that can be known, and yet it is also conceived as the subject of the act of knowing (though that too in a peculiar and not really satisfactory sense).[123] Both as substance and as subject, furthermore, the soul is limited, particular. It knows the world qua world, and knows it as other than itself, and yet "the soul presupposes the world, and itself as in the world"; each, soul and world, is a moment in the other, and as such is both free and subjected to necessity.[124] But even this soul-world correlation is not complete in itself, is not yet the totality; it is a "many," each side of which is composed of contingent individualities that both are and are not, that come to be and disappear. The subsistence of this "many" requires a "one" of which it is the "emanation": the highest being or highest essence that alone simply "is in itself," an all-inclusive "absolute genus," "the absolute existence, not a necessary being but necessity itself," and "the absolute ground" from which all distinctions proceed. This highest being is the Spinozistic "extension," or substance, but it is also "thought," really the substance that is subject in an absolute sense (unlike the soul, which unites substance and subject in a limited particular), in which "thought and extension or being are simply one."[125]

The soul–world–highest being triad, which in a summary way contains the whole of traditional metaphysics, is here presented as merely the second moment of metaphysics, the Metaphysic of Objectivity. It realizes the *Indifferenz* of thought and being, subject and object, but in a merely objective form: an objective subject-object. Precisely as an objective description of putative realities, the traditional content of metaphysics is not properly transcendental. Taken in itself it is naive, dogmatic. Far from being able, on its own terms, to resolve the dualities of subject and object, thought and being, it is itself still so riven by these dualities that Hegel will soon consider that its problems belong rather to the special propaedeutic science of phenomenology than to proper philosophy. Even now, Hegel concludes the section by observing that the highest being and the world remain separated: "the emanation of particularity from the highest being is an empty thought, for that with which it would be filled would only be a differentiation" *(Ungleich-heit)* that "the absolute unity of the genus" could not resolve.[126] Though he does not use the term here, the highest being is a *Jenseits* that resolves the dualities of thought and being, indeed of existence itself, only in a sphere "beyond" that in which they arise.

In order to grasp its absolute unity of thought and being in an absolute form, not set in opposition, Hegel must transmute the conception of highest being into that of transcendental ego and spirit, treated in the culminating section of the Metaphysics. Here it is evident that Fichte's influence on Hegel had grown as Schelling's had waned. The triad of theoretical ego–practical ego–absolute spirit is not differentiated as three apparently objective realities like that of soul–world–highest being, but as three modes in which the Idea comprehends itself in its totality; as consciousness, as active existence, and as the true infinite that recovers itself in its other or in negation. This Fichtean theoretical/practical ego is not a distinct particular like the soul nor a totality distinct from its diremptions like the highest being, but is the "absolute unity of particularity and universality."[127] Its envisagement and its existence are complete, all-encompassing, unsituated. As absolute spirit, finally, it comprehends all the moments of the Idea in itself, recovering the moments of the Logic again, as well as their "metaphysical" negation, in their necessity. Since the "construction" of the Idea in the development of the Logic and Metaphysics is necessary, "in absolute spirit construction and proof are absolutely one."[128] The culmination in spirit or mind, in Geist, is in fact a kind of return to the beginning of the Logic, constituting a completed circle that represents the Idea itself. This very self-enclosure, however, this circularity that lends necessity to all the moments of this Logic-Metaphysics, also marks off its limitation: "this entire Idea of spirit is only Idea." It is absolute spirit in virtue of having found itself in the content of its knowing, but it "has not known itself as absolute spirit. It is this for us, not for itself"; its infinite self-reflexiveness has not yet essentially come to include anything outside its own closed circle, and so it has not been able to recognize itself in something radically other, which it must do in order to be absolute spirit for itself. Its return to itself in the Metaphysics "is again simple connection, or infinity itself, and even in its highest peak it falls back into its first moment, into its beginning again."[129] The Subjective Metaphysic, which closes the circle of the Idea, is as deficient in its way as the Objective. It overcomes the apparent otherness of soul–world–highest being, but requires a genuine otherness if it is to be fulfilled as spirit. It will find this otherness in nature, and the Philosophy of Spirit will presumably mark its return to itself in this alien medium, as human consciousness, rooted in natural conditions, becomes aware of itself as spirit in the development of culture.

Still, it is clumsy to have something that both is and is not absolute spirit appearing already as the culmination of the Logic-Metaphysics, lacking precisely the economic, social, religious conditions that give content to absolute spirit and therefore lacking precisely the recognition-in-another that is the very definition of spirit. The redundancy of having the whole system culminate in a conception already in some sense contained in its first, purely ideal moment reveals some of the problems of systematic construction with which Hegel was wrestling. In the first place, it is a sign that the position of Metaphysics in this system is anomalous, a problem Hegel was to solve by eliminating it altogether and dispersing its contents into other parts of the system: developing the internal, circular structure of the Idea in a thoroughly speculative Logic; reserving the conception of absolute spirit until it could receive its proper content at the conclusion of the system, no longer presented under the aspect of a merely subjective subject-object; and indeed relegating the whole problem of subject-object dichotomy, so obsessively but confusingly treated in this Metaphysics, to the special pre-systematic science of phenomenology.

It was certainly a bold stroke, to break with tradition by developing a systematic philosophy without a metaphysics, but the new ordering did much better express the originality of Hegel's vision. It enabled him to become clearer to himself. But there is also a cluster of related problems in this Metaphysics, precisely because of the central position it occupies in the system of 1804–5, that needed to be resolved and not simply redistributed. To dispose of Metaphysics as a distinct section of the system leaves open the question of the degree to which the system may still be "metaphysical," in something like the sense the term receives here. The Logic surely became a metaphysical logic. And if in 1804–5 Hegel could present absolute spirit under the rubric of Metaphysics, as a more adequate mode of transcendental ego, then to what extent—for all its rich concreteness of content—are the *systematic* underpinnings of the Philosophy of Spirit also metaphysical, both then and later?

On the one hand Hegel clearly needed the concept of absolute spirit to complete this Logic-Metaphysics, despite the awkwardness of its premature appearance. Nothing less would decisively express the dialectical conception of identity in difference, which after all is the very meaning of absolute spirit: finding itself in its other. Without such a paradoxical concept neither the "phenomenological" dichotomy of subject-object nor the "objective metaphysical" dichotomies of inner and outer, soul and world, one and many (or highest being and soul/world), could be resolved. But this Metaphysics achieves this resolution by reducing the "differences" to purely ideal, internally related moments in an essential *Indifferenz:* they come to be defined purely by their position in a closed conceptual circle. Given this conception of metaphysics it could not be otherwise, for it must complete the ideal first moment of the system. The "otherness" of its moments must be recognized in the end to be only apparent, and the introduction of the concept of absolute spirit serves this purpose very well.

But then what sort of otherness can exist in the second and third moments of the system, in nature and in culture, if absolute spirit is to "find" itself there as well? If it, too, is in the end only an apparent otherness within an essentially circular systematic structure, then all the complaints of Hegel's critics about the "closed system" are valid. Well, so much the worse for the critics! But in this case, as Hegel recognized very well, there would be a fundamental contradiction in his conception of absolute spirit: if there is no genuine other there is no absolute spirit, by definition, but only a Neoplatonic Idea. That is why Hegel tries so hard (with questionable success) to distinguish the absolute spirit of the Metaphysics from that which was to appear in the Philosophy of Spirit. If, on the other hand, nature is indeed a genuine other, spirit cannot achieve identity with itself in the real world of nature and culture in the way that it does in the Metaphysics, in the manner of circular self-relation. But without that sort of admittedly ideal *Indifferenz,* what sort of identity can it find? The distinction Hegel mentions in the Metaphysics, that the spirit does not yet know itself as absolute spirit, while it presumably will in the Philosophy of Spirit, depends entirely on its recognizing itself in an unequivocal other in those later parts of the system. It does not explain how that self-recognition is to be achieved, in an essentially different manner than in the Metaphysics.

This technical problem that arises with respect to Hegel's systematic conception bears directly on some rather more concrete issues in his philosophy of religion, as we shall see. Of course it is not clear how he might have tried to resolve the dilemma at this time, since the Philosophy of Spirit for this system of 1804–5 was not written. It is indeed possible that Hegel could not finish this system because of unresolved dilemmas of just this sort concerning the relation of spirit to Idea. The writings of the next few years do not even attempt to articulate that relation systematically. Though he never again attempted to subsume spirit under Idea in the explicit if equivocal fashion of this Metaphysics, the dilemma that arises so clearly out of this single attempt to do so was not soon resolved, and perhaps not ever.

Of the 1804–5 Philosophy of Nature, it will be sufficient to observe that it differs materially from the version he had written during the previous year. It is much less Schellingian, much less theosophical, adhering much more rigorously to the scientific thinking of the times.[130] Still, the half-metaphysical, half-physical notion of aether is again exhaled into the system to accomplish the transition from Metaphysics to Philosophy of Nature. Indeed, as if the concept of absolute spirit were not already sufficiently confused by its introduction into the Metaphysics, it is here identified with this aether, which is also "the absolute material" and the pure indeterminate being that in its negation of all particularity is also "pure, absolute nothingness."[131]

It must be said that Hegel's systematic manuscripts of both 1803–4 and 1804–5 are crabbed, repetitious, and rambling, containing long patches that are stupefyingly obscure, partly because he was so preoccupied with systematic arrangement as such. Though the topic outline shows painstaking attention, the texts expounding some of the topics go in circles, with particularly turbid paragraphs devoted to showing why just this particular moment must be treated at just this point in the system, and straining to establish the connection with what came before. System-building was heavy labor.

Manuscripts of 1805–1806

At least by comparison, the systematic manuscript that has come down to us from the fourth and final Jena period, the *Realphilosophie,* is refreshingly clear of redundancies and stupefactions. This fourth period is coterminous with the composition of the *Phenomenology of Spirit,* which was begun by the spring of 1805 and appeared in January 1807. It is surprising Hegel could have put his mind to much of anything else, but he was if anything more venturesome than usual in the range of his teaching during this period, and again produced substantial lecture manuscripts. His announcement of lectures for winter 1805–6, committed him to three courses, two of them entirely new: For the first time he offered lectures in the history of philosophy, a subject that was to be one of his staples in later years; the manuscript is unfortunately lost.[132] The other new course was on "Pure Mathematics"; for these lectures Hegel was content to follow established textbooks. Even the third course was at least different from what he had done before, since he taught the philosophy of nature and the philosophy of spirit without the logic/metaphysics, under the title "philosophiam realem." The term was employed in distinction from "philosophiam speculativam," which since the previous year he had been restricting to the logic/metaphysics. The complete manuscript for this *Realphilosophie* has survived; it was not quite finished, but seems to have broken off much closer to the conclusion than earlier systematic manuscripts did.[133]

Treating nature and spirit separately from logic/metaphysics had obvious practical grounds: the whole system was far too much to present in a semester. Certainly the farthest thing from Hegel's intention was to imply that nature and spirit bore no relation to Idea, but their separate treatment as "real" sciences did permit Hegel to deal with them without systematically articulating their relation to the "speculative" groundwork, and it is notable that none of Hegel's courses or manuscripts during this period do deal with that relation. It is possible that Hegel deliberately suspended that nest of thorny questions for a while, in order to concentrate on other problems that were equally important to the basic structure of the system, namely, those related to its foundations: how the system should begin. For while he was elaborating and clarifying his philosophy of nature and philosophy of spirit, as the superstructure of the system, he was heavily preoccupied with the substructure, with the problems of "introduction" to the system, in two quite different senses: (1) He was developing a new, pre-speculative propaedeutic to the system in the *Phenomenology;* and (2) he was at the same time reconstructing the first, "speculative" moment of the system proper. The evidence on the second point suggests that during this period he already came to identify the speculative groundwork simply as logic. In summer 1805, after announcing lectures on the same vast topic as the preceding winter, on "the entire science of philosophy," he decided in fact to devote those lectures to logic alone. In summer 1806, his announced topic was "philosophiam speculativam sive logicam"; for this course he was able at last to put sections of a published work into his students' hands, since parts of the *Phenomenology* were already being printed. His lectures dealt with phenomenology and logic, in particular, according to Rosenkranz's report on the lost lecture manuscript, treating the transition between phenomenology, issuing in absolute knowledge, and Being, with which the logical grounding of the system proper began.[134] During that same semester, the last in which he taught at Jena, Hegel also repeated his separate lecture course on philosophy of nature and spirit.

That *Realphilosophie* opens, like the earlier versions of the Philosophy of Nature, with the Idea materializing as Aether.[135] This Philosophy of Nature, furthermore, is organized according to the same general outline as that of 1803–4 (the version of 1804–5 experimented with a very different organization of the material), moving from Mechanics through Chemism and Physics to the emergence of "The Organic," which presents that life process from which the transition to spirit arises. But the detailed content of these general topics evidences another thorough overhauling. The *Geistesphilosophie* differs both in its organization and in many of its details from earlier versions, though the range of phenomena treated is still traceable to the *System der Sittlichkeit* of the first period. It begins with Subjective Spirit, comprising Intelligence and Will, and then in the second section introduces the social dimension as Actual Spirit, comprising Recognition, Contract, Crime and Punishment, and Sovereign Law. The fragmentary final section, like that of the *System der Sittlichkeit,* treats political Constitution, but at the end of that section there appears for the first time as such the triad Art, Religion, and *Wissenschaft* or Philosophy. I shall have more to say about this triad in the next section.

To go much further than this admittedly sketchy presentation of our pilgrims' progress in Jena would plunge us into extraordinarily complicated problems in intellectual biography. Reconstructing Hegel's development during the 1790s, no easy task in itself, would still be nowhere near so difficult. His thinking is still in flux, but the one thing on which it is firmly fixed from the time he appears in Jena, the determination to construct a complete system of philosophy, makes the flux into a veritable whirlpool. For what others had pursued as specialized fields of inquiry, politics, nature, religion, the logical forms of thought, the metaphysical categories, epistemology, and so forth, Hegel was determined to comprehend from a unified point of view as interrelated moments within a single capacious philosophical science. The perennial cliche of Hegel criticism is, of course, that such ambitions were overweening. But nothing less would satisfy what Hegel had identified as early as the Introduction to the *Differenzschrift* as the "need" of philosophy: to bind up the fractured life of human consciousness in modern society, which could not become whole until it had the philosophical resources to comprehend things whole. Short of that, Hegel thought, there is no philosophy, but merely a chaotic intellectual reflection of the fractured culture itself. But it is admittedly easier to dismiss Hegel's ambitions than it is to understand the strenuous and often confusing measures he took to satisfy them. The determination to bring everything within the frame of a unified science required that his thinking about each thing be constantly subjected to criticism and reshaped in light of his changing conception of the whole, as well as his deepening insight into the matter at hand. In this universal flux nothing stays put for long.

We can only salute the courage of those scholars, chiefly the modern editors of the Jena writings, who have plunged into this morass and begun to reconstruct the course of Hegel's thinking in Jena. They proceed from the sound axiom, frequently expressed in their studies, that any view Hegel expressed in these writings must be interpreted in the context in which it appears, without reading in meanings derived from his later works. It appears to me to be equally axiomatic, however, and equally important methodologically, that there was no philosophy of Hegel in Jena, at least until 1805 (and none to which we have more than fragmentary access even then). To state the point positively, what we have are persistent efforts to develop a philosophy, from which it is altogether misleading to extract an early philosophy or series of philosophies. It is not simply a matter of Hegel's having changed his mind, and moved from one philosophical position to another. The very fact that he abandoned each attempt before it was finished, and began afresh, registers his dissatisfaction with what he had done; that is particularly clear in light of the great professional pressures on him to produce a philosophical system and the embarrassment of all those broken promises to do so. In spite of those pressures, he refused to complete and publish any of these manuscripts because none of them satisfied his sense of what it would mean to develop a philosophy. Instead, with amazing patience and energy, he would abandon hundreds of pages of manuscript to see whether he could not do better if he began with page one again. He was experimenting, always hopefully but also tentatively, always ready to judge an experiment a failure, and there is no reason to suppose he was committed to all the positions he took even at the time he tried to spell them out. Many passages seem to have been written in order to see where an idea would lead if it were developed a bit, and what could be said in defense of it. It is of course legitimate for an interpreter to find some views expressed in these early writings more attractive than contrary views developed in the later system, or even to judge that a line of reflection Hegel abandoned was more promising than what he later developed.[136] But it is not possible to prefer Hegel's early philosophy, or one of his early philosophies, to the later, because there is no early philosophy of Hegel, either in his own early or late understanding of the term or in any other reasonably rigorous sense. There is instead a powerfully committed early quest for a philosophy, and if the manuscripts in which this quest is carried on are not interpreted in that light one risks attributing to Hegel views to which he was never committed, constructions he never thought were satisfactory, and passing thoughts he would never have confused with philosophical ideas. An overzealous attempt to trace a philosopher's development in minute detail can have very misleading results.

The very modesty of our ambitions in that regard will spare us some of these pitfalls. Having introduced the mass of manuscript material in this section, in chronological order but very sketchily, in the next section I shall outline some of the persistent themes of the Jena writings that are most relevant to our subject. Again, as in our treatment of some of the Bern and Frankfurt manuscripts, we will be less interested in Hegel's shifting opinions than in the way he understands the problems, but in this case we will have to explore these problems particularly in light of his emerging systematic constructions. As in all our treatments of manuscript materials, we will not seize on isolated remarks, but will interpret materials that reflect fairly constant concerns through the Jena years.

5. Geist, Volk, and the Christian Religion in the Jena Manuscripts

It might be possible to put together a general philosophy of religion or an interpretation and assessment of Christianity out of the mass of Jena manuscript material, but it would be an altogether misleading contrivance. Not only was Hegel's point of view essentially in flux during these years; but he also approaches religious questions from very different points of view in different contexts. One purpose of a system, of course, is to bring the many sides of philosophical thinking into a single coherent scheme. But whether or not Hegel ever achieved this aim, he certainly had not done so in his various attempts at system-building in Jena. Another purpose of a system, furthermore, is to provide the appropriate context for discussing any particular issue, and once Hegel had set out in earnest to develop a system the question of context becomes all-important. The sort of speculative theological issues that emerge from the attempt to show how the Idea is exhaled as Nature, for instance, will be quite different from the more concrete religious issues that arise in Hegel's social theory, and some interesting puzzles will appear in our attempt to relate them. That second set of problems will return us to the sphere of Volksreligion; we will see how some of the related motifs of the 1790s were updated during the Jena years. But we will begin on the abstract end of the spectrum.

Toward a Speculative Doctrine of Divinity

We noted in the preceding section the dismaying regularity with which the notion of aether turns up in Hegel's various systematic efforts to mediate between the ideal and the real. As Hegel defines this antique notion it seems simply to be contrived for that mediating purpose. In an ungenerous mood we might even say that aether is the *problem* of mediating the ideal and the real masquerading as an *explanation* of that mediation. What may save it from being an entirely stipulative solution is the fact that Hegel does often invest it with the speculative logos doctrine we found him employing in the Jena critical writings. But then Hegel expresses himself poetically, in a frankly mythic vein to which it is difficult to assign a sober philosophical meaning and yet which cannot simply be dismissed in an interpretation of Hegel; it does most directly reflect a visionary enthusiasm that he never fully succeeded in suppressing.

On the one hand the aether is "absolute matter," undifferentiated, nonsensuous, not yet a natural universe of definite material entities. At rest in its unmoved self-identity *(Sichselbstgleichheit),* it is the whole in a state of pristine transparency. "Aether does not permeate all, but itself *is* all."[137] Sometimes Hegel identifies it with Being, anticipating the empty, undifferentiated Being of his mature Logic. But as absolute matter, aether is the "other" of absolute Geist; and since absolute Geist must by its very nature find itself in its other, the aether must therefore, on the other hand, be susceptible to Geist. So something is stirring in the aether after all! Everything is, in fact. While retaining its "rest" of self-identity it must also unfold itself into the "unrest" of its "fermentation-process," uniting the infinitude of its unfolding with its self-identity. That is, its unfolding is an example of the true infinite, not simply an endless proliferation, but a diremption in which it remains unchangeably itself: "In its unfolding it is not a movement proceeding outward or a voice calling out to another, but in its movement it remains just as much entirely at rest, in its utterance [*Aussprechen*] just as mute and sealed."[138]

Yet precisely as that other in which Geist is to find itself, it must indeed speak, if only in this paradoxical sense. Nature will finally materialize as the self-articulation of this mute voice: mute because in thus "uttering" the whole of nature it will still be speaking only to itself. The logos is entirely immanent, a creative activity that never passes outside its own source. Though Hegel does not in this context employ the language of *Indifferenz,* it is clear that the otherness constituted by this creative logos is just that sort of differentiation within the aethereal self-identity.

> This utterance is its otherness or its infinitude; what it utters is itself, what speaks is itself, and that to which it speaks is again itself; . . . the aether is the air that receives and absorbs the speech, the plastic material that takes the opposed fermentation into itself, and . . . its subsistence is a simple subsistence that is just as much simple nothingness.
>
> This speaking of the aether with itself is its reality, namely, that it is just as infinite as it is self-identical.[139]

There follows a complex play on the factors of speaking and awareness or hearing *(Vernehmen),* the one expressing infinity and the other self-identity. This extraordinary conversation then takes on a musical dimension: "the speaking is the articulation of the tones of infinitude," and is heard as the "absolute harmony of the universe." A natural universe permeated, so to speak, from its metaphysical source by an ideal harmony is an "other" in which Geist will be able to find itself without insuperable obstacles. Indeed, the aether itself can be said to be Geist in at least an anticipatory sense, in virtue of this very unity of speaking and hearing, or this harmonization of the infinitude, which are already expressions for Geist's "return to its self" in its other.[140] But that process will be complete only at the end of the Philosophy of Spirit, not at the beginning of the Philosophy of Nature. Hegel's immediate task, which we will not consider here, is to establish the self-articulation of aether, first into light (the star as an indivisible point of light is "the first limitless, inarticulate word of the aether"), and then into spatial and temporal dimensions. It all reads like an Orphic myth of creation.

We have been following the account of the aethereal substratum from the systematic manuscript of 1804–5, which is admittedly unique in some of its details, but in its general tendencies finds many parallels in the Jena writings. Hegel's primary aim here, of course, is to establish the transition from Idea to Nature. But a closely related purpose is to develop a speculative doctrine of divinity. As in the ancient creation-myths themselves these two purposes are quite inseparable: accounting for the existence of the world and forming a conception of deity, both understood in a way that will give a hint about human destiny. Furthermore, Hegel is attempting deliberately to displace another metaphysical (but not properly speculative) conception of God: that of the "highest being," which he had discussed in the section on Objective Metaphysics in this same manuscript. We recall that the notion of highest being was correlative with those of "soul" and "world," and while these objective-metaphysical conceptions were not judged simply false, their defect was precisely the objectified form assigned each: each is regarded as an independent and irreducible reality in itself. None of the three can pass over into the others, nor can they together make up an integrated totality; that is, each, even the highest being, is in the end a merely finite conception, limited by its opposition to the others.

Hegel recognizes that all three can be and have been understood in ways that strain these limits to the breaking-point. The very conception of the soul, for instance, as an encapsulated, determinate particular *(Bestimmtheit)* seems to require the transcendence of that limitation.

"This requirement expresses itself in the attempt to assert and to prove the immortality of the soul. But this determinateness can only be transcended"; that is, one can only overcome the predicament that has given rise to the yearning for immortality, insofar as the fundamental "ground" of this conception is transcended, "or insofar as it is transcended [*aufgehoben*] qua soul."[141] To understand immortality properly, I must free myself from my constricted identity as a self-enclosed "soul," and must become aware of a much richer, more inclusive identity. Similarly with the highest being. One wishes to speak of a being that transcends all limited, particular things, but the highest being "is itself particular," a limited existence precisely in its manner of transcending everything else, in its separation; it is "absolute being" only insofar as "this negative particularity" is itself transcended, that is, insofar as it is no longer conceived as highest being.[142] The point about the soul and the point about the highest being are the same; both are grasped in their truth in the conception of transcendental ego, and finally of Geist, treated in the Subjective Metaphysics. The conception of Geist unites self and deity, and does so in a form that is not estranged from the natural universe: it contains what is true in the conceptions of soul, world, and highest being, without the self-contradictory features that prevented them from realizing the very truth one wanted to express by means of these conceptions. Given the conception of Geist: "The yearning for immortality and the Beyond of the highest being are retrogressions of Geist into a lower sphere, for it is in itself immortal and highest being."[143]

But if we are to be referred to the conception of Geist to resolve the quandaries of speculative divinity, as we are in the Metaphysics of 1804–5, we are immediately sent on a much longer route. For the absolute Geist of that Metaphysics, we recall, is still Idea requiring embodiment in another. So the longer route will in fact lead us through the entire system, through the projection of Idea into its other, as Nature, and its return to itself in this other as Spirit. According to Rosenkranz, Hegel spoke in another manuscript of "the immanent dialectic of the Absolute" as the "*Lebenslauf Gottes*"—as God's career or life story, the divine curriculum vitae. The Idea is "the night of the divine mysterium," which mystery, however, is revealed in the visible world. Rosenkranz says that Hegel "loved" to speak of "the creation of the universe as the *utterance* of the absolute *word* and the return of the universe to itself as the *receiving* of it, . . . so that nature and history became . . . the disappearing medium between the speaking and the receiving."[144]

We have found Hegel writing in essentially the same terms in his dark meditations on the aether, though with the added paradox that the word remains enclosed within the divine taciturnity. Speculative divinity is already highly dynamic for Hegel, an immanent process, a *Lebenslauf,* but it still never breaks out of an essential identity. It represents an entirely internal, and I think essentially timeless metamorphosis, such as we found Hegel laboring to express in the language of total negation and transfiguration in the conclusion of *Glauben und Wissen.* But in the latter Jena periods the crucial speculative problem shifted to the relation of Idea and Nature. In order to displace the "objectivity" of the traditional metaphysics of soul–world–highest being, it must be shown how the natural universe that had been objectivized under the concept of "world" is in truth the immanent diremption of absolute Geist and the immanent dwelling-place of human selves; it cannot be the latter unless it is the former, for beings capable of expressing the return of spirit to itself cannot at the same time intrinsically inhere in an irreducibly alien world. Hegel must develop a speculative doctrine of divinity not only because of its own intrinsic interest, but because his whole scheme of things would be incoherent without it. Hence his struggle in 1804–5 to incorporate the notion of aether, as the transitional state between Idea and Nature, into such a doctrine. Aether expresses the indwelling Word; it is not itself, however, "the living God" but "only the idea of God," since the Word does not yet achieve self-recognition in aether as such; it speaks but does not hear. "The living [*lebendiger*] God" is that other in which absolute spirit can come to self-recognition as absolute spirit: it is Nature itself.[145]

Similarly, in the report by Rosenkranz to which we have already referred, Hegel is quoted as saying that "the eternal creation of the universe" is none other than *"das Anschauen Gottes"*—the vision or direct intuition of God—"as himself." Precisely in the natural universe, the night of the divine mysterium gives way to clear daylight, and Hegel ingeniously reinterprets a number of traditional attributes of deity to accord with this thoroughly immanent conception: the goodness of God is the procession of the manifold reality of things, his eternal wisdom is the "character of ideality" he retains even in the becoming of things, and so on. The judgment of God, though, takes a poignant turn: "Because he is the absolute universal totality, God as Judge of the world must break his heart. He cannot judge it, he can only have mercy on it."[146] For as the totality that encompasses even the splintering into particularity, this God cannot distance himself in the manner of a judge elevated high on his bench above the accused.

The pathos, that God's judgment is his broken heart, would be either a cynical or a sanctimonious stroke on Hegel's part if he were only playing the game of finding terms in which to explain the idea of God away. But it is not simply a matter of replacing God by the universe. Hegel is and will remain serious about these ventures in speculative theology. Divine spirit is sensitive subject as well as all-encompassing substance, and the motif of the suffering God is one that Hegel never thereafter abandoned. The very fact that a metaphysic of soul–world–highest being, set in objectified opposition, really cannot accommodate such a compellingly serious religious image as the suffering God furnishes grounds for seeking a speculative theology that can. That is one of the motives that kept Hegel at the task with such energy and perseverance, despite what he himself must have recognized at the time as the clumsiness of a good many of his efforts. He had long before broken with traditional theism, particularly in its supernaturalistic seventeenth- and eighteenth-century ossifications. But he was determined to find an adequate philosophical expression for what he perceived as the profoundest religious intuitions: that the universe, though without a beginning, is nevertheless in some significant sense a divine creation; that it is indeed still transparent to its divine source, which permeates it as an indwelling word; that human affairs are providentially guided toward a high destiny; that there is a significant sense in which deity speaks, moves, suffers, lives. A speculative theology needed to be both rationally coherent (i.e., integral to a total systematic conception of things) and at the same time faithful to a religious perception of the divine tragicomedy.

The Eternal Triangle

Hegel's Jena excursions in this vein led him into some first attempts at trinitarian speculation. Rosenkranz mentions a "significant fragment" treating "the divine triangle." Baader, among others, had recently employed this geometrical form speculatively, and of course the triangle is an ancient trinitarian symbol. But Rosenkranz says that Hegel was not satisfied with a simple triangle, but "constructed, in order to express the life of the Idea, a *triangle of triangles*."[147] In the excerpt from this lost fragment Rosenkranz published elsewhere, it appears that each interior triangle epitomizes the whole triangle, but is dominated by the side it shares with the larger one. I take it that Hegel had in mind a diagram something like that illustrated in Figure 1.

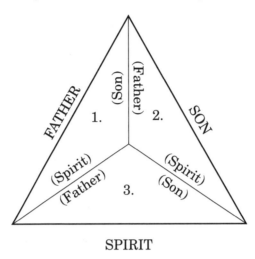

Fig. 1

Father, Son, and Spirit are contained in each interior triangle, but the first contains them in the mode of Idea, which Hegel identifies with "the Kingdom of the Father." In this first interior triangle, "which is at the same time only one side of the absolute eternal triangle, the Godhead is merely with itself in mutual intuition and recognition. It is its Idea, in which the pure light of unity is the center, and its sides are the pure radiation outward and the pure return of the rays into itself."[148]

The Son is already present as the "radiation outward" of the Idea, but in the second triangle, representing "the Kingdom of the Son of God," this movement dominates, the pure deity mixing with its opposite: "The Son must go forth through the earth, overcoming evil, and if on the one side he steps forth as victor, on the other there awakens the self-knowledge of God, as the Spirit of God: through which the center becomes a beautiful, free, divine center, the *Universe of God*."

The third triangle represents "the return of everything to God himself, or the pouring out of the Idea over everything. What was only a mixture [in the second triangle] is through this Spirit absolutely one with God and, as he recognizes himself in it, so it recognizes itself in

God."[149] According to Rosenkranz, Hegel suggested that this third step had been neglected in traditional trinitarian theology. Hegel was determined to make up for this neglect of the Spirit by treating the third triangle as the necessary completion of the other two: Godhead itself, in order to be complete, requires a "sanctified earth."

Though Hegel soon dropped the awkward geometrical figures, this fragment marks the beginning of his treatment of a motif that later became the speculative basis of his philosophy of religion. More than that, Hegel was evidently thinking already of this trinitarian construction as an alternative expression for that metaphysical foundation that he treated in more abstract terms in the system. Indeed, according to Rosenkranz, the fragment broke off only after Hegel had begun showing how the sun and the earth, light and water, were derived in relation to the great triangle! The procession and return, furthermore, that make up the life of God and the sanctification of earth in this trinitarian version of Hegel's metaphysics, remind us of the soundless word evoked in the systematic writings: again, no actual development seems envisaged. The great triangle of triangles, for all its apparent interior movement, is itself essentially changeless. There seems to be no decisive role assigned to history, and still no historical incarnation of the Son in this trinitarian construction, but only what Hegel had called the "eternal incarnation" in the critical writings, here expressed as the mixing of Godhead in its other, in nature.

As in the critical works, it is also more obvious in this fragment than in the systematic manuscripts that the problem of evil is a central preoccupation of Hegel's speculative theology. His later solution to the problem of evil is generally thought to be teleological,[150] an interpretation that may not stand close inspection. But at least in Jena, Hegel's speculative solution to tragedy and evil is no teleological development in which they are gradually overcome, but an indwelling logos that incorporates a suffering world into the divine life. Logos does not imply telos; if anything, it implies the suffering God who is reconciled in the eternal return to himself as Spirit. "For-itself," to be sure (i.e., considered as it appears among its suffering inhabitants), the world seems to exist in opposition to God; the divine "in-itself" seems its simple negation. But the Son is the other in which the ideal Father finds himself:

> In the Son God recognizes himself as God. He says to himself, I am God. The in-itself ceases to be something negative. . . . The

extended kingdom of the universe no longer has its being-for-itself in opposition, but rather its being-for-itself is a turning to God, which is God's turning to himself, his joy over the glory of the Son that he sees to be himself. Since *the earth's* being-in-itself is no longer the pure being-for-itself that is *evil,* it also ceases to be a mixture. . . . And for the sanctified earth *this self-consciousness of God* is *the Spirit* that proceeds from God, and in which it is made one with him and with the Son. This Spirit is here the eternal mediator between the Son who has returned to the Father and is now altogether at one with him, and the being of the Son in itself or the glory of the universe. The simplicity of the all-embracing Spirit is now in the center, and there is now no longer any distinction, for the earth as the self-consciousness of God is henceforth the Spirit; but it is also the eternal Son, that God beholds as himself. . . . Thus the sacred triangle of triangles is closed.[151]

What we find here is not only a radically "spiritualized" rendering of the Trinity, but also a rendering of Geist that clearly owes a great deal to a mystical vision of the union of all things in God. The fragment on the divine triangle sounds explicitly this significant overtone in the Philosophy of Spirit Hegel was straining to articulate in the systematic manuscripts. Though it must be discussed in other terms as well, Geist is always Holy Spirit.

But now we must shift our attention from the metaphysical heights to the other end of the spectrum, to the treatments of religion that emerge in Hegel's social thought. We shall then be able to ask whether they can be made to coincide.

The God of the Volk and the Deification of the Volk

If the speculative motifs we have been considering seem metaphysically remote, the themes to which we now turn are down-to-earth, and with a vengeance. They are also more fully developed, as they continue a line of reflection with which Hegel had been heavily preoccupied at least as early as his years in Bern. During the first Jena period his conception of Volksreligion (though he seldom used that term anymore) was sharpened to a new incisiveness in his writings on *Sittlichkeit* and natural law.

Contrary to Kant, Hegel united morality and ethics with the social bonds of custom, language, legal right, and culture in his concept of *Sittlichkeit*—"ethics" in the broadest sense, or "ethical life." It was the cornerstone of his early Jena conception of practical philosophy, and from that time on was indeed one of the pivotal conceptions in his thinking. "The absolute ethical totality," furthermore, as he declared in his treatise *Natural Law* in the *Critical Journal,* "is none other than a Volk."[152] That equation appears constantly in Hegel's unpublished manuscripts of the period as well. His sense of the overriding importance of this ethical unity of a people was made all the sharper by his bitter acknowledgment of its lack in his own land, expressed especially in *The German Constitution.* And when he discussed religion from this point of view, as in that treatise, it is not surprising that the emphasis falls on its function in unifying the Volk. In the Europe of earlier times, Christianity had provided the religious unity that was "always the basic condition for a state," the "primary unity" without which "no other unity or trust was possible." Religion was not confined, to be sure, to this political function; it could play such an important political role only because "people's innermost being expresses itself" in it.[153] But what had been the strongest unifying bond politically and culturally, was now, in a Germany divided between Catholic and Protestant, tearing the common life apart. In this situation a makeshift expedient had to be contrived:

> Since . . . religion has completely rent the state asunder, it has at the same time, in a marvelous manner, offered the hint of a few principles on which a state can be based. Since its rupture has torn people apart in their innermost being, and yet an association is still supposed to remain, they must therefore associate externally over external things, warmaking, and so forth: an association that is the principle of the modern state.[154]

Hegel goes on in the same paragraph to suggest that the principle of separation of church and state is another contrivance dictated by religious pluralism; indeed, he likely saw it as simply another aspect of that soulless association that is "the principle of the modern state."

Hegel forges his own political philosophy in vigorous reaction against this atomistic, mechanistically ordered modern state, still harking back as he had in the 1790s to what he perceived as an earlier, more organic political life that was integral to the ethical unity of the Volk. It is unthinkable without a common religion. We must, to be sure, beware of overstating that point, just because we cannot go into other aspects of this political theory in any detail. There are many factors Hegel finds essential to the ethical state, for example, a social class differentiation (nobility, bourgeoisie, peasantry) with complementary functions. With the ruling, warmaking nobility, however, as the conscious embodiment of Volk and Vaterland, without crass preoccupations with private wealth and material production, warmaking turns out not to be such an externality after all; it requires a radical sacrifice of private interest and even of life itself for the sake of the Volk.[155]

But the religious cultus undergirds the shared ethical life of society in a different, more ideal sense: according to the so-called Lecture Manuscript on Natural Law, "a Volk comes to its highest self-enjoyment" *(Selbstgenuss)* in its cultus. This "self-enjoyment" implies that the cultus not only serves other social ends, but is itself an ultimate end, a closure of communal consciousness with the life that has otherwise found only partial expression in it, the satisfaction of that need to comprehend itself without which there would be no Volk at all. Here it celebrates the spirit that is moving in it. But like the devotion of the aristocratic warrior-class to the Volk, this self-enjoyment of the whole Volk entails a sacrifice: not the material sacrifice of life and property in warfare, but the "Aufhebung of subjectivity," the "destruction" of people's "empirical individuality and through this purification" their elevation "to the absolute enjoyment" of the Volk's "absolute essence."[156] For the God of the Volk is precisely this essence in ideal, objectified form: "The most living God of a Volk is its *national God,* in which there appears to the Volk not only its pure spirit but also its empirical existence, with its untruth and uncertainty as a sum of details *transfigured.*"[157] In the cultus the individual members of the Volk sacrifice their special interests and desires in order to commune with and "enjoy" their own transfigured life as a people: "This act, the *irony* upon the moral and useful actions of humans, is the *reconciliation,* the ground-idea of religion."[158] In cultic life mortals resign their mortality as individuals and are reconciled to that immortal spirit, the Volksgeist, that binds the many into one.

This deification of the Volksgeist coincides with the culminating position Hegel gives to *Sittlichkeit* in the practical philosophy of his first Jena period. *Sittlichkeit* unites nature with intelligence, the one and the many, the idea and the actual; in fact, "intellectual intuition is something real through *Sittlichkeit* and in it alone, the eyes of the spirit and the bodily eyes perfectly coincide." Here the unification of opposites exists in actual practice. As Adam saw flesh of his flesh in woman, every person sees "spirit of his spirit" in the ethical life of his people.

> In *Sittlichkeit* the individual thus exists in an eternal manner; his empirical being and actions are altogether universal; for it is not individuality as such that acts, but the universal absolute spirit in him. Philosophy's insight concerning the world and ne- cessity, according to which all things are in God and no particu- larity exists, is perfectly realized for the empirical consciousness, since every detail of activity or thinking or being has its essence and significance in the whole alone.[159]

That was Hegel's special twist on the Schellingian Philosophy of Identity: to locate the ultimate identity in the social sphere of *Sittlich- keit*. It is of course present in nature as well, but only as "something internal," hidden, not brought to conscious expression. But in *Sittlich- keit* the absolute identity "steps forth into consciousness," as it must in order to be fully realized. "The intuition of this idea of *Sittlichkeit*," furthermore, "the form in which it appears from the side of its par- ticularity, is the Volk."[160] The universality adhering in principle to *Sitt- lichkeit* as such manifests itself intuitively (i.e., visibly) in this particularized form, uniting a community of people with the universal form of intelligent life. So the Volk is "the living *Indifferenz*," achieving the "highest subject-objectivity." Once Hegel has invested all the most loaded terms of the Philosophy of Identity in the Volk it seems a matter of course that he should deify it as well: "This universality, which has altogether united the particularity with itself, is the divinity [*Gottlich- keit*] of the Volk, and this universal intuited in the ideal form of particu- larity is the God of the Volk; he is an ideal manner of intuiting it."[161]

Here again Hegel suggests that the God worshiped by the Volk is none other than an ideal vision of its own common life. The Volk is not divine as a mere sum of its members, however, but precisely in the universality of its ethical life that it contemplates in worship. Precisely in its religious cultus the Volk achieves that ideal consciousness of itself without which it would not be a genuine Volk at all. That self- awareness, after all, is what distinguishes the Volk from a mere natural phenomenon. For all his stress, in *System der Sittlichkeit* and else- where, on the natural sources of social life, Hegel's social theory is not in the end naturalistic; the Volk is not the mere outgrowth of its biological conditions or of the forms of economic organization that arise in the struggle with its natural environment. In its cultus above all it rises above mere useful and self-serving activity to achieve a divine life of ethical universality. In his remarks on the deity of the Volksgeist, Hegel is more concerned with his conception of the Volk than he is with the idea of God as such.[162]

In the later Jena periods Hegel did not retain a special practical philosophy alongside the system on which he was laboring so mightily, but incorporated the main lines of this philosophy of *Sittlichkeit* into the culminating part of the system, as a Philosophy of Spirit. In the first version, the system of 1803–4, indeed, the absolute Geist that completes the system seems to be none other than the Volksgeist.[163] Placing his conception of Volksgeist in the context of a Logic/Metaphysics and Philosophy of Nature seemed simply to give Hegel some additional resources for expressing his exalted sense of its significance. The notion of aether, for instance, that we have found him putting to such imaginative use in the transition from Idea to Nature now gets called into service again to express the all-permeating spirit of the Volk, which is to consciousness as the earth's atmosphere is to organic life, the total medium in which it lives.[164] "The absolute Spirit of a Volk is the absolute universal element, the aether, that incorporates all the single consciousnesses into itself, the *absolute simple* living, *single substance;* it must thus be the *active substance*"[165] — of which the passive element seems to be the biological. To invoke the already overworked notion of aether in this way may seem simply a badly strained metaphor. But Hegel's point seems to be that the Volksgeist is precisely the return of spirit from its exile in otherness, as nature. The aether that was the pervasive but hidden logos in nature here steps forth as an actual, conscious life, the visible Spirit of the Volk.

The assignment of this culminating position to the Volksgeist, however, seems a pretty crude solution to the macrocosmic, speculative problems posed in the opening parts of the system. The very invocation of the universal aether to express it serves to call the incongruity to mind. For a Volksgeist is necessarily limited, the spirit of a particular community that must confront other such spirits. It is an inherently pluralistic notion. Once Hegel had presented his students the spectacle of the entire natural universe issuing from the Idea as its other, it could scarcely escape notice that no spirit of any particular people could retrieve the fullness of the Idea from those vasty deeps. Yet there may be a graceful, polytheistic sense in which every Volksgeist could be said to be divine, perfect in its own way and realizing within its limits something of the universal Idea, and Hegel might well have had something of the sort in mind even in those manuscripts that seem so to absolutize the Volksgeist. All those manuscripts, after all, break off unfinished, and already in the earlier Jena texts there are other notions introduced that are hardly congruent with an unqualified identification of absolute spirit as Volksgeist. In the conclusion to *Glauben und Wissen,* for instance, Hegel had conjured with a spirit that could only arise resurrected from the grave into which everything, actual or ideal, had descended in universal negation. But there were some positive expressions for this universality as well.

Spirit in the Volk and in World History

In Hegel's first systematic ventures the notion of Volksgeist that he had developed in his earlier ethical philosophy seemed to answer the need for the Idea to *exist* as spirit, actually, visibly, self-consciously. But in his essays for the *Critical Journal,* Hegel had employed the notion of Weltgeist[166]—world spirit—at least marginally. Though he did not elaborate upon this notion very fully at that time, he did bring it into direct conjunction with that of the Volksgeist in the remarkable closing pages of the last work he composed for the journal, the treatise *Natural Law.* In those same pages, furthermore, a conception of universal human history comes into view, in which a vast procession of Volksgeister are brought to birth and done to death.[167] For what Hegel will later call "world history" is clearly adumbrated here, as that "world" spanning all time, of which the Weltgeist is the living spirit. This transhistorical totality makes up a "chain" of which each ethically grounded Volk is a "single link," in its own time necessary to the whole, and yet, says Hegel, also necessarily passing away and being replaced by another. This strange image, of a chain the links of which are temporally related, serves to convey Hegel's sense of the necessity of the relation; in their very coming to be and passing away they together make up a rationally organized totality that requires even the weakest link.[168]

The Volksgeister are not simply relativized in playing this historical role in the life of the world's spirit. Precisely as a necessary stage in that life, a visible shape in which the Weltgeist exists, each Volksgeist in its ethical individuality unites its geographical and historical particularity with the universal *Sittlichkeit*. For this ethical universality is not a mere abstraction or cosmopolitan dream. It must, of its own necessity, be incarnate in the everyday details of an actual way of life. Hegel's sense of just how the universal and the particular are united, however, obviously shows his debt to the Schellingian Philosophy of Identity. Indeed, in these pages Hegel constantly draws analogies from the organicist philosophy of nature, according to which the vital force of nature is unconditionally present in every living thing, though of course some living things are higher than others.

> Just as the totality of life is just as much present in the nature of the polyp as it is in that of the nightingale and the lion, so the Weltgeist has in each of its shapes enjoyed a self-awareness that may be weaker or more developed, but is none the less absolute, and in every Volk, under every totality of customs and laws, has enjoyed its own essence and its self.[169]

The circle-closing, self-conscious awareness of spirit in its own ethical life can come to light even in a Volk that exists at a very modest level of development. Returning, in fact, to his old problem of positivity, Hegel goes on to argue that the customs, laws, and religion of a people cannot be regarded as merely positive, however barbarous and historically contingent they may seem, so long as the ethical individuality of that Volk finds necessary expression in them.[170]

It is likely that Hegel continued to have some such notion in mind when he assigned the Volksgeist such a culminating role in his first ventures in system-building, though the evidence is only fragmentary.[171] It is not clear, though, how he might have gone about uniting the universal with the particularity of each Volksgeist after he had laid down the magic wand of identity-philosophy. At any rate, by the time he composed the *Phenomenology of Spirit*, the accent fell on the historical relativity of each Volksgeist,[172] and in the systematic manuscript belonging to the same period, the *Realphilosophie* of 1805–6, the position of the Volksgeist is refined and considerably toned down.

A rich social philosophy is still invested in it. The power and legal authority of the state finds the "organization of its life" and its self-sufficiency, as an end in itself, in the spirit of its people. The Volksgeist is the universal life that flows through its members: as he had earlier spoken of it as the aether in which they carry on their conscious life, so now Hegel says that this spirit is "the *nature* of individuals, their immediate substance and its movement and necessity."[173] So the Volksgeist, as the living bearer of ethical life, continues to occupy an absolute position in relation to its individual members as such. That is, for instance, what keeps them from being debased to a purely economic relation with one another. Each person does have a private life, of course, and a sphere of private economic interest that places him in competition with others. The same individual "cares for himself and for his family, works, enters into contracts, and so forth, and also works just as much for the universal, has this as his aim. From the former side he is called *bourgeois,* from the latter *citizen.*"[174]

The bourgeois role is very demanding, and Hegel has no illusions about the enormous power the marketplace wields over the lives of individuals. In the merchant class, for instance, money—in itself "a great invention" into which all material needs are concentrated—becomes the measure of human worth. A person is only "so real as the money he has."

> Imagination has disappeared; meaning has immediate existence; the *essence* of anything is that thing itself; its worth is jingling coins. . . . The exchange must be honored no matter what is brought to its downfall, family, well-being, life, and so forth—utter mercilessness. Factories and manufacturers base their subsistence directly on the misery of a class. Spirit in its abstraction has thus become an object as interiority without selfhood.[175]

Hegel immediately goes on to say that the form of this inner being is not merely this "dead thing, *money,* but just as much *ego*"; and that spirit becomes a proper object to itself, not in this abject economic sphere but in the state. For he looks to the state to counteract the immense power of private interest and economic class. Elevated above the narrowness and conflict of such interest, the state preserves and enforces the overriding claim of the Volk as such in the life of all its members. Hence the importance of having a hereditary, classless monarch at its head, "the firm, *immediate* knot of the whole," to help preserve the state from itself becoming embroiled in class interests.[176]

Still, neither the state nor the Volksgeist it embodies is simply identical with the absolute spirit. Beyond the social sphere as such, though rooted in it, are three higher forms of the spirit: art, religion, and philosophy (identified more generally as *Wissenschaft*). The *Realphilo-sophie* ends, furthermore, with "world history" overarching the limits of any particular Volk. It is the comprehensive totality in which spirit comes to its perfect self-knowledge, with philosophy as that completed knowledge.

But before trying to explicate the relation of the Volksgeist to these new configurations it may prove useful to consider two closely related problems on which the conclusion to the *Realphilosophie* also contains some important new departures: the specific role of "religion" in the life of spirit, and the position Christianity occupies in "religion." We will take up the second of these problems first. But the relevance of both to our theme is obvious. Furthermore, like the kindred problem of defining the role of the Volksgeist, these two problems occupied Hegel throughout his Jena years, and received a treatment in the conclusion of the *Realphilosophie* that despite its sketchiness, clearly anticipates positions developed in detail in his later system.

Christianity Among the Religions

Although Hegel did not introduce the term "world history" into his writings until the final page of the *Realphilosophie,* there were adumbrations of this conception in earlier works, as we have seen. In fact, the speculative use of historical method, the incorporation of a bold kind of historical analysis into the attempt to extract speculative truth from a phenomenon, seems particularly to have developed early on in his treatment of religion. There are intimations of it already in Frankfurt, after Hegel had stopped confronting Christianity with Hellenic glory and Kantian moral philosophy and had begun sifting what was living from what was dead in it in relation to early and late phases of its own epoch. In Jena it became axiomatic for him that a religion could be understood and criticized only in relation to the Volk of which it was the expression. But he also began seeing a progression among historic religions, reflecting stages in the development of consciousness. What is more remarkable in its anticipation of later Hegelian method is the comprehension of historical progression as an unfolding of the essential truth of the matter.

We find this method most strikingly exhibited during the first Jena period in the treatment of religion in the so-called Lecture Manuscript on Natural Law, to which we referred earlier.[177] After speaking of the God of the Volk as the transfiguration of its own life, and of the sacrifice of private interest and bias in the cultic celebration of that common spirit, Hegel turned from these general characterizations of "religion" as such to a differentiation of three types of religion. Now this typology purports to reflect the three essential modes in the relation of identity and *Differenz*. These three rationally necessary modes are roughly those we have found turning up again and again in Hegel's Jena writings: an initial identity, a passing into differentiation and otherness, and a return, the recovery of identity *in* difference. But Hegel also finds that these three types of religion correspond, by remarkable coincidence, to three historic stages in the religions of the West![178]

The first type, called "religion of nature," is only sketchily characterized, but Hegel's understanding of Greek religion is clearly the model for it. It is an imaginative pantheism in which nature, encompassing all that is, is "in and for itself a spirit and holy." Individuals may bring a curse down upon their heads, but reconciliation is sure to follow, for the whole is reconciled through and through, an original identity uniting artistic beauty and ideal truth with the actual.[179] But in the religion of the second type this identity of the ideal and the actual is fractured. Here, "this beautiful world of the gods, with the spirit that animates it, must go under and can abide as a mere memorial. The unity of spirit with its reality must be torn asunder. The ideal principle must constitute itself in the form of universality, the real must be fixed as particularity, and nature lies prone between the two as a *desecrated corpse*."[180]

This polarization of the universal and the particular has its counterpart in a politics without *Sittlichkeit:* as a deified nature had bound together the ideal and the real, the ethical solidarity of the Volk had bound individuals together for higher purposes freely willed by each. With the breaking of the one bond the other broke as well, and it was every man for himself.

> The ethical organizations, the free states of antiquity in which reason had become objective in a shape of spirit, lost their vitality; as a result their gods fled from them as well. . . . On this godless earth now, and under a race that had lost all awe toward this godforsaken nature together with any vital national spirit and sense for the state, a feeling of infinite ethical pain has to arise. The time of this infinite pain had come when the Romans

shattered the vital individuality of the peoples [*Völker*], thereby uprooting their spirits, destroying their ethical life [*Sittlichkeit*], and extending the empty universality of their rule over the fragmentation.[181]

Early and late, Hegel saw in imperial Rome a rule of force without *Sittlichkeit* and thus without a genuine political life, pulverizing every Volk under its sway into a heterogeneous mass of private interests and enforcing, by sheer police power, a purely external conformity to law. Now he argues that Roman rule had consolidated those conditions that gave rise to the second type of religion: Out of "this fragmentation that found no reconciliation" and "this universality that had no life," in the aridity of "this *boredom of the world*," spirit had to take refuge in an "original identity" denuded of both nature and Volk but elevated "in its eternal power" over the pain of a dismembered life. Here again Hegel has a definite historical example in mind: the religion of the Hebrew people, identified only as "the most abject of peoples," in whom this "reawakened manifestation of aetherial reason" could occur, just because in this Volk the pain was the deepest.[182] This aetherial reason, of course, is the high God of Hebrew monotheism, transcending all human life and indeed transcending that "world which has ceased to be nature."

This brief characterization of Judaism recalls Hegel's harsh assessment of Hebrew religion in his Frankfurt manuscripts, but it is placed in a more clearly defined historical and systematic context. It represents a general type of religion, the description of which is echoed in Hegel's polemics against the current religion of the "beyond" and its philosophical counterpart, again associated with a fractured social life and the loss of the natural world. It will reappear in the *Phenomenology* in the generalized form of the Unhappy Consciousness. Even in the present manuscript it is clear that the Hebrew people provide only "the first arena" in which this type of spirituality manifests itself.

There follows immediately the treatment of Christianity, understood to be historically and essentially formed under the conditions of this second type of religion. It is likely, indeed, that the manuscript treats Christianity as a variation on the second type rather than as the model for the third; Rosenkranz, on whose report we are largely dependent, seemed to think so.[183] However that may be, there is no doubt about what Hegel thought historic Christianity did, and did not, accomplish. It certainly did not, and could not, restore the sort of integrated life in nature and society that Hegel had found in the first type. What did occur was the reconciliation of the divine and the human; that is, of the abstracted polar opposites thrown up by the collapse of the organic unities of nature and ethical Volk. That the physical and social environment did not share in that reconciliation indeed subjects Christianity to a limitation reminiscent of that ironical "fate" assigned it in the Frankfurt treatise on *The Spirit of Christianity*. For the debasement of nature and the destruction of *Sittlichkeit* casts what is left in their place into a hostile role, while Christianity for its part takes up a position of enmity to this degenerate environment—to what the New Testament calls the powers of "this world."

> *Christ* is the founder of a religion through the fact that he expressed out of its most inward depth the suffering of his entire age, and over it elevated the power of the divinity of spirit, the absolute certainty of reconciliation that he bore in himself, and through *his assurance* awakened the assurance of others. He expressed the suffering of his age, which had become unfaithful to nature, in his absolute *contempt* toward that world into which nature had degenerated [*zur Welt gewordenen Natur*], and expressed the absolute assurance of reconciliation in the *certainty that he was at one with God.* —The contempt that he expressed against the world had necessarily to be revenged upon him as his fate through death; and precisely this *death* had to justify the contempt for the world and make it into a fixed point. These two necessary elements had to become the hinge of the new religion: the godforsakenness of nature, thus the contempt for the world, and that in this infinite separation a human being yet bore in himself the assurance of being at one with the Absolute. In this human being the world was again reconciled with spirit.[184]

Christianity is at once the religion of "infinite pain" and of reconciliation. That is another way of stating its two "necessary elements." The infinite pain is the loss, for divine and human alike, of natural unity with the cosmos and ethical unity with the Volk, of which the Christian "contempt for the world" is the reaction and of which the cross is the symbol. If Christ had been done to death in modern times, Hegel points out, the gallows would have been placed on the Christian banner. Death as a natural necessity would imply no such total degradation and rejection, no such "infinite pain." But to be done to death by the state as a criminal outcast registers the dismemberment into which the human race itself has fallen. That is why the other "necessary element," the reconciliation, also takes on a universal significance. Christ can reconcile the human race to the absolute spirit precisely because he bears that "infinite pain" which is the universal human condition. He is "at one with God," furthermore, because the divine spirit itself shares this same "infinite pain" that unites all humankind. Hegel has come to understand Christianity as a religion of the cross, emblematic of what he elsewhere calls absolute negativity even in its work of salvation.

He does make the point he had repeatedly made in Bern and Frankfurt, that Christ first appears to be uniquely identical with God. People who knew themselves to be utterly "undivine" "perceived divinity in him *alone,* and had to attach the unity of individuality with absolute spirit to his *personality,* so that his existence itself became the starting-point of this religion."[185] But Hegel no longer finds in this starting-point the source of a fatal "positivity." It is precisely in his crucifixion that Christ suffers the universal condition and history of the race: its "absolute separation" from the actual world it inhabits. That is one side of his universality, his share in universal dismemberment.

> The other side of the infinite pain of this absolute separation was its reconciliation in the faith that *God* has appeared *in human form* [Gestalt], and human nature is thus reconciled with itself in this single figure [*Gestalt*] as representative of the race. This single human figure expresses in *his* history the *entire* history of the empirical existence of the human race, as he had to in order to be able to be the *national God of the race.* But he expresses this history only because it is at the same time God's. For the principle is infinite pain, nature absolutely torn apart [*absolute Zerrissenheit der Natur*]. Without this pain the reconciliation has no meaning and no truth.[186]

The paradoxical expression, "national God of the race," recalls the remark earlier in the manuscript (where Hegel was speaking of religious cultus generally) that the national God of a Volk is its "most living God," indeed, is its own spirit and the transfiguration of its "empirical existence."[187] But now the Volk is no longer the point of reference; we are presented a "national God" essentially without nation or Volk, arising in that history in which human beings have been

denuded of any integral political life. He is the God of the great negation—and he is a man! a man, in fact, in whom the desolated history
of the race finds its epitome. As the bearer of infinite pain his life is
the all-inclusive history, human and divine: his life and his death.
His crucifixion is the death of humankind and the death of God; his
resurrection is the transfiguration, not of a Volk, but of the divine life
and the human life into a single life.

Before striking that tremendous chord, however, Hegel suggests that
the Christian religion is so bound up with that infinite pain that this
religion as such could scarcely survive an actual historical cure for that
pain. Christianity "must eternally produce this pain in order eternally
to reconcile it"—which reminds us of Hegel's remark many years earlier
about giving people the itch in order to be able to scratch them! (see
Chapter 2).

But Hegel does not think the infinite pain began with Christianity,
but with that divine/human history that the gospel so readily epitomizes. Yet he suggests that Christianity might well succeed in its work
of reconciliation to the point of rendering itself obsolete!

> The empirical condition of the world out of which this religion
> began must itself be transcended [*aufgehoben*] through the strug-
> gle of this reconciling religion, wherewith the world would really
> become happier and more reconciled and the religion would thus
> transcend itself. It must therefore at the same time bear in itself
> the very principle for arousing the infinite suffering in order
> infinitely to reconcile it.

In fact that dialectic of pain and reconciliation is woven into the gospel:
into the essential Christian drama itself, or what we might call its
mythos. Here God and humankind alike are crucified—and resurrected.
This religion, Hegel continues,

> possesses that principle, the fate of the world, necessarily in the
> history of its God, who has died the death of a criminal. The
> death of a criminal would of itself be only a particularity. The
> view of death as universal necessity can arouse no infinite reli-
> gious pain, but he who died on the cross is at the same time the
> God of this religion and as such his history expresses the infinite
> pain of a godforsaken nature. The divine was plunged into the
> *sordidness of life, the divine had itself died.* The thought that

God was dead upon the earth could alone express the feeling of this infinite pain: so too his reconciliation, that he is resurrected from the grave. Through his life and death God is degraded, through his resurrection the human becomes deified.[188]

This passage contains an unusually sharp statement of Hegel's understanding of the gospel, and from now on this essential drama of the dying and rising God-man is of overriding importance in Hegel's consideration of Christianity. The teachings of Jesus are now important only to the extent that they reflect the awesome significance attached to his crucifixion, and the spirit and fate of the community he founded have world-historical significance precisely because that community is the bearer, in its innermost consciousness, of this gospel. Here Hegel reveals not only his understanding of that gospel, but also the form in which it had come to shape his own thinking. Not only do a number of expressions in this passage turn up in that conclusion to *Glauben und Wissen* on which we commented earlier—enough to suggest that it was likely written at about the same time—but the pattern of images is strikingly similar: the "infinite pain" of universal negation expressed in the feeling that God is dead, crucified in order to make way for the resurrection of a new divine-human totality. There the pattern expressed speculative truth, and incidentally the culture of modern times. Here it is the meaning of the Christian religion. The essential Christian mythos contains what Hegel was to call, in a related context in the Preface to the *Phenomenology,* "the tremendous power of the negative."[189] This mythos negates even when it affirms.

Hegel finds a good deal of affirmation in the historical development of Christian cultus and culture, to which the present manuscript now turns. A number of familiar themes are touched on. The cultus moves beyond the particularity of Christ's person as such by finding in the sacrament of his body and blood the means by which all believers share in his union with God; through this cultic act each individual makes the history of God and of the race his own story. Furthermore, as the "religion of nature" had expressed itself in art, so this religion realizes "the ideality of spirit in the *form of thought.*" Here "the highest ideas of speculation" are articulated "not merely as a *mythology,* but in the *form of ideas.*"[190] There follows a brief statement of the doctrine of the Trinity, not, to be sure, quite as the Nicene fathers had defined it, but in the terms in which Hegel himself treats it in his fragment on the divine triangle (pp. 220 ff above). But to the Trinity of Father, Son, and Holy Spirit, in which Christianity rises to speculative truth, Hegel now adds the "Mother of God" as a form of divinity in which that love arising from the infinite pain finds its objective expression and its satisfaction.

From this tantalizingly cryptic remark about the Mother of God Hegel turns to a comparison, also brief, of the Catholic and Protestant forms of Christianity. "In *Catholicism* the Christian religion has become a 'beautiful religion,'" of which Marian piety is presumably an example. Hegel finds in it "the poesy of consecration," "the individualization of sanctity," a "religious elevation and sanctification of empirical existence, the *Sabbath of the world*." Protestantism swept all that away in favor of a "commoner, unholy working-day." The Protestant is reconciled to an ordinary, disenchanted existence. On the one hand there is the recovery of nature and of the empirical world generally, but on the other hand the Catholic sense of the cultic presence of deity is lost, and God becomes an object of unsatisfied longing. That dualism, we recall, is what Hegel had found at the heart of modern Protestant culture, not least among its philosophical expressions. Protestantism

> has again poured the color of universality over a nature sanctified as fatherland and has again banished the religious fatherland and the manifestation of God out of its own fatherland into a far distance. It has transformed the infinite pain, the vitality, the assurance and the peace of reconciliation into an infinite longing. It has impressed upon the religion the whole character of *northern* subjectivity.[191]

If for Catholics deity becomes accessible only at the cost of either despising empirical and social reality or covering them with a patina of enchantment, for Protestants deity disappears into the Beyond. Neither form of Christianity can seem to recover a living unity of divinity with the actual world; to the extent that a Christian knows himself to belong either to God or to the world, the other is lost to him—the seed in Hegel's thinking of the fatal dilemma of unhappy consciousness in the *Phenomenology*.

That is why the infinite pain is endlessly self-perpetuating. Hegel points repeatedly in the manuscript to a recovery of the sacredness of nature in Christianity, but only on terms that perpetuate the "absolute separation" with which it began. Insofar as Christ alone was known to be divine and nature was considered ungodly, "nature could only again become consecrated by extension from him" *(von ihm aus)*.[192] To the extent that all believers came to share sacramentally in his divine life, nature, too, and also the state, could have a derivative part in this reconciliation.

> By extension from reconsecrated human beings the whole of nature will again become sanctified, a temple of reawakened life. *Everything will be given the new consecration.* The authority of the monarch will be consecrated by extension from religion: his scepter contains a piece of the holy cross. . . . the old curse that lay upon all is resolved, the whole of nature is appropriated to grace and its pain reconciled.[193]

But this extension of grace is quite different than treating nature and political life as if they were sacred in themselves; in fact it implies quite the reverse. That is especially clear in Hegel's remarks on Protestantism, under whose aegis the world of nature and politics seem to enjoy the highest possible dignity—but it is a dignity that is bestowed:

> for nature is sanctified, but not through its own spirit; it is reconciled, but it remains of itself something unholy, as before. The hallowing comes from something external. The entire spiritual sphere does not ascend on its own basis [*aus eignem Grund und Boden*]. The infinite pain is permanent in this sanctification and the reconciliation is itself a mere sign toward heaven.[194]

In this context Hegel may have added[195] his old point that the very imagination of the Volk is divested of its indigenous contents and filled with stories and figures from alien sources. What seems native to Christianity, even at its best, is precisely alienation.

To resolve this impasse Hegel invokes, as a kind of deus ex machina, the appearance of a new religion. It is not clear just how this new religion is to be related to the old; our sources are confusing and somewhat conflicting on that point,[196] but the new religion seems in some sense to be an outgrowth of Protestantism. What is clear from all accounts is that philosophy is to be instrumental in the formation of the new religion. As in *Glauben und Wissen,* Hegel here calls upon philosophy to resolve religious dualism and to lead religious life into the integral truth lying at its depths. Philosophy must provide that "knowledge" *(Erkenntnis)* by which the "magic word" may be spoken that will overcome "the entire energy of suffering and of opposition that has dominated the world and all the forms of its civilization for a few thousand years."[197] As for the new religion itself, however, Hegel packs all he has to say about it in one overloaded sentence:

> Now after Protestantism has thrown off its alien consecration, spirit can dare to sanctify itself as spirit in its own form and to produce the original reconciliation with itself in a *new religion,* in which the infinite pain and the entire gravity of its opposition is absorbed, but also resolved, unbeclouded and pure. . . .

The new religion will mark the great return, not of course to the religion of nature, but to the encompassing identity Hegel at that time saw as the Absolute. Hegel does not use the term *Indifferenz* in this manuscript, but that conception of identity-in-difference is clearly what he has in mind. The new religion will appropriate even the dualistic pain of the old, but only as a necessary phase in its own wholeness, its oppositions reconciled not in yearning but in actuality; it will contain the opposites, but in their resolution, not in their opposition. To bring such a new religion into existence, however, requires not only philosophical illumination but also a radical social transformation: the rise of a free Volk! Geist can produce this new religion constituted by its own life, Hegel continues,

> if, that is, there will be a *free people* and reason will have recovered its reality as an ethical spirit, that can have the boldness *to take on its religious form on its own basis and out of its own majesty.*[198]

Thus the manuscript ends as it began, by reclaiming religion as a vital aspect of *Sittlichkeit.*

We might wish that Hegel had told us more about the new religion. We have every reason to believe that he took this possibility seriously for a time, given his dissatisfaction with Christianity and the vivid sense he expressed on a number of occasions in Jena of standing on the threshold of a new age. The *Critical Journal,* after all, issued a public call for such a new religion wedded to philosophy; though it was likely written by Schelling,[199] there is no reason to doubt that he was speaking for his co-editor as well.

It is therefore striking that we hear nothing more from Hegel about a new religion. That possibility drops out of his thinking entirely. He certainly continued to think that there was an essential progression among world religions, a conception vastly elaborated in his mature Philosophy of Religion and already adumbrated in the later Jena writings. Indeed, this conception of a progressive religious "development," both in history and in essence, seems to have supplied the seed for a similar interpretation of culture generally, to be worked out in the popular Philosophy of History of Hegel's mature years. But at least from 1805–6 on, the religious progression culminated in Christianity. Hegel later articulated a considerable "development" within Christianity itself, but no *religious* development beyond it. Already in the *Phenomenology* we find a sketchy progression from Nature Religion through the Religion of Art to Revelatory Religion, and under Revelatory Religion we are presented with what is basically an interpretation of Christianity. The major manuscript produced during the same period, the *Realphilosophie,* introduces the religion of the incarnate God as "the absolute religion," beyond which there is and can be no other. That is the first time Hegel uses this expression, with which he was to characterize Christianity in his later Philosophy of Religion. It implies that this religion is at once the culmination of religious development and the essential realization of the very idea of religion. It is not merely another relative stage, but "absolute." There is no longer room for a higher religion to come.

It must immediately be said that the very idea of religion now seems to Hegel to suffer an insuperable formal deficiency, insuperable, that is, within the terms of any possible religion. We will look closely at this limitation in the next subsection, and in the chapter on the *Phenomenology.* Briefly stated, Geist itself is grasped in religion, but grasped in the form of object, something presented to consciousness; religion cannot entirely overcome the gulf between the conscious subject and the (divine) objectivity presented to it. Even the absolute religion manifests this formal deficiency, though it moves as far toward the remedy as it can without ceasing to be a religion at all.

Still, to anyone familiar with Hegel's development, this absolutizing of Christianity among the religions is a most startling turn in his thinking. In the first, brief statement of it, in the *Realphilosophie* of 1805–6, it is clear that belief in the full incarnation of the Godhead is what gives the Christian religion this special position. In other respects Hegel is still critical of it. Many of his earlier criticisms come out in appropriate contexts in the *Phenomenology,* and some of them are touched on even in the brief statement in the *Realphilosophie.* The terms, in fact, in which he speaks of the religion of incarnation as absolute are consistent with the most serious lines of criticism developed earlier, for instance in the Lecture Manuscript on Natural Law to which we have devoted major attention in this subsection. But now, within the context of his developing Philosophy of Spirit, the central problem has changed for Hegel: it is not so important that nature and society be recognized immediately as sacred in their own right. The crucial task of religion is that Geist itself should be consciously confronted in some approximation of its naked truth. It must, so to speak, be lifted out of its ambiguous presence in nature and society, to be grasped directly. Then its presence in nature and society will become recognizable; not that it will be conferred externally upon them, as Hegel had complained in the earlier Lecture Manuscript, but its actual presence will become transparent in them. In traditional Christian dogmatics, after all, the universal logos is disclosed, not conferred, in its particular incarnation. That, for Hegel, now appears a fair approximation of speculative insight.

The Absolute Religion

For in the Philosophy of Spirit constructed in the *Realphilosophie* it is critical that Geist become conscious of itself. It already exists in nature, but in a doubly unconscious mode: it is neither articulated there, nor is it itself articulate, which is to say that it is not yet complete as Geist. In the Volk as such it not only exists but is conscious, yet it is not conscious of *itself* qua Geist. To put the point the other way around: The Volk does in fact have a spirit, the Volksgeist, but it does not directly *know* this spirit. We have already seen the way Hegel had regarded the God of the Volk as the objectification for and by the Volk of its own spirit. But the Volk as such is not yet aware that its God *is* in fact its own immanent spirit. It worships its God as something other.

   Now "recognition"—*Anerkanntsein*—is precisely "the spiritual [*geistige*] element,"[200] Geist's own essential medium. Spirit takes form in self-recognition, though the realization that the recognized and the recognizing are one and the same does not dawn all at once. In its religion the Volk does recognize Geist; that is, Geist does recognize itself, if only through a veil. But in religion generally, Geist is known in objectivized form; it is "object [*Gegenstand*] as absolute universal, or as the essence of all nature, of being and act, and in the form of immediate self." Its return from nature into itself qua Geist occurs precisely in this developing knowledge, which is crowned in the absolute religion:

> The self is universal knowledge, and thereby the return into itself. The absolute religion is this knowledge, *that God is the depth of spirit certain of itself* [die Tiefe des seiner selbst gewissen Geistes]. Thereby he is the self of all. It is the *essence,* pure thought; *but this abstraction is externalized* [entäussert], *he is an actual self.* He is a *human being,* that *has an ordinary spatial and temporal existence.*

Here Hegel is no longer speaking merely of an "eternal incarnation," the logos inherent in the natural world, but of the concentration of the logos into the life of a historical human individual. We recall that that had always been a stumbling-block for Hegel, because it was not clear how human beings generally could share in this particularized incarnation. That step was still to take considerable explaining in the *Phenomenology.* But here he simply takes the step by bare assertion; the passage continues:

> And *all individuals* are *this individual. The divine nature is not an other than the human.*

From this time on, Hegel regularly asserted the identity of the divine and human natures as the general speculative upshot of the Christian religion. Here the formula is introduced for the first time. It constitutes a very problematical interpretation of the gospel, to say the least! It had to be elaborated in later writings and lectures, but always remained Hegel's most questionable thesis from the point of view of Christian orthodoxy. But in this context even the bare assertion is clear enough: the selfsame Geist is both the deity that is the object of religion and the human beings who are the religious subjects. Recognizing that identity is the supreme aim of religion. Hegel can affirm the particular incarnation in one human being now, to the extent that it can be regarded as the point of disclosure from which the subjective and the objective poles of Geist can be consciously resolved into identity. That is what makes this religion, beyond all others, absolute.

> *All other religions* are incomplete [*unvollkommen*]—either only essential being [*Wesen*], the awfulness of the force of nature, in which the self is only null, or beautiful religion, the mythic, a play that is not worthy of essential being. . . .

Even in these sketchy notes we can detect an antinomy on which Hegel's thinking often dwells. One finds many variations on this dilemma. Either we affirm an austere, impersonal sublimity, in which humanistic values have no place, or we affirm a colorful scene, congenial to human experience and human needs, but remaining on the surface; the Lord Jehova or the Olympians; inaccessible substance or accessible appearance. The latter, Hegel says, lacks "*Gründlichkeit* and depth," or displaces its depth to an "inscrutable fate," which is not itself part of the storylike play of powers.

> *But the absolute religion is the depth, that comes forth into the daylight.* This depth is the Ego; it is the concept, the absolute pure power.[201]

The incarnation religion resolves these antinomies. "In it," Hegel says in the next paragraph, "Geist is therefore reconciled with its world." The ultimate depth is disclosed in selfhood, in personal ego—which is also to say that the ego is not to be identified with its psychological appearance, but is the divine depth.

In what follows the passage we have been examining, Hegel goes on to assert the resolution of other fundamental antinomies in the absolute religion. He does not trouble to explain himself much. It is enough that he finds in the incarnation a general principle of reconciliation. Heaven and earth, inner and outer, Idea and actuality, Nature and Geist, Being and Essence, God and Volksgeist—all are seen to converge, the already familiar Hegelian litany of reconciliation, to which other paired terms could be added ad libitum.

Hegel could hardly go further, on his grounds, in bedecking the Christian incarnation with treasures from the speculative vaults. Yet it is to be emphasized that this section of the *Realphilosophie* betrays not the slightest interest in any apologetic for Christianity as such. There is no effort to accommodate to orthodox interpretations and no sign that Hegel has abandoned his earlier criticisms of church belief and practice. Indeed, he still complains of Christian otherworldliness, and on the other hand pours scorn on "the fanaticism of the church" in supposing that the kingdom of heaven can ever be realized on earth in any pure, unpolitical fashion. Indeed, the state is "the *actuality* of the *kingdom of heaven*," while the church only grasps the reconciliation in thought; the state therefore has no obligation to respect the rights of Christian conscience.[202] But the church's attitudes and social policies are no longer central to what Hegel finds in Christianity. Neither is the teaching of Jesus, nor what his immediate and remote followers made of it, nor the way Christian otherworldliness so neatly fit the abject political situation of the late Roman Empire—and of modern Germany. The evidence is that Hegel had not changed his mind about any of those things.

But now the overriding issue about Christianity concerns its dogmatic center, and here, in the doctrine of the Incarnation in particular, Hegel finds a religious approximation of speculative truth. Indeed, I suggest that Hegel has come to acknowledge the extent to which the fundamental systematic structure of his thinking reflects the traditional dogmatic structure of Christianity, what we have called the basic Christian drama: the immanence of the logos in creation, the fall of man and of nature, their reconciliation with the logos through its incarnation, the dialectic of death and transfiguration, the immanence of the spirit. Hegel is not conciliatory toward the church in the way he interprets this dogmatic structure. In fact, we find in Hegel the crucial historical point at which the dogmatic structure of Christianity, the abstract rendering of its Gospel, pulls away from the church's characteristic forms of spirituality as such. From now on this "liberated" rendering of the Gospel will inform modern ideas and social movements that have no explicit relation to recognized forms of Christianity, and indeed could even turn antagonistic toward them.

Only in this ambiguous sense can "the absolute religion" be identified with Christianity. Yet of course it is vitally important to Hegel that this absolute religion inheres in an actual, socially shared consciousness. Through it the speculative truth not only takes root in the Volk, but is itself made complete: Geist recognizing itself qua Geist.

> The thought, the inner, the idea of the absolute religion is this
> speculative idea, that the self, the actual, is thought, essence and
> being are the same. This is so presented *that God, the absolute*

> *essential-Being from beyond,* has *become a human being* [das jenseitige absolute Wesen Mensch geworden], this *actual one,* but equally that this actual one has been transcended [aufgehoben], has become something past.

The point here is that this particular man, Christ, must pass away in order that the Incarnation may extend beyond him to the community at large, as Volksgeist. (Hegel stresses on the following page the importance of this "sacrifice of the divine human being" as such.) God, no longer in the beyond, is not confined within this individual either. So the passage continues:

> and this God, the actuality and its transcendence, i.e. universal actuality, is the same as the Volksgeist, existing only in the immediacy of the spirit in the community. *That God is spirit* [der Geist], *this is the content* of this religion and the object of this consciousness.[203]

In no other work does Hegel so baldly identify the incarnate God with the Volksgeist. So to interpret his later thinking would certainly be an oversimplification. But there is no question that this identification is what originally made it possible for him, in Jena, to conclude that the religion of incarnation is absolute. He goes on, as we have noted, to stress the necessity that the divine man be sacrificed as such, and cultically shared by the community through the sacrament. For that matter, "the sacrifice of Godhead, i.e. the abstract essential-Being beyond, has already occurred in his becoming actual."[204] In this sense "God appears in nature as an actuality," but this actual man is sacrificed in turn, his divinity to be shared by the community. Hegel added in the margin: *"Alles Jenseits ist entflohen"* (everything Beyond has fled away).

Vorstellung and Its Limits

Well, not quite all beyond-ness had fled away after all. There remains the formal deficiency attaching to religion as such, which we noted earlier, and a certain alien tendency toward the Beyond remains as a consequence of this deficiency. In the *Realphilosophie,* Hegel delineates this inherent religious limitation immediately after he has introduced that conception of the absolute religion we have been considering. This discussion leads, in turn, to the treatment of philosophical science *(Wissenschaft)* with which the manuscript concludes. In order to move beyond the limits of religion one must turn to philosophy.

Hegel says that the church has indeed made the spirit of the community or congregation *(Gemeinde)* into its object qua spirit. That is why it embodies the absolute religion. Though it is "an existing, actual Geist," however, which is made its object, namely the spirit of the *Gemeinde* itself, it is so objectified only "as representation and faith."[205] Now this word "representation"—*Vorstellung*—is another term introduced in the *Realphilosophie* that Hegel was to continue using systematically ever thereafter. *Vorstellung* is from now on Hegel's systematic codeword for the distinctively religious mode of apprehension. In ordinary German usage it does not have a peculiarly religious meaning. The verb *vorstellen* simply means to bring something to mind, to imagine or visualize or think about something: to place *(stellen)* it before *(vor)* your mind's eye. One may begin describing a situation to a friend by saying "stelle dir vor!" ("just imagine this!" or "try to picture this!"). A *Vorstellung,* then, is that "representation" of something that appears in imagination; generally a concrete object, not directly seen but *visualized.* In an extended sense one can speak of a performance or a picture or even an abstract conception as a *Vorstellung,* something placed before a spectator or a hearer or an audience. That is what Hegel thought was the characteristically *religious* way of apprehending Geist, as an imaginative object: the image of a god, a tableau, a narrative, even an idea in a loose, popular sense. In later works this category of *Vorstellung* comes in for an elaborate and refined exposition, but we must be cautious about reading his more mature understanding of the term into his thinking in 1805–6.

Here he simply uses the word as if it were more or less self-explanatory, as that form of objectification characteristic of a faith-relation. It defines the religious mode of apprehension, but also defines the limits of that mode, the deficiency to which we have alluded. So when Hegel says that "the existing, actual Geist" of the community itself is confronted as an object in the mode of "*Vorstellung* and faith," the point is that the community does not realize that this Geist is its *own* immanent spirit. In the absolute religion God becomes man, but this incarnation is itself apprehended in the mode of *Vorstellung,* as an imagined event occurring independent of the community as such. The spirit apprehended in faith *is* the spirit of the community, but in its representation it takes flight beyond itself, far away from it. That immediate knowledge and this otherness are not combined. Everything has the form of representation, of Beyond [*Jenseits*], without concept, without necessity, mere event, accident. The Word is indeed the eternal decree and will of God, but it is only said, not seen into, not concept, not self [*nicht eingesehen, nicht Begriff, nicht Selbst*].[206]

The representational mode still relegates Geist to a "beyond," not necessarily in the sense that it locates God in a heaven above or another metaphysical dimension, but at least in the sense that it preserves an imaginative distance between the social existence of the believer and the object of his faith.The very fact that the Incarnation is told in the form of a story, for example, or treated as an event in the past, or celebrated in a ritual drama, seems to Hegel to leave the believer in the position of a spectator to something happening independent of him and of his community as such. The problem is akin to that of positivity, with which Hegel had been wrestling as early as his Bern writings. But the problem is no longer the arbitrary givenness of the object of faith, on the basis of authority; as Hegel has long since recognized, an object or a commandment positively given can be appropriated in a manner fully expressive of the believer's own life. He certainly thinks that is true of the absolute religion. But even the highest religious manner of appropriation still employs a representational form, which prevents the believer from *recognizing* that the object is in truth expressive of his own life. Or, to state the matter more precisely, in a way less subject to a simple humanistic reduction: Geist is prevented from becoming fully transparent to itself in the religious believer.

Hegel then turns to his treatment of the distinction between church and state, to which we have already referred. To the church, with its apprehension of spirit in the mode of imaginative representation, there is juxtaposed the state, "the *existing* Geist." The church *thinks* eternity in its fashion, while "*this eternal has its existence* [Dasein] *in the Volksgeist.*" The state is the actualized, living articulation of the Volksgeist, but the state does not recognize the absolute Geist in the Volksgeist. The church knows and celebrates absolute Geist, but does not recognize its actuality in the Volksgeist.

The human being lives in two worlds: In the one he has *his actuality, which disappears,* his natural being, his sacrifice, his transitoriness; in the other he has his absolute subsistence, knows himself as absolute *essence* [Wesen].[207]

Church and state are therefore complementary; each is defective, incomplete, when not in harmony with the other. The very distinction between church and state argues against their separation. So Hegel reiterates, on these new grounds, his support for an established, national church. At the same time, just because the state actually *is* (without quite knowing it) what the church can only *think* or *imagine* (without quite realizing what it is thinking), Hegel emphatically insists that the state's authority is superior. Theocracy does not tempt him.

Then Hegel turns to the relation between religion and philosophy. Reiterating the identification of religion with *Vorstellung,* he also makes it clear that he is not speaking of religion in an otherworldly, pre-incarnational sense. What is being compared with philosophy is the absolute religion. The *Vorstellung* set before the imagination presents no supernatural, aethereal beings, but putatively historical events, above all, the supreme event of God becoming an actual human being.

> Religion flees from heaven into actual consciousness: the human being falls down onto the earth and finds the religious in it, only in imagination. Or this selfless factor in religion is in itself such that it is only the representing [*vorstellende*] spirit, i.e. that its moments have for it the form of *immediacy* and of *event,* that they are not conceptualized, not seen into. The content of religion is indeed *true,* but this *being-true* is an assurance without insight.
> This *insight* is philosophy, absolute *science* [Wissenschaft]— the same content as that of religion, but in the form of concept.[208]

This formula, that religion and philosophy have the same content, but differ only in form, is unfortunately another expression that was to become canonical for Hegel. He resorted to it virtually every time he spoke of the relation of philosophy and religion.[209] Religion grasps the true content in the form of *Vorstellung,* philosophy in the form of *Begriff* (concept).

That he should have stuck so tenaciously to this formula is all the more remarkable in that the separability of form and content which it seems to assume is scarcely coherent on Hegel's own grounds. A content is not an isolated thing-in-itself that remains self-identical through every change in the way it is grasped; the constitutive role of consciousness in forming its object leaves no "content" subsisting in indifference to its form. That is one of the most characteristically Hegelian insights. Change the form in which something is apprehended and you materially alter the content as well. The *Phenomenology* provides the massive evidence that Hegel was thoroughly aware of the correlation between form and content even when he first coined this formula in the *Realphilosophie*. We shall in fact confront the problem again in the *Phenomenology,* which is where it most appropriately belongs. For on Hegel's terms the relation of philosophical knowing to other forms of consciousness, such as religion, is properly a phenomenological issue.

In the *Realphilosophie,* however, which as a systematic work is supposed to be an act of philosophical knowing from beginning to end, what Hegel *wants* to say is clear enough: it is that Geist is the *true* content of both philosophy and religion, and of art as well. The conception of Geist, to be sure, is so thoroughly reflexive that it would seem to be least of all susceptible to the form-content distinction. Geist *is* by definition self-apprehension, and the form of that self-apprehension is integral to its very reality. But the reality of Geist is not in question here. A systematic work, as Hegel conceived it, is devoted simply to its explication. Geist does not come to birth and develop through the various moments of the system. These moments subsist simultaneously, and Geist is fully present in the whole. Of course societies develop, art and religion develop, even philosophy develops. The system may take note of that development, as it does in contrasting the absolute religion with less adequate types of religion. But the subsisting reality of Geist precisely supplies the criterion of such adequacy. It is the measure of their truth; it is the measure, for instance, not only of the truth of this religion and that, but of the adequacy of religion generally. That is how Hegel seemed to conceive a systematic work, at least at that time.

The Structure of Philosophy of Spirit in the *Realphilosophie*

The treatment of religion we have been considering in the last several pages appears in the concluding section of a Philosophy of Spirit. The *Realphilosophie,* we recall, is made up of a Philosophy of Nature and this particular Philosophy of Spirit. This systematic context fundamentally determines what Hegel chooses to say about religion here; all the topics are presented with the primary aim of articulating the concept of spirit. Having looked at the details of this treatment of religion in the last two subsections, we shall now step back and see it in its larger systematic context: to see how it arises within the conceptual structure of Hegel's idea of spirit, and where it leads. We shall begin with the master outline of this Philosophy of Spirit as a whole, and then gradually focus in again on its concluding section.

The habit of triplicity having already seized Hegel, this Philosophy of Spirit has three main parts, titled as follows:

1. Subjective Spirit
2. Actual Spirit
3. Constitution

The first part, treating such topics as intelligence and will, is psychological. Under the second, "Actual Spirit," we are presented a social philosophy, more particularly a philosophy of law. The third is oddly titled, "Constitution." By this term *Konstitution,* Hegel did not seem to have in mind the charter or the fundamental law of the state (for which the German word *Verfassung* would have been the more common usage), but rather, judging by the contents of this third chapter, he had in mind the "constituent" factors that "constitute" the life of Geist in society. It is devoted, in particular, to the way in which the Volksgeist is constituted, or more precisely to the three quite different ways in which the Volksgeist may be said to be constituted.

The chapter on Constitution opens with several introductory pages dealing in general with the conception of Volksgeist on which the analysis to follow will turn.[210] I referred to these same pages above in introducing the questions that have occupied us ever since. I promised at that juncture to explain how art, religion, and philosophy are related to the Volksgeist in the *Realphilosophie,* and the time has come to try to keep that promise.

The Volksgeist, we recall, is the universal spirit animating the individual members of a society. In these introductory pages Hegel employs Rousseau's expression, "the general will," as its rough equivalent. It is made up of the wills of individuals, but they achieve common direction in it to the extent that it comes to take on the sort of unity that the will of an individual person has. In fact it becomes a universal self:

> The general will is the will of all and of each, but as will it is simply this self, the action of the universal is a One [*ein Eins*]: the general will has to gather itself together into this One. It has to *constitute itself in the first instance out of the wills of individuals* ... but on the other hand it is *the first* and *the essence;* and individuals have to make themselves into the universal through their *negation,* their externalization and education [*Bildung*]. It is earlier than they, *it exists absolutely* for them.[211]

In the margin Hegel cites Aristotle to the effect that according to nature the whole is prior to the parts. Hegel does concern himself in the following pages with the way such a whole may be formed, an urgent political issue for him given Germany's fragmented condition. But when he turns to systematic analysis he is concerned only with the nature, the "constitution," of the whole as such, regardless of the politics of bringing it into existence.

The topics are arranged as follows:

3. Constitution
    A. The Social Classes, or the Nature of Spirit Organizing Itself Within Its Self
        1. The Lower Classes and Their Disposition
        2. The Class of Universality
    B. Government, the Spirit of Nature Certain of Itself
    C. Art, Religion, and Science *(Wissenschaft)*
        Synthetic Connection of the State and the Church

These three moments make up the "constitution" of Hegel's extraordinary notion of the corporate individual, the Volksgeist or the general will. But they do not all "constitute" it in the same sense. Since the Volksgeist is an individual it bears, after all, some analogy to an ordinary individual person: an analogy that is at least as old as Plato's *Republic.* It must provide for its subsistence; it must impose its singleness of will against internal and external forces tending to its dissolution; and its thought and imagination must take wing in order to comprehend its own meaning and destiny. All three conditions are equally essential to it qua self: qua spirit. But each constitutes it in a different sense.

A. The differentiation of society into social classes provides the necessary conditions for the very subsistence of the Volk. The lower classes (i.e., the peasantry, the craftsmen, and the merchants) extract from nature the material conditions for life and convert and market them in a form that will sustain a complex social order.[212] The so-called universal class, an unlikely conglomerate of police, men of affairs, scholars, and soldiers, has in common the service of the Volk as a whole.[213] The Volk exists in virtue of this class differentiation; each role is necessary for the health of the whole, though not all who play them are consciously concerned about the whole. All of them are imbued with the Volksgeist, but they are not necessarily conscious of it as such, nor do they necessarily articulate the general will as such.

B. It falls to the government to articulate and enforce the general will. In a surprisingly brief section—three short paragraphs—and in some hints expressed elsewhere, Hegel suggests that the Volksgeist expresses its corporate will and enforces it, through the administration of laws and public policies. It also mobilizes the population for warfare. By preventing the "falling-apart of the whole into atoms" (i.e., an aggregate of self-seeking private operators), the government provides the conditions for that true freedom of individuals that consists in the accomplishment of shared aims in the real world.[214] This political freedom of the Volk, furthermore, is the point of departure for the third sphere, the point of entry into another region of free accomplishment.

C. Art, religion, and philosophical *Wissenschaft* make up this highest sphere, which also "constitutes" the Volksgeist in an entirely different sense than the class structure or the government as such can be said to constitute it. Class structure and government provide the conditions for the existence of the Volk as a complex unity, and they find their ultimate purpose in its common life. But the Volk, in turn, finds its highest, transcendent purposes in the sphere of art, religion, and philosophical science. For this, above all, it exists: to contemplate spirit, and in that contemplation to become a fully self-conscious spirit itself. For here "recognition," the distinctively "spiritual [*geistige*] element," directly occurs: the Volk generates objects and activities that serve no utilitarian function, but that hold up a kind of ideal mirror in which the Volk is brought face to face with its true self, spirit recognizing spirit.

> The absolutely free spirit, having appropriated its qualities back into itself, now brings forth another world—a world that has the

> *form* of its self, where its work is complete in itself, and it achieves
> the intuition of *its own* as *its own*.[215]

Here the Volk realizes its most liberated possibilities. In thought and imagination it "brings forth another world," an ideal world that is not, however, alien to its own life.

Interpreting the relation of this sphere to the life of the Volk is full of pitfalls. In no way is this sphere, with its other world, separable from the common life of the Volk; it is the Volk's supreme sphere of activity. On the other hand, no more fundamental error can be committed in interpreting Hegel than to treat this sphere of activity in a reductive manner. It is not the ministry of propaganda. It is not designed merely for the aggrandizement of the Volk. It does not *serve* the Volk in the sense that the government and the economic life of the social classes do. Hegel can speak of the Volksgeist in the exalted fashion he does precisely because it is the conscious life in which these "spiritual"—imaginative or intellectual—activities develop. Art, religion, and *Wissenschaft* are not reducible to their economic and political functions. They are ends in themselves. But just in their liberation from mundane social functions they are the most perfect self-expressions of the Volk, its Geist become articulate and free.

Neither in Jena nor later on does Hegel fit the popular caricature of him as an ideologist of the absolute state. When he does speak of the state in exalted terms he has in mind the nation, or the Volk in its public, political life, and not the government as such, which serves the state and does so within definite limits. But even the political life of the Volk, important as it is, is incomplete apart from the cultural life in which a people is nourished and fulfilled. The culminating position of art, religion, and intellectual life is evident in the systematic structure, not only of the *Realphilosophie* but of the mature system as well. Not, of course, that a people exists as a mere platform from which to pursue these higher aims; it is vital to Hegel that the spirit is ingredient in the entire practical sphere of an actual nation's activity, in its "ethical life." At the end of the brief section on government in the *Realphilosophie* Hegel speaks of Geist as "fulfilled freedom" in a double sense: It achieves in the Volk and its classes a "definite character as reality," through which there is a structure with "twigs of power" in which individuals can subsist. But this Geist is "equally the freedom from the subsisting as such," the freedom to achieve a more exalted destiny.[216]

Further: Hegel is concerned with art, religion, *Wissenschaft* as cultural activities in a general sense, and takes no systematic interest in the persons or groups we might identify with them: artists, priests, philosophers and other scholars and scientists. They do not make up an elite caste within society, corresponding to the elevated position assigned their characteristic activities. They all belong to ordinary social classes, not generally the highest, and they are ordinary citizens; we do encounter them in the earlier sections on social class. But the Volk as such, and not merely these special functionaries, participates in the artistic culture, the religious cultus, and even, no doubt with varying degrees of accomplishment, in the intellectual life. When Hegel speaks of this sphere he refers to a dimension that permeates the whole life of the Volk. Here that almighty power in society, the Volksgeist, at once expresses the spirits of all its members and reaches out beyond its own cultural relativity toward what is unconditionally true.

While art, religion, and philosophical science together make up this distinct sphere, they are also related to one another on an ascending scale of transparency to the truth, with philosophy at the top. This ascending triad, too, was hereafter canonical for Hegel. The mature system culminates in art, religion, and philosophy, as the moments of absolute Geist; Hegel was later to devote one of his celebrated lecture series to each of them, the lectures on aesthetics, on philosophy of religion, and on the history of philosophy. This final triad was in some respects already anticipated, we recall, in the *Differenzschrift* of 1801, though there religion was treated as a mode of art, and art/religion was related to speculation as variant forms of *Indifferenz*. But in the *Realphilosophie* the ascending movement, from art to religion to philosophy, replaces the balanced symmetries he had constructed among them in the *Differenzschrift,* and more recognizable historical content is introduced into the treatment of each.

Art, Religion, and *Wissenschaft*

Now we shall focus in again on this concluding section of the *Realphilosophie,* beginning with the treatment of art. The various art forms, to be sure, are given only fairly perfunctory mention, with the rudiments of a schema to relate them. Music and sculpture, for instance, make up the extremes of motion and of rest, and between them fall dance, poetry, and painting.[217] But Hegel seems chiefly concerned with the systematic position of art in general, particularly in relation to religion. In art the supremely important step is taken in which consciousness directly confronts its own imaginative activity: here conscious Geist first presents itself as a comprehensible object *(Gegenstand)*, directly accessible to the senses. In particular, it presents itself as an object of "intuition" *(Anschauung)*, a term that became canonical for Hegel in connection with art, just as "representation" *(Vorstellung)* was thereafter the characteristic mode of religion and "concept" *(Begriff)* of philosophy.[218] The English word "intuition" unfortunately has some misleading connotations but it seems the best translation we have for *Anschauung*. Here it generally denotes a direct apprehension through the senses. Hegel is troubled, in fact, by the phenomenon he calls the "modern formalism of art," which seems to present a "pure intellectual beauty" through a nonsensuous intuition; but an art of nonsensuous intuition seems to him to be a self-contradiction.[219] Sensuous intuition remains the characteristic mode in which Geist presents itself in art.

For that very reason art is not an entirely adequate medium for the self-comprehension of Geist. A problem of the incommensurability of form and content arises, paralleling that which is characteristic of religion, but in art the problem is more severe. An artistic medium achieves its absolute satisfaction in rendering a content that is entirely appropriate to its form. A landscape, for instance, can be directly apprehended in a painting, while a poet can only describe it through a tedious recital of details that are taken in at a glance in the painting; "nature poetry is therefore the poorest . . ." because its subject can only imperfectly and laboriously be rendered in language.[220] Now every sensuous medium employed in the arts presumably has a content to which it is most perfectly suited. But there is no sensuous medium, no mode of intuition, that can render the infinitude of absolute Geist. Here, to be sure, as we have seen, Geist already "brings forth another world . . . which has the *form* of its self." But in art this form cannot contain its fullness.

> Art begets the world as spiritual and for *intuition*. It is the Indian Bacchus, which is not the clear spirit that knows itself, but the inspired spirit [*der begeisterte Geist*] that envelopes itself in sentiment and image, under which something terrible is concealed. Its element is intuition; but it is the *immediacy* that is not mediated. This element is therefore inadequate to spirit. Art

can therefore give its forms only to a limited spirit. . . . This medium of finitude, intuition, cannot grasp the infinite. It is only as *intended* infinitude. . . . Beauty is the veil that covers up the truth rather than its manifestation.[221]

Plastic images of the gods, for instance, render "the universal essence in mythic, individual form." In order to realize an infinite content, art must pass over into religion. In religion the immediate particularity to which sensuous intuition is confined is mediated through its incorporation into a properly infinite universality.

> Art in its truth is more properly *religion,* the elevation of the world of art into the unity of absolute spirit. In art each *particular* wins through beauty a free life of its own, but the truth of each particular spirit is to be a moment in the movement of the whole, *absolute* spirit's knowledge of itself as absolute *spirit.* It is itself the *content of art,* which in general is only its self-production as self-conscious life reflected into itself.[222]

If Hegel had earlier, in the *Differenzschrift,* treated religion as a mode of art, now in the *Realphilosophie* art is treated as a preliminary mode of religion. That is also the case in the *Phenomenology,* where art appears as such only in the section on "Religion in the Form of Art."

The movement is from direct sensuous intuition to imaginative representation, from *Anschauung* to *Vorstellung.* For what must be represented to consciousness is the infinite Geist itself, the infinitude of which consists ultimately in its incarnation in a conscious human existence. That self-reflexive movement is above all what cannot be directly intuited in a sensuous medium as such. But it can be "represented" in the religious mode. We must be cautious in suggesting just how this is so, for the category of *Vorstellung* is still a little vague in the *Realphilosophie.* But at least it is clear that religious *Vorstellung* makes an advance on artistic *Anschauung* in that it is capable of reflexivity. In a very sketchy schematic statement of the matter Hegel suggests that there is, to be sure, something universal in art: "the universal intuition of beauty." But that universality, he seems to say, is not a self. Selfhood belongs only to the artist, who is a particular self. The content of his work is also particular. What is needed is a union of the universal and the particular with selfhood on both sides of the equation; or more

precisely a unity of universal and particular precisely qua self. That
does not occur in the aesthetic distance of intuition.

> But in religion spirit becomes object to itself as absolute univer-
> sal, or as the essence of all nature, of being and action, and in
> the *form* of the immediate self. The self is universal knowledge,
> and thereby the return into itself. The absolute religion is this
> knowledge.[223]

There follows the discussion of the absolute religion, which I treated
earlier. We need only add, in our present context, that in absolute
religion Geist and self become, at least in principle, interchangeable.
Geist having come to self-recognition in a human self, it is particular
as well as universal; and the self is universal as well as particular. To
that extent they are one.

But the unity is religious. It is achieved, that is, in the mode of
Vorstellung. The limitation of this distinctively religious mode of representation has also been discussed already in some detail, but we are
now in a position to clarify that discussion by seeing how Hegel places
religious *Vorstellung* on a continuum between artistic *Anschauung* and
philosophical *Begriff*. Like artistic intuition, religious representation
still makes use of sensuous images; indeed, its limitation is that it
cannot entirely free itself of them. But what it expresses, iconographi-
cally for instance, or in the sensuous language of hymn and story, is
not itself entirely sensuous. It combines thought and imagination in a
rather confusing mixture. *Vorstellung* is already thought: unlike mere
Anschauung, it can grasp the reflexive idea of spirit recognizing itself
in its other. But *Vorstellung* is also imagination: unlike the philosophical
Begriff, it can grasp this idea only in a kind of narrative, as the event
of incarnation.

Now this event is sacramentally incorporated into the cultic life of
the church. To that extent the believer participates in the movement
of spirit. He does not merely behold an image. There is no longer the
hiatus that existed between the intuiting self and the work of art. But
the hiatus has shifted into the very life of the self. Art, Hegel had said,
is Geist, not "the clear spirit that knows itself, but the inspired spirit
that envelopes itself in sentiment and image."[224] Paralleling that formula, Hegel has this to say about religion: "Religion . . . is the represented spirit [*der vorgestellte Geist*], the self that does not bring together
its pure consciousness and its actual consciousness, the self to which

the content of the former appears in the latter as an other, opposed to it."[225] *Vorstellung* is not merely a mode of apprehension still infected with sensuous imagery. It is rather the manifestation of a divided self, a single selfhood divided between divine self and human self.

Hegel gives pithier expression to the same point a few pages later, in contrasting religion to philosophy: "Religion is the thinking spirit which, however, does *not* think *itself*—not its own self, therefore not the sameness with itself, not the immediacy."[226]

The reflexiveness of religious *Vorstellung* is not complete, for although it recognizes that there is nothing in the divine-human relation that is not self, it does not recognize its own self in the divine self-activity. The name for the spirit that does think its self is philosophy. This thoroughly self-reflexive thought is what Hegel calls the concept *(Begriff)*.

> In philosophy it is *ego* as such which is knowledge of absolute spirit, in the concept in itself, as *this* that is universal. Here it is not an *other* nature, not the *non-present* [ungegenwärtige] unity, not a reconciliation the enjoyment and existence of which is beyond and future, but *here: here* ego knows the absolute. It knows, it *grasps* [begreift]; it is none other—*immediate; it is this* self. Ego is this inseparable relation of the particular and the universal, and the particularity as universally of all nature and of the universal, of all *essentiality,* of all *thought.* The *immediacy* of spirit is the Volksgeist or it is the *existing* absolute spirit.[227]

To put it the other way around, the absolute spirit *exists* as the Volksgeist, the collective self of a people. It recognizes itself already in art and religion, but only mediated through intuited and represented objects. In the third distinctively spiritual mode, philosophy, this collective self, in principle universal, achieves an articulated universality, as knowledge, indeed as self-knowledge, which Hegel goes on to describe as "the restored immediacy." It is immediate in that no alien object stands between it and its direct recognition of itself. This immediacy, to be sure, is mediated, but it is mediated purely through self-reflexive concepts. "It is itself the form of mediation, of the *concept.*"

The knowledge with which the *Realphilosophie* concludes, in fact, takes the form of the very treatise itself. That seems implicit in its long, difficult final paragraph. For, as Hegel reminds us, the spirit that philosophy knows in this new, mediated immediacy has passed into otherness as nature and has returned to itself in human consciousness. This return, of course, is consummated in philosophical knowing itself, but it has presumably been under way in the other moments of the Philosophy of Spirit as well. For these moments have been presented precisely as they are philosophically known. Philosophical knowing comprises the whole Philosophy of Spirit and, as Hegel has pointed out two paragraphs earlier, it comprises Speculative Philosophy (as he then called his Logic and Metaphysics) and Philosophy of Nature as well. The philosophical *Wissenschaft* with which the book culminates is not some other work of knowing, but precisely the one that has been presented. The philosophical knowledge of nature *is* spirit's full recovery of itself in the otherness of nature.

Similarly, the Philosophy of Spirit is that knowledge of *itself* that spirit secures in world history. (*Weltgeschichte* as a systematic term is first introduced into Hegel's writings in this closing paragraph of the *Realphilosophie*.) Along with its knowledge of nature, philosophy also comprehends human being, first of all as "*immediate,* sensuous consciousness, that in the form of an entity [*Seienden*] is an other to itself, something divided into *nature* and *knowledge of itself*." The human being, that is, is a microcosm, an epitome of the whole, sundered into body and mind, nature and consciousness. Just as spirit, in the macrocosm, passes into otherness as nature and recovers itself in that otherness, so in the human microcosm spirit passes into its natural immediacy, dividing itself, and recovering its unity in self-knowledge. Macrocosm and microcosm are not merely parallel, however. The human sphere completes the macrocosmic self-recovery of spirit. This "self-knowing spirit" *(sich wissende Geist)* knows itself at least dimly in every sphere of human activity, and knows itself fully in philosophy. Self-knowing spirit "is its own work of art *in repose,* the *subsisting universe,* and *world history.* Philosophy externalizes its own self, comes to its beginning, to immediate consciousness that is as such divided. Philosophy is thus human being generally; and as this human point is, so is the world, and as the world is, so is he: *one* stroke creates them both."[228] Human being epitomizes and completes the world, and philosophy comprehends both, in a state of timeless repose, as total system.

There follows in this same final paragraph a little meditation on time and eternity. The human and his world, point and parameter, "created" *(erschafft)* in one stroke, are temporal. How can they be grasped in the philosophical concept, which is timeless? That seems to be the underlying question in this little meditation, but the answer is not entirely clear. In fact, it contains an ambiguity that I shall presently spell out.

Reviving and updating an old problem that Augustine had pondered,[229] Hegel asks, What existed before the time of that single stroke in which macrocosm and microcosm were created? Like Augustine, he replies that there is not another time, before all time. Nothing *exists* before time. There is only "eternity, the thought of time." Of course, the priority of this eternal thought of time is not itself a temporal priority, as if "eternity itself" were "in time." Hegel labors this point a bit but does not say very clearly just what sort of priority we are in fact talking about. The text, to be sure, is very compressed and rather fragmentary; it is not always easy to tell whether a particular statement expresses Hegel's own view or presents a view he is opposing. But I think he does mean to affirm that eternity is the ontological ground of time: "*Time* is the pure concept, the empty *self* intuited in its movement," just as "space" is the concept or self "in its rest." The relation between the concept and the eternal thought is ambiguous here. Assuming that eternity, the thought of time, is another term for the concept, it follows that philosophy proceeds from a reflection on space (nature) and time (history) to penetrate their eternal ground. This eternal ground is itself a thought, the concept, in which thinking recovers its own proper subject in its own medium. "The thought of time," Hegel says, is "just the thinking, the reflected-in-itself. It is necessary to go out over this time, each period, but into the thought of time." Otherwise we would have a "bad infinite, that never reaches what it is moving toward." So eternity is not only the ontological ground of time, but also its ultimate purpose: at once logos and telos. What is "grasped" in the philosophical *Begriff* is none other than this eternity.

Yet this eternity is not simply abstracted from time, nor is it a mere construct of the philosopher. The concluding sentences of the *Realphilosophie* treat eternity and time as moments in the movement of spirit. First there is the "division" *(Entzweiung)* between time and eternity. Now Hegel tells us that this division of time from eternity is precisely creation, not of course a creation in time, but an "eternal" creation in which, presumably, that "one stroke" occurs constituting human being and world.

> This division is the *eternal* creation, i.e., the creation of the *concept* of spirit, this substance of the concept bearing both itself and its opposite. The universe is thus, in its immediacy, free

from spirit, but it must return to it, or rather the *action,* this movement, is the spirit's; it has to establish the unity, also in the form of immediacy. It is *world history.* In world history the situation is transcended in which nature and history are only *implicitly* [an sich] one *essence.* Spirit comes to the knowledge of this essential unity.

The human being cannot become master over nature until he is master over himself. *Nature* is *in itself* [an sich] a becoming toward *spirit;* in order for this "in itself" to *exist,* spirit must comprehend itself.[230]

Thus the manuscript ends, or breaks off. The general drift of this conclusion is clear enough: The breach between time and eternity, which is the "eternal creation," has constituted the spatiotemporal reality of nature in its independent immediacy. This "division" is immediate, real, though "in itself," implicitly or in principle, time and eternity are one. That, I take it, is simply another way of stating the division: temporarily they are divided, but in the eternal "thought of time" they are one. How can the implicit unity assert itself in the sphere of immediate reality? Through world history, itself a temporal immediacy, which accomplishes precisely in time, indeed over a long period of time, the "return" of temporal reality into its eternal thought. Now the specific world-historical medium of this return is the sphere of art, religion, and philosophical science. In aesthetic intuition, in religious representation, and, supremely, in philosophical concept, that thought develops historically, in time, which recovers the eternal thought of time itself, and thus bridges the division between time and eternity. "Spirit" comprises this entire process of division and return, becoming itself fully actualized only in the philosophical recovery of the concept in time. The implicit presence of spirit throughout now becomes "immediately" manifest in that self-knowledge it achieves in philosophy.

That much is clearly what Hegel intends. The achievement of philosophical system is so important to him because it must forge precisely that connecting link in which spirit recovers itself. A Philosophy of Spirit is not merely a treatise about spirit, but a culminating movement in the very life of spirit.

An Ambiguity in the System

There are two ways, however, of construing this self-recovery, either of which is congruent with the conclusion of the *Realphilosophie.* Spirit is the recovery of eternity, the thought of time, in the alien medium of real time. By this excursion into the real world of becoming, the eternal thought gains the necessary condition for its existence as spirit. But has it also gained specific content? On one reading it has not, since its content is true only insofar as it is ideal, not contaminated by that excursion into otherness. Already determinate apart from real time, its true content constituted precisely in its ideality, it expresses itself in time as the element of truth in what is otherwise a senseless flux, and is to be recovered in its purity by thought. On the other reading, the thought of time is empty of content, purely formal, indeterminate apart from that real temporality in which it is "fulfilled." It achieves its truth only insofar as it is "filled" with real content in time.[231]

The issue between these two readings may seem rather arcane, but it directly affects the content of the philosophical concept: what is grasped in this *Begriff*? On the first reading the philosopher must deal with nature and history only as the point of departure for grasping the timeless thought expressed in them. In that case philosophy, as it were, reverses the "division" of time from eternity (the eternal creation), discovering the eternal truth behind the apparent contingency and temporality of the real world. On the other reading the very content of the philosophical concept is essentially derived from the real world of experience in time and space. It grasps eternity and time together, thus filling the emptiness of the former and giving intelligible form to the apparently meaningless flux of the latter.

Another way of stating our issue places in the foreground the relation of philosophical *Begriff* to aesthetic *Anschauung* and religious *Vorstellung*. The formal deficiency of the aesthetic and religious modes, we recall, consists in the fact that they remain in varying degrees infected with the kinds of apprehension characteristic of experience. Religious representation retains something of the particularity of spatiotemporal experience even in the form in which it represents what is not literally spatiotemporal. Does this mean that art, religion, and philosophy are three independent, alternative ways of transcending experience, achieved in an ascending order of adequacy? Or does the philosophical concept simply mediate more completely what must first present itself in aesthetic and religious forms? Are the aesthetic and religious forms, that is, indispensable sources of philosophical insight, precisely because they are closer to the immediacies of experience? How dependent is the philosophical concept on the world that presents itself in experience, and on the aesthetic and religious modes of mediating it?

Let us expand the alternative answers to such questions that follow from the two readings of the conclusion of the *Realphilosophie* that we have identified:

(1) In time, in history, there arises a science that is capable of penetrating through time and history to that eternal "thought of time" that is ontologically antecedent. In this case what we have in the treatment of nature and spirit in the *Realphilosophie* is their interpretation in light of that "thought" that is itself neither natural nor historical in its basis. Religion, in particular, in its systematic comprehension by philosophy, can be true only to the extent that it "represents" in its limited form that truth that is adequately expressed in the timeless comprehension of "speculative" philosophy. Not actual incarnation, for instance, the manifest content of "absolute religion," but the *thought* of incarnation, the metaphysical necessity of spirit expressing itself in nature and history, will be that truth of religion that only philosophy, and not religion itself, can recognize in religion. Religion, then, is only a superfluous point of departure for speculative insight, which is purely ideal in essence.

The other way of reading the conclusion is this: (2) that the mere thought of time (logic/metaphysics) is itself empty apart from that manifestation in nature and history that gives it its specific content. Time, that is, is "necessary" not only in the sense that its historical course leads inevitably to its comprehension in philosophy, its representation in religion, its intuition in art, but also in the sense that the logico-metaphysical "thought of time" itself requires actualization in time in order to have concrete meaning. What is actualized, that is, cannot be a thought that is already articulated apart from the actualization. This thought, as it were, discovers its own content only under the actual conditions of nature and history, because the content is constituted under these conditions.

Philosophy, in this case, has no truth that is purely its own. It does not confer an a priori truth on nature and history, and systematize them accordingly. It grasps as self-reflexive insight what is presented to it under conditions of contingency and otherness. It comprehends conceptually, that is, what is first presented to it in the otherness of nature, actualized in world history, intuited in art, represented in religion. Spirit, then, is not identical with Idea, which remains as spiritless without nature and history as they do apart from it, in meaningless contingency. Idea itself requires that spirit appear only *in* the contingent other. In this case the philosophical *Begriff* can comprehend the truth of religion, for instance, only insofar as it is first represented in religion, under actual historical conditions. Without religious *Vorstellung* spirit cannot comprehend itself, because it has not yet actualized itself, and it cannot actualize itself because it has not comprehended itself. The incarnate union of the ideal and the real, the divine and the human, in particular, can be comprehended only because it has first been "represented."

Each of these readings is idealistic. At stake in the conflict between them is the sort of idealism Hegel's system is to express. It will be convenient for present reference to label them, though no label is free of misleading connotations. I propose with some misgivings to call the first reading experience-negating, the second experience-appropriating. I have in mind the notorious double meaning of the Hegelian term *aufheben,* which signifies both negation and appropriation, and indeed, both movements are at work in both types of idealism we have sought to identify. But the accent falls differently: in the first type, experience—its world, its categories, its aesthetic and religious formations—is provisionally appropriated only in order, in the end, to be subjected to speculative negation. In the second type, experience is negated as such in order to be distilled into a form that can be speculatively appropriated.

I have argued that the conclusion of the *Realphilosophie* can be read either way. Nor is the ambiguity resolved elsewhere in the Jena manuscripts. Some passages in these manuscript materials point one way, some the other, and some can be read either way, but nowhere is the ambiguity directly faced and resolved. It extends to a number of problems we have encountered along the way that indeed are variations on the same problem. We encountered it, for instance, in discussing the systematic relation of "speculative" philosophy (Logic/Metaphysics) to the "real" Philosophy of Nature and Philosophy of Spirit, regarding which we found such puzzles in the systematic manuscripts generally. A parallel problem, if not the same problem, concerns the relation of the speculative doctrine of divinity, with which we began this long section, to the content of "religion" as it is treated in the *Realphilosophie* and in other renderings of the Philosophy of Spirit. Is the concrete content of historic religion a representation of what is presented in proper conceptual form in the speculative doctrine, perhaps in the divine triangle? But the latter never extends so far as historical concreteness, while concrete religion is too integrally related to its cultural roots in the life of the Volk to incorporate the speculative doctrine fully.

The "absolute religion" appears to bridge the two poles, but in fact it becomes a primary locus of the dilemma. To the extent that the absolute religion expresses speculative truth, it begins to pass over into philosophy, attenuating both the historical content of its doctrine and its roots in the religious practice of a historic community; to the extent that it retains its doctrinal and communal identity, it falls short of speculative truth. If we are not easily pacified by the facile formula that religion and philosophy have the same content, but differ only in form, our problem arises again with respect to the precise relation of the two. Do religious representations provide an indispensable source for philosophical insight? Or does philosophy find in religious life only what it is independently, speculatively programmed to find there? A parallel issue arises with respect to art, and to world history generally.

The system must reconcile the ideal and the real, but there appear to be these two quite different kinds of idealism contending through all the systematic ventures of Hegel's Jena years. Perhaps the issue would have been resolved if Hegel had ever managed, after he abandoned the Schellingian identity-philosophy, to present the whole system within a single, self-consistent frame. More likely, as I have already suggested, his failure to resolve this central systematic issue was a factor that prevented him from accomplishing that presentation of the whole system that he so ardently desired throughout his Jena years.

But Hegel was determined to embark once again on the composition of the whole system when he began writing the *Phenomenology of Spirit* in 1805. The *Phenomenology* was designed as a propaedeutic to the system that was immediately to follow. But the *Phenomenology* turned out to be a much longer work than Hegel had originally intended, and by the time he finished it in autumn 1806, Napoleon had intervened: World History interfering with the constructions of speculative wisdom! The University of Jena was soon in a state of collapse, Hegel fled, and during most of 1807–8 he had to support himself as a newspaper editor in Bamberg, complaining frequently of the "newspaper yoke." He secured a position as a teacher of secondary school students and rector of the school in Nuremberg in November 1808. The first, "speculative" part of the system appeared with the publication of his *Science of Logic*, in three volumes (1812, 1813, 1816) while he was still employed as a schoolmaster. So that urgent piece of unfinished business, the completion of the system, had to wait for several years: it was outlined in the three editions of the *Encyclopaedia of the Philosophical Sciences* (1817, 1827, 1830) and spelled out in the famous lectures he delivered in

Heidelberg and Berlin during the last fifteen years of his life (1816–31). It is absurd to speculate how much of that later system Hegel may have had in mind when he wrote the *Phenomenology*. A system does not exist in its full articulation until it is written. It is certain that the three main divisions had already evolved, that the system was to consist in a Logic or speculative part, and a Philosophy of Nature and a Philosophy of Spirit, and we have noted along the way several features of the Jena manuscripts, of the *Realphilosophie* in particular, that were retained in the later system. But beyond this broad outline and a few such details, plus the hints in the concluding chapter of the *Phenomenology* itself and in its Preface (designed as a preface to the whole system to come), we cannot go.

Now it is obvious that Hegel's intent in the *Phenomenology* is affected in important respects by his conception of the system of which it was designed to serve as the propaedeutic. But that system never got written! To follow the usual practice, and read the *Phenomenology* as if it were the propaedeutic to the system that finally did get written, is dangerously misleading. The later system pointedly omits any phenomenological pathway into it, as if it were superfluous, and incorporates a truncated "Phenomenology of Spirit" into the system proper (outlined in the *Encyclopaedia*) as a segment of the section on Subjective Mind. We shall discuss the importance of this change in more detail in the next chapter. My present point is that there was an ambiguity about the position of the *Phenomenology,* even when he wrote it, in relation to his conception of the system. It was designed to be pre-systematic, and yet have an integral function in the system. Does this integral function testify that the system he envisaged at that time would articulate an experience-appropriating type of idealism? Or does its position as a kind of vestibule suggest that the system itself, its appropriation of experience done, could have a markedly experience-negating design? The fact that this *Science of the Experience of Consciousness*—Hegel's original title for the *Phenomenology*—was placed in this ambiguous limbo, this anteroom, suggests to me that he had not resolved the ambiguity between the experience-negating and the experience-appropriating types of idealism in his conception of the system at that time. That judgment is supported by the additional fact that the ambiguity still exists in the conclusion to the *Realphilosophie,* written while he was already at work on the *Phenomenology.*

The question whether the later system resolves this ambiguity would carry us beyond the scope of the present study. The fact that it dispenses with a phenomenological propaedeutic, at any rate, is a warning against reading the *Phenomenology* in light of the later system. It is safer to read it in light of the Jena essays and manuscripts that precede it. That is a primary reason for my having devoted this long chapter to those writings, pointing up especially those themes and problems that will figure most directly in the sections of the *Phenomenology* which we shall discuss in the following chapter.

Notes

1. *Briefe* (cited in Chapter 1, note 19) 1:58–60 (*Letters* cited in Chapter 1, note 51, 63–64). Also Rosenkranz, *Leben,* (cited in Chapter 1, note 1). 142–44.

2. Generations of Hegel scholars were led astray in this respect by the fact that Rosenkranz assigned a rather elaborate system, which he summarized at length (*Leben,* 99–141), to the latter part of Hegel's Frankfurt period. But the manuscript on which his summary was based in fact dates from well into Hegel's career as a lecturer in Jena. Rosenkranz's error caused great confusion. One finds Haym, for instance, resorting to the most ingenious expedients to explain how Hegel, coming to Jena with the manuscript of a system in hand that so clearly bore the seeds of his mature system, should then have abandoned it to become largely a spokesman for Schelling during his first Jena years (e.g., Haym, *Hegel und seine Zeit* [cited in Chapter 1, note 1], 150ff.). Haym had, to be sure, corrected Rosenkranz's even more serious error in assigning the manuscripts on the *Verfassung Deutschlands* to 1806–8 (Rosenkranz, *Leben,* 235ff.; Haym, *Hegel und seine Zeit,* 70, 159, and notes, 485, 496). But only the work of Heinz Kimmerle and his colleagues at the Hegel-Archiv has fully corrected the mistaken impression of Hegel's course of development as a systematic thinker.

My interpretation in this chapter is indebted to Kimmerle's reconstructions of the course of Hegel's career in Jena, which have been published in a series of articles in *Hegel-Studien* (vols. 4 and 5, 1967 and 1969, and Beiheft 4, 1969) and elaborated in *Das Problem der Abgeschlossenheit des Denkens: Hegels 'System der Philosophie' in den Jahren 1800–1804* (*Hegel-Studien,* Beiheft 8, 1970). This book combines the fruits of Kimmerle's philological research with a deep-going philosophical investigation of the problem of systematic conception, as it arises already in Hegel's earliest ventures into system-building in Jena.

But Kimmerle makes it clear that when Hegel came to Jena he had no full-blown system in hand at all, though he had begun to conduct some studies in logic and metaphysics that were given expression in his earliest Jena lectures. Even the fragment that Nohl entitled "Systemfragment von 1800" is probably not really part of a system; as Kroner points out (*Early Theological Writings* [cited in Chapter 1, note 2], 309 n), this fragment "contains some of the seeds of the later system, but there is nothing to indicate that Hegel was writing the sketch of a system rather than a theological essay"—akin to *The Spirit of Christianity.*

3. *Briefe*, 1:60 (*Letters*, 64). The letter closes on a guarded but unmistakable note of appeal for some assistance in launching Hegel's career.

4. Both the monograph on the Fichtean and Schellingian systems (1801) and the complete text of the six issues of the *Kritisches Journal der Philosophie* (1802–3), including Schelling's contributions as well as Hegel's, are included in volume 4 of the latest edition of Hegel's *Gesammelte Werke*. This volume is entitled *Jenaer kritische Schriften*, ed. Hartmut Buchner and Otto Pöggeler (Hamburg: Felix Meiner, 1968); that is the edition of these texts I shall be citing here, as *JkS*.

The monograph and two of the journal articles have been translated. The full titles of these important pieces, and their translations, are as follows:

Differenz des Fichte'schen und Schelling'schen Systems der Philosophie in Bezeihung auf Reinhold's Beyträge zur leichtern Übersicht des Zustands der Philosophy zu Anfang des neunzehnten Jahrhunderts (Jena, 1801). *The Difference Between Fichte's and Schelling's System of Philosophy*, trans. H. S. Harris and Walter Cerf (Albany: State University of New York Press, 1977).

Glauben und Wissen oder die Reflexionsphilosophie der Subjectivität, in der Vollständigkeit ihrer Formen, als Kantische, Jacobische, und Fichtesche Philosophie (Tübingen, 1802). *Faith and Knowledge*, trans. Walter Cerf and H. S. Harris (Albany: State University of New York Press, 1977).

Über die wissenschaftlichen Behandlungsarten des Naturrechts, seine Stelle in der praktischen Philosophie, und sein Verhältniss zu den positiven Rechtswissenschaften (Tübingen, 1802). *Natural Law*, trans. T. M. Knox, introduction by H. G. Acton (Philadelphia: University of Pennsylvania Press, 1975).

All three of these translations indicate the pagination of the German texts as they appear in *Jenaer kritische Schriften*, so it will be unnecessary to cite them separately here. These early published works of Hegel's also appeared in Hegel, *Erste Druckschriften*, ed. Georg Lasson (Leipzig: Felix Meiner, 1928). A photographic reprint of the entire *Kritisches Journal der Philosophie* in the original edition has also appeared, with an attached essay by Hartmut Buchner (Hildesheim: Georg Olms, 1967).

Schelling had attempted for some time to found a new philosophical journal, in collaboration with Fichte and/or the Schlegel brothers, Schleiermacher, or others, but party disputes frustrated these various efforts (see the account in the Editorischer Bericht of *JkS*, 533ff.). Even after he and Hegel decided to launch their *Kritisches Journal der Philosophie* it was hoped that others in the Jena circle would join in the venture, at least by contributing articles; Schelling tried, for instance, to get Schleiermacher to write a critique of Jacobi. But in fact all the articles in the six issues of the journal that appeared during 1802–3 were written by the co-editors. Indeed, Schelling was at the same time editing the *Neue Zeitschrift für speculative Physik*, and since he was chiefly devoting himself to his philosophy of nature at that time, he was writing more for that journal than for the *Kritisches Journal*. So most of the essays that appeared in the latter were written by Hegel. But articles in the *Kritisches Journal* were unsigned, Hegel and Schelling were in the closest association with one another, and the degree of collaboration between them on some of the articles is difficult to determine. An acrimonious dispute erupted in the 1830s between the editors of Hegel's collected works and Schelling's circle over authorship of some of these essays (*JkS*, 540ff.).

5. Rosenkranz, *Leben*, 151.

6. Ibid., 142.

7. F. Köppen, *Schellings Lehre oder das Ganze der Philosophie des absoluten Nichts* (Hamburg, 1803), 145. Quoted in the Editorischer Bericht to *JkS*, 541. The essay to which Köppen refers is *Glauben und Wissen*, which includes a lengthy and not gentle

critique of Jacobi. A report in a Stuttgart newspaper that Schelling had brought "a doughty defender" to Jena from his native land to do battle for him roused Hegel to an indignant reply in the *Kritisches Journal* (*JkS*, 190 n; Rosenkranz, *Leben*, 162–63).

8. Quoted from a letter by Schleiermacher to K. G. v. Brinkmann in *Hegel in Berichten seiner Zeitgenossen*, ed. Günther Nicolin (Hamburg: Felix Meiner, 1970), 53; hereafter cited as *Berichten*. The primary targets of these remarks about the evils of *Jüngersucht* are Jacobi and Köppen, and they are occasioned by Köppen's book, cited in the previous note, defending his master against the Schelling-Hegel phalanx. But he also mentions as an example "wie sich Schelling behängt mit dem Hegel."

9. *Briefe*, 1:69–76 (*Letters*, 65–68 [excerpts]).

10. *Briefe*, 1:71–72, 73–74. Schelling had been a frequent guest in the Schlegel home, and had been in love with Caroline's daughter, Auguste Böhmer, who was taken fatally ill. There were indeed rumors that Schelling's efforts to cure her had hastened her death; an insinuation to that effect found its way into print in an anonymous attack on Schelling published in the *Allgemeine Literatur-Zeitung* in 1804, which caused Schelling, with August Schlegel's support, to sue the editor. Meanwhile, Schelling had transferred his affections to the mother of his former sweetheart, and early in 1802 Schelling and the Schlegels had already decided during a trip to Berlin on the divorce and remarriage. The Schlegels were divorced in May 1803. Schelling married Caroline that summer, and began lecturing in Würzburg during the following winter semester.

11. *Briefe*, 1:71, 73 (*Letters*, 75, 76). Hölderlin had been sent to France, Schelling thinks under false pretenses, but his condition had so worsened that he had to be brought back. Schelling considers him utterly deranged "since this fatal journey," though he reports that the poet is still able to do some translation from the Greek—doubtless the haunting translations of Sophocles that belong to this period.

12. Quoted from a letter dated November 9, 1803, in *Berichten*, 53.

13. See entries quoted from the Goethe-Schiller correspondence and from Goethe's *Tagebuch*, ibid., 54–55.

14. Rosenkranz, *Leben*, 217. Rosenkranz followed an eyewitness report prepared for him by G. A. Gabler in relating some vivid stories from the latter part of Hegel's tenure in Jena; Gabler, later a leading thinker of the Hegelian right wing, had been Hegel's student at that time. His report, first published in *Hegel-Studien* 4 (1967), has been reprinted in *Berichten*, 59–70. Rosenkranz places the episode with the indignant auditor after Hegel's lecture criticizing Schelling in particular, but Gabler (*Berichten*, 65) does not imply that, though he does report that "we" had not recognized any difference between Hegel and Schelling until Hegel presented detailed criticisms of Schelling in the historical lectures.

15. Gabler's report in *Berichten*, 62; Rosenkranz, *Leben*, 216.

16. *Briefe*, 1:65 (*Letters*, 89).

17. "Brief von Zettel an Squenz," *JkS*, 191. "Squenz" seems to be C. G. Bardili, with whom Reinhold had associated himself in his *Beiträge zu leichtern Übersicht des Zustandes der Philosophie beim Anfange des 19. Jahrhunderts* (erstes Heft, 1801), on which Hegel poured scorn in the *Differenzschrift*. See Pöggeler's discussion of Reinhold and Bardili in his essay, "Hegels Jenaer Systemkonzeption," in *Hegels Idee einer Phänomenologie des Geistes* (Freiburg: Karl Alber, 1973), 128–33. Pöggeler points out (132) that Hegel did not even wait for the appearance of the second volume of the *Beiträge*, in which Reinhold specifically treated the philosophies of Fichte and Schelling, before attacking him for misunderstanding the relation between them! "Zettel" and "Squenz" are the German names for two of the rustic players in Schlegel's translation of Shakespeare's *Midsummer Night's Dream*.

18. *Berichten,* 43–44. The letter is dated January 15, 1802.

19. Ibid., 45. Letter dated March 22, 1802.

20. Ibid., 50. Letter dated December 12, 1802.

21. Haym, *Hegel und seine Zeit,* 152.

22. See *Differenzschrift, JkS,* 5, 62–63, 77–78; and also, more indirectly, in the critique of Fichte in *Glauben und Wissen, JkS,* 387ff. In letters to August Schlegel, Schelling himself expressed reservations about the interpretation of Fichte in *Glauben und Wissen,* and asked on grounds of friendship that Schlegel not show the piece to Fichte. While he does defend some of Hegel's analysis, he also complains of the quarrelsome and cloudy style, particularly in the critique of Jacobi (ibid., 538–39, 539 n). Haym, on the other hand, suggests (*Hegel und seine Zeit,* 153) that Schelling himself simply did not understand the profound differences between himself and Fichte until Hegel pointed them out to him! Claiming that Hegel's contributions to the *Kritisches Journal* were embarrassingly superior to Schelling's, Haym goes so far as to argue that Schelling did not even understand his own philosophy until it had been "verdolmetscht" for him by Hegel (157).

23. See Klaus Düsing, "Spekulation und Reflexion. Zur Zusammenarbeit Schellings und Hegels in Jena," *Hegel-Studien,* 1969, 5:95–128. Düsing makes a plausible case for the mutual influence of the two friends during this period. He argues, for instance, that in Schelling's writings of 1802–3, the concept of "speculation" is derived originally from Hegel.

24. *Einleitung. Über das Wesen der philosophischen Kritik überhaupt, und ihr Verhältniss zum gegenwärtigen Zustand der Philosophie insbesondere,* in *JkS,* 119.

25. Ibid., 117.

26. Ibid., 9. The target here is Reinhold, against whose confounding of the Fichtean and Schellingian systems the *Differenzschrift* is directed.

27. Ibid., 10. Cf. 84ff.

28. Cf. the famous remark in the Vorrede of *Grundlinien der Philosophie des Rechts* (1821; ed. Hoffmeister [Hamburg: Felix Meiner, 1955], 16), that philosophy is "its age apprehended in thought." But earlier in the same Vorrede he has distinguished in a manner that reminds us of the present passage between the "core" of philosophy, which is one with the Idea, and its "colorful peel" (15).

29. *JkS,* 117.

30. Ibid., 118.

31. Ibid.

32. Ibid., 121.

33. Ibid., 126. In particular, Hegel remarks that the ascendancy of this "reason-abandoned understanding" has in the end "ruined theology."

34. *Differenzschrift,* in *JkS,* 64; cf. 25–26, 38, 62–64. Compare the formulation in the *Systemfragment* of 1800, quoted in Chapter 2: "Life is the union of union and non-union."

35. David Hume, *An Inquiry Concerning Human Understanding,* ed. with an Introduction by Charles W. Hendel (New York: Liberal Arts Press, 1955), 83.

36. Immanuel Kant, *Kritik der reinen Vernunft,* B 75.

37. Ibid., B 218; see B 294, 303, 308f., 730.

38. Ibid., B 237ff., 262ff., 280ff., 528ff.

39. Ibid., B 87, 170, 309, 314. Already in his Inaugural Dissertation *(De mundi sensibilis atque intelligibilis forma et principiis),* sec. 24, Kant had declared that the most important rule of metaphysical method is: "sollicite cavendum esse, ne principia sensitivae cognitionis domestica terminos suos migrent ac intellectualia afficiant."

40. Ibid., B 85f., 308, 310.

41. Ibid., B 432ff.

42. Ibid., B 350ff., 397, 595f. While we are not concerned here with Kant's philosophy as such, in order to avoid one-sidedness we should notice that there is another danger on his terms, the opposite of "transcendental illusion." Kant also denies what we may call the "empirical illusion," that the boundaries of empirical knowledge are cogently to be regarded as the boundaries of all reality. There is a great deal that we cannot properly know, an area embracing morality and religion, to which reason is related only in its practical employment. Ibid., B 499 and passim.

43. W. T. Stace, *The Philosophy of Hegel: A Systematic Exposition* (Mineola, N.Y.: Dover, 1955), 43.

44. This point is convincingly made in relation to "onto-theology" by Dieter Henrich in *Der Ontologische Gottesbeweis* (Tübingen: J. C. B. Mohr, 1960), 194–219. Henrich shows that Hegel accepted Kant's critique of previous onto-theology, and in large measure accepted also Kant's formulation of what must be accomplished if onto-theology were to be reconstituted. But Kant did not think it could be, and Hegel did, frequently defending the proofs for God's existence against Kant's critique. Cf. Hegel's remarks, already in *Glauben und Wissen,* on Kant's critique of speculative theology, *JkS,* 338, 344–45.

45. *Enzyklopädie der philosophischen Wissenschaften im Grundrisse* (1830; ed. Nicolin and Pöggeler [Hamburg: Felix Meiner, 1959]), Zusatz and sec. 41, following Wallace's translation. See also secs. 25, 40–45.

46. Vorerinnerung to the *Differenzschrift, JkS,* 5. Hegel goes on to draw a similar discrimination within the Fichtean system, 6–7; also 36–38. For Hegel's critique of Jacobi's "raisonnirenden" treatment of Spinoza, see *Glauben und Wissen, JkS,* 352ff.

47. *Glauben und Wissen,* 328. See 326–30.

48. *Differenzschrift,* 13–14. Cf. *Glauben und Wissen,* 325–26.

49. *Differenzschrift,* 14. See 15–16 for a further development of this motif.

50. *Differenzschrift,* 48–54; *Glauben und Wissen,* 404–5.

51. *Glauben und Wissen,* 332.

52. Ibid., 338–43.

53. Ibid., 339. Cf. Kant's *Kritik der Urteilskraft,* sec. 57, Anm. I.

54. Ibid., 344–45. A few pages earlier (338) Hegel has dismissed Kant's refutation of the ontological proof for God's existence as based on a trivial version of the proof.

55. Ibid., 345–46.

56. Ibid., 324. See also 358–59, 372.

57. Ibid., 346. Hegel goes on to summarize what seems to him distinctive about Kant's version of reflection-philosophy, preparing the reader for the contrasting versions of Jacobi and Fichte. For Kant the "absolute subjectivity is presented in objective form, namely as concept and law." The moral law does, after all, have an objective form, though it has no basis in objective knowledge. For summaries of the comparison with Jacobi and Fichte, see 321 and 387.

These three systems represent variations on the subjective form of reflection. In the *Differenzschrift* Hegel classifies such absolutizing of subjectivity as the mark of dogmatic idealism, in contrast to a dogmatic realism, which absolutizes objectivity (ibid., 32). He suggests, however, that dogmatic idealism or realism is characteristic of *systems,* and that a genuine philosophy may only imperfectly be expressed in its systematic form (30–34).

58. See Günter Rohrmoser's excellent monograph, *Subjektivität und Verdinglichung: Theologie und Gesellschaft im Denken des jungen Hegel* (Gütersloh: Gütersloher Verlagshaus Gerd Mohn, 1961), which traces this fundamental problem in its different forms from Hegel's early writings through the Jena writings, with a concluding chapter on the *Phenomenology.* On the Jena critique of reification and reflection, see 61–74.

See also the aforementioned study by Heinz Kimmerle, *Das Problem der Abgeschlossenheit des Denkens,* 49–66, for a discussion of the relation between "reflection" and Hegel's conception of logic in his lectures of 1801–3. As Kimmerle points out, in the *Differenzschrift* Hegel still uses the term "Reflexion" in a more general sense; reflection can be either speculative or "raisonnierend." In *Glauben und Wissen,* however, and in the early lectures on logic, the term is limited by being related to "the understanding as the epistemological organ of reflection" (50). For reflection is the proper sphere of logic, while speculative reason defines the sphere of metaphysics: reflection has a productive function insofar as it prepares the way for reason and passes over into reason. The reconstruction of logic into a discipline that is already speculative, that can indeed replace metaphysics, had to await further developments in Hegel's conception of his system.

59. Rosenkranz, *Leben,* 156.

60. This notorious refusal to acknowledge the law of (non-)contradiction as a rule of truth, which later scandalized Hegel's critics, is discussed in his essay on skepticism published in the *Critical Journal* in 1802, the year after he had defended his theses: *Das Verhältniss des Skepticismus zur Philosophie, Darstellung seiner verschiedenen Modificationen und Vergleichung des neuesten mit dem alten.* In Spinoza's proposition, for instance, that God is the immanent cause of the world, the notion of an immanent cause seems to Hegel to be deliberately paradoxical; for a cause is ordinarily understood to be different from its effect, but here cause and effect are also one. "God is cause and not cause, he is one and not one, many and not many. . . . The so-called law of contradiction has therefore so little of even merely formal truth for reason that, on the contrary, every law of reason, in view of the concept, must contain a thrust against the law; that a law is *merely* formal *(formell)* means for reason that it is posited for itself alone, without asserting precisely the opposite, its contradiction, and precisely for that reason is false." Since every genuine philosophy has this negative, skeptical side, it necessarily violates the merely *formell* law of contradiction—not promiscuously, to be sure, but precisely when it moves toward some encompassing truth. *JkS,* 208–9.

61. Ibid., 158.

62. See the letter of November 2, 1800, to Schelling, quoted above.

63. *Differenzschrift,* 58. See 54ff. The language of *Herrschaft und Knechtschaft* (lordship and bondage), treated in the most famous passage in the *Phenomenology,* also appears on 55 and 59 of this treatise.

64. Einleitung to the *Kritisches Journal,* in *JkS,* 124–25. There is an interesting allusion in this passage to a story about Aristotle and Alexander the Great. When he heard that Aristotle was publishing philosophical writings, Alexander took his old teacher to task for making "common" the wisdom that had passed between them; to which Aristotle replied that his philosophy had been published, but also not published. Then follows Hegel's remark about elevating the people to philosophy but not lowering philosophy to them.

Though Kimmerle does not cite this particular passage, he does seem to think that Hegel's hope for philosophy to have effect in the world is based on some contemporary Alexander, trained in philosophy, establishing his rule over modern European society. Kimmerle therefore takes Hegel to task for betraying his youthful ideal of a society transformed from its roots. This line of criticism is part of the overarching thesis of *Das Problem der Abgeschlossenheit des Denkens:* that Hegel's turn to systematic philosophy in Jena, indeed to the construction of a closed system, is a fatal reversal of the vital social and religious concerns and the historical orientation of his youth (see 41–44, 47, 104, and passim). This thesis is advanced along with Kimmerle's splendid reconstruction of the development of the Jena system.

As Kimmerle points out, Hegel concludes his unpublished manuscript *Die Verfassung Deutschlands* (1801) by calling for a new Theseus to end the disarray of the German people, and he praises Machiavelli for his effort to instruct a prince in a way that might have helped put an end to a similar disarray in the Italy of his time (*Schriften zur Politik und Rechtsphilosophie*, 110–17, 135–36). It is even possible, but barely possible, that Hegel may have composed *Die Verfassung Deutschlands* in the hope of playing Machiavelli to some German "prince." But it is not at all plausible to suppose that the austere ideal of "philosophy" that Hegel propounded and then developed in detail in Jena could have been set forth with any such aim in mind, or that Hegel might have hoped that philosophy could gain entrance into human affairs by his becoming an Aristotle to some current Alexander. Certainly the context of the Alexander-Aristotle passage cited above gives it quite a different point.

Kimmerle reflects, much more guardedly than Harris and others, a tendency in recent Hegel scholarship to exaggerate the breach between the Frankfurt and the Jena works: to read into the early writings a program for an activist and even revolutionary role for Hegel himself, and then to find in the Jena years a retirement into theoretical philosophy, with nothing more than an outlandish Aristotle-Alexander dream for some return by the philosopher into "engagement in the life of men." But Hegel knew perfectly well that the greatest contribution of an Aristotle to "the life of men" is hardly made through his Alexander!

65. Ibid., 126. The "spirit" in this passage may refer back specifically to "the German spirit" referred to in the preceding paragraph.

66. Ibid., 12–16. Of course the problem of dualism had existed long before the modern age, but Hegel saw his own age as riven by this problem in its most refined and exacerbated forms, as we have seen. We shall attend more closely to his remarks on "the need of philosophy" below.

67. The expression is Pöggeler's, in "Hegels Jenaer Systemkonzeption," *Hegels Idee einer Phänomenologie des Geistes*, 136–39. Pöggeler and other current scholars have connected this passage in the *Differenzschrift* with the cryptic remark Hegel made about his own "wissenschaftliche Bildung" in the letter to Schelling, and have also seen it as the key to that important transition in Hegel's thinking from his view of religion as the reconciler of opposites to his view of philosophy as the remedy for this "need." See Pöggeler, 139ff., 151ff., and also Hartmut Buchner, "Hegel im Übergang von Religion zu Philosophie," *Philosophisches Jahrbuch* (1971): 82–97, esp. 89, 93–97; and J. H. Trede, "Hegels frühe Logik (1801–1803/04)," *Hegel-Studien* 1972, 7:132–35. Buchner's essay takes the form of a very deep-going exposition of the crucial passage in Hegel's letter to Schelling, setting its cryptic terms in the context of Hegel's writings at the end of the Frankfurt period and the beginning of the Jena period.

68. *HtJ* (cited in Chapter 1, note 2), 348.

69. Hegel expresses this new position in Fichtean language in the *Differenzschrift*, 27–28, 35–36.

70. Ibid., 77. Intellectual intuition (the term is used interchangeably with transcendental intuition) is said to be "the absolute principle, the single real basis, and firm standpoint of philosophy" for both Fichte and Schelling, 76.

71. *Kritik der reinen Vernunft*, B 310; *Kritik der Urteilskraft*, sec. 77.

72. Nicholas Cusanus, for instance, did speak explicitly of a "visio intellectualis" (*De Possest*, 38), and expressed this motif with the elegant suggestion that the term "visio dei" employs both the subjective and the objective genitive *(De visione Dei);* that is, God's vision, and the human vision of God.

73. *Differenzschrift,* 77. See also 35–37 for Hegel's exposition of the Fichtean doctrine of transcendental intuition; also in *Glauben und Wissen,* 389ff. Hegel first presents his own understanding of transcendental intuition in the Introducation to the *Differenzschrift,* 27–28.

74. Ibid., 73.

75. Ibid., 28; cf. 32–33 for the characterizations of dogmatic idealism and materialism, both dominated by causal relations likewise aufgehoben in transcendental intuition. In the last major treatise Hegel wrote for the *Critical Journal, Über die wissenschaftlichen Behandlungsarten des Naturrechts,* Hegel again addressed himself to these two standpoints, in terms of the one and the many: with "physical" nature we begin with the many in the relation of necessity, with "ethical" nature with the one in freedom. These are also two different ways of relating "relation" to *Indifferenz;* and the Absolute is the identity of *Indifferenz* and relation. *JkS,* 432–33 (Knox trans., *Natural Law,* 71–74).

76. Ibid., 74.

77. Ibid., 74–75. The Schellingian legerdemain, by which the notion of light plays this mediating role, had been introduced a couple of paragraphs earlier (73).

78. Ibid., 75.

79. Ibid., 32–33.

80. For some examples of Hölderlin's suggestive employment of intellectual intuition, see Friedrich Hölderlin, *Sämtliche Werke und Briefe,* ed. Günter Mieth (Darmstädt: Wissenschaftliche Buchgesellschaft, 1970), 1:840–41, 889–96, and letters to Schiller and Niethammer, in 2:667, 689–90. Dieter Henrich discusses the influence of Hölderlin's philosophical thinking on Hegel in the first two essays of *Hegel im Kontext* (Frankfurt am Main: Suhrkamp, 1967), entitled "Hegel und Hölderlin" and "Historische Voraussetzungen von Hegels System." Henrich also details Hegel's break with the somewhat Fichtean conception of identity adopted by Hölderlin, 35–40, 64–72.

81. "Womit muss der Anfang der Wissenschaft gemacht werden?" *Wissenschaft der Logik,* ed. Georg Lasson (Leipzig: Felix Meiner, 1934, reprinted, 1951), 1:51–52, 62–63. The notion of "absolute Indifferenz," however, finds a place in the *Logik,* in the transition from Being to Essence, as the final effort to conceive an ultimate substratum in the manner of Spinoza, to resolve all apparent differentiations by referring them to a single prior identity (ibid., 387–98). The failure of this attempt gives rise to the category of Essence, with its network of paired terms (called *Reflexions Bestimmungen!* 2:7) such as reality and appearance, thing and properties.

82. *Glauben und Wissen,* 404. The quotation is compiled from Fichte's *Bestimmung des Menschen,* 106 in the original edition (or *Werke,* 2:214). For other passages in which Hegel details the Kantian-Fichtean sin against nature, some *Differenzschrift,* 48–54, 69ff., and *Glauben und Wissen,* 342ff.

83. *Differenzschrift,* 72. In the preceding paragraph (71–72) Hegel has explained that the ideal and the real themselves form a polarity: the ideal, as the form of knowledge, predominates in intelligence; the real, as the form of being, predominates in nature. But both poles manifest themselves in both intelligence and nature, in intelligence as a "subjective subject-object" in nature as an "objective subject-object."

84. Ibid., 72–73. In this passage I have translated the verb *entzweien (entzweyen)* simply as "to divide," though it was already becoming a heavily loaded technical term in Hegel's vocabulary. It is after all this *Entzweiung,* this bifurcation or diremption or estrangement, that produces the proliferating oppositions: as polar concepts in thought, or as the *Aussereinander* of distinct things spatially "outside one another" in nature.

85. *Über die wissenschaftlichen Behandlungsarten des Naturrechts,* 462–64 (Knox trans., 108–112).

86. Ibid., 464. As the distinction is made in this passage, the Absolute does indeed intuit or behold itself *(es sich selbst anschaut)* in its "infinite expansion" in nature, but it comes to conscious recognition "as its self" only in its infinite reintegration *(Zurücknehmen)* in spirit.

87. *Differenzschrift,* 8. Schleiermacher's *Reden über die Religion* had already created something of a sensation. Since Hegel does not refer to the author by name, either here or in *Glauben und Wissen,* it is not certain whether he knew who had written it.

88. *Glauben und Wissen,* 316–17; cf. 323.

89. Ibid., 385.

90. Ibid., 385–86. Regarding the splintering effect of this religious subjectivism, Hegel further points out that the resulting "allgemeinen Atomistik" is nicely suited to the principle of the separation of church and state that was so dear to the Enlightenment. Protestant subjectivism and Protestant sectarianism go hand in hand. I shall have occasion to comment in more detail on Hegel's opposition to both. He never abandoned the "catholicity" and public efficacy of his ideal of Volksreligion. That, and not merely his well-known scorn of mere "feeling" that could not attain rational form, lay behind his continued animus against the theological position of Schleiermacher.

91. Ibid., 379.

92. Ibid. Hegel speaks of "faith" in similar terms in the *Differenzschrift:* "This relation or connection of limitation applied to the absolute, a connection in which only the placing in opposition is present in consciousness, while being totally unconscious of the identity, is called *faith.*" Faith in this sense can grasp "the holy and the divine . . . only as object" (21).

93. *Glauben und Wissen,* 399. Hegel goes on to say that this "third position"—"which is truly the first and only"—is no more to be found in the Fichtean system than in Jacobi's. The quotation is from Jacobi's *Werke,* 3:49.

94. Ibid., 407.

95. *Differenzschrift,* 75. The "original identity" referred to in this rather obscure passage already has in its "unconscious contraction" both subjective and objective forms: feeling and matter. But that contraction should not be confused with the "self-constituting contraction in the self-knowing point of (subjective) reason," which negates or stands in opposition to the "expansion" into nature.

96. *Glauben und Wissen,* 407. I have added italics to emphasize the polarities: possibility/actuality, subjective/objective. The italicizing of "in itself" is Hegel's, and significantly points up his quarrel with Fichte, which is the chief concern in this passage: According to the "ideal of the moral world-order," lampooned a bit in examples of volcanos burning out, earthquakes becoming tamer and people less warlike, the redemption is a process of progressive improvement, and blessedness or sanctification is *jenseits;* whereas for Hegel the world is already *an sich* redeemed. One should not read the technical meaning Hegel later gave this term into its present use, as if he were saying that the redemption is implicit, in essence, rather than manifest; for his point, contra Fichte, is the opposite.

97. Ibid., 75–76. While this particular formulation of the relation among art, religion, and speculation is by no means a casual passing thought, still in its details it represents a transitional position in the development of Hegel's thinking. He did not long regard religion as he does here, under Schelling's influence, as a mode of art, nor did he continue for long to balance this religion-art with speculation in such precise equilibrium. In the mature system, of course, art, religion, and philosophy are arranged in an ascending order of adequacy to the Idea. Yet even in his lectures on the philosophy of religion, delivered during the last decade of his life, Hegel still spoke of philosophy as a form of worship *(Vorlesungen über die Philosophie der Religion,* ed. Lasson [Hamburg: Felix

Meiner, 1966], I-1, pp. 29, 30); and the essential affinity of the three forms of absolute spirit, so carefully detailed in this early work, was an insight that found a permanent place in his thinking. The ascending order, art, religion, philosophy, lends itself so well to a kind of schoolroom recitation that among many of his interpreters the easy formula of this ein, zwei, drei has eclipsed the more subtle point that all three are internally conjoined as modes of absolute spirit.

98. *Das Verhältniss des Skepticismus zur Philosophie*, in *JkS*, 207–8. The concepts expressed in every speculative proposition must be so understood that they are at the same time aufgehoben, "or are unified in such a manner that they contradict themselves; otherwise it would not be a proposition of reason but of the understanding." There are of course also types of skepticism that do not retain this inherent relation to reason, but simply negate without elevating to a higher truth.

99. *Differenzschrift*, 15–16. The passage appears in the section on "The Need of Philosophy." The source of this need, we recall, is dualism, *Entzweiung* in its many forms. Pouring scorn on the notion that philosophy must have presuppositions, Hegel argues that the only thing presupposed in philosophy is the problem created by dualistic thinking, though such dualism is itself presupposed by *Reflexionsphilosophie*. In this ironical sense there are two opposing presuppositions: the absolute itself, and "the division into being and non-being, into concept and being, into finitude and infinitude." Thus "the task of philosophy" (according to the passage omitted in the quotation) is to unite these two presuppositions, to posit being in the non-being, as becoming, and so forth.

See also 20 for another passage in which Hegel employs this imagery of light and darkness.

100. According to reminiscences of one Bernhard Abeken, who complains of the banishment of God, faith, redemption, and immortality in the new teachings, Hegel opened his first course of lectures that way, "die Worte Dantes zugerufen, Lasciate ogui speranza voi ch' entrate." To which Abeken adds, his worst fears confirmed, "I wept the bitterest tears." Quoted in *Berichten*, 41. Abeken was clearly in no condition to notice whether Hegel uttered these words with a twinkle in his eye.

101. *Glauben und Wissen*, 413.

102. Cf. the systematic use of "intuition" and "concept" (*Anschauung* and *Begriff*) in *System der Sittlichkeit*, an unpublished treatise dating from the same period, that I shall introduce in the next section. In the opening sentence Hegel remarks that the Idea is none other than the identity of *Anschauung* and *Begriff*.

103. *Glauben und Wissen*, 413–14.

104. One of the essays in the *Critical Journal*, *Über das Verhältniss der Naturphilosophie zue Philosophie überhaupt*, declares that "we" do not recognize as a genuine philosophy any philosophy "that is not in principle already religion." But at the same time, it calls for a new religion with an "absolute gospel," synthesizing the painful earnestness of the Christian quest for redemption with the already reconciled beauty of Greek paganism (*JkS*, 271–74). Paganism raised the finite to the infinite; Christianity, particularly in that mystical side of it that not even Protestantism entirely succeeded in expunging, had grasped the descent of the infinite to the finite. Put the two together, their mutual opposition reconciled, and "then is heaven truly won again, and the absolute gospel proclaimed." "Philosophy" already celebrates this reconciliation, indeed "the life of the newly-risen Godhead" is already recognizable in philosophy itself (ibid., 274).

The authorship of this essay, however, was the subject of a particularly bitter dispute in the 1830s between the followers of Schelling and the original editors of Hegel's works. Schelling himself claimed it at that time, declaring that Hegel had not written a single letter of it; but some of the Hegelian circle were still not convinced, including Michelet, who had set off the dispute by including it in the first volume of Hegel's works and claimed that Hegel had assured him in a conversation some years before that he had written it (see Editorischer Bericht, ibid., 543–46). The Hegelian contenders in this rather childish dispute wanted to claim for the master as much independence from Schelling as possible in the formative years of German idealism, indeed to claim that Hegel had primarily influenced Schelling at that time rather than the reverse, as had always been supposed. Why Michelet thought that Hegel's independence would have been proven by his having written an essay in Schelling's very *style* is not clear. Anyway, Hegel's modern editors concede authorship to Schelling. The views sketched above, however, are consonant with some of those expressed in Hegel's unpublished manuscripts during this period, if in rather less facile form.

105. Heinz Kimmerle, "Jenaer Dokumente—B. Erläuterungen," *Hegel-Studien*, 1967, 4:85–87, presents the data on Hegel's publishing plans during the Jena years. Throughout this section I shall be presupposing and sometimes reporting the important information Kimmerle presents in the assembled documents and his *Erläuterungen*, and also in his establishment of the order in which Hegel's Jena manuscripts, published and unpublished, were written, in his numbered list and commentary, "Zur Chronologie von Hegels Jenaer Schriften," in the same volume of *Hegel-Studien*, 125–76.

106. Rosenkranz, *Leben*, 132–41. Haym also refers to this manuscript (*Hegel und seine Zeit*, 159–67, 414–46, 509), and a composite text of the fragment following Rosenkranz but with additions and corrections by Haym appears in *Dokumente*, 314–25.

Die Verfassung Deutschlands and *System der Sittlichkeit* are both scheduled for publication in volume 5 of the new *Gesammelte Werke: Schriften und Entwürfe, 1799–1808.* They were both published in Hegel, *Schriften zur Politik und Rechtsphilosophie*, edited by Georg Lasson (2d ed. [Leipzig: Felix Meiner, 1923]), and *System der Sittlichkeit* alone has appeared in a small volume reprinted from the Lasson edition (Hamburg: Felix Meiner, 1967); this reprint is the text I shall cite here. A translation under the title *System of Ethical Life*, with pagination based on the 1923 edition, has been published with a detailed introduction by H. S. Harris in *System of Ethical Life (1802/03) and First Philosophy of Spirit* (Part 3 of the System of Speculative Philosophy 1803/4), trans. H. S. Harris and T. M. Knox (Albany: State University of New York Press, 1979). The edition of *Die Verfassung Deutschlands* I shall cite appears in Hegel, *Politische Schriften,* Nachwort von Jürgen Habermas (Frankfurt am Main: Suhrkamp, 1966). It is translated by Sir Malcolm Knox in Knox and Pelczynski, *Hegel's Political Writings* (Oxford: Oxford University Press, 1964), 143–242.

107. Quoted from a lost lecture manuscript in Rosenkranz, *Leben*, 190–91. Actually Rosenkranz put together a long section (178–98) out of diverse materials dating from various periods, but these remarks on logic and metaphysics very likely stem from the lectures of winter 1802–3, or even as early as those of winter 1801–2. (See Kimmerle, "Zur Chronologie von Hegels Jenaer Schriften," *Hegel-Studien* 4:140, 150.) Their language and premises certainly seem to belong to the period of the *Differenzschrift* and the *Critical Journal*.

Hegel's early conception of logic as a science of the reflective understanding, metaphysics as the rational science, is represented in his lecture announcement for summer 1802: "*Logicam et Metaphysicam* sive systema reflexionis et rationis" ("Jenaer Dokumente," *Hegel-Studien* 4:53).

108. For a splendid treatment of this parallel, see the essay by Johann Heinrich Trede, "Hegels frühe Logik (1801–1803/4). Versuch einer systematischen Rekonstruktion," *Hegel-Studien* (Bonn: 1972), 7:123–68. On the basis of admittedly fragmentary evidence,

Trede argues that this early logic differs radically, in both content and method from the conception of logic Hegel began to develop in the manuscripts of 1804–5.

109. Rosenkranz, 191–92. This sense of the identity of all genuine philosophy echoes the section in the Introduction to the *Differenzschrift* discussed above.

110. These manuscripts constitute volume 6 of the new *Gesammelte Werke: Jenaer Systementwürfe I*, ed. Klaus Düsing and Heinz Kimmerle (Hamburg: Felix Meiner, 1975), to which I shall refer here. They had previously been collected under the title, *Jenenser Realphilosophie I*, ed. Johannes Hoffmeister (Leipzig: Felix Meiner, 1932), under the impression that they paralleled the "philosophia realis" that was the subject of Hegel's lectures in the winter semester of 1805–6, the manuscript for which Hoffmeister edited under the title *Jenenser Realphilosophie II*. But unlike that "real-philosophy" the scope of these lectures clearly includes a logic and metaphysics. Besides eliminating the misleading title, the new edition significantly reorders the manuscripts and presents many details more accurately.

A translation of the Philosophy of Spirit from these lecture manuscripts, with pagination correlated with *Jenaer Systementwürfe I*, trans. H. S. Harris, has been published with an introduction by Harris in *System of Ethical Life and First Philosophy of Spirit*, cited in note 106.

111. *Jenaer Systementwürfe I*, 268.

112. Ibid., 265.

113. Ibid., 264–66.

114. Ibid., 273.

115. Ibid., 277ff. Yet here too, consciousness is said to have aether as its "absolute element" (277), and "the absolute spirit of a people is the absolute, universal element, aether" (315).

116. *Logik, Metaphysik, Naturphilosophie: Fragment einer Reinschrift, 1804–05*, has been published in volume 7 of *Gesammelte Werke: Jenaer Systementwürfe II*, Rolf-Peter Horstmann and Johann Heinrich Trede (Hamburg: Felix Meiner, 1971). This is the manuscript that comprises most of that "first system" Rosenkranz thought Hegel brought with him to Jena from Frankfurt, thus introducing untold confusion into earlier efforts to reconstruct Hegel's intellectual development. See note 2.

The first two parts of this manuscript have been translated in G. W. F. Hegel, *The Jena System, 1804–5: Logic and Metaphysics*, translation edited by John W. Burbidge and George di Giovanni, introduction and explanatory notes by H. S. Harris (Kingston and Montreal: McGill-Queen's University Press, 1986). This translation, a collaborative effort by a team of scholars, indicates the pagination of *Systementwürfe II*.

117. E.g., *Systementwürfe II*, 120, 175. The problem of reconstructing the structure of this Logic is discussed in the Editorischer Bericht.

118. Ibid., 120–27. Hegel still frequently resorted to the notion of *Indifferenz*, with which he had expressed the transcendental intuition in his earlier critical writings, e.g, 139, 160–61, and *Systementwürfe I*, 264, 273.

119. *Systementwürfe II*, 127. Certain oft-used terms in Hegel's vocabulary, e.g. aufheben, Volk, Geist, Volksgeist, Weltgeist, have turned up so often in our study that there seems little point in italicizing them any more. Perhaps the reader will join me in welcoming them as resident aliens in the English language.

120. *Phänomenologie des Geistes*, ed. Hoffmeister, 19 (Miller trans., 9; Baillie trans., 79), and 26, 42–43 for further polemics against such "formalism" and against "the enthusiasm which begins immediately with absolute knowledge" as if it were shot "out of a pistol." See also Chapter 1, note 24.

121. Already in the *Differenzschrift* Hegel had claimed that the whole of philosophy is speculatively derived from a single "absolute ground principle," the identity of identity and nonidentity (*JkS*, 23–27). Trede argues that in the earlier treatments of logic, the principles of the reflective Understanding were aufgehoben by being transmuted into antinomies, the identity and nonidentity that were disclosed as identical by the invoking of this principle in the concluding section of the Logic (Trede, "Hegels frühe Logik," 139–43, 159–61, 165–66). Here, however, "Knowing" is the totality that completes the Logic, and is then articulated in the first part of the Metaphysics as a "System von Grundsätzen"; but each ground principle within this system expresses the "ground," the essential *(an sich)* identity of the speculative antinomies, identity/contradiction, one/many. *Systementwürfe II*, 134.

122. *Systementwürfe II*, 138–39.

123. Ibid., 140–41. Precisely in the *Indifferenz* of subject and substance the meaning of both "subject" and "substance" changes. But the identity is still invested in single souls, each one among many. It is not yet the absolute identity of substance and subject.

124. Ibid., 142–43.

125. Ibid., 150–53.

126. Ibid., 154.

127. Ibid., 157. See 157–60.

128. Ibid., 174.

129. Ibid., 176–77. See also 174–75.

130. Rosenkranz, *Leben*, 198–99, reports that in what he calls "Hegel's Wastebook 1803–1806" there are copious excerpts from works in diverse fields of natural science, and also some polemical remarks against the "formlessness" of Jakob Böhme's writings on nature and against the unscientific character of the Schellingian philosophy of nature, particularly as it was developed by some of Schelling's followers. (The manuscript of this "Wastebook" has been lost, though Rosenkranz preserved some "aphorisms" from it in an appendix to his biography of Hegel and elsewhere.) Rosenkranz also quotes, 181–87, extensive excerpts from a lost lecture manuscript that likely dates from this period, in which Hegel inveighs against the "alien terminology," the "empty formalism," the Romanticism and apparent arbitrariness of the language of Schellingian natural philosophy, particularly in its use among Schelling's followers.

131. *Systementwürfe II*, 177–78, 188–92.

132. For scholars interested in the minute details of Hegel's intellectual development, the loss of this manuscript is particularly frustrating, because his famous lectures on the subject during the 1820s really founded the subject as a modern philosophical discipline. Rosenkranz's report on the manuscript is very sketchy, mentioning what he thought were a few high points (201–2), and Michelet mentioned it and used it as a source, together with later materials from which it is impossible to sort it out, in his edition of the *Vorlesungen über die Geschichte der Philosophie* in the original *Werke*, vol. 13.

133. The *Realphilosophie* of 1805–6 is included in volume 8 of the *Gesammelte Werke, Jenaer Systementwürfe III*, ed. Rolf-Peter Horstmann in collaboration with Johann Heinrich Trede, together with an updated "Chronologie der Manuskripte Hegels in den Bänden 4 bis 9," by Heinz Kimmerle (Hamburg: Felix Meiner, 1976). The text is also available under the title *Jenaer Realphilosophie*, ed. Johannes Hoffmeister (Hamburg: Felix Meiner, 1969), a reprint of the edition Hoffmeister published in 1931 under the misleading title *Jenenser Realphilosophie II*. See note 110 above; the manuscript of 1805–6 is not the second *Realphilosophie*, but the only one Hegel ever composed as such.

134. Rosenkranz, *Leben*, 214; also Gabler, who was present at these and other lecture courses during the fourth period, in *Berichten*, 66–67. For the announcements of courses,

and class lists compiled as the semester began, that sometimes registered the change in subject, see Kimmerle, "Jenaer Dokumente," *Hegel-Studien,* 4:54–55, 62–63. The reference to metaphysics did not yet drop out of the notices altogether. Though the class list for summer 1805, is headed "*Collegium privatum* von *Prof. Hegel über die Logik,*" the one for summer 1806, which had been announced as speculative philosophy or logic was headed "*Collegium privatum* über Logik und Metaphysik oder speculative Philosophie"—though Hegel went on to lecture, in fact, on phenomenology and logic.

135. *Jenaer Realphilosophie,* 3–4; also *Jenaer Systementwürfe III,* 3–4.

136. E.g., Pöggeler, as one among many recent interpreters who express a preference for one or another "early" Hegel over the Hegel of the later system, in part 4 of his essay on "Hegels Jenaer Systemkonzeption," *Hegels Idee einer Phänomenologie des Geistes,* 158ff. Pöggeler is surely correct in distinguishing the philosophical writings of the Jena period from the "pre- and extra-philosophical cogitations" of the 1790s (110–114). But to call the Jena writings philosophical still should not imply that they contain a philosophy or a succession of philosophies.

137. *Systementwürfe II,* 189; repeated verbatim in the *Jenaer Realphilosophie* of 1805–6, 3, which adds, "for it is Being." (Also in *Jenaer Systementwürfe III,* 3.) We are generally following here the account given in the *Logik, Metaphysik, Naturphilosophie* of 1804–5, *Systementwürfe II,* 187ff., but many of the same expressions turn up in the opening pages of the *Realphilosophie* of the following year.

138. *Systementwürfe II,* 189.

139. Ibid., 190. Though this confusing notion of aether mercifully drops out of the later system, it marks the beginning of a line of thinking that issued in that equivocal doctrine of Being with which the *Logik* of 1812 opened. Its identity with Nothing, that Hegel mentions here and had stressed on the previous page, reminds one of that identity of Sein and Nichts that requires the more determinate categories of the Logic.

140. Ibid., 190–91.

141. Ibid., 141; see also 150, 158.

142. Ibid., 160, 170, and variations on this point are made in numerous references to the highest being in this manuscript.

143. Ibid., 171. Considering that the section on "world" in the Objective Metaphysics opens with an extended argument for the essential identity of freedom and necessity (142–43), it is likely correct to see in Hegel's critique of Objective Metaphysics not only an assessment of traditional metaphysical notions but also a criticism of the form in which Kant expressed his three postulates of practical reason: a freedom of the will contradicting natural necessity, the immortality of the soul, and the existence of God as the highest being.

144. Rosenkranz, *Leben,* 192–93. It is not clear what manuscript Rosenkranz is referring to here. It is evidently not the manuscript of 1804–5, to which we referred in our account of the aether above, despite the similarity of the language. For Rosenkranz thought that manuscript was the one Hegel brought with him from Frankfurt to Jena, and says that Hegel still loved, as he had in that "first exposition of metaphysics," to speak this way. Rosenkranz introduces his reference to this whole theme (192) by referring to the lectures on *Realphilosophie* of summer, 1806, but there is nothing of quite this sort in the text we have of the *Realphilosophie* of 1805–6, so one cannot date these remarks with much certainty.

145. *Systementwürfe II,* 187–88.

146. Rosenkranz, *Leben,* 192–93.

147. Rosenkranz, *Leben,* 101–2, contains a brief discussion of this lost fragment, but he had published an excerpt from it in Prutz's *Literarhistorischem Taschenbuch,* 1844, 159–64, substantially reprinted in *Dokumente,* 303–6.

148. *Dokumente,* 304–5.

149. Ibid., 305.

150. Pöggeler, for instance, seems to prefer Hegel's thinking in Jena to his mature philosophy because of what seems to Pöggeler the facile use of teleology in the latter to deny the ultimate truth of tragedy. See "Hegel und die griechische Tragödie," *Hegels Idee einer Phänomenologie des Geistes,* particularly 104–9.

151. *Dokumente,* 304. Actually the rather forced geometrical design is further complicated by the fact that the second internal triangle is also somehow a rectangle, representing the provisional opposition between the world's evil and the divine purity in the movement into otherness.

A mysterious and possibly related drawing that may or may not have been drawn by Hegel himself has been found among his Jena papers: an equilateral triangle, blank within and with the word "Spiritus" appearing on each side followed by several signs or figures (moon, stars, cross, and so forth), and a smaller equilateral triangle drawn outside each of its three angles; it differs most importantly in that respect from the triangle of internal triangles Hegel seems to have had in mind in our fragment. This drawing is reproduced and discussed in relation not only to our fragment and to Christian symbolism, but also to occult, magical uses of such signs, in Helmut Schneider, "Zur Dreiecks-Symbolik bei Hegel," *Hegel-Studien,* 1973, 8:55–77. The drawing certainly is intriguing, but with so little known about it or how it found its way among Hegel's effects, Schneider's suggestion (75) that it must be included at least conditionally in the "corpus hegelianum" is surely the nethermost extremity of the solemn attention given Hegel's manuscript materials.

152. *JkS,* 449.

153. *Die Verfassung Deutschlands, Politische Schriften* (ed. Habermas), 37. (*Hegel's Political Writings,* trans. T. M. Knox with an introductory essay by Z. A. Pelczynski [Oxford: Oxford University Press, 1964], 158–59.)

154. *Die Verfassung Deutschlands,* 82; see 74–84 (Knox trans., 193; 189–95).

155. *System der Sittlichkeit,* 56–68. The glorification of the nobility one finds in this work was greatly modified in the *Realphilosophie* of 1805–6, but one finds aspects of it in Hegel's later argument for monarchy, which is also based on the need for someone in the society to wield supreme authority on behalf of the society as a whole, apart from private, commercial, or narrow class interests.

156. Rosenkranz, *Leben,* 133. As I remarked in note 106, this important lecture manuscript is available only in Rosenkranz's report, but Haym, who seems to have been the last to see it before it was lost, assures us that Rosenkranz quoted most of it almost verbatim. Hoffmeister reprinted it with a few additions and corrections by Haym in *Dokumente,* 314–25. This document does not directly draw the parallel between religious renunciation and the sacrifice of the warrior, but Hegel does so in *System der Sittlichkeit.*

157. Rosenkranz, *Leben,* 134.

158. Ibid.

159. *System der Sittlichkeit,* 53.

160. Ibid., 54.

161. Ibid., 54–55.

162. Hegel particularly speaks in this document of the priests and the elders (the aged nobility) as persons peculiarly free of the special economic class interests that divide the Volk, and therefore as figures who are able purely to celebrate its universal life (ibid.,

71–73). In this sanguine view of the priests and elders, and of the ruling class generally, Hegel appears to have dismissed the lessons of the Enlightenment too easily, in particular the element of simple realism in its diatribes against grasping aristocracy and priestcraft.

163. *Systementwürfe I,* 274, 314ff.

164. Ibid., 276–77. See also the Treatise on *Naturrecht,* in *JkS,* 463.

165. Ibid., 315.

166. E.g., in the passage from *Glauben und Wissen* quoted above.

167. Hegel did not introduce the term "world history" into his writings until the *Realphilosophie* of 1805–6. But as H. B. Acton observes in his introduction to the Knox translation of *Natural Law,* 43, the concept is present in this treatise "in all but name."

168. Treatise on *Naturrecht,* 481–82; the chain metaphor is also employed, 479.

169. Ibid., 479.

170. Ibid., 480, 482–83. Hegel goes on in these passages, in a way that again reminds us of the reflections on religious positivity during the 1790s, to argue that such laws and customs do become positive when they are merely an arbitrarily enforced legacy of a dead past; the manner in which the living is distinguished from the dead is remarkably reminiscent of the earliest Bern fragments. But laws that at their inception represent a negation and dissolution of the "sittlichen Totalität" are dead from the start.

171. There is a very short fragment that the editors of *Systementwürfe I* have appended, 330–31, to the manuscript of 1803–4, which treats the historical displacement of the Volk and its decline, under the rubric of comedy—but divine comedy! In this connection the fragment contains a reference, rare in the Jena manuscripts, to the Weltgeist.

172. E.g., *Phänomenologie des Geistes,* 506–7 (Miller trans., 439–40; Baillie trans., 729–32), but implicitly in the whole chapter on Spirit. The *Rechtsphilosophie* of 1821 concludes with world history as the higher moment into which every Volksgeist was aufgehoben; see especially §340, but also the section on world history that immediately follows.

173. *Jenaer Realphilosophie,* 242, also 243–44; *Systementwürfe III,* 254, also 255–56.

174. *Jenaer Realphilosophie,* 249.

175. Ibid., 256–57. The anticipation of Marx is obvious here, particularly the treatment of money and the victimization of the proletarian class in Marx's manuscripts of 1844. But far from regarding the state as any sort of solution to this dehumanization, Marx considered it together with all Hegel's higher forms of the spirit as mere superstructure built on and determined by this economic foundation.

176. Ibid., 250.

177. This is the striking manuscript only preserved in the quotations and/or paraphrases of Rosenkranz and Haym, not to be confused with the treatise on *Natural Law* published in the *Critical Journal.*

178. Rosenkranz, *Leben,* introduces this typology with a paragraph, 135, in which it is impossible to disentangle quotation from paraphrase, offering general speculative characterizations of the three forms. He remarks that Hegel employed the language of current philosophy of nature in showing how religion had to follow "the general three dimensions of reason," and at the same time proceeded "world-historically."

Rosenkranz may have used this paragraph to splice together what Haym suggests were two different manuscripts, the one containing the general characterization of religious cultus to which we referred earlier, and the other containing the historical-typological construction presently under discussion.

179. Ibid., 135–36; reprinted without alteration in *Dokumente,* 317.

180. Rosenkranz, *Leben,* 136; *Dokumente,* 317–18.

181. Following the version in *Dokumente,* 318, which supplements Rosenkranz's account, *Leben,* 136, with a passage quoted from the manuscript by Haym, *Hegel und seine Zeit,* 415.

182. Rosenkranz, *Leben,* 136; *Dokumente,* 318.

183. In the opening sentence to the final paragraph of his report, 140, a sentence in which he is paraphrasing rather than directly quoting, Rosenkranz *(Leben)* reserves the third type for a form of religious life that is yet to appear. "Hegel at that time . . . believed," he says, "that out of Christianity through the *mediation of philosophy* a *third* form of religion would take shape." He then proceeds to quote a passage to which we will shortly refer, in which Hegel prophesies the rise of a new religion; that concluding passage, in fact, is the only one in his report on this manuscript that Rosenkranz does place in quotation marks, though Haym *(Hegel und seine Zeit)* tells us that the whole report is taken almost verbatim from the manuscript. While it is probably safe to conclude, therefore, that Hegel did indeed hold that the third type must await the appearance of this new religion, that point is not made in the material that seems to have been directly quoted, so it may be still safer to suspend judgment on the point, as the missing manuscript may chance to turn up! For the extended treatment of Christianity does in certain respects seem to furnish what is needed for a third type distinct from the second, while the remarks on the new religion are brief and understandably sketchy, and Rosenkranz's own comment on the relation to Christianity of the third form of religion is not very precise. Is Christianity only its point of departure, or is the new religion in fact only a third form of Christianity, beyond Catholicism and Protestantism?

184. Rosenkranz, *Leben,* 136–37; *Dokumente,* 319. Hoffmeister, the editor of *Dokumente,* regarded the phrase, "which had become unfaithful to nature," as an addition by Rosenkranz, and relegated it to a footnote.

185. Rosenkranz, *Leben,* 137; *Dokumente,* 319.

186. Rosenkranz, *Leben,* 137; *Dokumente,* 320.

187. See Rosenkranz, *Leben,* 134. There is, we recall, some question whether that section of Rosenkranz's report really referred to the same manuscript as these systematic/historical sections before us now. But Rosenkranz treated them as one manuscript, and the use in both sections of this same unusual term, *Nationalgott,* and also the reference in the former to reconciliation as the "ground-idea of religion" support that.

188. Rosenkranz, *Leben,* 137–38; *Dokumente,* 320. The word *Geschichte* here for the sake of consistency translated "history," might in this context better be rendered as "story."

189. *Phänomenologie des Geistes,* 29 (Miller trans., 19; Baillie trans., 93).

190. Rosenkranz, *Leben,* 139; *Dokumente,* 322. In this passage Hegel refers to Christianity, rather anomalously, as a *Volksreligion.*

191. Rosenkranz, *Leben,* 139–40; *Dokumente,* 323.

192. Rosenkranz, *Leben,* 137; *Dokumente,* 319.

193. Rosenkranz, *Leben,* 138–39; *Dokumente,* 322.

194. Rosenkranz, *Leben,* 140; *Dokumente,* 324.

195. *Dokumente,* 324, places here a remark quoted by Haym, *Hegel und seine Zeit,* 165; it is not found in Rosenkranz's report.

196. Rosenkranz speaks *(Leben,* 140; see note 184) of "a third form of religion" issuing "from Christianity through the mediation of philosophy." Haym *(Hegel und seine Zeit,* 165, quoted in *Dokumente,* 324) says that "in Protestantism consciousness comes through philosophy to a breakthrough" that will carry it over the impasse. Through philosophy, he says, apparently quoting directly from the manuscript, "reason" receives "its vitality and nature its spirit back."

197. Rosenkranz, *Leben*, 141; *Dokumente*, 325. The concluding two sentences of Rosenkranz's report, from which the quoted material is taken, speak more particularly of this knowledge as insight into the "chain of absolute necessity" in which every individual is a link. The individual gains "mastery over a greater length of this chain" to the extent that he knows where "the great necessity" is moving. Nothing in the report quite prepares for this particular characterization of philosophical *Erkenntnis*, and the relation of this passage to the rest is a little puzzling, though it is characteristic enough of Hegel's thinking during this period. The same term, *Erkennen* (knowing), occupies the pivotal position between Logic and Metaphysics in the system of 1804–5, and Hegel may still have had something of the sort in mind in linking philosophy to world-historical *Wissen* (knowledge, with perhaps a more scientific connotation) at the conclusion of the *Realphilosophie* of 1805–6.

198. Following the version of this sentence in *Dokumente*, 324. Rosenkranz's original version (*Leben*, 140–41) reads, "reason will have its reality reborn as an ethical spirit, that can have the boldness to take on its pure form."

199. See note 104.

200. *Jenaer Realphilosophie* (ed. Hoffmeister), 263; *Systementwürfe III*, 278. Recognition *(Anerkanntsein)* as the "spiritual element" is a central concept in the *Phenomenology*, and will receive major attention in the next chapter. See the splendid monograph by Robert R. Williams, *Recognition: Fichte and Hegel on the Other* (Albany: State University of New York Press, 1992). Williams traces this motif to Fichte, but points up Hegel's very different development of it as a crucial concept in Hegel's theory of intersubjectivity and social philosophy in the *Phenomenology* and elsewhere. A fascinating final chapter treats the engagement with this Hegelian motif in Husserl, Sartre, and Levinas.

201. *Realphilosophie*, 266–67; *Systementwürfe III*, 280–81.

202. *Realphilosophie*, 270; *Systementwürfe III*, 284. In the context, Hegel is attacking the separation of church and state, and remarks that *both* are incomplete to the extent that they are unreconciled. He does attempt to do justice to the church's function, for example, in cultivating the "inner" life. But he is quite explicit that it is the state which rules, and that the church must serve the state (*Realphilosophie*, 271; *Systementwürfe III*, 285).

203. *Realphilosophie*, 268; *Systementwürfe III*, 282.

204. *Realphilosophie*, 269; *Systementwürfe III*, 283.

205. *Realphilosophie*, 269; *Systementwürfe III*, 284. Hegel opens the final subsection of the manuscript with this remark. The heading of this subsection, "Synthetic Connection of the State and the Church," does not suggest all that is included in it, since the subsection is as much concerned with the relation of philosophy and religion as state and church. The entire final section we have been and will be interpreting here is entitled "Art, Religion and Science [*Wissenschaft*]."

206. *Realphilosophie*, 269–70; *Systementwürfe III*, 284. The word *eingesehen* is awkwardly rendered, "seen into," in order to preserve the etymological connection with *Einsicht*, "insight," which is important in what follows.

207. *Realphilosophie*, 270; *Systementwürfe III*, 284.

208. *Realphilosophie*, 271–72; *Systementwürfe III*, 285–86.

209. For example, *Phänomenologie des Geistes*, 553–56 (Miller trans., 483–86; Baillie trans., 794–98); *Enzyklopädie* (1830), §§ 24, Zusatz, and 571–73; *Einleitung in die Geschichte der Philosophie*, 191–92; *Philosophie der Religion*, I-1, 28–32, 291–98.

210. *Realphilosophie*, 242–53; *Systementwürfe III*, 253–65.

211. *Realphilosophie*, 244–45; *Systementwürfe III*, 256–57. Apparently with Rousseau still in mind, though without anywhere directly mentioning him, Hegel goes on to discuss

the notion of social contract as an account of how this general will arises from the wills of individuals. But he himself gives more credence to the ability of "great men" to impose their will on others, not through physical strength but through a certain psychic power that makes others acknowledge the great man as their master: "They obey him against their will; against their will his will is their will"—even without their recognizing it consciously (246). In this connection Hegel mentions Theseus and the French Revolution, and praises Machiavelli's *Prince*.

212. *Realphilosophie*, 254–57; *Systementwürfe III*, 267–70. Needless to say, I am presenting here the barest essentials of the analysis. I noted above the baleful effects Hegel saw in the ascent of the merchant class and its values into control of an industrial order concerned solely with profit, thus creating a new class of unrivaled misery at the bottom of the social order.

213. *Realphilosophie*, 257–62; *Systementwürfe III*, 270–75.

214. *Realphilosophie*, 262–63; *Systementwürfe III*, 276–77. This section is presented in a very rough sketch that is hard to summarize, but I think that is the gist of it.

215. *Realphilosophie*, 263; *Systementwürfe III*, 277–78.

216. *Realphilosophie*, 263; *Systementwürfe III*, 277.

217. *Realphilosophie*, 264; *Systementwürfe III*, 278. Actually there are some intriguing hints about the relation of the various artistic media to time and (implicitly) to space, to hearing and (implicitly) to seeing, and to various contents. But it is all very sketchy. The influence of Lessing's *Laokoon* seems to be in the background.

218. E.g., see the *Enzyklopädie* of 1830, §§ 556–57.

219. *Realphilosophie*, 264–65; *Systementwürfe III*, 278–79.

220. *Realphilosophie*, 264; *Systementwürfe III*, 278–79. Cf. Lessing's *Laokoon*, chap. 17. Kierkegaard proceeds on the same premises in his essay on "The Musical Erotic" in *Either/Or*, vol. 1.

221. *Realphilosophie*, 265; *Systementwürfe III*, 279.

222. *Realphilosophie*, 266; *Systementwürfe III*, 280.

223. *Realphilosophie*, 266; *Systementwürfe III*, 280.

224. *Realphilosophie*, 265; *Systementwürfe III*, 279.

225. *Realphilosophie*, 268; *Systementwürfe III*, 282.

226. *Realphilosophie*, 272; *Systementwürfe III*, 286.

227. *Realphilosophie*, 272; *Systementwürfe III*, 286.

228. *Realphilosophie*, 273; *Systementwürfe III*, 287.

229. *Confessions*, book XI, x–xiv. Augustine's remarks on the subject were provoked by the impudence of those who doubted the doctrine of creation, and demanded that Christians explain what God was doing before he created heaven and earth.

230. *Realphilosophie*, 273; *Systementwürfe III*, 287. The passage I have placed in a separate, final paragraph is a marginal addition in Hegel's manuscript.

231. In a confusing passage in Hegel's discussion of time and eternity to which we have referred, he uses the word *Erfüllung* to designate what is achieved in actual time. The context is his Augustinian argument that there is no previous state of affairs before the creation of time: "Previously, before *erfüllte* time exists, there is no time at all." Now *Erfüllung* can mean both "fulfillment" and, literally, "filling up." This fulfillment or filling up, Hegel says, "is the actual returned into itself out of empty time." This empty time seems identical with "no time at all," but Hegel also writes in a way that could be construed as identifying it with "the thought of time." "But if we say, *before* the world—time without *Erfüllung*—the thought of time, just the thinking, the reflected-in-itself." The punctuation, however, is ambiguous. The dashes in the manuscript often cover considerable leaps in meaning and syntax. Furthermore, even if Hegel does mean to say that the

thought of time, previously identified with eternity, is without *Erfüllung,* the ambiguity concerning *Erfüllung* remains: he may mean only that the thought of time requires the fulfillment of expression in real time in order for spirit to exist; or he might mean in addition that it is filled up with determinate content only in virtue of its passage into real time. *Realphilosophie,* 273; *Systementwürfe III,* 287.

IV

"The Recollection and the Golgotha of Absolute Spirit" in Hegel's *Phenomenology*

1. The Unhappy Consciousness

Hegel's discussion of the unhappy consciousness concludes the chapter of the *Phenomenology of Spirit* entitled "Self-Consciousness." I shall have some things to say about the design of that monumental work, and some more particular things to say about this enigmatic chapter. But let us begin by plunging into the text at this crucial point, and work out from there.

It soon becomes apparent that the unhappy consciousness is not the affliction of some person in particular, or of an identifiable community, or generation, or historical epoch. It is a universal crisis of self-conscious life, that occurs everywhere and always whenever spirit is being born. This unhappiness is the travail of conscious life giving birth to spirit. It is suffered not once but many times historically. In fact it is not so much a historical phenomenon as the precondition of self-consciously historical life, appearing in many different guises. Every person, every culture preserves at least a dark memory of this unhappiness or a dark premonition of it on the horizon, or both.

This unhappiness is no accidental misfortune. Human beings suffer many kinds of pain without thereby being unhappy in this sense. On the other hand a life can be relatively free of pain, successful in its undertakings, robust in health, and yet unhappy. A love affair, a military campaign, a painting, a commercial enterprise, the rearing of a child, can be unhappy regardless of success or failure, insofar as this psychic crisis has in some manner been invested in it. At first glance, indeed, this unhappiness seems to have little to do with what people ordinarily mean by the term. It appears to be a very peculiar, downright esoteric sort of unhappiness. But it is arguable that Hegel has actually identified the deep root of psychic misery in all unhappy conditions. The love affair, for instance, can be unsuccessful without being unhappy. The lovers can shrug their shoulders, nurse their hurt a little, and find other partners, as all their sensible elders advise. Plenty of fish in the sea. But if a lover invests the full passion of her hope for psychic fulfillment in just this love affair, its failure will be unhappy beyond consolation. So, perhaps, will its success. Conquering young Alexander, said to have died yearning for new worlds to conquer, is perhaps as unhappy as the monk, exhausted by austerities, who dies of unrequited longing for God.

The unhappy consciousness is infinite longing unsatisfied. Its longing is infinite, unlimited, because the subject of this longing is incomplete within itself so long as it is not united with its object. It experiences itself as a mere fragment of a psyche, yet sensitive enough to suffer its lack. It is bereft of itself. Yet for that very reason its longing necessarily remains unsatisfied. Who can supply a psyche with itself? The irony of this situation, according to Hegel, is that the object of this longing is indeed itself, and that is why it is always tantalizingly beyond reach: its predicament is that its "essential being" *(Wesen)* is "doubled," "contradictory." This internal rupture will be expressed in every project the unhappy consciousness undertakes, even if it seems to succeed; it is inherently divided against itself, yearning for its other half, really its true self, in every object of its longing. For only the subject and the object of this longing together make up a complete psychic life:

> This *unhappy, internally divided* consciousness, because this contradiction in its essential being is itself [present in] a *single*

consciousness, must therefore always have in the one consciousness the other as well, and so it is immediately driven out of
each in turn whenever it supposes it has achieved success and
has been brought to rest in unity. (H 158–59; M 126; B 251)[1]

The unhappy consciousness is essentially a unity, its two sides making
up a single psychic field, but it does not experience itself as a unity. In
Hegel's jargon, it is a unity "in itself" *(an sich),* but not "for itself" *(für
sich);* that is, for itself it does not yet so appear. To complete this
comment on terminological practice, which is uniform in the *Phenomenology:* We, who observe its ordeal, recognize that the two opposing
selves into which it is divided are in fact two sides of a single consciousness. That is, what it is "in itself" it is "for us" *(für uns)* who observe
it under the guidance of our phenomenologist. Hegel and we know,
furthermore, that it is the destiny of this divided consciousness to
realize its unity, to recognize it "for itself." For its destiny is to become
Geist—spirit. This unhappiness is in fact the ordeal through which
conscious life must pass in order to become spirit. Unhappy consciousness is the premonition and precondition of spirit; spirit is its fulfillment
and essential being. In itself it is already spirit, but it is spirit still at
odds with itself. It will eventually recognize what is true of it "in itself
" and "for us," when as spirit it will grasp its own concept. Then it will
be spirit in-and-for-itself. Hegel continues:

> Its true return into itself, however, or its reconciliation with
> itself, will exhibit the concept of spirit when it has come alive
> and stepped into existence, for what has already happened to it
> is this, that as a single undivided consciousness it is a double
> consciousness: it itself *is* the beholding of one self-consciousness
> in another, and it itself *is* both, and the unity of both is in its
> eyes also the essence; but *for itself* it is not yet itself this essence,
> not yet the unity of both. (H 159; M 126; B 251)

That is its unhappiness: that it does not seem to itself to be in possession
of its own true being. It is bereft of its animating force, like an ampu-
tated limb. What is left to it is spiritually dead, inessential.

Again we must remind ourselves that we are not dealing here with
anyone in particular. The unhappy consciousness is an odd sort of
archetype, the archetype of every form of alienated existence, instanti-
ated in quite diverse ways. Its true life is alien to it. Yet it is not some

other life. If the alien essence were not its own, the rupture would not cause it unhappiness. Though it does not recognize this essence as its own, its very unhappiness testifies that it is. That is the predicament, abstractly stated, but it can take endlessly varied forms.

Hegel goes on to suggest that the unhappy consciousness characteristically identifies this essence as "the simple unchangeable." It is simple in the antique metaphysical sense: indivisible, without parts, and therefore irrefragable and incorruptible. It is unchangeable because it is perfect, like the Aristotelian or Scholastic deity. In such a form the object of highest psychic desire might present itself, but it is a desire that cannot be fulfilled. What is left for the unessential, with which in its hopeless yearning the unhappy consciousness identifies itself, is the "manifold changeable." It is vulnerable from every side, threatened indeed with inner dissolution, carried up and down on the wheel of fortune. It is flawed, expendable, painfully limited: unessential. In its eyes, its own unessential being is utterly cut off from the essential.

> Both are *for it* beings alien to one another; it itself, because it is the consciousness of this contradiction, places itself on the side of the changeable consciousness and is itself the unessential; but as consciousness of the unchangeable, or the simple essential being, it must at the same time undertake to free itself from the unessential, i.e. to free itself from itself. For even though it is indeed *for itself* only the changeable, and the unchangeable is something alien to it, yet *it* is *itself* simple and thus unchangeable consciousness, of which it is thus conscious as *its* essence, yet still in such a way that *it itself* is again for itself not this essence. (H 159; M 127; B 252)

The dialectical point in this apparent doubletalk is that the changeable, finite consciousness is alienated from its own essential being. It recognizes its own true being in the unchangeable; were that not so it would simply be a different entity, minding its own business and in a position to be indifferent to the unchangeable. A hawk is not alienated from the mountain over which it flies, or from the heavens above. It has its own life. But the unhappiness of the changeable consciousness arises precisely from the fact that it recognizes its own life substance in the unchangeable, which is beyond its reach precisely in being its conscious object. It is the peculiar capacity of a self-conscious being, its glory and its pain, to be able to objectify its own life substance. But to make an object of its own essential life, as if its essence were indeed like a mountain or the sky, is to set it at a psychic distance from the conscious subject. Its only recourse is yearning, yearning to be taken up into the unchangeable.

But here the dialectic of unhappy consciousness takes a turn: if this yearning for union with the unchangeable were to be satisfied, it could only be through loss of its own changeable existence. It would gain its substance at cost of its personal identity. So the unhappy consciousness finds itself suspended between these two irreconcilable opposites. Hegel continues:

> The position which it assigns both sides can therefore not be one of mutual indifference, i.e. not an indifference of itself toward the unchangeable; but it is itself immediately both, and it is for it *the relation of the two* as a relation of essence toward nonessence, so that the latter is to be transcended *(aufzuheben ist)*; but since from its point of view both are equally essential and contradictory, the unhappy consciousness is merely the contradictory movement in which each opposite fails to come to rest in its opposite, but is engendered in it anew as its opposite. (H 159; M 127; B 252)

A person afflicted with the unhappy consciousness may seem to be confronted with a simple dilemma: he can have himself, vulnerable, changeable, poor forked thing, driven from pillar to post, unfulfilled but still in possession of a certain personal identity, with memories and worldly prospects and perhaps a circle of intimacy with others with whom he shares the earth for a precarious time. Or he can throw himself onto the bosom of unchangeable being and find his substantial life there, at the loss of the child his mother bore. But in fact it is a false dilemma; he cannot have either without having both. In any particular case one could find psychological reasons why that is so, but the deeper reason why it is impossible for unhappy consciousness to come to rest in either horn of the dilemma is dialectical: that in truth ("in itself") it *is* both. This dual identity, present in itself and evident to us phenomenological observers, asserts itself coercively in the unhappy consciousness only by making life impossible for its sufferers, cast on the horns of a dilemma they are powerless to resolve.

Thus we have before us a battle with an enemy, against whom victory turns out to be a defeat, to have achieved the one is rather its loss in its opposite. Consciousness of life, of its existence and act, is merely the pain caused by this existence and act, for therein it finds only the consciousness of its opposite as its essence, and its own nullity. In elevating itself out of this consciousness it goes over into the unchangeable. But this elevation is itself this same consciousness; it is therefore immediately the consciousness of the opposite, namely of itself as a particular individual. The unchangeable that enters into consciousness is just thereby also affected by the particularity and is only present with this particularity; instead of being destroyed in the consciousness of the unchangeable, the particularity only continues coming forth in it. (H 159–60; M 127; B 252–53)

There are precedents for this analysis, particularly in the Augustinian psychology that has dominated traditional Christian thought: Human being is formed in the image of God and created for life with its creator, the image directly mirroring its great original, face to face. Therefore the loss or perversion of this divine image in sin produces a predicament from which the sinner, bereft of the image in which he is created, can find no way out. One thinks of the prayer of the restless heart that opens Augustine's *Confessions:* he can find no satisfaction in his innermost being so long as he is turned away from his creator. Every worldly project, from the most debased to the most exalted, will peter out uncompleted, abandoned in futility and impatience, "for you have made us for yourself, and our hearts are restless till they find their rest in you." It is noteworthy that Augustine's restless heart cannot finally find rest even in the Plotinian ecstasies of mystical union, though the symmetry of this predicament, that neither the changeable nor the unchangeable can resolve it, is brought out more clearly in Hegel's analysis. For Hegel, indeed, it seems evident that the Augustinian psychology furnishes not only a precedent for but also an illustration of the dialectic of unhappy consciousness. The sense of the lost image of God, afflicting the entire race of Adam, is one important self-diagnosis of the unhappy consciousness itself. Still, it is far from offering the only illustration of this predicament. Hegel's analysis does remind us of his own interpretations of traditional Christianity that go back to the youthful manuscripts of the 1790s, but we are equally reminded of the interpretation of Judaism dating from that period (in *The Spirit of Christianity)*, and also of Hegel's critique of Kant and of post-Kantian Romanticism and *Reflexionsphilosophie* during his earlier Jena years. Hyppolite points out, for instance, that Fichte's early *Wissenschaftslehre*, as Hegel interpreted it in the *Differenzschrift*, culminates in a clear example of unhappy consciousness, with an unbridgeable gulf between the absolute ego and any phenomenal self.[2]

But any self-understanding, religious, philosophical, psychological, or in popular culture, that positions the limited self-conscious identity of the self over against some Beyond *(Jenseits)* as the repository of its psychic vitality, would be an instance of unhappy consciousness. It would not be difficult to apply Hegel's analysis to widely held readings of the human situation dating from more recent times. One thinks of Marxist and neo-Marxist ideologies that locate the true wellsprings of human motivation in impersonal social forces beyond the control if not the understanding of the conscious personal agents who are driven by them. Hegel's own critique of revolutionary ideology later in the *Phenomenology,* in the section on "Absolute Freedom and Terror" already goes a long way toward such an application. But recent psychoanalytic theories and therapies, that presuppose a vast reservoir of libidinal and/or aggressive vitality beneath the surface of conscious life and supplying its psychic energies, would provide yet another guise for the unchangeable Beyond. Whether the "civilized" ego attempts to suppress this prodigious energy or to give it free expression the result is equally self-destructive. According to the hydraulic metaphors of this psychology, the ego is moved at the behest of impersonal vitalities that are its own and yet not owned. No one has expressed this predicament, which is cultural as well as personal, more eloquently than Freud himself, in *Civilization and Its Discontents,* surely one of the great modern tracts on unhappy consciousness. There seems no solution, no happiness, in either Freud's view or Hegel's, for a conscious being whose own essential life is in some manner beyond and at odds with it.

It may be objected that such examples imply no commerce with anything literally unchangeable. But such an objection would overlook the fact that Hegel's analysis is phenomenological, not metaphysical. It is not that the unhappy consciousness necessarily confronts anything truly unchangeable, like the Scholastic deity, but that it appears so to it. For that matter, a great deal of traditional metaphysics, widely discredited because of its pretensions to present literal truth, would, if divested of such pretensions, make excellent phenomenology.

Be that as it may, as Hegel proceeds to spell out typical permutations of the unhappy consciousness his analysis is modeled unmistakably on some types of Jewish and Christian piety. In fact one could find Christian analogues for the entire analysis. It is therefore tempting for a commentator simply to identify unhappy consciousness with the Christian self-understanding, or with some combination of the Jewish and Christian: tempting and also convenient, because it avoids the cumbersomeness of many of Hegel's apparent circumlocutions. For "the unchangeable" or "simple essential being" read "God"; for "changeable consciousness" read "man" or "Jew" or "Christian"; for Hegel's barbarism, "the figurated unchangeable," let's just say "incarnation"; and so on.[3] But then one can only be puzzled that Hegel appears to go over so much of the same ground in his later chapter on Religion. Hegel in fact nowhere speaks directly of religion here, much less of God, Judaism, Christianity, and so forth, though if that were what he had meant he could have spared himself a great deal of trouble by doing so. He adopts no explicitly Christian language at all. Such identifications are always misleading, especially in treating early chapters of the *Phenomenology;* while Hegel usually has historical examples in mind he pointedly refuses to name them, not in order to play guessing games with his reader, but because they are only limited approximations of categories subject to much wider application. That is especially the case with the unhappy consciousness, which is one of his most basic statements of the problem addressed by the *Phenomenology* as a whole. Unhappy consciousness is an archetype of such vast ramification because Hegel introduces it as an unavoidable crisis of spirit on its way to fulfillment. One may indeed question whether that is so, or whether Hegel has been misled by his Judeo-Christian background to assume that it is necessarily so; nonetheless, it is important to recognize (and is incidentally the thesis of this study) that in Hegel's hands Christian categories are dialectically "purified" and transmuted into forms that he thought universally applicable.

From that point of view it is useful to view unhappy consciousness, not as the affliction of an individual or group, but as a kind of psychic field, very roughly analogous to a magnetic field, with many elements within it that are capable of shifting about and being redistributed through permutations that are in principle endless, but always retaining a certain basic polarity. "In itself," after all, it is one, on the analogue of the total magnetic field; but "for itself" it is first concentrated at one pole, but then turns out to be capable of endless fluctuation. Hegel undertakes to chart its characteristic fluctuations, ringing the changes on the multiple positions assumed by this consciousness, restless as an insomniac in its irresolvable tension. In its original position, polarized in its stark, poor particularity, it confronts the unchangeable as the object of helpless yearning; it then shifts position, redistributing itself at the other pole, the universal and unchangeable, as if in a fitful dream, only to find its individual particularity appearing at the other pole as the inescapable counterpart of the unchangeable. Such shifts occur, strictly speaking, in the *experience* of the unhappy consciousness, and as such cannot escape the subject/object structure of experience generally. Wherever this conscious subject positions itself, an object will appear confronting it. "In this movement," therefore, consciousness

> experiences just this *coming forth of the particularity in the unchangeable, and of the unchangeable in the particularity. For it,* particularity *in general* appears *in* the unchangeable being, and at the same time its *own* particularity in the unchangeable being. For the truth of this movement is just the *oneness* of this double consciousness. *This unity,* however, will *at first* be *to it* of a kind *in which the difference* between the two is *still* predominant. (H 160; M 127–28; B 253)

Wherever consciousness positions itself within this essential unity, it will experience an aspect of itself at the other pole, as if it were something other. Abstractly considered, these are the two conditions that constitute unhappy consciousness: an essential identity, and a form of experience in which it necessarily appears divided against itself.

At this point Hegel introduces the characteristic permutations through which unhappy consciousness redistributes itself in its restless effort to overcome this basic bipolarity. He identifies the three moments into which his analysis is basically organized. The first is the simple opposition with which we began, and into which unhappy consciousness tends always to regress. But in the second moment the unchangeable itself appears to the changeable consciousness in an individuated form; that is, it comes into existence, for to exist is to be particularized. Indeed, it takes on the figure *(Gestalt)* of an existing individual like the changeable consciousness itself, but a *different* individual. In the third moment, however, the changeable consciousness "finds *its own self* as this individual in the unchangeable." Hegel recapitulates these three moments as a kind of metamorphosis undergone by the unchangeable as it appears to the changeable consciousness:

> The *first* unchangeable is to it merely the *alien* being passing judgment on individuality; but since *the second* is a *figure* of *individuality* like itself, so *thirdly* it becomes spirit, and rejoicing to find itself therein, consciousness becomes aware that its own individuality is reconciled with the universal. (H 160; M 128; B 253)

This last step, a kind of mystical union, seems to promise the cure for its unhappiness. But it is, alas, only a promise, and an empty one at that. Hegel reminds us that all these permutations occur only in "the *experience* through which the divided self-consciousness passes in its unhappiness." Through all its movements it is unable to pass beyond the essential division of subject and object implicit in the structure of experience. To experience its individuality in union with the universal is still to find its experiencing consciousness standing outside that unity.

Indeed, the second and third moments of this basic triad generate their own submoments, but the apparent advance through these moments and submoments is reminiscent of the "third man" problem in Platonic dialectic: to reconcile A and B we postulate a third term, C, in which the two will presumably be united. But then the problem arises of relating C both to A and to B. For this purpose we postulate a D (between C and A) and E (between C and B), but then we must unite D with both C and A, for which purpose we postulate an F and G; and must also unite E with C and B, spawning H and I, and so on and so forth. Presumably we could go on projecting intermediate moments indefinitely, without ever resolving the basic polarity with which we began. Hegel gives us some samples of this fruitless effort, and I shall rehearse some of them briefly. But they are only samples. It is a mistake to suppose, as many commentators do, either that unhappy consciousness assumes just these forms, or that any real progress is achieved through these forms in resolving the predicament.

In the second moment of the basic triad, for instance, in which the unchangeable appears in individuated "figuration" *(Gestaltung),* it continues to present itself in opposition to the changeable consciousness despite its apparent affinity. Though of course Hegel does not refer directly to the Christian doctrine of incarnation, he is clearly rehearsing the old problem about the "positivity" of that doctrine that exercised him in the manuscripts of the 1790s: The changeable consciousness is obliged to regard this new "formation" of the unchangeable as a contingent "happening" *(Geschehen)* that it merely discovers, like any other external event in its experience. Furthermore, this individual figure remains that of the unchangeable, still "belongs" to it, so that "the opposition remains even in this unity." The unhappy consciousness is no more able to unite itself with this figure than it was with the simple unchangeable: even less so, in fact, for

> through this *figuration* of the unchangeable the moment of the Beyond not only persists but is even more entrenched; if on the one hand it does indeed appear to be brought nearer to consciousness through this individuated, actual figure, still on the other hand it now confronts him as an opaque sensuous *unit,* with all the impermeability of something *actual.* The hope of becoming one with it must remain a hope, that is, without fulfillment or presentness, for between the hope and its fulfillment there stands precisely the absolute contingency or immovable indifference that inheres in the very figuration on which the hope was founded. (H 161–62; M 129; B 255)

In fact the unhappy consciousness is further stymied in its effort to unite itself with the mediating figure by the fact that this figure, like any historical individual, has the property of becoming ever more distant, receding in space and time.

> Because of the nature of the *existing unit,* because of the actuality with which it is clothed, it necessarily transpires that it disappears in time and becomes remote in space, and remains utterly remote. (H 162; M 129; B 255)

Here we are reminded unmistakably of the young Hegel's treatment of the plight of the latter-day Christian, whose savior is utterly alien, having existed long ago and far away. Only his grave is present. In every respect, the mediating figure turns out to be no mediator after all. Like the Platonic third man, he simply creates the need for yet further mediations, placing the unhappy consciousness ever further from his goal.

As a result, the unhappy consciousness must simply recapitulate, in relation to this individual figuration of the unchangeable, a version of the same three moves it undertakes in relation to the simple unchangeable itself. Indeed, insofar as the mediating individual has vanished he is as if swallowed up again in the abyss of the unchangeable. Now he is, in the first place, a mere memory, a pure object of yearning, as the unhappy consciousness nurses the pain of its loss in sorrowful feelings, which Hegel compares to a random tolling of bells or a mist of incense, "a musical thinking" that lacks conceptual form (H 163; M 131; B 257). Hegel hints that the error of unhappy consciousness consists in its having sought the mediating individual as a particular object, the very nature of which is to disappear, and not a "*universal individuality in the form of thought, not a concept.*" This error is unavoidable because it is inherent in unhappy consciousness to seek satisfaction "where . . . it cannot be found," in a Beyond the very nature of which is to be inaccessible. But when consciousness has finally "learned from experience" the futility of morbid preoccupation with a grave from which life has already flown, it collapses back into itself in feeling: feels in itself that individuality it has lost in the mediating figure (H 164; M 131–32; B 258–59).

Though this return to itself only occurs in feeling, to us who observe the ordeal of the unhappy consciousness this second moment appears to promise a genuine advance.

> It is the *pure heart* (Gemüt), which *for us* or *in itself* has found itself and is inwardly satiated, for although *for it* the essential being is still separated from it in feeling, still this feeling is in itself a feeling of *self* (Selbst*gefühl*), it has felt the object of its pure feeling and this object is itself. . . . In this return into itself its *second relationship* comes into play for us, that of desire and labor, in which consciousness is confirmed in that inner certainty of itself which it has for us, through overcoming (Aufheben) and enjoying the alien being, specifically in the form of independent things. (H 164–65; M 132; B 259)

These independent things are real, natural, consumable goods of the earth, to be worked on and cultivated, and also desired and enjoyed, as food for instance. That the alien being should now appear in such a form suggests a sacramental relationship, which no doubt provides Hegel's model for this second moment. This laboring, desiring, and enjoying, furthermore, is something the conscious being actually does himself, in his newly achieved *Selbstgefühl*. But unfortunately it is only we phenomenological observers who recognize that in itself the unhappy consciousness has now attained this independent, reality-oriented status. For itself the hapless subject of these strivings has only pushed his way into a new cul-de-sac. "The unhappy consciousness . . . *finds* itself only as *desiring* and *laboring*," is otherwise unaware of the self-certainty it has achieved, and indeed seems bent on denying itself even this achievement. Instead of finding its self-certainty confirmed in the fact that it is the one who desires and labors, and enjoys, it "finds only the confirmation of what it is for itself, namely its dividedness." Precisely in finding its old nemesis, the unchangeable, expressed in the things it desires and works upon, the unhappy consciousness remains unaware of the independence it has achieved in these very activities. Now, indeed, for itself divided between its own desiring, laboring self and the unchangeable to which it seeks access through these immediate objects of its desire and work, it comes to regard the world of actuality itself as divided. It comes, that is, to find in the actual world something "such as it itself is, an actuality broken in two, which . . . on one hand is a nullity, but on the other hand is also a sanctified *world;* it is the form of the unchangeable" (H 165; M 132–33; B 259–60). The unchangeable, in its appearance in the ensemble of sanctified, sacramental things, is no more at the disposal of the unhappy consciousness than it was in its appearance as a conscious individual. The world that consciousness can deal with and enjoy at its own pleasure is as empty as it is, while the sanctified world becomes the domain of the unchangeable.

The sanctified world, to be sure, is also given to our hapless antihero, but as an "alien gift," not as his own independently earned possession. Therefore in his work and enjoyment of it he still remains unaware of his own identity with the alien benefactor. On the contrary, he explicitly disclaims both his independent right to the gift and his identity with the giver by giving thanks for it. Only in this posture of gratitude is it given him to participate in the sanctified world. He can in fact unite with the sanctified actuality only on condition that he renounce any sense of independent achievement, any claim on behalf of his own efforts; finally he must renounce even the autonomous self-worth that this moment seemed to promise. As the receiver of the gift assumes this posture of gratitude and self-renunciation, the giver withdraws again into a "beyond" behind its gift. The result is the renewed splitting-apart of the two poles (H 165–67; M 133–35; B 260–62).

This result appears to bring us back more or less to square one, but the self-renunciation entailed in this second moment does lead to a third attempt to unite with the unchangeable. The unhappy consciousness does, after all, know himself to be something actual. It is he who works, enjoys, gives thanks, renounces, and he experiences himself in these activities. "But just therein is the enemy now encountered in his most characteristic form." For it is evident that the unhappy consciousness can unite with the unchangeable only by the effective annihilation of this self-actuality. "This third relationship, in which this true actuality is the one extreme, is the linking of itself, as nothingness, to the universal essence" (H 168; M 135; B 263). In order that the unchangeable can be everything, the unhappy consciousness must become nothing, through a psychic self-immolation so complete that he attempts to divest himself even of those "animal functions" in which a residual independence remains. Rather than being matters of indifference, these "functions" (unnamed, but presumably eating, drinking, sexual activity, and the like) now become "the enemy" against which relentless war must be waged. The aim of this ascetic repression is to become nothing, and so to disappear into the unchangeable. But becoming nothing is not so easy. Suppose this battle against one's own flesh succeeds for a time:

> Since, however, this enemy renews itself in its very defeat, consciousness, being fixated on it, constantly lingers over it instead of getting free of it, and constantly considers itself defiled. At the same time, this content of its efforts, far from being anything essential, is of the meanest sort, the most particular rather than anything universal, and so we see here a personality closed in on itself and its petty activity, brooding on itself, as unhappy as it is destitute. (H 168–69; M 136; B 263–64)

Obviously this petty obsession cannot as such secure unity with the unchangeable, so the unhappy consciousness seeks out a mediating figure between itself and the unchangeable, perhaps a priest, an abbot, a therapist, a mystagogue, a leader, and puts itself totally in his hands. This mediator, of course, desires only to serve; indeed, he installs himself as the servant alike of the unhappy consciousness and the unchangeable. He serves the former by assuming total control. In this way the unhappy consciousness seeks at last to be rid of itself, in a self-emptying of which the monastic vows of poverty, chastity, and absolute obedience are emblematic.[4] By letting the mediator stand in for the unchangeable, the unhappy consciousness is able to complete its self-renunciation in minutest detail. It gives up its own will, "and transfers to the mediator or servant the owning and freedom of decision, and therewith the *guilt* for its action" (H 169; M 136; B 265). The fruit of its labor and its enjoyment thereof it also renounces, the former through giving up its property, the latter through "fastings and mortifications."

> Through these moments of giving up its own decision, then its property and enjoyment, and finally through the positive moment of pursuing tasks it does not understand, it truly and completely divests itself of the consciousness of inner and outer freedom, the actuality of its being-for-itself; it possesses the certainty of having in truth exteriorized its *I,* of having made its immediate self-consciousness into a *thing,* into an objective being. (H 170; M 137; B 265–66)

Here the unhappy consciousness has reached a kind of terminus, having carried out its project to the bitter end. In another sense, of course, for all its efforts it has never stirred from the irresolvable predicament with which it began.

We will return to the conclusion of Hegel's treatment of unhappy consciousness when we survey its wider prospects in the *Phenomenology* as a whole, which is much taken up with its plight. But the next item on our agenda will be to discover how self-consciousness got into this fix in the first place.

2. The Mythos of Hegel's *Phenomenology*:

The Chapter on Self-Consciousness

The chapter that concludes with the dialectic of unhappy consciousness is surely one of the most uncanny in philosophical literature. The impasse described in that concluding section is a pathology peculiar to self-consciousness, yet in introducing this chapter Hegel declares that with our arrival at the theme of self-consciousness we have entered "the native kingdom of truth" (H 134; M 104; B 219). Self-consciousness is already spirit in embryo. But the truth into which "we" are to be initiated in this kingdom will not be apparent to any of the figures we will meet there. It certainly eludes the unhappy consciousness. But it is in general hard to know what to make of such figures. They are not historical persons, nor are they types, nor are they fictional characters such as one might meet in a novel or a romance. The "kingdom" they inhabit, truth's own native land, is no less strange. We encountered something of this strangeness when we had to resort to the image of a restless play of forces in a magnetic field in order to suggest the region of unhappy consciousness. Of course that was only an image, and not Hegel's own, but without some such device we would have been misled into supposing we were dealing with fixed entities in some natural or supernatural environment. But this entire chapter proceeds as if nothing of the sort were given; Hegel attempts here to evoke the manner in which consciousness evolves a sense of itself and a correlative sense of an environing whole. It does not simply discover either a self or a larger whole already in place prior to the discovery. Nor, on the other hand, does it simply invent them. Self and world are correlative, in process of formation together.

Hegel lets this process materialize for us in an odd sort of narrative. He makes no effort to prove anything in any formal sense. The account is not psychological, as if the psyche were presupposed as given in its various states and functions, and needed only to be explained. Nor is the narrative historical; though there are veiled historical allusions, Hegel deliberately refuses to be explicit about them (a reticence not shared by some of his commentators), because the primal dimension of psychic life being uncovered is not yet historical at all. History is too concrete, both too rich and too particular to provide more than very confused examples. But this strange story is not "prehistorical" either, in the sense of describing conditions chronologically prior to history. Rather, as this story unfolds we find ourselves in an esoteric region of everywhere-and-nowhere, always-and-never, simple, nebulous, yet full of resonance. Though Hegel does not so describe it, it is the region of philosophical myth: not the region of cosmogonic origins and theophany characteristic of folk myth, but that equally dreamlike terrain to which some philosophers have repaired in order to view the vivid scenes that can only be presupposed and finally perhaps validated in argument and systematic analysis. Here Hobbes's humanoids do anarchic battle until they consent to forgo lives "solitary, poor, nasty, brutish, and short" to join in the civilizing restrictions of social contract. Here Rousseau's solitary savage lopes through lush forests in primal freedom, confronting his kind only in brief episodes of fighting and mating, until he is seduced by the illusory claims of that same social contract. Here the Platonic soul, at rest between earthly lives, enjoys the direct vision of those ideal forms he must struggle to divine in the flux of earthly experience. Here we find that gateway at which two mountain paths meet where Nietzsche's Zarathustra discovers the secret of eternal recurrence. As interpreted and rationalized by Christian theologians, Genesis 2–11 tells a story that transpires in these regions; in some ways Hegel's chapter on Self-Consciousness provides a revisionist version of that story, and some of the others mentioned as well.

Not that Hegel deliberately set out to compose a philosophical myth in this chapter. Hardly anyone does. Hegel does not use the term, but the peculiar character of the chapter and the way its moments are connected, unique in the *Phenomenology,* as well as the way it functions in the work as a whole, make this description appropriate. The term is certainly subject to misunderstanding, but much less so than the various historical, psychological, socioeconomic interpretations it serves to guard against. We of course do not intend by the term "myth" merely a fabulous falsehood. A myth aims to communicate a complex truth of highest generality, but the factors that make up this complexity are presented successively, in a kind of narrative. It does not literally describe a series of events that occurred once upon a time. Taken as a whole the philosophical myth tells a story of primal foundations, but its priority is not in time but in the structure of things. It discloses the bedrock on which everything essential rests, and for Hegel that foundation is the birth of the psyche as the chrysalis of spirit. It underlies historical life, society, cultural expression, not in the sense of being their cause, but in the sense of being a primary dimension that actually exists only in and through them. Though this story is told by means of individual figures, it certainly is not implied that social, historical, cultural life is only an ensemble of individual expressions. The use of individual figures is due to the abstractness with which this dimension must be discussed when it is isolated and lifted out of the complex texture of self-conscious life in the actual world. That Hegel locates the birth of the self-conscious psyche at the mythic foundation of his phenomenology of spirit establishes the primary orientation of the entire text, and its crucial problem: the multiform duality inherent in self-consciousness. The psyche is entirely reflexive. To become conscious of itself is not merely to discover a preexistent entity: the psyche is born in the process of becoming aware of itself. That is why this mythic region is the native land of Hegelian truth.

I shall present the strange narrative that moves through this chapter in a series of nine tableaux, strong visual scenes appearing in the mythic mist. Hegel himself organizes the chapter into an introductory part, untitled but comprising several paragraphs, followed by two titled sections. The entire chapter is given two titles: it is an oddity of the *Phenomenology* as a whole that it is arranged in two distinct tables of contents, on which I shall comment later. The first title, "Self-Consciousness," is elaborated in the other, literally "The Truth of [Con-sciousness's] Certainty of Itself." The series of tableaux and comments into which I shall arrange my discussion fits into Hegel's organization of the chapter as follows:

> B. *Self-Consciousness*
> IV. *The Truth of Self-Certainty*
>   i.   the life cycle
>   ii. the intelligent predator
>   recognition and the concept of self-consciousness
> A. *Independence and Dependence of Self-Consciousness: Lord-ship and Bondage*
>   iii. the life and death struggle
>   iv.   the surrender
>   v.   the master and the slave
>   vi.   the self-mastery of the slave
>   is the master-slave dialectic a historical paradigm?
> B. *Freedom of Self-Consciousness: Stoicism, Skepticism, and the Unhappy Consciousness*
>   vii. stoicism: the contentment of pure thought
>   viii. skepticism: the polemic of thought against actuality
>   ix.   unhappy consciousness and the problem of Hegel's *Phenomenology*

i. The Life Cycle

The first scene to appear in the Wagnerian mist seems little more than the undulating mist itself, but closer inspection reveals a free-floating vitality constantly taking shape and constantly dissolving its shape in the "universal fluidity." It is reminiscent of the watery chaos with which the cosmogonic myths generally begin. The "essence" characterizing this all-encompassing, fluid field

> is infinity as the *being superseded (Aufgehobensein)* of all distinctions, pure rotational movement at rest in itself but a rest that is absolute restless infinity; an *independent subsistence* into which the distinctions within the movement are dissolved; the simple essence of time, which in this self-identity has the solid form of space. (H 136; M 106; B 221)

The temporality referred to is merely random movement, spatial displacement without direction, in which nothing is stable except the scene as a whole. It differs from the chaos of the cosmogonic myths, however, in that it already has a dialectical character within itself. No god, no demiourgos standing well formed apart from this chaos will shape it into intelligible forms. It is not, after all, an inert matter. Hegel stresses the "negative nature" of "this universal fluidity." But, as he points out, something must stand forth, however fleetingly, or there would be nothing to negate. So in fact we have two dialectical moments constantly asserting themselves in this infinite broth: "the standing-forth of subsistent shapes" and their constant dissolution or negation (H 136–37; M 106; B 222). The scene can also be expressed as a dialectic of one and many, with the one totality constantly negating the many particular forms that just as constantly take shape in it.

Out of this deceptively simple dialectic all the other moments in the development of self-consciousness will follow. This basic dyad, indeed, is still recognizable in the dialectic of unhappy consciousness with which the chapter ends, translated from the externality of nature to psychic inner space. This dyad of unity and division, *Einheit* and *Entzweiung*, furthermore, establishes the primal conditions for all the episodes between.

The fluid whole takes on the character of "life," as a kind of universal "process." For life is a great digestive tract, constituting itself by consuming. But insofar as distinct living entities appear on the scene, the universal life process must take on a new aspect, the inverse of its active character as all-consuming negation: it must also give itself as a "passive medium," a horn of nutrient to nourish the distinct organism. So from this point of view the differentiated "other" consumes, and thus is able to live for a while, while the universal fluidity provides the consumables. The organism, to be sure, is itself part of the universal life process, and will finally be consumed by it, but so long as it is able to succeed in its own gastronomic adventures it will continue to enjoy its relative and temporary independence. This "inversion" *(Verkehrung)* of the negativity attending the whole, so that the subsistent organism maintains its hold on existence by negating "at the expense of the universal," is again the moment of division *(Entzweiung)*

> and this division of the undifferentiated fluidity is precisely the establishment of individuality. The simple substance of life is therefore the division of itself into shapes and at the same time the dissolution of these subsisting differences; and this dissolution of the division is itself just as much a division and a formation of new members. (H 137–38; M 108; B 223)

It is now clear, in fact, that the universal fluidity as such is merely an "*abstraction* of the essence," which is "actual" only in the constant procession of distinct members that take form in it.

> It is this entire cycle which constitutes life, not what was first expressed, the immediate continuity and solidity of its essence, nor the enduring shape and discreteness subsisting for itself, nor their pure process, nor even the simple combination of these moments, but the self-developing whole which dissolves its own development and in this movement simply preserves itself. (H 138; M 108; B 224)

With this evocation of the great cycle of life the curtain falls on the first tableau.

The account owes a good deal to Hegel's still-developing philosophy of nature, though a detailed description of natural processes would be superfluous in a myth of psychic birth. But by beginning as he does, Hegel does firmly situate the birth of the psyche in the encompassing world of living nature generally. Indeed, this tableau presents a thoroughly vitalistic vision of nature. The entire field with which we begin exhibits the essential dialectic features of life, a cyclical play of vital powers and living organisms. This field is the whole within which an intelligent organism must become aware of itself as a separate identity, but even in so separating itself off in self-awareness it remains rooted in the common soil to which all living things must eventually return. The very possibility of self-consciousness depends upon the dialectic of one and many, subsistence and negation, that characterizes living nature.

ii. The Intelligent Predator

But now a remarkable organism appears on the scene, himself of course a child of nature, who is able to confer a new kind of unity on the living whole that has spawned him. He is able to reflect: he possesses an intelligent consciousness that internally registers and in a manner mirrors his environment. He is capable, that is, of experience. The emergence within the living whole of such an experiencing organism creates a new relationship within that whole. The whole has existed in its "immediate" unity, as "being," but now, mirrored in an intelligent consciousness, it becomes a "reflected unity" in which all the successive moments of the life process are gathered up, aufgehobene, into a simultaneous, "universal" totality. In the comprehending vision of this organism, which is part of and a "result" of the life process, the living whole exists "for itself" as a universal genus *(Gattung):*

> In this *result* life points to something other than itself, namely to consciousness, for which it exists as this unity or genus.
> But this other life, for which the *genus* exists as such and which is for itself genus, i.e. self-consciousness, exists at first only as this simple creature *(Wesen),* and has itself for its object as *pure I;* in its experience, which is not to be considered, this abstract I-object will become ever richer for him and will undergo the unfolding which we have seen in the sphere of life. (H 138; M 109; B 224–25)

This experiencing subject is not yet self-conscious. The "pure I" is part of his field of consciousness only as an object among others, the object closest to him. It is not yet himself as the subject of the experience he undergoes. Yet in this active though as yet undiscovered consciousness an entire field of experience becomes a reflected whole, registering in this new medium. That he experiences means that the great sphere of life does not merely subsist, but registers in his consciousness, which is itself universal as the medium in which the generic whole finds reflected repose.

But the subject who comes into view in this new tableau is no contemplative, no theorist enjoying the pure spectacle that presents itself to him. So far as he is concerned, his awareness of his environment is incidental to the predatory designs he has on it. He is hungry. Like other living things his primary relation to the world is digestive, securing his own existence by consuming. He bears the power of negation characteristic of all life,

> and self-consciousness is thus certain of itself only through the absorption *(Aufheben)* of this other that presents itself to him as an independent life; self-consciousness is *desire.* (H 139; M 109; B 225)

"Desire" *(Begierde)* has here the force of sheer, unsublimated appetite, and it is the primal relation of self-consciousness to its environment. In introducing the entire chapter, Hegel emphasizes the primary role of desire in establishing the active, driving movement of the self-conscious organism toward the world, that results in its self-awareness. For self-consciousness implies an achieved identity with itself that must be actively forged. It is brought into touch with sensuous objects by desiring them, indeed by desiring actively to negate them, and in this negative activity it secures its own self-certainty (H 135; M 105; B 220). This active exercise of desire is what distinguishes self-consciousness from abstract "consciousness" treated in the previous chapter, "consciousness" regarded as a passive epistemological subject of sensation, perception, and understanding. In his critique of empiricism contained in that first chapter Hegel attacks both the notion that sensation is primitive in experience and the supposed independent reality of sensuous objects as such. He suggests that empiricists

> go back to the most elementary school of wisdom, namely into the old Eleusinian mysteries of Ceres and Bacchus . . . [in order] to learn the secret of eating bread and drinking wine; for he who is initiated into these secrets comes not only to doubt the being of sensuous things but to despair of it, partly himself bringing about their nothingness and partly seeing them bring it about themselves. Even the animals are not excluded from this wisdom, but show themselves rather to be most profoundly initiated into it; for they do not stand still in the presence of sensuous things as if these things possessed intrinsic being, but despairing of this reality and in complete assurance of the nothingness of such

things, they grab them without further ado and eat them up. (H 87; M 65; B 159)

And so it is with the intelligent organism on the way to self-consciousness. No empiricist, he shows himself perfectly initiated into these mysteries from birth.

Desiring, hungering, consuming he moves through the world. He attains satisfaction and secure self-certainty only insofar as he destroys the independent reality of the other living things that confront him, nourishing himself by converting them into food. There are other forms of raw desire, of course: the sexual, for instance, which does not generally destroy its object; but insofar as it is merely an object of desire, the desire seeks its own satisfaction with hardly more respect for the independent life of the object than a diner has for a sausage.[5]

It may be objected that an intelligent organism cannot exist in pure desire. But once we get curious about the concrete life of our predator we will be hopelessly misled. What does he do for shelter? How does he protect himself in cold or foul weather? Does he really go foraging alone through the world, or do these predators run in packs? And so on. Such questions ought only to remind us of the mythic abstractness of the entire analysis. There is no effort to deal concretely with actual humanoids. What we have is an imaginative construction that, taken as a whole, will disclose the characteristic human feature, self-consciousness, as it arises everywhere and always in the larger stream of life, and the primary feature of its rise is desire, the experience of other lives as a means to its own satisfaction.

Richly satisfying as such experiences are, however, they do have their limitations. As Hegel's ironical remark about animals being initiated into the Eleusinian mysteries suggests, it is possible to pursue this primary relation to the world without ever becoming self-conscious. Even the self-conscious animal, to be sure, can never simply abandon this negative relation to other living things without forfeiting its own life. The certainty of self that comes with desiring and consuming, furthermore, is an essential step toward self-consciousness. Yet insofar as desiring and consuming make up our predator's exclusive comportment in the world, he will never become self-conscious. Self-consciousness can in fact remain a potentiality unfulfilled, in which case our little mythic drama would end with its second tableau.[6]

Recognition and the Concept of Self-Consciousness

If a new episode is to occur, the desiring-consuming relation to other lives cannot be the exclusive one. Life is satisfied thereby, the sheer animal vitality of this potentially self-conscious organism, but precisely not its potentiality for self-consciousness. Here Hegel breaks into his odd narrative to offer a philosophical gloss on the concept of self-consciousness. The explanation of this concept must be distinguished from the narrative account of how self-consciousness emerges, but it is presented at this point to alert us to the condition that must somehow be met if it is to emerge fully. It is one of the *Phenomenology*'s primary principles: that a self becomes conscious of itself only in being recognized as a self by another self. A self-consciousness needs another self-consciousness in whom to find itself reflected. It does not need this recognition in the sense that it cannot exist without it, but without recognition it cannot be a self-conscious self. So this requirement is of quite a different sort than the desire of a living organism for other living things to consume. Indeed, that organic need is at cross-purposes with the need for recognition. For recognition is mutual: The other self-consciousness can confer a reflexive self-awareness on me only insofar as I recognize that he or she is also a self-conscious self. I must recognize the other person's recognition of me, and that is possible only to the extent that I see in that person a being capable of divining the existence of a self. But I fulfill my organic need as a living organism by desiring and consuming the other—which is not a very promising basis for mutual self-recognition! You cannot get much recognition from someone you regard only as a piece of meat or a sexual object. One is recognized as a self only insofar as one recognizes the other as a self: and only so can one become a self-conscious self. A self-centered consciousness is, paradoxically, not yet a self at all.

Yet all life-relationship begins in desire. Hegel points out that even in the satisfaction of desire consciousness "makes experience of the independence of its object." For I cannot desire and consume the other without first experiencing it as an independent entity. But this independence is just what I negate in converting it into sustenance for myself. But I negate the otherness of the other in an entirely different sense if, instead of consuming the other, I recognize in it a conscious nature akin to my own. Then it is no longer entirely other, no longer alien, and my relation to it is not simply desire, but a conscious awareness of another consciousness, that is, of the same genus *(Gattung)*. Then I experience its independence in a new sense, in recognizing that it, too, is a conscious negativity.

> But this universal, independent nature, in which negation exists as absolute, is the genus as such, or as *self-consciousness. Self-consciousness achieves its satisfaction only in another self-consciousness.* (H 139; M 110; B 226)

This satisfaction, however, unlike the satisfaction of desire, is not achieved by negating the experienced independence of the other, by which consciousness first secured the certainty of itself. The self-certain "truth" of conscious existence "is rather the doubled reflection, the doubling of self-consciousness." This necessary doubling, as we have seen, will finally lead to unhappy consciousness, for it is inherent in the very structure of self-conscious existence. Here, however, it has the consequence that one either becomes self-conscious through another self-consciousness or not at all. A "living self-consciousness"

> is *a self-consciousness for a self-consciousness.* Only thereby can it be such in fact; for only here does it become for itself the unity of its self in its otherness. . . . When a self-consciousness is the object, it is just as much I as object. —The concept *of spirit* is thereby already present for us. What still lies ahead for consciousness is the experience of what spirit is, this absolute substance, which in complete freedom and independence of its opposing subjects, namely the different self-consciousness existing for themselves, is their unity: the *I* that is *we,* and the *we* that is *I.* (H 140; M 110; B 226–27)

Self-consciousness is intersubjective, and as such already contains the basic structure of spirit. Indeed, in this prophetic mood Hegel goes on to anticipate the culmination of the entire phenomenological ordeal:

> Consciousness first finds in self-consciousness, as the concept of spirit, its turning-point, from which it steps forth out of the colorful illusion of the sensuous here and now *(Diesseits)* and out of the empty night of the supersensuous Beyond *(Jenseits)* into the spiritual daylight of the present. (H 140; M 110–11; B 227)

Certainly this point is not reached in the chapter "Self-Consciousness." Since we have taken more than a peek at the conclusion of this chapter, at the unhappy consciousness torn between *Diesseits* and *Jenseits,* we know that this consummation still lies far ahead. In fact it receives only scant adumbration even in the final chapter, on "Absolute Knowledge."

The striking expression, "spiritual daylight of the present," for the condition beyond the duality of *Diesseits* and *Jenseits,* suggests that only self-conscious spirit achieves the clarity and personal integration necessary to occupy the present. What is lacking in the various dissipations of psychic energy diagnosed in *Phenomenology* is precisely full presence and the temporality focused in that experience of presentness. The expression is echoed fifteen years later in the famous Preface to the *Philosophy of Right* (1821), where Hegel says that it is only the "fetter of some abstraction" that stands "between reason as self-conscious spirit and reason as the actuality at hand." But philosophical insight enables us "to know reason as the rose in the cross of the present and thereby to enjoy the present."[7] From this point of view the affliction common to all the figures that appear in the *Phenomenology* is the inability to enjoy the present; they only suffer the cross. If that is so, an important question in interpreting the chapter "Self-Consciousness" is whether self-consciousness can be fully achieved under the conditions described in it; whether, indeed, there can be more than a fragmentary, variously flawed, at most incipient self-consciousness so long as it falls short of spirit. Considering that Hegel regarded the *Phenomenology,* at the time he wrote it, as a propaedeutic to the system, do we not have to await the system proper before we can find self-consciousness presented in adequate form? In the present chapter, the question turns on the concept of mutual recognition, which Hegel introduces in opening the first main section of the chapter. As the fundamental condition for achieving self-consciousness, mutual recognition is a basic principle that informs the *Phenomenology.* But we find that this principle had already taken root in earlier Jena manuscripts. It appears as early as the *System der Sittlichkeit* (1802–3)[8] and receives extended treatment in the systematic manuscript of 1803–4[9] and again in the *Realphilosophie* of 1805–6;[10] in each case Hegel devotes to it an analysis that clearly anticipates that of our chapter in the *Phenomenology.* In introducing the section on art, religion, and *Wissenschaft* in the *Realphilosophie,* Hegel declares that "*recognition* is the spiritual element."[11] So it is not merely a phenomenological principle, but a systematic principle that informs the *Phenomenology,* perhaps without finding fully adequate realization there.

As he introduces the principle of recognition here, as the key to the intersubjective nature of self-consciousness, Hegel already seems to be preparing us for a description of peace and concord. Self-consciousness "exists only as something recognized." Its concept requires mutuality, a "unity" within a "doubled" structure (H 141; M 111; B 229). As we have seen, the self-conscious "I" entails a "we," and vice versa. Each must transcend its self-centered existence toward the other, in order in that other to find its own self in truth. Presented in the syllogistic form Hegel likes to employ during this period, self-consciousness is assigned to neither self as such; it is the "middle term," of which the two selves constitute the extremes (H 142–43; M 112; B 230–31). Self-consciousness is the mediating whole in which the two are united.

> Each is for the other the middle term, through which each medi-
> ates and brings itself together with itself; and each is to itself
> and to the other an immediately existing being for itself, which
> at the same time is such for itself only through this mediation.
> They *recognize* themselves as *mutually recognizing* one another.
> (H 143; M 112; B 231)

The student of Hegel's earlier writings finds himself on familiar ground in this remarkable evocation of intersubjective recognition. Indeed, what seems called for now is the introduction of the great theme of love, already so richly developed during the Frankfurt years, which would seem to answer perfectly to the concept of self-consciousness presented here: "The beloved is not opposed to us, he is one with our essence; we see ourselves only in him."[12] Also in the *Realphilosophie,* produced while Hegel was at work on the *Phenomenology,* the concept of mutual recognition is introduced as the essence of love, fulfilled in marriage and embodied in the children who are its fruit.[13] The earlier tableaux in the present chapter have presented our nascent self-consciousness in a mode that differs little from that of a beast of prey. How is he to be transformed into a creature possessed of that mutuality that will transform the brute into a self? How but in the manner of the fairy tales, at the touch of love's magic wand? Surely desire is to be at once consummated and sublimated, transfigured into love. We await the next tableau with the mellow confidence of the theatergoer when he resumes his seat for the last act in a romantic comedy: *omnia vincit amor.*

iii. The Life and Death Struggle

This tableau, however, turns out to be a rude surprise. Now two nascent selves do indeed emerge from the mists to confront one another. But instead of clasping one another in mutual embrace they do furious battle, fighting to the death. Each must kill or be killed.

We were not simply mistaken in thinking that love would fulfill the condition of mutual recognition. Many pages later in the *Phenomenology*, in the first section of the chapter entitled "Spirit," Hegel does point to marriage and the family circle as an intimate bond in which it occurs. In "the relation of *husband* and *wife*" we first find, in its immediate form, "the knowledge by the one consciousness of itself in the other and the knowledge of mutual recognition" (H 325; M 273; B 474). Between husband and wife, to be sure, this mutual recognition has not entirely freed itself of desire! Because of this biological bond, Hegel suggests that this relationship offers "only the *representation* and *image* of spirit, not the actual spirit itself." He goes on to propose that mutual recognition is achieved in its more perfect ethical form, without the admixture of animal libido, in the relation of brother and sister (H 325–27; M 274–75; B 475–77). This curiously innocent conclusion (which, to be sure, is advanced partly to set the stage for some allusions to Sophocles' *Antigone*) does shed a certain light on the passage before us. In order to become self-conscious, the nascent self must in a manner achieve detachment from the sheer biological life process in which it is embedded. For the self is not as such a biological entity. The two combatants do become aware of this free selfhood in the life-and-death struggle, as we shall see, though they do not yet achieve mutual recognition, and so this freedom does not yet entail self-consciousness. In Hegel's syllogistic language, what develops "at first" is "the displacement of the middle term"—self-consciousness—"into the extremes, which as extremes stand in opposition" (H 143; M 112–13; B 231).

Love, on the other hand, except in its most sublimated expressions, submerges the two partners too fully in life's warm stream for this detached, individuated freedom to develop fully, though it does provide mutual recognition of a sort.[14] Love, at any rate, is not mentioned at all in the chapter on Self-Consciousness. In the *Realphilosophie,* on the contrary, which articulates several forms of recognition, love is the first, but it has its limitations:

> Recognition is thus the first thing that must happen; or the individuals are *love,* this being-recognized without opposition of wills . . . in which they emerge only as characters, not as free wills. That is what they have to become. They have to become for themselves what they are in themselves. Their being for one another is the beginning of that process.[15]

So in the *Realphilosophie* we begin with the sweet peace of mutual recognition in love but proceed to a complication of the plot, including the life-and-death struggle,[16] out of which free individuality develops. But in our chapter in the *Phenomenology,* the life-and-death struggle is waged as a struggle for recognition on each side, a recognition that has not yet been secured.

The demand for recognition motivates both combatants, though it is not in fact achieved in the struggle. It cannot be, because each party is trying to force the other to recognize him, without bestowing any recognition in return. That is the essential impasse. To demand the esteem due a spiritual being is to be brought into conflict with the one to whom this demand is directed, so long as there is no reciprocity; the other simply poses the same one-sided demand.

On these terms the demand cannot be met, and yet it motivates the conflict. To compound this irony, however, something else is achieved through the conflict, something that is not intended by the combatants, but is destined to be an essential element in a higher form of self-consciousness than could have been secured even by an immediate recognition. What is achieved is the sense of possessing a free self that is more than its life. This sense of self is produced precisely by the fact that the combatants *risk* their lives as biological organisms. In this tableau self-consciousness "shows itself to be the pure negation of its objective mode, or shows that it is attached to no limited *existence* (*bestimmtes* Dasein), is not attached to the universal singularity of existence generally, not to life."

Only in this form is there anything like a dialectic of mutuality in this scene, that each sees in the action of the other the mirror of his own act, the one as murderous and heedless of his life as the other.

> This presentation is a *doubled* action: action of the other and action through himself. Insofar as it is the action of *the other,* each is bent on the death of the other. But the second aspect also comes into view thereby, *action through himself;* for that implies the staking of his own life in the act. The relation of the two self-consciousnesses is thus so defined that they put themselves and one another *to the test* through the struggle of life and death. (H 144; M 113–14; B 232)

In this ironical turn given the concept of mutual recognition it is tempting to see the germ of Hegel's tragic conception of history: that a distinctively human selfhood can emerge from the great cycle of natural "life" only through bitter conflict. This battle is not to be confused with the merely predatory struggles of natural life, where every organism including the human can exist only by consuming others. Precisely in the demand to be recognized by the other, each is prepared to risk his merely natural life. That risk is both the precondition of historical existence and the grim prospect of which historical existence provides constant opportunity. Contrary to Marxist and Freudian interpretations, this struggle is motivated by no natural necessity, nor is the demand for recognition merely a sublimated desire, though competition for food, sex, territory, and so forth, might well provide its occasion. So long as the fight is no more than such a competition, it is simply a matter of risking life in order to defend one's life, in which case strategic retreat is the prudent course when one's objective appears unattainable. The life-and-death struggle is also avoidable, in quite another sense, and happy the person who avoids it: happy, but not yet a free self. But if our nascent selves are to realize their freedom, they "must" fly at each other's throats.

> They must enter this struggle, for each must raise the certainty of himself, *to exist for himself,* to the truth of the other and of himself. And it is alone through this staking of one's life that freedom is secured, that it is established that self-consciousness is not in essence mere *being,* not the *immediate* manner in which it appears, not the submergence in the mere extension of life—but that nothing is present to it that would not be a vanishing moment for it, that it is only pure *being-for-itself.* The individual who has not risked his life can certainly be recognized

as a *person,* but he has not achieved the truth of this recognition as an independent self-consciousness. (H 144; M 114; B 232–33)

Even in ordinary German the term *Person* is generally used much more restrictively than in English, for instance to imply a primarily legal status; to be called a mere "person" is something of a slur, like calling someone a "character." In fact a character in a play is also called a "person" (cf. *dramatis personae*). Here Hegel uses the term for an intelligent, human life that is not yet an autonomous self. In his *System der Sittlichkeit* (1802–3), where for the first time he introduced the category of master and slave, and implicitly the life-and-death struggle leading to it, he introduces the term "person" in that context as designating one who receives merely "formal" recognition, an abstract "recognition of life" such as even a slave might be granted.[17] Later in the *Phenomenology,* mere "personality" is the status to which the ethical self is reduced in the destruction of his ethnic identity under imperial power, where every individual is isolated and atomized, being granted only legal recognition (H 342–43; M 290; B 501–2). There too we find merely a submissive security, without risk, and therefore without freedom. From such a "recognition" self-consciousness does not arise. I become a self by being recognized as more than a "life." In fact my life as a mere intelligent organism in the biosphere must be transcended before there can be any question of becoming an autonomous self, and in the struggle this biological status is transcended in the most dramatic way, by being deliberately put on the line. The free self is a negativity, arising from the negation, in principle, of his natural life.

So what is at stake in the life-and-death struggle is a transcendence of mere organic life after all, though in quite a different sense than was intended by the demand for recognition that motivated it. It is misleading to make the struggle seem more plausible by assigning economic or other more fashionable motives for it. Gadamer, in a splendid exposition of this chapter, suggests that the institution of the duel, for "the restoration of violated honor," offers at least an analogy if not an example. If we assume that one's honor is a purely psychological possession, that suggestion at least seems closer to the mark than competition for food or goods. But Hegel explicitly rejects the example of the duel many years later in a comment on the life-and-death struggle in his *Enzyklopädie,* on the grounds that dueling is a feudal institution that "does not belong to the natural state of human beings, but to a more or less developed form of civil society and the state," where "the recognition for which the combatants fought"—in the life-and-death struggle—"already exists."[18] A duel is a highly defined cultural phenomenon, whereas the struggle that occurs at this mythic level cannot presuppose any cultural life since the very possibility of culture is precariously balanced on the shoulders of free and autonomous individuals who have suppressed the most urgent demands of nature to risk their lives.

But what still does not occur in the life-and-death struggle is mutual recognition. Demanding recognition for himself, each combatant enters the struggle to wrest it from the other, while refusing to recognize in the other more than the means to his own recognition. Since the recognition must be mutual if either party is to become self-aware, this demand for recognition that motivates the combat cannot be achieved in it. What is achieved is an independent formation of self in each through the risk of death. But the free self is not yet the self-conscious self. Indeed, self-consciousness, which according to its concept had been described as the middle term between two individuals as extremes, now collapses into the extremes, which confront each other as free but self-enclosed consciousnesses, each of which sees in the other merely a "thing" to be destroyed.

If one of them does in fact kill the other, there is of course no question of mutual recognition. The victor destroys in the vanquished the power that might have conferred self-consciousness on him. But another conclusion to the struggle is possible, which is dramatized in the next tableau.

iv. The Surrender

The players in our little mythic drama learn (i.e., develop psychically) by experience. Out of the experience of risking his life, there dawns in the consciousness of each combatant the awareness that he is free: which is to say that he becomes free, for the activation of psychic power is inseparable from the awareness of it. Breaking free of biological determination he has seized his destiny in his own hands. But as the fight begins to go against him, one of the combatants now learns by experience the peril of this freedom, discovers "that life is as essential to him as pure self-consciousness" (H 145; M 115; B 234). If life is lost all is lost, so the heady but fleeting experience of freedom must be renounced. Out of the life-and-death struggle life becomes more precious than freedom, and fear of its irremediable loss leads him to bend the knee to the victor: Spare my life and I shall renounce my freedom and serve you. But his humiliation is profound. For in his surrender the loser accepts for himself the reduction to mere "thingness" that he has suffered in the eyes of the victor. He becomes a mere thing in his own eyes as well.

v. The Master and the Slave

Now the scene changes drastically. The victor in the life-and-death struggle can take his ease. His life is no longer at risk, and he need no longer seek out the objects of his desire by his own efforts. In this sense his transcendence of the life cycle is permanent. He need but speak his desire and his erstwhile opponent, now his slave, will hasten to see that it is satisfied. We might most characteristically picture the master at table, with the slave waiting on him, serving up the food that he has prepared and trembling lest it not meet the demands of the master's discriminating palate.

Probably no section of the *Phenomenology* has been so much commented on as this tableau and the one to follow, both comprised under Hegel's title "Lordship and Bondage." So it will suffice to call attention briefly to a few points.

In this tableau the master is a free and independent self. The slave is reduced to a mere instrument for fulfilling the master's desires. Since for the master the world exists only to satisfy his desires, through the mediating efforts of the slave, he exists as the only autonomous self in a world of things. Indeed for the master the things have lost all their independence, their resistance to his desires; he has the slave to labor at overcoming this resistance, serving things up to him already prepared for his enjoyment. The slave, for his part, performs no action on his own behalf. What he does, the master does through him.

Recognition is entirely one-sided. The slave must recognize the master, who thus enjoys recognition through another consciousness. But the slave enjoys no such recognition. In the eyes of the master he is a mere instrument of the master's will. As Hegel spells the situation out, two aspects or "moments" of recognition are present, but not the crucial aspect of reciprocity:

> Thus there is this moment of recognition present, that the second consciousness denies its own being-for-itself, and thereby does

what the first does to it. The other moment is present also, that
this action of the second is the first's own action; for what the
slave does is really the action of the master, who is solely the
being-for-himself, the essence. He is the pure negative power for
whom the thing is nothing, and therefore is the pure essential
action in this relationship, while the action of the slave is not
pure, but unessential. But the moment needed for genuine recognition is lacking, that what the master does to the other he also
does to himself, and what the slave does to himself he also does
to the other. For this reason there is only a one-sided and unequal
recognition. (H 147; M 116; B 236)

The consequence of this lack of reciprocity is not only that the slave
receives no recognition, and thus no self-consciousness, but that he
cannot bestow a genuine recognition either. The master cannot find
his own self reflected in a slave who has no self. From the slave, as a
mere tool, he can receive only the identity of master, just as a man
becomes a woodsman through his ax, or a soldier through his sword,
or a plowman through his plow. So the slave, reduced to "thingness,"
confers on the master a fixed identity that generates no further psychic
development. The identity "master" is an undialectical dead end. Not
that the slave shows any guile in conferring this fixed identity. It is
the only one that he can confer, because he is only a slave. Of course
the master is well compensated for this lack of psychic development
by having a high old time for himself. But the happy life is stultifying,
just as the happy times, Hegel says many years later, are the blank
pages in history.[19] So the master enjoys no genuine being-for-himself
after all: because of the one-sidedness of the relation his identity is in
fact determined by the slave; his truth is "the unessential consciousness, and its unessential action" (H 147; M 117; B 237).

The irony of this turn in the story, in which the master's reduction
of the slave to a merely instrumental, thinglike person is made to recoil
on the master himself, introduces one of the masterstrokes of Hegelian
dialectic. It is no wonder the commentators have dwelt on it so lovingly.
The master-slave dialectic is completed in the essential inversion of
their positions, not that the slave becomes the master of his former
lord, but that he achieves a far more significant mastery, while the
master enjoys his torpidly good life at the cost of utter dependence on
the slave. For this reason we can now bid farewell to the master,
with best wishes for a long and pleasantly boring life, since he now

essentially drops out of the picture. In order to do justice to this remarkable inversion we introduce a new tableau to complete the dialectic of *Herrschaft und Knechtschaft*.

vi. The Self-Mastery of the Slave

Now both lordship and bondage are invested in the single figure of the slave, who alone occupies the stage. It is he, precisely through his bondage, who becomes the autonomous self and the cultivator of nature. We see him at his work, like a sculptor reshaping given natural materials into forms in which he finds his own psychic life reflected. To that extent he is as close to a fully self-conscious being as Hegel's chapter "Self-Consciousness" offers us. This ironic inversion of the slave's abject condition transpires through two converging relationships, one to the master, the other to the real things on which he labors. He becomes a self precisely as the mediator between the master's will and the real world.

To this extent the master remains a shadowy presence in the scene, though only as the transparent image of a more absolute master. In relation to the master the slave experiences a total anxiety, the terror of death, in which he makes discovery of a total self. In fact the life-and-death struggle remains, for the slave, the hidden ground of the whole relationship. His work is spurred by the terror that forced him into his enslaved condition in the first place. But the slave, who chose life above free selfhood in the mortal combat, now finds a still fuller sense of selfhood in the terror of his servitude.

With this analysis Hegel introduces the theme of "anxiety" into philosophical literature, as a medium of self-disclosure.[20] The slave, he says, has discovered autonomous self-consciousness in the master, but is not yet aware that he himself possesses it. He makes this discovery through the experience of anxiety. The slave

> has this truth of pure negativity and of *being-for-itself in fact within himself;* for he has *experienced* this essential being in himself. For this consciousness has experienced anxiety, not over this or that, nor for this or that instant, but encompassing his entire being; for he has felt the fear of death, the absolute master. (H 148; M 117;[21] B 237)

The master whom he is forced to serve is in fact a kind of surrogate for this absolute master; the slave is terrorized by his master only because the master wields this power of death over him. In this mortal terror the slave makes experience of his entire self as a whole; it is threatened as a whole, and also rendered totally fluid and malleable. As if in consonance with this negativity in himself, furthermore, he finds his world rendered in the same condition. In this experience of anxiety, Hegel continues, the slave's consciousness

> has been inwardly dissolved, he has trembled in every fiber of his being, and everything fixed and secure in him has been shaken. This pure universal movement, in which everything stable has become absolutely fluid, is the simple essence of self-consciousness, the absolute negativity, *the pure being-for-itself,* that is thereby *in* this consciousness. This moment of pure being-for-itself is also *for him,* because in the master it presents itself as the slave's *object.* Furthermore, he is not merely this universal dissolution *in general,* but in his service he brings it about *in actuality;* he transcends thereby his dependency on natural existence in every single detail, getting rid of it by his labor. (H 148; M 117; B 237–38)

The slave had renounced his freedom because his natural life had become too precious for him to risk. But now, ironically, in his bondage, not only is he shaken loose from the moorings of his own natural life, but in his terror he is induced to interfere with the givenness of natural life generally. He transforms the natural world by laboring over it.

This new relation to the natural world through labor is the second aspect of the slave's achievement of mastery. This second aspect is the consequence of the first, for he is driven to it by his mortal anxiety. He makes tools, cultivates fields and vineyards, cooks, builds shelters and furnishes them: he reshapes nature for human use, negating it as it is and reconstituting it. It is fundamental to Hegel's analysis that he does so only at the behest of another will. Ironically, he is forced into the dialectical role, which bears the seed of the higher consciousness, by his lord and master who, for his part, luxuriates in all the material benefits of the slave's labor. There is nothing to *drive* his Lordship into self-transformation, and for Hegel consciousness overcomes its own inertia only when it is driven to do so. So the bondage the slave suffers is the means of his liberation, which in the first instance is a liberation from the limits of his own self-will. The child whose whims are indulged is so confined within the fixed limits of his own desires that he never submits to the profoundly educative process of coming to terms with a world. That is the condition of the master, who remains related to the world purely through desiring and consuming, undisturbed in the psychic bondage of his narcissism. Yet it is he, ironically, who imposes the discipline on the slave that enables the slave to achieve that actual autonomy of which the master's independence is the illusory image.

Hegel summarizes the outcome of the master-slave relation in an outrageous pun on Psalm 111, "the fear of the lord is the beginning of wisdom." But the labor induced by this fear is what moves the slave forward from this anxious beginning to a measure of real wisdom. Desire simply consumes its object, at no great gain for wisdom. Deferred satisfaction is more frustrating, but more liberating in the end.

> Desire has reserved to itself the pure negating of the object and thus the unalloyed feeling of self. But this satisfaction is therefore only a disappearance, lacking the side of *objectivity* or *permanence*. Labor on the contrary is *restrained* desire, *delayed* disappearance; that is, labor *cultivates*. The negative relation to the object becomes the object's *form* and what is *abiding* in it, for precisely to the laborer does the object have independence.

This independence of which Hegel speaks is not merely the object's natural perdurability, but the new reality into which it has been transformed by the laborer. Out of the given, natural material he *makes* a new enduring thing, and this new, stable object, bearing the mark of his labor, reflects his own psychic life. Precisely because he has had to cope with real things, in their resistance and otherness, in his labor the slave overcomes the alienation that had existed between consciousness and the reality that confronts it. He finds himself mirrored in the thing he has made. Hegel continues:

> This *negative* middle term or formative *activity* is at the same time *the singularity* or the pure being-for-itself of consciousness, which now in labor passes out of consciousness into an enduring element. The laboring consciousness comes in this manner to perceive the independent being *as its own self*. (H 148–49; M 118; B 238)

The slave does not, to be sure, achieve recognition in another self-consciousness, as the concept of self-consciousness prescribes. But he does come to recognize his own objectified image in the work of his hands, and in this image he recognizes himself.

Hegel concludes this remarkable dénouement of the master-slave dialectic by suggesting that in this process the slave finally overcomes that fear for his life that had reduced him to servitude in the first place. Not that he has become invulnerable, but that in asserting his own power to fashion the things in his environment he has achieved a psychic detachment from that entire natural, given life cycle in which his own animal life is embedded. Self-consciousness, secure in its autonomous being-for-itself, has asserted its own higher order against that order of dumb nature. The negativity of the natural order against that life which is its mere part has been superseded by the negativity of active, laboring self-consciousness. In the "fashioning" or "cultivating" *(Bilden)* of a natural entity into a new object suffused with his own intention,

> the slave's own negativity, his being-for-itself, only becomes an object for him through overcoming the subsistent *form* that stood in opposition to him. But this objective negativity is precisely the alien essence before which he had trembled. But now he destroys this alien negativity, establishing *himself* as the abiding negativity, and thus *for himself* becomes an existence-for-itself. (H 149; M 118; B 239)

The erstwhile slave, that is, now assumes an autonomous dignity in his own eyes, as the master of nature and the possessor of a transcending selfhood that is more than his own mere natural life. Now the Sartrean formula for the self that is for-itself *(pour-soi)* becomes appropriate: he is the being who is not what he is, and is what he is not. Contrary to Sartre, however, he is not confronted by an alien world as a sheer impermeable in-itself. He has achieved his sense of self not only through mortal anxiety, but in the fashioning of the world into a human environment, a wheatfield, a well-furnished home, a city, coming to self-discovery in the mirror of his own works. He has given it a form that is the reflection of himself.

> In virtue of the fact that the form is *established* by him, it is to him no longer something other than he; for it is just his pure being-for-itself that comes to the truth in it. Thus through this rediscovery of himself through himself, precisely in his labor, he

comes to his *own meaning* in what had seemed to have only an *alien meaning.*

Having overcome the natural givenness of things, the slave has also transcended the mere natural givenness of his own life, and can no longer be enslaved by threats against his life. Thus he has negated even the predicament that had originally forced him onto the path to this truth. But as Kojève points out, this achievement required the moment of enslavement: "The complete, absolutely free man . . . will be the Slave who has 'overcome' his Slavery."[22] Hegel concludes his section "Lordship and Bondage" by carefully underlining this essential irony: In order for this reflection to occur, in which the slave finds his free and autonomous existence mirrored in the things he has formed, the discipline of his bondage and the terror of death together with his formative activity *(Bilden)* are necessary conditions:

> For this reflection both moments are necessary, the moments of fear and of service in general, together with that of formative activity, and both at the same time in universal fashion. Without the discipline of service and obedience the fear would remain merely formal and would not extend over the known actuality of existence. Without the formative activity the fear would remain inward and dumb, and consciousness would not come to exist for itself. If consciousness performed its formative activity without the original absolute fear it would be merely a vain self-centeredness; then its form or negativity would not be negativity *in itself;* and its formative activity could therefore not give him the consciousness of himself as essential being. If he did not experience the absolute fear, but only a bit of anxiety here and there, the negative essence would remain external to him and his substance would not be infected by it through and through. (H 149–50; M 119; B 239–40)

In that case, Hegel goes on to suggest, his mastery both of the world and of himself would be incomplete, willful, and episodic. All three of these elements must be in place for autonomous self-consciousness to arise. Terror, discipline, and labor, among the more unwelcome conditions of existence, give rise to a new self-mastery and a mastery of the world of which the original master could scarcely conceive.

Is the Master-Slave Dialectic a Historical Paradigm?

It is not surprising that this ironical dialectic of the master and slave
has provided one of the seminal documents of Marxist philosophy of
history. It is characteristic of Marxist readings of the *Phenomenology*
to treat this section as the key to the entire work. It is also characteristic
of Marxist thinkers to find in its central themes—the oppression of
slaves by masters and their triumph in the reflexive transformation of
world and self through labor—not only the key to a book, but a paradigm
for understanding history generally. In 1844 Marx himself criticizes
the idealistic premises he sees informing the *Phenomenology* as a whole,
yet he singles out the theme of transformation through labor as its
great contribution: "The great thing in Hegel's *Phenomenology* and its
end result—the dialectic of negativity as the moving and generative
principle—is simply that Hegel grasps human self-generation as a process, objectification as opposition, as externalization *(Entäusserung)* and
as the overcoming of this externalization; that he therefore grasps the
essence of *labor* and comprehends the objective human being, the true
because actual human being, as the result of his own labor."[23]

Kojève, the great Marxist interpreter of the *Phenomenology* (though
his Marxism is of a very independent sort!), in fact interprets the entire
work as the elaboration of this insight, thus treating the dialectic of
master and slave as the central problem addressed by the work as a
whole, and indeed its solution. In this way, Kojève offers a reading that
effectively eliminates the idealism to which Marx objected, treating not
only the present section but the entire *Phenomenology* as a historically
grounded paradigm of historical conflict. This brilliantly executed tour
de force is not only the most philosophically serious interpretation of
the *Phenomenology* in our century, but was an important political event
in its own right. Its critics, who have an easy time showing that Kojève
takes impossible liberties from the standpoint of Hegel's own intentions,
seem not to recognize that for Kojève interpreting a philosophical text
is not necessarily the same as compiling the opinions and intentions
of its author. One suspects that Kojève took a good deal of pleasure in
showing how some of Hegel's ideas, particularly those developed in the
master-slave section, could be carried to logical conclusions that might
have horrified Hegel. But in a *philosophical* interpretation the important thing is to read the text according to its truth. The truth in
the present case, for Kojève, lies in its application to history. A very
general statement of his thesis is as follows:

In fine, then, we can say this: Man was born and History began with the first Fight that ended in the appearance of a Master and a Slave. That is to say that Man—at his origin—is always either Master or Slave; and that true Man can exist only where there is a Master *and* a Slave. (If they are to be *human,* they must be at least *two* in number.) And universal history, the history of the interaction between men and of their interaction with Nature, is the history of the interaction between warlike Masters and working Slaves. Consequently, History stops at the moment when the difference, the opposition, between Master and Slave disappears.[24]

Kojève goes on to suggest that this moment had arrived, in principle, with the French Revolution and the Napoleonic Wars, with the Battle of Jena in particular, so that Hegel actually *heard* its arrival as he completed the *Phenomenology!* Hegel's achievement of a total comprehension of history was assured by this experience in which the master-slave dialectic was brought to a triumphant close on his doorstep. Kojève later suggests that Hegel completed the achievement of Napoleon by doing the one thing Napoleon was not equipped to do: comprehending its universal significance. Thus Hegel becomes "somehow Napoleon's Self-Consciousness," and the two together, the man of action and the man of thought, make up one complete personal identity.

The phenomenon that completes the historical evolution and thus makes the absolute Science possible, therefore, is the "conception" *(Begreifen)* of Napoleon by Hegel. This dyad, formed by Napoleon and Hegel, is the perfect Man, fully and definitively "satisfied" by what he *is* and what he *knows* himself to be. *This* is the realization of the ideal revealed by the myth of Jesus Christ, of the God-Man.[25]

That, according to Kojève, is why there is also so much theology in Hegel's thought, developing the significance of this event from its religious side.

We shall certainly want to return to this startling conclusion, which does, with a vengeance, offer one reading of the "transformation of Christian themes" in Hegel's thought. I have introduced it at this point just to indicate how far Kojève is prepared to carry his thesis that the key to universal history is the master-slave dialectic and its dénouement. Our interest here is in this "motive principle of the historical process" presented in the present chapter of the *Phenomenology* and elaborated in the chapter on Spirit through "the analysis of the historical process itself." Indeed, the entire *Phenomenology* is devoted to the articulation of this theme, in the interest of an interpretation of "universal history," that "is nothing but the history of the *dialectical*—i.e., *active*—relation between Mastery and Slavery."[26]

In an article containing perhaps the most astute criticism to which Kojève's interpretation has been subjected, George Armstrong Kelly registers his chief objection at just this point. He does not object, however, to the historicizing of the master-slave dialectic, but to what he argues is its one-sided historicizing: the historical interpretation must be balanced by and integrated with a psychological interpretation.

> Lordship and bondage is properly seen from three angles that are equally valid and interpenetrable. One of these angles is necessarily the social, of which Kojève has given such a dazzling reading. Another regards the shifting pattern of psychological domination and servitude within the individual ego. The third then becomes a fusion of the other two processes: the interior consequences wrought by the external confrontation of the Self and the Other, the Other and the Self, which has commenced in the struggle for recognition. . . . On the overtly social plane there are, at a given point in history, slaves and masters. In the interior of consciousness, each man possesses faculties of slavery and mastery in his own regard that he struggles to bring into harmony. . . .
>
> In brief, man remits the tensions of his being upon the world of fellow beings and is himself changed in the process. This relationship should be stressed, since it furnishes the bridge between psychology and history.[27]

But this view seems to me to be quite consonant with Kojève's interpretation, elaborating the use of the master-slave dialectic as a historical paradigm into a historico-psychological paradigm.

I should say that the master-slave dialectic can be forced into service as a historical paradigm only at great violence both to historical interpretation and to the reading of Hegel's *Phenomenology*. To apply it without further ado directly to the rest of the *Phenomenology,* much less to universal history, is to place a burden on it much too great for it to bear. Masters are not invariably reduced to torpor. Slaves and other bondsmen do not always achieve mastery over nature or over themselves; indeed, according to Marx's own reading of history the slaves, especially in their modern incarnation as proletariat, are brutalized and dehumanized, only roused to change their condition when they have nothing to lose but their chains. But it is doubtful whether the tangled web of history can be explained purely by reference to the relation of "slaves" and "masters" anyway, even if we allow the widest possible latitude in our use of these terms. To propose, furthermore, that the inadequacy of this analysis as an interpretation of history might be corrected by interiorizing it, so that it would also do service as a psychology, is simply to extend to psychology the violence done to history. Nor can any of these theses be attributed to Hegel without equal violence to the *Phenomenology* itself, the great virtue of which is that its application to history and psychology, not to speak of theology, is indirect and nonreductive. We do learn something about social relations and the inner life, and particularly about their interpenetration, by pondering Hegel's master-slave dialectic, but we do not thereby "explain" these relations in any quasi-scientific sense, nor would Hegel even have supposed that we could. When Hegel does venture to develop a philosophy of history, and also a psychology, the attempt does not remotely resemble the reductive simplicities to which such a paradigm would lead us. Of course one may argue, as Marx quite straightforwardly does, that Hegel did not grasp the full import of his most fruitful ideas. But without arguing that question, the deeper issue concerns the reductive employment of ideas the dialectical design of which is calculated to challenge all forms of reductionism. Our suggestion that the entire chapter on Self-Consciousness (though not the whole *Phenomenology*) has a mythic character at least has the negative advantage of forestalling that particular error. A serviceable myth does indeed provide a certain depth dimension to historical and psychological understanding, but it never provides direct and exhaustive explanations precisely because this dimension is always qualified by the particular historical and psychological conditions under which it finds expression.

But here we are less concerned with the use of the master-slave dialectic as a paradigm for historical understanding than with the obverse of that effort, with historical and/or psychological interpretations of the section of the *Phenomenology* in which it appears. Such interpretations fly in the face of the context Hegel has provided in this chapter. The conclusion of the master-slave dialectic is precisely the point at which a transcending form of self-consciousness arises, detaching itself qualitatively from the material and social (really intersubjective) conditions that gave rise to it. Hegel's concluding remarks in that section, to which we have called attention, are as if designed to forestall both the existentialist interpretation of this autonomous self, based on absolute anxiety alone, and the Marxist interpretation based on labor and the discipline of servitude alone. The three factors together produce, and can alone produce, a self whose self-mastery finally liberates it from the terror, the material dependency, and the servitude alike that had produced it. That is the full irony of that triumphant conclusion. Just at this point in our myth a new region of psychic space takes shape, detached from the conditions of its natural life. The entire chapter up to this point has described the tortuous formation of this new region, above the horizon of the natural life process and asserting its mastery over that process. Here self-consciousness breathes the uncontaminated air of its pure freedom, and the remainder of the chapter ("Part B. Freedom of Self-Consciousness: Stoicism, Skepticism, and the Unhappy Consciousness") will unfold entirely within this new inner space.

But as we know, from having dipped into the conclusion, this new region of free self-consciousness, having disentangled itself from its material conditions, will generate some new entanglements of its own.

vii. Stoicism: The Contentment of Pure Thought

In this tableau the dramatic element is distinctly subdued. In fact nothing is happening at all. The curtain rises on a man sitting and thinking. Rodin's "Thinker" is as if designed for this tableau. If there is anything else lying about on the stage he does not permit it to distract him. Still, a person lost in deep thought is, in its way, quite a remarkable sight. One thinks of Augustine's astonishment when he came upon Ambrose silently reading. Perhaps, as Melville suggests, a faint undulation of steam arises, of which the whale's spout is prototype, from the head of all ponderous and profound creatures in the act of deep thought, but no other motion is disclosed in this tableau. What is uncanny is that a sensuous creature has withdrawn his attention from the sensuous world. He has directed the most concentrated attention to the invisible inner space that has taken form in his thoughts.

So the interest in this scene is entirely inward, in the mind. But even an inscape would reveal no sensuous images, or memories of things past, or objects of desire, or other such perturbations to disturb the contemplations of our thinker, for nothing that derives from experience has any place there. He thinks pure concepts, of the good, the true, and the beautiful, for instance, purely rational in form and without concrete content. Hence his sublime self-contentment: his thought is entirely engendered in the mind itself. That is his perfect freedom. Mere sensuous images must be impressed upon my mind from the outside world, through experience; "however, the concept is to me immediately *my* concept. In thinking I *am* quite *free,* because I am not in another but abide entirely within myself, and the object that is essential to me is my being-for-myself in inseparable unity" (H 152; M 120; B 243).

The pure mind, indeed, that enjoys this perfect unity, is only incidentally attached to a particular person; his biographical details are irrelevant to his thought. For here we have *"thinking* consciousness *in general,"* uncontaminated alike by external objects and by whatever psychological development may have brought it to this plateau.

So it is useless to ask for some story that would show how the erstwhile slave of our previous tableau, having become master of his world and of himself, has further progressed to the enjoyment of this mental state. He would not be able to recognize "for himself" how this transition occurs. But it occurs "in itself" and "for us" who observe. *We* see (don't we?) that "in the concept of autonomous consciousness the being-*in-itself* is consciousness, and thus the side of being-*in-itself* or *thinghood,* which received its form in labor, has become no other substance than consciousness, and has become for us a new form of self-consciousness" (H 151; M 120; B 242). The world and the conscious self, which still remain distinct for the self-liberated slave, are conjoined for us in this new tableau. The essential world is contained in consciousness itself.

This new moment has been exemplified historically in Stoicism, if only loosely, and without implying all the details of that philosophical system. Yet this form of consciousness is one of the few in the *Phenomenology* that can be directly referred to a philosophical school at all. The moments in this work represent shapes of consciousness we might encounter in ordinary, active life, and that is true of this one as well, but it is precisely characteristic of it to have achieved philosophical detachment from the snares and delusions of experience. Stoicism is what popular understanding recognizes as a "philosophical" temper of mind, in the actual world to be sure, but not of it, perhaps coping with it according to need but beyond desire for anything it can provide. Even the distinction between master and slave, which dominated the previous section, here becomes a matter of indifference on both sides. Hegel doubtless has in mind the Emperor Marcus Aurelius and Epictetus the slave, Stoic sages both and alike indifferent to the enormous social gulf that separates them. What is essential

> is solely the distinction that is *thought,* or immediately indistinguishable from myself. This consciousness is accordingly negative toward the relation of lordship and bondage; its activity is neither in the master to have its truth in the slave, nor in the slave to have its truth in the master's will and service, but whether on the throne or in chains to be free in all the dependency of its particular existence and to maintain itself in that lifelessness which constantly returns out of the movement of existence, out of productive activity as well as suffering, into *the simple essentiality of thought.* (H 153; M 121; B 244)

Hegel cannot suppress a little historical note at this point, of which the chapter on Self-Consciousness is otherwise free. Historically, after all, Stoicism was a phenomenon of late Roman antiquity, and the fearful leveling of ethical life that Hegel attributed, early and late, to the Roman order (that *"boredom of the world,"* he called it a few years before),[28] provides the sort of ravaged field that spawns the unworldly wisdom of Stoicism, like a cactus in the desert. The radical turn inward occurs historically when active political life becomes insupportable. The Stoic phenomenon "could come forth as a universal form of the World-Spirit only in a time of universal fear and slavery, but also of universal culture which had ascended to the level of thought" (H 153; M 121; B 245).

This historical explanation of the rise of Stoicism is more pointedly (and appropriately) drawn in the section of the chapter on Spirit entitled "Legal Status," obviously modeled on the Roman world, where a spiritless order has reduced human community to a homogeneous aggregate of atomized individuals possessing merely legal "personhood." There Hegel alludes directly to the present section, suggesting that this desolated condition gives rise to the form of thinking divorced from actual life characteristic of Stoicism. Stoicism

> is nothing else but the consciousness which brings the principles of legal status, spiritless autonomy, to abstract form; through its flight from *actuality* it achieves only the thought of autonomy;

it is absolutely for *itself* in that its essence is not attached to any existing thing, but renounces everything that exists and locates its essence in the unity of pure thought alone. (H 343; M 290–91; B 502)

It is important to note that Hegel goes on to discuss skepticism and unhappy consciousness again in this section on Legal Status, placing them along with Stoicism in this recognizably historical context. The difference this context makes will be of interest to us in connection with the larger question that has troubled us about the relation to history of the rather abstract, ahistorical, "mythic" treatment of these themes in the chapter on Self-Consciousness. We will return to this nest of issues shortly, in our reconsideration of unhappy consciousness.

Returning to our present section, Hegel remarks that Stoic freedom, just as an achievement of uncontaminated thought, is necessarily lifeless. Real freedom must be achieved *in* actual life, not in detachment from it. But here we have "only the concept of freedom, not the living freedom itself," and however "uplifting" the Stoic pronouncements about Truth, Goodness, Wisdom, or Virtue may be, in the end they are in their abstractness merely boring (H 153–54; M 122; B 245–46). The curtain falls on this tableau with our philosopher nodding off, his index finger still on his brow.

viii. Skepticism: The Polemic of Thought Against Actuality

If the Stoic sage was indifferent to the world of experience, this new scene pictures a thinker actively presenting proofs against it, perhaps thrusting his stick in the water to show how the senses deceive when the stick appears bent. Again, as in the case of Stoicism, we have a rare case in which a philosophical school is named to epitomize a much more general attitude, though it does usually involve some intellectual sophistication, or at least sophistical pretension. Here the negativity of reflective self-consciousness toward the empirical world becomes polemical, actively denying it any claim to truth. So skepticism is "the realization of that position of which Stoicism is merely the concept — and the actual experience of what the freedom of thought is." Pure thought is complete in itself, "infinite" in its self-sufficiency, and thus indifferent to anything outside itself. For whatever is finite, limited in itself, confronting the free consciousness as something other which would place

a limit on its own completeness, can have no truth. That was already
the case in principle with Stoicism;

> in skepticism, now, there develops *for consciousness* the com-
> pletely unessential and nonindependent status of this other;
> thought becomes the completed thinking that annihilates the
> being of the world in its *complex determinacy,* and the negativity
> of free self-consciousness becomes the real negating of this mani-
> fold configuration of life. —Just as Stoicism fulfills the *concept*
> of *autonomous* consciousness that appeared as the relation of
> Lordship and Bondage, so it is clear that skepticism fulfills its
> *realization* as the negative attitude directed against otherness
> in desire and labor. (H 155; M 123; B 246–47)

Desire and labor were the partial negativities introduced earlier, desire
directed to the consumption of the natural object (by the master), labor
to its transformation into an artifact (by the slave). But as Hegel goes
on to say, with self-conscious thought the negativity is complete, denying any independent validity to anything in the world of experience.
For the thinking consciousness nothing is essential except itself. Using
its own self-evident validity as the measure, it finds everything outside
itself so questionable as to dissolve before its eyes. By this measure
not only the world of the senses is cast into doubt, but supposed ethical
laws as well, anything that would impose some external claim on thinking consciousness.

What gives this description of skepticism a special interest is its
superficial resemblance to Hegel's own phenomenological method,
which serves to bring out important differences. Negativity is the skeptical moment in dialectic, and in the *Phenomenology* this skeptical
negativity prevails over every positive form presented to it. The entire
Phenomenology, according to the Preface, exhibits "the tremendous
power of the negative," which is "the energy of thinking, of the pure
ego" that both presupposes and validates the absolute freedom of spirit
(H 29; M 19; B 93). Again, as a "pathway of doubt" and of "despair,"
the method of the *Phenomenology* is described in the Introduction as
a "thoroughgoing skepticism." But in that context Hegel distinguishes
sharply between his phenomenological use of this skeptical method
and a skeptical form of thinking that pretends "to produce everything
itself and to regard only its own deed as true." There are two related
differences: the skeptical method of phenomenology is as critical of the

thinker's own form of consciousness as it is of the phenomena of ordinary experience; and this skeptical method is the negativity that clears the way and propels thinking toward a systematic science of wisdom. "The series of its own configurations through which consciousness passes on this pathway is . . . the detailed history of the *education* [*Bildung*] of consciousness itself into science" (H 67; M 50; B 136). Here skepticism has the function Hegel had assigned it in his essay in the *Critical Journal* on "The Relation of Skepticism to Philosophy" (1802), as a propaedeutic to speculative truth; Plato and Spinoza were said to be "skeptics" in this sense. In Hegel's view, spirit is not locked into the inner space of consciousness, in opposition to the actual world. That opposition between inner and outer is one of the dualisms against which the skeptical method of the *Phenomenology* is directed, in order that spirit may emerge as their unity.

But the skepticism being passed in review in the chapter on Self-Consciousness is predicated on that opposition. It is clearly of the undialectical sort that is critical of everything but its own purely inward truth. Secure in its own absolute freedom and self-sufficiency, the skeptical self-consciousness lets everything definite or determinate *(bestimmt)* disappear; "it is this ataraxy of thinking that thinks itself, the unchangeable and *genuine certainty of itself.*" "Ataraxy" is the stoic indifference toward everything not under the control of the mind itself. So this self-certainty is not the consequence of a dialectical movement from outer to inner, that incorporates and reflects in itself a development in the sensuous world. Instead, sensuous images that had supposedly been dismissed simply crop up in the mind thinly disguised, as if the mind had generated them itself. Whether the skeptic in question is one who marshals philosophical arguments against common experience and social convention, or is a streetwise cynic who consigns the world to filth and folly, and so maintains a frosty integrity by refusing to be taken in by it, a certain inner disorder arises by virtue of the impossibility of keeping the region of delusion safely at arm's length.

He discovers the delusion creeping into his own inner space, like fog through a window. And so the division he has clung to between his own rational identity and the world of illusion outside now comes to reside in himself. The skeptical self-consciousness must confess that alongside his free and uncontaminated mind he *also* finds

> an utterly accidental, particular consciousness—a consciousness that is *empirical,* directed toward things that have no reality for

him, which obeys what has no essential being for him, which
acts and brings to actuality what has no truth for him. But even
so, while he admits in this way to being a *particular, accidental*
and in fact brutish life and *lost* self-consciousness, he also takes
himself, on the contrary, again to be a *universal, self-identical*
self-consciousness; for it is the negativity of all particularity and
all difference. (H 157; M 125; B 249)

The reader who has glanced ahead, as we have, to the next section,
will recognize that the unhappy consciousness is beginning to take
shape in the skeptic, who has no sooner rejected the unessential world
outside than he finds that the division between the essential and the
unessential, the unchangeable and the changeable, the pristine and
the mottled, has taken up a painful joint residence in his own inner
being. Hegel is not necessarily committed to the claim that unhappy
consciousness can only develop out of a prior skepticism, but there is
more than a casual association, both in the history of philosophy[29]
and in everyday life between the kinds of quasi-religious absolutism
represented by unhappy consciousness and a skeptical disillusionment
with the sensuous, the relative, and the worldly. If I experience the
world as *Dreck,* if I am "repelled" by it, the energy of that repulsion
will carry me some distance in search of an absolute perfection; or if I
have found such an absolute the world will seem a poor thing by
comparison.

   In Hegel's analysis the stoic has found such an absolute in himself,
in his own inner space, and the skeptic, in turn, has found the actual
world wanting. But as the analysis proceeds, the entire repellant relation between *Dreck* and perfection has been relocated in the skeptic's
inner space. Hegel completes the analysis by pointing up the logical
and psychological contradictions into which the skeptic falls as a result.
The skeptic

> lets the unessential content in his thinking disappear, but in
> that very act his consciousness is an unessential; he declares
> the absolute *disappearance,* but this declaration *is,* and this
> consciousness is the declared disappearance; he declares the
> nothingness of seeing, hearing, etc., and yet he *himself* sees,
> hears, and so forth; he declares the nothingness of ethical prin-
> ciples and yet subjects his own behavior to their rule. His actions
> and his words constantly contradict, and in the same way he

has the doubly contradictory consciousness of his own unchange-
ability and identity together with that of being completely accidental and without identity. (H 157–58; M 125; B 249–50)

Finding it impossible to bring the two sides of this contradiction together, the skeptic resorts typically to a posture of childish polemic
that attacks whichever side of the contradiction anyone else chances
to defend. Against worldly common sense he unfurls his absolutism,
against absolutism he counters with shrewd cynicism: "His chatter is
in fact like the bickering of wilful boys, one of whom says A if the other
says B, and again says B when the other says A, and who at cost of
contradicting *themselves* purchase the pleasure of constantly contradicting each other" (H 158; M 126; B 250).

　But this experience of self-contradiction gives rise to "a *new shape*" of
consciousness, "which brings together the two thoughts that skepticism
holds apart." This new moment is the unhappy consciousness, which
affirms both sides of the contradiction, finding both the essential and
the unessential present in that inner, psychic space that has arisen
with the subjugation and subsequent denial of the actual world.

ix.　Unhappy Consciousness and the Problem of Hegel's
　　Phenomenology

Now that we have come full circle, returning to the topic with which
we began this chapter, we will reconsider our earlier analysis in context,
as the final tableau in the series we have reviewed. Here, indeed, our
plan of presenting the chapter on Self-Consciousness in a series of
tableaux falls into some embarrassment. It becomes impossible to render this final moment visually, but this embarrassment may itself suggest how this moment is related to the preceding ones. Beginning with
the tableau representing Stoicism, what was directly visible on our
stage began to be attenuated, while the significant activity receded
more and more to that invisible, psychic region of inner space that
opened up at the conclusion of the master-slave dialectic. With skepticism we began with a conflict between the flux and illusion of the
external world and the stability and truth of the inner region of thought,
but then this very distinction was transferred into inner space. With
unhappy consciousness the visible world has been reduced to nullity,
and attention is fixed upon the polarity between the changeable and
the unchangeable that is located entirely in the psychic interior. "For

itself," to be sure, unhappy consciousness does not recognize that this conflict transpires entirely within itself. Since the subject-object structure of consciousness requires at least an imaginative object, unhappy consciousness finds a ghost of the exteriority it has lost in the unchangeable it has projected into the Beyond. But there is nothing anthropomorphic about this particular ghost. If the tableau representing this situation is to be anything more than an empty stage, we must resort to some such metaphor as we proposed in our earlier discussion of unhappy consciousness, of elements in a magnetic field constantly changing their configurations between the two poles. But a better image would highlight the primacy of the single field rather than its two poles.

In fact such an image lies close at hand, one that rounds off the chapter in particularly handsome fashion: it is the tableau with which we began, representing the great cycle of life, organic nature as a universal fluidity, perpetually constituting individuated forms and absorbing them again, yet remaining ever the same as a whole. In our discussion of that tableau we remarked upon its formal resemblance to the restlessly shifting configuration that makes up unhappy consciousness. But with unhappy consciousness the configuration has passed entirely out of nature, to be reconstituted in this aethereal intrapsychic region containing not so much as a smudge of real protoplasm. Its image is a kind of photographic negative, as its concept is the dialectical negative, of the organic flux. The entire chapter is in fact the story of this displacement from pure nature to pure ideality. Its series of tableaux makes up a myth, not of creation, but of aetherealization.

So we should not be surprised to find many formal resemblances from one episode of this myth to another despite dramatic changes of scene. Hegel himself points out that something very like the relation of master and slave is recapitulated in the unhappy consciousness. He makes that connection in locating unhappy consciousness as the extreme point in the latter half of this continuum from outer to inner.

> In Stoicism self-consciousness is simple freedom within its own self; in skepticism this freedom becomes a reality, annihilating the other side, that of determinate existence, but then it doubles *itself,* and is now in its own eyes a duality. In this fashion the doubling that earlier distributed itself between two single figures, the master and the slave, is now lodged in one; the doubling of self-consciousness within itself, which is essential in the con-

cept of spirit, is thus at hand, but not yet its unity: and the *unhappy consciousness* is the consciousness of itself as the doubled, merely contradictory being. (H 158; M 126; B 250–51)

That is how Hegel introduces unhappy consciousness. The statement deserves close attention. The formal resemblance of unhappy consciousness to the master-slave dialectic does not imply that it is merely a psychological sublimation of the condition of servitude, as Marxists tend to view it. Rather, both are instances of the "doubling" *(Verdopplung)* inherent in self-consciousness. This "doubling" is the formal equivalent of the principle of recognition. That is why Hegel can say that it is "essential in the concept of spirit." Self-consciousness will be completely realized only when the principle of recognition is perfectly fulfilled, in spirit. But even in these defective realizations of the principle, without mutual recognition, *we* can see that in each moment there is both unity and doubleness or division. In the life-and-death struggle and in lordship and bondage self-consciousness exists only in a state of dispersion between two figures, neither of whom is self-conscious: self-consciousness, in itself and for us, is the "middle term" that joins the two "extremes" of the relationship. It is like the common literary device of representing the two psychological sides of a character by providing him with an inseparable companion, his alter ego, so that the duality is exteriorized and made more poetically available. Goethe made an especially rich use of this device, of which the pairing of Faust and Mephistopheles is only the most familiar of many examples.[30] The two combatants in the struggle, and then the master and the slave, make up similar pairings that together express the concept of self-consciousness. In the sections on Stoicism and skepticism, on the other hand, "we" see how the doubleness comes to reassert itself even within a single, free consciousness that has severed its reflexive relation with an actual other, and unhappy consciousness is the result, mirroring both the failed struggle for recognition (Hegel refers more than once to the "unchangeable" as the "enemy") and the master-slave relation despite the decisive turn inward. In this ironical sense the "concept" of self-consciousness does assert itself after all, through the entire course of the chapter: the relationship between two is mirrored in each consciousness, though not "for itself," but only "in itself" and "for us." The concept of self-consciousness asserts itself either as the unity of the two, or the division of the one, but in neither case is mutual recognition actually achieved. In the struggle and in the master-slave relation each is aware of the other, but does not recognize himself in the other. Unhappy consciousness recognizes itself without being aware that it *is* itself it recognizes in the apparent other. In either case there is in truth both identity and division, the "we" that is an "I" and then the "I" that is a "we," and that condition is not only inherent in self-consciousness, but is the necessary condition for the emergence of spirit.

So this moment of psychic laceration—the unhappy consciousness that is "for itself" two but "in itself" one—is a necessary ordeal of self-consciousness in the course of what Mark Taylor felicitously calls its "journey to selfhood" as spirit.[31] Indeed, it represents the fundamental problem of the *Phenomenology,* of which spirit is the solution. From this point of view what has come before in the chapter, including the master-slave dialectic, requires the moment of unhappy consciousness to culminate the myth of the self. Only in unhappy consciousness do we arrive at a form of self-consciousness that recognizes the self in its absolute, unconditional form (though, to be sure, without recognizing *itself* in this absolute self). For Hegel this absolute identity, this un-changeable essence, is an essential moment in the truth of spirit. It *is* not yet spirit: the vital cycle of life, at the other pole, must also be incorporated into spirit's fullness, as well as a form of individuality that recognizes itself both in the absolute essence and in nature, and is recognized in turn. Spirit requires this last moment in the myth of the self as well as the first moment of which the last is the negative image; spirit requires as well the entire development by which we have proceeded from the one to the other. The struggle for recognition and the master-slave dialectic constitute at once the break in the natural totality with which we began and the prefiguration of and preparation for the ideal totality that arises in unhappy consciousness.

But before discussing further this relation of unhappy consciousness to spirit, I must acknowledge that the alternative Marxist reading, according to which the master-slave dialectic is itself the definitive statement of the problem, of which unhappy consciousness is merely a secondary growth, does enjoy textual support in the later section on Legal Status to which we referred in discussing Stoicism. For there, in a transparently historical context in the chapter on Spirit, referring to Roman rule, the transition from Stoicism to unhappy consciousness is recapitulated as the direct outcome of the reduction of all to mere legal "personhood," really to universal bondage under the will of a single imperial "master." In that section Hegel carefully underlines the parallel, that as Stoicism arises in the chapter on Self-Consciousness "out of Lordship and Bondage, as the immediate existence of *self-consciousness,* so personality"—the atomized individual bereft of ethical community or free political life—"proceeds out of the immediate *spirit* which is the universally dominating will over all and is concurrently the servile obedience to it" (H 343; M 290; B 502). This "immediate spirit" is composed, that is, of the symbiosis between the single "Lord of the World" and the universal bondage of these abject "persons."

This desolate pattern in the actual world, this haggard "spirit" that has replaced the many Volksgeister of ethnic/ethical communities destroyed by the might of the new master, has left consciousness with no politically effective alternative: it must retreat from the public space of the actual world into the inner space in which the futile procession Stoicism–skepticism–unhappy consciousness unfolds. "The *consciousness driven back* out of this actuality *into itself*" now, with unhappy consciousness, contemplates "its unessential nature," which corresponds to its condition in the actual world. This is the context in the *Phenomenology* in which Hegel introduces the concept of self-alienation. Here is disclosed the "*actual* truth" of unhappy consciousness, lost in the contemplation of its unessential nature: its truth, that is, from the point of view of the "actual" political world. This truth

> consists in the fact that this *universal valuation* [*Gelten*] of self-consciousness is its alienated reality. This *valuation* is the universal actuality of the self, but it is immediately the perversion of the self as well; it is the loss of its essence. —The actuality of the self, which was not present in the Ethical World, is achieved through its regression into the *person;* . . . it emerges in developed form, but alienated from itself. (H 346; M 293; B 506)

This brief recapitulation of the transition from lordship and bondage to unhappy consciousness accordingly introduces the long section of the chapter on Spirit entitled "Self-Alienated Spirit."

Now this recapitulation in the section "Legal Status" is accented in a dramatically different way than the original development in the chapter on Self-Consciousness. Here we have no ironic triumph of the slave over his master, but a retreat from the world over which the imperial master holds complete and terrible sway. Here the development issuing in unhappy consciousness is no myth of the self becoming lost in the newly discovered topography of inner-psychic life, but a fundamentally political phenomenon: the impotent reaction to universal tyranny. Unhappy consciousness is the pathetic recourse of the slave who, far from finding inner liberation, simply transfers to his inner world the same abject bondage to a tyrannical master that he had suffered in the actual, public world. Even if we follow the Marxist commentators and identify unhappy consciousness with religion, we find here no "opium of the people," no "heart of a heartless world," no "expression of" and "protest against real suffering,"[32] but an inner landscape as harsh and heartless as the actual world it reflects. There is admittedly a harder Marxist line on religion, according to which it is the ideological mirror and legitimation of a society's power structure, to which this interpretation of unhappy consciousness is more consonant. It is still closer to Nietzsche's diagnosis of religion as the servile inner life of slaves. But none of that is implied in the chapter on Self-Consciousness.

So the issue for the interpreter of the *Phenomenology* concerns the relation between these two quite different versions of the transition from lordship and bondage to unhappy consciousness. The second puts this transition into a definite historical, political context. The first does not. Does the second version therefore provide the definitive interpretation of the first? But then the first version, in the chapter on Self-Consciousness, could not have the universality Hegel appears to invest in it. Unhappy consciousness would *merely* be a neurotic reaction to a particular set of historical circumstances, and not an essential crisis of self-consciousness under way to becoming spirit (it could be the latter and still sometimes be the former, but it cannot merely be the former and still be the latter). But in fact unhappy consciousness keeps turning up explicitly in several other sections of the *Phenomenology* (e.g., "Faith and Pure Insight," "The Beautiful Soul") and implicitly in many more. Its appearance under the rubric of legal status may well represent its historical locus classicus, that prompted Hegel to recognize its general significance. We found Christian otherworldliness interpreted as a reaction to Roman rule already in the Frankfurt manuscripts (especially in *The Spirit of Christianity and Its Fate*), and this motif is further developed in Jena (especially in the Lecture Manuscript on Natural Law); even in Bern, both in his manuscripts and in his correspondence, we have found him alert to the general link between authoritarian religion and political oppression.[33] This motif is enshrined in the *Phenomenology* in the section on Legal Status. But it is characteristic of Hegel to press his historical insights on into their universal ground, and that, I think, is what has led to the much more detailed and much more general treatment of unhappy consciousness in the chapter on Self-Consciousness.

In this chapter generally, Hegel has distilled motifs that are among the most thoroughly and frequently considered, and also among the most original, that had developed in his thinking over the preceding ten years. Here he has distilled them into a series of moments of the highest generality and abstractness. That he is able to present them in a kind of simple mythic narrative that seems so concrete is in fact a function of that abstractness; for what is really concrete could never be so simple. Having achieved this distillation he could then proceed, in the remaining chapters, to more concrete developments in the life of the mind, in the history of culture, and in the history of religion, applying and providing relevant contexts for the hard-won insights displayed in his myth of the self. For of course there necessarily *are* particular conditions that qualify and redefine the quite abstract presentation of the myth of the self. That is always true of a myth, philosophical or otherwise: it is recapitulated everywhere, yet never found in its purity under actual historical conditions. To a historical determinist the historical explanation is of course exhaustive, but Hegel's analysis is multidimensional.

One of the things that is useful about the myth presented in the present chapter is, as we have suggested, that it confronts us with such a transparent statement of the central problem of the entire *Phenomenology*. We are now in a position to elaborate that claim a bit.

In a passage already quoted, Hegel says that self-consciousness already contains "the concept of spirit," and constitutes the "turning point" from which consciousness "steps forth out of the colorful illusion of the sensuous here and now and out of the empty night of the supersensuous Beyond into the spiritual daylight of the present" (H 140; M 110–11; B 227). Now our chapter does not extend into that spiritual daylight. Remaining in the shadows throughout, it begins with the self sunk in that "colorful illusion of the sensuous *Diesseits*," submerged in "life's" warm biosphere, and it ends with the self yearning hopelessly for "the empty night of the supersensuous *Jenseits*." The chapter traces its course from the one predicament to the other. There is progress through the episodes of this myth only in the sense that it proceeds from the one pole to the other, which must also be developed in its full identity to balance the purely natural "life" of the self. Both poles must be in place before the spiritual "daylight" can dawn. That is why that consummation cannot follow directly upon the ironical triumph of the slave. That, I think, is also why love is not invoked in Hegel's myth of the self, even though it so obviously answers to the criterion of mutual recognition (which in fact probably was developed out of Hegel's early reflections on love). That would be a resolution that would *not* lead to unhappy consciousness, and to the ideality developed in it. Instead, Hegel introduces the life-negating risk of freedom, out of which that ideality does grow.

The concept of self-consciousness is presupposed in each of these partial realizations, and is expressed in the entire succession among them, but it is not merely a golden mean between the polar extremes. Viewed synchronically, we do find the entire concept of self-consciousness surveyed through this succession of moments, but without the movement into the spiritual daylight that would unite them. Viewed diachronically, the myth of the self exhibits the successive efforts to become a self without becoming spirit, which as such are doomed to failure. The failure will take different forms under different historical conditions, such as those suggested in the section on Legal Status, but the fundamental ground for that failure is the impossibility of becoming a complete self without becoming spirit, and that is the problem of the entire *Phenomenology*.

The dialectic of unhappy consciousness that completes the chapter not only carries the ideality of the self to its ultimate exacerbation, but itself expresses the fundamental predicament in its most transparent form. Here all the conditions are present for a self that is completed in spirit, at once universal and particular, unchangeable and changeable, essence and appearance, identity and difference. Its exquisite unhappiness consists in the fact that these conditions remain polarized. Whether it identifies itself with the changeable and is confronted by an unchangeable Beyond, or whether it achieves identification with the unchangeable by actively denying its own actual life, it cannot *recognize* itself in its other. "For itself" it can only apprehend its polar opposite *as* an other, though "in itself" it is in truth its own self.

This peculiar predicament of unhappy consciousness is created by its suppression of the "actual"; that is, its suppression of natural life both in itself and in its world, and also its suppression of that cultivated or cultural world formed out of nature by labor. Having only with its inner self to do, in the medium of free self-consciousness, it constantly objectifies its own essential selfhood. The master and the slave, who did comport themselves toward the actual world, in desire and enjoyment on the part of the master, in labor on the part of the slave, had not yet developed that inner freedom, that transcendence of material conditions achieved through Stoicism and skepticism. But in unhappy consciousness we see that this freedom has been purchased through loss of the actual, of life with others, in which mutual recognition might occur. It can only objectify its own essentiality, without the material or social medium in which it might discover itself in that other.

"We" found it a hopeful sign when in the recovery of a certain *Selbstgefühl* that inner freedom did begin to address its other through desire and labor. But as we recall, it no sooner became involved with the actual world than it sanctified that world, consigning it to the unchangeable and denying both the independent reality of the world and its own role as the one who desires, labors, and enjoys. Given what modern phenomenologists call the intentional structure of consciousness, that it exists only in relation to an object, this alienation from the actual is what compels unhappy consciousness to fabricate an objectified other out of the fullness of its own autonomous inner life. Now even its involvement with the actual world, in desire and labor, in support of its natural life, is incorporated into the hopeless inner struggle with its own objectified fullness. The liberated slave could recognize himself in the actual world he had fashioned and cultivated, but unhappy consciousness cannot, because his activity is so locked up in his ideal other that he finds that ideal other reflected in the objects of his desire and labor: an inaccessible God in the world sanctified by his presence, the eternal feminine in the real woman he desires, a utopian future in the political struggles of the present, and so forth—and he suffers the consequent inability to achieve self-recognition in the actual world, the actual woman, the actual political process. With the effluvium of his own mind no reciprocity, no mutual recognition, is possible.

But also at stake in this dialectic of unhappy consciousness is a more strictly philosophical issue, with which Hegel had wrestled at least since the beginning of his philosophical career in Jena. In order to bring out this issue I must consider the opposition between the changeable and the unchangeable from the other side, from the side of the unchangeable essence. In a famous passage in the Preface to the *Phenomenology*, Hegel declares that "the true is not to be apprehended and expressed as *substance*, but equally as *subject*" (H 19; M 10; B 80). Hegel does not directly apply the term "substance" to that unchangeable essence that emerges with unhappy consciousness, but there are many other terms that do link the dialectic of unhappy consciousness with the issue Hegel introduces with that remark in the Preface. There

Hegel clearly has in mind the One Substance of Spinoza, which he goes on to criticize in the following terms: "If God, interpreted as the One Substance, shocked the age in which this definition was pronounced, the reason for this reaction lay in part in the instinctive sense that self-consciousness was thereby submerged, and not preserved" (H 19; M 10; B 80).

Here what distinguishes the Hegelian subject from the Spinozistic substance is the pivotal position of self-consciousness. Self-consciousness, of course, is not simply a matter of knowledge. Hegel notes that "substantiality includes within itself the universal or the *immediacy of knowledge itself,* as well as that which is *being* or immediacy *for* knowledge." That was certainly true of the idealistic versions of Spinozism with which Hegel had struggled in the *Differenzschrift* and in *Glauben und Wissen.* But the position that identifies "thinking qua thinking" as the universal is equally sunk in "undifferentiated, immobile substantiality."[34] The Schellingian unity of thought and being in intellectual intuition, however, which Hegel had earlier defended, no longer seems satisfactory either: "there is still a question whether this intellectual intuition does not again fall back into inert simplicity, and present actuality itself in an unactual manner" (H 19–20; M 10; B 80). What is still missing in the *Indifferenzpunkt* uniting being and knowing is precisely the self-conscious self. That is why the chapter on Self-Consciousness occupies such a central position in the *Phenomenology:* here we find the emergence of an actual self-conscious self, which as unhappy consciousness finally confronts its absolute ground. Without that confrontation absolute substance cannot bestir itself from its dead simplicity, cannot relate itself to the actual in mutual recognition, cannot itself be alive.

In the next paragraph of the Preface, Hegel underlines the crucial importance of this opposition, this otherness, in a "living" truth. "Living substance . . . is the being which is in truth *subject,*" but this absolute subjectivity consists in "the movement of constituting itself" *(Sichselbstsetzens),* "the mediation of becoming-other with itself." In language reminiscent of the dialectic of unhappy consciousness (the Preface was written later), Hegel says that the living substance

> is as subject the pure *simple negativity,* and just thereby the division [*Entzweiung*] of the simple; or the doubling [*Verdopplung*] that sets things in opposition, and which is again the negation of this indifferent unlikeness and is its opposite: only

this self-*reconstituting* identity or the reflection in otherness within its own self—not an *original* unity as such, or *immediate* as such—is the true. (H 20; M 10; B 80–81)

In this general statement in which Hegel attempts to summarize the difference between his own view of the absolute and the Spinozism of other absolute idealists, the importance of that "division" and "doubling" that occurs with unhappy consciousness is evident. It is the indispensable moment of opposition that confronts substance with the self-conscious self. The absolute "subject," of course, will be spirit, in which each side of this opposition will achieve recognition in its other. In the next paragraph Hegel further develops both the affinity of his view with Spinozism and also the difference: "Thus the life of God and divine cognition may well be spoken of as a play of love with itself."

This apparent allusion to Spinoza's *Amor dei intellectualis*[35] may suggest that it is an adequate statement of divine cognition *(Erkennen)*, but not yet of divine re-cognition *(Anerkennen)*, for which the antecedent moment of otherness and negativity is necessary. Suggestive though this characterization of divine life may be, Hegel continues, "this idea sinks into mere edification and even into insipidity, if the seriousness, the pain, the patience and labor of the negative are lacking in it." Hegel elaborates this oft-quoted remark in terms unmistakably reminiscent of his description of unhappy consciousness as "in itself" one but "for itself" bifurcated and contradictory: "*In itself* that life is indeed an untroubled likeness and unity with itself, for which otherness and alienation are not serious, nor is the overcoming of this alienation. But this *in-itself* is abstract universality, in which we abstract from its nature *to be for itself,* and thereby neglect the self-movement of the form generally" (H 20; M 10; B 81).

This "nature" of the divine life "to be for itself" implies that it too, like self-consciousness, becomes self-aware in mutual recognition with an other: that is how it becomes "subject." So what we find in unhappy consciousness is the necessary moment in which substance or absolute essence, again like self-consciousness, is "for itself" the negating opposition of its other, of self-consciousness in fact, with which it is "in itself" in unity. Unhappy consciousness epitomizes precisely the moment of "seriousness," "pain," "the patience and labor of the negative." The entire *Phenomenology,* until its final chapter, unfolds under the spell of this negativity that receives its general definition in unhappy consciousness. The problem of the entire work is to show the actual process by which spirit recovers "for itself" that identity with its other that is already implicit "in itself" in its concept: to show how substance becomes subject, not "submerging" the subjectivity that self-consciousness, for its part, brings to this initial confrontation, but "containing" it in mutual recognition, itself becoming in this sense subjective. Hegel's speculations on the Trinity had already convinced him that the divine life is subjective in itself, in its very concept. But to be an actual subject, it must *"be for itself,"* in "self-movement" through the definite forms that stand in opposition to it.

Hegel therefore goes on in this paragraph to deny the Schellingian position that "cognition can content itself with the in-itself or essence." In introducing this entire discussion of subject versus substance, Hegel has poked some fun at that absolute which is "the night" in which "all the cows are black" (H 19; M 9; B 79). It is not enough to say that all things are one and the same in the absolute, nor is the issue that separates Hegel from his erstwhile collaborator merely that of whether things need to be worked out in detail, in systematic form (though Hegel is certainly committed to doing so, even in a work that is in some respects pre-systematic). The reason that the definite forms have to be articulated in detail is precisely to bring out their opposition and mutual negativity, and it must be *shown* how the absolute becomes subject by recognizing itself in them. That task is dramatized in the predicament of unhappy consciousness. But as Hegel's treatment of that predicament makes abundantly clear, the movement into mutual recognition does not follow of itself from the ordeal of mutual negativity and opposition.

I have steadily insisted that this predicament is not peculiar to the Christian religion, but there is no doubt that Hegel's formulation of it does directly arise out of his long-standing preoccupation with Christian "positivity," in particular with the plight of the believer confronted by an absolute Object in the Beyond or by its incarnation in the past. Yet we have also seen how Hegel came to find the living image of negativity in the Christian drama of incarnation and crucifixion. Both as a predicament and as an image of that moment of negativity necessary to the achievement of spirit, the dogmatic structure of Christianity has been universalized in unhappy consciousness. Its central irony is that for unhappy consciousness itself, even an incarnation of its ideal other is necessarily just another disappointing delusion, as we have seen.

Precisely because the unchangeable essence is not a genuine other, but the absolute ground of his own psychic life, unhappy consciousness finds that its incarnation in a historical individual renders that figure as inaccessible to mutual recognition as its ideality had proven to be. The unchangeable cannot unite with living flesh, but simply recedes into an unrecoverable past. On these terms it is yet another fantasy, like the investment of a real woman with the eternal feminine, in which the living presence of the actual woman is volatilized into the ideal prototype. That is perhaps the deepest, and certainly the most theologically interesting predicament of unhappy consciousness: that incarnation is its need, but there can be no incarnation in this myth of the self. Yet Mark Taylor is correct: "For Hegel, the Mediator represents the inherently rational reintegration of the opposites that rend unhappy consciousness. The central symbol of Christian faith neither obscures the reality of conflicting contraries nor denies the passion of spiritual tension. Christ reveals reconciliation *in the midst of* estrangement."[36] In this sense incarnation has indeed been incorporated into the speculative heart of Hegel's philosophy, again in universalized form, but its articulation awaits the chapter on Religion. But in the myth of the self the incarnational principle can only be expressed as absolute negativity. Unhappy consciousness cannot recognize itself in its ideal other, precisely because in the myth of the self this absolute other can be nothing but the ideal fullness of its own psychic life, with which no mutuality is possible. Its desire to enter into relationship with this specious other is necessarily a frustrated yearning. Its longing for union is masturbatory, because unhappy consciousness is in truth locked within the confines of its own psychic life, with no actual other in whom to recognize itself. Its *lack* of a genuine other is, ironically, the measure of its descent into pure otherness and negativity; for it incarnation can only be another psychic fantasy. It does, after all, need an actual world, a life of nature and society in which to achieve self-recognition; it cannot recognize itself, and therefore cannot become a self, without recognizing an actual other. Spirit is actual only insofar as it is incarnate. For self to become spirit and spirit to become subject (i.e., for self and spirit to be one), mutual recognition in the actual world is necessary.

That appears to me to be the most cogent reading of the predicament of unhappy consciousness. Still, a critical problem arises at just this point. In Hegel's first Jena years he had adopted the Schellingian intellectual intuition as the ineffable *Indifferenzpunkt* in which both identity and difference or otherness could be affirmed. Having consigned this solution to the nocturnal cows, it is still necessary for him to assert that there is actual difference, otherness, negativity, in the divine life. We see that in unhappy consciousness; "for it," indeed, there is no solution, no recovery of identity in this difference. But "for us" phenomenological observers, and "in itself," this moment of otherness presupposes an identity of these opposites, without which the actual identity to be achieved by spirit would presumably be impossible. But this identity is also what makes it impossible for unhappy consciousness to achieve recognition, since there can be no mutuality without actual otherness. So is this otherness merely apparent? In that case, of course, the achievement of unity in which the absolute becomes subject will be an empty charade, an *Indifferenz* of the sort that Hegel has consigned to the bovine darkness. But can the otherness be actual without being irreducible, *unaufhebbar?*

That, for Hegel himself, is the dilemma presented by unhappy consciousness, which poses in the most transparent form the central problem to which the entire *Phenomenology* is addressed.[37] He articulates here, furthermore, the central predicament that had been embedded like a thorn in the entire development of his own thought, particularly since he had begun his serious effort to construct a systematic philosophy. We have encountered it earlier, in systematic form, in what I described as the unresolved tension in Hegel's thought between an experience-negating and an experience-appropriating type of idealism, and also in the related dilemmas in Hegel's systematic manuscript of 1804–5 concerning the "otherness" in which absolute spirit was to find itself (see Chapter 3).

Of course unhappy consciousness is not primarily a philosophical position, although it can take philosophical form: for instance, in the Kantian-Fichtean and Romantic philosophies of "reflection" Hegel had assailed in the critical writings of his earlier Jena years. It is the existential posture of infinite yearning that cannot be satisfied because it is invested in what is in principle Beyond. That was the problem he had encountered in a variety of guises even in the 1790s, and here he gives it the most general, far-reaching expression. When he calls this unchangeable Beyond "the enemy," he is speaking not only for the unhappy consciousness but for himself, for he had spent his adult life assailing it in all its guises. But he has come to see that this enemy is spawned by autonomous self-consciousness itself, not in the trivial Feuerbachian sense that the mind has "projected" it, but in the sense that the unchangeable Beyond is precisely the mind itself in its aseity, in that absolute plenitude that Hegel wants to claim for it.

That it now arises to confront consciousness as an inaccessible Beyond is not merely an unaccountable psychological trick the mind plays on itself. Unhappy consciousness cannot recognize itself in this specious other, precisely because this "other" *is* its own mind or spirit in its aseity, and not a genuine other to which it might be related in mutual recognition or in labor. The self has achieved its absolute ideality by prescinding from the actual, with the ironical result that its identity with its absolute essence does not exist "for *it*." The self can either achieve self-consciousness in relation to the actual: but then it is not absolute; it lacks its universal "essence." Or, it can achieve an ideal identity with the absolute essence: but then it cannot recognize itself in this identity; essence cannot become spirit, substance cannot become subject.

Of course Hegel is confident that he has the solution to this dilemma in hand, and he gives us reassuring hints of it along the way. Spirit is not complete in its ideality. It must find itself in its actual other, in the natural world, in political life, in intersubjective recognition. That, to be sure, will solve the problem, unless "spirit" should simply be another name for the problem, masquerading as its solution. It is easy enough to square the circle: all you need is a square circle. But simply to postulate an identity of the ideal and the actual in spirit would be the night of the black cows, or the absolute produced as if shot "out of a pistol," like the Schellingian *Indifferenz* that Hegel derides in the Preface (H 19, 26; M 9, 16; B 79, 89). Whether such a resolution can be developed "immanently," out of the phenomenological inquiry itself, as Hegel insists it must be if it is to be valid, remains to be seen. His myth of the self simply concludes with a masterly evocation of the predicament.

In the concluding paragraph of that chapter and the opening paragraph of the next, Hegel announces that some relief is already in sight from the predicament of unhappy consciousness. The unhappy consciousness itself, to be sure, will not be in a position to enjoy this relief, but at least "we" phenomenological observers will be rid of it for a while. Because, in itself and for us, the particular/changeable and the universal/unchangeable make up one psychic field, this totality steps before us in a new guise, as reason. We will not follow Hegel through the lengthy analysis contained in the chapter on Reason, but I shall have a bit to say about it in the next section. Here it will suffice to say that the title, "Reason," bears an ironical relation to its contents similar to that we have found in the chapter on Self-Consciousness. As the

chapter we have surveyed presents a myth of the self that never fulfills
the concept of self-consciousness, so the moments of the new chapter,
though no longer mythic in form, will just as persistently fail to embody
reason as Hegel had come to understand the term. Nor will it resolve
the predicament of unhappy consciousness. This "reason" will simply
forget that predicament, in generating new problems of its own.

3. A Synoptic View of the *Phenomenology of Spirit*

Now that we have begun to penetrate the *Phenomenology* at a central
point, it may be useful to offer some observations about the composition,
design, and systematic placement of the work as a whole. Probably we
cannot put that off much longer in any case. We have proceeded as we
have because our interests take us more into the details, where Hegel
insists that the real work is done, rather than into matters that are
usually treated in prefaces and introductions, which Hegel generally
disparaged. Fortunately there are a number of works available that
address the larger questions about the design and purpose of the *Phenomenology,* including some commentaries on the entire text,[38] so we
need not try to be exhaustive. It is a dense and many-sided work, which
can usefully be analyzed from many different angles of vision. Our
special interest in the interpretation and transformation of Christian
themes will determine what is singled out for comment here. That is
a central interest of the text itself, but there are others, and I do not
claim that this interest provides a privileged position from which to
analyze the work. Many important matters will be left undiscussed or
only alluded to, but the comments on the chapter on Self-Consciousness
will provide us with a reference point in discussing the remainder of
the book.

On the Composition of the *Phenomenology*

As a little relief from the heavy going of commentary, let us first survey
a few known facts about the composition of this text. When it was

published, in March or early April 1807, it bore the title *System der Wissenschaft: Erster Theil, die Phänomenologie des Geistes*. As the "First Part" of the "System of Science," this volume was intended to be part of a larger whole, comprising the entire system. So this work represented the launching of Hegel's fourth effort in Jena to write his system: an effort, like the first three, that ended in frustration. After the Preface another title page stands: *I. Wissenschaft der Phänomenologie des Geistes*. So the Preface, which was written last (numbered with Roman numerals) was to introduce not merely the first part but the entire projected System of Science. The Introduction, which follows this second title page, is specifically addressed to the *Phenomenology*. In some extant copies, however, a different title stands on the page between Preface and Introduction: *Erster Theil. Wissenschaft der Erfahrung des Bewusstseins*. "Science of the Experience of Consciousness" had evidently been the original title for this first part of the system, but Hegel later directed the publisher to cut this original page out of the text and to substitute one bearing the new title. Through carelessness this change was not made in some copies, and there are even copies extant with *both* title pages.[39] A much-discussed question, to which we shall return, is whether this change in the title registers an important change in Hegel's conception of the work. Since the Introduction still refers to this "first" science as the "science of the experience of consciousness" (H 74; M 56; B 144), the question about the change in titles also implies the question of whether there is some tension between the conception of the work projected in the Introduction and the conception of the completed work as it stands.

A further feature of the text that may indicate some change in its conception, if not tension among competing conceptions, is the confusing double organization of the table of contents. On the one hand we seem to have a work in eight chapters, numbered with Roman numerals. That numeration of the chapters is also followed in the actual text. But the table of contents (though not the text) *also* contains a system of parts and subparts organized under capital letters. The two systems line up as follows:

(A)   Consciousness

I. Sense-Certainty, the This and Meaning

II. Perception, the Thing and Deception

The tension in the early parts of this double arrangement seems to clear up in the chapter on Reason, and in the last three chapters the double arrangement becomes redundant. It is also noteworthy that part (C) in the capital letter arrangement comprises not merely Reason, but Reason, Spirit, Religion, and Absolute Knowledge, distinguished as subparts with double capitals. Part (C) includes pp. 162–765 in the original edition, making for quite a remarkable disproportion among the three parts of the text.

In practice commentators often treat the text as if it were composed of six chapters: Consciousness, Self-Consciousness, Reason, Spirit, Religion, and Absolute Knowledge. We will generally proceed on that arrangement in what follows, though it is admittedly quite different from either of those employed in Hegel's table of contents. But it has some textual justification: By the time Hegel reaches the chapter on Religion he also appears to be thinking of his work as falling into six parts. He speaks of the moments antecedent to Religion as "Consciousness, Self-Consciousness, Reason and Spirit" (H 473, 476–77; M 410, 412–13; B 685, 689–90), without treating the three moments of Consciousness as if they were major divisions corresponding to the others,[40] and without treating the entire development from Reason on as if it were a third division paralleling Consciousness and Self-Consciousness. The eight-chapter division of the text, in fact, may well be a relic of an early arrangement that was superseded as the conception of the entire work developed in the actual writing, but that could not be expunged as part of the book had already been printed. There is, in general, reason to suspect that the confusion of these different arrangements is created by changing conceptions while the work was in progress, though the tripartite arrangement does offer an important way of viewing the work. But there are in fact many more than three overlapping interconnections among the main parts of the text, each illuminating an aspect of the whole. This work is a multitextured fabric.

Let us now step behind these confusing textual facts to consider some of the known facts of the work's composition. On August 6, 1806, Hegel wrote his friend Niethammer that the publisher, J. A. Goebhardt of Bamberg, had begun printing a "part" of the text during the preceding February.[41] This "part" which he had sent the publisher at that time cannot have been the First Part of the System of Science (i.e., the entire *Phenomenology*), since Hegel was still working on that into October. He seems to have sent large sections of the manuscript to the publisher as he completed them, the final installment being sent on October 20[42] (except for the Preface, completed in January 1807). But in the August letter, Hegel complained to Niethammer of delays in completing the printing of "this part" which was begun in February; "according to the original contract this part was supposed to be finished before Easter," then it was promised by the beginning of his lectures for the summer semester, which began in May, but "this was also not fulfilled." Hegel had been promising published works as the basis of his lectures for some years in the printed catalogue of courses, and he hoped at last to be able to keep this promise. He did in fact put printed portions into the hands of his students as they appeared that summer, but the catalogue had promised much more for the summer semester: "Philosophiam speculativam s. logicam ex libro suo: System der Wissenschaft, proxime prodituro."[43] It is evident that at the time Hegel submitted this announcement (probably in March), he still expected that the promised text would contain not only Part One, still entitled Science of the Experience of Consciousness, but at least part of the Logic, which was to comprise the speculative part of the total system. As it turned out, he lectured that summer on the Logic from rough notes, in relation to the parts of the *Phenomenology* that appeared.

Still, the "part" the publisher had begun printing in February must have been considerable. If Rosenkranz is correct in saying that Hegel had begun writing in 1804,[44] the part in the publisher's hands in February 1806 represents more than a year's work. Furthermore, by September 29, 1806, twenty-one sheets, comprising 336 pages, had been printed, carrying the text almost to the end of the chapter on Reason.

Earlier in the summer a dispute had arisen between Hegel and the publisher: According to the original contract the publisher had agreed to pay Hegel eighteen florins per sheet after half the manuscript was printed, and Hegel claimed that honorarium. The publisher denied this claim on the ground that he had not yet seen the whole manuscript, and therefore could not tell whether the printed portion amounted to half![45] The publisher had a point. The state of the project was surely not very stable. Hegel's plan, earlier that year, to publish the "speculative" part of the system, Logic, along with Part One, his Science of the Experience of Consciousness, presumably in the same volume, had evidently been abandoned as that first part continued to grow under his hands, and it was not yet clear how large a volume would be required for the still-expanding Part One alone. This rather comical result of the expansive development of a philosopher's thoughts was not at all funny to Hegel, who was in desperate need of money, and felt ill-used. For us, at any rate, the important point is that the precise design of the great project was still in quite a fluid state through at least the first half of 1806.

Furthermore, the work took shape under conditions not calculated to induce philosophical calm. Hegel had yet to write a book, and was under great professional pressure to do so. He was dangerously short of money, and the political situation was becoming ever more threatening even as he wrote. He finished it with Napoleon at the gates, with buildings burning and considerable looting. Indeed, writing Schelling the following May, he asked him to excuse the shapelessness ("Die grossere Unform") of the last parts on the grounds that he had finished editing them the night before the Battle of Jena (October 13, 1806).[46] The university was clearly threatened by this turn of events, and in fact closed down shortly thereafter, leaving Hegel without an academic position. His private life was hardly in less turmoil: since the spring a local woman, Christiana Charlotte Burkhardt, abandoned by her husband, had been pregnant with Hegel's illegitimate child. After this child, a boy named Ludwig, was born in February 1807, Hegel assumed financial responsibility for him and offered such support as he could to the mother. His letters show that he did not treat the matter lightly.[47] Yet despite Napoleon's advancing armies, Frau Burkhardt's advancing pregnancy, and his own declining fortunes, Hegel's book was somehow completed. If he was scornful of Stoic philosophizing in detachment from reality, he himself had quite enough reality on his hands.

The first extant reference to the work under the title, *Phenomenology of Spirit*, is in the announcement Hegel submitted, perhaps in August, for the course catalogue for the winter semester, 1806–7: "Logicam et Metaphysicam, praemissa Phaenomenologia Mentis ex libro suo: System der Wissenschaft, erster Theil (Bamb. u. Würtzb. bey Goebhardt 1807)."[48] The new title registers the fact that Part One had outgrown the original plan, certainly in bulk, and perhaps in conception as well, even while its early chapters were already being printed. By that time the work had assumed proportions that required a large volume devoted to Part One alone. Now the Logic, together with "the two remaining parts of philosophy, the Sciences of Nature and of Spirit," were consigned to a second volume,[49] which of course never appeared.

So much for the facts. There has been considerable scholarly debate on whether the new plan, and the new title, entailed an expansion of the scope of Part One, as well as its length. Theodor Haering, for instance, in an influential article published in 1934, argued that Hegel had originally intended to end the work with the chapter on Reason, and only decided to go on to the later chapters as the earlier chapters were being printed.[50] Haering combined this view of the original plan of the *Phenomenology* with an assumption that Hegel's decision to compose such an "introduction" to the system was suddenly formed in winter 1805–6, and flew in the face of his previous "energetic" opposition to the possibility or value of any such introductory path into the system. That assumption is certainly wrong. We have seen that Hegel planned some such critical and "skeptical" work as a pathway to systematic science for almost as long as he had planned to write the system itself; and he was certainly at work on it well before winter 1805–6. Pöggeler has demolished not only Haering's argument about the suddenness of Hegel's decision to compose the work, but also his grounds for arguing that it was first intended to end with the chapter on Reason.[51] At least Pöggeler has swept away the admittedly indirect external evidence Haering had offered in support of this argument. Still, it remains an open question whether, as Pöggeler appears to think, Hegel had originally (say, when the publisher began the printing in February 1806) envisaged a work comprising the present eight chapters, or whether the design evolved in the writing, as Haering had argued. We need not be convinced by Haering's argument that the work was to end with the chapter on Reason[52] to consider that the latter thesis is more likely. As I have suggested, it is hard to believe that the eight-chapter scheme, with three devoted to Consciousness, can be more than a relic of a design that could not be changed because the early chapters were already in press. The sheer disproportion in size between the three early chapters and the massive chapters on Reason and Spirit, indeed the very confusion of the dual or triple arrangement of chapters, appears to support Haering's general impression that Hegel's book developed "under his hands," as does Hegel's abandonment, by mid-1806, of the plan to combine the First Part with the Logic in a single volume. The evidence points to an astonishing burst of intellectual energy from February to October, during which the work took on quite an unforeseen shape, certainly in the articulation of the final chapters, if not in their design.

The result was a dense and bewildering masterpiece, brilliantly original, penetrating and effervescent, obscure and chaotic, sometimes sublime, rather like "the true" itself, according to the Preface: a "Bacchanalian revel, in which not a member is not drunk," and yet "transparent and simple repose" (H 39; M 27; B 105). Hegel himself recognized that this marvelous offspring was somewhat ungainly. A number of his letters, written while the work was appearing, such as the one to Schelling confessing "the greater shapelessness of the latter parts," are apologetic about the work's defects. He was already looking forward to a revised edition. Even as he was finishing work on it, he wrote Niethammer on January 16, 1807, that as he read through it for typographical errors, "I did indeed often have the wish to be able to clear the ship of ballast here and there and make it more seaworthy. —With a 2nd edition soon to follow—si diis placet?! everything will be improved, with that I will console myself and others."[53]

Under the circumstances of social and personal upheaval the improved version was in fact out of the question, but the imperfections of the work were a lasting irritant to Hegel, so much so that twenty-four years later, in the last months of his life, he actually did begin a revision without getting very far before death overtook him. So the *Phenomenology* has come down to us in its original condition, ballast, barnacles, and all. We should not exaggerate these imperfections. Recalling the huge piles of manuscript that he had let accumulate since the 1790s, with no effort to publish them, particularly the succession of abandoned systematic manuscripts in Jena, it is evident that Hegel was too severe a critic of his own work to let anything appear in print that was simply unsatisfactory, and he did, after all, judge that here at last was a work that was fit to appear, to say the least! Still, Hegel's reservations about the work ought at least to make us cautious about insisting that every jot and tittle of the *Phenomenology* is coherently worked out. One cannot dismiss it, with Haym, as a confused mixture of history and psychology,[54] and there is certainly design in the work, indeed a dense network of interlocking designs. But Hegel himself aptly describes the problem in the letter to Schelling from which we have already quoted:

> The working in of detail has, as I feel, done damage to the overview of the whole; but this itself is, by its very nature, such an interlaced shifting back and forth [*ein so verschränktes Herüber- und Hinübergehen*] that it itself, were it to be better edited, would still cost me a great deal of time to make it clearer and more finished.[55]

I shall have more to say about this complex design shortly.

The deeper question that is raised by this account of the work's composition is whether the abandonment, midway, of a "Science of the Experience of Consciousness" in favor of a "Phenomenology of Spirit" introduces a fundamental structural incoherence in the work. Haym had suggested that the *Phenomenology* is a "palimpsest: above and between the first text we discover a second."[56] Pöggeler suggests that this remark was truer than Haym knew:

> The talk about a palimpsest . . . is with Haym nothing more than a glittering turn of phrase, a pretty word about which he is not serious: Haym had not at all intended actually to read the *Phen.* as a palimpsest—as a work behind the beginning of which quite another conception is visible than that expressed in the completed work; as a work the Introduction of which bears quite another conception than the conclusion and the Preface written still later.[57]

Pöggeler does find just such a palimpsest in the *Phenomenology,* and to that extent he does after all follow the lead, not of Haym, but of Haering, despite his critique of Haering's conclusions about the original plan of the work: Haering's "merit" is "that he began in earnest to read the *Phen.* as a palimpsest: as a text under which an older, different text is still visible."[58] Pöggeler evidently thinks this perception is quite fundamental to the interpretation of the work. He goes almost so far as to deny that "the idea of Hegel's *Phen.* can be understood without explaining how it is related to the ambiguities in the *Phen.*, to the change of title, to the contradictions between the 'Introduction' on the one hand and the Conclusion and Preface on the other."[59]

To speak of "contradictions" is at best an exaggeration, yet the Introduction sets in motion a dialectical interplay between "certainty" of knowledge and "truth" in the "experience of consciousness," and that dialectic governs the organization of the early chapters of the work through the chapter on Reason. Thereafter, as Pöggeler points out, this way of posing the problem of the work recedes; even the concept of experience becomes less prominent, and when it is employed it is the "experience of spirit" rather than of consciousness as such.[60] In fact as Hegel wrote the latter chapters he had decided to change the name of the work, using the more objective language of phenomena or appearances (cf. the Greek *phainomena*) of spirit rather than the more subjective language of experience. Accordingly, the dialectic of cognitive "certainty" and "truth" articulated in the Introduction gives way to, or I would say develops into, the dialectic of "substance" and "subject" articulated in the Preface.

What I suspect troubles Pöggeler the most, however, though he does not relate it very directly to the "palimpsest" problem, is that the "new" conception appears to be teleological, introducing a necessary progression from natural consciousness to spirit. Indeed, as he points out, Hegel speaks in the Preface of reason as "purposive activity," harking back to Aristotle's concept of "nature as purposive activity" (H 22; M 12; B 83). This "turn to teleological thinking," says Pöggeler, "is a return to the metaphysical tradition," and furthermore is for Hegel also a way of appropriating "the historical teleology of the Christian concept of providence."[61]

This alleged introduction of teleology into the *Phenomenology*, with its alleged theological ramifications, seems to me to be the serious problem entailed in reading the work as a palimpsest, and it will be important for us to address it presently. For the rest, I cannot see that the evolution of the work from a Science of the Experience of Consciousness to a Phenomenology of Spirit introduces any serious problem of incoherence, much less contradiction, into the work as it stands. In a passage in the Preface that reads as if it were designed to address this very issue, Hegel explicitly relates consciousness and its "experience" to spirit with its transformation of substance into subject: *"Consciousness,"* he says, is "the immediate existence of spirit," and as such its knowledge is always separated from the "negative objectivity" that is presented to it. This antithesis, between knowing subject and object known, is characteristic of all forms of consciousness, which can be scientifically arranged in sequence. Hegel goes on, in language reminiscent of the Introduction:

> The science of this pathway is the science of *experience* that consciousness undergoes; the substance is observed as it and its movement make up the object of consciousness. Consciousness knows and comprehends nothing except what is in its experience; for what is in this experience is only the spiritual substance, and indeed as the *object* of its self. But spirit becomes object because it is this movement of *itself* into an *other*, i.e. of becoming an *object of its own self,* and of transcending this otherness.

Actually Hegel is saying nothing more here than he had said in the chapter on Self-Consciousness. As we have seen, the "concept" of self-consciousness entails precisely this overcoming of the separation of subject and object, such that selfhood becomes object to itself and so finds itself on both sides of the equation: and as such it is already implicitly spirit. That is to say that this understanding of the matter is already clear in those early chapters Hegel delivered to his publisher when he still conceived of this work as a Science of the Experience of Consciousness. He argues there, as here, that this overcoming of the "antithesis" implicit in consciousness is entailed by the very concept of experience. The present passage continues: "And just this movement is what is called experience, in which the immediate, the unexperienced, i.e. the abstract, whether it is sensuous being or merely something simple that is thought, alienates itself and then returns to itself from this alienation and is only then presented in its actuality and truth, in the way in which it is also a property of consciousness" (H 32; M 21; B 96).

Hegel goes on in the next paragraphs to argue that the disparity between consciousness and its object is also the disparity of objectified "substance" with itself. From this point of view (i.e., proceeding from the "objective" side of the antithesis between subject and object), it is more cogent to speak of "appearances" (i.e., *phainomena*), rather than of "experience," though the movement of self-overcoming is precisely the same, proceeding from the opposite pole. Objectified substance becomes subject. Again it is important to stress that this dialectic of substance-becoming-subject is entirely consonant with the position developed in the early chapters, in the chapter on Self-Consciousness in particular. We have seen how it is implicit in Hegel's treatment of unhappy consciousness, the impasse of which is precisely that it can *not* overcome the objectification of substance as unchangeable essence "beyond" itself. "We," meanwhile, already know that "in itself" unhappy consciousness and its object are already one, and spirit will be their mutual self-recognition in one another.

It is noteworthy that Pöggeler develops the dire implications of his palimpsest in entirely general terms, scarcely descending into the text at all. *If* there is a teleological understanding at work in the *Phenomenology*, it is already present in the necessity for consciousness to become self-conscious, and for self-consciousness to achieve its "concept" by becoming spirit. That necessity is not imposed on the early chapters from the point of view of a later conception of the work.

I suspect that it simply became clear to Hegel, in the actual writing, even while the early chapters were in press, that he could not complete his Science of the Experience of Consciousness without showing how spirit, which had been implicit in consciousness from the beginning, comes to more and more decisive expression in its appearances: that Hegel himself experienced the need for an Aufhebung of consciousness into spirit, in order to complete the analysis of consciousness itself. It is not surprising that all efforts to pinpoint just where the one conception was abandoned and the other adopted have failed, since from beginning to end they are two sides of the same coin.

Notes on the Design of the *Phenomenology*

Still, the *Phenomenology* is a dense and tangled work, pursuing many aims simultaneously, as Hegel attempts to overcome all the forms of dualism that he had turned up in his earlier critical works: epistemic, psychological, moral, cultural, religious, metaphysical, political. No simple schema can accommodate all these interwoven motifs, but the commentaries contain a number of alternative ways to divine some coherent order in the whole. Without rehearsing those efforts, I want to offer some suggestions of my own about the design of the work. These suggestions are hardly definitive, but they may be serviceable in providing some general orientation for the parts of the work on which I have chosen to comment in previous and subsequent sections of this chapter. Treating it as a work in six parts, and also making use of the tripartite division in Hegel's table of contents, I want to concentrate on certain formal features in the composition of each part that will be useful in showing how they are related.

I have already offered my reasons for suggesting that the chapter on Self-Consciousness takes the form of a philosophical myth of the self. Certainly its style and atmosphere are radically different from those of the first chapter(s), on Consciousness. Whether we regard the treatment of consciousness as falling into one chapter or three (and hereafter for convenience sake we will refer to it as one, though if our interest were epistemological it would be important to discriminate among the three), it shows a pronounced unity of style and method. It is a dialogue. The dialogue is philosophical, treating the abstract issue that since Descartes had been the philosophical issue par excellence: how consciousness could be certain of its knowledge. Consciousness therefore presents itself as a pure epistemological subject: "Consciousness, for its part, exists in this certainty only as pure *I*" (H 79; M 58; B 150). "We," on the other hand, interrogate it in a Socratic manner, bringing out what it claims to be certain of, and bringing it step by step to see that its claim cannot be coherently maintained. What it claims to "mean" by knowledge is steadily undermined by being shown to be self-contradictory, to require a different meaning that in its turn is also no sooner articulated than *its* incoherence becomes apparent. As for "us," who interrogate, Kenley Dove points up very well "our" peculiar role in this procedure:

> The way out of consciousness' meaning-solipsism cannot be simply "pointed out"; it must be worked through. In doing so, the reader must note Hegel's peculiar use of the word "we" in this section. For it is only in "Consciousness" (and in subsequent references back to *Phen.* I–III) that the "we" is seen to play the role *(zum Bei-spiel)* of the consciousness presented, to *speak* for it and *write* for it[a], immediately and passively *observe* for it[b], as well as perceive for it[c], and actively participate in its Concept[d]. Moreover, "we" are able so to relate ourselves, not because it is some primordial experience and the "we" is the Absoluteness of the Absolute (with Heidegger), or because the "we" is a speculative Hegelian philosopher (with Hyppolite), or because the "we" enjoys the privileged access of Absolute Knowledge (with Kroner). Both the consciousness in question and "we" ourselves are already in the element of *pre*-Hegelian philosophy. Indeed, the

section called "Consciousness" is the most clearly philosophical of the entire work—when philosophy is understood as the theory of knowledge. And this is so because it must enable its readers to get beyond "philosophy," beyond the "love of knowledge" and thus to begin to know.[e] [62]

In this last sentence Dove alludes to Hegel's distinction (H 12; M 3; B 70) between philo-sophia or love of knowledge and the actual knowledge, or "science" that is its goal. So on this reading we begin with a philosophical dialogue, which gives way, in the chapter on Self-Consciousness, where the concept of spirit is disclosed, to a dialogue between consciousness and spirit—the "I" that is a "we." The initial dialogue, in the chapter on Consciousness, "is consciousness'... voyage to the discovery that it *is* Spirit.... The 'I' of consciousness must ... be grasped as constituted through the 'we' of Spirit."[63] The "we" in this new sense is the basis of actual sophia, Hegel's science of wisdom. But then, I suggest, we no longer have an actual dialogue, as we do under the rubric of Consciousness. Already in the chapter on Self-Consciousness, "we" no longer speak for, or directly address, the protagonist figures, but simply observe and comment on them.

But in the "philosophical" dialogue of the opening chapter, "consciousness" is driven, in a succinct recapitulation of modern epistemology, from naive realism to a pure empiricism to a critical empiricism on the Kantian model, being made ever more aware of its own role in shaping its apparent knowledge, until it can no longer avoid the question, What, then, am *I?* But when that question arises it becomes evident that self-consciousness is its truth, and it is ready to learn "from experience" that self-consciousness begins not in sensations or perceptions or understanding by an epistemological subject but in desire, and is constituted by intersubjective transaction.[64] Pure consciousness clings as long as it can, however, to the epistemological dualism of subject and object in its various forms, confronted with some objective "other" independent of itself. As we will see, that paradigm returns again and again in the *Phenomenology,* though with each reappearance it assumes a more complex form. The other fundamental paradigm, which again returns throughout the *Phenomenology,* is supplied by the chapter on Self-Consciousness, where the "other" encountered by consciousness is another *self,* and "we" discover that its other is in truth its own self, though in its "unhappiness" it is not yet aware of this identity.

Now I think we can begin to consider the significance of the tripartite arrangement of the *Phenomenology* that Hegel introduced into the table of contents after the entire work was written. The first of these capital-lettered parts is "(A) Consciousness," the second is "(B) Self-Consciousness," and the third is the untitled "(C)" which contains the four remaining chapters, comprising almost four-fifths of the work.[65] That oddly disproportionate arrangement does serve to bring out the paradigmatic role assigned the chapters on Consciousness and Self-Consciousness. In a manner that I shall spell out presently, part (C) will continue to oscillate between these two paradigms until the position of "science" is achieved in the final chapter, with the paradigm of self-consciousness triumphant in absolute spirit. It is already tempting, upon confronting the chapter on Reason, to resort to the facile formula that it is the synthesis of consciousness and self-consciousness. The formula does have this limited validity, that reason is consciousness that has become self-conscious, is in fact "the certainty of consciousness that it is all reality" (H 176; M 140; B 276).

But with this basic premise of idealism the chapter on Reason returns fundamentally to the position of consciousness, in the sense that it is a subject confronting a succession of objects, but with a rational consonance between them: both the subject and its world of objects are assumed to be rational. The return to the position of "consciousness" is particularly evident in the first part of the chapter, on Observing Reason. In fact Hegel finds the three moments of consciousness recapitulated in the "pure category" of this idealistic reason (H 180–81; M 144–45; B 279–80). But consciousness has been enriched by its newfound self-awareness: it is now a self-conscious consciousness, aware of the rational consonance between itself and the objects it confronts. It moves from theoretical to practical reason, from observing reason to the actualization of rational self-consciousness through its own self, and finally to individuality, actively impressing its moral intuitions and principles on the world, no longer merely observing its objects but constituting them practically.

So the chapter on Reason is more straightforwardly discursive than the preceding chapters. It is a systematic treatise on theoretical and practical reason. Yet there is still an ironical duplicity in this treatment. We still find the distinction between the for-itself, now reason's own self-understanding, and the in-itself to which "we" are privy. The title, indeed, is no less ironical than that of the preceding chapter; this is reason that does not yet comprehend its own ultimate basis. Hyppolite indicates this limitation by calling it "Reason in Its Phenomenological Aspect." This "reason" suffers, after all, like "consciousness," from a certain solipsistic self-enclosure, since the individual subject, for all his formal universality as the embodiment of reason, is not yet self-consciously rooted in an actual, social self. Therefore it cannot be "reason" as Hegel himself understands the term: it is reason under the limits of "understanding," or what Hegel had called "raisonnieren" or "reflexion" in his earlier critical essays. Toward the end of the chapter we begin to get hints of this deficiency: Reason requires history, the social development of selfhood in time, in order to be complete; that is, reason must become spirit if it is to transcend mere "understanding." The chapter on Spirit accordingly opens with the assertion that "reason is spirit when its certainty of being all reality has been elevated to truth, and it is conscious of its own self as its world, and of the world as its own self" (H 313; M 263; B 457).[66] The "world" referred to is a cultural, historical world.

After elaborating this relation of reason to spirit, and recapitulating the chapter on Reason from this point of view, Hegel enunciates what I take to be one of his most fundamental pointers on the design of the entire work: "Spirit is thereby the absolutely real essence, bearing its own self. All the previous forms of consciousness are abstractions from spirit; they result from spirit analyzing itself, distinguishing its moments and lingering a while with each" (H 314; M 264; B 459). In the social, historical, cultural configurations of spirit's "world" we find the actuality of psychic life, contextualized and concrete. The previous chapters have lifted out certain aspects of this living whole in order to articulate special features and problems ingredient in it. But their moments are abstractions. The epistemological subject does not exist as such, nor do the figures that appeared in our tableaux in the myth of the self, nor does the rational man in his theoretical and practical activity. In this passage, if not before, it is evident that the "experiences of consciousness" have been shadows cast by the appearances—phenomena—of spirit. Spirit can be regarded as a new entry in the series of "forms of consciousness" only because consciousness is actually an appearance of spirit. Hegel continues this central orienting passage, recapitulating the three previous chapters from this perspective: This "isolating" of abstracted moments from the concreteness of spirit has spirit itself

as its *presupposition* and *subsistence,* or this isolation exists only in spirit, which is actual existence. In this isolation they create an illusion, as if they actually *were* as such; but how they are only moments or disappearing magnitudes is shown in their advance and retreat into their ground and essence; and this essence is just this movement and resolution of these moments. Here, where spirit or its reflection into itself is constituted, our reflection can briefly recollect them from this side: they were consciousness, self-consciousness, and reason. Thus spirit is *consciousness* generally, which comprehends sense certainty, perception, and understanding in it, insofar as spirit holds fast in the analysis of itself the moment in which it is an *objective, existing* actuality to itself, and abstracts from the fact that this actuality is its own being-for-itself. If on the contrary it holds fast the other moment of the analysis, that its object is its own being-for-itself, then it is self-consciousness. But as immediate consciousness *of being-in-and-for-itself,* as the unity of consciousness and self-consciousness it is the consciousness that *has* reason. . . . When this reason, which consciousness *has,* is finally perceived by it to be such that reason *is,* or the reason that is *actual* in spirit and that is its world, then it exists in its truth; it *is* spirit, it is the *actual ethical* essence.

Spirit is the *ethical life* of a *people,* insofar as it is the *immediate truth*—the individual that is a world. (H 314–15; M 264–65; B 459–60)

The appearances of spirit in the three preceding moments show their abstractness in being individuated, isolated: As an epistemological subject, consciousness stands alone confronting its various objects. Even self-consciousness, though inherently intersubjective, seems to itself to be locked in itself, as does the self-conscious consciousness that merely "has" reason. Spirit examines itself, in all these abstract appearances, only from the depth of an individuated life. But now it appears objectively as a "world," that "*is*" rational. Echoing his earlier manuscripts on ethics and social philosophy, Hegel speaks of the ethical life *(Sittlichkeit)* of a Volk as a collective individual, who is also a phenomenological world.

This newly achieved concreteness registers in the style and method of the chapter on Spirit, which takes the form of an idealized historical narrative. It is idealized in the sense that it does not recount actual historical events, nor does it attempt to offer a complete chronicle of Western culture. But it attends to certain definite cultural moments, linked to one another in a narrative in which each develops out of its predecessor in historical fashion.

So this chapter marks a new beginning to the work, a second half in which the appearances of spirit are concrete. But it also completes a pair, with the chapter Reason, paralleling the first pair of Consciousness and Self-Consciousness. In the chapter on Reason a multidimensional world is viewed from the standpoint of a single consciousness that "has" reason. In the chapter on Spirit that world appears from its inside; it "is" rational, and the figures that appear in it have internalized that world. So these two chapters recapitulate, in relation to a much more complex natural and social world, the distinction between consciousness and self-consciousness: the "synthesis" of that first paradigmatic pair is itself distributed into a new form of the original antithesis. As reason returns us fundamentally to the subject-object standpoint of consciousness, so Spirit returns us to the intersubjective standpoint of self-consciousness.

Now I want to suggest that the chapters on Religion and Absolute Knowledge make up a similar pair. So the following scheme emerges in relation to the arrangement Hegel introduced into his table of contents under capital letters (see Table 1).

Table 1.

	A-Series		B-Series
(A)	Consciousness		(B) Self-Consciousness
		C	
(AA)	Reason		(BB) Spirit
(CC)	Religion		(DD) Absolute Knowledge

Part (C) reiterates in new pairs, at richer levels, the original antithesis between (A) and (B). The horizontal relation between each set of pairs is one significant feature of this scheme, but another is the vertical relation among the three moments making up the first term of each pair and among those making up the second term of each pair. For convenience sake I have labeled these two vertical sets the A-series and the B-series. The formal resemblance among the moments making up the A-series is constituted by a mutual otherness or opposition between subject and object, of which the structure established in "(A) Consciousness" is the paradigm. That among moments making up the B-series is constituted by mutual recognition or identity-in-difference, of which the concept of recognition and its ironical articulations in "(B) Self-Consciousness" is the paradigm. If the tendency in the A-series is to set subject and object in opposition, the tendency in the B-series is to lose the integrity of the "other"; for example, of the actual, as we saw in the concluding moments (Stoicism, skepticism, unhappy consciousness) of the chapter on Self-Consciousness.

Each horizontal pairing represents a certain sphere of reality, which creates a difference among the members of each vertical series. In both consciousness and self-consciousness, for instance, we have particular subjects or selves coming to terms with particular objects or others in their experience. In the next pair, reason and spirit, the protagonists come to terms with an entire natural and social world in its cultural transformations. Here we deal with the "actual" *(Wirklichkeit)* as it is comprehended or acted upon rationally, or as it is inhabited by spirit in its ethical, cultural concreteness. Hegel speaks of spirit in this sphere as "actual" spirit, a term he also uses in the *Realphilosophie* for the sphere of social philosophy and akin to what he was to call "objective" spirit in his later system: comprising the politically, culturally, historically actual. We have noted that the rational subject in the chapter on Reason still takes an individuated form, though its rationality is putatively universal. But in general the subject in the A-series undergoes transformation correlative to the nature of its object. The subject of reason is again consciousness, an "I," but conceived already as a universal individual capable of "understanding" a world. That correlation between subject and object is what is transformed in its counterpart in the B-series, actual spirit, into a vast pattern of mutual recognition, a collective individual that is a world.

Admittedly, Hegel's articulation of each of these moments is more complex than this simple scheme suggests, but I think it is useful in helping us keep the general line of advance through the *Phenomenology* clear. There are, to be sure, submoments of "consciousness" within the moments of the B-series, and vice versa. We have seen, for instance, that unhappy consciousness is splayed across an unbridgeable gulf between a finite subject and its infinite object; it is an unhappy *consciousness*. And yet its divided existence "for itself" is based on what "we" recognize as an identity "in itself" that is a form of self-consciousness after all. Similarly, the second moment in Reason is entitled "The Actualization of Rational Self-Consciousness through its own Self," and indeed the rational subject presented in the entire chapter is constituted by the flawed realization of self-consciousness in the preceding chapter. Yet this rational and self-conscious ego confronts its world, theoretically and practically, in a manner that bears the unmistakable stamp of the A-series. Its recognition of itself *in* its world awaits the chapter on Spirit. Each moment, furthermore, prepares for the next by turning into its opposite.

This interplay between A and B becomes still more complex in the final pairing. I shall have more to say about the relation between religion and absolute knowledge further on, so I shall content myself with some simple schematic observations here: In this pair we rise from "actual" spirit existing in *time,* under the condition of its dispersion in the actual world, to confront spirit in its timeless, transparent unity. But this new elevation from actual spirit to absolute spirit is achieved in the chapter on Religion under the basic conditions of the A-series: spirit appears as a divine other, with the religious devotee or community standing over against it. In this chapter, however, we find a steady overcoming of this otherness, in accordance with Hegel's long-standing definition of "religion" (as opposed to "faith") as the elevation of the finite to the infinite. The chapter Religion accordingly takes the form of an odd kind of mystical theology, like its medieval models moving stage by stage from otherness to union; but unlike the medieval models this movement transpires among entire religious traditions, and not as the pure ascent of an individual soul to God. Furthermore, as we shall see, this Hegelian *itinerarium mentis in deum* stops just short of total union. For so long as it transpires under the conditions of religion it cannot escape a certain *formal* otherness that we have already encountered in the treatment of religion in the *Realphilosophie,* and that is characteristic of the A-series generally. The completion of this mutual recognition in the sphere of the absolute must await the final moment of "absolute" self-knowledge, in which divine substance itself becomes self-knowing subject in its finite other. Here, too, as in the earlier pairings, the subject-object dichotomy of the first member of the pair (the A-series) terminates in the overcoming of this dichotomy in its counterpart from the B-series. But in this case the mutual recognition takes the form of a kind of Platonic *anemnesis,* the external relation of self and other transformed into the "inwardness" of *Er-innerung* (recollection).

Taken as a whole, the six moments, alternating between A-series and B-series, moves from Socratic dialogue on the possibility of knowledge to that final self-knowledge in Platonic recollection, in which the original interlocutors, consciousness for-itself and "we" who have comprehended its ordeals, become one, spirit in-and-for-itself. So our schema is elaborated in Table 2.

Table 2.

	A-Series		B-Series
Abstract Particularity:	(A) Consciousness (Dialogue)	(B)	Self-Consciousness (Myth)
		(C)	
Worldly Actuality:	(AA) Reason (Treatise)	(BB)	Spirit (Ideal History)
The Absolute:	(CC) Religion (Mystical Theology)	(DD)	Absolute Knowledge (Recollection)

Hegel repeatedly speaks of the work in the Introduction as a "pathway" *(Weg)*. It can, for instance, "be taken as the pathway of the natural consciousness that presses forward to true knowledge, or as the pathway of the soul that journeys through the series of its own configurations as through stations appointed for it by its own nature, in order that it may refine itself into spirit" (H 67; M 49; B 135).

To that "natural consciousness," however, that suffers the negation of each of its forms of experience as such, the work will appear as a skeptical "pathway of doubt . . . or more strictly as the pathway of despair" (ibid.). But the metaphor of the path should not mislead us into expecting a simple linear series of ascending moments from beginning to end. Within each chapter one may find such a continuous path, but each chapter in a sense begins afresh at a higher plateau, affording a more capacious view of the course that has been traveled. At least "we" enjoy this longer perspective, but the protagonist consciousness that occupies the higher plateau has a distressing way of "forgetting" how it got there. It is not only that it is too occupied by its present adventures on the path to look back, or down. It really is such a different form of consciousness that only "we" can see its continuity with its predecessors. Furthermore, as our characterization of the formal differences among the various chapters indicates, the path is constructed very differently in each chapter. The ideal historical narrative of the chapter on Spirit, for instance, will connect its successive moments very differently than we found to be the case in the chapter on Self-Consciousness, where each tableau in the myth of the self seemed to take form afresh out of the mists. Narrative connection, even in that looser sense, is not present at all in the chapters on Consciousness and Reason, where more logical types of connection prevail, dialogical in the one case and discursive in the other.

An odd pathway! Not only does the journey seem to start over with each chapter, but the chapters are related to each other in ways that the metaphor of the path can scarcely accommodate at all. They are like six successive impressions of a block print, each contributing a new dimension of color and form while radically altering the impression left by its predecessor. Each contributes to the same picture, which is complete only when the last block has been impressed on it. That last impression is the contribution of "science," which in principle brings the entire System of Science into the picture. That metaphor has its limits, too, but at least it may help to bring out how misleading it is for Pöggeler to speak of a "teleological" process at work in the *Phenomenology.* "Science" is not so much the goal or telos of this series of six moments as it is the most adequate reorganization of the same picture to which the other five have contributed. But each contribution is necessary. Each chapter contributes an interpretation of the *same* life of experience, the *same* appearance of spirit, and at once negates and builds upon the previous interpretation. For reasons that we will discuss shortly, at the time he wrote the *Phenomenology* Hegel thought that one could not dispense with the first five moments and simply present the point of view of "science," because science itself derives its content through the appropriation of what must first be presented in the earlier forms. If "absolute knowledge" as the position of science is an ideal re-collection, it requires the earlier moments in order to have anything to recollect.

Since, however, Hegel's phenomenological enterprise is conceived in relation to a System of Science, further issues about its conception and design, including the issue about teleology, can best be addressed by considering the nature of that relation.

The *Phenomenology* and the System

We saw in the preceding chapter how persistently Hegel labored in Jena to produce a system. He arrived in Jena with that aim already firmly in mind, and in its pursuit he wrote and abandoned a succession of massive manuscripts. This prodigious effort was fueled by two deeply held convictions: that something was basically awry with modern life, and that he was living on the edge of a revolutionary change that would transform it. The murderous collision between reactionary and revolutionary politics, in the wake of the French Revolution, was merely the most conspicuous sign that the modern world was coming apart at the seams. Other signs of modern alienation were religious sectarianism and otherworldliness, a compartmentalization of intellectual life into many sciences having nothing to do with each other in method or content, a mechanistic interpretation of nature and a moralistic interpretation of spirit that projected spiritual fulfillment in an unachievable "beyond" outside the natural realm and left the latter as a mere field for exploitation, conflict between the public and the private, and so on and on. Now Hegel had come to think that the various aspects of this diagnostic were interrelated, dimensions of a single lacerated whole, at once cultural, political, religious, intellectual, personal. He never supposed that a philosopher could set all this right, but he did set about his philosophical work buoyed by an optimism exuberantly expressed on a number of occasions in Jena and earlier that the world was on the edge of a new age. The following paragraph from the Preface to the *Phenomenology* shows that this youthful confidence was still vividly alive when he wrote that work:

> It is furthermore not difficult to see that our time is a time of birth and of transition to a new period. Spirit has broken with the previous world of its existence and thought, and is of a mind to let it sink down into the past, while spirit engages in the labor of its own transformation. Spirit, to be sure, is never grasped at rest, but in its constant forward movement. But as a child after its long, quiet nourishment breaks with its first breath the gradualness of its merely cumulative growth—a qualitative leap—and now the child is born: so the spirit forming itself matures slowly and quietly into its new shape, dissolving one bit after another of the structure of its previous world, whose tottering is only indicated by isolated symptoms; the frivolity as well as the boredom which unsettle the established order, the vague premonition of something unknown, are harbingers that something else is approaching. This gradual crumbling that did not alter the physiognomy of the whole is interrupted by the dawning that in a single flash discloses the features of the new world. (H 15–16; M 6–7; B 75)

One is reminded of the quotation from Diderot's *Rameau's Nephew* that appears in the chapter on Spirit: After spirit has infiltrated the "unconscious idol" through and through, then "one fine morning it gives its comrade a nudge with its elbow and bang! crash! the idol lies on the floor" (H 388; M 332; B 564–65). The sudden appearance of the

newborn child after its steady gestation in the womb provides a metaphor (of which, as we have seen, Hegel had a prototype nearer at hand!)
for this same bursting on the scene of a new age that has been invisibly
taking form. Hegel's thought had been developing for some years with
a vivid sense that this "qualitative leap" was soon to appear.[67] Hegel's
own response to this expectation was to address himself with astonishing energy and persistence to the composition of a total system.

That may seem an odd thing to do to herald the birth of a new age,
but one must sound whatever trumpet God has given one to blow.
Furthermore, what Hegel saw as the philosophical pathologies of the
passing age, the dualisms of post-Kantian *Reflexionsphilosophie* in particular, were integrally related to its other pathologies. As he said much
later, in the Preface to the *Philosophy of Right,* the philosophy of an
age is "its age comprehended in thought"; not in the sense that culture
causes philosophy but in the sense that intellectual understanding is
symbiotic with other aspects of the life of an age. And so it must be
with the philosophizing attendant upon and integral to an age in which
a reconciling spirit is to be born: it will both negate and bind together.
It will expose the false assumptions of the age of dualism and will leave
them with no philosophical ground on which to stand, and it will disclose
the underlying harmony of things. Not that there will be no conflicts
or tensions, but the system will show that despite all the eruptions on
the periphery the center holds.

The system was to articulate a synoptic vision of spirit in all its
dimensions: political, personal, religious, aesthetic, biological, historical, and so on and so forth. But the system was not to be merely a work
about spirit. In this work of the human mind, spirit was to achieve a
self-conscious recognition of itself in all its dimensions, as an inherent
part of the achievement of wholeness it was to celebrate. The *Phenomenology* was an integral part of the plan: it would exhibit spirit's own
appearances in that "previous world" of spirit's past "existence and
thought" *(seines Daseins und Vorstellens),* and also its break with that
world, its negation of these superseded appearances. Through this path
of negation, spirit would be seen moving toward that reconciling fulfillment that was the task of the new age, in which all those aspects
of its life that had led more or less independent careers during the
time of spirit's diaspora, and were generally at odds with one another,
will be united in their depths: art, religion, political life, the several
sciences, even philosophy itself, will cease to be unrelated activities
and will achieve their completeness in the one life of spirit. The system

on its positive side, as an integrated science of wisdom, will articulate this totality and complete it. That double task, addressed respectively to the old age and the new, was what kept our indefatigable system-builder at his desk. In the dogmas of Christianity, as we shall see, he found not merely an approximation of an outdated metaphysics, with its teleology doing service for providential history, but precisely a religious expression of this break between the old and the new, in particular the negativity and Aufhebung, the death and transfiguration of religion itself, in which it ceases to be "religion" and becomes spirit. As such, these dogmas have an integral place—properly interpreted!—in that system which reflects spirit's negation of its fragmented past, its diaspora, and its triumphant reintegration and return to Jerusalem!

So when Hegel wrote his *Phenomenology* he was gathering his energies to attempt yet again the construction of a total system, of which this work was to be a first, introductory part, a way of negation into strict science. But as we have seen, world history intervened in the person of Napoleon. The University of Jena was closed down and Hegel had to seek nonacademic employment. So his burning desire to publish a system was frustrated yet again. The *Phenomenology,* published even while he was negotiating for a newspaper editorship in Bamberg, was in a singular way left stranded, as the propaedeutic Part One of a system that never got written.

It is important to realize that when Hegel did finally publish the outline of a system ten years later (the Heidelberg *Encyclopedia*), his conception of the system had changed so radically that he could no longer regard his Jena masterpiece as its propaedeutic, and to an extent disowned it. In all his earlier efforts to write a system in Jena, he considered that some such negative propaedeutic was to be an integral part of it.[68] That was certainly his view when he wrote the *Phenomenology,* in a strong sense that we will elaborate shortly. But in the 1817 edition of the *Encyclopedia,* as well as subsequent editions (1827, 1830), the system outlined required no such propaedeutic. The Introduction to the *Encyclopedia* may be a relic of the earlier conception, with its useful survey of various philosophical "positions of thought toward objectivity," but this brief survey bears no integral relation to the system it introduces, and is in any case a pale shadow of the Jena masterwork.

A more curious relic is the section in the third part of the *Encyclopedia,* the Philosophy of Spirit, under "Subjective Spirit," entitled "Phenomenology of Spirit." Already included in the Heidelberg edition of 1817, it comprises twenty-six numbered paragraphs of the final edition of 1830.[69] It clearly derives from the Jena *Phenomenology,* and yet the resemblance between the two is entirely superficial. This so-called Berlin Phenomenology has been displaced from the propaedeutic role of the Jena *Phenomenology* and limited to the topic of "Consciousness," which is its subtitle. It is divided into three parts: A. Consciousness as Such (§§ 417–23), B. Self-Consciousness (§§ 424–37), and C. Reason (§§ 438–39). The reduction of the entire part C of the *Phenomenology* of 1807 to the two paragraphs on reason is only the most conspicuous example of how Hegel has truncated his earlier work. The paragraphs on self-consciousness are divided into three subparts entitled "Desire," "Recognitive Self-Consciousness," and "Universal Self-Consciousness." The first two subparts follow the chapter in the Jena work in topic outline up to the Master and Slave dialectic. There is no treatment of Stoicism, skepticism, unhappy consciousness.

But even when the same topic is treated it is presented from a markedly different point of view.[70] For this Berlin Phenomenology is like a patch cut from a rich old garment and sewn into a new quilt: it is trimmed to serve an essentially different purpose in the design of the later system. It treats the doctrine of consciousness in a limited sense defined by its position in this larger scheme, without undertaking the extraordinary act of divination by which Hegel had attempted in Jena to present a form of consciousness from within, for itself, in counterpoint to its comprehension in itself. Here we find only a summary of the systematic upshot, with no treatment of actual spirit or religion since these topics are given their philosophical definitions later. There is, as Petry argues, a gain in cohesion, clarity, and certainly in conciseness,[71] but a fearful loss in the treatment of the dynamics of experience, not to speak of the poetry of spirit.

At any rate, the *Phenomenology* of 1807 survives as a relic of a conception Hegel later abandoned. In the Preface written in 1812 to the *Science of Logic,* he still spoke of the *Phenomenology* as "the first part of the *System of Science,*" of which the "second part" was comprised of the Logic, the Philosophy of Nature, and the Philosophy of Spirit; and in that Preface he indicated "the relation of the science which I call the Phenomenology of Spirit to Logic." But he added a note to this Preface in a new edition in 1831 saying that "this title will not be repeated in the second edition" of the *Phenomenology* on which he was at work: it was no longer to be regarded as the first part of the system.[72] Instead of that projected second part of the *System of Science* he had written his *Encyclopedia.* Because the *Encyclopedia* proceeds through three moments with the same titles as those he had projected for Part 2 of *System of Science,* it is easy to miss the significance of the change: the latter was conceived in integral relation to Part 1, the *Phenomenology,* while the *Encyclopedia* is self-contained. Indeed, there are few references to the *Phenomenology* in Hegel's work after those remarks in the Preface to the *Logic,* though the very fact that he was at work at the end of his life on a revision of this work he had written twenty-five years earlier suggests that he did not simply disown it.[73] Still, the work was left stranded in this anomalous position because its author was no longer convinced that the system had to confront the wayward luxuriance of experience on its own terms. It is therefore very difficult to interpret the *Phenomenology* of 1807 if we approach it from the point of view of the later system.[74] It is a relic of a conception of "science" quite different from that realized in the *Encyclopedia,* really an alternative, a road not taken.

At the time he wrote the *Phenomenology,* Hegel was convinced that any systematic position had to be earned by showing how it is the immanent outcome of a critical process in which each form of experience criticized was first allowed to speak for itself. In the Preface to that unwritten system, which survives anomalously as the Preface to the *Phenomenology,* Hegel speaks in general terms of the system as the articulation of that truth that is constituted by the life of spirit through all its expressions: "That the true is actual only as system, or that substance is essentially subject, is expressed in the representation which pronounces the absolute to be *spirit*—the most sublime concept, and that which belongs to the more recent age and its religion." It is noteworthy that this sublime concept of the absolute as spirit is to be expressed both in the system and, as the equivalent or really the condition of this scientific system, in the insight that "substance is essentially subject." This insight belongs to the religion as well as to the philosophy of the age that is being ushered in. Hegel goes on to say that "the spiritual," which "is alone the actual," is both "the essence or being-in-itself" and "*being-other* and *being-for-itself.*" In fact spirit is not actual at all unless it incorporates both. The essential must unite itself with that otherness if spirit is to become actual or if the system of science is to be achieved. But it is not yet enough for science to recognize this unity independently: "This being-in-and-for-itself . . . is first for us or *in itself,* it is the spiritual *substance.*"

But substance must become subject: The other

must also be this *for its own self,* must be the knowledge of the spiritual and the knowledge of itself as spirit; that is, it must be itself as object, but just as immediately as transcended object, reflected into itself. It is *for-itself* only for us, insofar as its spiritual content is engendered through its own self; but insofar as it is also for-itself for its own self, this self-engendering, the pure concept, is at the same time the objective element in which it has its existence, and it is in this manner in its existence for its own self the object reflected into itself. (H 24; M 14; B 85–86)

The point of this tortured language is that spirit, and the science of spirit, is only achieved in dialectical engagement with the other, whose experience "for itself" must develop to embrace the position of science: but the position of science is not already fixed, but itself takes form in this engagement with the experience of the other! Otherness is the "objective element" in which the self-engendering of spirit must transpire. "Spirit that knows itself to be so developed as spirit is *science.*" Science is spirit's "actuality and the realm which it builds for itself in its own element."

Hegel makes a distinction between what science is in principle, according to its definition, and science in its detailed content, which must incorporate all the "appearances" of spirit. For this first general statement defining science, Hegel employs the notion of "aether" that he had found so handy in his systematic manuscripts of the Jena period,[75] to signify a pure material medium not differentiated into actual objects, a generalized "otherness" in which the Idea is actualized in principle, sometimes identified with "being." Here it expresses the pure definition of science: "*Pure self-cognition* in absolute otherness, this aether *as such,* is the basis of science or is *knowledge in general.* The beginning of philosophy presupposes or demands that consciousness find its way in this *element.*" Yet it is not as if science were merely this aethereal element in which the unscientific consciousness must sink or swim. That would be so if the spirit that is articulated in science were already complete in itself, independent of this not-yet-scientific consciousness: "But this element achieves its own completion and transparency only through the movement of its becoming" (H 24; M 14; B 86).

Science is incomplete and opaque so long as the movement of consciousness into it is not explicitly contained in it. Consciousness must be brought to the point of disporting itself in this aethereal medium, but for its part consciousness may make its own claim on science in return: "Science, from its side, demands of self-consciousness that it should have elevated itself into this aether in order to be able to live with it and in it. . . . On the other hand the individual has the right to demand that science should at least extend him a ladder into this standpoint, showing him this standpoint within himself." The point is not simply that science benignly drops a ladder down into the murk and confusion in which the individual dwells. The unscientific individual has the standpoint of science in some manner "within himself," and the ladder will consist in showing how this is so. That the individual has a "right" to this ladder, furthermore, implies that the extending of it is no mere act of charity or pedagogical zeal on the part of "science": "His right is based on his absolute independence, which he knows himself to possess in every form of his knowledge, for in each form, whether it is recognized by science or not, and whatever its content, it is the absolute form; that is, he is the *immediate certainty* of himself and, if this expression be preferred, he is thereby unconditional *being*." The individual is that actual other in which science must comprehend itself in order to pass beyond its general definition and achieve genuine content. Whatever the state of his own knowledge, the actual individual has at least *this* decisive relation to a science of spirit: he is in his existential immediacy, in his "being," that "other" in which spirit must find itself in order to exist as spirit. Without mutual recognition between spirit and precisely this recalcitrant bundle of prejudices, spirit will remain an unrealized possibility, and science with it. His existence as the opposite of science is precisely the opposition that must be reconciled, and not merely for the sake of his own enlightenment: lost as he is in manifold dualism or opposition, the unity of science must come to terms with him, as *its* opposite, in order to be anything but a castle in the air, aethereal indeed: "If the standpoint of consciousness, which knows objective things in opposition to itself, and itself in opposition to them, is regarded by science as its *other* . . . so on the other hand is the element of science for him a remote beyond in which he is no longer in possession of himself" (H 25; M 14–15; B 87).

This mutual opposition between science and the individual provides the context for the famous and often misunderstood remark about science requiring a person to walk "on his head," upside down.[76] Hegel is not recommending this inconvenient posture. It rather expresses the impossibility of an individual's adopting straightway the standpoint of science: it is like demanding that he should walk on his head. But such a contradictory demand is not only frustrating for the individual: it is inherently self-defeating for science itself.

> Each of these two parties appears to the other to be the inversion of truth. That the natural consciousness should entrust itself to science is an attempt, it knows not under what provocation, just once to walk on its head; the compulsion to assume this unaccustomed posture and to move about in it is a violence that appears as unprepared for as it is unnecessary, that it is expected to inflict on itself. —Let science be in itself what it will; in relation to the immediate self-consciousness it presents itself as an inversion to him, or since he in the certainty of himself possesses the principle of his actuality, it bears the form of unactuality, since he for himself is outside science. (H 25; M 15; B 87–88)

If this impasse were allowed to stand, the relation between science and consciousness would be precisely that satirized by Kierkegaard's comical pseudonym, Nicholaus Notabene in *Prefaces:* "I am so stupid that I cannot understand philosophy; the antithesis of this is that philosophy is so clever that it cannot comprehend my stupidity. These antitheses are mediated in a higher unity: in our common stupidity."[77] Such mutual incomprehension, Hegel agrees, would have to exist if science were a closed in-itself, a science merely of absolute substance. But in fact philosophical science must comprehend Nicholaus's stupidity insofar as Nicholaus too, in his witty self-assurance, is after all an appearance of spirit. "Science," Hegel continues, "must therefore unite this element" of subjective self-certainty "with itself, or rather must show that and how it belongs to itself. So long as it dispenses with such actuality, science only consists in its content as the *in-itself,* the *purpose* that is still something *inward,* not as spirit but only as spiritual substance." So the necessity for extending a ladder to the unscientific individual, and his right to such a ladder, is finally grounded on the most basic need of science itself to articulate the subjectivity of spirit. Short of that it merely reflects a Spinozistic "substance," has not yet comprehended the subject, is not yet spirit.

> This *in-itself* must externalize itself and become *for-itself,* which means that it has to establish the self-consciousness as one with itself.

This becoming of *science in general* or of *knowledge* is what this *Phenomenology* of Spirit describes. (H 25–26; M 15; B 88)

The "for-itself" (the various forms of consciousness described on their own terms in the *Phenomenology*) is thus not merely the falsehood that must be confronted with the truth of the in-itself.[78] It furnishes the very medium through which the in-itself, substance, becomes subjective, spiritual. "Science" is not fixed in stone. Science must "become," and this development is achieved in apprehending the way consciousness, positioned for-itself, proceeds through the series of its forms to unite itself with the developing standpoint of science, which itself takes form in just this process. The experiences of consciousness are themselves appearances, *phainomena,* of spirit. That *spirit* for-itself, in these appearances, does not yet recognize itself as spirit (e.g., most poignantly, in unhappy consciousness) is the impasse, from its side, that must be overcome. But it is the same impasse that prevents science, from the other side, from recognizing itself in the experiences of consciousness. The special science of phenomenology must not only articulate the forms of this impasse but achieve the mutual recognition in which it will be overcome. The very possibility of science, as Hegel then conceived it, depended upon the success of this propaedeutic science.

So it is evident that the *Phenomenology* was indeed conceived as an essential part of the system: as Part 1 of the *System of Science,* without which Part 2, comprised of Logic, Science of Nature and Science of Spirit, could not be written.

This conception of science or of philosophical system was quite novel. Implicit in it is a fundamental critique of other systematic philosophies before and since, and this critique has implications for every branch of philosophy. There are abundant examples, for instance, of philosophies of religion developed in a systematic vacuum, without ever coming to terms with any actual religion as it appears for itself. Hegel's own later *Encyclopedia,* for that matter, treats religion from the standpoint of a philosophical science that is assumed to be already achieved. Actual religious life is already distilled into the philosophy or science of religion. In practice, to be sure, when Hegel *lectured* on the philosophy of religion in the 1820s, he freely introduced the phenomenological element notably missing from the paragraphs devoted to the subject in the *Encyclopedia.* That was also true of the lectures on aesthetics. Still the question arises in principle with respect to all forms of "pre-scientific" consciousness: what does it mean when the propaedeutic science of phenomenology is banished from the system? Certainly it means disowning the conception of science expressed in the Preface to the *Phenomenology,* so far as its intrinsic dependence on the forms of experience is concerned.

We may lament the fact that the system Hegel had in view in that Preface never got written, but the further question arises whether Hegel was able to compose a system on these terms. If there was in the Jena systematic manuscripts the ambivalence we have suggested between an experience-negating and an experience-appropriating conception of the system, it may well be that the firm commitment to the experience-appropriating type expressed in that Preface was a commitment he found impossible to execute. In that case Napoleon's intervention may have been timely, sparing Hegel the embarrassment of an inability to follow through on his announced conception of science. It is possible, indeed, that the science of phenomenology is inimical to any sort of putatively final systematization: that Hegel's *Phenomenology* is an *alternative* to the system, implying quite a different conception both of spirit and of a science of spirit. In that case Hegel's actual accomplishment in the *Phenomenology* will have a significance quite different from what he intended for it when he wrote it as a propaedeutic to the system. Such a divergence between intention and actual accomplishment is, after all, a characteristic Hegelian irony, particularly if the accomplishment should turn out to be more significant than the intention that informed it.

The intention, at any rate, is clear enough: Hegel goes on in the Preface to speak of the "long path" that "immediate spirit" or "sensuous consciousness" must "work through" in order "to engender the element of science." The "absolute knowledge" that lies at the end of this long path, will differ fundamentally from "the enthusiasm which begins immediately with absolute knowledge, as if shot out of a pistol, and disposes of other standpoints by declaring that it will take no notice of them" (H 26; M 15–16; B 88–89). Yet at the end of this path will be the goal articulated earlier in the Preface: that we will "lay aside the title of love of knowledge"—philo-sophia—and achieve "actual knowledge." This actual knowledge *(Wissen)* is described as "science" *(Wissenschaft)* or "the scientific system," characterized by "the inner necessity" of its moments (H 12; M 3–4; B 70). That is the position to be won at the conclusion of the *Phenomenology:* the chapter on Absolute Knowledge can be so brief because it represents the consummating experience of consciousness or appearance of spirit, spirit in-and-for-itself, to be articulated in the remaining parts of the System of Science. But this position must be *won,* and not merely "shot out of a pistol" in disregard of "other standpoints." A science of spirit is a "becoming" that is only "actual" (absolute) to the extent that it unites itself with spirit "for itself" as represented by these other standpoints.

That was not only the view of the phenomenological task that Hegel expressed in the Preface to the System of Science, written after he had completed the *Phenomenology.* He expressed the same position on the central methodological issue in the Introduction, when he still conceived the work as the "Science of the Experience of Consciousness." This propaedeutic science is already considered to be a genuine science; indeed, the "First Part" of the System of Science, in virtue of the "necessity" by which consciousness is shown to proceed through the series of its forms of experience until it achieves that form of experience that is identical with science itself. But Hegel devotes a considerable part of this Introduction to showing that science brings no independent criterion (*Masstab;* literally, "measuring stick") of its own to measure the adequacy of the various forms of experience being passed in review. There is, to be sure, a constant tension between the form of consciousness "for itself" and what it is "in itself" or "for us" (H 70–71; M 52–53; B 139–40), as we have seen in the chapter on Self-Consciousness. But Hegel insists that this distinction does not imply that "we" apply any extrinsic criterion or "measuring stick" to the experience of consciousness for itself. "Consciousness gives its criterion to its own self, and the investigation becomes thereby a comparison of consciousness with itself; for the distinction made above"—between the in-itself and the for-itself—"falls within" consciousness (H 71; M 53; B 140). Consciousness for-itself simply experiences its own intentional object. What it does not recognize is the intentional structure of its experience, as a subject-object relation. But that intentional structure also "falls within" consciousness. Unhappy consciousness, for instance, recognizes the unchangeable, but not the inherent correlation between itself and this unchangeable object. "We" do recognize the latter, but in doing so we simply see what is inherent in its own predicament. We do not bring an independent metaphysical truth or other superior standpoint to bear on it.

"We" simply observe and describe. That may seem a disingenuous description of "our" role, since we observe the subject-object correlation as a whole and not from the standpoint of the subject himself—already no inconsiderable advantage over the consciousness in question—and we observe this correlation within a connected series of such intentional structures. Still, the two moments,

> *concept and object, being-for-another* and *being-in-itself,* fall within that knowledge itself that we are investigating, and thus it is not necessary for us to bring criteria with us and to apply *our* conjectures and thoughts to the investigation; just by leaving these aside do we succeed in observing the situation as it is *in* and *for* itself.
>
> But any contribution by us is superfluous, not only in virtue of the fact that concept and object, criterion and what is to be tested, are present in the consciousness itself, but we are also spared the trouble of comparing the two and the actual *testing,* so that also in this respect all that remains to us is purely to look on, since consciousness tests itself. (H 71–72; M 53–54; B 141)

Precisely because consciousness *intends* to grasp what is really the case in its knowledge of its object, however mistaken it may turn out to be, the distinction between in-itself and for-itself is implicit in its own experience. We find in the experience of consciousness that dialectic between truth and subjective certainty that is to be investigated in this work. Indeed, consciousness learns by experience that it has been deceived in its knowledge of the object.

> Simply because consciousness does after all know an object, the distinction is already present between something that *to consciousness* is *in itself,* and the other moment in which this knowledge or being of the object is, however, *for* consciousness. Upon this distinction, which is already present, the testing proceeds. If this comparison of the two moments shows that they do not correspond, it seems that consciousness has to alter its knowledge in order to make it adequate to the object; but in the alteration of its knowledge it in fact alters the object as well, since the knowledge that was present was essentially knowledge of the object . . . or the criterion of the testing changes, if what was to have been the criterion does not hold up in the testing; and the testing is not only a testing of knowledge, but also of its criterion. (H 72–73; M 54–55; B 142)

This entire process, in which consciousness learns by experience the inadequacy of its previous form of knowledge, is what we observe. Object, criterion, and the subject himself, are transformed before our eyes. A new subject-object configuration arises out of the negation of the previous one, and the series of such transformations is the content of our science of the experience of consciousness.

> This *dialectical* movement which consciousness practices on it-self, on its knowledge as well as on its object, *insofar as a new true object arises from it,* is just what is called *experience.* . . . This new object contains the nullification of the first, it is the experience made out of the first. (H 73; M 55; B 142–43)

Consciousness itself undergoes this metamorphosis in the "dialectical movement" called "experience." Experience, that is, is dialectical in itself; "we" do not impose a dialectical pattern on it.

Yet Hegel goes on to admit that there is, after all, something that is "our contribution" (*unser Zutat,* which might be translated by its possible cognate, "our doodad": the term is used for the garnishing of food, or the trim or decoration of clothes, nothing very essential). When consciousness replaces a previous construction of its object with a new one, this change appears to it to occur in a "fortuitous manner and externally." Consciousness for itself does not recognize the dialectical character of its own experience, or that "the new object shows itself to have come about through a *transformation of consciousness* itself." Intent on its object, consciousness does not recognize that a transformation has occurred in its entire intentional structure, including itself.

> This observation of the situation is our contribution, through which the series of experiences of consciousness is raised to a scientific progression, which does not exist for the consciousness we observe. This is in fact the same circumstance of which we already spoke above in regard to the relation of our presentation to skepticism, namely that the result produced in each case by an untrue knowing is not to collapse into an empty nothing, but must necessarily be apprehended as the nothing of that *of which it is the result,* a result which contains what is true in the previous knowledge. (H 74; M 55–56; B 143–44)

We noted this important difference between Hegel's phenomenological procedure and outright skepticism in our treatment of the section on skepticism. Though our science can be described as a "thoroughgoing skepticism," its negativity consists in recognizing that the "nothing" of what is negated is "the nothing of that out of which it proceeds"—not the "pure nothing" of skepticism, but productive of a "genuine result" which "is itself something determinate and has a *content*." This result Hegel calls the "*determinate* negation" of the preceding moment (H 67, 68–69; M 50–51; B 136–37). That is the discussion Hegel alludes to in the present passage. What we observe, and consciousness for itself does not, is that the new state of consciousness and the object it intends are the necessary result of what has been negated. There is therefore a "scientific" progression in the series of determinate negations: we can see how each subject-object structure proceeds from and is constituted by its predecessor. But the sequence arises out of the consideration of experience itself, in *its* dialectical movement, and not out of any superior wisdom derived, say, from the System of Science, to which we are privy. Systematic science, on the contrary, takes form on this very pathway of experience. That each negation leads to a new position containing the truth of what is negated is the "circumstance"

> which guides the entire progression of the forms of consciousness in their necessity. Only this necessity itself, or the *origination* of the new object that presents itself to consciousness, without its knowing how it occurs, is what proceeds for us behind the back of consciousness, so to speak. In its movement there occurs thereby a moment of *being-in-itself or for us,* which is not for the consciousness comprehended in the experience itself: but the *content* of what presents itself to us exists *for it,* and we grasp only its formal aspect or its pure origination; *for it* this originated object exists only qua object, *for us* at the same time as movement and becoming.
>
> Through this necessity this pathway to science is itself already *science,* and thus in virtue of its content it is the science of the *experience of consciousness.* (H 74; M 56; B 144)

Hegel certainly does not mean that this propaedeutic to genuine science might at a pinch be regarded as itself scientific despite its commerce with the illusions of experience. That is how we might read the passage if we were to make the later system, with its quite different assumptions, the norm for proper science. Hegel came to think that the later system needed no such "pathway to science." But when he wrote these words he was explaining why this pathway is intrinsic to proper science, indeed is its sine qua non. He was no less convinced of that when he had finished the work, despite whatever truth there may be in the palimpsest theory, as our discussion of the passage in the Preface about the "ladder" to science shows.

"We," who observe each new intentional structure originating out of the debris of its antecedent, can therefore comprehend the necessity of the entire sequence and can see why it must be a pathway of "doubt" and "despair." But the protagonist consciousness must himself *experience* this doubt and despair, and must learn, step by step, from this experience. "We" are simply a tragic chorus witnessing and commenting on his ordeal, recognizing that the upheavals that drive him to despair are not accidental, but are in the nature of experience itself. Its relentless dialectical movement transpires "behind the back of consciousness," because consciousness is *in* the experience, constituted by it. Recognizing this process is our role, as the chorus that is neither protagonist nor victim of the tragedy but is fated to be its commentator.

In the next paragraph, which concludes the Introduction, Hegel suggests that the tragic protagonist will himself finally be brought to the "point" at which this process no longer occurs behind his back: tragedy culminates, according to the Sophoclean model, in self-knowledge. As consciousness

> presses forward to its true existence, it will reach a point at which it gets rid of its illusion of being burdened with something foreign to it, that simply exists for it as an other, or a point at which appearance coincides with essence, so that its presentation will at just this point come together with the genuine science of spirit; and finally, when consciousness grasps this its own essence, it will disclose the nature of absolute knowledge itself. (H 75; M 56–57; B 145)

This passage has excited discussion about just where this "point" occurs. The traditional view, which despite recent challenges[79] seems to me correct, is that it occurs with the concluding chapter of the work, which initiates consciousness and "us" alike into the more strictly systematic Part 2 of the System of Science. At the time Hegel wrote the Introduction, after all, he expected to move directly from the Science of the

Experience of Consciousness into the Logic, probably in the same volume; and it is noteworthy that he actually speaks of "absolute knowledge" as the disclosure resulting from this coincidence of essence and appearance. Of course it is anticipated at many "points" in the *Phenomenology,* beginning with the concept of spirit as mutual recognition in the chapter on Self-Consciousness. As we have seen, furthermore, there is reason to doubt that Hegel anticipated the full scope of the text at the time he wrote the Introduction; he could hardly have expected to reach this "point" in a chapter he did not yet know he was going to write! But the present passage does give clear evidence that he intends the text to culminate in "absolute knowledge," and that, I think, is where he intends the convergence of essence with appearance, in-itself and for-itself, to occur.

But there is a more important question than that of locating just where this "point" occurs: What does this projected convergence of essence and appearance imply about the relation of systematic science to experience? We introduced this query earlier, in asking whether Hegel's system was to be of an experience-negating or an experience-appropriating type (see Chapter 3). I have argued that as the system was taking shape in Jena this issue remained unresolved. The passages we have reviewed from the Preface and the Introduction to the *Phenomenology* suggest that the issue was clearly on Hegel's mind, and that he intended to resolve it in favor of a system of the experience-appropriating type. But just how is the rest of the system to be affected by its phenomenological basis? Does the cryptic comment at the conclusion of the Introduction imply that when the essence or systematic form of our science converges with appearance (already, contra the palimpsest theory, identified with experience), in the chapter on Absolute Knowledge if not before, "science" will be finished with its critical appropriation of experience? After this "point" will it turn dogmatic after all? In that case the system would merely enshrine the memory and the yellowed bones of subjective experience. Such a system would not be the science of living spirit that the passages we have been examining from the Preface and Introduction seem to promise. In this science there might well be a point at which the systematic "essence" determines the form of the exposition, but there could not be a point at which it ceases being informed by the phenomenological appropriation of experience.

This formal issue directly affects the interpretation of religion, even in the *Phenomenology* itself, since every living religion is, in these terms, an appearance of spirit under the conditions of experience. If the relation of the *Phenomenology* to the rest of the system were to be so conceived that the science of these appearances gives way to a science articulating the immutable plenitude of a spirit that no longer appears under the conditions of experience, then there would after all be a teleological principle at work even in the *Phenomenology* itself, the progression of which would represent, despite his evident intentions, Hegel's regression into metaphysics. But the issue closer to our own inquiry would not be whether this teleology is theologically inspired, a form of the Christian belief in providence, as Pöggeler suggests. As for that, Hegel did, early and late, consider the doctrine of providence to be an existentially serious belief, but he did not confuse it with teleology, certainly not in the period we have surveyed. He believed, after all, in the suffering God, whose heart was broken by the world (see Chapter 3). The issue is whether the achievement of science presupposes a terminal coronary attack, the death of God, and implies the replacement of living religion with the scientific Aufhebung of religion.

Religion in the *Phenomenology*

In introducing the chapter on Religion, Hegel surveys the various earlier parts of the *Phenomenology* in which "religion, as consciousness of the *absolute being: being* had already been treated. He immediately adds that these previous appearances of spirit in religious form have exhibited a significant formal deficiency. They have been presented "from the *standpoint of consciousness* alone, that is conscious of the absolute being; but the absolute being has not appeared *in and for its own self,* not as the self-consciousness of spirit, in those forms" (H 473; M 410; B 685). If religion, properly considered, is the mutual recognition characteristic of spirit between finite and absolute being, these previous appearances are not yet properly religious. In other words, they have transpired (with a single exception to be discussed) under the conditions of the unhappy consciousness, for whom the absolute being is objectified and cast into the Beyond. Even when these appearances have been treated under the conditions of what we have called the B-series, the mutual recognition characteristic of the B-series has not extended to absolute being. They have taken the form characteristic of the A-series, as in the case of the section on unhappy consciousness itself.

In this connection Hegel speaks of what is in fact only a brief allusion in the chapter on Consciousness, the paradigm of the A-series: "*Con-*

sciousness, insofar as it is *understanding,* is already consciousness of the *supersensuous* or *inner* side of objective existence. But the supersensuous, eternal, or whatever else one might call it, is *devoid of self."* This allusion we shall therefore ignore, though it is characteristic of Hegel, in treating the distinction between the sensible *Diesseits* and the supersensible *Jenseits* in the chapter on force and understanding, suddenly to introduce the "holy" form of this empty Beyond (H 111–13; M 87–89; B 190–93). Instead, let us return to Hegel's recapitulation that introduces the chapter Religion, where he goes on to remark that this supersensuous Object of the understanding, being "devoid of self,"

> is at first only the *universal,* that is still far from being spirit that knows itself as spirit. —Then there was *Self-Consciousness,* that reached its culmination in the form of *unhappy* consciousness, that was only the *pain* of spirit struggling to get itself out into objectivity again, but without reaching it. The unity of the *single* self-consciousness and its unchangeable *essence* that it confronts remains therefore a Beyond to it. —The immediate existence of Reason and its characteristic forms, which for us proceeded from that pain, have no religion, because its self-consciousness knows or seeks *itself* in the *immediate* present. (H 473; M 410; B 685)

So the chapter on Reason we shall also largely ignore in what follows, and the chapter on Self-Consciousness has received sufficient attention. But the sections of the chapter on Spirit that Hegel goes on to discuss will assign us our task in the next section: The Ethical World, the Religion of Enlightenment (presumably including the section Faith and Pure Insight as well as the one on The Struggle of Enlightenment with Superstition), and the Religion of Morality. In the subsequent section we shall consider the chapter on Religion proper, culminating in the presentation of Christianity under the rubric of Revelatory Religion. The final section will discuss the relation of Revelatory Religion to Absolute Knowledge, where we shall reconsider some of the issues raised in the present section from the standpoint of Hegel's transformation of Christian themes.

4. Religion Under the Conditions of Actual Spirit

Actual spirit is social, historical, self-conscious. As appearances of actual spirit, human beings recognize themselves, achieve personal identity, in the communities to which they belong: which they recognize as their own, and which recognize them. But these communities and their members are subject to radical metamorphosis; actual spirit exists in time. "All previous forms of consciousness" surveyed in the *Phenomenology* "are abstractions" from this spirit in history (H 314; M 264; B 459), their moments have been abstractly related, but here the moments represent actual shapes of existence, historically connected.

The chapter devoted to actual spirit is a long one, and we shall have to adhere rather strictly to our program, ignoring many interesting features in order to pay close attention to what is a recessive motif in this chapter, that only becomes dominant in the one to follow. It is important to note, furthermore, that all the religious intimations in this chapter are somewhat skewed, viewed from a historical standpoint rather than from the standpoint of religion itself, with its supreme interest in divine spirit. Here we are concerned with the religious subject, with spirit in its all-too-human historical appearances. With a single important exception, furthermore, all of these moments of actual spirit appear to some degree under the baleful spell of unhappy consciousness. Their protagonists are separated, in their own eyes, from the divine spirit that "we" know is in truth expressing itself in this entire historical succession.

The single clear exception to this subjection of actual spirit to unhappy consciousness is treated in the opening section, devoted to the ethical world. Subsequent sections trace the alienation of actual spirit, an alienation that is its tragic necessity if it is to achieve a reintegration at a higher level. The unified, unalienated life of the ethical world is "immediate," lacking any critical perspective on itself and lacking independent individuals; it is a traditional society secure in its integrated worldview, its customs, social structure, and cultural life, all of a piece. It is a world, its natural environment and its Volk making up a rationally coherent whole. It is a collective individual, unified by its indwelling Volkgeist.

> Spirit is the *ethical life* of a *people* [*das* sittliche Leben *eines* Volks], insofar as it is the immediate truth: the individual that

is a world. It must advance to the consciousness of that which it immediately is, must transcend the beautiful ethical life and through a series of shapes achieve knowledge of itself. These shapes, however, are distinguished from the previous ones by the fact that they are real spirits, genuine actualities, and instead of being merely shapes of consciousness are shapes of a world.

The *living ethical* world is spirit in its truth. (H 315; M 265; B 460)

Though its subsequent alienation is a tragic necessity, through which it will be brought to self-knowledge, this untroubled moment of spirit's living truth is a central landmark of the entire phenomenological journey. Here we find a happy consciousness, indeed a world that is healthy and whole. We shall look back to it wistfully as we proceed through the unhappy ages and divided worlds to come, measuring both gains and losses against this moment.

And the reader will have anticipated this happy consciousness in previous moments, abstracted from this one moment and finding only in the ethical world their concrete wholeness. The chapter on Reason, for instance, concludes with words of scorn for the Kantian moral individual, testing his moral law through the abstract, empty universality of reason. The moral law that is merely an "ought" must give way to the ethical substance that "is" and is unconditionally valid, permeating the entire life of a world (H 310–11; M 260–61; B 451–52). The tormented moral conscience (which comes later historically, but here the ordering is systematic, from abstract to concrete) is made whole in the "immediate self-consciousness of the ethical substance," whose distinguishing forms imply no tension between what is and what ought to be. These distinct forms simply consist of different social "masses,"

articulated into groups by the life that permeates them, undivided spirits transparent to themselves, spotless heavenly shapes that preserve in their differences the unprofaned innocence and harmony of their being. —Self-consciousness is likewise the simple, transparent *relationship* to them. They *are,* and nothing more—that is how consciousness is related to them. Thus Sophocles's *Antigone* acknowledges them as the *unwritten* and *infallible* law of the gods.

not of today and yesterday, but everlastingly
it lives, and no one knows from whence it appears.

They *are.* (H 311; M 261; B 452; *Antigone,* act 1, lines 456–57)

The sheer givenness of the ethical world, grounded significantly in the divine law of the gods below, distinguishes it fundamentally from that moral calculation by which the moral individual attempts to legislate the right for himself. Theft, for instance, is wrong, not because it contradicts a right to property that I could will to be a universal law: "Something is right, not because I find it not to be contradictory; but it is right because it is right. That something *is* the property of another, this is the basis; I need not calculate [*räsonnieren*] about it." Indeed, "when I begin to test" the law, "I am already on an unethical path" (H 312; M 262; B 453).

For the basis of law *(Gesetz),* moral as well as civil, is that "right" *(Recht)* that is ingredient in an actual world. Here the great theme of *Sittlichkeit* (ethical life), which has been developing in Hegel's thinking since his Frankfurt writings, is made the centerpiece of his *Phenomenology of Spirit,* dramatizing his rejection of Kantian moralism. This "appearance" of spirit is not merely one among others. It is the definitive appearance of actual spirit, to which and from which all other appearances proceed. It is the prototype of spirit, of which unhappy consciousness is the anti-type, and the "beyond" of the Kantian "ought" adheres to that anti-type. Indeed, a moralism of the Kantian type will reappear at the end of the chapter as a moral worldview, a final appearance of actual spirit in a state of acute alienation. The chapter proceeds from prototype to anti-type, from *sittliche Welt* through a type of alienated faith to *moralische Weltanschauung,* with its outgrowth in the self-congratulatory beautiful soul. The sources of this progression lie deep in Hegel's thinking, in the early conflict between Christian "positivity" or Kantian moralism and the wholeness of that Greek spirit of which Hegel and Hölderlin dreamt their happiest dreams.

The latter is, again, clearly the model for the treatment of the ethical world. It is an ethnic world, the exhalation of a particular Volksgeist. The ethical world signifies, in principle, any one of the many traditional societies out of which historical life develops, but the details of the exposition reflect that classical Greek culture that Hegel always recalled so warmly. Even now, when he is more ready to acknowledge its limitations, it is treated with unmistakable nostalgia. But the systematic point is not merely a nostalgic effusion: the organic traditional society is the touchstone for the existence of actual spirit in the world; even in its dissolution, when actual spirit passes into self-alienation, its roots in the ethical world give it the vestigial cohesion that makes its alienation painful.

i. The Domestic, Subterranean Religion of the Ethical World

With Actual Spirit we have returned to what I called the B-series, to the structure of self-consciousness. But here the identity of the self-conscious man or woman is secured by mutual recognition with the community, all for one and one for all. Indeed, Hegel carefully avoids calling this man or woman an individual, so integrally is he or she incorporated in the community, in the Volk, with which each man or woman achieves mutual recognition. This single member *(Einzelheit)* has here

> the status of *self-consciousness* in general, not of a single acciden-
> tal consciousness. The ethical substance is therefore . . . the *ac-
> tual* substance, absolute spirit *realized* in the plurality of existing
> *consciousnesses;* it is the *community* [Gemeinwesen]. . . . It is
> spirit which is *for itself,* since it maintains itself in being *reflected
> in individuals,* and it is *in itself* or substance since it contains
> them in itself. As *actual substance* it is *one* people [Volk], as
> *actual consciousness* it is a *citizen* of this people. (H 318–19;
> M 267; B 466–67)

The ethical Volk, then, is an organic unity, expressed in the life of all its members, who are conscious of themselves precisely as members of the Volk, performing the roles assigned them in its common life.

Still, Hegel immediately points out, there is after all a distinction within this apparently seamless unity. He makes the distinction in terms of two laws, human and divine, but each law has its source in a different sphere of the common life and a different authority-structure. Human law governs the public sphere, broadly speaking, the sphere of political life. Here the Volksgeist expresses itself in legal statutes and customary practices generally agreed to, based on the clearly per-ceivable public good, the needs and aspirations of the entire Volk. Its "truth" is its acknowledged "validity, open to the light of day" (H 319; M 268; B 467). Metaphors of openness and light turn up regularly in references to this human law. Divine law, on the other hand, is no less an expression of the Volksgeist, but its basis is obscure, dark and somewhat damp, unconditional. Divine law governs the private sphere, the sphere of household and family life. Its divinities are underground, not subject to inspection in the light of day; they enforce the age-old duties and taboos of blood kinship. Divine law, in particular, has the character of sheer givenness that Hegel contrasted with reasoned morality. It simply "is," and it communicates its unconditional reality to the ethical world generally. There is in fact something akin to biological necessity about divine law, associated with the life cycle that transpires within the family, of desire and procreation, nourishment and shelter, death and burial. Family life, too, is an ethical sphere, that entails more than this biological basis, but its roots remain sunk, out of sight, in that natural soil, from which the biological force of blood kinship derives.

Indeed, the family is the life-support system of the entire ethical world. Here the young are engendered, born, nourished, protected, trained, and sent forth to assume the duties of citizenship; here they continue to be sustained even when they have entered public life, and here they are returned in death for the ceremonies of burial on which Hegel lays great emphasis. So the entire human life cycle transpires under the aegis of the subterranean deities and their divine law: from dust we come and to dust we shall return. This proximity of the family to the earth gives it its life-supporting role in the ethical world generally. We have already seen that the self-conscious self is more than its "life"; the life cycle as such is not ethical, and yet the entire ethical world must be sustained by the life forces that flow into it and out of it through the family.

It is odd that these gods of the earth are not balanced by gods of the sky, presiding over the public sphere. Given the warmth with which Hegel always recalled the Olympians, early and late in his career, it is surprising that nothing is said about these political gods of the air in this section. Perhaps it was more important to emphasize the human basis of the public sphere. At any rate the ethical world is divided into an upper and a lower part, and the divine is the earthy, primarily the old chthonian deities who were more ancient and less civilized than the Olympians. But since the entire ethical world is so organic, there is a kind of circulatory system that joins these upper and lower regions. The "ethical substance" exists in both regions, each of which "contains it entirely and all the moments of its content." In the public life of the community this substance is conscious of its activities, while in the lower region this same substance exists in its most concentrated imme-diacy, inscrutable but immovable. The latter is the unshakable founda-tion of the ethical world, "the inner concept or the universal possibility of ethical life generally," and yet it does after all possess "the moment of self-consciousness equally within it."

> In this element of *immediacy* or of *being* expressing ethical life,
> . . . that is, as a *natural ethical* community, it is the *family*. The
> family is the *unconscious,* still inner concept juxtaposed to its
> self-conscious actuality, it is the element of actuality of the nation
> [Volk] juxtaposed to the nation itself, the immediate ethical *being*
> juxtaposed to that ethical life cultivated and maintained through
> *labor* for the universal—it is the Penates juxtaposed to the uni-
> versal spirit. (H 319–20; M 268; B 468)

The Penates—literally "dwellers in the store-room" *(penus),* old Roman household deities who watched over the family food supply—here repre-sent the gods of hearth and home generally, that nourish the universal spirit of the public sphere to which they are juxtaposed. But it is equally the case that an ethical order could not exist within the confines of family life alone; to gain the ethical expression appropriate to family life itself its mysterious life processes must express themselves in the daylight of conscious, political speech and action.

This circulatory flow links the conscious to the unconscious, in the life of society and its members alike. Consciousness flowers in the public sphere, the daylight where all is open and transparent. Here human awareness is in command, to decide and control. The shaded region of the private sphere, on the other hand, harbors the unconscious life forces that animate the public sphere, but the intimacy of family life itself is not deliberately arranged, nor is its basis subject to questioning. It is given, and here that given character of the ethical world generally, such that it simply is what it is, finds its wellsprings. Like a plant, the ethical Volk has its roots in this dark, elemental soil, whence its vital juices well up into the sunlit sphere of consciousness, its flowers turned toward the sun, and then return.

The public sphere is typically male, the private sphere female. Of course the man and woman both share in family life; indeed, the love of husband and wife exhibits both a biological and an ethical character. We have seen already, in discussing love as the element of mutual recognition, how this double character creates a certain ambiguity. Husband and wife do achieve that mutual recognition that is the essence of the self-conscious, spiritual relation, and yet because of its biological basis in sexual desire this recognition is not unequivocally ethical.

The biological bond between parent and child also tinctures the purity of their reciprocity. The purely ethical relation does exist in the family between brother and sister, precisely because, Hegel assumes, this bond is free of both biological dependency and sexual desire (H 325–26; M 273–75; B 474–77). The mutual recognition of brother and sister, as the point at which family life transcends its biological root,

> is at the same time the boundary line at which the self-contained life of the family dissolves and passes outside itself. The brother is the side of the family in which its spirit proceeds toward individuality, which turns toward another sphere and passes over into consciousness of universality. The brother abandons the *immediate, elemental* and thereby in fact *negative* ethical life of the family in order to acquire and bring forth its self-conscious, actual ethical life.
>
> He passes out of the divine law, in whose sphere he lived, over into the human. But the sister becomes, or the wife remains, the head of the household and the guardian of divine law. In this way the two sexes overcome their natural being and proceed to their ethical significance as diverging characters who share between them the two distinct spheres that make up the ethical substance. (H 327; M 275; B 477–78)

A sexist arrangement, no doubt, but after all Hegel has not arranged it. Such, typically, is the traditional society after which the ethical world is modeled, and despite his emphasis on the necessary reciprocity of the two sexes it is clearly the male who enters the public sphere while enjoying the benefits of the private. The wife is even denied "the right of desire" that the husband enjoys, because for her the household is the ethical universal to which she is related as a vocation, rather than in the particularity of her feeling. Of course she does not necessarily suppress her desire, whether she has a right to it or not, so on both sides there is the ambiguity that prevents the mutual recognition of husband and wife from being quite pure. But between brother and sister is a meeting of equals, between whom reciprocal recognition is possible "pure and unalloyed by natural connection." Indeed, "the moment of *single selves* recognizing and being recognized can here assert its right." But the salient point in this curious insistence on the sanctity of the brother-sister relation is that "the loss of the brother is therefore for the sister irreparable, and her duty toward him is the highest" (H 326–27; M 274–75; B 476–77).

The allusions to Sophocles's *Antigone,* which stud this section and the next, give away Hegel's most important reason for singling out the brother-sister bond in this way. The tragedy focuses the conflict of divine and human law on Antigone's insistence on burying her brother, fallen in the effort to overthrow the government of their uncle Creon, despite Creon's prohibition of this burial. It must be said that many details in the depiction of the ethical world are designed to set the stage for this tragic conflict, which is spelled out in the next section. Not only is the brother-sister bond said to be the purest ethical expression of family life, with the sister's duty to the brother the highest, but the solemnities surrounding the death of a family member seem to provide the ultimate ethical function of family life generally (H 321–23; M 269–71; B 469–72).

Doubtless the divine law entails many family responsibilities, and also many taboos (e.g., against matricide, patricide, and incest). But Hegel insists that it concerns burial of the dead above all: "This last duty . . . constitutes the perfect *divine* law, or the positive *ethical* action toward the individual." In fact his absolute right as an individual only arises in his death. While he lives his individuality is subordinated to his membership in the family and, in the public sphere, to his citizenship in the body politic. In the latter he works, or fights, for the universal, and it is his ethical duty to suppress his individual interests for the common good. So "every other relation to him that does not limit itself to love, yet is ethical, belongs to human law," in which he transcends his individuality. Only in death has he an unconditional right as an individual, under the terms of divine law, for this law has its "content and power" in "the individual who is beyond the actual world." In fact, as we shall see presently, the divine is here the power of the dead exerted among the living through the blood-bond of kinship:

> His power is the *abstract,* pure *universal,* the *elemental* individual, whose individuality, having been detached from its element to constitute the self-conscious actuality of the nation, now with-

draws back into its pure abstraction as into the essence which is its ground. (H 323; M 271–72; B 472–73)

Having been reduced to this elemental individuality, the dead man is sacred to his family, above all to his sister, whose relation to him is the purest ethical expression of family life.

So all the conditions are in place for the tragic conflict that erupts in Sophocles's *Antigone*. If this analysis seems contrived to prepare the ground for that conflict, Hegel would doubtless insist that the contrivance is not arbitrary, that the Sophoclean tragedy offers an inspired insight into the structural tension inherent in the ethical world. But until this tension breaks, destroying the ethical world with it, the spheres of divine and human law are symbiotic, and the circulatory system that joins them functions smoothly: happily.

> The distinction of the sexes and their ethical content thus abides in the unity of substance, and its movement is precisely the steady becoming of that substance. The man is sent forth from the family spirit into the community and finds there his self-conscious being; just as the family thereby possesses in the community its universal substance and preservation, so conversely the community possesses in the family the formal element of its actuality and in the divine law its power and authority. Neither of the two is alone in-and-for-itself; the human law proceeds in its vital movement from the divine, that which is valid on earth from the subterranean, the conscious from the unconscious, mediation from immediacy, and returns again from whence it came. The subterranean power, conversely, has its *actuality* on the earth; through consciousness it achieves existence and activity. (H 327–28; M 276; B 478–79; cf. also H 330; M 278; B 481–82)

So while the sphere of divine law is "other," rooted in the natural world, it is not an inaccessible "beyond." Unhappy consciousness has no place in the ethical world, with its free circulation among mutually dependent spheres: "The whole is a stable equilibrium of all its parts, and each part is a native spirit that does not seek its satisfaction beyond its own self, but has it within itself, because it itself is in this equilibrium with the whole" (H 329; M 277; B 480).

Here we find Hegel's old ideal of *Sittlichkeit* in an integral community, expressed with the ardor he always invested in it. Nor is it an empty ideal. It has existed, and still furnishes the deep foundation of social life, though subsequent developments have produced variously alienated structures on the original foundation, like an archeological deposit in which the remains of iron and brass cities are found layered above the original city of gold. Whether a new equilibrium, with its own integral spirit, is achievable under modern conditions, out of the debris of the unhappy cities: that was the vital issue. Hegel's sense of standing on the edge of a new age was animated by just such a hope.

The subterranean religion of the original golden city, at any rate, is not a religion of unhappy consciousness, for all its fierce energies. It is a religion of blood, expressed among men and women joined in blood-kinship. Its divine law is not prescribed from without, but is, so to speak, in their blood, in that blood they share, and it demands blood-vengeance against transgressors of divine law. Even if the transgression is unintended, as in the case of Oedipus, or is itself an act of vengeance for a prior transgression as in the case of Orestes, the subterranean Erinnyes are not interested in mitigating circumstances. The peaceful gods of family solidarity are roused to implacable fury by its trespass, its violators not so much judged as simply destroyed, like a man stepping in quicksand. Divine justice is not arbitrary, but it is unconditional. As Hegel says, it simply is. It recoils, indeed, against the violator in the very blood of his victim. This justice, exercised even against the universal power of the state on behalf of the one it has wronged, "is the simple spirit of the one who has suffered wrong—it is not broken up into two forces, the sufferer and an essential being beyond [ein jenseitiges Wesen]; he himself is the subterranean power, and it is his Erinnye which wreaks vengeance; for his individuality, his blood, lives on in the household; his substance has an enduring actuality" (H 329; M 277; B 480–81).

Justice is not delivered from the Beyond, any more than it is in the sphere of human law, of which Hegel gives a parallel account. Under divine law it is the victim's own blood that works justice. Indeed that life force that circulates through the ethical world, from the darkness underground to the daylight of the forum and back, is in fact blood, the blood of the living bound in one blood with the dead. Hegel says it is the victim's own Erinnye that wreaks vengeance, and in his summary of the "religion of the underworld" in the chapter on Religion he emphasizes this identity of subterranean divinity with the dead, even in its benign form as Eumenides. He yokes this spirit of the dead, furthermore, with fate. The religion of the underworld "is the belief in the terrible, unknown night of *fate,* and in the Eumenides of the *departed spirit;* —the former is pure negativity in the form of universality, the latter this same negativity in the form of particularity" (H 473–74; M 410; B 685–86).

Fate is not mentioned in the section on the Ethical World, but it does appear in the next section as the "abyss" into which the ethical world dissolves, again linked to a fatal individuality (H 331; M 279; B 484). Fate, after all, unlike "destiny," is a purely negative force, the necessity of death that overtakes the living. As a universal force it is faceless, but to the family it bears the individual face of the dead kinsman, whose blood his family shares. Fortunate the family that can fulfill its absolute obligation to him in quiet solemnities, blessed by his Eumenides. But where there is transgression the family itself is possessed by "his Erinnye," and fatal powers are abroad in the ethical world.

ii. The Dissolution of the Ethical World and the Rise of Self-Alienated Spirit

The ethical world is, after all, a world, coherent and comprehensive. Its worldview is implicit in its language, its myths and traditions, its institutions and customs. It expresses the ethical life of an ethnic community, its Volksgeist. A man or woman who achieves recognition in this world has a definite role and personal identity. Situated in a reliable world, he or she can lay plans and direct actions accordingly, and generally the outcome will confirm a happy confidence in the order of this world. There seems to be no reality except that which is disclosed in the transparency of this ethical order. If reality has some concealed aspect, an intractable, one-sided "being-for-itself" that cannot be assimilated into the ethical world, the ethical consciousness cannot recognize it.

> The ethical consciousness . . . has drunk from the cup of absolute [ethical] substance the forgetfulness of all the one-sidedness of being-for-itself, of its purposes and peculiar concepts, and has therefore at the same time drowned in this Stygian water all of the objective actuality's own essentiality and independent meaning. The absolute right of ethical consciousness is therefore that when it acts in accordance with the ethical law it shall find nothing in the actual consequence except just the fulfillment of this law itself, and the deed shall manifest nothing but the ethical

> doing. . . . The absolute right of the ethical consciousness is there-
> fore that the *deed*, the *shape* of its *actuality*, shall be none other
> than what it *knows*. (H 333; M 281; B 487)

The "right" of this somewhat myopic expectation, however, is subject
to disappointment, even catastrophic violation, through unforeseen
consesquences of the deed. According to the theory of tragedy implicit
in the second section of our chapter, on Ethical Action, tragedy is precisely this catastrophic recoiling of the ethical agent's own deed against
him. It is undeserved. The agent is motivated by his ethical right, and
the self-destructive consequence of his deed puts him in the wrong. In
the first place, actuality turns out to have its little secrets. The ethical
world exists, it is no mere "ought," but it does not include everything
that is; its "in-itself" is merely "for" its inhabitants. Actuality has a
being of its own that may, after all, contain some dangerous possibilities.
In the second place, there is inherent in the fact that the ethical world
contains two laws, human and divine, the possibility that an agent
may run afoul of one of the laws while observing the other.

The Oedipus tragedy dramatizes the first of these dark possibilities,
and finally both. Oedipus, a public man, behaves blamelessly according
to the "side" of human law. But his action activates something "other"
than he intended, calls forth something "alien," an unknown
counterforce.

> Actuality thus contains another side concealed in itself, alien to
> knowledge, and does not show itself to consciousness as it is in
> and for itself, —does not show the son his father in his attacker,
> whom he slays, nor his mother in the queen he takes as his wife.
> The ethical consciousness is in this way ambushed by a light-
> shunning power, which only bursts forth when the deed is done
> and seizes the doer in the act; for in the completed deed the
> opposition between the knowing self and the actuality confront-
> ing him is removed. (H 335–36; M 283; B 490)

The tragedy consists in the fact that the ethical agent is destroyed by
his own well-meant deeds. Nor is this ironical consequence merely an
outward misfortune: by his act he has run afoul of divine law, has
become guilty of its most monstrous transgressions. He "cannot deny
the crime or his own guilt." Ambushed by that unknown side of reality
that lay, so to speak, concealed in the bushes along the ethical path,

the public man who appears blameless under human law finds himself at once condemned and fearfully punished by those "light-shunning" powers that turn out to be the implacable furies of divine law.

But the classic tragedy of conflict between divine and human law is of course the *Antigone,* which receives most of Hegel's attention. Here, Hegel suggests, the guilt is "purer," because the guardian of each law is fully aware of his or her transgression of the other law. We will not go into the details of Hegel's penetrating analysis of this tragedy (especially H 337–41; M 285–88; B 493–97), but certain features of this conflict illustrate the deeper tragedy of the dissolution of the ethical world generally. In the first place, the conflict is not merely between two moral principles, both supposedly absolute, that a Kantian moral agent might have to choose between (cf. the concluding sections of the chapter on Reason). That "collision of duties" is merely "comic," because it "expresses the contradiction of an absolute opposed to itself" (H 331; M 279–80; B 285).

But *Sittlichkeit* is reality. To each protagonist it seems that his or her duty is determined by nature itself. "Nature, not the accident of circumstance or of choice, assigns the one sex to the one law, the other to the other," and these roles are so perfectly interiorized that they make up the "character" of each. The ethical, not to be confused with the morality of choice, is a formation of "character," expressed in an unreflective certainty of what is to be done. So if a conflict arises, it will not appear to either protagonist to be a conflict of two rights, as it appears for us who witness the tragic collision, but a conflict of simple right against wilful force. Each may recognize that he or she is violating the other law, but will not consider that law valid in the present case. Just because "the ethical consciousness" is *"determined"* to express one law, it "is essentially *character;* for it the two laws do not have the same *essentiality;* the opposition appears therefore merely as an *unhappy* collision of duty with an *actuality* that has no right" (H 332; M 280; B 485–86). For Antigone, Creon's denial of her brother's right of burial is simply a tyrannical sacrilege. When she flouts this decree, her act seems to Creon to be a treasonous interference with the punishment of a man who has committed the ultimate crime against the state.

The doom this tragic collision brings down on the heads of all parties, however, represents a victory of an "absolute right" against the partiality of those rights invoked by the protagonists. The inclusive "ethical substance" takes on the aspect of "the negative power which devours both sides." Ethical substance, that is, comes on the scene as "the almighty and righteous *fate*" (H 337; M 285; B 492–93). To this extent the ethical world appears to remain intact, precisely through the tragic downfall of all the protagonists. Their fate is the reassertion of the total ethical order against them, when they break themselves against it.

They break with the ethical world through their *acts*. When the ethical self-consciousness asserts itself in action, it already "raises itself out of the simple immediacy" of its harmonious ethical world and creates "division" *(Entzweiung)* between itself and its world. Its deed separates it from that "simple certainty of immediate truth" it has enjoyed as a member of the ethical world. "Through the deed it becomes *guilt.* For this deed is its doing, and doing is its innermost nature; and the guilt also contains the significance of *crime:* for as simple ethical consciousness it has embraced the one law but has denied the other, which it violates by its deed" (H 334; M 282; B 488). Here is the essential tragedy of the ethical world: that it plainly requires action, and yet action disrupts its equilibrium, not accidentally but necessarily. Not because of the intention of the doer, but in the very nature of action, "the deed is itself this division" between "itself for itself and an alien external actuality confronting it": "Innocence therefore consists only in nonaction, like the being of a stone, not even that of a child" (H 334; M 282; B 488).

This is not to say that all routine behavior qualifies as action. A deed asserts the will of the doer, bearing the seed of an incipient individuality. That is the potentially destructive element in the ethical world. Still, we have a paradox: the ethical world remains all right, while every member of it is in the wrong insofar as he or she is a doer of a deed. The ethical world can survive this paradox, as Hegel goes on to point out, only because individuality remains incomplete and shadowy. The ethical consciousness remains rooted in its harmonious world, and accepts its breach of this harmony merely as its own guilt. Hegel quotes in this connection the poignant line (act 1, 926) from *Antigone:* "Because we suffer we acknowledge that we have erred" (H 336; M 284; B 491). The ethical world cannot accommodate fully developed individuality. That, for "us," is what necessitates its downfall. With many sighs for its beauty and happiness, "we" recognize the need to move on into ugliness and unhappiness, to the ordeals in which the individual subject will be born, of which the tragic deed is the first premonition.

"For itself," however, Hegel suggests, the overthrow of the ethical world is initiated through the assertion by the woman of the right of this incipient individuality against the universality of human law. She, acting on behalf of the family and divine law, asserts her claim on a particular man as her son, her brother, her husband, against the demand of the state that he should exist to serve the collective aims of the community. She values him, in particular, in the virile power of his youth. Public life has pressed the common interest to the disregard of "family happiness," and thus ironically

> produces its internal enemy in the one that it suppresses and that is at the same time essential to it, in womankind in general. Womankind—that everlasting irony of community life—changes the universal aim of the government into a private aim through intrigue, transforms its universal activity into a work of this particular individual, and turns the universal property of the state into a possession and ornament of the family. She makes fun of the earnest wisdom of mature age which, dead to the pleasures and enjoyments of private pursuits [*Einzelheit*] . . . , thinks and cares only about the universal. (H 340; M 288; B 496)

She even incites "ridicule" and "contempt" for aged wisdom among the young men themselves, whom she recognizes only as sons, brothers, husbands.

> But the community can maintain itself only through the suppression of this spirit of singularity, and yet, because it is an essential moment, the community engenders it all the same, indeed just through its repressive attitude toward it as a hostile principle. (H 341; M 288; B 497)

Hegel still avoids the word "individuality" here, choosing the more equivocal term, *Einzelheit* (private "singularity") for this spirit, but individuality is incipient in it. The state must depend on its virile young men who, if not yet "individuals," still have a livelier interest in those private pleasures and pursuits the graybeards have renounced than in those graver aims they uphold. So this "singularity" encouraged by the women cannot really be snuffed out, and the effort to do so only has the effect of consolidating its opposition.

But there is another sense in which this spirit of singularity is an "essential moment" in the life of the community: that the Volksgeist is itself, after all, an individual (and here Hegel does use the word *Individualität*)—a world that is an individual. Furthermore, it excludes and opposes other such collective individuals, other communities. War-fare, for instance, which is the event in the community's life that most radically subordinates private interest to the public (H 324; M 272–73; B 474), also pits its own collective individuality directly against others. It has the ironical effect, furthermore, of maximizing its dependence on those wilful young men, on the "brave youth in which womankind has its pleasure."

> Now it is their natural strength and what appears as the accident of luck that determines the very existence of the ethical essence and its spiritual necessity; because the existence of the ethical essence rests on strength and luck, it is *already determined* that it has run aground. (H 341; M 289; B 498)

The community is undone, within and without, by that individualizing principle that is inimical to its cohesion as an ethical collectivity, and yet is inherent in its life. Its downfall is an ironical triumph of the very principle that divine law had asserted, and that human law had suppressed.

But this principle now asserts itself in a more universal and much more baleful form, which capitalizes on the inner disintegration of the ethical world and its mutually destructive conflict with other ethical communities. Indeed, Hegel seems to press the analogy between the individual Volksgeist and the particular member of a community in the following way: As these members, when they emerge from family life, are subordinated to the collective life of the community, so the ethical communities themselves come to be subordinated to the still more universal collectivity of empire. The analogy, to be sure, cannot be pressed too far: The ethical communities are subdued and incorpo-rated into the empire by force, and are effectively destroyed in the process. Ethical community does not survive to continue carrying on a rich life of its own or playing a vital role in the harmony of the whole, as the family had in the ethical community itself.

In fact, there is nothing to ground the empire in the intimate life of its subject peoples in the way that the family rooted the ethical world in the vital cycle of birth, nourishment, nurture, love, and death. There is no ethical life to mediate between the empire, as a concentration of political and military power, and the individuals it rules. The family presumably survives, but its lifeblood does not circulate through the imperial order as it did through the ethical world. The empire is indifferent to the languages, customs, traditions, religions, and cultural life of its subject peoples. It rules by force, pulverizing the many ethical communities into a mere aggregate of undifferentiated individual "persons." In this sense it represents the ironical triumph of the individualizing principle. As the Penates, the domestic gods "had run aground in the Volksgeist, so the *living* Volksgeister now run aground through their individuality in a *universal* community whose *simple universality* is spiritless and dead, and whose remnant of life is the *single* individual qua single. The ethical shape of spirit has disappeared, and another steps forth in its place" (H 341–42; M 289; B 498). This new collectivity that bulldozes all the ethical/ethnic Volksgeister into oblivion produces the spirit of what Hegel calls "legal status," since its "formal universality" atomizes community life into an aggregate of merely legal "persons."

We have referred earlier to the section on Legal Status, as the desolate political order in reaction to which the sequence of Stoicism, skepticism, and unhappy consciousness emerged historically. These three moments constitute the retreat of spirit from an intolerable social reality into pure thought, pure inwardness. That bleak political order, too, is of course an appearance of spirit, but it is no longer an "indwelling" spirit permeating an actual world. The indwelling Volksgeister have "sunk into the simple necessity of an empty *fate*," which turns out to be simply the "*I* of self-consciousness" devoid of ethical substance and atomized into a self-enclosed and dissociated "person" or "negative universal self" (H 343; M 290; B 501). All power is concentrated in one person, "the lord of the world" who is a "monstrous self-consciousness who knows himself as the actual god." All other persons are "unactual," "powerless," possessing only that "legal status" conferred on them by the ruling power (H 345; M 292–93; B 504–5).

They have lost their spiritual home in the actual world, and can pursue a life of the spirit only in abstraction from it, finally in the pure but fatally divided interiority of unhappy consciousness. Still, in this melancholy form there emerges what was lacking in the happy harmony of the ethical world: "The actuality of the self, which was not present in the ethical world, is achieved through its regression into the *person;* what was there submerged in unity now emerges in developed form, but alienated from itself" (H 346; M 294; B 506). Self-conscious selfhood had emerged, after all, from mutual recognition in a culturally cohesive world, where the sense of self was inseparable from the world in which it was born. But now it is aware of itself in a different way, as an interiority isolated from the actual world in which it is in fact grounded. So this new self-awareness is achieved at the price of alienation from itself. Furthermore, the self that has retreated into its individual isolation, and thus has become actual to itself as a self, now confronts the actual world, including other selves, as something external, opposed to it. "Self" and "world" are still correlative: they made up a unity in the ethical world, and now they emerge together in mutual opposition: For "that spirit whose self is absolutely discrete has as its content an equally hard actuality opposed to it, and the world has here the character of being something external, the negative of self-consciousness."

But this world, that "for" self-consciousness appears so unyielding and external, is still "in itself" expressive of this new spirit the self-conscious self has taken on. *He,* in fact, has projected it into this alien otherness, though he does not recognize that this alienation is his own "work." For him it seems simply the actuality that confronts him; for us, however, this creation of a hostile reality is the expression of his own spirit. That is why his alienation from the world is also self-alienation, in which he becomes a stranger to himself. Hegel continues: "But this world is a spiritual creation [*Wesen*], it is in itself the interpenetration of being and individuality; this existence it has is the *work* of self-consciousness, but it is equally an immediately given actuality alien to him, which has a being of its own in which he does not recognize himself." In truth this external actuality is his own "negative" work.

> It obtains its existence through self-consciousness's *own* exteriorization and loss of essence [*Entäusserung und Entwesung*], which in the desolation that reigns in the world of legal right appears to inflict on self-consciousness the external violence of the unleashed elements. This violence is for him just pure devastation and self-dissolution; but this dissolution, this negative nature of the elements, is precisely the self; he is their subject, their activity and becoming. This activity and becoming, however, through which this substance becomes actual, is the alienation of personality. (H 347–48; M 294–95; B 509–10)

Hegel's thought here is difficult, but crucial to his phenomenological project. The unalienated life of the ethical world admits no psychic interiority distinct from that world. The flight into this interiority constitutes the pure self that was lacking in the ethical world, but this interiorization entails the "exteriorization" *(Entäusserung)* of an entirely material world outside the self; it entails, that is, the splitting of the ethical world, that was the substantial, shared ground of selfhood, into the pure but empty interiority of the individual self and a pure exteriority that contains all determinate content. This exteriorization of the world is the self's own act; for him, however, it appears as a brute, alien facticity that confronts him. That is not to say that its reality is merely subjective, but that its alien objectivity and his subjectivity are alike the consequence of his self-alienation, which is the price he has paid for his individuality.

This alienation is a tragic necessity; without it the individual cannot be born. Here the great systematic problem of the *Phenomenology*, how the metaphysical substance of Spinoza becomes spiritual subject, receives its concrete expression: Ethical *substance* (the ethical world) develops into spiritual *subject* by incorporating the experience of a fully developed individual, its "other." So an alienated world must come into existence, which occurs when self-conscious personality, exteriorizing itself, creates this alien reality to which it will be subjected. "Or," as Hegel writes a few pages later, "self-consciousness is only *something*, it only has *reality*, insofar as it alienates itself" (H 351; M 297; B 514). Until then it is only part of the substantial, ethical whole.

What Hegel is struggling to comprehend is the transition, historically, from a traditional society to the modern. The ancients did not have to deal with what he later called "the principle of subjective freedom."[80] That was their blessing, but also their limitation. The spirit of traditional society was ethical substance, but not yet subject. The modern ordeals of fragmentation and unhappy consciousness, alienated from its essential substance, are the birth pangs of spiritual subjectivity. Hegel did not invent the ordeals of modernity. He simply observed them, and surely also recognized the great risk that they would prove to be merely destructive. But then again they might prove to be worth the pain. Such was his optimism when in the Preface he declared that a new age was being born.

Returning to our text, we must recognize even at this juncture that "in itself" spirit remains one and undivided, as it appeared in the ethical world: "Substance is in this way *spirit*, the self-conscious *unity* of the self and essence; but each also has for the other the character of alienation" (H 348; M 295; B 510). As with unhappy consciousness, there is "in itself" an abiding unity, within which the process of alienation occurs; the self and its world continue to belong together, though the self has alienated itself into a pure interiority confronting an exteriorized world. This process of alienation, furthermore, continues to produce new divisions. The self, divided from its world, now divides within itself in turn, into an "actual" and a "pure" consciousness. The "actual" consciousness is the subject confronted by the ensemble of objects that make up the exteriorized actual world; it presumably resides in the sensuous life of the body. The "pure" consciousness exists only in relation to its interiorized essence, having transcended both its actual or empirical consciousness and the objectified world.

But still the process of alienation is not complete: the pure consciousness, alienated from the exterior actuality, now produces, in its own inner space "beyond" the actual, a world of thought that is the "thinking" of the actual and its "being-thought." The familiar Hegelian duality of *Jenseits* and *Diesseits* now takes the form of an external actuality and an internal thinking about it within pure consciousness. "So this spirit fashions not only *one* world, but a doubled, separated, and self-opposed world." The divided self exists in a divided world, or in two worlds, the actual world and the world of thought. What makes it difficult to see the point of this distinction is that modern thought so takes it for granted. Of course the actual world, including our own organic processes, is simply "out there," a pure objectivity "beyond" our thought, and of course the world as we know it is our own mental construct. To bring out the strangeness of this all too familiar assumption of our alienated culture, Hegel contrasts it with the situation of the ethical world.

> The world of the ethical spirit is its own *present* world; and therefore each of its powers exists in this unity, and insofar as they are distinguished they exist in equilibrium with the whole. Nothing has the significance of being the negative of self-consciousness; even the departed spirit is present in the *blood* of his kin, in the *self* of the family, and the universal *power* of the government is the *will*, the self of the entire people. But here what is present is only objective *actuality*, the consciousness of which lies beyond it; each particular moment as *essence* receives this essence, and its actuality as well, from an other, and insofar as it is actual its essence is other than its actuality. Nothing has a spirit grounded within itself and indwelling, but everything is outside itself in something alien. . . . The whole is therefore, like each single moment, a reality alienated from itself. (H 348–49; M 295–96; B 510–11)

So this new, alienated spirit will continue to engender new forms of alienation, each built on the others like a house of cards.

This doubled world is the context for the second major division of the chapter on Spirit. The first division consisted of the three moments we have reviewed:

A. *True* Spirit: Ethical Life
    a. The Ethical World. Human and Divine Law, Man and Woman
    b. Ethical Action. Human and Divine Knowledge, Guilt and Fate
    c. Legal Status

The second division of the chapter has a more complex arrangement:

B. Self-Alienated Spirit. Culture
    I.   The World of Self-Alienated Spirit
        a. Culture and Its Realm of Actuality
        b. Faith and Pure Insight
    II. The Enlightenment
        a. The Struggle of Enlightenment with Superstition
        b. The Truth of the Enlightenment
    III. Absolute Freedom and Terror

Our interest, again following Hegel's introductory remarks in the chapter on Religion, will focus on I.b. and II.a, which treat the pseudo-religious expression of "faith." What precedes these sections is a capsule history of "culture," in an ironical sense of the term: the word is *Bildung,* which literally means something formed or cultivated. It is the world human selves have made, human selves in the state of alienation we have described. It is an *artificial* world, with no organic relation either to nature or to social solidarity. Its characteristic form is the courtly world of warring, accumulating lords and their service vassals. The individual in this artificial "culture," is no longer a mere legal "person," equal to all others in his servitude simply as a member of the human species. In order to count, the individual must be "cultured," must divest himself of his "personality" and be trained to comport himself appropriately in this artificial world that human beings have made, which thereby achieves the status of a specious "realm of actuality." The individual's natural being and spontaneity must be suppressed so that he can trade in the complex system of signals and mannerisms prescribed by courtly life (H 350–53; M 297–99; B 514–17).

We will not follow Hegel into his analysis of this "culture and its realm of actuality," which follows a rough historical order. But before passing to the form of "faith" that appears in this alienated culture we will pause over one motif that from this point on becomes a major theme in the *Phenomenology,* particularly in its later treatment of religion: the role of language. Language in alienated culture epitomizes the artificiality of that culture. Its "state power," for instance, exists only to the extent that its public servants make it exist, since it has no organic relation to nature and society as a whole. They make it exist through the force of their own commitment to it: through their willingness to renounce their own self-will, their own "being-for-self," in order to serve state power without reservation. It is a renunciation, Hegel says, as complete as the self-immolation of those who die in defense of the state's interests, but it is accomplished by a psychic alienation, which transfers their psychic energies from their own being-for-self and invests them in the state, which thereby gains the selfhood its subjects have lost. Severed from the subject's own distinct existence, this "separated inner spirit, the self as such, comes to the fore and alienates itself, so that the state power is raised thereby to the possession of a self of its own" (H 362; M 308; B 529).

Now "this alienation," Hegel goes on to say, "occurs solely in *language,* which here appears in its own distinctive significance" (H 362; M 308; B 529–30). This last phrase, "in ihrer eigentümlichen Bedeutung," is an important qualification of this surprising claim. Not all language is the medium of self-alienation. When it is simply referential, for instance, indicating a state of affairs that exists independent of language, or when it is expressive, the utterance of a self that exists independent of language, language is simply a medium. In the ethical world it is the medium in which a shared reality is communicated, for instance (Hegel's example) in "*law* and *command.*" But here language displays its prodigious power to constitute a reality out of its own resources. No longer a mere medium, a form in which an independent content is expressed, "the form which language is contains itself for its content, and is valid simply qua *language.* It is the power of speech as something which performs whatever is to be performed."

In fact, self-alienated selfhood, the "pure" self severed from its own organic being and floating in the void at the behest of state power or some other artificial construct, has its own thin subsistence purely in language. For language, Hegel continues, is the *existence* [*Dasein*] of the pure self qua self; in language the *singularity* of self-consciousness *subsisting for itself* comes into existence, so that it exists *for others*. The *"I"* as this *pure* "I" is otherwise simply not *there* [*ist sonst nicht* da]. (H 362; M 308; B 530)

Here, to borrow a Heideggerian expression, language languages a self, a pure artifice that only is there *(ist da)* in language. It does, to be sure, reside in a body that has a certain appearance and performs organic functions, walks, feels pain when it stubs its toe. But as a self, it exists for itself and for others, in detachment from its organic life, in what it *says*. Its existence "for others" is essential. In its speech it gives itself over to these others and hovers with them in a shared cultural empyrean that gains its actuality in their talk. Hegel compares this linguistically formed culture to an infection or contagion *(Ansteckung)* that is passed from one pure self to another in language, and thus gains a certain universality. Language, he says, contains this pure self's existence *(Dasein)*

in its purity, it alone expresses the "I," its very existence. This *existence* it has is qua *existence* an objectivity, which contains its true nature in it. *"I"* is *this* "I"—but it is equally *universal;* its appearance is just as immediately the exteriorized utterance [*Entäusserung*] and disappearance of *this* "I," and thereby its continuation in its universality. *"I,"* that expresses itself, is *heard;* it is a contagion in which the "I" has passed at once into union with those for whom it is there, and is a universal self-consciousness. (H 262–63; M 308–9; B 530)

Thus we find a culture—also in the medical sense—that is not only an artifice of language but a kind of linguistic epidemic. Words that may once have meant something (e.g., "good" and "bad," "noble" and "base") lose all consistent definition, freely reversing their meanings at will and thus redefining this tenuous realm of actuality to suit the interests of the speakers (H 371–72; M 316–17; B 542). Even the monarch, who does have considerable real power, is made to soar far above all common clay on the hot air of courtly flattery (H 364–65; M 310–11; B 533).

Diderot's satirical dialogue, *Rameau's Nephew,* published for the first time in Goethe's translation (1805) while Hegel was writing the

Phenomenology, is assigned a role in this section like that of the *Antigone* in earlier sections of the chapter, with many allusions and quotations; Hegel found in it the epitome of the alienated culture in its most decadent phase, awash in language that even the speakers and hearers no longer take seriously. The nephew of the composer, himself a man of erratic brilliance, has subsisted as a constant dinner guest at the table of a noble patron on the strength of his capacity for flattery, gossip, and witty chatter. He is expelled from the household when, for the first time, he tells the truth! At this point language has degenerated into sheer self-sustaining frivolity, deployed with pathetic cynicism by the very self that is constituted by it. Here we find "pure culture" unalloyed, a "universal inversion and alienation of actuality and of thought" (H 371; M 316; B 541). Yet this decadent culture, too, is an appearance of spirit. What this spirit speaks about itself is "the perversion of all concepts and realities, the universal deception of itself and of others," but "the shamelessness that speaks this deception is just thereby the greatest truth" (H 372; M 317; B 543). It is the self-disclosure of the alienated spirit.

The stage is set for the appearance of another spirit, which is at once the horrified reaction against this debased "realm of actuality" and another manifestation of its alienation.

iii. Faith

For several years Hegel had consistently distinguished "faith" from proper "religion." Religion not only animates an entire community, but is a dynamic movement of its spirit, uniting finite, actual spirit with infinite, absolute spirit. But faith is fixated on its divine "object," which faith locates in an inaccessible Beyond. Faith is trapped in this objectifying posture.

The structure of the *Phenomenology* enables Hegel to spell out this distinction between religion and faith in detail, and to clarify the dialectical conditions of each. "Religion" is assigned the penultimate chapter of the work, paired with absolute knowledge, with which it comprises the appearance of absolute spirit. Faith, on the other hand, is the purest expression of unhappy consciousness. It is treated in the second part of the chapter on actual, historical spirit, as an appearance of self-alienated spirit. Faith is a reaction to an alienated world, but precisely as a reaction it tragically reproduces the self-alienation it seeks to escape. In introducing "The World of Self-Alienated Spirit," Hegel tells us that "the world of this spirit breaks up into a doubled world; the first is the world of actuality or of its alienation itself; but the other is the world which spirit, rising above the first, builds for itself in the aether of pure consciousness" (H 350; M 296–97; B 513).

That first world is the artificial world of culture, the "actuality" of which is precariously constructed from the language and trappings with which its servants have invested it. It is already an alienated world, from the untruth of which spirit takes flight into a second world, in search of some solid ground on which to stand, something not made of gilded paper and flattering words. But this second world, "*set in opposition* to that alienation, is just for that reason not free from it, but is rather merely the other form of alienation, which consists precisely in having one's consciousness in two worlds, and embracing them both."

Just because it is a reaction against the alienated world of culture, faith defines itself in relation to that world: defines itself negatively. The God it seeks must be radically *other* than the alienated actuality of that world, not enmired in its decadence and duplicity; so its God cannot be the indwelling spirit of the actual world. But this radical otherness also sets its God at a distance from faith itself. So even though faith is an appearance of actual spirit, with its feet, so to speak, in the actual world it disdains, it directs its consciousness to another world that it cannot itself actually occupy. Faith exhibits the subject-object duality of consciousness, characteristic of the A-series. For spirit has "built" faith's world "in the aether of pure consciousness": "What is under consideration here is therefore not the self-consciousness of the absolute being as it is *in* and *for itself*, not religion, but *faith*, insofar as faith is the *flight* out of the actual world."

This striking identification of religion with God's self-consciousness is simply the reverse side of Hegel's more typical definition of religion as the elevation, in an actual community, of the finite to the infinite. Religion is the mutual self-recognition of finite and infinite spirit, actual and absolute spirit, each in the other. Faith, however, as the flight from the only "actuality" available, cannot be the locus of this in-and-for-itself, this mutual recognition. Proper "religion" is not really possible in an alienated culture, while "faith" is tragically destined for an escapist role in such a culture. Indeed, Hegel goes on to suggest, faith reflects its own alienated condition by itself splitting apart into two sides, neither of which can recognize itself in the other.

> This flight out of the realm of the present is therefore in its own self immediately a doubled one. Pure consciousness is the element in which spirit rises, but it is not only the element of *faith,* but also of the *concept;* both together therefore enter the scene simultaneously, and the latter comes under consideration only in opposition to the former. (H 350; M 297; B 513)

This element of the concept, that makes its appearance alongside faith, is what Hegel calls "pure insight." It is, generally speaking, the philosophy of the Enlightenment, which also arises in reaction against the artificiality of culture. It is one of Hegel's most ironical strokes to present modern supernaturalism and Enlightenment as twins, their bitter quarrels as a kind of sibling rivalry.

They are an unfleshly pair of twins. Both faith and pure insight traffic in their own thoughts. Like the "I" of the alienated world, they are detached from any actuality that they have not produced themselves, in language and thought, but that "I" did create its own artificial actuality, while faith and pure insight, at least at the outset, produce nothing but thoughts. Now faith (leaving its twin aside for the moment) produces thoughts that still retain the *form* of actualities, though they have no empirical existence. Louis XIV presided over an artificial world, but at least you could see him ride by in his golden coach. Not so the objects of faith. Yet faith does not realize that its objects are only thoughts. They resemble images of real things: anthropomorphic figures, a heavenly landscape. In this sense faith does indeed direct itself to another world, standing above and in some ways duplicating the actual world. Faith of course knows that God and his angels are not really like human beings and that heaven's streets are not paved with gold, or even with cobblestones. Yet it is sure that *some* such invisible objects do exist. The problem is not merely that these thoughts are "representations"—*Vorstellungen*—rather than abstractions or proper concepts. That is characteristic of religious ideas generally (see Chapter 3). But faith is a pure consciousness that has turned from the actual world to objectify its representations in a duplicate world beyond. That alienation of thought is not characteristic of all religious representations. The religion of the underworld, for instance, that we encountered in the ethical world, is not a faith in that sense, because its "element" is not "pure consciousness beyond the actual," but "it has an immediate presence: its element is the family." Faith's representations, on the other hand, have no such concrete presence in the actual world. They are merely "beliefs." Nor can the believing consciousness recognize itself in its objects, as the family member could in the indwelling family deities. Faith's *"pure consciousness* of the absolute Being is an *alienated* consciousness" (H 376–78; M 321–22; B 549–51).

As a pure *consciousness,* faith has a formally objective, positive content. Pure insight, on the other hand, not only has no object (since it is a pure *self-*consciousness): at least at the outset it has no content at all, either actual or representational. As an empty form of thought, pure insight is "the certainty which immediately knows itself to be the truth, pure thought as *absolute concept* that is present in the might of its *negativity,* which annihilates everything objective that supposedly stands over against consciousness, and makes it into a being of consciousness itself" (H 378; M 323; B 552).

Pure insight is the universal form of thought itself, indifferent to its locus in any particular thinker or situation. No less than faith a reaction against the artificial actuality of culture, it is thought withdrawn into itself, like Stoicism and skepticism, dismissing that arbitrarily contrived world as unreal because it has no rationally justified ground on which to stand. Only the empty universality of thought is true. So as faith is pure consciousness of absolute being, pure insight is pure self-consciousness, regarding its own universality as absolute. These ghostly twins, furthermore, are alienated from one another. Pure insight

> is the spiritual *process* comprehended in *self-*consciousness, which has as its opposite the consciousness of the positive, the form of objectivity or of representation, and pits itself against it; pure insight's own object, however, is only the *pure "I."* . . . Pure insight therefore has at first no content of its own, because it is negative being-for-itself; to faith, on the other hand, belongs the content, but without insight. (H 379; M 323–24; B 552–53; cf. H 385; M 329; B 561)

Quentin Lauer, borrowing a well-known Kantian formula, neatly expresses this opposition: "Insight without belief is empty; belief without insight is blind."[81] Since each has what the other lacks, there might seem to be a beautiful symbiosis in the making. But since faith's content and pure insight's rationality are alike alienated from anything actual, since, that is, their common element is alienation, there can be no recognition between them. Insight negates all positive content (we recall Hegel's own early polemic against religious positivity), and faith rejects the proud pretensions of human understanding.

We phenomenological observers, to be sure, can see in this opposition a recapitulation of Stoicism and skepticism, on the one hand, and unhappy consciousness on the other. We can also recognize in these two moments a foreshadowing of the relation between religion and absolute knowledge, where the distinction between *Vorstellung* and *Begriff* will be merely formal, without this intractable opposition, because each side will have recovered its actuality. But for faith and pure insight themselves no such harmony is possible. Faith is, "to be sure, pure consciousness of *essence,* that is, of simple inwardness, and *is* therefore thought—the cardinal moment in the nature of faith, that is usually overlooked. The *immediacy* with which the essence is in faith consists in the fact that its object is *essence,* that is, is *pure thought.*"

In fact, unfortunately, only "we" seem not to have overlooked this cardinal moment, which might serve to make faith entirely consonant with pure insight. Faith, for itself, sets this immediacy at a distance, as an object of consciousness, so that it signifies

> an objective *being* that lies beyond the consciousness of the self. Through this signification . . . the *essence* of faith falls away from thought into *representation* and becomes a supersensible world which is essentially an *other* of self-consciousness. —In pure insight, on the contrary, the passing of pure thought into consciousness has the opposite consequence: objectivity signifies a merely negative content, that overcomes itself and returns into the self, that is, only the self is really the object, or the object only has truth insofar as it has the form of the self. (H 379; M 324; B 553)

So our two twins are in fact locked in combat from the womb, like Romulus and Remus or Jacob and Esau.

Pure insight furnishes the fundamental principle of the Enlightenment, which pits its rational self-confidence against the corruptions of a decadent culture, but especially against faith, which it perceives to be the superstitious legitimation of the very culture that faith loathes. To this enlightened insight, faith is merely "a tissue of superstition, prejudice, and error" that leads the masses astray and opposes "reason and truth." Far from seeing in faith its own alter ego, Enlightenment regards it as an invention of "priestcraft" in unholy alliance with "despotism" (H 385–86; M 329–30; B 561–62). Faith, for its part, sees nothing but wilful sacrilege, "lies, unreason and bad intentions," in Enlightenment, especially in its calumnies against faith itself (H 390; M 333; B 566–67). We see in this exchange of insults merely the pathos of two mutually uncomprehending positions. It is not even tragic, like the conflict between divine and human law in the ethical world, since it is not a conflict between two actual rights, but a polemic between blindness and emptiness, the two sides of an alienated mind.

The section entitled "Faith [*Glauben*] and Pure Insight," and the following section, entitled "The Struggle of Enlightenment with Superstition" *(Aberglauben),* present an intricate, many-sided debate between the two positions. Particularly in the latter section we perhaps find some of that "ballast" that Hegel admitted to Niethammer tended to weigh down the latter part of the *Phenomenology.* He undertakes to reproduce and systematize the many lines of argument that philosophers of the Enlightenment directed against contemporary supernaturalistic religion. Some of these polemics he pronounces grossly unfair, some on target—and some of the best-aimed shots ironically recoil on the Enlightenment itself. Hegel's analysis is further complicated by the fact that both faith and pure insight undergo development, each within itself and in relation to the other.

All these developments just happen to be triadic, beginning with the abstract moment that defines each, the absolute *Wesen* (essence) either as faith's universal object or pure insight's universal self. In the second moment this absolute *Wesen* expresses itself in some fashion in its other, in the actual world. In the third moment the particular consciousness or self-consciousness is partially united with its absolute essence. While the variations on this basic triad receive their content from historical developments in modern Protestantism and Enlightenment, the triad itself, of course, derives from the dialectic of spirit, since faith and pure insight do, after all, make up an appearance of spirit. Here, however, spirit appears under the conditions of its alienation, so the triad is always flawed and incomplete. The triad most directly resembles the three positions unhappy consciousness assumes in relation to the unchangeable, since both faith and pure insight are "unhappy," pursuing an absolute being or essence *(Wesen)* that is itself a "bad infinite," excluding the actual world. In the details of the analysis are many echoes of Hegel's long-standing critique of religious positivity and of *raisonnieren, Reflexion, Verstand.* Through this interlocking system of triads he settles his accounts with both, coolly pronouncing a plague on both their houses.

An example of the way the triad is applied refers to faith's object. It is at first (1) simple absolute Being, in reaction to, but ironically duplicating, the position of state power in the actual world. It undergoes (2) a kenotic movement in which the absolute Being sacrifices its universal substance to appear as an actual, perishable self. Finally (3) there is "the return of this alienated self and the humbled substance into their original simplicity." Thus, Hegel says, spirit appears, though in representational form. For us this sequence appears "necessary," as it does after all represent the dialectic of spirit. But for faith it appears to be a series of actual events. Furthermore, the believing consciousness, despite its renunciation of the world, still does not achieve unity with its divine object. The absolute Being remains a Beyond, and its appearance as an actual self simply gives "the Beyond . . . the character of remoteness in space and time"—an old motif for Hegel. The third moment, "the present actuality of spirit," remains for faith an ineffectual "inner" truth (H 380–81; M 324–26; B 554–56). Pure insight's concept, on the other hand, is (1) an absolute self containing all truth, in opposition to the world's falsehood. (2) Pure insight itself is merely a partial, finite consciousness, but it adopts for its "purpose" the dissemination of this rational truth in the world. (3) In virtue of its rationality, the particular consciousness perceives itself to be united with the absolute self. "This pure insight is therefore the spirit that calls out to *every* consciousness: *be for your own selves* what all of you are *in yourselves—rational.*" But this cry merely expresses an empty imperative and a distant goal (H 381–83; M 326–28; B 556–58). Pure insight, no less than faith, is a form of unhappy consciousness.

There is no point in our reporting on the entire battle between these twin positions. But one polemical fusillade is of particular interest, since it represents perhaps the most persistent modern critique of religion, and at the same time is the clearest example of the way Hegel applies his analysis of faith and pure insight as two sides of the same coin. This line of criticism, simply stated, has two points: that religious faith is a form of spiritual slavery to an alien being, and that this alien being together with all the figures in which it is represented are in fact products of human consciousness. Human beings invent the gods that enslave them. Hegel presents this argument in a form that seems to have been derived from Holbach in particular,[82] but it also anticipates the "projectionist" theory of Feuerbach in *The Essence of Christianity*

(1840). As Hegel reconstructs the polemic, Enlightenment seems simply to be applying its own primary assumption—in Hegel's view a vacuous assumption: that consciousness essentially confronts only itself in any of its putative objects. In other words, the subject-object structure of what we have called the A-series can be reduced without remainder to that of the B-series. Thus: "What is not rational has no *truth,* or what is not comprehended *is* not; when, therefore, reason speaks of anything *other* than itself, it in fact speaks only of itself; it takes not a step beyond itself" (H 389; M 333; B 566).[83]

In this case, as Hegel points out, one can hardly label the objects of consciousness as lies and illusions! What can be truer than reason's own self-contemplation? But in fact Enlightenment does not recognize its own rational principle in what it declares to be the irrationality of faith. It simply sees in faith's object an illusion generated by consciousness itself. That in fact is Enlightenment's pure "insight" into such putative objects: "In *insight* as such consciousness grasps an object in such a way that it becomes of the essence of consciousness or becomes an object that consciousness permeates, in which it preserves itself, remaining with its own self and present to itself, and, since it is therefore the object's movement, produces it." Since consciousness cannot be aware of anything it has not itself "produced" in this sense, it follows that faith's consciousness must have produced its God. For on these terms, Enlightenment can "correctly" say of faith "that what it regards as the absolute being is a being of its own consciousness, of its own thoughts, a product of consciousness." So it pronounces this absolute being "an error and a fiction" that perverts Enlightenment's own principle of the absolute self. But this "insight" turns out to be only an invidious version of a testimony that faith offers about itself. When Enlightenment

> wishes to instruct faith in this new wisdom, it does not thereby tell faith anything new. For faith's object is also to faith precisely this, namely the pure essence of faith's own consciousness, so that this consciousness does not regard itself as lost and negated in its object, but rather puts its trust in it; that is, just *in this* object does faith find itself *as this* consciousness or as *self*-consciousness. When I trust someone, his *certainty of his own* self is for me the *certainty of my* self. I am aware of [*erkenne*] my being-for-myself in him, in that he recognizes [*anerkennt*] it. . . . Trust, however, is faith, because its consciousness *relates*

itself *immediately* to its object, and thus also perceives that it is *one* with its object and in it. (H 390; M 334; B 567–68)

This comment attributes to faith the salient quality of mutual recognition, characteristic of spirit. The mutual recognition is flawed, since its absolute being is still an "object" for faith, which remains a "consciousness." Yet in the believer's worship there is an active and trustful communion that makes his own identity inseparable from God. That is the truth in the "insight" that faith's object expresses its own consciousness, but it does not follow that faith simply "produces" it. The "new wisdom" of Enlightenment reduces the mutuality to mere autism, as if consciousness itself were "the *mediating* movement" whose own "act" is the "production" *(Hervorbringen)* of the object (H 391; M 334–35; B 568).

It is in fact noteworthy that "faith" has begun to assume a form more characteristic of "religion," and there are two additional factors in which this religious dynamic is visible. First, it expresses its certainty of the existence of God actively, in "obedience and action," though this "action of faith does not, to be sure, appear to be such that the absolute being itself is produced thereby." Second, this absolute being "is essentially not the *abstract* essence existing beyond the believing consciousness, but it is the spirit of the congregation, it is the unity of abstract essence and self-consciousness." Hegel goes on to emphasize that this immanence, as the indwelling spirit of the believing community, is "an essential moment," but "is only one moment," in the existence of the absolute being. Qua indwelling spirit "it exists *only through being produced* by consciousness; or rather"—an important qualification—"it does *not* exist *without* being produced by consciousness." Yet that is only one essential moment. Absolute being "is at the same time in and for itself" (H 391; M 334–35; B 568–69).

Now there is a problem for faith in simultaneously asserting that absolute being is self-subsistent and that it is the indwelling spirit of the congregation: the first and third moments of faith's dialectic. The problem deepens when we add the second moment, of absolute being's appearance in a historical person. But Enlightenment, in the full cry of its polemic against faith, itself falls into self-contradiction. It declares that faith creates its God, and also that faith's object is an absolute Other, a being "*alien* to self-consciousness, that is not *its* essence but a changling foisted on it," presumably by the priests.

But here the Enlightenment is utterly foolish; faith regards it as just talk that does not know what it is saying, and does not understand the matter when it speaks of clerical deception and deluding the people. It talks about this as if through some hocus-pocus of conjuring priests consciousness had had something absolutely *alien* and *other* foisted on it in place of its own nature [*Wesen*] and says at the same time that this is a creature [*Wesen*] of consciousness that it believes in, trusts, and seeks to please. . . . It says in the same breath that what it asserts to be a being *alien* to consciousness is the *innermost nature* of consciousness. —So how can it talk about deception and delusion? (H 391–92; M 335; B 569–70)

Hegel here seems to be presenting faith's protest and counter-polemic against Enlightenment. He agrees, at least to the extent of finding it contradictory to suppose that consciousness can be deluded about what belongs to its own "immediate certainty of itself." Still, the fact that Enlightenment falls into self-contradiction does not imply that faith, for its part, is entirely coherent. As Hegel knows perfectly well, beyond superficial polemics there is still the question whether the absolute essence is entirely within self-consciousness or whether it is an object to which consciousness is inseparably bound.

We have considered only one line of argument among the many reviewed in the two sections before us, but that example may suffice to put us in a position to appreciate the general conclusions that "we" are led to reach about Enlightenment's theoretical arguments against faith. There are three such general conclusions. The first is that when Enlightenment *separates* the three moments of faith's dialectic, and attacks each one singly, its arguments tend to be point-missing if not perverse; furthermore, they contradict one another. The second judgment to which we are led, however, is more damaging to faith: When Enlightenment *combines* the three moments of faith's dialectic, and forces faith to confront them together, it becomes apparent that they do not make up a coherent concept. The third conclusion is that Enlightenment falls into similar embarrassment in trying to combine the moments of its own dialectic. Let us review these conclusions one by one.

First, the result when Enlightenment *separates* faith's three moments is well illustrated in our consideration of the projectionist argument. When Enlightenment charges that faith is subjected to an alien being, faith justifiably points to its trustful communion and to God's immanence as the indwelling spirit of the congregation. Aha! says Enlightenment: This means that faith has "produced" its God. But this argument overlooks not only faith's testimony to the self-subsistence of its absolute being, but Enlightenment's own claim that faith's God is utterly alien. In other words, when Enlightenment attacks the first moment of faith's dialectic, faith appeals to the third, which Enlightenment had overlooked. And when it attacks the third moment, faith indignantly reminds it of the first.

Similarly with Enlightenment's attack on the second moment. It regards faith's claim that the absolute being is incarnate in a historical personage, attested to by scripture, as evidence that faith bases its "certainty on a few particular historical witnesses," without even the basis in evidence that we would expect of a routine newspaper report. In fact, Enlightenment charges that faith's certainty in the end seems based on purely documentary evidence that is all too easy to explode. But here again faith appeals from the second moment to the third, with some justification denying that faith's certainty is based on anything so uncertain as historical evidence alone. In fact its certainty is based on the witness of the spirit to itself in faith's own individual inwardness and in the believing community. In this connection Hegel suggests that if faith's apologists let themselves be tempted to meet this critique on its own terms, and try to prove that faith's claims can be established on purely historical grounds, then faith "has already let itself be seduced by the Enlightenment" (H 394–95; M 338; B 572–73). In general, arguments of this sort, that attack a single point torn from the total context of belief, are not, so to speak, offered in good faith.

Second, pure insight proves more insightful when it confronts faith with all three of faith's own moments together. Faith tends to keep them separate, for instance, meeting Enlightenment's polemic against one moment by appealing to another. But in fact the contradictions into which Enlightenment falls when it attacks each moment singly turn out to be the reverse image of contradictions that faith suffers when it has to bring them together. When Enlightenment exploits this insight its critique is far more damaging.

> For the Enlightenment directs itself against the believing consciousness, not with Enlightenment's own principles, but with those that faith itself possesses. It merely brings faith's *own thoughts* together for it, which faith unconsciously lets fall apart; when faith dwells on *one* of its modes of thought it reminds faith

of the *others* which it *also* has, but which it always forgets when it dwells on the other one. (H 401; M 344; B 581)

In other words, as Hegel goes on to suggest, Enlightenment confronts faith with faith's own "concept," for the concept is precisely the grasp *(Begriff)* of the whole in each of the parts.

But faith's concept is incoherent. For instance, when faith insists on the existence of its object independent of consciousness, Enlightenment confronts faith with its claim that its absolute being is *not* an alien "thing," but the object of its absolute trust. In that case what is absolute in the relation appears to be faith's own unconditional "act" of service and trustful obedience. In this sense faith does indeed appear to "produce" its object, "*its* absolute being, through its own *action*. Here Enlightenment really only reminds faith of this factor when faith declares purely the *in-itself* of absolute being *beyond* the *action* of consciousness" (H 402–3; M 345; B 583). We are also reminded that Enlightenment has here merely turned the tables on faith's claim that Enlightenment has fallen into self-contradiction when it "isolates the pure moment of *action* and asserts of the *in-itself* of faith that it is *only* a *product* of consciousness," and yet maintains that the absolute being is for faith something "*beyond* consciousness, alien and unknown to it" (H 403; M 345–46; B 584). This self-contradiction merely echoes faith's own self-contradictory assertion.

Such ironical echoes run throughout the analysis, as we would expect in view of the symmetry of the two positions. Each finds the concept, the entire triad grasped as a whole, an effective critical instrument for use against the other, but neither seems to recognize the "necessity" of the concept. For faith it is composed of three separate moments linked only in an external, quasi-historical way, while Enlightenment appropriates the concept as something it simply "finds . . . at hand," as if by accident, and therefore cannot recognize that the same conceptual structure is as applicable to its own position as it is to faith's.

Third, Enlightenment is as devoid of conceptual coherence as faith is. Not only does it echo faith's own contradictions in its critique of faith, it also separates the three moments of its own concept, just as faith does, and is equally unsuccessful in establishing any necessary relation among them. Accordingly, in keeping with his contention that Enlightenment is faith's mirror image, Hegel follows his account of the contradictions among faith's moments by pointing out the corresponding contradictions among the moments of Enlightenment's own concept.

Without repeating all these correspondences in detail, we can see how the problem arises in general by rehearsing what Enlightenment's own positive program is, according to Hegel. That is, "if all prejudices and superstitions have been banished, the question arises, *so what now? What is the truth which Enlightenment has propagated in their place?*" (H 397; M 340; B 576). The first moment, as we have seen, posits an absolute self-consciousness without content or finite subjectivity: a universal "vacuum" without predicates, that is, the pure negation of finite content. The second moment, however, affirms the particular, sensuous objects of finite consciousness, affirms, that is, the irreducible reality of empirical "things" (H 397–98; M 340–41; B 576–77). Here we can already see a pattern emerging that seems to correspond to the contradiction between faith's absolute being and its all too particular *Vorstellungen* and historical appearances: "The Enlightenment, for its part, equally isolates *actuality,* as an essential nature abandoned by spirit, isolates determinacy as unalloyed finitude, as if it were not itself a moment in the spiritual movement of essence" (H 403–4; M 346; B 585). Again like faith, Enlightenment must undertake in its third moment to find a way of mediating this stark opposition.

How it sets about doing so is complex: In the first place, Enlightenment engenders two apparently irreconcilable metaphysical positions. Sensuous reality can be regarded as irreducibly true in itself (materialism), or it may have no truth in itself, but may exist only in relation to an "other," that is, to self-consciousness (idealism). Here Enlightenment seems to divide theoretically into two parties (H 398–99; M 341–42; B 577–78). But the two positions can be united practically in the principle of utility, which asserts both the irreducibility of sensuous reality and that it finds its value in being serviceable for another. Sensuous things are valued for their usefulness to human beings, and even human reason is valued for its usefulness in preventing the human enjoyment of sensuous things from falling into self-destructive excess. In the end, in fact, the human being himself is valued for his usefulness as a "member of the troop." In this generous utilitarian spirit some use is even found for religion! Indeed, as "*relation* to absolute being . . . religion is . . . of all useful things the most useful of all," since in their relation to an absolute being or "*Être suprême* or the void," presumably conceived in deistic fashion, all things both exist in themselves and are available for use by others (H 399–400; M 342–43; B 578–80). God is now the Engineer of a mechanical universe.

Hegel goes on to remark how "horrendous" faith finds all this, particularly the platitudinous wisdom whereby absolute being is an empty void to which finite things stand in a purely external relation, without communion. But the crucial point, for Hegel, is that the principle of utility has no intrinsic relation to Enlightenment's own starting-point in absolute self-consciousness. The first and third moments fall apart, just as they do for faith, the active, practical relation of consciousness to a definite object being wholly inadequate to express the supposed commitment to an absolute self-consciousness.

Indeed, there seems in principle no end to the self-contradictory course of this dispute between faith and Enlightenment, just because each is directed at its own reverse image. Even in Hegel's text the quarrel is sufficiently prolonged to make the reader feel it will never stop. But in fact it does. Though the two parties may reach a draw in principle, in fact it is only faith that is decisively undermined; faith is forced to confront the incoherence of its own concept, and can no longer sustain its double bookkeeping. Its heavenly kingdom seems to be "plundered," all its supposed riches are reclaimed by the earth "as its property." Faith has lost its content. Believing consciousness is left with a purely empirical world of particular things, with which it is wholly dissatisfied. This reality is devoid of spirit, while its absolute being has receded into a distant void, empty of determinate content, a pure object of unsatisfied longing.

> Since faith is without content and cannot abide in this emptiness, or since in proceeding out over the finite that alone does have content it finds only emptiness, faith becomes a *pure yearning,* its truth an empty Beyond, for which no fitting content can any longer be found, since everything has passed into a different relation. —Faith has in fact become the same as Enlightenment, namely the consciousness of the relation of self-subsistent finite things to an absolute that is without predicates, unknown and unknowable; except that Enlightenment itself is satisfied, while *faith* is the *dissatisfied* Enlightenment. (H 406–7; M 349; B 588–89)

Faith has now become in fact what Enlightenment had charged it with being all along: a sorry state of pure longing for what is hopelessly Beyond.

The concept of Enlightenment is in principle as incoherent as that of faith, and as empty of spirit, but it is in point of historical fact untroubled by its own vacuity. Its ascendancy over faith, quite independent of all their hairsplitting and rather comic wrangling, has in practice been assured all along. Hegel had compared pure insight at the outset with "a quiet expansion or *diffusion* like a perfume in the unresistant atmosphere," or a "contagion" that goes unnoticed until it has reached such epidemic proportions that it is too late to check it. It moves through that inner medium of consciousness that is the native element of pure insight. This "diffusion," this "contagion" is precisely the Enlightenment (H 387; M 331–32; B 563–64). Finally it penetrates faith itself. This

> invisible and unnoticed spirit infiltrates the noble parts through and through, and soon has taken complete possession of the vitals and members of the unconscious idol, until "on one fine morning it gives its comrade a shove with the elbow and bang! crash! the idol lies on the floor." —On *one fine morning* whose noon is not bloody if the infection has penetrated all the organs of spiritual life. (H 388; M 332; B 564–65; the quotation is from *Rameau's Nephew*)

Enlightenment's polemics against faith seem to be no more than the shove of the elbow, at least to the extent that faith's object is the unconscious idol whose arterial linkage with an actual world has already been severed. No blood needs to be shed in its overthrow because it is bloodless to begin with, drained of any vital fluid circulating between it and an actual world. Though faith continues to lurk rather ominously "in the background," "mourning the loss of its spiritual world," ascendant Enlightenment has moved on to do battle with alienated culture, under the all-conquering banner of utility, the principle of useful things devoid of selfhood (H 407; M 349; B 589). But that battle will be bloody.

Our program does not permit us to follow Enlightenment through these further adventures, treated in the sections entitled "The Truth of the Enlightenment" (which of course is the principle of utility) and "Absolute Freedom and Terror." In the latter section Hegel shows how the bloodless dialectical battle against faith gives way to revolutionary violence against a decadent culture. Again Enlightenment will demonstrate the essential vacuity of its own principle, now called "absolute freedom." Absolute freedom is unrealizable because it has no positive content at all, but is again only the name for the negativity it pits against its adversary. It can only destroy.

iv. The Religion of Conscience

With the passage from the second part of this long chapter on actual spirit to the third, we steer away from the turbulent sea of world history to navigate the quiet channels of the human heart. "Morality," "the spirit certain of itself," which is the subject of this third part, is a far more introverted spirit than those spirits we have met in the first two parts, such as the ethical world or the alienated world of culture, or Enlightenment, with its dénouement in a historic storm of revolutionary violence. Morality represents a rather homely, gentle spirit, which in fact comes on the scene in direct reaction to the world-historical turmoil created by its predecessors, a return to inwardness, a withdrawal into self-consciousness from the abortive effort to impose an empty ideal of freedom on the actual world. As an inward reaction to a desolated actuality, it resembles the reaction of faith and pure insight to alienated culture: "As the realm of the actual world passes over into that of faith and insight, so absolute freedom passes from its self-destructive actuality into another land of self-conscious spirit in which freedom is regarded in this unreality as the true" (H 422; M 363; B 610). This new land of purely inner freedom is surveyed in the third major division of the chapter under the following headings:

    C. Spirit Certain of Itself. Morality
        a. The Moral Worldview
        b. Pretense
        c. Conscience. The Beautiful Soul, Evil and Its Forgiveness

Our attention will focus on the third moment of this division, which is also the third "religious" formation treated in the chapter, offering a contrast to the subterranean religion of the ethical world and to faith.

But before turning to conscience as the primary locus of the religion of morality, we must note that the sections entitled "The Moral Worldview" and "Pretense" also exhibit religious interest of a sort, indeed a religious interest with heavy resonance in Hegel's own past. These two sections are largely devoted to an interpretation and ever more biting critique of Kant's postulates of practical reason. It is noteworthy that the only protracted critiques of specific philosophical positions in the *Phenome-nology* are all directed at Kant,[84] and it is odd to have the sort of intramural criticism Hegel had delivered against "unphilosophy" in his writings of 1800–1802 turning up in the *Phenomenology*. At any rate, what is expounded here as moral worldview and denounced as pretense or dissemblance *(die Verstellung)* is Kant's effort in the second critique to find in morality the basis for the sort of speculative assertions con-cerning God, freedom, and immortality that Kant had denied could be based on proper knowledge. We have seen how Hegel and his friends in the 1790s, following Fichte, had seized on the Kantian postulates as the bridge to the new speculative program of German Idealism. But here Hegel thoroughly burns that bridge behind him, confident that he is building a much more secure bridge to speculative wisdom in the *Phenomenology* itself. Of course he had already criticized Kant's postulates in the earlier Jena writings, but here the critique is far more fully developed and more thoroughly negative. Furthermore, Hegel scarcely takes it seriously at all as a religious position; in its reduction of God to the conclusion of a weak inference, it seems only to be a variation on the deistic religion of the Enlightenment.

According to Hegel's reading of the Kantian moral worldview, perfect morality is not achievable by a finite moral agent, who must struggle to do his duty against the grain of his sensuous nature. Moral purity is possible only for the "holy will" of God, whose existence is a postulate of a moral faith. Only as part of a moral world order, likewise postulated in face of all empirical evidence to the contrary, can the troubled moral agent hope that his ultimate moral intentions will be fulfilled. His own moral perfectibility depends on the extension of his life beyond the grave, which is accordingly also postulated. All these postulations, like the object of "faith," are in the mode of representation *(Vorstellung),* having the form of empirical objects without being based on possible experience, and they project all moral fulfillment into the Beyond (H 430–33; M 370–73; B 621–27). Hegel disposes of this moral *Weltan-schauung,* to his own satisfaction at least, as "a *whole nest* of thought-less contradictions," sarcastically adopting "a Kantian expression . . . where it is most appropriate" (H 434; M 374; B 629; in the first critique Kant had called the cosmological argument for God's existence "a whole nest of dialectical presumptions").

Hegel then turns, in the section on conscience that will chiefly occupy us here, to a new moral position differing radically from that Kantian effort to construct a worldview on practical reason. The new position, concentrated on the inner voice of conscience, implies no worldview, no general speculative postulates. In fact it rejects the moral rationalism on which such postulates might be based. The duty of conscience, furthermore, can actually be performed. "*Pure conscience* despises such a moral representation of the world [*Weltvorstellung*]; it is *in its own self* the simple, self-certain spirit that, without the mediation of those representations, immediately acts conscientiously and in this immediacy has its truth" (H 444; M 383; B 641). The moral perfection of conscience is self-contained, complete here and now, without reference to an external lawgiver or a quasi-objective world order.

Hegel introduces a nice play on the German word for conscience, *Gewissen:* This conscience is "certain [*gewiss*] of itself," autonomous. It needs no postulated God or immortality, and its freedom is an immediate certainty to itself, not an uncertain postulate. It is not assigned its duty by an allegedly universal reason that contradicts its sensuous nature. Rather, its knowledge of its duty has the immediacy of "sense-certainty," like a direct perception. Upon finding a situation in which action is called for, it knows just what to do with no hesitation, no fatal hiatus between the perceiving, willing, and doing of the deed (H 447; M 385; B 646–47). Nor does it experience any conflict of duties, as if each duty were an independent moral "substance" of a general sort that must be applied to a specific situation in the face of contrary duties: "Conscience is rather the negative unity or absolute self, which sweeps away these various moral substances; it is simple dutiful action, which does not fulfill this duty or that, but knows and does what is concretely right" (H 447; M 386; B 647).

In other words, duty itself is not a general principle but something definite, something specific to be done, out of a "conviction" lodged in the conscience of the particular self as such. Like the citizen of the ethical world, he knows just what is right, though unlike that citizen he knows it individually, without reference to community norms. This particular self with his particular conviction gives irreducible content to the claim of duty: "Duty is no longer the universal standing opposed to the self, but rather is known to have no validity when it is separated in this way." Like the Gospel dictum about man and the Sabbath, "it is now the law that exists for the sake of the self, not the self for the sake of the law" (H 449; M 387; B 649).[85]

Indeed, this conscientious self acknowledges no other law than his own inner conviction. His duty consists in his "pure *conviction* of duty," which is given content by the individual himself as a "natural," "sensuous" consciousness driven by its own "drives and impulses" (H 452–53; M 390; B 653). When Kant claimed that the moral agent legislates his duty for himself, he meant that the agent did so as the locus of that universal reason shared by all rational beings. In Kantian terms duty is the same for all, universally. But for the conscientious self the "truth" of *Gewissen* is sheer *Gewissheit*, his certainty of himself, and his duty is given in the urgent promptings "of his unconscious natural being." Duty is only formally the same for all, in the sense that every person should do his or her duty. Duty, that is, is no more than "a predicate, which has its subject in the individual, whose arbitrary will [*Willkür*] gives it content, who can attach any content to this form and can invest his conscientiousness in it" (H 453; M 391; B 654). This arbitrariness will of course turn out to be the fatal weakness of the conscientious spirit.

Nevertheless, this spirit is of special interest to our study because it is the locus of a significant new form of religious life. In fact it provides the third important religious moment in Hegel's chapter on the historic pilgrimage of actual spirit, alongside the cult of the family and the supernatural "faith." It is characteristically modern, a type of worship [*Gottesdienst*] concentrated on the self-certain individual himself, without any objectified representation of deity beyond him. In its own sublime "majesty," requiring no external authority, conscience "is the moral genius which knows the inner voice of its immediate knowledge to be a divine voice." Since in this knowledge it grasps its own reality-producing deed, "it is the divine power of creation that has vitality in its very concept. It is equally within itself a divine worship; for its action is the intuition of its own divinity" (H 460; M 397; B 663). Hegel immediately adds that "this solitary worship is at the same time essentially the worship of a community."

For even though his duty and his very God have been reduced to predicates of his entirely subjective and autonomous conscience, the conscientious self does nevertheless necessarily exist with other conscientious selves. That is because the principle of recognition applies most obviously at this point: Such certainty of self requires the confirmation of others. "In the power of its certainty of itself," conscience, to be sure, enjoys "the majesty of absolute autarky, to bind and to loose." Yet just in the apparently Petrine infallibility of the promptings of his conscience, this moral agent is after all a *"being for others"* (H 456; M 393–94; B 658; see also H 449–50; M 387; B 649–50). In fact, "conscience" claims at least a formal universality, such that every man or woman of conscience respects the conscience of every other, even if they totally disagree about what conscience demands in a particular case. Precisely as a highly developed form of self-consciousness, conscience exhibits "the spiritual element" of mutual recognition. It has abandoned the Kantian claim to be acting on moral laws that prescribe the same duties for every rational being. Yet it is still dutiful.

> Conscience has not given up pure duty or the *abstract in-itself,* which is rather the essential moment of relating itself, as *universality,* to others. Conscience is the communal element of self-consciousness, and this element is the substance in which the deed possesses *abiding* worth and *actuality:* the moment of *being recognized* by others. . . . The *subsistent actuality* of conscience . . . is such that it is a *self;* that is, a particular existence [*Dasein*] conscious of itself, in the spiritual element of being recognized. (H 450; M 388; B 650)

What is recognized is sincere moral conviction, and this recognition occurs through language. It cannot occur simply in the deed itself. One and the same deed may be performed on any number of grounds besides those of conscience. If I choose to bear arms in warfare—and for the conscientious person such a course is a matter of personal choice and conviction, not as for the citizen of the ethical world a duty simply entailed in citizenship—such an act is subject to multiple interpretations. You may suspect that I am naturally bloodthirsty, or an adventure-seeker, or that I want to impress susceptible women, and so on and so forth. You can never know, on the basis of my deed, whether I am acting conscientiously or not. Suppose you refuse to bear arms, a refusal subject to an equal variety of possible motives. Still, if you refuse on grounds of conscience you may respect my decision if you believe that it, too, is based on honest conviction, and I may reciprocate with the same understanding. But how can we be sure one another's motives are pure? The situation is in principle the same even if we both follow the same course of action. "The last temptation," says a poet,

> is the greatest treason:
> To do the right deed for the wrong reason.[86]

How can either of us be sure that the other is acting for the right reason, or, for that matter, that I myself am? Answer: I must tell you that I am defending my country as a matter of conscience, and you must likewise speak the conviction according to which you refuse. Of equal importance, furthermore, is the condition that we must believe each other. It is not a matter of arguing our respective cases. It is sufficient to convince each other of the sincerity of our convictions (H 453–58; M 391–95; B 654–61).

Our mutual recognition occurs in the language in which we voice our conviction. This deceptively simple answer is implicit in the very idea of conscience, whose rectitude cannot consist in objective knowledge of the rightness of its deed as such. The "circumstances" of any act are manifold, "endlessly" dividing and extending "backward into their conditions, sideways into their accompanying factors, forward into their consequences," beyond any possible knowledge (H 452; M 389–90; B 652). On this basis the agent has no firm ground on which to stand. Yet my conscience is certain, not only subjectively but intersubjectively, requiring only that I be recognized as a man of conscience on the basis of my self-testimony as such.

What is recognized is not only the conscientiousness of my action, but my conscientious *self.* Now a "self" is an elusive and problematic entity. It is not purely self-subsistent, like a stone or a human body. The *Phenomenology* consistently maintains that its very existence, its "being-there" *(Da-sein)* occurs in mutual recognition. Even this most radically individualistic, conscientious self can come into existence as such only when it is acknowledged by another whom it recognizes to be a conscientious self. "What ought to *be there,"* the conscientious self in the deed,

> is here an essentiality solely through being *known* to be a self-expressive individuality, and this *being-known* is what is recognized and what, *as such,* is to have *existence* [Dasein].
>
> The self steps into existence *as self;* the spirit certain of itself exists as such for others; its *immediate* action is not what is valid and actual; what is recognized is not the determinate *being-in-itself* of the action, but solely the self-knowing *self* as such. The element of abiding presence is the universal self-consciousness; what enters into this element cannot be the *effect* of the action; this effect cannot endure in it and acquires no permanence, but only self-consciousness is what is recognized and achieves actuality.

Here again we see *language* as the existence [*Dasein*] of spirit.
(H 458; M 395; B 660)

Spirit "is there" in language. We shall see in the chapter on religion
how important this general proposition is for the program of the *Phenomenology*. Here Hegel is reminding us that it was already introduced
in relation to the self-alienated spirit of "culture," as the medium in
which a pure self "is there," detached from its organic existence. That
pure self was constituted by language in its vanity and alienation. Here
the form of language is different, the language of mutual recognition
in which the conscientious self, equally intangible, comes into existence,
apart from its specific deeds as well as from its organic life, as a pure
I=I.

The content of the language of conscience is *the self that knows
itself as essence.* This alone is what it declares, and this declaration is the true actuality of its deed and the validity of its action.
Consciousness declares its *conviction;* it is in this conviction
alone that the action is duty; only because the conviction is
declared is the action valid as duty. (H 459; M 396; B 661)

It makes no sense to ask whether this conviction is correct, independent
of the declaration, since the conscientious self "is there" precisely when
it declares itself and is recognized. The bare objective fact of the deed
is from this point of view drained of all moral significance, which resides
entirely in the acknowledged good intentions of the conscientious agent.
The tree is not known by its fruits, but the fruits by the tree.

The crucial role of recognition in establishing the conscientious self
is the key to the paradox that his "solitary worship" of the God within
"is at the same time essentially the worship of a *community*" (H 460;
M 397; B 663). Like his certainty that he is doing his duty, his secure
possession of the God-within requires the confirmatory recognition of
those also so constituted. Together they make up an elite community
of sublime spirits, each worshiping at the shrine of his own divinity
and celebrating the unfalsifiable rectitude of his peers: "The spirit and
the substance of their association is thus the mutual assurance of their
conscientiousness, good intentions, the rejoicing over this reciprocal
purity and refreshment in the glory of knowing and declaring, of nurs-
ing and nourishing, such a splendid state of affairs" (H 461; M 398;
B 664). The unmistakable sarcasm of this description suggests that

this cult of the God-within has rather the aspect of a particularly self-satisfied secret society, whose members consider that they are conferring the loftiest honor on anyone who is fitted, by their recognition of his or her sterling qualities, to join them. If, Hegel goes on to say, the conscientious spirit were just a little less certain of itself, if it were troubled by some disjunction between its "abstract," pure consciousness and its actual self-consciousness, it might claim that its essential life is mystically "*hidden* in God." But nothing is hidden for the conscientious spirit, since it "is there" precisely in its self-congratulatory speech, where it is all of a piece. It is simply identical with its own inner God.

It might seem that at least unhappy consciousness is overcome in this mutually reinforced self-satisfaction. But in fact unhappy consciousness appears in a new guise precisely as this fraternity of self-congratulatory spirits soars above all objective conditions, as if everything real were beneath its collective notice. For their perfect mutual recognition is not mediated by anything actual at all, but exists purely in the element of language, with perhaps a few deeply significant pressures of the hand. The loss of objectivity is the tendency of the self-conscious forms of spirit that we have called the B-series. They incorporate everything significant within the self. With the Romantic conscience that tendency appears in its most extreme form historically. That is why it is the last stop on the pilgrimage of actual spirit, having achieved a purity of individual self-consciousness opposed at 180 degrees to the corporate self-consciousness of the ethical world, entailing the loss of any world at all. Here "self-consciousness has withdrawn into its innermost, for which all exteriority as such has disappeared—in the intuition of I=I, wherein this 'I' is all essentiality and existence" (H 461; M 398; B 665). The very structure of consciousness, in its intentional relation to objects, has disappeared with this exteriority. Pure self-consciousness is everything: and nothing: "Refined to this purity, consciousness exists in its most impoverished form, and the poverty which constitutes its sole possession is itself a vanishing; this absolute *certainty* into which substance has dissolved is absolute *untruth,* which collapses into itself; it is the absolute *self-consciousness* into which consciousness is submerged" (H 462; M 399; B 665).

This submergence of consciousness with its objective world is precisely a new refinement of unhappy consciousness. Loss of the actual is always characteristic of unhappy consciousness, but in all earlier forms, for instance in the moment of "faith," or in the moral worldview, unhappy consciousness was not aware that its representations of absolute being or moral world order were really its own inner self appearing under the aspect of a specious objectification. But now, for the pure self-consciousness, "all life and all spiritual essentiality is withdrawn into this self, and has lost its difference from the 'I' itself." The consequence is that this self knows that its apparent objects are only ephemeral "abstractions" that constantly arise from and disappear into itself; "it is the revolving circuit of unhappy consciousness with itself." Unhappy consciousness is the deliberate project of this self! Indeed, since it is only "there" in language, these ephemera are merely sounds that are uttered and die away: Its "created world is its *speech*," the mere "echo" of which returns to it. Like all forms of unhappy consciousness, this pure self "lacks the power to exteriorize itself, to make itself into a thing and to endure being. It lives in anxiety that it might soil the glory of its inwardness through action and existence; and in order to preserve the purity of its heart it flees from contact with actuality" (H 462–63; M 399–400; B 666). Unable to recognize itself in any enduring expression in the actual world, it has only a kind of ghostly presence, whose "deed is a yearning," presumably yearning for its lost world, which it cannot recover without staining the purity of its inner deity. "In this transparent purity of its moments" the conscientious self becomes "an unhappy, so-called *beautiful soul,* flickers away within itself and vanishes like a shapeless vapor that dissolves into the air" (H 463; M 400; B 666–67).

This reference to the beautiful soul is another literary allusion. Goethe's *Bildungsroman* of 1795, *Wilhelm Meisters Lehrjahre* includes a section (Book 6) entitled "Confessions of a Beautiful Soul," really a distinct novella within the novel purporting to be the memoir of a woman who became a spiritual guide to an intimate little company practicing a Romantic pietism. Goethe already employed the expression, "beautiful soul," with some irony, and the following pages in Hegel's text contain his own heavily ironical analysis of this spiritual type, with many allusions to Goethe's portrait and to the much more earnest portrait of such a figure in Jacobi's *Woldemar.*[87] Since no real action can express the purity of the beautiful soul's intention, he or she lives in retirement from the world, making the highest virtue of abstention from any worldly involvement. Here "duty consists only in words," which the beautiful soul bestows rather freely in sadness over the crassness of things. To the beautiful soul Hegel juxtaposes another conscientious self of slightly more robust disposition, that still takes the risk of committing itself to some actual course of action. The psychological maneuvering between these two figures occupies the rest of the chapter.

I shall not rehearse in detail the course of this relationship, which Hegel describes with slightly sardonic humor. With the arrival of this "unhappy, so-called beautiful soul," the progression of actual spirit is essentially complete, for here actual spirit achieves an extreme of introversion that completes the unraveling of the ethical world. The exquisite unhappiness of the beautiful soul consists in an individual's inner identification with an abstract ideal of perfect universality, really "the unchangeable" pole of unhappy consciousness, to the degree that any particular expression in the actual world is impossible.

The beautiful soul can only talk, passing harsh judgment on the more active conscience which, just because it acts, commits many a breach of the universal perfection that the beautiful soul preserves in pure inwardness. This conflict creates a comedy of thwarted recognition. The doer needs to be recognized as possessing a conscience of the same purity as that of the beautiful soul, in order to know himself as conscientious. But this recognition the beautiful soul refuses to confer. For the sake of linguistic convenience, and in conformity with Goethe's prototype, let us refer to the beautiful soul in the feminine, though Hegel does not, and of course in practice this role is as likely to be played by a man as by a woman. So "she" withholds recognition from the doer, because she regards his deeds as evil: They violate the perfection that can only be preserved by not acting at all. Furthermore, she finds it hypocritical that this evildoer should claim to act out of conscience (H 464–65; M 401–2; B 668–70). Actually the beautiful soul is equally hypocritical. Her hypocrisy consists in wanting her "judgment to be taken for an *actual* deed, and instead of proving [her] rectitude through action does so through the utterance of splendid sentiments." But the necessity to act "is entailed in the very talk of duty, since duty without deeds has no meaning at all" (H 466; M 403; B 671).

Realizing this fact, the doer makes another abortive attempt to achieve mutual recognition with the beautiful soul who sits in judgment on him: Let both admit their common hypocrisy, so that they will recognize in each other kindred, morally earnest but troubled spirits. So he confesses his evildoing and hypocrisy, not in order to abase himself, but "because language is the existence [*Dasein*] of spirit *qua* immediate self"; he naturally expects the beautiful soul—the judging consciousness—to "contribute" her share to spirit's being there in this common admission of moral failure: "But this avowal of the evildoer: *That is what I am!* does not produce the same admission in response. That was not what the judging consciousness meant at all; quite the contrary! It repudiates this common ground and becomes the hard heart that exists for itself and rejects any continuity with the other" (H 469; M 405; B 674).

Stung by this refusal, the evildoer now attempts to turn the tables: He accuses his judge of being in the wrong, and of being hard-hearted and unrepentant besides. She is the one who is guilty of the refusal of spirit; she "is not aware that spirit in the absolute certainty of itself is master over every deed and actuality, and can cast them off and make them not to have happened" (H 469; M 406; B 675). Withholding the words by which the evildoer could be healed, the beautiful soul dooms not only him but herself to an existence forsaken by spirit. Because she is forced to see this mutually destructive consequence of her self-righteousness, the beautiful soul in her "unreconciled immediacy" is driven to madness and "wastes away in yearning consumption" (H 470; M 407; B 676).

The solution to this tragicomic impasse is evident in the nature of the impasse: At last the two protagonists embrace in mutual forgiveness. The hard heart relents, confessing her own wronging of the wrongdoer, and "the wounds of the spirit heal, without leaving any scars" (H 470; M 407; B 676). Indeed, in this mutual forgiveness on the part of both these final protagonists of actual spirit, a new spirit appears on the scene, no longer subject to the polarizations and historical limitations of actual spirit at all: "The word of reconciliation is the spirit *that is there* [*der* daseiende *Geist*], which beholds the pure knowledge of its own self as *universal* essence in its opposite, in the pure knowledge of itself as the absolute *particularity* existing in itself—a mutual recognition which is *absolute* spirit" (H 471; M 408; B 677).

At just this "point" of mutual forgiveness absolute spirit appears at last. This is not at all to say that active conscience becomes absolute spirit, much less the beautiful soul. Absolute spirit spreads its wings just when both protagonists abandon their moralistic pretensions, reconciling the universal and the particular in an identity that transcends the merely historical sphere altogether.

v. Religion Under the Conditions of Actual Spirit: Reprise

The three religious moments we have highlighted in this long chapter on historical Geist stand in a quasi-spatial relation to one another. The religion of the ethical world is subterranean, of the earth *beneath,* expressing itself in the blood-kinship of the family. The religious reaction to the alienated world, on the other hand, is a faith directed *above,* indeed a *"faith* in *heaven,"* as Hegel calls it in the summary that introduces his chapter on religion.[88] From the family's devotion to deities below we have turned to faith's worship of the absolute being in heaven above. Finally we have encountered the conscientious self's spontaneous expression of the God-*within.* Here the self lays claim to being itself the sole content of divinity, and acknowledges no other essential truth to which it is subjected. Now these three appearances of deity in the development of actual spirit—God-beneath, God-above, God-within—nicely register the course of development traced in this chapter. Actual spirit proceeds from its all-encompassing collective identity in the ethical world to its essentially individual moral identity. Appearing at the outset, in the ethical world, the God-beneath joins the natural to the social actuality of that world. It inheres substantially in the family. Appearing at the end, the God-within again unites the divine and the human, but now in an individual self, for whom all natural and social actuality have disappeared. Here we find subjectivity without substance. The entire historical life of actual spirit unfolds between these two extremes, in the midpoint of which arises the God-above of faith, distanced in its objectification from collective and individual spirit alike. It is the reflective object of a spirit doubly alienated from itself. The moment of alienation marks the necessary transition in the pilgrimage of actual spirit from corporate substance to individual subject: Spirit had to disengage itself from its natural and social actuality in order to recover its actuality in the morally developed individual.

Actual spirit unfolds historically, in time. It is never complete in any single moment, nor is its unfolding simply progressive or cumulative. Every gain is accompanied by losses. In fact the later moments seem to represent such a decline in social happiness and solidarity from the ethical world that we have to keep reminding ourselves that there is a compensating gain in the development of individual autonomy, culminating in the conscientious self. But however we calculate gains and losses, none of these appearances of actual spirit achieves spiritual plenitude, since it is the nature of this historical spirit to unfold its moments in a series of fragmentary temporal appearances; only in the whole course of these appearances can "we" see the whole of actual spirit in its many sides. Similarly, we should not expect to find in the three religious moments that punctuate this series of appearances anything more than the dissociated fragments of an authentic religion, its divine life dispersed below, above, within. They are all pseudoreligions, none a full realization of absolute spirit, but each a one-sided appearance of actual spirit reflecting a particular historical form of self-consciousness. Each is the reflex of a human reality of its historical moment. Nor can the three be synthesized, as if the combination would yield a true religion, since each is a characteristic result of the limitations of its historical moment.

The religion of the conscientious self and the beautiful soul, directed to the God-within, is the purest example in the *Phenomenology* of the self-referential form characteristic of the B-series, of self-consciousness. Conscience knows its divinity to be its own spirit. The conscientious self may, to be sure, give his own self-consciousness the form of a representational object, as "the universal self . . . which contains all essence and actuality in itself"; but he attributes no independent subsistence to this actuality. Even if he does objectify this universal spirit, in the form characteristic of the A-series, this objectification "is constituted in the essential character of being *self*-consciousness," so that it is reduced finally to the purest form of the B-series. The objective form "is completely transparent; and the actuality it contains is enclosed within him and is transcended in him" (H 475; M 411–12; B 687). Hence it exhibits in the highest degree the characteristic problem of the B-series generally: the essential disappearance of all objectivity, all independent otherness.

It is in fact notable that each major division of the chapter on Spirit ends with a moment in which otherness, objective actuality, is essentially lost. In legal status, at the end of the first division, this loss of the other takes the form of the political destruction of all the ethical/ethnic worlds, and issues in Stoicism, skepticism, and unhappy consciousness, in which this loss of the actual is rendered in thought. In absolute freedom and terror, at the end of the second division, revolutionary violence undertakes the destruction of all existing social structures. This loss of the other occurs in "Conscience" and "Beautiful Soul," at the end of the chapter, in a very different, psychological manner: with the assertion of the self as the sole spiritual actuality.

For Hegel the appearance of this fatal defect at the close of each division of the chapter reveals an inherent problem in the phenomenological structure of self-consciousness that must be addressed in the final chapters. This refusal of the actual other given in nature and in the "ethical substance" of society, this assertion of the omnipotent human will and deed against it, also poses the deep challenge of modernity. The challenge is not met by taking sides in the war between the ancients and the moderns. For all his love of classical antiquity and the cultural nostalgia that tempted him from the time he entered adulthood, Hegel was convinced that this challenge of modernity had to be accepted as a necessary aspect of any complete life of the spirit.

The two primary forms of this modern challenge are, indeed, the revolutionary right of rational control and the right of individual subjectivity. That the modern world has been rent, in Hegel's time and since, by the tragic collision of these two rights simply lends urgency to the need to find a common ground beyond the resources of either. Left to themselves they generate totalitarian tyranny on the one hand and egocentric decadence on the other. Hegel already saw that these were the characteristic deformities of the two aspects of modernity that he epitomized phenomenologically as the ascendancy of self-consciousness. Yet the rights of rational control and of individuality are in themselves vital aspects of that life of the spirit that had been disclosed piecemeal in the four millennia of recorded history. Irreconcilable on their own grounds, they require the deeper ground, also available in the life of the spirit, that can reconcile them not only with one another but with the ethical solidarity and fidelity to the earth of the ancients: all of them together or not at all.

This deeper ground of reconciliation, the availability of which is the source of Hegel's optimism about the modern prospect, is what he called absolute spirit. It is, at best, only fitfully disclosed in the pseudoreligions of the ancient and modern world, with their deities below, above, within. Unhappy consciousness, the pervasive malaise that expresses itself especially in the modern pseudoreligions and in the modern political and psychological violence against the actual world, is also the rite of passage into the absolute ground. The ethical substance which is the legacy of antiquity must be aufgehoben, taken up and transformed, into spiritual subject, through the manifold ordeals of unhappy consciousness.

However one judges Hegel's solution, one can only salute his scarcely surpassed grasp of the problem.

5. The Religious Recognition of Absolute Spirit

The final pair of chapters in the *Phenomenology,* mercifully much briefer than the preceding pair, treat the appearance of absolute spirit. The later system also ends with absolute spirit. That is probably the point at which most contemporary readers of Hegel lose interest, but it is consummatory for Hegel himself, for much the same reason: that with absolute spirit we poor mortals are beckoned beyond our everyday concerns as children of nature and history and are invited to move to that deeper ground that sounds suspiciously metaphysical, theological, speculative. At this point philosophy does become unabashedly speculative, the mirror—*speculum*—of an all-encompassing truth. Here, indeed, the cloven hoof of the notorious systematizer peeps from under the phenomenological veil. The *Phenomenology,* after all, is the pathway into the system proper, and in these consummatory chapters the phenomenological project begins to shade into that science of wisdom we were promised in the Preface. That the penultimate station on this pathway looks all too suspiciously like an account of the Christian gospel seems, furthermore, to justify the currently fashionable dismissal of this science of wisdom under the facile label of "onto-theology."

But this project in fact remains phenomenological to the end, what we have called an experience-appropriating construction of thought. What Hegel calls "spirit" is not so diaphanous as it sounds, nor is its absoluteness so conversation-stopping. An original thinker, after all, has two terminological choices: He can coin new words to express his new ideas, or he can invest available terminologies with new meanings. Hegel opts for putting his new wine in the old wineskins, and if they burst, so much the better! This practice extends even to his appropriation of the gospel, as we shall see.

Absolute spirit is not a *different* spirit than we have encountered in the earlier chapters. It has a physical body, and a history. It is the life's breath *(pneuma, spiritus)* of living things and the selfhood of selves who, however imperfectly, recognize one another as such. It is the collective identity of communities *and* the unhappiness of their alienation *and* the self-deifying conscience of individual men and women. Hegel has taken this word "Geist," already luxuriant in connotation, and has made it the name for all these diverse phenomena. Spirit exists: ist *da,* has its particularities in space and time. This multifarious

Dasein of spirit is what we have encountered in earlier chapters. This "spirit in its world or the actual *existence* of spirit . . . consists . . . in the whole of spirit insofar as its moments express themselves in fragmentary fashion [*auseinandertretend*] and each for itself" (H 476; M 412; B 689).

This diaspora into distinct localizations and historical episodes, this ensemble of appearances, contains in its sum "the whole of spirit." Without these appearances spirit would not exist at all. For there *is* no spirit except insofar as it "is there" in space and time. The dialectical "moments" of this fragmentary existence, Hegel says, "are *consciousness, self-consciousness, reason,* and *spirit*—spirit, that is, as immediate spirit, that is not yet the consciousness of spirit. Their totality *taken together* constitutes spirit in its worldly existence generally; spirit as such contains the previous formations in universal determinations, the moments just named" (H 476; M 412–13; B 689).

The reason actual spirit is singled out for comment is that it already contains the other three, not consciously but in the mode of historical time. Consciousness, self-consciousness, and reason are, as we have seen, "abstractions" from this historical spirit. It is in a dialectical sense the ground into which they proceed; for dialectic differs from formal logic in that it does not proceed from ground to consequences, but from consequential particulars to their ground. That is the movement that occurred when these three "abstract" moments found their actual existence in history, in the entire historical progression from the collectivity of the ethical world to the individuality of the conscientious self. But because actual spirit, which grounds the first three moments, does not disclose its totality in any one of these historical appearances, but only in their entire progression, this disclosure is known only to us who observe it, but not to its protagonists as such. They *are* the appearances of spirit, but are not conscious of being so, because they are not aware of the whole of which they are the fragmentary appearance. Another step must be taken if actual spirit is to become conscious of the spiritual whole, a step that again proceeds into its ground, but in a different sense: not of course into its historical-existential ground, but from its episodic and localized existence into its timeless totality.

This dialectical movement occurs, first, in religion. Religion, of course, has a history, but this historical aspect now becomes incidental. Nor is this movement into religion a new historical episode added to the history of actual spirit. Essentially it has been present all the while, but its significance has not been historical, nor are its own moments historically related. The religious moments, as we have suggested, borrowing a title from Bonaventura, make up a mystical journey of the mind into God—or into that absolute spirit which is spirit's comprehensive totality—and its moments constitute stages in that ascending journey. As such, the spirit in religion is distinguished formally from spirit in its historical being-*there,* but it is not separated from it. "Religion presupposes the entire course" of the preceding moments (consciousness, self-consciousness, reason, actual spirit), "and is their *simple* totality or absolute self." It is the seamless unity of spirit recovered from its historical diaspora in the preceding moments.

> Their procession in relation to religion, moreover, is not to be represented as occurring in time. The entire spirit only exists in time, and the forms, which are the forms of the entire *spirit* as such, exhibit themselves in a sequence; for only the whole has genuine actuality and thus the form of pure freedom over against others, which is expressed in time. But the *moments* of the whole, consciousness, self-consciousness, reason, and spirit, just because they are moments, have no existence separated from one another. (H 476; M 413; B 689)

Hegel is making an important distinction in this somewhat confusing passage: On the one hand, the concrete existence of spirit is splayed across its temporal appearances. Otherwise spirit would be ghostly indeed, merely an abstraction without the power freely to express itself, to be one thing and not another, in spatiotemporal contingency. "Time," Hegel tells us in the final chapter, "is the *concept* itself, that *exists*" (da ist) (H 558; M 487; B 800).

On the other hand, spirit in its merely episodic being-there does not yet grasp itself as spirit, does not confront itself in its totality, in which all its moments inseparably cohere. This confrontation occurs in religion, where spirit in its entirety appears as object of worship. I must immediately add that the object of worship itself undergoes development, though its development is not essentially historical, and what begins as object of worship becomes the goal of the self-transformation of the worshipers. Strictly speaking, "religion" is the whole, the process of uniting the divine and the human, and in religion this whole presents itself to consciousness. So there are two parallel developments. One development is historical, in which spirit necessarily appears but is not conscious of itself as spirit. The other development is religious, the mystical ascent that is only incidentally historical, in which spirit actually presents itself to consciousness.

In turning to the final two chapters of the *Phenomenology,* it is useful to recall two remarks in the Preface: "The true is the whole" and "the true is not to be grasped and expressed as *substance* but just as much as *subject*" (H 21, 19; M 11, 10; B 81, 80). If the whole were Spinozistic substance, a changeless truth the spatiotemporal appearances of which are merely the illusions of perception, it would be a good example of what William James called a "block universe," against which James protested on behalf of the validity of experience with its contingency and open-endedness. But the temporal appearances of spiritual subject are not illusory. It is the very nature of spirit to appear in time. Yet folk who are immersed in their own historical moment are apt to ignore precisely its temporality. They recognize themselves and everything of value to them only in the conditions of their own age, and if they see it passing away the loss will seem total: "after me, the deluge." It is customary to refer such folk, enduring the loss of everything in the storms of history and in their own mortality, to the consolations of religion. Prominent among these consolations, for Hegel, is a new dimension of self-recognition, recognizing themselves in relation to a whole that transcends each historical moment because it is its nature to exist in the entire progression of such moments.

That an age turns out to be ephemeral is no catastrophic accident. It is as it should and must be, in the very nature of the larger life of the spirit that expresses itself in every age. The citizen of the ethical world, for instance, knows the ethical substance enshrined in its customs, beliefs, institutions. Through the ordeal of history this ethical substance is transformed into the dynamic life of spiritual subject. That is the whole, and it is in principle always available to consciousness in the transcendent religious vision.

Religion, Hegel says, is at once "the fulfillment of spirit" and the *"ground"* into which the dialectically antecedent moments of spirit *"return* and have *returned."* The relation of this ground and fulfillment to the historical moments in which it necessarily appears is not itself essentially temporal. The relation perdures, just because its distinct dialectical moments "together constitute the *existing actuality* of the entire spirit, which only *is* as the movement of its two sides," at once "differentiating and returning into itself" (H 477; M 413; B 690). In a hoary analogy, not Hegel's but apt, it is like the relation between the ocean and the drops, waves, and currents that compose it. But the oceanic side of the relation is not unchanging divinity but "religion," comprehending both human experience of the divine and divine appearance as two sides of the same phenomenological coin.

"Religion" in fact denotes the dynamic process, a living whole, that overcomes this distinction; it is a name for absolute spirit: "The entire spirit, the spirit of religion, is again the movement out of its immediacy to achieve the *knowledge* of what it is immediately or *in itself,* and to reach the point at which the *form* in which it appears for its consciousness is perfectly identical with its essence, and it beholds itself as it is" (H 477; M 414; B 690). This point of convergence is reached in what Hegel calls "revelatory" religion, where spirit reveals itself as the union of divine and human. The further step, beyond religion, will not merely reveal this identity *to* consciousness, but will embrace consciousness itself in the identity. In absolute knowledge, that is, spirit will be fully *self*-conscious.

So religion, as we have suggested, is assigned to the A-series, retaining the subject-object structure of consciousness. It is consciousness of absolute spirit, while absolute knowledge, which perfects the B-series, is absolute spirit's self-consciousness. The religious subject is self-conscious in other respects, and the divine object likewise appears, in the Religion of Art, as a self-conscious god, recognized by its devotees as self-conscious, in that respect like themselves. Furthermore, as there were moments in the chapter on actual Spirit (belonging in general to the B-series) in which the subject-object structure of the A-series asserted itself (e.g., in supernatural "faith"), so in the present chapter there are points at which self-consciousness is ascendant. Hegel even suggests that there is a systematic development in this respect through the chapter: In natural religion spirit "generally" takes the form of consciousness, in the religion of art the form of self-consciousness. In revelatory religion spirit is manifested "in the form of the unity of both; it has the form of being-in-and-for-itself" (H 480; M 416; B 694). Still, this development transpires, wheels within wheels, within a structure essentially defined by the A-series. Even the consummatory in-and-for-itself merely strains at the limits of religious representation *(Vorstellung),* without quite surpassing them. This representational form, in which the divine is objectively "placed-before" *(vor-gestellt)* consciousness, formally defines and limits the nature of religion. That view of the nature of religion is also consistent with the treatment in the *Realphilosophie.*

Still, the religious spirit moves toward absolute self-consciousness, and its ascent toward this goal also defines the nature of religion. The spirit "that knows itself in its truth" will have surpassed all earlier forms of A-series and B-series alike: "Its consciousness and self-consciousness are equivalent." But to achieve this equivalence is the *task* of religion, which is not completed in the religious ascent as such. Since "here religion is first *immediate,* this distinction has not yet returned into spirit. What is posited is only the *concept* of religion, which contains the essence of *self-consciousness* that is itself all truth and contains all actuality within this truth. This self-consciousness has, as consciousness, itself for its object" (H 479; M 415; B 692–93).

The religious spirit, in what Meister Eckhart called its wayfaring condition, objectifies this absolute self-consciousness as the "being" of God. For this pilgrim spirit, its own "essence" is still hidden, "not the same as its consciousness. . . . It is first actual as absolute spirit when it is also in its *truth* as it is in the *certainty of its own self,* or the extremes into which it is divided qua consciousness are for-one-another in the form of spirit" (H 479; M 415; B 693; see also H 481; M 416–17; B 696). The pilgrimage will not be complete until this wayfaring spirit has surpassed its own limits. This self-surpassing movement is the "concept" of religion.

Hegel divides this religious pilgrimage into three chief moments, of which the first two are subdivided into three subordinate moments, making up seven steps in all—an auspicious number!

A. *Natural* Religion
    a. The Light-Essence
    b. Plant and Animal
    c. The Craftsman
B. *Art*-Religion
    a. The Abstract Work of Art
    b. The Living Work of Art
    c. The Spiritual Work of Art
C. *Revelatory* Religion

This series of moments is no capsule history of religion. Even the Lectures on the Philosophy of Religion presented during the 1820s are not intended to offer a history of religions, though the analysis is far more fully developed, with more attention paid to historical foundations and circumstances. By that time Hegel did know more about the history of religions, including non-Western religions, of which he understood little in 1806. Here the seven moments can easily be associated with historic religions, but they are very impressionistically rendered, generally with only a single interest: distilling some feature from each that can furnish a stage in the ascent of spirit from a pure religious consciousness to a self-conscious science of wisdom. Each moment does loosely represent "one religion" that "distinguishes itself . . . from another" according to the specific manner "in which spirit knows itself" in it.

Admittedly, "the exposition of this self-knowledge according to this *single emphasis* does not in fact exhaust the whole of any actual religion." Any historic religion will exhibit many significant features that are not relevant to this nonhistorical schematization. Furthermore, from this standpoint "religion" constitutes a single continuous movement through these seven steps that can in principle be ascended any time and anywhere, rather than a procession of distinct religions as such: "The series of diverse religions . . . exhibit just as much again merely the diverse sides of a single religion, indeed of *every single* religion, and the representations which appear to characterize one actual religion by contrast with another occur in each one" (H 481; M 417; B 696). Now this conception is both questionable and ingenious: "Religion," from this point of view, is not merely a generic name we attach to essentially different patterns of belief and practice in diverse cultures. "Religion" denotes a single life of the spirit, so self-identical in essence that it may reproduce its moments, in principle, within *any* historical religion. Since Hegel's exposition of these moments is obviously modeled on particular historic religions—notably on classical Greek religion in the religion of art, on Christianity in revelatory religion—it is important to emphasize the universality that he is claiming for this scheme, which at once embraces all religions and is present in each. It will not do, any more than in earlier chapters of the *Phenomenology*, to identify a phenomenological moment with some historical episode that may merely provide its locus classicus. If, for instance, on the one hand there is a great deal in historic Christianity that is ignored in Hegel's section on revelatory religion, on the other hand the fundamental achievement of revelatory religion could in principle be replicated in other religions. In fact Christianity, or any other religion, could exhibit all seven moments.

That seems generous enough. But this universal conception of "religion" should alert us to the fact that no religion is being presented strictly on its own terms. To the extent that Christianity is represented in the scheme it is incorporated into a mythos quite different from its own.

Hegel immediately adds, to be sure, that the diverse moments of the scheme must "also be regarded as a diversity of religion." In fact the historical development of religions is such that even if some feature of a "lower" religion remains present in a "higher," it will have receded into an "unessential" vestige. More likely it will disappear with the ascendancy of the higher. On the other hand, "where the lower is still dominant, but the higher is also present," this intimation of something higher will still be "devoid of self"; that is, it may already be an object of that religious *consciousness,* but it is not yet appropriated by the *self-consciousness* of that historical community (of its "actual spirit"). To bring out this point Hegel uses the example of the incarnation of God found in Oriental religions, claiming that it "has no truth, because its actual spirit is without this reconciliation"; that is, the religious community is not itself self-consciously reconciled with deity in the manner that the divine-become-human strictly implies, even though images and stories of divine humans may be a lively part of its lore (H 481–82; M 417–18; B 696–98). So there may be a strictly historical ground, in the developing self-consciousness of a religious community, for finding its dominant representations unique. But that is a far cry from its unique claims of divine favor, which are by definition irrelevant to the phenomenological reconstruction of "religion."

In that reconstruction the interest is in the movement from consciousness to self-consciousness, in the appropriation of what had been objectively "represented" or "placed-before" consciousness: "For the represented ceases to be represented and alien to the self's knowledge only when the self has brought it forth, and therefore perceives the determination of the object as its *own,* as well as perceiving itself in the object" (H 482; M 417; B 697). Selfhood, of course, only arises through mutual recognition. "Self" is in fact the name for a relationship, not for an independent subject; it is the relationship that confers selfhood on both parties. Selfhood can in this sense develop in some respects and not in others, depending on the measure of selfhood in the "other" in whom a self recognizes itself. One may, for instance, become a self-consciously finite self in relation to other such selves. But in Hegel's view the testimony of the world's religions implies the further possibility that this finite self may come to recognize itself as infinite. The religious pilgrimage is the progressive fulfillment of that possibility, the gradual dawning of mutual recognition between human and divine, finite and absolute spirit.

But enough of the skeleton; now for the meat of this dialectic, which is language.

i. Dumb Awe: Natural Religion

We have been told that language is the existence *(Dasein)* of self, or of spirit. To be sure, the two earlier contexts in which this assertion has been developed have cast it in a somewhat uncertain light. Language was said to play this extraordinary role with respect to culture in its state of self-alienation, and then with respect to the self-congratulatory fellowship of conscientious spirits. In both cases the self "is there" *only* in language, and this strange existence arises only when it is alienated from nature, from its ethical/ethnic identity, and from its own actual deed. It appeared to be a singularly disembodied existence. While these two alienated ways of being-there were necessary appearances of spirit, integral to the great historical circuit through which it had to pass in encompassing the fullness of its possibilities, these two appearances hardly seemed to warrant the general assertion that language is the *Dasein* of spirit, nor was there anything said previously in the *Phenomenology* that directly prepared us for this assertion. Nor was language assigned any such role in the philosophy of spirit that consummated the *Realphilosophie*. So far as Hegel's intellectual biography is concerned, the significance of language may have become apparent to him in the very process of writing the latter half of the *Phenomenology;* at least there is no documentary evidence to the contrary.

What is certain is that language comes to play a central role in the chapter on Religion. It seems in retrospect that the general significance attributed to language is implicit in the principle of mutual recognition. At least that seems now to be Hegel's assumption, for which he all too characteristically offers no arguments. Still, it can be plausibly maintained. Hegel had rejected the claim that the self is a metaphysically given, irreducible, subsistent entity, as in some traditional conceptions of the soul. We recall his critique of the correlative metaphysical notions of soul, world, and highest being in the systematic manuscript of 1804–5 (see Chapter 3). So how account for the undeniable experience of self, simply as a phenomenon? Hegel's answer seems to be that it takes form in the invisible and intangible medium of language, where meaning, intention, interrogation can arise and be communicated intersubjectively.

No doubt language has an "actual," even physiological basis, but what takes wing in this medium is no quasi-physical entity but an elusive and ephemeral locus of intentional activity, at once constituting a publicly shared sense of world and creating the resources for intimate interchange and even the most private inwardness. It is difficult to see how mutual recognition could occur without this resource of language, assuming that language is inherent in the capacity for symbolic communication and even for symbolic representation and understanding. It is notable that Hegel does not explicitly refer to language in the chapter on Self-Consciousness, where he first expounds the principle of recognition. But the linguistic capacity both to communicate and to conceive what is not palpably manifest seems necessary in order to recognize and so to constitute the elusive inwardness of self.

Now selfhood in just this sense is the root from which the more capacious inwardness of spirit grows. Hegelian *Geist,* to be sure, embraces material reality, together with everything in heaven and on earth. Earlier in this section, I emphasized the sense in which nature and history can be described as the *Dasein* of spirit, its concrete material existence. Language is the *Dasein* of spirit in the sense that precisely *within* its necessary material conditions there arises a self-activity that is not reducible to its material or biological basis. This self-activity is the mutual recognition in which the *self*-conscious existence of the mutually recognizing and recognized takes form. For now Hegel is suggesting that this mutual recognition is linguistic. In the earlier passages in which language was said to be the *Dasein* of spirit, this linguistically constituted existence was alienated from the "actual" conditions that supported it. In the dialectic of absolute spirit this alienation will be overcome, a process that begins under the rubric of religion. Here, too, the existence of spirit will emerge as a linguistic phenomenon, a type of selfhood that is both divine and human. Its full reconciliation with the actual must await the chapter on absolute knowledge, but religion, being an explicit affair of the spirit, is already ordered dialectically, from "lower" to "higher" moments, according to the presence and increasingly sophisticated role of language in the divine-human relation. This increasing role of language signals the development from consciousness of the divine to *self*-conscious identity of the divine and human. The organization of these religious moments in terms of language also distinguishes this schema from Hegel's earlier efforts, in the Jena manuscripts, to comprehend religion as an ascending series of forms.

So "natural religion," comprising the first three of the seven moments, can be characterized negatively by the absence of language as an integral feature of the divine-human relation. Successive moments of natural religion are "higher" to the extent that the preconditions of language become more apparent. The positive role of language comes into its own in the religion of art.

Of course the presence or absence of language is not the only factor that figures in the schema. Hegel is more resourceful than that! The three moments of natural religion, for instance, recapitulate the three moments of the chapter(s) on Consciousness: sense certainty, perception, and understanding. But selfhood was initially introduced in the chapter on Self-Consciousness. The reiteration of the schema of the chapter on Consciousness reinforces the point that natural religion unfolds strictly under the conditions of the A-series, where the object, in this case a divine object, appears to unself-conscious subjects. They are of course language-users in other respects, but they stand before the divine in dumb adoration.

There is no point in our rehearsing these three moments in detail; Hegel's own exposition is sketchy enough, just a few bold strokes. But we may pause a bit over the first, just because it brings out most clearly what it would mean for a religious moment to be devoid of any effective role for language, and so for self. Hegel uses the odd term, "Das Lichtwesen," for this moment, literally "The Light-Essence" or "The Light-Being." At the simplest level this essence signifies the light of the rising sun, gradually illuminating the entire visible world, bringing everything into sharp visual clarity, but itself formless and aimless, extending indeterminately into the heavenly sublime. But to the dialectical eye this appearance is far from simple; it contains the essential concept of religion, though still in an entirely latent manner.

> Spirit, as the *essence* which is *self-consciousness*—or the self-conscious essence which is all truth and knows all actuality to be itself—is at first merely *its concept,* in contrast to the reality which it gives itself in the movement of its consciousness; and in contrast to the day of this unfolding this concept is the night of its essence, the creative secret of its birth in contrast to the concrete existence of its moments as independent forms. (H 483; M 418; B 699)

The equation suggested is that the concept of absolute spirit is to its actual unfolding in the following moments as the darkness is to the light of the rising sun. This equation does not express merely a loose analogy, but the double-sided significance of this first moment of natural religion. The "creative secret" of the light is the darkness from which it arises. Here light signifies all being, which it illuminates without discrimination, darkness the "simple negative" that is the abyss from which and into which everything proceeds (H 484; M 419; B 700).

Now this endless play of light and darkness is the objective correlate of the consciousness that beholds it in a manner analogous to simple sense-certainty, unaware of the negative depth of its own concept, which contains its ultimate truth as self-conscious spirit. Yet just because spirit is the truth of both sides of this subject-object correlation, the consciousness that sees this universal light beholds there the dawning of the life of spirit that it does not yet recognize as its own. So this beholding is already more than simple sense-certainty, which sees only the exteriority that presents itself. Absolute spirit "perceives itself in the form of *being,* though not in the form of spiritless *being* filled with the accidental determinations of sensation that belong to sense certainty; rather it is being that is filled with spirit" (H 483; M 419; B 699).

The conscious subject is not yet aware that it itself is spirit; Hegel goes on to compare it with the servile consciousness of the master-slave relation, standing in abject awe of its lord. But in both cases the principle holds: only spirit can recognize spirit. The very recognition that the light is spiritual, divine, attests to the spirituality of the one who recognizes. This truth, however, is hidden from the conscious subject; as the mirror reflex of the rising sun, this consciousness likewise leaves the depths of its truth in the darkness from which it proceeds. Yet consciousness like its object is "in truth the *self;* and spirit therefore presses on to know itself in the form of self" (H 484; M 420; B 701).

This spiritual self-knowledge, however, is not achieved within the limits of the religion of nature; here spirit appears only in the form of natural objects. The self-reflexive "concept" of spirit remains shrouded in darkness. In the second moment, "Plant and Animal," the indeterminate unity of light gives way to diverse forms existing side by side, first innocently ("flower religion"—San Francisco, 1967) and then in conflict as the totem animals of warring Volksgeister (e.g., panthers and eagles). The third moment, "The Craftsman," is transitional; here the finite spirit does not behold absolute spirit in the natural environment as such, but fashions the objects of its worship with its own hands. Nature supplies merely his materials, which the craftsman shapes into solid forms never beheld in nature as such, first geometrical solids, pyramids and obelisks, then highly stylized images of organic forms or fantastic composites like the sphinx. Of course the craftsman does not yet recognize himself as spirit in these works he has made.

The religions of nature are dumb. In the first two moments consciousness confronts the divine as an exterior surface the spiritual interiority of which is left in darkness, because it cannot find utterance. It is without language. This silent, dark abyss, however, provides a depth-dimension to the dialectic of religion generally, an unutterable depth that will be recalled at later moments. Still, the dominant movement of this dialectic is toward the external expression of this inwardness, in language. The craftsman, for instance, beginning to act like an artist, deliberately stylizes the animal form in his work, asserting his own productive power over the natural shape and vitality of the animal and knowing it "as *his* work," invested with "the hieroglyph of another meaning, of a thought." This thought, to be sure, still remains unuttered: "The work still lacks the form and concrete being-there in which the self exists as self—it still fails in its own self to declare that it contains within itself an inner meaning, it lacks language, the element in which the sense that fills it is present" (H 488; M 423; B 706). The center of gravity is nevertheless already shifting away from the tacit, merely latent presence of spirit in nature to its self-conscious appearance in art.

This transition is epitomized when the craftsman fashions the half-human, half-animal figure of the sphinx, which is also, in legend, the propounder of the famous riddle. Speech, properly, is "the outer being-there that is in its own self inward." But the riddle is ambiguous in this respect. This crafty form of speech, designed to trap the unwary (even if, like Oedipus, he seems to give the right answer), suggests to Hegel an inwardness still separated from its outward aspect.

> The craftsman therefore unites both in a confusion of the natural and the self-conscious shape, and this ambiguous creature that ' is a riddle to itself, the conscious contending with the nonconscious, the simple inner with the multiform outer, the darkness of thought paired with the clarity of utterance, break into the speech of a deep but scarcely intelligible wisdom. (H 489; M 423–24; B 707)

The monster is clearly a borderline case! Still it does speak, and thereby breaks the silence of nature. In such a work the craftsman becomes self-conscious, confronting "an equally self-conscious, self-expressive interiority" (H 489; M 424; B 707). Spirit has met spirit, for the craftsman has become an artist, able to recognize himself in his work.

ii. The Religious Spirit Finds Its Voice in Art

"Spirit is *artist*" (H 489; M 424; B 708). Indeed, in the *Realphilosophie,* the systematic work roughly contemporaneous with the *Phenomenology,* art is presented as one of the three forms of absolute Geist: spirit expressed in the mode of *Anschauung,* as religion in the mode of *Vorstellung* and philosophical science in the mode of *Begriff* (see Chapter 3). It is an oddity of the *Phenomenology* that art is given no independent treatment in its pages. This oddity cannot be accounted for by the difference between phenomenological and strictly systematic analysis, though that difference would call for another sort of treatment in all three cases. Perhaps the philosopher's hand grew weary. To be sure, in earlier Jena manuscripts Hegel always treated art and religion in close conjunction. In *Glauben und Wissen* (1802) he had even treated religion as a mode of art (see Chapter 3), and in his later lectures on Aesthetics the subject is given a markedly religious interpretation. But in the *Phenomenology* we hear only of the religion of art, and our interest is restricted, as Hegel tells us at the outset of that section, to artistic developments historically located in the ethical world. So classical Greek forms of art provide the models. Only a "free people" will give its religious life an essentially artistic character, and in art-religion will find "consciousness of its absolute essence." Here ethical custom *(Sitte)* "constitutes the substance of all, the actuality and concrete existence of which everyone knows to be his own will and deed" (H 490; M 424–25; B 709). For such a people religion, too, will be inseparable from its own will and deed, not dominated by dumb nature but artful, a human work.

A few years before, Hegel had been prepared virtually to identify the God of such a Volk with that Volk's own spirit objectified (see Chapter 3). We have seen how he struggled with that equation and eventually backed away from it, at least in its strongest form. In the structure of the *Phenomenology,* with its distinction between actual spirit and the religious spirit, the Volksgeist clearly occupies the region of actual spirit. So how is it related to a people's strictly religious recognition of absolute spirit? For a free ethical Volk, to be sure, religion will express its own "will and deed."

> But the religion of the ethical spirit is its elevation over its actuality, the withdrawal *out of its truth* into the pure *knowledge of itself.* Since the ethical people lives in immediate unity with substance and lacks the principle of the individuality of self-consciousness, so its religion first proceeds toward its fulfillment in its *separation* from this people's *real life* [Bestehen]. (H 490–91; M 425; B 709–10)

A primary feature of this religious distancing is that its gods and goddesses will appear in individuated form, at odds with the collectivity of its ethical life. We have seen how the ethical Volk rested content in the stable equilibrium of its customs, its prescribed rights and duties, its social class organization, so that the individual member "had not yet grasped the boundless thought of his free self" (H 491; M 425; B 710). Individuality, as we have also seen, came to the ethical Volk only in the traumatic ordeal of its dissolution, which Hegel also recalls in introducing art-religion. When its trust in the ethical substance is broken, this spirit "mourns over the loss of its world and now brings forth its essence, elevated above the actual world, out of the purity of self." "In such an epoch," Hegel goes on to say, "absolute art steps forth" (H 491–92; M 426; B 711). But before this final apotheosis of the self-conscious individual in art, the more "instinctive working" of the artistic spirit already anticipates this discovery of the individual in its presentation of the gods and goddesses. Art-religion, though a product of the ethical Volksgeist, is not merely a rendering of its actual life, but its transfiguration into individuated divinity, in which finally, in the trauma of historical catastrophe, the Volk comes to recognize itself. Ethical substance becomes subject, "ethical spirit is resurrected as a form liberated from nature and from its immediate existence" (H 492; M 426; B 712). This pure form of self-consciousness, preserved in the work of art itself, will be the permanent legacy of the ethical Volk to the life of the religious spirit generally.

The first unambiguous work of art-religion is the statue of the god or goddess, an idealized human figure that Hegel always considered to be a superb achievement, perfect of its kind. In his later lectures on aesthetics he treats it as the classic work par excellence. Here absolute spirit has appeared in perfect human shape, free of the monstrous ambiguity of the sphinx. The beast has been suppressed; nature itself has been reduced to the supplier of the material medium, the stone, transformed into the anthropomorphic figure. Hegel handsomely suggests that the artistic labor of bringing this form out of the natural state of the stone recapitulates the process by which the old natural deities have undergone their metamorphosis into the Olympians.

> The *essence* of the god . . . is the unity of the universal existence of nature and of self-conscious spirit, which in its actuality appears opposed to the natural. . . . But nature is in this unity the element reflected into spirit, which is transfigured by thought and united with self-conscious life. The form of the gods has therefore the natural element within it as something transcended [*ein aufgehobnes*], as a dark recollection.

Even as the stone is preserved but transformed in the statue, so the primal, savage deities of nature are tamed and consigned to the margins of the new, becalmed world of the spirit. Begotten of the original play of light and darkness, these deified natural powers, "Sky, Earth, Ocean, the Sun, the blind Typhonic fire of earth, and so forth, are supplanted by forms that still possess only the dimly recalled hints of these Titans, and are no longer natural beings but the clear ethical spirits of self-conscious peoples" (H 494; M 428; B 714–15). That is the serene figure of the god or goddess, at rest in stone, in which the Volksgeist presents itself to the ethical Volk, like a city shining in the morning sunlight after a stormy night.

The statue, however, has only the anthropomorphic external shape of self-consciousness, without its interiority: it does not speak. The god in stone lacks the "higher element" of "*language:* a being-there that is immediate self-conscious existence," the inwardness that can exteriorize itself (H 496; M 430; B 716). This deficiency is somewhat remedied by two forms of divine utterance that are not directly associated with the statue as such: the oracle and the eternal law. The oracle is contingent, a happening like a chance event of nature, reflecting the dual nature of the god as a being "of nature as well as of spirit" (H 496; M 430; B 717). Hegel compares it to the throw of the dice or the drawing of lots or the warnings of the Socratic daemon (H 497–98; M 431–32; B 719), settling particular matters that have to be decided without general ethical criteria. On the other hand, what Sophocles, whom

Hegel quotes, calls "the certain and unwritten law of the gods, a law which lives eternally, and of which no one knows whence it appeared," is also language of the gods, upon which the ethical world is founded (H 497; M 431; B 718). Here the god does not speak episodically, with that touch of whimsy for which the oracles are famous. The law always has been spoken primordially; the silent statue stands serene in the fullness of one who has spoken definitively and has nothing to add.

Somewhat surprisingly, given the obvious dialectical possibilities of this pairing of the particular and the universal, Hegel no sooner introduces these two forms of divine speech than he drops them from discussion. He indicates that the oracle is a rather primitive way to make decisions, rightly superseded by the "higher" method of rational deliberation. If the oracle is somewhat unsettling and alien, the law, on which the rocklike assurance of the community rests, had its significance in the community-formation of the ethical world.

The form of language presented as though it were of far greater religious significance is the hymn. This shared, musical speech is discussed in our text in a way that highlights several important features of religious language. The hymn is of course intoned by the god's devotees, in contrast to the silence of the statue to which the hymn is offered. But the beautiful individuality of the god and the collective devotion of the community make up a single religious spirit. However the community may be otherwise occupied and identified, in this act it is inspired by the god, with whom it is thereby at one, and in this oneness it is forged into a single soul. For language is both individual and collective. Indeed, a "*single* self-consciousness . . . is there" *(da ist)* only in its speech. But language is at the same time "a universal contagion," in which those who share it also become concretely present as a distinct *Dasein:* "the complete isolation of the being-for-itself of the many selves is at the same time their fluidity and universally shared unity; language is the soul existing as soul" (H 496; M 430; B 717).

The linguistically constituted corporate self-consciousness of the devotees is at the same time the extended self-consciousness of the god. Existing as a "thing" of stone, the god "who has language as an element of his form is in himself the ensouled work of art." The existence of the god, abiding in himself, requires this unison expression of the community's devotion for his ensoulment. This collective self-consciousness, human and divine, "thus abiding in its essence with itself, is *pure thought* or the devotion the *inwardness* of which has at the same time its *being-there* in the hymn."

This exterior *Dasein* of the inward is not only, in general, the nature of language, but is also the very concept of spirit. That is why language is given such prominence in Hegel's exposition of the religious spirit. The hymn provides a particularly simple and transparent instance of this central role of language. It is the living unity of the one and the many, the inner and the outer, the god and the community. The hymn "retains the singleness of self-consciousness within it, and this singleness is at the same time heard there as the universal; the devotion kindled in all is the spiritual current which in the manifold presence of self-consciousness is conscious of its act as the same *act* of all and as *simple being*" (H 496; M 430; B 717). Like all works of language the hymn is a medium of thought, admittedly of rather modest value in that respect, and soon to be surpassed by other forms of language. Yet it is presented as the significant starting-point for a development of language that will finally give rise to the cognitive concept. It is already a linguistic form that joins all, spirit's "pure inwardness as well as the being-for-others and the being-for-itself of individuals," in one vocalized breath *(spiritus),* as a single religious identity.

This fundamental achievement of spirit in the hymn, furthermore, is the basis for the next significant development, which Hegel calls the cultus, the entire ritual practice of the community in its celebration of the life of the god. In the cultus, the god will also enter the common life of the celebrants. The cultus will in fact bring together the two achievements of art-religion that we have discussed: the appearance of the god in statue as object of consciousness and the stirring of collective self-consciousness "in the current of hymnodic song." The statue is an enduring thing at rest, the accented and inflected language of the hymn is a movement whose being-there constantly disappears "like time, which is no sooner there than it is immediately there no longer." Now these two "sides" of divinity, "the divine form *in motion* in the pure sensitive element of self-consciousness and *at rest* in the element of thingness," begin to converge, so that "there comes into existence the unity of both which is the concept of their common essence." This converging movement, Hegel says, "constitutes the cultus." The cultus comprises both sides of this apparent polarity between one and many, outer and inner, divine and human, rest and motion, and recovers the essential unity that had all the while been the hidden truth of both poles.

> In the cultus the self gives itself the consciousness of the descent of divine being to the self out of its remoteness Beyond [*Jenseitig-*

keit], and divine being, which previously was not actual and was merely objective, obtains thereby the genuine actuality of self-consciousness. (H 498–99; M 432; B 720)

Hegel immediately suggests that this convergence was already implicit in the collective soul constituted by the hymn. But the cultus gives the union with the god a perduring life in a steady cycle of ritual acts, invocations, purifications, sacrifices, hymns, and celebrations.

The phenomenon of the cultus spans the transition from the "abstract" to the "living" work of art. The cultus remains "abstract" in all its works insofar as the divine-human unity is not fully realized in its own present life: insofar, for instance, as it proceeds upon a "path of works, punishments and rewards" in external fashion, to prepare itself for a purified existence "in the dwellings and the community of blessedness" (H 499; M 433; B 720–21). The god with whom it seeks union remains at a distance, propitiated by sacrifice. But suppose that the god also sacrifices his independent divine substance to be present in the sacrificial animals or the grain and wine offerings, "the *living* Ceres and Bacchus *themselves*," ritually offered to the gods but actually consumed by the human celebrants (H 500; M 434; B 722). Then the divine is incorporated, ingested, into the life of the community. To the extent that the blessed life, indeed the divine itself, is fully immanent in the present existence of the cultus, the cultus has become the living work of art. The god or goddess dwells in human beings and their works.

The dwellings and halls of the gods are for the use of human beings, the treasures preserved in them are theirs in case of need; the glory enjoyed by the god in his adornment is the glory of the artistically cultivated and great-souled people. . . . The people receives . . . a return for its gifts from the grateful god and the proof of his favor, in which it was bound together with him in its labor, not in hope and later actuality, but it has immediately in its witness to his glory and in the presentation of its gifts the enjoyment of its own riches and adornment. (H 501–2; M 435; B 724)

Here indeed the god of the Volk is the Volk's own spirit. In the living work of art the god dwells harmoniously in the national cultus and culture.

It must immediately be said that there is a certain superficiality in this harmonization achieved in the life of the cultus. There is, for instance, no awareness of radical evil or, more generally, of the psychological depths or the spiritual heights in this union of the human and the divine. It is a middling sort of union, but it anticipates a more capacious one and already achieves a significant advance in self-consciousness along that road. The living work, indeed, is the "self-conscious" moment of the religion of art, with a characteristic loss of otherness.

The immanent god of the cultus no longer manifests the "simplicity" and "depth" of the austere play of light and darkness in the primordial religion of nature. But Hegel suggestively reintroduces the motif of the rising and setting sun in interpreting the living work of art. The emergence of self-consciousness is the going down of the sun in its sheer objectivity as the object of religious consciousness. Yet it continues to express itself in two parallel ways, in relation to self-conscious religion. In the first place, in the sunset of "its pure essentiality" it becomes "an objective force of nature" that supports the organic existence of "the self by which it is consumed." Nature provides food and drink for god-bearing life.

> The still essence of self-less nature achieves in its fruits the stage in which it offers itself, prepared and digested, to self-bearing life; in its usefulness as food and drink it reaches its highest perfection; for it is therein the possibility of a higher existence, and is in touch with spiritual being-there. (H 503; M 436–37; B 726)

The all-engendering light has become the earth-spirit that nourishes and energizes self-conscious existence. Nature, perfected by spirit, is directly enjoyed.

> In this enjoyment is thus disclosed what that rising light-essence really is: enjoyment is its mysterium. For the mystical is not concealment of a secret or ignorance. It rather consists in the self knowing itself to be One with that essential being, which is thus revealed. (H 503; M 437; B 726–27)

We recall how desiring and consuming, the basis of all life, was shown in the chapter on Self-Consciousness to be the basis of selfhood as well—contrary to the assumption of the empiricist that perception lay at the foundation of consciousness. In fact, Hegel proposed sending the empiricist for schooling in the Eleusinian mysteries to learn that for living creatures the mere perception of what is placed before them is quite incidental to their desire for its consumption. Now the cultus of art-religion shows itself well schooled in these mysteries of Ceres and Bacchus. Its mysticism consists in uniting itself with the fruits of the earth in the most direct and unsublimated fashion. Such a consumable thing has "not only the existence that can be seen, felt, smelled and tasted, but is also object of desire, and through its actual enjoyment becomes one with the self and thereby completely disclosed and revealed to it" (H 503–4; M 437; B 727). What is merely revealed to reason or to the heart, Hegel goes on to say, never has the "actual certainty of immediate existence" enjoyed in this gastronomic consummation of the mysterium. In its engendering of the life cycle, which is also the food-chain, the sun is revealed to the self-conscious beneficiary in its bountiful truth.

But it also inspires the cultus of eaters and drinkers who enjoy its fruits. They partake of its own nature, in a manner resembling the diffusion of the rising sun through the world. Hegel obviously has in mind the Bacchantes, self-conscious beings who represent "the transparent impulse" of "the many-named light-essence of the dawn and its tumultuous life." Having offered the cultists its fruits, this life force now "roves about as a crowd of frenzied women, the untamed revel of nature in self-conscious form" (H 504; M 437–38; B 727). The Bacchantes furnish an example of the collective enthusiasm that expresses the life force of nature itself, which moves among them and binds them into a single dancing organism. Again we recall from the chapter on Self-Consciousness that "life" signifies a kind of animal vitality, reacting immediately in desire and enjoyment, without the hesitations of reflection. Such direct desire and enjoyment are precisely what unhappy consciousness cannot express, receiving even its food and drink sacramentally, as an "alien gift" from a higher being. But the living work of art achieves a direct celebration of life, its Dionysian god fully present in its eating and drinking and in its ecstatic dance. Dionysius is the light-essence, the all-permeating earth-spirit, incarnate in his dancing devotees. That ecstasy is at once the total *unio mystica* of self with nature and a crucial moment in the mystical ascent to absolute spirit. "The true" itself, after all, according to a famous remark in the Preface, is "the Bacchanalian revel, in which not a member is not drunk" (H 39;

M 27; B 105). But it is also the "transparent and simple rest" of recollection, of inner knowledge *(Erinnerung)*, which is yet to come.

Though such as the Bacchantes express the life force "in self-conscious form," they are not in their ecstasy self-conscious. In fact they are self-conscious beings forgetful of self. "Life," according to the chapter on Self-Consciousness, is the foundation of selfhood but not yet its achievement. The living work of art is of course no longer a merely potential self, like the intelligent predator of that earlier chapter. It is a self that achieves self-forgetful reunion with nature, and as such it recapitulates that earlier dialectic at a higher level. The Geist that discloses itself in the Bacchanalian revel

> is only the *immediate* spirit, the spirit of nature. Its self-conscious life is therefore only the mysterium of bread and wine, of Ceres and Bacchus, not that of the other, properly higher gods, whose individuality inherently includes self-consciousness as such as an essential moment. So spirit has not yet sacrificed itself . . . as *self-conscious* spirit, and the mysterium of bread and wine is not yet the mysterium of flesh and blood. (H 504; M 438; B 728)

Here Hegel anticipates the crucial point of "revelatory religion," where the incarnation of the god also entails sacrifice: the sacrifice, however, not only of the fruits of the earth but of self-conscious flesh and blood, into which those fruits of the earth are sacramentally transfigured. The higher mysterium will occur when even this sacrifice is directly "enjoyed" in the bread and wine, finite and infinite united in the consumed and consummating union of nature and spirit. But that sacrifice is possible only for an incarnation of the spirit "that *essentially* takes on the human form" (H 505; M 438; B 728); that is, that entails self-consciousness in its very nature.

Still, the cultus of living art "lays the foundation for this revelation" of incarnate spirit, though it "lays its moments out separately." The cultus involves not only the collective Bacchantic revel, but also an individuated expression, the god-bearing warrior-athlete celebrated in "the festival that human being holds in his own honor." This pairing of Bacchantes and Olympic hero as living works parallels that of the chanting chorus and the statue in the "abstract" work of art, but now the sedate hymn to the god is intensified into the wild dance of the god-possessed, and the statue of the god becomes living and mobile: "an ensouled, living work of art that matches strength with his beauty, and on whom is bestowed, as the prize for his might, the adornment with which the statue was honored, and the glory of being, in place of the god in stone, the highest bodily expression among his people of their essence" (H 505; M 438; B 728–29). The crowned warrior-athlete is the embodied spirit of the Volk, its living god, the incarnation of the Volksgeist as the Bacchantes are the incarnation of the *Erdgeist*. Together they offer an intimation of the higher incarnation to come.

But the living work of art is deficient in a crucial aspect. Like sheer animal vitality as such, this dual incarnation into "life" lacks any significant component of language. Again, the conditions for speech are present, but divided between the two living works: "The stupor of consciousness and its wild stammering" among the revelers "must be taken up into the clear being-there" of the champion's corporeal beauty, and his "spiritless clarity" into their "inwardness." The Bacchic enthusiasts are all ecstatic inwardness impervious to outward appearances, the champion all magnificent surface. A synthesis is clearly in the making! "The perfect element in which inwardness is just as external as externality is inward is again language; but neither that of the oracle, wholly fortuitous and particular in content, nor the deep-felt hymn in praise merely of a particular god, nor the contentless stammer of Bacchic raving" (H 505; M 439; B 729).

If religious self-consciousness is to move beyond the plateau of the "living" work, the embodiment of *Erdgeist* and Volksgeist, it must find expression in a new use of language, lucid in form and of universal content. This new speech will still be artful, a human shaping of a natural medium, but it will assume a form no longer limited ultimately either by natural models or by the specific interests and biases of the Volk. Hegel suggests that the "beautiful warrior" of the folk festival already paradoxically transcends these limits, at least implicitly: Just in its exteriorization into his "complete corporeality," the particular Volk contemplates "the universality of its human existence" (H 506; M 439; B 729–30). But this universal humanity now takes on spiritual form by being rendered in a poetry that makes the transcendence of the Volk explicit. Here the various Volksgeister coalesce into a common Geist, "into a single pantheon, the element and habitation of which is language" (H 506; M 439; B 731). This poetic language, of which the epic narrative provides the first instance, is what Hegel calls "the spiritual work of art."

This use of the epic is clearly modeled on the *Iliad,* the theme of which already conveniently involves the mobilizing of a number of diverse peoples in a grand common enterprise. But in the epic narrative the uniting of diverse national Volksgeister finds a poetic form that fully reflects this universalizing movement. Not only diverse peoples, but also gods and goddesses and the natural world all mingle in complex interaction within the single frame of the poetic narrative. The divine, the natural, the human appear, of course, only as "re-presented" in language, placed before the hearer or reader not in their reality but in a phonetic code: *vor-gestellt. Vorstellung,* Hegel's own codeword for religious expression generally, is thus introduced as the artful work of language capable of rendering "the universal content, at least as regards the *completeness* of the world, though not, to be sure, as regards *universality* of *thought.*" The epic does not take the form of concept *(Begriff),* but of imaginative representation. Here human and divine figures and natural phenomena are represented in their distinct particularity, but are united by their interaction within the inclusive texture of the poetic narrative. This inclusive narrative is spun from the single point of view of the singer who chants the tale: "The *singer* is the individual and actual subject of this world, out of whom it is engendered and borne. His pathos is not the stupefying force of nature but Mnemosyne, the calling to mind and interiorization, the recollection of what was once directly present [*die Erinnerung des vorhin unmittelbaren Wesens*]" (H 507; M 441; B 732).

In this passage Hegel introduces a term crucial to the remainder of the text: *Erinnerung,* rendered "recollection," but also bearing the literal sense it is given in this passage of the interiorization of what had existed in external reality. It is a term Hegel will use, following Plato, for the conceptual knowledge that completes this interiorization. In fact, the transition from *Vorstellung* to *Begriff* can be characterized as the inner re-collection of what has first been placed-before consciousness imaginatively. So it is worth noticing that this imaginative placing-before in epic narrative is already an inner re-collection of what may presumptively have been presented in reality (whether it actually did occur in reality is irrelevant to this crucial formal distinction). From the putative "presentation" in external reality to the imaginative "re-presentation" in narrative language the movement into inwardness has already begun to occur, which will be completed in conceptual knowledge. In the epic representation things still unfold in temporal sequence and distributed in the narrative space created by the singer. But this representational form is nevertheless the starting-point for a continuous development *within language* that will issue in conceptual knowledge.

The distinction between *Vorstellung* and *Begriff* is illustrated in the discussion of the epic that follows in the text. First Hegel carefully distinguishes between the way "the relation of the divine to the human" is placed-before consciousness in the epic and the way that relation is ecstatically experienced in the cultus. The cultic experience of being possessed by the god does not occur among hearers or readers of the epic. Instead, in his narrating the singer places the interactions between the immortal divinities and human mortals objectively before the consciousness of his audience. *Action* is what is rendered in narrative. But incongruities begin to appear when the relations of mortals and immortals are narrated as specific actions. The shifting course of the battle before Troy, for instance, is represented as the result of actions among the warriors on both sides. But it is also said to be determined by the actions of the gods who have chosen up sides because of past gifts and offenses.

> Thus one and the same thing has been done both by the gods and by the human beings. The earnestness of these divine powers is a laughable superfluity, since they are nothing in fact but the exertion and labor of the individuality that performs the action—and the exertion and labor of this individuality is just as useless an effort, since it is rather the divine powers who control everything. (H 508; M 441–42; B 734)

Hegel suggests that this incongruity, that disturbs every literal-minded modern reader of the epic, is partly due to the fact that the gods are themselves represented as anthropomorphic individualities (as they must be in order to function as characters in the story), though they are at the same time understood to be universal powers. They therefore seem both to transcend the form of existence presented by the moral antagonists and yet to face off against them on the same plane.

This incongruity also creates odd conflicts within the divine nature itself, as when the gods do battle against one another in "comic self-forgetfulness of their eternal nature" (H 509; M 442; B 735). As a result, Hegel suggests, this forgotten universality is relegated to "the irrational void of Necessity," to the fate which hovers over "this entire world of representation," over gods and humans alike (H 510; M 443; B 735). From this point of view fate seems to arise in the epic as a solution to a problem created by the exigencies of narrative form, which require even gods to appear as individual agents capable of action in the story. Unlike this fate that *Vorstellung* must posit beyond the narrated world proper to it, the necessity of philosophical *Begriff* is of course inherent.

Tragic drama, a "higher" form of language than the epic, also falls short of the philosophical *Begriff* in this respect, but it does already resolve some of the incongruities in epic representation. Speech, which had been concentrated entirely in the continuous narrative of the singer, is now distributed among the actors on the stage, where it enters more directly into the content of the drama. Here language does not merely narrate action, but expresses the inwardness of the characters themselves. Their speech is not that of everyday life, in which the actors might chat offstage. Hegel even suggests that this elevated speech, the high style of tragedy, follows the nature of the concept, where universal and particular are united.

This is not to say that we have already passed beyond the limits of *Vorstellung*. In the drama, if anything, the action of definite human and divine characters is placed-before the audience with maximum vividness. Still, in their speech the characters give utterance to universal powers that constitute their "character" in an ethical sense, and not merely to their personal quirks and accidental circumstances. Tragic drama is not a slice of everyday life. What its characters "utter" or literally "exteriorize" *(äussern)* is not merely "the external" *(das Äussere)*, but "their inner essence." They take their stand on universal ethical grounds, "they prove the rightness of their actions, and the pathos to which they belong . . . is thoughtfully asserted in its universal individuality" (H 611; M 444; B 737). Hegel recalls the analysis of tragedy already offered in the section on ethical action, according to which tragedy is a conflict of two rights, each protagonist (e.g., Antigone and Creon) expressing one universal order (divine law, human law) in her or his action, and thereby violating the other order, with calamitous results all around. Now, in its religion the ethical world "expresses itself to its consciousness in its purer form and simpler embodiment." Its gods no longer have the arbitrary individuality they exhibit in the epic, but appear as properly universal powers that are only superficially anthropomorphic (H 512–13; M 445–46; B 739).

Illustrating from both classical Greek and Shakespearean tragedy this concept of tragedy as the collision of such universal powers, Hegel goes on to argue that in the deep structure of tragedy these universal powers are themselves dethroned and crushed under the absolute negativity represented either as fate or as Zeus, who has been elevated beyond the pantheon to all-embracing unity and simplicity. Offstage, dimly comprehended by the protagonists under the aspect of one or another power, Zeus or fate is the negativity in which all sides of the tragic action come to rest, and this negativity "completes the depopulation of heaven," the fading out of those gods and goddesses who had populated the lively but superficial world of epic *Vorstellung*.

> The expulsion of such representations without essence, which was demanded by the philosophers of antiquity, thus already begins in tragedy generally, through the fact that the distribution of substance is dominated by the concept, so that individuality is of the essential sort and its qualities are absolute characters. The self-consciousness represented in tragedy therefore knows and recognizes only a single supreme power. (H 516; M 449; B 743–44)

This first decisive influence of the concept, however, which anticipates philosophical insight, contributes to the tragic vision in two quite different ways: On the one hand, it leads each of the conflicting protagonists to universalize his or her own standpoint, as if it alone provided the ultimate ethical ground of action. "The self-consciousness represented in tragedy [i.e., a protagonist in the drama] recognizes only a single supreme power," on which, for instance, an Antigone grounds the claims of family loyalty, a Creon, the authority of the state. On the other hand, the tragic vision that informs the drama as a whole recognizes, precisely in this conflict of absolutes, the universal negativity of Zeus or of fate into which all such polarities, even that between good and evil, ultimately dissolve. The particularized self-consciousness of the characters on the stage cannot recognize this universal negativity, and thus cannot recognize themselves in reflexive relation to it, and so they perish. But the universal self-consciousness, the bearer of the tragic vision itself, "is in fact the negative force, the unity of Zeus, the *substantial* essence and the *abstract* necessity; it is the spiritual unity into which everything returns" (H 517; M 449–50; B 744). For the protagonists, each of whom invests it in his or her own point of view, the protophilosophical *Begriff* simply makes the conflict irreconcilable. But from the point of view of the drama as a whole, the *Begriff* discloses the universal negativity in which all the protagonists are consumed.

There is of course one other significant element in the tragedy: the audience that beholds this inescapable catastrophe. Hegel suggests that the common folk who see and hear the action are represented on the stage by the chorus. Without deep insight into its tragic necessity and without participating in its awful negativity, the chorus simply expresses its terror before such forces and its pity for the living individuals like themselves who are destroyed by these forces. To this marginal role Hegel relegates the catharsis of terror and pity that Aristotle had considered the essence of tragedy (H 511–12, 517; M 444–45, 450; B 737–39, 744–45). There is no comfort for the beholders, or for the chorus that speaks for them, in the high style of tragedy. They must seek a word of cheer from another quarter, and in another idiom.

iii. The Comic Dénouement of Art-Religion and Its Aufhebung in Revelatory Religion

Before we spread this word of cheer, let us pause to get our bearings. The chapter on Religion belongs as a whole to what I have called the A-series, dominated by the subject-object duality of consciousness. But the religion of art, as the second moment in the dialectic of religion, constitutes a temporary excursion into the structure of the B-series, dominated by self-consciousness. In previous moments determined by the B-series, the ascendancy of self-consciousness has invariably reached an extreme in which objective otherness is altogether lost. So it is with the religion of art. The utter loss of objective structure occurs in this case in the transition from tragic drama to the low style of comic theater. That is good news for the plebeian audience, which has been frightened out of its wits by the relentless negativity of objective forces exhibited in tragedy.

Hegel, showing a dash of theatrical flair himself, epitomizes this transition from tragedy to comedy by an actor's removal of his tragic mask, to show his audience of groundlings that he is not a god or a hero after all, but just an ordinary fellow like themselves. What a relief! No tragic hero buffeted by inscrutable powers, no god personifying an awful negativity; he is just a hired artist who in ordinary life complains about his wages, quarrels with his spouse, and finds surcease from such everyday trials in his cups, as all commonplace mortals do. Gods and heroes were nothing but the masks he wore, and when with a wink at the audience he drops his mask the gods and heroes fall as well, doubtless to a rousing round of applause. In this ironical sense the ordinary fellow, an "actual self-consciousness," whether on the stage or in the audience, "shows himself to be the fate of the gods" (H 517; M 450; B 745). His own utterly happenstance appearance on the scene is, indeed, the "fate" of supposedly omnipotent necessity itself, whether that of fate or of Zeus. Ethical substance dissolves into this same "fate."

> The pretensions of universal essentiality are exposed in the self; it shows itself to be entangled in an actual life, and lets the mask fall just because it wants to be something in its own right. The self, stepping forth here in its significance as something actual, plays with the mask that it once put on to play its part, —but from this illusory role it just as quickly differentiates itself in its own nakedness and ordinariness, which it shows to be indistinguishable from the real self of actor and spectator alike. (H 518; M 450; B 745)

The comic spirit, earthy, irreverent, and plebeian, has literally come on the stage to replace the fateful terrors and solemnity of tragedy. Playing with its mask, it demystifies the entire region of the sacred. It consumes the bread and wine for its own unsanctified pleasure, it parodies the high style with absurd effect, it claims for "*Demos*, the general mass," all political authority, it lampoons the highfalutin ideas of the wise as nothing but clouds, and it toys with them as mere opinions, such as any honest citizen is entitled to (H 518–20; M 450–52; B 746–48).

The comic spirit is concentrated without remainder into the demystified self. Whatever has been presented as possessing "the form of essentiality over against it" is "dissolved into its thinking, its existence and act"—dissolved, indeed, in laughter. It seems a uniquely happy moment, in which the self finds complete repose and well-being in its own certainty of itself; that is, in "complete loss of fear and loss of essence in anything alien" (H 520; M 452–53; B 748–49). Here substance has become subject in the most radical and frivolous sense: Capering subject has simply replaced substance, reducing it to a predicate of itself.

> The proposition that expresses this frivolity runs thus: *the self is the absolute being* [*Wesen*]; essential being, the substance of which the self had been mere accidentality, has sunk down to being the predicate, and in *this self-consciousness,* over against

which nothing appears in the form of essence, spirit has lost its *consciousness.* (H 521; M 453; B 750)

In this cocky, comic self-consciousness that arrogates absolute being to itself the structure of the B-series asserts itself in its most extreme form, and Hegel goes on to remark that with this proposition spirit reverts to its "nonreligious, actual" form; that is, to a type of spirit that had been treated in the preceding chapter, in fact to a particular moment in the historical dialectic of actual spirit: to legal status. There, we recall, the ethical/ethnic worlds of the various Volksgeister had been pulverized into a vast aggregate of merely legal "persons." It is just such "persons" who appear, grinning amiably, from behind the masks of high tragedy's dramatis personae, and now implicitly claim to be the reality of which all spiritual substance is the illusory shadow. Welcome to the desacralized world of lighthearted nonentities!

There is a splendidly comic scene in Fielding's *Tom Jones,* in which a voluptuous older woman who has taken lusty young Tom to bed learns that her new lover is her son. The shrug and grimace with which she greets this intelligence are all that are left of the Oedipal agonies of high tragedy. It is paradoxical that the penultimate moment in the religious ascent to absolute spirit should entail this total collapse of the sacred order, in which the "eternal law" of the gods can be so egregiously flouted. But we are reminded that the religion of art "belongs to the ethical spirit, of which we earlier witnessed the downfall into legal status; that is, into the proposition: *the self as such, the abstract person is absolute being*" (H 522; M 454; B 751). This portentous claim, which surely no comedian ever actually uttered, seems to Hegel to epitomize all that is in fact said in the low style of this new language of comedy. Here the linguistic progress of the religious self-consciousness has run full course: The sacred powers that had expressed themselves in more elevated language take their exit amid universal laughter. This comic *Götterdämmerung,* too, is a moment through which the religious spirit must pass, a purge that purifies it for a higher self-disclosure.

Of course the comic spirit is not aware that it is a transitional moment in that long pilgrimage. It appears *for itself* to be the last word on the truth of religion, the definitive transformation of substance into subject, but that is not the case "*in itself* or *for us*" (H 521–22; M 453; B 750–51). *We* recognize that this abstract, legal "person" who claims to have reduced everything substantial to a mere predicate of himself has already suffered the most fearful diminution in the loss of his ethical/ ethnic identity. His hollow claim is only the other side of its opposite, the reduction of his subjectivity to an atomized fragment of an impersonal substance.

In other words we see, yet again, the familiar passage from Stoicism to skepticism to unhappy consciousness, as the direct expression of the abject condition of this legal "person." Stoicism is the last heroic effort, necessarily doomed to failure, to exist as a spiritual self in a world that has been divested of ethical spirit. The happy repose of comedy is the obverse side of unhappy self-consciousness, which "knows" that the self-sufficient "validity of the abstract person . . . is rather a complete loss." The laughter of the clown expresses the pathos of this loss. He has lost not only his gods and goddesses but also the ethical world in which everything of substantial spiritual value was immanent: He has lost his very self, as a spiritual being. Any claim that he has incorporated essential substance as a predicate of himself is in fact empty, since in his parting with or alienation from *(Entäusserung)* the divine, he has also parted with his own selfhood. His *self-consciousness,* his certainty of self, is that of a comic-strip character: I yam what I yam and that's all I yam, I'm Popeye the sailorman. Like the comic-strip character he has become two-dimensional. His dimension of depth he possesses only in *consciousness,* as something lost.

Thus the dialectic of unhappy consciousness is in full swing. "We see that this unhappy consciousness constitutes the obverse side and the consummation of the comic consciousness that is completely happy within itself." Unhappy consciousness is "the tragic fate" of its *"certainty of its own self.* . . . It is the consciousness that all essentiality is lost in *this certainty* it possesses, and that just this knowledge of itself, of the substance as well as the self, is lost: it is the pain that expresses itself as the hard saying that *God is dead"* (H 523; M 454–55; B 752–53). For Hegel, as for Nietzsche's madman who declares that God is dead, the hard saying implies the death of the ethical world and the spiritual self as well.

This hard saying, which appears in the *Phenomenology* for the first time in this passage, is not new to Hegel's thought. *Glauben und Wissen* (1802) concluded, in a passage we have examined in some detail (see Chapter 3), by invoking the death of God, both as a cultural phenomenon and as a "speculative Good Friday" to be followed by an odd sort of Easter. The hard saying will reappear in the *Phenomenology* in another speculative idealization of the crucifixion/resurrection pattern.

In all three cases it implies a dissolution of the divine in its representational form, as an objectified figure. Here what is dissolved is the entire pantheon of the religion of art, and all ethical substance with it. It is also notable that in the present passage this hard saying is specifically attributed to the unhappy consciousness. That is new. Unhappy consciousness had originally been presented as splayed irresolvably between the changeable and the unchangeable, between finite self and infinite substance. Here the tension is in a manner resolved, by the total loss of substance and self alike, which stand or fall together.

To that ironical resolution there corresponds an ironical inversion of the "religion" of "art." The disappearance of the gods and of ethical personality alike, for whom art had been the medium of religion, is followed by their reappearance simply as artistic objects, as artifacts. The old religion is made available to consciousness purely as art. The paragraph in which Hegel describes this transformation, a gloss on the death of God, is central to the dialectical structure of the two concluding chapters of the *Phenomenology*. The reconstitution of "revelatory religion" as "absolute knowledge" will parallel this reconstitution of "the religion of art" as art pure and simple. Each of these parallel developments is described as the recollection or interiorization—*Erinnerung*—of what had appeared outwardly in representations of deity.

In the present context this process is described, appropriately enough, in a rather fanciful poetic metaphor. The gods and goddesses are gone, with their oracles and their eternal laws that had proven all too transient. Their statues are "corpses" from which the "animating soul" has fled, as has "belief" from the words of the hymns, and spirit from the divine food and drink and from the works of the muses, and human being is no longer united with divine being in his games and festivals. All these forms through which the gods had dwelt with human beings have already become "what they still are for us: beautiful fruit broken from the tree, which a friendly destiny has offered us, as a maiden might present such fruit" to guests of the house (H 523–24; M 455; B 753). Hegel develops this suggestive metaphor at some length: What is left of these religious forms are works of art, statuary and poetry, placed before us to sample like fruit picked and polished and arranged in an attractive bowl. But our hospitable maiden cannot offer us, with these fruits,

> the actual life in which they existed, not the tree that bore them, nor the earth and the elements that provided their substance,

nor the climate that gave them their particular flavor or the changing seasons that governed the process of their growth. —So this destiny can give us the works of antique art but not their world with them, not the springtime and summer of the ethical life in which they blossomed and ripened, but only the shrouded recollection of this actuality. —Our action in enjoying them is therefore not an act of worship through which our consciousness might come to its perfected truth and fulfillment; rather, it is only an outward act, that perhaps wipes raindrops or a speck of dust from these fruits, and, in place of the ethical actuality that environed, engendered and inspired them, erects the elaborate scaffolding of the dead elements of their external existence, of their language and historical circumstances, and so forth, not in order to live in them but only so as to represent them within consciousness.

Here Hegel expresses more eloquently than usual the wistfulness by which he was always moved when considering the passing away of the classical Greek spirit. If the passage stopped at this point, our only recourse would be romantic nostalgia for what is lost, reminiscent of Hölderlin's laments for the withdrawal of the gods and goddesses, but without his passionate hope that they might return. For Hegel that loss is irretrievable. All that is left of the religion of art are the works of art, presented to consciousness for purely aesthetic appreciation.

It turns out, however, that this aesthetic representation is no pallid consolation for what is lost, despite Hegel's remarks about its externality. When he says that our enjoyment of these works is not a consummatory act of worship, the reason is not only that the life and cultus of the ethical community are no longer available. Even if the ethical world were available, it would be retrogressive for us to enter into it. Beautiful as it is, it is not the ultimate fulfillment of spirit. Its contribution to the higher consummation is precisely its purely aesthetic legacy. This legacy may appear truncated, mere fruit from the tree that bore it. But the passage continues:

But just as the maiden who offers us the plucked fruit is more than the nature that immediately displayed them, extended into their conditions and elements, the trees, atmosphere, light, and so forth, because she gathers all this together in a higher manner in the gleam of her self-conscious eye and in the gesture with which she offers them: so is the spirit of destiny that displays this artwork to us more than the ethical life and actuality of that people, for it is the *inner re-collection* [Er-innerung] of the spirit that was still *exteriorized* [veräusserten] in that people—it is the spirit of the tragic destiny, which gathers all those individual gods and attributes of their substance into the One pantheon, into the spirit that is conscious of its own self as spirit. (H 524; M 455–56; B 753–54)

Here the metaphor becomes a burdened analogy: A spiritual act is higher than a natural growth, and as the self-conscious offering of the fruit by the maiden is higher than the dumb nature that originally offered it, so is the spirit that comes to self-awareness in the inner act of recollection higher than the unself-conscious Volksgeist.

What becomes of worn-out religions? They become art. Their arterial connection with a living community severed, the divine life in them dies. That is not because the gods were nonexistent human projections all the while, as Hegel's Enlightenment predecessors and his own left-wing disciples argued. But the divine exists only in reciprocity, finite/infinite, mortal/immortal. Once the specific human order of things passes through which the gods had found the finite expression necessary to them, they die as well. Without ears to hear them or offerings to nourish them, they fall silent and waste away. With Hegel the old issue of their existence or nonexistence had long been historicized: What was once living is now dead. Even in his earliest "theological" writings of the 1790s he had framed the issue that way. The residue of the religion of art, in which mortals and immortals existed in reciprocity, consists in words and artifacts and music through which that religion is re-collected into purely objective form, that exists only for consciousness. When we recall that this account applies in principle to all religious development, it provides a powerful and attractive interpretation of the fate of dead religions generally. Any archeological museum furnishes many examples. The remains of Mayan, old Asian, or African or Nordic religions, for instance, are available for purely aesthetic wonder.

The relation of religion to art, furthermore, had long been a preoccupation of Hegel's, as we have seen. Quite apart from the way he resolves it in the *Phenomenology,* the issue itself as it develops in his thinking is suggestive. Already in the *Realphilosophie,* as in the later system, religion is presented as a higher moment of absolute spirit than art.

But he had once, in the *Differenzschrift* of 1801, presented religion as a mode of art, and other ways of relating the two surely occurred to him, including that suggested by the present passage: that it is the destiny of religion, quite generally, to pass over into art, that this aesthetic transfiguration of religion is indeed its "higher" destiny.[89] It would not be difficult to argue that this process is well advanced with respect to Christianity, and already was in Hegel's day. Christian icons and altarpieces are presented to the general public as *objets d'art* in museums, musical renderings of the Mass are played in concert halls, carols and evangelical hymns are sung as folk music, and the Bible is read in university courses on world literature. If an aesthetic moment belongs to religion generally and, in principle, to the historical development of any historic religion, why not also the "higher" moment in which it passes over into pure art?

While this possibility is certainly latent in the *Phenomenology,* in point of fact Hegel's own analysis takes a different turn: "Revelatory religion," of which Christianity furnishes the obvious model, represents a higher spirit than that of the religion of art, and it is precisely this higher spirit that recollects the artistic legacy of the religion of art.

This new spirit, "conscious of its own self as spirit," is in the first place capable of re-collecting its own inner life out of the works of classical art that a friendly destiny has retrieved from the debris of antiquity. This re-collection is a form of spiritual recognition. It recognizes itself, not in the spirit of the antique Volk as such, nor in the gods and goddesses of the Volk, but in their distillation as works of art. With its recollection of the religion of art, purely as art, this new spirit will consummate the entire dialectic of religion. It is notable, furthermore, that the route into this "revelatory religion" does not pass through a religious form reminiscent of Judaism. In Hegel's later Lectures on the Philosophy of Religion, the Jewish legacy is represented under the rubric of "the religion of sublimity." In the *Phenomenology* it is ignored.[90] Not only is the contemporary existence of the Jewish religion ignored, as was common enough among writers of Christian background; Hegel does not even follow the common Christian practice of acknowledging the Hebrew religion of biblical times as the essential precursor of Christianity. Not the "sublime," transcendent God of Hebrew scripture, but the aesthetic recollection of the religions of classical paganism furnishes the transition to "revelatory religion."

A poetic mood being upon him, appropriate in spinning his metaphor of works of art as a bowl of fruit offered by a graceful servant girl,

Hegel goes on to imagine another rather fanciful scene: Around the "birthplace" of the new spirit are ranged all the "productions of art" in which the gods and goddesses had appeared, to make up one side of a circle: the individuated statue, the oracle, the collective cultus, the hero-athlete, the tragic and comic actors. Their presence in this circle signifies not only that they are in a manner witnesses of the newborn spirit, witnesses in the conventional double sense that they both behold and testify, but also that they each represent fragmentary aspects of this incarnate spirit. Like the statue, he bears "the form of individuality . . . as the *existing* object of sensuous consciousness." Like the oracle, he will express himself in language, in that pure objectivity that constantly disappears with its utterance. Like the cultus, he exists in "immediate *unity* with universal *self-consciousness* in its inspiration." He is "beautiful *self-like corporeality*" like the athlete, and as an existence "elevated to *representation*" and extended into "a world that finally collects itself into a universality which is at the same time a pure self-certainty" he embodies the transition from epic to comedy. So all these artistic forms are in a manner present at the birth of incarnate spirit, which draws together into its own personal unity the special features of each (H 524–25; M 456; B 754–55).

These "productions of art" are not the only figures that attend this extraordinary birth.The circle gathered, as it were, around the manger in Bethlehem is completed by figures representing the desolated world of legal status as its aftermath. For the historical preconditions of this birth are drawn from that world. So the forms of the religion of art on the one side of the circle, "and on the other side the *world* of the *person* and of law, the destructive wildness of the elements of the content that have been let loose, as well as the person as *thought* in Stoicism and the endless unrest of the skeptical consciousness, constitute the periphery of forms which stand expectantly and impatiently around the birthplace of spirit as it becomes self-consciousness."

It is a motley and grotesque crowd that replaces the shepherds and magi of the traditional crèche, but it signifies the entire condition of spirit in the pulverized, exhausted state in which it awaits its rebirth. More than that: This strange scene recapitulates the recurrent nightmare of the *Phenomenology* in order at last to dispel it. For when Stoicism and skepticism appear on the scene can unhappy consciousness be far behind? It is present indeed, not among the witnesses, but in more intimate participation in the event. The passage continues: "the pain and longing of unhappy consciousness, that permeates them all, is their center and is the corporate birthpang of the new spirit's emergence—the simplicity of the pure concept that contains these forms as its moments" (H 525; M 456–57; B 755). Unhappy consciousness, which has haunted the dialectic of art-religion, as it has the entire *Phenomenology*, now inflicts its pain on the scene of new birth. But the ordeal, this time, is productive.

The scene is an elaborate allegory. The birthpang of unhappy consciousness, "corporate" because it afflicts all the figures in the scene, is the familiar dualism between divine and human, infinite and finite, that spirit must suffer as the precondition for overcoming this dualism when spirit is reborn incarnate in self-consciousness. The various figures of the religion of art that range themselves in the circle around its birthplace had been encountered as diachronic stages in the development and dissolution of the divinity that was "there" in language: Divine substance gradually came to utterance in speech and then fell silent. But now all these stages present themselves synchronically, simultaneously, in a common conceptual space. Taken together, as pure dialectical moments of a single concept, they make up a whole, that now emerges in "the simplicity of the pure concept." The other figures, that greeted the death of God first with ludic cheer and then with bereavement, constitute the moments of disillusionment that must precede the new birth if it is to be really new. For the mystical ascent, upon which the entire dialectic of religion is patterned, must have its purgative moment of desolation, in which all worldly illusions and otherworldly fantasies of the past are abandoned. The six stages in the mystical ascent of the religious spirit, from divine substance as all-pervading light to the comic and pathetic subjectivity abandoned by all vestige of divine substance, makes up the diachronic continuum canvassing the moments in the religious recognition of absolute spirit. This recognition is not complete in any one of these moments, but only in their ensemble, which is recollected as a unified whole in the mystically auspicious seventh stage. This culminating stage does not merely complete the continuum, but is complete in itself, the recognition of absolute spirit "revealed" in its incarnation as self-conscious self.

One can, in a manner of speaking, say that this incarnate spirit has "two sides": Divine substance passes outside *(entäussert)* itself to become self-consciousness and, on the other hand, self-consciousness in its *Entäusserung* becomes "universal self." But Hegel stresses the "necessity" of this reciprocal movement into identity, in the sense that this kenosis of divine substance is no accidental metamorphosis, but reveals that it is its very nature to "exteriorize" itself in this way; that is to say, it is *"in itself* self-consciousness," while self-consciousness is *"in itself* the universal essence." So while one can say, again in a manner of speaking, that incarnate spirit "has an *actual mother,* but a father subsisting-*in-itself,*" or as substance, the truth of this dual parenthood is the irreducible immediacy of his simple self-identical existence (H 525–26; M 457; B 755–56). This immediate identity is not merely an appearance to the religious consciousness as previous moments were, not a mere work of enthusiastic imagination or of "mythical representation" in which the appearance is one thing, the reality another (H 526; M 457–58; B 756). The simple truth is that divine substance *is* in itself self-conscious subject, self-consciousness in its natural and historical actuality *is* divine spirit. There is no discarnate spirit, nor is the actual ever devoid of spirit. Here every veil seems to fall away that had concealed this identity, and its simple truth is "revealed": The very concept of absolute spirit is disclosed to the religious consciousness.

> The *immediate in-itself* of spirit, that gives itself the form of self-consciousness, means none other than that the actual world spirit [*Weltgeist*] has attained this knowledge of itself. . . .
>
> That absolute spirit has given itself the form of self-consciousness *in itself* and thus also for its *consciousness:* this now appears in such a way that it is the *faith of the world* that spirit *is there* as a self-consciousness, that is, as an actual human being, that it exists for immediate certainty, that the believing consciousness *sees* and *feels* and *hears* this divinity. (H 527; M 458; B 757; cf. 1 John 1:1)

It is this sensuous immediacy of incarnate spirit that constitutes the revelation. Consciousness does not project its inner "thought" of God onto an existing person, but *recognizes* God in his "immediate contemporaneous existence." Here the religious ascent has reached its goal: It confronts deity in a *"simple* positive self," that

> has thereby the form of complete immediacy: it is neither as something thought or represented nor as something produced, as is the case with the immediate self in the religion of nature and also in the religion of art. Rather, this God is sensuously,

directly beheld as self, as an actual particular human being; only so *is* he self-consciousness.

This becoming-human [*Menschwerdung*] of the divine being, or the fact that it has essentially and immediately the form of self-consciousness, is the simple content of the absolute religion. (H 527–28; M 459; B 758)

Hegel, who had criticized the "positivity" of the Christian religion in the 1790s, has not forgotten that there can be problems with this assertion of the sheer sensuous immediacy of God's incarnation in a particular human being, as we shall see. Still he ascribes immense importance to this essential content of what he here calls "absolute religion." Correctly grasped, it expresses the very concept of spirit: "For spirit is the knowledge of its own self in its exteriorization [*Entäusserung*]; the essence that is the movement of maintaining, in its otherness, its identity with itself" (H 528; M 459; B 758).

In principle, this identity-in-otherness is the solution to the central predicament diagnosed by the *Phenomenology,* the unhappy consciousness. Unhappy consciousness is the self alienated from its own spiritual ground, and constantly negated by this alien spirit. But now what is disclosed is that the divine spirit *is* the self, that it is not absolute *unless* it is the self. Nor is the self entirely self-conscious, and therefore fully a self, unless it recognizes itself in absolute spirit. To that extent this two-sided revelation coincides in the sheer positivity of the *"simple positive self."* That relentless negativity that has been the moving force of the phenomenological development seems in principle to be overcome. Indeed, introducing this *"simple* positive self" Hegel draws a cryptic parallel: "the religious spirit, in the return of all essentiality into consciousness, has become *simple* positive self, just as actual spirit as such in unhappy consciousness was just this *simple* self-conscious negativity" (H 527; M 458–59; B 758). The actual self referred to is what he had called the changeable, unessential consciousness, unhappy in its alienation from its unchangeable essence and reduced in its own eyes to *"simple* self-conscious negativity." The *"simple* positive self" is its opposite, a fullness in contrast with the emptiness of unhappy consciousness, possession in contrast with its unfulfilled yearning.

The impasse of unhappy consciousness is overcome precisely in the mutual recognition that is the essence of selfhood or spirit. The two sides that had opposed one another in so many guises now recognize one another, and each recognizes itself in the other. This mutual recog-

nition of divine and human is precisely revelation, the content of absolute religion: "In this religion the divine being is therefore *revealed*. Its
being-revelatory consists obviously in the fact that what it is becomes
known. But it becomes known just because it becomes known as spirit,
as the essential being that is essentially *self-consciousness*" (H 528;
M 459; B 758–59). What the self knows when it sees, hears, touches
its incarnate God is precisely a self: not, to be sure, its own self, but a
self like its own, recognizing and recognized by its own self. To that
extent this moment is indeed the promised land that rewards our long
and arduous trek through the phenomenological wilderness.

As for the universal attributes of God that had seemed to make God
an Other, "the good, righteous, holy, creator of heaven and earth," these
"are predicates of a subject" that have their sole locus in this subject
(H 528; M 459–60; B 759). If we abstract from this subject-self and
deify these traditional attributes as such, we remain in the impasse of
unhappy consciousness, longing for an unreachable other.

> The *subject* itself, and thereby also *this pure universal* is, how-
> ever, revelatory as *self,* for this is precisely this inwardness re-
> flected in itself which is immediately there, and the certainty
> possessed by that self for which it is there. This—to be revelatory
> according to its concept—is therefore the true form of spirit, and
> this form it has, the concept, it likewise alone its essence and
> substance. (H 529; M 460; B 759)

We cannot prescind from the God-revealing to postulate what God must
be apart from this revelation. For God is only God in being revelatory.
If we should adopt a merely representational manner of speaking, and
say that this God revealed as self is a condescension from his "eternal
simplicity," we would have to insist, paradoxically, that only in this
incarnation has God become "highest being."

But strictly speaking, according to the concept, this talk of divine
condescension is illegitimate. To be "revealing" is, if it accords with the
concept, just what divine spirit truly and always *is*. That is the difference between a conceptual and a merely representational rendering of
this revelation, of which I shall have much more to say shortly. According to the concept, it is not that an abstractly imagined highest
being becomes lowly. "The lowliest is at the same time the highest; the
revealing that has stepped forth entirely on the *surface* is just thereby
the *deepest*" (H 529; M 460; B 760). With this disclosure of the very

concept of spirit on the surface, where it can be seen, heard, felt, the dialectic of religion is in principle completed—and aufgehoben.

ir. Revelatory Religion in Concept and in Representation

Hegel's insistence that divinity is known fully and irreducibly in its incarnation is oddly reminiscent of Luther's frequent assertion that we know God only in Jesus Christ. From this unconditionally Christocentric standpoint Luther inveighed against the entire Scholastic tradition of speculation about the nature and attributes of deity. Luther, to be sure, was a hero of Hegel's, but orthodox Lutheran theologians of the nineteenth century and neo-orthodox theologians of the twentieth have been among the harshest critics of Hegel's interpretations of Christianity, particularly as these interpretations have influenced liberal Protestantism. Kierkegaard, whose Climacus literature *(Philosophical Fragments, Concluding Unscientific Postscript)* is radically Christocentric, earned his reputation as an anti-Hegelian particularly in his polemics against Hegel's treatment of the Christian gospel, and was a major inspiration of neo-orthodoxy. Karl Barth, the outstanding neo-orthodox theologian, whose massive, multivolume *Kirchliche Dogmatik* reconstituted the whole of Christian theology on rigorously Christocentric lines, and who was the equal of Luther and Kierkegaard in polemic vehemence, steadily directed his thunder against the intrusion of philosophical speculation into theology, of which the Hegelian influence was a prime instance. But how could Hegel be so wrong in the eyes of the Christocentric theologians, despite differences on many other issues, when like Luther he insisted that the only true God was revealed, without reservation or remainder, in his incarnation?

There is a short answer to that question, and a longer answer. The longer will be implicit in the remainder of this study. For the short answer, I return to the paragraphs I was expounding at the end of the preceding section, where Hegel presents the essential content of revelatory religion. In the incarnation of God in a self-conscious self, the divine "becomes known" as it truly is, according to the concept of spirit. But this *Menschwerdung* is a *becoming* human only, in the strict sense, in that it "becomes known." That is not an insignificant sense of becoming for Hegel, since it marks the moment of mutual self-recognition in which spiritual selfhood is complete. But what becomes known in this revelation, including this crucial moment of self-recognitive selfhood, is precisely the concept, in which, strictly speaking, there is no becoming. When grasped according to the concept, incarnation is not an event, but a general truth. Spirit "becomes known as self-consciousness and to this self-consciousness it is immediately revealing, for it is this self-consciousness itself; the divine nature is the same as the human, and this unity is what is beheld" (H 529; M 460; B 759–60). This equation of divine and human nature, already enunciated in the *Realphilosophie* of 1805–6, had become for Hegel a standard formula for expressing the essential message of Christianity, retained in his later work as well. It also summarizes everything in the Hegelian rendition of Christianity that the Christocentric theologians have found objectionable.

For the formula implies the denial of divine transcendence. It is only, as we have suggested, in a manner of speaking, a concession to representational thinking, that Hegel could speak of the transcendent God becoming incarnate: What is revealed, according to the concept, is that deity and humanity are timelessly identical. This disclosure is the overcoming of unhappy consciousness, to which Hegel consigns all continuing insistence on the Otherness of God. For a Kierkegaard or a Barth, or for Luther, of course, there is nothing unhappy about an existence that celebrates the God of Isaiah's vision, high and lifted up in holiness, or a mystery of grace in which just this transcendent God appears redemptively as a human being among humankind in Jesus Christ. Nor is faith in this *mysterium* a belief in a general proposition. For Kierkegaard:

> Christianity is no doctrine concerning the unity of the divine and the human, or concerning the subject-object, not to speak of other logical transcriptions of Christianity. If Christianity were a doctrine, the relation to it would not be faith, for to a doctrine there can be only an intellectual relation. Christianity is therefore no doctrine, but the fact that God has come into existence.[91]

For all Barth's differences with Kierkegaard in other respects, he might have said the same. Luther, far from thinking that God's self-disclosure in Christ had been designed to clarify the relation of the divine and human natures, often suggested that God was even more hidden in this revelation than he was in creation. Luther's paradox, that God is *deus absconditus* precisely in being *deus revelatus,* could not be more foreign to Hegel.

But there is no point in piling up quotations from Christian thinkers concerning this issue. Traditional Catholic and Protestant divines have hardly spoken with one voice over the years, but it is difficult to find any who did not, with the Council of Chalcedon (451 C.E.), consider the incarnation to be a unique mystery of grace, a paradoxical union of divine and human natures, in the language of Chalcedon, "without confusion" of those natures. Only the God with the self-subsistence to *act,* as both Hebrew scripture and the New Testament assume, could have *become* a human being. The only notable interpreters of the gospel who had denied this active being of a God distinct from the human spirit were denounced as heretics; the early Gnostics, for instance, like Hegel, also proceeded from an understanding of the gospel either unrelated to or negatively related to Hebrew scripture.

So much for the short answer to the question why Hegel's rendering of revelatory religion has seemed so objectionable to more orthodox Christians, despite his apparent Christocentrism. It should not surprise us that Hegel, for his part, was not intent upon repeating the catechism. His placement of "revelatory religion" at the penultimate stage in the *Phenomenology* was not intended to be any sort of bow to traditional Christianity. He is as uninterested in Christian apologetic here as we have always found him to be. In spite of what this rendering of "revelatory religion" obviously does owe to the Christian gospel, Hegel's own interest in this gospel is not evangelical and his use of what he has borrowed from it is quite independent. For Christocentric theologians the human predicament addressed by the gospel is sin, the wilful rebellion of the creature against the creator, who is, axiomatically, the Holy One of Israel. The Christocentric theologian ponders the implications of the claims that the high God of Hebrew scripture has been born of woman and become one of us for the salvation of sinners, and his strictly theological problem is how the high God is to be understood in light of this event; that is, how the creator of heaven and earth is to be understood from the standpoint of faith's Christological center. Hegel's problems are quite different. Granted that unhappy consciousness is a necessary ordeal in the birth of the self, and ultimately in the self-recognition of absolute spirit, how can the phenomenological path finally emerge from the shadow of this unhappy consciousness? How, from this fearful negativity that has driven self-consciousness along this path, can absolute spirit be born precisely in this self-consciousness? Assuming, furthermore, that "religion" is a penultimate stage in this pathway, how is this *itinerarium mentis in deum* to be

completed? It is notable, on the other hand, how suspicious the Christocentric theologians are of "religion" in this universalistic sense. Even
the Christian "religion" is something of an embarrassment to them.
When Luther placed "justification by faith" on his theological escutch-
eon, he meant an unqualified, unmediated trust in God's forgiveness
through the redeeming grace of Christ crucified. Any hint that "justification by religion" might serve as an equivalent would have set him
railing against works righteousness and pagan subversion of the gospel.
We have seen what Hegel, for his part, thought of "faith," and while
the Lutheran, Kierkegaardian, or Barthian "faith" is a far cry from the
early modern supernaturalism that furnished the model for Hegel's
use of the term, the divine transcendence that they did avow as the
correlative of faith, precisely in the redeeming work of Christ, would
for Hegel have been a retrogression from the comic dénouement of
religion and yet another form of unhappy consciousness.

So different are the problems that they addressed that it is again
difficult to join the issue squarely. Just as the "faith" Hegel repudiated
was not quite what the Christocentric theologians had in mind, so
"religion" does not bear for Hegel the reductionistic implications that
they imputed to it, or that Hegel's left-wing followers invested in it. It
is not a merely "human" phenomenon. When Hegel epitomizes the
content of revelatory religion with the formula that the divine nature
is the same as the human, any traditional understanding of the "human" is altered by the equation as fundamentally as is the traditional
understanding of the divine. According to the concept, both terms of
the equation are aufgehoben into absolute spirit. It is not as if "spirit"
were merely a mystified manner of speaking that could be replaced,
as Bruno Bauer or Ludwig Feuerbach thought, by "criticism" or "humanity." "Religion," for Hegel, had always implied the uniting of the
human with the divine, and it culminated in the transfiguration of
both into spirit.

Yet Hegel had had a theological education, however sullen he had
been about it at the time. He knew very well what traditional Christianity had made of the content of "revelatory religion," and in the remainder of his treatment of it he directly contrasts this theological
appropriation of the gospel with its authentic "religious" meaning. The
former he consigns to *Vorstellung*, while the latter is informed by
Begriff.

This contrast between *Vorstellung* and *Begriff*, furthermore, none too
neatly divides Hegel's treatment of revelatory religion into two quite

distinct levels, creating some formidable obstacles in understanding this section, which is one of the most confusing in the *Phenomenology*. The treatment of *Vorstellung* is particularly entangled. Before undertaking to untangle that, let us complete our exposition of the pure *Begriff* of incarnation. From this standpoint, as we have seen, what is revealed is the reducible identity of divine substance with self-conscious self, and it is revealed *to* self-conscious self. In this mutual recognition unhappy consciousness is overcome, the religious ascent is completed in divine-human identity, and the passage to absolute knowledge seems smooth. All that is needed is for mutual recognition to be complete: for the identity of absolute substance with self to be not merely revealed to the self, but to arise from the self's own self-knowledge.

Self-knowledge, really the ultimate form of recognition, is already implicit in revelatory religion, insofar as we adhere strictly to the standpoint of *Begriff*. The pure concept of highest being or essence *(Wesen)*, of divine substance, is consummated when it is "seen, heard, etc., as an existing self-consciousness . . . and through this consummation this essence is just as immediately *there* as it is essence" (H 529; M 460; B 760). This being-there *(Dasein)* of divine essence is precisely absolute spirit. In revelatory religion absolute spirit is disclosed to "religious consciousness," just as it is to "us" phenomenological observers. Here, then, may be that "point" to which Hegel had referred in the closing paragraph of the Introduction, at which the consciousness of the phenomenological protagonist "for itself" converges with "our" standpoint, the awareness of spirit "in itself" and "for us." As I have suggested, this "point" is reached decisively and unambiguously in the chapter on Absolute Knowledge, but it is clearly anticipated here, to the extent that revelation is grasped according to the concept.

> What we ourselves are conscious of in our concept, that *being* is *essence*, is what the religious consciousness is conscious of. This *unity* of being and essence, of *thinking* that is immediate *being-there,* is both the *thought* of this religious consciousness or its *mediated* knowledge and equally *its immediate knowledge;* for this unity of being and thinking is *self*-consciousness, and is itself *there.* . . . God is therefore *revealed* here as *he is;* he is *there* such as he is *in himself;* he is there as spirit.

Here Hegel states more rigorously the sense of his formula that divine and human nature are identical. It is in the fulfillment and transfiguration of self-consciousness, in the God who is "there" as a self-conscious self, that this identity is revealed. The other troublesome and facile formula, that religion and philosophical knowledge have the same content, differing only in form, is also placed in a more illuminating context: What is revealed in absolute religion is already speculative wisdom insofar as it is grasped according to the concept of spirit. Hegel continues:

> God is reachable in pure speculative knowing alone, and is only in that knowing and is that knowing itself, for he is spirit; and this speculative knowing is the knowing of revelatory religion. Speculative knowing knows God as *thought* or pure essence, and this thought as being and as being-there, and this being-there as the negativity of itself, hence as self, *this* self and universal self; precisely this is what revelatory religion knows. (H 530; M 461; B 760–61)

When Hegel says that God is reachable *(erreichbar)* solely in speculative knowing, the knowing is recognitive, not in any restrictive sense merely cognitive. In recognizing God "there" as a self, the knower also appropriates his own selfhood. For the knowing is "speculative" in the pregnant metaphor of mystical theology: The knower is the mirror *(speculuum)* in which God sees himself ever more perfectly reflected as the mirroring soul ascends to union with its divine original. God has been ever more directly "there" in language, the *Da-sein* of self-conscious self. In this consummatory moment the union is complete: Divine and human are brought to mutual recognition in a self that is both seen as an existing being and heard in the linguistic mode of spiritual being-there. Here self-recognitive speculation and revelatory religion are one, the completion of the religious ascent for which, as Hegel goes on to say in the same paragraph, in an unmistakable echo of Saint Paul (Romans 8:19–23), "the hopes and expectations of the entire preceding world had pressed forward."

So what is missing? What more can the fulfillment of absolute spirit require? As so often before in the *Phenomenology,* the deficiency is implicit in the achievement. In the incarnate God the concept of spirit is actualized, as Hegel has steadily emphasized, in the mode of pure immediacy. But it is "not yet developed"; that is, the immediacy must be mediated, articulated. Why is this mediation necessary? Because "spirit in the immediacy of self-consciousness is *this single* self-consciousness, set over against the universal; it is an exclusive One, that has the still unresolved form of a sensuous other for the consciousness for which it is there; this consciousness does not yet know spirit as its own, or spirit is not yet there as the self of all, as the universal self as well as the individual self" (H 530–31; M 461–62; B 762).

The problem Hegel is formulating here, articulated already in early fragments and essays of the 1790s, has two aspects: First, the religious consciousness sees, hears, feels deity in a self *like* his own, but it is not yet a self he knows to *be* his own. The second aspect is more fundamental, because it goes to the root of the first, which is the exclusiveness of the individual self, with its locus confined to a single body. One individuated self must confront another as a "sensuous other," with which it cannot enter fully into unity. Precisely because the religious consciousness is necessarily distanced from the divine-human self it sees and hears by the sensuous otherness of this self, it cannot appropriate this incarnate spirit as its own. If incarnate spirit is to be shared, its locus must be the "universal self"; that is, the collective self of a community. The *single* God-incarnate must pass away, and spirit must come to reside in the entire religious community.[92] The immediate singularity of the incarnate God must be universalized in two senses: It must be translated from its sensuous immediacy into the form of thought, and it must be extended to the entire community.

First, the single God-bearing self must become past, the object of memory rather than of sensuous immediacy. It is of course the nature of what has sensuous presence that it must pass away: "This single human being . . . is the *immediately* present God; his *being* passes over thereby into *having-been*. The consciousness for which he has this sensuous presence ceases to see him, to hear him; it *has* seen and heard him; and only in this way, that it merely *has* seen and heard him, does this consciousness itself become spiritual" (H 531; M 462; B 762).

Here Hegel is applying to the incarnate God of revelatory religion the principle enunciated with respect to the religion of art when all that was left of it was the inner recollection: The recollected form is of a higher spirituality than the immediate; it now assumes the form of *thought*. We must add at once that this thought-form is not strictly conceptual: an important point to which we will return shortly. Still, if the religious consciousness is to know this unity of divine and human as its *own* self, it must first be interiorized. The immediate, sensuous consciousness that sees and hears cannot as such transcend "the unlikeness of objectivity." It can "know this objective individual as spirit, but not its own self as spirit."

When this sensuous objectivity passes into recollection, into thought, however, the second development can occur: The lost immediacy of the single divine-human self can be recovered in the religious community itself, the collective self: "In the disappearance of the immediate being-there of the one known to be absolute being, the immediate receives its negative moment; spirit remains the immediate self of actuality, but as *the universal self-consciousness* of the community that reposes in its own substance" (H 431; M 462; B 763). So now we have a community that recollects, and in this recollection comes to recover the lost immediacy of the divine presence by recognizing it in the community's own collective identity.

With this twofold universalization, which is characteristic of Hegel's treatment of the gospel, early and late, we enter a dialectical thicket that we must clear up as best we can. It is precisely here that the interplay of *Begriff* and *Vorstellung* occurs. Revelatory religion, according to its pure concept, is the disclosure of the incarnate God in its pure immediacy, as a self. But in "developing" this immediate concept we find that it must take the re-collective form of thought and the collective form of spirit-in-community. In this "development" of the concept, however, the strict conceptual form is paradoxically abandoned, and in its place another form of thought is employed, that of representation *(Vorstellung)*. We are already familiar with this representational form; it was also employed in the religion of art (for instance, in the epic) as a kind of speech in which the story of bygone gods and heroes was told. Now it arises again as soon as the religious consciousness gets beyond direct seeing and hearing.

It might seem that "we," at least, could avoid this detour into representation, could move directly from the disclosure of the concept in revelatory religion to its appropriation as absolute knowledge. Perhaps "we" could make this move, but not the religious consciousness that is the phenomenological protagonist in this section of our text. If "we" were to attempt, as it were, to go on without our protagonist, leaving the religious consciousness behind, the promised point of juncture between phenomenological observer and protagonist would not occur. Which is to say that at this penultimate point in our "science of the experience of consciousness," we would be abandoning the standpoint of experience. And that, as Hegel has conceived his phenomenological project, simply will not do. The concept of spirit, already "revealed" in its immediate purity, must be "developed" through yet another excursion into experience before the concept can be recovered in its full concreteness. If as a result we seem to be following our phenomenological pathway two steps forward, one step back, that, after all, has been characteristic of the entire journey.

In this final excursion into experience, the religious consciousness must revert to the form of *Vorstellung*. It must. The concept itself, which only develops through the vagaries of experience, requires this reversion. Representation, the form of thought that recollects by way of narrative, image, metaphor, approximates the life of experience itself. Necessary as it is, however, it is also a deficient form of thought. Its use is perilous. Those who employ it, for instance, may become Christo-centric theologians! It is an unstable compound of thought and sensuous image. At its best it may be directed by the concept, approximating the concept in a metaphorical mode. At its worst it may literalize its metaphors and ossify into a mere positive "faith," even regenerating the unhappy consciousness that revelatory religion had in principle overcome. Such is the representational pilgrimage of religious con-sciousness. In the remainder of Hegel's section on revelatory religion we will follow its unsteady course, with its many side comments about its progression and retrogression, now following the straight path of the concept, now lurching into the ditch. Trying to track its course between these conflicting tendencies makes for difficult reading.

The perils are already apparent. The religious consciousness has universalized the revelation by rendering the incarnate individual, who has died, in the recollective mode of representational thought, but at the cost of placing itself at a distance in space and time from what was revealed in him. This will create difficulties for the other form of universalization, the embodiment of spirit in the community, as we shall see. At any rate, the recollected revelation is long ago and far away.

> *Pastness* and *distancing,* however, constitute only the incomplete form in which the immediate mode is mediated or rendered universal; this form is only superficially dipped into the element of thought, is preserved in this element *as* a sensuous mode and is not made at one with the nature of thought itself. It is only raised into representation, for representation is the synthetic combination of sensuous immediacy and its universality or thought. (H 531–32; M 462; B 763)

This combination does still reflect the unity of universal and particular, ideal and actual, that is achieved in the concept of spirit, but it is synthetic in the sense that it expresses this unity in sensuous guise, as if its moment were related as a series of physical events in space and time. *Vorstellung* provides only an artificial, confused mixture of the elements united in the concept. We have discussed this confused mode of mediation as Hegel had introduced it in the *Realphilosophie* of 1805–6, where it appears as transitional between the pure sensuous *Anschauung* of Art and the *Begriff* of philosophical science, and is something of a mixture of both. There the representational mode is treated as the formal limitation of religion generally. It comprehends the self-reflexive nature of spirit, which only a form of thought can do, but it employs for this purpose the sensuous images characteristic of art. It is, broadly speaking, an imaginative mode. Now this mode is characteristic of the way the religious community comprehends the indwelling spirit that is in-itself present in its own life. Consequently the community cannot fully *recognize* this indwelling spirit as its own. It comprehends the spirit, but only by placing it at a spatiotemporal distance. The "mediation" of the incarnate God through the community is therefore "still incomplete." "In this combination of being and thought there is therefore the defect that the spiritual essence is still burdened with an unreconciled division between a this-side and a Beyond" (H 532; M 463; B 763–74).

The familiar formula generally associated with unhappy consciousness, the division of psychic space into *"Diesseits und Jenseits,"* signals that the relapse into *Vorstellung* is not merely an innocuous formal defect. Yet Hegel insists that the use of representational thinking does not necessarily imply unhappy consciousness. He does admit, a few paragraphs later, that the content of this *Vorstellung* is "partly" what we have encountered in considering "the unhappy and *believing* consciousness." But he is at pains to distinguish the position of the properly religious community from both unhappy consciousness and from the "faith" that is a primary locus of unhappy consciousness. The object of unhappy consciousness, he reminds us, is one for which finite spirit "yearns" without "satiation" or "rest," "because it is not yet its own content *in itself* or as its Substance." Faith, for its part, has as its content an objectified "essence of the world" lacking a self, "a representation that altogether flees actuality and thus is without the *certainty of self-consciousness*." But the consciousness of the religious community actually possesses the content of its representations "for its *substance*" and as the "certainty of its own spirit" (H 533–34; M 464; B 765–66).

It is difficult to be quite satisfied with this distinction, since the basis of unhappy consciousness is the fact that its apparent other is in truth its own depth; faith, we recall, was subject to the charge that it had "produced" its absolute being precisely because in its third moment it claimed that this absolute being was the indwelling spirit of its community. The truly *religious* community, on the other hand, possesses the divine substance as its own spirit *in itself* but not *for itself;* that is, it does not yet recognize its own common life in its *Vorstellung* of the divine. Still, the crucial point of the distinction seems to be that the properly religious community is still sufficiently in touch with its own actual social life that it is not volatilized into mere yearning for what is Beyond.

At any rate, the intent of our text is clear on this important point: Hegel dissociates the community created by revelatory religion both from unhappy consciousness and from the otherworldly objectifications of faith. No doubt he would acknowledge that it is at least threatened by both as perversions of its authentic life; indeed there are points at which the threat becomes all too vivid, as we will see. But unhappy consciousness and otherworldly "faith" are not inherent in the community's relapse into representational thinking as such. *Vorstellung,* precisely by "placing" the content of revelatory religion objectively "before" the religious consciousness implies the *Diesseits / Jenseits* distinction, but in itself it is in secure possession of this content as its own.

> The *content* is the true, but placed in the element of representation all its moments have the character of not being conceptually grasped, but appear as completely independent sides that are *externally* related to one another. For the true content to receive its true form for consciousness as well, a higher cultivation of consciousness is necessary, elevating its intuition of absolute substance into the concept, and making its consciousness *for its own self* the equivalent of its self-consciousness, as is already the case for us or *in itself.* (H 532; M 463; B 764)

In order to complete this elevation the community must not only possess absolute spirit as the unrecognized "substance of the community" in itself, but must recognize it as the community's own indwelling spirit. Only so can absolute spirit, for its part, transcend its status as substance "to become actual self, to reflect itself into itself and to be subject. This is therefore the movement that spirit accomplishes in its community, or this is the community's life" (H 532; M 463; B 764).

This movement in the community's life is in fact a necessary development in the life of absolute spirit as well, by which, as Hegel had promised in the Preface, substance becomes spiritual subject. The fact that the religious community plays such an essential role in the inner development of absolute spirit is what gives it its special penultimate status in the *Phenomenology*. This role is what distinguishes it by definition from an objectifying faith or from any other form of unhappy consciousness, however much these elements may plague its life in a historical sense.

For there are three essential moments in the inner development of spirit: First it must present itself to consciousness "in the form of *pure substance.*" But it must "descend" into the particularity of being-there. "The middle term" between pure substance and its incarnate being-there "is their synthetic combination, consciousness of passing into otherness or representation as such." The *Vorstellung* that is characteristic of the thinking of the religious community is therefore not merely an accidental formal relapse, but is itself inherent in the dialectical development of absolute spirit, its second moment or its moment of otherness. The third moment, which will transcend this essential limitation of religion altogether, is of course

> the return out of representation and otherness or the element of self-consciousness itself. —These three moments constitute spirit; its falling asunder [*Auseinandertreten*] into representation consists in its existing in a definite manner; but this definiteness is nothing else than one of its moments.... *Representation* constitutes the middle term between pure thinking and self-consciousness as such. (H 533; M 464; B 765)

Just because it is the mediating movement into otherness, this "synthetic combination" of apparently external events and images in *Vorstellung* has its necessity within the inner development of absolute spirit, despite all its formal deficiencies. It occurs in the picturesque, narrative thinking of the religious community.

Now since the community does, after all, represent for itself the true content of spirit in this necessary but deficient mode, it must comprehend these same three essential moments in its own way. But it comprehends them, not in their conceptual necessity, but as events in a great story. Indeed, its instinct is to found its thinking on the testimony of the primitive community, the early church, and the teachings of that "actual human being" in whom God had been revealed to it. This "instinct" to go back to its origins is in fact an instinctive groping for the concept, "but it confuses the *origin* as the *immediate being-there* of the first appearance with the *simplicity* of the *concept.*" This confusion is characteristic of representational thinking. Like mythic thinking it represents the essential nature of a movement as its primitive origin, which it attempts to recover in its "sheer externality and particularity" (H 532–33; M 463; B 764–65). This tendency to grasp the concept, not in its necessity, but as a series of events or episodes in a story, is characteristic not only of the way the community founds itself on the source of its tradition, but in the way it represents for itself the actual content of its message.

v. The Christian Mythos and the Hegelian Myth of the Self: The Gospel Reinterpreted

There follows in our text an extraordinary interpretation and critique of this message taught by the community constituted by revelatory religion. The community presents the message as a series of episodes in a narrative, and Hegel follows this order, commenting cryptically on each in turn. The series of episodes obviously reflects the traditional mythos of the Christian religion, its sacred story. But the traditional significance invested in the episodes of this story, as the story of salvation, is regularly construed as due to the inevitable distortions of representational thinking.

The first episode stands rather apart, reflecting for Hegel the first moment in the inner development of spirit as it presents itself to consciousness. This moment is represented as the doctrine of the Trinity, in its abstract majesty, apart from the world. The following episodes represent the second moment, the movement into otherness. Here we pass in review the representations of creation, fall, incarnation, crucifixion and resurrection, and finally the immanence of the Holy Spirit in the church that Hegel treats as the transition to the third and consummatory moment. Of last judgment we do not hear, except implicitly, since the truly eschatological moment, from Hegel's phenomenological standpoint, is the community's recognition of the spirit in its own life; this is the "end" of religion as such: both its telos and its Aufhebung. With this significantly different ending, we are presented the basic drama of the Christian credo, what I have called the Christian mythos. The interpretation is not merely dismissive or perfunctory. It is interesting in its own right. We shall see, in fact, that in this rendering the familiar Christian mythos is interpreted in terms of quite a different mythos, which I have called Hegel's myth of the self, presented in its essential elements in the chapter on Self-Consciousness, the dynamic of which is mutual recognition. That is how "the concept" of spirit guides the interpretation of the representational mythos. What cannot be assimilated to the concept, or to the Hegelian myth of the self in which the concept is articulated, is relegated to "faith" and dismissed as such.

At any rate, the following topics are presented as the effort of the religious community to comprehend its revelation in representational form. There are frequent side-glances at the way the scene represented may be grasped conceptually. At the same time Hegel cannot resist getting in some polemical strokes against the egregious perversions of "faith," even while he is trying to show how the religious community proceeds through its own representational path as an intuitive reflection of the concept with which, in its final self-surpassing moment, it culminates. There is no point in summarizing all that Hegel says under each of these headings, but I shall in each case attempt to track this tension in its representational form, guided by the structure of the concept and yet constantly tending to harden into the positive objectivity of faith, taking us back to the self-alienated moment of actual spirit that has been demolished by Enlightenment. And we will take note of the way Hegel's own myth of the self is invested in that guidance attributed to the concept.

The Trinity   Historically, the doctrine of the Trinity emerged as the orthodox statement of the Christian understanding of God only after an extremely complicated process of speculation and controversy in the early church. Given definition at the Council of Nicaea (325 C.E.) and ratified in an expanded version, after having been subjected to a great deal more controversy, at the Council of Constantinople two generations later (381 C.E.), the Creed declared that the second person of the Trinity, the eternal Son or logos, being of the same substance *(homoousia)* as the Father, was "begotten of the Father before all worlds." The biological metaphor of begetting was chosen to distinguish the ontological status of the Son from that of anything created. "Begotten, not made" or created, the Son belonged essentially and eternally to the Godhead, and it was this Son or logos that was incarnate in Jesus Christ and suffered on the cross for the salvation of the fallen human race. Let us say simply that this doctrine developed in the effort to rationalize the Christian understanding of the divine nature in light of what Christian orthodoxy had come to believe about the work of salvation: The Redeemer of the human race was unequivocally divine, of the same substance as the Creator, indeed he was the logos "through whom" the Father had made all things in the beginning. Yet the Father Himself had not suffered and died on Calvary. In these terms the fourth-century church undertook to rationalize what we have called the Christian mythos into a paradoxical but self-consistent story that culminated in a divine work of salvation.

In Hegel's terms, the religious community thus represents even the first moment in the self-development of spirit as a kind of primordial event in which "the eternal essence *begets* for itself an other." It recognizes that this talk of begetting is metaphorical: "in this otherness it has at the same time immediately returned into itself; for the difference is the difference *in itself;* that is, it is immediately differentiated only from itself, it is therefore the identity that returns into itself" (H 534; M 465; B 767). In this trinitarian representation of the primordial Godhead, the community "has the content without its necessity, and instead of the form of the concept it brings the natural relation of father and son into the realm of pure consciousness" (H 535; M 465–66; B 767). The Trinity, so understood (cf. Hegel's own trinitarian speculations, discussed in Chapter 3), is a good example of the peculiar mixture of thought and sensuous image that constitutes *Vorstellung.* The religious consciousness knows perfectly well that the biological relation of begetting is a metaphor, a sensuous image doing service where it might seem least appropriate, to represent an utterly nonsensuous relation within the divine life. But since it *thinks* in such terms, the religious consciousness remains in irreducible ambiguity concerning its deity. The divine essence is indeed "revealed" to consciousness, but since it thinks *"representationally"* the moments of this essence fall apart into distinct entities, and consciousness itself, for its part, "retreats from its own pure object, relating itself only externally to this object; it is revealed to consciousness by something alien, and in this thought of spirit consciousness does not recognize itself, not the nature of pure self-consciousness" (H 535; M 466; B 768).

To this extent, the religious consciousness dissipates into mere faith, an objectifying consciousness that does not self-consciously recognize itself in its object; it loses the content as well as the form of the concept, relegating the content "to a historical representation and an heirloom of tradition; in this way only the pure externality of faith is retained . . . as something dead and unknowable" (H 535; M 466; B 768). So here we have an example of revelatory religion succumbing to faith and unhappy consciousness. This occurs when the "externality" of the representation is itself treated as the object of its devotion (e.g., as a supernatural father who has a son).

What Hegel's own phenomenological program cannot permit him to acknowledge is the possibility that this incorporation by the community of a story of God into the story of its own salvation may be precisely the means by which it appropriates its God as its own: not as its possession, but as its creator eternally bound to his creatures. For this representational mythos cannot be accommodated to the Hegelian myth of the self qua spirit.

That is especially true, of course, of the representation of spirit itself, considered as yet another substantial entity that completes the traditional trio. It is not the purely "abstract" element (the Father), but implies an element of otherness in the pure thought of divine being: not the *actual* otherness, the relation to an actual world, implied in the concept, but a kind of aethereal other in the medium of mere thought. "It is the difference which in pure thought immediately is *no* difference; a recognition *of love* in which the two elements do not according to their essence *stand over against* one another" (H 536; M 466–67; B 769). Love is invoked, as in Hegel's own writings of the late 1790s to unite entities that seem otherwise both differentiated and yet not differentiated. The ambiguity of this simultaneous assertion and denial of differentiation is again characteristic of representational thinking. Spirit, in Hegel's own view, far from being such a pseudoentity in the sphere of abstraction apart from the actual world, is the encompassing identity that unites essence and actuality.

Creation has two sides, the creation of an actual world and of the self, of which the second is far more significant in Hegel's interpretation. The "merely eternal or abstract spirit," the Trinity, "becomes *an other* to itself, or comes into existence and immediately into *immediate being-there*. Thus it *creates* a world." Hegel wastes no time drawing out the mere *Vorstellung* of creation, but relates it at once to the *Begriff:* "This *creating* is the representational word for the *concept* itself in its absolute movement, or for the fact that the simple, or pure thought, that has been asserted as absolute, is rather, because it is abstract, the negative and thereby the self-opposed or *other* of itself" (H 536; M 467; B 769–70).

The "absolute movement" of the concept of spirit inherently contains otherness, an actual world that is at the same time incorporated in spirit itself. But the representation separates these dialectical moments out into the abstraction of an absolute being existing in pure thought apart from the world, and then a world that it plants out as something other than itself. Thus all selfhood is thought to be concentrated in the absolute being, the trinitarian God, and the world is an other *without* selfhood, containing no active agency of its own. It is merely a passive "being for another"; that is, it exists only in its dependence on the divine. Having in this way represented a world without selfhood, the religious consciousness must introduce a self into it, as if by a separate act of creation. But this single self, Adam, is thus also a dependent being, "not yet spirit for itself," and because it does not yet exist "*as* spirit, it can be called *innocent* but not really good" (H 537; M 467; B 770). A "self" that lacks the spiritual condition of selfhood is merely a happy humanoid, like the intelligent predator in Hegel's own myth of the self. It lives sensuously in the moment, without self-consciousness.

The Fall   But according to the concept, self-conscious spirit is in fact implicit in the existence of even such a poor sort of self as this. That is why the religious consciousness, which is unwittingly guided by the concept, cannot represent the self as existing for long in the sensuous paradise of its innocence. The story must add a new episode, in which the immediate sensuous consciousness of its Adam is initiated into self-conscious thought. He must generate a region of otherness within, through a movement of introspection or introversion *(Insichgehen)* in thought, a thought that contains mutually exclusive alternatives. For his sheer sensuous being-there was all of a piece, but since this introverted movement introduces an internal other, the thought that constitutes it must be "the thought that has otherness within it, and is thus the self-opposed thought of good and evil." This particular thought-polarity is hardly chosen at random. Of course Hegel does, after all, know the story! But this particular polarity, represented by the tree of the knowledge of good and evil, does suit his purpose by introducing the counterfactual region of value into Adam's hitherto untroubled immersion in sensuous immediacy. According to the concept this self-differentiation is crucial to the achievement of self-consciousness. But representation, as usual, renders this necessity as if it were accidental, and a most unfortunate accident at that.

> The human being is represented such that it happened, as something not necessary, that he lost the form of being at one with himself [*Sichselbstgleichheit*] through picking from the tree of the knowledge of *good* and *evil,* and was driven out of the condition of innocent consciousness, out of the nature that provided for him without toil, out of paradise, the garden of beasts. (H 537; M 468; B 770–71)

This fall will, of course, turn out to be fortunate in the long run, though not for precisely Miltonian reasons: The happy humanoid must leave the garden of the beasts behind in order ultimately to become a true self.

Two observations before we follow Hegel's interpretation of the fall further: First, thumbing through the opening chapters of the Bible, we note that some important details of the Genesis account are missing in Hegel's rendering: above all, Adam's companionship with God and with the woman in whom he recognizes "flesh of his flesh," and so forth. Eden is not, after all, simply a garden of beasts. God walks there in the cool of the evening, presumably chatting with Adam about the affairs of the day, and the covenant of marriage is also prelapsarian. Both details might seem ready-made for Hegelian exegesis, except that mutual recognition between human beings and between human being and God occur too early in the biblical story for Hegel's myth of the self to accommodate at this juncture. One must begin with the happy humanoid in a garden of beasts, existing like them in immediate desire and enjoyment. For—our second observation—this reading of the prelapsarian paradise and its disruption does bear more than a faint resemblance to the first moments in the chapter on Self-Consciousness. The resemblance may be quite unconscious on Hegel's part, and his interpretation is in any case not so heavy-handed as to make it exact. Here there is no life-and-death struggle, but a polarization does occur that does radically change the conditions of existence, introducing both servitude and a measure of self-consciousness.

The polarization is more abstract than in the life-and-death struggle, at least at the outset: The polarity of good and evil now comes, in the postlapsarian condition of the man routed from the garden, to determine his self-awareness. Having become introverted, the existing consciousness becomes *"unlike,"* discordant within itself:

So *evil* appears as the primary being-there of the introverted consciousness; and because the thoughts of *good* and *evil* are set in utter opposition and this opposition is not yet resolved, this consciousness is essentially just the evil. But at the same time, precisely because of this opposition the *good* consciousness that opposes it is also present, and their relation to one another. (H 538; M 468; B 771)

Since the postlapsarian Adam has become a man of thought, the good and evil spirits confront each other, in the first instance, not in existence but in an ideal region of thought, represented as a kind of heavenly landscape. Lucifer, the son of light, presents a primordial image of Adam's own fall; he asserts his own introverted existence, centered in himself, against the most high. That is the essence of his evil. But Hegel adds, in a startling mixture of angelology with trinitarian theology, that "in the place" of Lucifer, the fallen son of light, "another is immediately begotten" (H 538; M 468; B 771).

This symmetry between fallen Lucifer and the heavenly Christ as prototypes of evil and good, which may owe something to Jacob Böhme,[93] is not entirely foreign to the Christian imagination, which has tended to picture Christ and Lucifer at the head of contending armies of light and darkness. Of course Hegel steadily protests against such fanciful representations as "fall" and "Son," which generate the absurd effort to get an accurate count of such pseudoentities as these faithful and fallen sons of light. To entertain these representational figures of good and evil, furthermore, reifying them as unresolved opposites, each with an independent existence of its own, reduces the actual human being to the status of "self without essence and the synthetic field for their existence and for their battle" (H 539; M 469; B 773). So there is indeed a curious life-and-death struggle between these "universal powers," which in fact have their "actuality" in the self; but the self regards itself as their mere battleground.

Noting this passive and subservient role assumed by the self, and recalling that Hegel had called attention to the way unhappy consciousness creates a mental "doubling" within itself similar to the master-slave relation, it is tempting to suggest that this account of the fall bears an uncanny structural resemblance to the predicament of unhappy consciousness. Our text does not directly refer here to a master-slave relation, nor to unhappy consciousness, and it is futile to speculate about whether Hegel intended to draw the parallel. But it seems implicit in the analysis, intended or not: The Christian mythos of the fall has in fact been interpreted through the supreme negative moment in Hegel's own myth of the self. That the postlapsarian Adam is identified, in his introverted existence, with the fallen angel of light makes all the more striking his resemblance to unhappy consciousness, alienated from his own essential ground.

Incarnation   Evil has already found ready residence in fallen human nature, in particular in the self-centered "introversion" *(Insichgehen)* "of the natural existence of spirit." The divine, on the other hand, has excluded evil from its nature. So the goodness of God confronts the evil of the fallen human's merely natural existence: a division, in truth, within spirit itself, but represented as a simple confrontation between human and divine. But since evil is thus represented as having found its locus within the actual self, so "conversely the good enters into actuality and appears as an existing self-consciousness." We have already seen how the incarnation has been understood in accordance with the *Begriff.* Now it reappears as *Vorstellung:* "It consists in the self-abasement of the divine being, that renounces his abstraction and nonactuality" (H 539; M 469–70; B 773).

Hegel makes the interesting suggestion that, strictly speaking, the divine ought to express itself in evil as well as in good. But since evil has been represented as "alien" to God, this suppressed aspect of the divine has been grasped in an attenuated way *"as his wrath":* The thought of God's wrath "is the highest, hardest exertion of self-confined representation, which, since it lacks the concept, remains unfruitful" (H 539; M 470; B 773).[94] It is not simply that Hegel means to identify good and evil; it is as false to assert their undialectical identity as to represent them in stark opposition. The concept grasps the dialectical "movement" between their identity and their difference (H 542; M 472–73; B 776–77). But since good and evil are here treated, not in their interplay, but as reified opposites, pure thoughts regarded as opposing entities, God can be represented only in his goodness. Evil, on the other hand, is represented as the legacy of fallen human being, in the concentration of its selfhood in its natural existence opposed to the divine.

Under these circumstances an incarnation of the divine seems a paradox indeed. Representational thinking declares "that the divine being [*Wesen*] takes on human nature"; that is, that two natures that are by definition incompatible are somehow united. But the paradox is created by the initial assumption that they are opposites, that the pure ideality of divine being is good, the actually existing self-consciousness evil. We can see, on the contrary, that there is no paradox, that the very assertion "that the divine being takes on human nature" implies "that *in itself* the two are not separated," not really incompatible at all. That "the divine being externalizes [*entäussert*] itself *from the beginning*," which is to say, by its very nature qua spirit, that "its being-there proceeds into itself and becomes evil" likewise implies "that *in itself* this evil being-there is not something alien to it." "Absolute being" is according to the concept all-inclusive; there is nothing inherently alien to it, least of all that actual "being-in-itself" in which it is materially "there."

> The moment of *being-in-itself* rather constitutes the essential moment of the *self* of spirit. —That the *being-in-itself* and thus *actuality* belong to absolute being itself: this, which for us is the *concept* . . . appears to the representational consciousness as an inconceivable *happening*. (H 541; M 471; B 775)

It cannot be otherwise than a paradoxical event, given the tendency of representational thinking to objectify dialectical moments into independent entities—a tendency it shares with what Hegel elsewhere calls "the abstract understanding."

But to assert the union of apparently separate and incompatible entities as a sheer incomprehensible happening simply introduces the incompatibility into their union. Now we have an empirical, existing "self" in union with the "simple thought" of spirit, that is, with the divine as a pure ideality. Spirit is, to be sure, "the absolute unity," of which these two forms, self and pure thought, are dialectical moments. But representational thinking treats the two moments as if they had a prior independence: "The alienation of the divine being . . . consists in the fact that they fall apart from one another and the one has a value unequal to the other" (H 539; M 470; B 773). That is, the presumed union of the divine and the self still retains, for representation, their essential difference. Their difference in value can be assigned in two fatefully disparate ways:

> In the one, the *divine being* is regarded as the essential, the natural being-there and the self as the unessential that is to be transcended [*Aufzuhebende*]; in the other, on the contrary, the

being-for-itself is regarded as the essential, and the simple divine as the unessential. Their still empty middle term is being-there in general, the sheer commonality of their two moments. (H 539–40; M 470; B 773–74)

Though Hegel again does not speak here of unhappy consciousness, the language in which he describes these two alternative renderings of the relation suggests that this familiar impasse has been introduced by representational thinking into the incarnate God itself. Either the finite self is the unessential element, or if, in the typical inversion of unhappy consciousness, it becomes the essential it renders the divine unessential. The latter is the atheistic-humanistic reduction of Christology. The former, the theistic Christology of the church, is what Hegel goes on to analyze. But both are undialectical errors, in which the authentic movement of spirit is lost. Neither is able to "resolve" the impasse except in a reductive manner.

The Christology of the religious consciousness, having prescinded from the spiritual unity of the self, resolves its self-created impasse by treating both the divine being and the existing self as representational "thoughts," as a pair of images deployed in a story. As a free act of the divine being, according to this mythos, it unites itself with the unessential, with a human self. Thus the religious consciousness does not grasp the necessity, in the very concept of spirit, for the spirit to "exteriorize" itself in its other as self. And since in the representational mythos this exteriorization *(Entäusserung),* this coming into existence, is an alienation *(Entfremdung)* of divine being, it can overcome this alienation only in the obliteration of the existing self as such, so that divine being withdraws into its original simplicity. Having "simple" divinity as its essence, the existing self "exteriorizes" its own exterior existence, and in the double negative of this exteriorization-exteriorized razzmatazz it "proceeds into death, and thereby reconciles the absolute being with itself" (H 540; M 471; B 774–75).

Christ's Death and Resurrection   On this reading, Christ's death and resurrection seem not so much the completion of his incarnation as its nullification. But in fact the concept of spirit does assert itself, even under the representational veil. The death of the particular divine-human self, and the consequent return of divinity into its primordial simplicity, will result in the appearance of a *universal* divine-human selfhood. Now the "immediate being-there" of that actual self, which had seemed in its representation to be at odds with its divinity, "has ceased to be alien or external" to the divine essence, "since it is transcended [*aufgehobnes*], universal; this death is thus its arising as spirit" (H 540; M 471; B 775). The resurrected Christ, in other words, is no longer the single individual who died, but is now a collective self, universal spirit.

To follow Hegel's reading of the Christian mythos at this crucial point, we must bear in mind that the collective thought of the community has been the locus of this drama throughout. To say that the resurrected Christ is this very community in its transfiguration into spirit is another way of saying that the community comes to recognize, through the death of the individual Christ, that it itself is now spirit incarnate. Of course, the religious consciousness has from the start represented the "true content" in a manner that was "still *immediate* and thus not spiritual." So it has spoken of the necessary exteriorization of divine essence into its other as God becoming flesh: it "knows the human form of the essence first merely as a particular, not yet as universal." But the *Vorstellung*

> becomes spiritual for this consciousness in the movement of the figurated essence to sacrifice its immediate being-there again and to return to the essence; only the essence *reflected into itself* is spirit. —The *reconciliation* of the divine essence with the *other* generally, and specifically with the *thought* of otherness, with *evil*, is therefore represented herein. (H 541; M 472; B 776)

The linking in this passage of Christ's sacrifice with the divine reconciliation of evil may seem odd. Traditionally, of course, Christians have believed that a sinful world, specifically the human race that had sinfully rebelled against its creator, had in principle been reconciled with God on the cross. For Hegel, however, the evil of the world consists precisely in its being other than its divine essence. The religious representation becomes "spiritual" to the extent that it recognizes in Christ's sacrifice of his own otherness a reconciliation of the most general sort between essence and other.

We have already seen how Hegel regards this reconciliation with evil: not as if evil were simply the same as good, but reconciliation is the "movement" that recovers the dynamic unity in their abstract opposition. It is the same with the abstract opposition between divine being and "nature in its entire range," or that between the divine and the human. To say of any of these opposing terms that the one "is" the other—"the spiritless 'is'"—is as misleading as to pose them in stark opposition. "Essence" and "other"—to state the opposition in its most general form—belong essentially together in spirit; the opposition, however, is not simply false, since the opposed otherness is a dialectical moment in spirit's movement of unification with its other. For instance,

> nature is *nothing apart from* its essence; but this "nothing" itself still *is;* it is the absolute abstraction, thus the pure thinking or being-in-itself, and with the moment of its opposition to the spiritual unity it is the evil. The difficulty that arises in these concepts is solely the holding fast to the "is," and the forgetfulness of the thinking in which the moments just as much *are* as they *are not*—are only the movement which is spirit. (H 543; M 473; B 777)

This general insight concerning the play of essence and other seems a far cry from the church's naively hopeful story. But to the extent that the religious consciousness has grasped this insight in its *Vorstellung* of Christ's sacrifice for the world's sin, it has itself become spiritual: "The dead divine human or human God is *in itself* the universal self-consciousness; it has to become this *for this self-consciousness*" (H 543; M 473; B 778). The religious community, that is, must recognize *itself* as the universal incarnation of deity. But where the concept flies fast as a thought, the community comes to this recognition only through the most maddeningly slow progress, plodding step by step. Its story must bring it to this insight, for that is the representational means by which it can be incorporated self-consciously into the spiritual truth that is its destiny. Precisely by means of that *Vorstellung* in which it grasps the death of the savior as an objectified event, the community must rise to its own spiritual self-consciousness in which objective event as such is aufgehoben in the unity of self and other, identity and difference. Its story must culminate in the Aufhebung of narrative sequence itself into corporate mystical self-recognition.

Our phenomenological interest has accordingly already shifted from the figure of the single divine-human being to the mode in which his story is apprehended by the community. This seemingly formal issue is crucial to the dawning self-consciousness of the community. The Christian mythos, in other words, is already subordinated to the unfolding of our phenomenological myth of the self.

The community already knows that it is a collective spirit; it is self-conscious as a community that has formed around the figure of its dead savior. But it knows itself to be the merely "natural spirit," juxtaposed to the pure negativity of divine spirit. This "natural spirit" withdraws into itself, and knows this avowedly self-centered collective self to be evil: "But it is already *in itself* evil; the withdrawal-into-itself [*Insichgehen*] consists therefore in *convincing itself* that natural being-there is evil" (H 543; M 473–74; B 778). The irony is that the community becomes evil by this withdrawal out of its natural existence into itself. But the crucial step is the grasp of this evil being-there in thought. Now this thought may either be represented to consciousness or known as self-conscious concept. In the former, representational mode, there is the familiar dualism of an existing evil of worldly being-there juxtaposed to the existing reconciliation in divine or absolute being-there. In the latter—conceptual—mode what has been dualistically represented is already aufgehoben, "for the *self* is the negative." This negativity consists in its self-knowledge, in which it is already reconciled, the duality created by representation already reduced to dialectical moments in its reconciliation. So

> each part of the representation receives here the *opposite* meaning from what it had before; each meaning thereby completes itself through the other, and the content is only then a spiritual one . . . just as the opposed meanings were previously united for us or *in itself,* and even the abstract forms of the same and not-*the same, identity* and *non-identity* were transcended. (H 544; M 474; B 779)

The religious consciousness is beginning to catch on! It is even approximating *our* understanding. In particular, it begins to grasp the way a meaning turns into its opposite: The "thought of evil" is "recognized as the first moment of the reconciliation." Confession is the prelude to repentance. To recognize the evil of natural being-there is already "an abandonment of it" qua evil "and the dying away of sin" (H 544; M 474; B 779). As Hegel immediately adds, what is renounced is not "natural being-there as such," but its identification as evil. What transpires, that is, is a change in the self-understanding of the religious consciousness, the abandonment of its self-centered withdrawal *(Insichgehen)*—which is its real evil—and the reconciliation of its natural being with its communal, spiritual identity.

This purely inward drama is what is "represented" outwardly as the story of the death and resurrection of Christ. The representational consciousness, always several steps behind, gradually becomes aware of this equation as well, but in its own way. Its representational grasp *(Begreifen)*

> is therefore not the apprehension of this concept, which knows the transcended natural existence as universal, and thus as reconciled with itself, but is an apprehension of that *representation,* that through the *happening* of the divine being's own exteriorization, through his incarnation and his death that have happened, the divine being is reconciled with his being-there.—The apprehension of this representation now expresses more definitely what in this connection was previously called the spiritual resurrection, or the becoming universal of God's single self-consciousness, or his becoming the community. (H 545; M 475; B 780)[95]

Christ's death relegates his mere particularity to the status of the "natural universality" of humus. It is the destiny of particularity as such to vanish into the common soil from which it sprang. But incarnate deity, spirit, is thereby merely liberated from its particularization. By its death it becomes "transfigured into the *universality* of spirit, which dwells in its community, dies in it daily and is daily resurrected" (H 545; M 475; B 780). In this death-and-transfiguration the divine becomes, without remainder, the indwelling spirit of the community. That is not simply the culmination of the story as such. Insofar as the story does reach this culmination it surpasses itself as a story narrated by and for the community about objectified figures and events: It undergoes metamorphosis into the life of the community itself. It is as if a reader of a romance were interrupted in his reading by the sudden appearance and embrace of the heroine herself. Insofar as the community now knows itself to be the locus of spirit the objectified mode of *Vorstellung* will have died away, together with its central figure, in spiritual self-knowledge. Hegel describes this converging double movement with handsome symmetry: The particular self-consciousness of "the Mediator" has become universal, and the universal, the community, "has just thereby become self-consciousness, and the pure or nonactual spirit of mere thought has become *actual*" (H 545; M 476; B 781).

In describing this metamorphosis it is necessary to employ the cautious qualifiers "insofar as" or "to the extent that." For we are not necessarily describing what has happened historically in the church or in any other actual religious community. Perhaps so, perhaps not, perhaps in part. The description is hypothetical: This is what must occur *if* religious experience is to pass over into self-recognitive knowledge, *Vorstellung* into *Begriff*. *To the extent that* an actual community formed around something like the Christian mythos undergoes this metamorphosis, it transcends the formal limitations of religion itself, just as the mystical ascent, with the soul's progressively clearer mirroring of deity, culminates in the dissolution of the soul as such in its union with God.

Again, however, *insofar as* the community achieves this self-consciousness it will be driven to radical conclusions scarcely dreamt of within the limits of the religious consciousness: There is no God except the community's own indwelling spirit. The individual Mediator has mediated between the natural self and the divine. But his death signifies not only the death of his particular organism but the death of "abstract" or self-subsistent divinity: "The death of the Mediator is the death not only of his *natural* side or his particular being-for-self, there dies not only the already dead husk stripped of its essential being, but there dies also the *abstraction* of the divine being" (H 546; M 476; B 781). In fact, Hegel suggests, the representation of the Mediator in the "one-sidedness" of a particular self is deficient, just because "abstract" divinity cannot dissolve without remainder into a single self. We have seen the contradictions that arise in asserting their union. This "reconciliation" can occur only in a "universal" self, that is, in the spirit of a community. That corporate self is the God-solvent. "The *abstraction* of the divine being" in fact signifies any representation of deity altogether transcending the sphere of social life and the actual world in which it is conducted. Insofar as divine spirit is entirely immanent in that social sphere and its world, any such "abstraction" of divine being becomes superfluous. The death of that one-sidedly individuated Mediator implies at once the death of self-subsistent divinity and its resurrection as spirit-in-community.

> The death of this representation implies, therefore, at the same time, the death of the *abstraction of the divine being* that is not posited as self. This death is the painful feeling of the unhappy consciousness that *God himself is dead*. This harsh expression

is the expression of the innermost simple self-knowledge, the
return of consciousness into the depth of the night of I=I, that
distinguishes and knows nothing outside itself. (H 546; M 476;
B 781–82)

The Fichtean formula, "I=I," signifies here the identity with itself of
all that this collective self recognizes as spirit. Hegel will continue to
use this formula in the final chapter for this ultimate self-recognitive
knowledge.

This all-encompassing corporate life of the spirit and the death of
God are two sides of the same coin. The existence of a community that
has appropriated all spiritual substance into its own life would imply
the death of God. Unhappy consciousness, as we have seen, has already
bemoaned the death of its God. But what for unhappy consciousness
is a feeling of loss and a truth cruelly harsh is for the spiritual community the simple truth implicit in its own self-affirmation. For the spiritual community, beyond the toils of unhappy consciousness, there is
nothing harsh about this truth at all. The king is dead, long live the
republic! Already in the conclusion to *Glauben und Wissen* (1802) Hegel
had affirmed a "speculative Good Friday" consisting not merely of the
crucifixion of Christ but of the death of God, and there, too, this event
was followed by an Easter in which divine spirit was resurrected in an
entirely different form.[96] Here that "abstraction" of divine being is
precisely the "substance" that must be transfigured into "subject." The
self-recognitive knowledge of the spiritual community "is therefore the
inspiration through which substance has become subject; its abstraction and lifelessness have died, and substance has thus become *actual*
and simple and universal self-consciousness" (H 546; M 476; B 782).

The Indwelling of the Spirit   Only superficially is there any
resemblance between the church's teaching about the gift of the Holy
Spirit and our phenomenological reading of this indwelling spirit. In
the traditional Christian mythos, to be sure, the gift of the spirit to
the church was the promised consequence of the death of the savior,
the next act in the drama of salvation. But both the crucifixion of Christ,
the second person of the Trinity incarnate, and the descent of the third
person into the church's corporate life were safely interpreted within
the framework of trinitarian theology. Hegel of course recognizes that
the church had never drawn conclusions so subversive of its belief in

God from the crucifixion of Christ. *To that extent,* Hegel is insisting, the Christian community has failed to confront its own harsh truth, and thereby has failed to appropriate the indwelling spirit.

We have seen how the text identifies three essential moments in the inner development of spirit. The first has been represented by the religious community in its doctrine of the Trinity. The second, the objectification of spirit into the particularities of concrete existence, was represented in the intervening moments we have reviewed. The third, the return out of the objectified sphere into the element of self-consciousness, is the indwelling of the spirit. "Spirit is thus established in its third element, in *universal self-consciousness;* it is its community" (H 543; M 473; B 778).

Now the spirit's own community is still a religious community; its thought is still representational. That is a matter of some systematic importance, since it is what distinguishes even this consummatory moment of revelatory religion from absolute knowledge. But this lingering employment of *Vorstellung* is also somewhat paradoxical, since this third moment consists in spirit's "return" out of *Vorstellung.* Hegel acknowledges this paradox: The "content" of the community's knowledge "is in general in the form of representation for it," even in "its return out of its representation" (H 547; M 477; B 783). The solution to the paradox is the fact that the second moment, comprising creation, fall, incarnation, crucifixion and resurrection, is necessarily represented in image and narrative; it is the moment of otherness, of objectified experience, required by the concept itself. But the religious consciousness has also grasped the first moment in a representational manner and, more important, continues to do so even with respect to the third moment, objectifying even spirit's "return" into the community that is the locus of the religious consciousness itself.

It could not, by definition, do otherwise and still remain within the confines of "religion." But the result is crucial to the design of the *Phenomenology.* The religious community's *Vorstellung* expresses the true content, which is spirit; to this extent spirit can already be said to be "self-knowing." And the community itself *is* self-conscious spirit. But it does not yet know that it itself is the very content that it knows. Upon this seemingly rather hairsplitting distinction, this remaining hiatus between the community's consciousness and its self-consciousness, is hung the last veil that prevents the community's transcendence of religion altogether. But the two sides of the distinction are fully developed in the community, lacking only their fusion in self-recognitive knowledge. On the one hand, self-knowing spirit "knows itself"—though it does not yet know that the spirit it knows is in fact itself:

> That which is object for it *is,* or its representation is the true absolute *content;* it expresses . . . spirit itself. It is at the same time not merely the content of self-consciousness and not merely the object *for it,* but it is also *actual spirit.* It is actual spirit because it passes through the three elements of its nature; this movement through its own self constitutes its actuality; —what moves itself is spirit, it is the subject of the movement and it is equally *the movement* itself, or the substance through which the subject proceeds. (H 546–47; M 476–77; B 782)

Precisely in its excursion into the representational form of its mythos, which culminates in its return into itself, the community fulfills the conditions of spiritual actuality. And what it knows, precisely as the culminating episode in its mythos, is the true content: spirit-in-its-community. But the representational route it has necessarily followed to this spiritual self-knowledge prevents it from recognizing that it itself is, beyond the need of further fulfillment, precisely this spirit-in-community. In other words, its truth is still "revealed" to it, rather than arising out of its own self-knowledge. It still awaits the kingdom of God.

Hegel's rather sparse remarks about the spiritual community are largely devoted to spelling out this fine-grained dialectical distinction. He does not, as in other cases, evoke something of the concreteness of this moment in the life of experience, letting us feel what it is like, for itself, to step into this frame of mind. But the reader who has followed these preceding moments closely can project some aspects of the spiritual community's life. For instance, the contrasting case of the comic consciousness is suggestive. The contrast is relevant, because the comic consciousness, too, experiences the death of all gods as a liberating development, and recognizes all remaining spiritual substance to be concentrated in itself. But for the comedian and his audience there is scarcely any spiritual substance left, only so much as is needed to support this poor forked thing in his isolation, as he struts and capers about the stage. The self-important claim of this figure, who is in every sense disenfranchised, is rather an admission of loss, not only of the divine but of any significant community. What you see is what you get:

an emptiness. But the spiritual community is a fullness. Revelatory religion has in fact brought a new community into existence out of the desolation, with all the corporate solidarity of the ethical world. Yet it is not ethnically based, not animated by a Volksgeist, but is in principle universal, without national limits, the locus of absolute spirit. It is the Weltgeist's own community, in principle wracked neither by internal contradiction (divine versus human law, and so forth) nor by any necessary opposition to other communities. Furthermore, we recall that revelatory religion also recovers the entire spiritual legacy of the past in a new spirit of aesthetic inwardness that sounds, to be sure, suspiciously Romantic, but at any rate abjures the harsh iconoclasm of the Enlightenment, and might be expected to express its universality in new forms of art.

If there is in this picture more than a hint of the imperialistic claims of Christianity in the heyday of Christendom, it is also the case that the particularity of the Christian mythos has been thoroughly subordinated to an essentially nonsectarian myth of the self. If Hegel were correct in thinking that this new myth is in principle universal, incorporating into itself on its own terms the world's entire spiritual inheritance, this putative universalism would produce a cosmopolitan outlook quite without precedent. Unlike the comic spirit it would not be a cosmopolitanism of universal loss and impoverishment, nor would its receptivity be cramped by divisions of Volk, race, social class, or gender. Just the universal emptiness of legal status and Enlightenment would have cleared the field for this new fullness. No doubt a more convinced Hegelian than the author of this book could draw out even more wondrous implications of this universalism.

Finally, it is safe to say that the new spiritual community would have synthesized the rich corporate solidarity of the ethical world with the moral individualism of the self-certain spirit. As the "actual spirit" that has progressed through the essential moments in the development of spirit generally, it would unite in itself the polarity between ethical solidarity and moral individuality developed in the chapter on actual Spirit. In fact Hegel himself does call attention to the incorporation into the spiritual community of that conscientious "spirit certain of itself" that provided the transition from actual Spirit to religion, in particular to the fact that this conscientious spirit finally "forgives evil and thereby renounces its own simplicity and rigid unchangeableness." In other respects the arbitrariness and pretension of the conscientious spirit and the sentimentality of the beautiful soul hardly provide a

very promising model. But the posture of mutual forgiveness that finally melts the hard-hearted moralism of the protagonists is a necessary if not sufficient condition for a spiritual community as Hegel
conceives it. Because the religious consciousness incorporates

> the movement that acknowledges the absolutely *opposed* as *the
> same* and this acknowledgment breaks forth as the *Yes* between
> these extremes, —the religious consciousness, to which the abso-
> lute being is revealed, *beholds* this concept, and transcends the
> *difference* between its own *self* and *what it beholds;* as it is the
> subject, so also is it the substance, and *is* therefore itself the
> spirit, just because and insofar as it is this movement. (H 547;
> M 477; B 782–83)

The power to forgive evil is the crowning sign of the indwelling of the
all-reconciling spirit in this community.

Still, still, still: "This community, however, is not yet perfected in
this its self-consciousness." The long final paragraph is devoted to spelling out this remaining imperfection. We have already seen that its
flaw, insurpassable so long as it remains a religious community, lies
in the fact that *Vorstellung* is its characteristic form of thought. The
aesthetic richness it exhibits in its receptivity to stories and images
constitutes the threshold it cannot cross so long as its consciousness
is fundamentally religious. It cannot bring its consciousness to rest in
its own self-consciousness. The community "does not also possess the
consciousness of that which it is; it is the spiritual self-consciousness
that is not an object to itself as this self-consciousness, or which does
not unfold itself to a consciousness of itself; rather, insofar as it is
consciousness it has the representations that we have considered"
(H 547; M 477; B 783).

This formal hiatus between its consciousness and its self-
consciousness, which Hegel goes on to elaborate, necessarily has definite material consequences as regards the actual content of the representations that are placed before the religious consciousness. Its actual
self-consciousness, its existence as a community with divine spirit totally immanent in its own life, implies the death of God, but its consciousness continues to entertain representations of an alien deity that
is the agent of its own story of salvation. So it does not grasp "for itself
. . . that this depth of the pure self is the force through which the
abstract divine *being* is drawn down from its abstraction and through

the power of this pure devotion is elevated to a self" (H 547–48; M 477–78; B 783–84).

It does not recognize in this indwelling of the divine in the corporate selfhood of the community "its *own* action as such." It therefore does not consciously lay hold of its ultimate reconciliation with divine spirit as its own present possession, but projects it into an indefinite future: into the *Jenseits*.

> Since this unity of essential being and self has *in itself* been achieved, consciousness also still has this *representation* of its reconciliation, but only as a representation. . . . Its satisfaction therefore remains burdened with the opposition of a Beyond. Its own reconciliation therefore enters into its consciousness as something *distant,* as something distant in the *future,* just as the reconciliation that the other *self* fulfilled appears as something distant in the *past.* So just as that *single* divine human has a father subsisting-*in-itself* and only an *actual* mother, so also the universal divine human, the community, has for its father its *own action* and *knowledge,* but for its mother the *eternal love* that it only *feels,* but does not behold in its consciousness as an actual, immediate *object.* Its reconciliation is therefore in its heart, but with its consciousness it is still divided, and its actuality is still broken. (H 548; M 478; B 784)

So the religious consciousness is, even in its highest form, splayed between the specious past of its Christology and its specious eschatological future. One more lesson of experience still lies ahead: Spirit must learn how to occupy the fullness of the present in which self-consciousness is already "in itself" reconciled. But then it will cease to be religious. The religious elevation of finite spirit to absolute spirit can only be completed when it passes beyond religion as such: when it becomes wisdom.

6. Inconclusions

The *Phenomenology* ends with a bundle of distinctively Hegelian ironies, not all of them intended by Hegel himself. The central irony is that the final chapter of the work seems to offer a positive conclusion to the epic tale of relentless negativity that has preceded it, but is in fact overtaken by this negativity. Explaining this central irony, and commenting on some of the others, will enable us to say as much as we need to about the concluding chapter of the *Phenomenology,* and at the same time to conclude the present study. If both conclusions prove inconclusive, perhaps spirit itself is an ironist. Still, this final chapter of Hegel's text does in a manner complete the dialectical unfolding of Hegel's myth of the self, into which gospel religion is aufgehoben: is dissolved and distilled.

"Absolute Knowledge" may well be the most grandiose title ever assigned the concluding chapter of a philosophical book. It surely seems to promise quite a lot, particularly for a chapter only twenty pages long in the original edition, much the briefest of the six major parts of the text. Certainly the chapter does not offer a consummatory journey's end commensurate with such a long pathway of doubt and despair. In fact it was written as a transitional chapter. As we have seen, the *Phenomenology* was not intended to stand alone. It was published as the "First Part" of a "System of Science," and this concluding chapter of our text was designed to furnish a transition to the "speculative" and "real" parts of that projected *System der Wissenschaft.* The full conclusion was to be a science of wisdom built on the phenomenological foundations laid by our text. That, of course, was left unwritten, so the first irony connected with the concluding chapter of the *Phenomenology* is that these few pages have instead had to ring the curtain down on this monumental work. The chapter is sketchy, very suggestive but hardly consummatory. An "absolute knowledge," a wisdom transcending philo-sophia's wistful love of wisdom, is described but not articulated in any systematic way.

Not that this knowledge entails any vast catalogue of information. It is not definitive cosmology or metaphysics, nor does its absoluteness imply that the omniscience imputed to the God of religion devolves upon human wisdom instead. Something of the sort may be what one might expect from "absolute knowledge," but Hegel's use of the term ironically inverts that expectation. It is, in the first place, that knowledge of human fallibility of which the *Phenomenology* provides an ample introduction. It is characteristic, after all, of all those protagonists we have met along the way to assume that they are in possession of some sort of unsurpassable knowledge. It scarcely occurs to the slave's master, or to the skeptic, or to the phrenologist or the ethical citizen or the beautiful soul, even to claim they know it all, so secure are they all in the implicit confidence that they do. Nor, of course, are the various devotees of religion far behind in such confidence. All of these protagonists do have their pennyworth of insight, which is not simply proven false when each in turn is dismissed from the stage. But all of them do betray a fallibility they never suspected. That is what "we" learn, who make up the tragicomic chorus beholding their travails. If our knowledge is superior to theirs it is not because it is infallible. It is rather because we know, like Socrates, that we do not know. Fallibility is the root of our absolute knowledge, nourished by experience. As described in the final chapter of our text, absolute knowledge adds nothing to what we have already learned from experience. To that extent it still remains within the phenomenological project.

But if self-conscious fallibility is its root, the knowledge that grows from this root appropriates experience in a particular way. There is indeed an ascent from and through experience to knowledge, to the hard-won region of clarity, but it is only achieved episodically, before it gives way again to the vital obscurity of experience. This ascent is Sisyphean. Every act of knowing is itself a clarification of the specific course of experience that is its source. It is like the flowering phase in the life cycle of a plant, its typical form describable in general terms, but in its detail never predictably the same in every growth. In the life of experience it is the phase of lucidity. The ensemble of such flowerings can be organized, systematized, but such a systematic *Wissenschaft* can never be more certain nor more perduring than the moments that compose it, and it can always be dissolved, in whole or in part, through the continuing onrush of experience. Particularly in a science of self-knowledge, different in kind from all positive sciences in that experience is not merely the medium of discovery but the very stuff to be grasped, any organized body of knowledge is always in motion.

Such is the odd position of the science that crowns the Hegelian phenomenological project. If this absolute knowledge is made to appear, on this showing, all too radically relative, indeed evanescent, the apparent contradiction arises only because of a long-standing habit of mind that identifies the absolute with the static. That is an assumption from which Hegel attempts again and again to wean us, insisting that what is absolute is always dynamic, self-transformative, never locked into any single unchanging form. Readers have always found it difficult to believe he means what he says. Perhaps he does not always remember it himself. But to quote merely one passage of many, a famous one from the Preface to the *Phenomenology:*

> The evanescent is . . . itself to be regarded as essential, not in the determination of something fixed, cut off from the true and left lying outside it, who knows where, any more than the true is to be regarded as resting on the other side, a dead positive. Appearance is the arising and passing away that does not itself arise and pass away, but is in itself and constitutes the actuality and movement of the life of truth. The true is thus the Bacchanalian revel in which no member is not drunk, and because each member no sooner withdraws than he dissolves, the revel is just as much transparent and simple repose. (H 39; M 27; B 105)

In this sense, to be sure, knowledge is always true! The constancy in which it reposes is just the steady commotion of the revel where nothing stays in place for long. The only thing that does not arise and pass away in the revelers' field of vision is the mad flux of the arising and passing away of each thing that meets his eyes; the only tune that does not die away almost as soon as it begins consists in the striking and dying away of every note. Only the evanescent is the true, and the folk who insist on something that will last are the ones who thereby drop out of truth's Bacchanalia and dissolve, presumably onto the spurious peace of the sodden floorboards. Can "the true" really be as mad as this perpetual topsy-turvy? Has not Hegel roundly declared, a few pages earlier in the Preface, that "the truth is the whole," perhaps evoking for the learned reader the Spinozistic *amor dei intellectus* to which the wise of every age ascend? But Spinoza's unchanging substance is precisely what has been superseded by the yeasty "subject" of the Hegelian Geist. "The truth is the whole." But to this other oft-quoted statement in the Preface, Hegel immediately adds: "But the whole is only the essence perfecting itself through its development" (H 21; M 11; B 81). He goes on to explain that this whole, the absolute, is only an abstract word apart from its constant passing into concrete otherness and its mediation of this otherness. Here the essential is the evanescent. The unending process of experience and its clarification furnish the dynamic element in this whole. Its "perfecting itself" does not imply that it is proceeding, teleologically, toward a final perfection. Its self-perfecting is an unending process, nourished by fresh experience. Phenomenology, the science of the *phainomena* of experience, can never be a superseded moment in a science of wisdom.

Let us look more closely at this science of wisdom, by connecting some of the pivotal terms employed in the chapter entitled "Absolute Knowledge," together with others that have played a central role in our analysis of earlier chapters.

i. Recognition and the Spiritual Self: The I That Is a We

Hegel's phenomenological project is in the Socratic tradition. Wisdom is self-knowledge, the hard-won fruit of the dialectical art. The self that knows becomes identical with the self that is known, but the locus of this identity is not a single psycho-physical organism. The knowing self is a dialogue with others, in which it does not immediately recognize itself. We have observed the many phases of this dialogue in the *Phenomenology,* in which self achieves this recognition in one mode after another, shedding spurious identities in the process. Identifying itself in the beginning with a bare epistemological subject (consciousness), it undergoes a Socratic interrogation that undermines the very subject-object duality that had been the assumed presupposition of all cognition. It then learns to know itself in mutual recognition with other individual selves (self-consciousness), so that self is intersubjective, the I that is a we, the we that is an I. Self-knowledge, then, is not merely cognitive, but recognitive, reflexive. These two basic structures of selfhood (consciousness and self-consciousness) are then reiterated in alternate chapters at ever richer and more capacious levels of self-identity. The subject-object structure of consciousness reappears as reason and as religion, to make up what we have called the A-series. The reflexive or recognitive structure of self-consciousness reappears as actual or historical spirit and now as absolute self-knowledge, to make up what we have called the B-series.

"We" who have witnessed and commented on this hard passage to self-knowledge through doubt and despair, we too have learned something from it, though our sufferings, aside from the pain of reading an excruciatingly dense text, have been vicarious. Lacking the immediacy of self-discovery experienced by the text's suffering protagonists, we have by way of compensation enjoyed the retrospective insight that permitted us to recognize coherent patterns in the entire progress of their metamorphoses, and we have also been given some little hints along the way. We have been told, for instance, as early as the chapter on Self-Consciousness, that the self-recognitive self is in fact spirit, a term that implies the collective and self-transcending dimensions of which the protagonist selves were quite unaware. The last three chapters trace the course of their enlightenment. Self is recognitive spirit, but even in the chapter on actual Spirit this spirit has recognized itself as ethical world, as culture, as morality, and so forth without yet recognizing the spirit that encompasses all of these historical appearances. In the chapter on Religion, finite spirit does recognize this all-encompassing spirit, in representations of divine spirit, but does so in the manner of the A-series: it is *conscious* of spirit, but does not recognize *itself* as spirit. In the final chapter spirit does recognize itself as spirit. With this recognition the distinction, scrupulously observed before, between protagonist self and "we" who have witnessed its ordeals, breaks down, at least in principle. Our text is itself a work of self-recognitive spirit. It is at once both a kind of biography and autobiography of self coming to recognition of itself as spirit, a self-referential work that is itself an eminent instance of what it describes. In its final chapter "we" too appear in the text together with its other protagonists. We are both knowing and known.

"Absolute Knowledge" is admittedly a bloated and misleading name for this surprising self-knowledge, which actually is modest as can be. It implies, after all, an utter abnegation of psychological egoism, Volk chauvinism, pretensions to cultural superiority, and the like, which are nothing but the bad jokes of deformed spirits. Of course they continue to overtake us, often in new and more alluring guises, and then the joke is on us! For the personal ego, lodged in a single physical organism, does not disappear. To recognize itself in an infinite spirit is to recognize just how limited that personal ego is, and all its works and filiations. Self-recognitive knowledge is humbling. The self that knows the limitless horizon of its spirit is content with its personal limitations. It does not, like the unhappy consciousness, yearn to be more than it is. It has found fulfillment in an expansive life of the spirit in which it recognizes itself. The recognition is mutual: The very contingency, localization, and momentariness of the self is essential to the dynamism of the spirit. Self-recognitive knowledge "knows not only itself, but also the negative of itself, or its limit. To know its limit means to know how to sacrifice itself. This sacrifice is the externalization in which spirit displays its process of becoming spirit in the form of *free accidental happening,* viewing its pure *self* as *time* outside it, and equally its *being* as space" (H 563; M 492; B 806–7).

Self-recognitive knowledge constantly gives way to the obscurity and vitality of experience, where spirit is plunged into space and time, nature and history, a "sacrifice" through which it recovers itself in fresh configurations. Knowledge is in this sense no less vital than the experience that engenders it. The term "sacrifice," furthermore, has an unmistakable religious resonance. Four years earlier, in the conclusion to *Glauben und Wissen* that we have analyzed in some detail (see Chapter 3), Hegel had spoken of a "speculative Good Friday" as the dialectical precondition for the resurrection of that "highest totality" that would constitute true knowledge. Here the pattern is in a sense reversed, since spirit must perpetually sacrifice the provisional coherence and specious ideality of its knowledge to the vital obscurity, suffering, and contingency of experience in order to know and be known afresh, in a knowledge that keeps pace with its life.

To call this knowledge "absolute" does not imply the knower's domination of the known, or possession of a completed body of truth, or any final word to end the dialectical conversation. The implication is quite the contrary. There is no final knowledge that can surpass this unending process of learning from experience. Still, self-recognitive knowledge is "absolute" in two respects: Here, in the first place, the spirit in which I recognize myself is all-encompassing, like the divine in revelatory religion. That is why the two final chapters of the *Phenomenology* make up a pair, each grasping spirit in its most comprehensive manifestation. But the pairing also brings out the crucial difference between religion and self-knowledge, as they complete the A-series and the B-series respectively. Religion presents me with the universal spirit, but so long as I confront it in the representational mode of religion it is an Object in which I do not recognize myself. Furthermore, the divine is usually represented as immutable. Absolute knowledge, however, is self-recognitive, and in its reflexivity the integral relation of the encompassing spirit to the contingencies of experience render the encompassing spirit as mutable as the experiencing self. Spirit is universal, but the "whole" is changing, open to novelty.

So there is a second way in which self-recognitive knowledge is "absolute": the reflexivity in which I recognize myself in universal spirit is itself absolute, an unbroken circle of mutual recognition that abides through all its transformations, for which Hegel uses the Fichtean formula "I=I": "this *single* self that is immediately a pure knowing or universal [self]" (H 553; M 482; B 793). Absolute spirit, unlike the divine in its religious manifestation, is not simply the universal self, but is the mutually recognizing single and universal self.

So self-recognitive knowledge, in this expansive sense, completes one of the trajectories that has unfolded through the entire *Phenomenology*, with its alternating and ever more capacious moments of Consciousness and Self-Consciousness, A-series and B-series. That much seems clear. But in the concluding chapter Hegel describes this apparent moment of closure in a confusing variety of ways. Sometimes self-recognitive knowledge seems scarcely cognitive at all, or is so only incidentally, as the ensemble of experienced objects or images furnish the mirror in which the self comes to recognize itself. At one point, for instance, Hegel seems to acknowledge, if only in a rather muddled and embarrassed way, that this knowledge has little to do with anything strictly or soberly cognitive: True, "nothing becomes *known* that is not in *experience*"; that is the phenomenological principle, but Hegel goes on to paraphrase it in quasi-religious terms, and ends by appearing to throw up his hands altogether: "nothing becomes *known* that is not in *experience, or as the same thing can also be expressed, that is not present as felt truth, as inwardly revealed* eternal, as *believed* holy, or whatever expressions may otherwise be used" (H 558; M 487; B 800).

The expressions that Hegel does use seem to evoke a kind of *unio mystica,* and that would complete another trajectory that runs through the chapter on Religion, where the religious experience of the human race is epitomized as a mystical ascent. Hegel loosely follows late classical pagan and medieval Christian prototypes of the mystical way, but rather than being typified by an individual journey, the ascending path for Hegel is collective, within and among entire religious traditions, though in principle it can be pursued within any historic tradition. For many mystical writers, notably Meister Eckhart, whom Hegel had admired from his earliest days, the culmination of the mystical path lay beyond religious belief and practice as such, as not only the soul, with all natural things, but correlatively God himself as an independent being disappeared together into the abyss of an all-embracing *Gottheit*. It would not have occurred to an Eckhart to describe this culmination, beyond religion, as a kind of knowledge, but it seems here to be the sort of experience on which self-recognitive knowledge is based.

Of course this knowledge is not empirical either, in the sense disposed of to Hegel's satisfaction in the opening chapter of the text. Here he goes on to say that this "experience" which he has described in quasi-mystical terms, is such that its "content—and it is spirit—is *in itself* substance, and thus *object* of *consciousness*." But he no sooner invokes the Spinozistic language of substance than he speaks, as he does in the Preface, of substance becoming subject: For

> this substance, which is spirit, is its *becoming* what it is *in itself;* and only as this becoming reflecting itself into itself is it in itself truly *spirit*. It is in itself the movement that is cognition [*Erkennen*]—the metamorphosis of that *in itself* into the *for itself,* of the *substance* into the *subject,* of the object of *consciousness* into the object of *self-consciousness,* that is, into the object that is just as much transcended [*aufgehoben*], or into the *concept*. It is the circle returning into itself, that presupposes its beginning and only reaches it at the end. (H 558–59; M 487–88; B 801)

This process can be described from two standpoints, though the point is that the two are finally the same. We can say that the spiritual substance must develop until it encompasses the historical self that has known it only in the mode of consciousness, only as object. Or we can say that the historical self, individual or collective, must develop until it recognizes itself in the spiritual substance.

But the process within the life of spiritual substance is complete only when the self achieves this self-recognition. Though Hegel does not use the word "recognition" here, I take it that only then, when the movement from cognition to re-cognition is complete, can it be described as the circle returning into itself, like the serpent biting its tail. Historically an end can be discerned in its beginning, or indeed that a beginning has been made, only retrospectively. Such retrospective insight has been epitomized in the long chapter on historical Spirit, to which Hegel harks back in the earlier part of the present chapter. But it is not completed in its ideal circularity on the historical plane as such. These last two chapters, Religion and Absolute Knowledge, define the region in which the social self of historical spirit recognizes the absolute spirit, and then recognizes itself in this absolute spirit. For the local spirits of the historical process are distributed over time, fragmented. "Therefore, so long as spirit has not completed itself *in itself,* not as world spirit [*Weltgeist*], it cannot attain its completion as *self-conscious* spirit. The content of religion therefore declares what *spirit is* earlier in time than science [*Wissenschaft*] does; but science is alone its true knowledge of itself" (H 559; M 488; B 802). Religion and the science of wisdom are the spheres of absolute spirit, where end and beginning make up the circle returning to itself. But this science comprises the self-recognitive knowledge in which absolute spirit is complete not only "in itself" but "for itself."

That sounds like consummation. But in order to continue our scrutiny of this science of wisdom, let us examine the "concept"—*Begriff*—that is its medium. For that purpose we will need to recall another trajectory that runs through our text.

ii. Language and the Concept

In his discussion of "Culture and Its Realm of Actuality" Hegel declares that language "is the *being-there* [Dasein] of the pure self qua self" (H 362; M 308; B 530). Nothing that came earlier in our text quite prepared us for this sudden statement about the significance of language, and it seemed at first to be limited to the immediate context, as a statement about that "pure self" that is an alienated product of the artificiality of "culture." Perhaps that is what Hegel himself originally intended, and he may only have recognized as he proceeded that he had stumbled upon a principle of vast ramification. In the section on "Conscience, the Beautiful Soul, etc." that concludes the chapter on Spirit, he harks back to this principle to explain the mutual recognition that occurs between two conscientious selves: "Here again we see *language* as the being-there of spirit" (H 458; M 395; B 660). It has now become clear that language is, in a perfectly general sense, the medium of that recognition that constitutes the mutuality of spiritual entities or selves in their evanescent reality. The emergence and development of various linguistic forms is central, in particular, to the analysis of the types of divine-human reciprocity treated in the chapter on Religion, and so the significance of language was given major attention in our interpretation of that chapter.

Spirit "is there" in language. This *Dasein* of spirit denotes the specific localizations in which selves or spirits recognize one another, and come to some particular self-recognition in the process. Spirit takes many forms, some of them quite limited and even perverse (e.g., in alienated culture or among "beautiful souls"), but in each case there is some mode of mutual recognition mediated by language. The localizations and epiphanies of spirit are always occasions of language, and are limited by the form of language employed. Spirit also involves material embodiment, but these materializations are recognized as epiphanies of spirit or of self because some kind of speech is exchanged. To that extent a self is not reducible to its organic life, nor a community to its physical environment, though the existence of any form of spirit both requires and reflects its specific material conditions. For that matter, language itself necessarily has material conditions, such as voice or inscription or gesture. But the prodigious range of what can be said and how it can be said, and thus the multitude of ways in which spirit can "be there," reflects the formal modes of language. Spirit is there in one way in epic narrative, in quite a different way in dramatic dialogue, and in still other ways in different kinds of religious representation. Presumably it is also there in specific linguistic conventions of political debate or courtship rituals or gatherings at the corner pub. There is in principle no end to the specific formations in which spirit can be *there,* in particular times and places, in language. History, Hegel says, is "a slow movement and succession of spirits, a gallery of images, each endowed with the complete richness of spirit" (H 563; M 492; B 807).

However, although there may be no end to this historical proliferation of spirits, our selective phenomenological account introduces a certain order into their succession, and in this formal ordering there is an end. There is no suggestion that it puts a stop to the historical proliferation, but it does culminate the phenomenological ordering in a manner that gives it a privileged position among all possible modes of spirit's being there. It is constituted by that mode of spirit's *Dasein* that Hegel calls *der Begriff:* the concept. But what distinguishes the concept among all the ways that spirit can be there? Is it, too, a kind of language? Hegel does not explicitly say that it is, though it is closely associated in the final chapter with *Wissenschaft,* with scientific or systematic-dialectical knowing *(Wissen).* One is tempted to think that it is the characteristic language of philosophy, or the philosophical language employed by Hegel. That hardly offers us much of a definition! Deferring the issue of definition, however, we can still be fairly clear about the functional position occupied by the concept in the *Phenomenology:* Whether it is itself a type of language or not, it does seem to complete the succession of linguistic forms in which spirit has been found to be localized in the later portions of our text. It is explicitly distinguished from the figurative, representational forms of language in which absolute spirit has been recognized in religion. The knowing self recognizes absolute spirit in the concept. "This last form of the spirit, the spirit that gives its complete and true content the form of the self, and at the same time precisely realizes its concept thereby, as it remains within its concept in this realizing, is absolute knowing; it is the spirit knowing itself in the form of spirit or *conceptual knowing* [begriefende Wissen]" (H 556; M 485; B 797–98).

Knowing through concept is reflexive; its "content" has the very form of self that characterizes the knower, who indeed directly recognizes himself in it. Hegel goes on to speak of this conceptual knowing as the *Dasein* of spirit, but it is not merely one mode of being there among others. It is specifically the *Dasein* of knowing spirit "in the form of self-knowledge." The concept is that privileged form of self-knowledge in which spirit recognizing and spirit recognized are one and the same. Other appearances of spirit are inadequate anticipations of it. In religion, for instance, the "truth" of the "content" is not identical with the self-certainty of the religious subject. This truth, as we have seen, is something the religious subject merely represents to itself. But in conceptual knowledge this identity of content with subjective certainty is achieved, in that "the content has received the form of the self" (H 556; M 485; B 798).

A rather basic problem arises at just this point. Hegel immediately adds that in this identity "what is the very essence, namely the *concept, . . .* has become the element of being-there, or has taken on the *form of objectivity* for consciousness. Spirit *appearing* in this element to consciousness . . . *is science*" (H 556; M 485–86; B 798). Hegel abruptly abandons the language of intersubjectivity which we have learned to associate with self-consciousness (the B-series), and transmutes the concept into the subject-object structure of consciousness (the A-series). Obviously that is necessary if the concept is to take on "the form of objectivity," for objectivity is the correlate of consciousness.

What motivates this reversion to the structure of consciousness is clear enough. If there is to be a *Wissenschaft* (science) of spirit, Hegel suggests, spirit must appear to consciousness in the element of objectivity. The very term, *Gegenständlichkeit* (objectivity) implies the opposition of an object projected against *(gegen)* the subject, that has characterized consciousness. Hegel continues to insist, to be sure, that the self-knowledge that crowns the phenomenological project takes the form of self-consciousness. In the very next paragraph, for instance, he reminds us that the "nature, moments and movement of this knowing" are such that it is "the pure *being-for-itself* of self-consciousness." This locus in self-consciousness, after all, is what decisively differentiates this knowing from religious representation, though it is just as encompassing. The being-for-itself of self-consciousness, Hegel continues, is both localized, a being-there, and beyond spatial or temporal limit: "it is I, that is *this* and no other *I* and that is just as immediately *mediated* or transcended *universal* I" (H 556; M 586; B 798). Yet this universal-particular "I" "has a *content* that it differentiates from itself; for it is pure negativity or self-division; it is *consciousness*. This content is in its difference itself the I, for it is the movement of transcending itself, or the same pure negativity that the I is. In it, as differentiated, I is reflected into itself; the content is *conceived* [begriffen] solely in that I in its being-other abides with itself." Puzzles continue to mount, because the structure of consciousness, with its objectified content, can only express the concept insofar as the self-transcending movement of *self-consciousness* is invested in it. But how then can it still be objectified? Or how can the I that abides dialectically with itself in its other be reduced to an object of consciousness?

Hegel tries again: "More precisely stated, this content is none other than the very movement just spoken of; for it is the spirit that traverses its own self and indeed does so *for itself* as spirit, through the fact that it has the form of the concept in its objectivity" (H 556–57; M 486; B 798). This last phrase seems rather to obscure the puzzles than to resolve them. For if the concept embraces the movement through which spirit circumambiates itself, how can it be objectified for consciousness? The objective structure of consciousness would seem rather to be a moment in the circumambiation of self-conscious spirit. Self-consciousness is not merely consciousness that has the self for its object, nor can the self that can be objectified be the self-conscious self: not unless we forget everything Hegel has taught us about the categorial difference between consciousness and self-consciousness. Both the chapter on Self-Consciousness and the chapter on actual Spirit, in expounding the B-series, have unfolded a view of the self-conscious self as intersubjective, recognizing itself in recognizing another as self. Its reduction to a mere complex object of consciousness is another of those facile equations in which Hegel betrays his best insights.

To be sure, Hegel obviously wants to claim that absolute knowledge culminates both the A-series and the B-series, by in some manner reconciling them. He says as much in the next paragraph: "As the spirit that knows what it is" this final epiphany of spirit achieves the hitherto impossible condition in which it "secures for consciousness the form of its essence" and in this manner identifies "its *self-consciousness* with its *consciousness*" (H 557; M 486; B 798–99). The form of its essence is presumably the concept, so the identification of consciousness with self-consciousness still seems to mean that the concept becomes the object of consciousness. Two paragraphs later, in a passage I have already quoted, where Hegel again speaks of this consummation, he says that spirit "is in itself the movement that is cognition—the metamorphosis of that *in itself* into the *for itself*, of the *substance* into the *subject*, of the object of *consciousness* into the object of *self-consciousness*." But this last is an oxymoron, since self-consciousness precisely has no *Gegenstand*—as Hegel clearly recognizes, since he immediately adds what appears to be a paraphrase, but is in fact a crucial correction: "that is, into the object that is just as much transcended, or into the *concept*" (H 558–59; M 488; B 801). So the concept is in fact the object aufgehoben, related to self-consciousness in a way that may formally parallel the relation of consciousness to its object, but is in substance quite different. Here the subordination of consciousness to self-consciousness is clear, as a mere objectivizing moment in the concept of self-conscious spirit.

Terminology in this final chapter of the *Phenomenology* is admittedly loose. But I have belabored the wavering in Hegel's use of the term *Begriff* because it occupies such a central place in this chapter. Absolute knowing is conceptual, but Hegel's difficulty in locating it with respect to the systematically crucial distinction between consciousness and self-consciousness reflects an ambiguity at this central point that he perhaps never entirely overcame. Certainly the distinction is at the heart of the phenomenological project, in the dialectical analysis of experience. Broadly stated, experience requires that the experiencing subject both engage something outside itself and bring it in some manner within the horizon of its awareness. In the latter respect experience is mediated by language, or more broadly by signs, generated by the subject or subjects, that bring the object into different proximities. So the process of experiencing is capable of making the object ever more available. This we have seen in the chapter on Religion, the ascending order of which is due to differences in "language," and this ascending series of linguistic mediations culminate in the concept.

The problem is not that the "other" is utterly opaque, inconceivable, as some of our postmodernists appear to think. Instead, for Hegel there are two problems, that of the A-series and the B-series respectively. In the A-series, in which the subject-object structure of consciousness predominates, the problem is that the object is always in some measure alienated from the subject; mutual recognition, the spiritual element, either cannot occur at all or is incomplete. We saw that characteristic problem emerge in the chapter on Religion, where absolute spirit appears in an objectified form that is never entirely overcome. The problem of the B-series, on the other hand, is that its moments tend to succeed all too well in overcoming the subject-object dualism, at the expense of losing the other altogether: not only the gods, but the ethical order, other selves, the social sphere, even the natural world, have a way of dissolving into the self-conscious self when the B-series is ascendant.

These two tendencies constitute the most general formal dilemma of the *Phenomenology*. In either case a fundamental feature of experience is lost, and the phenomenological project falls to the ground, for the central nerve of this project is the appropriation of experience. To conceive such a project as an integral part of the philosophical task was one of Hegel's supreme achievements, and his peculiar genius was never more brilliantly exhibited than in the sustained interrogation of experience he conducted in our text. The courses of lectures he delivered in the 1820s show that he had not lost his touch in this respect; in these lectures the phenomenological aspect of his thinking is still on display. Still, as I have pointed out, the systematic design of his later philosophy no longer called for a distinct phenomenological project integral to it. So our text stands on its own, and the critical question with respect to it is whether in the end he resolves the basic dilemma regarding the systematic appropriation of experience.

Now, however ambiguous the meaning of the term *Begriff* may be in the final chapter of the work, at least its purpose is clear: it is assigned the task of resolving the dilemma created by the A-series and the B-series, consciousness and self-consciousness. The puzzles we have encountered in our dogged effort to track the usage of the term through a few paragraphs suggest that the work it had to do may have overtaxed it. It has appeared that the dilemma the concept was supposed to resolve has been reproduced within its own systematic usage. But we must examine the concept more systematically, in order to inquire into a closely related problem that has also continued to dog Hegelian philosophy.

iii. The Concept in Time and the Concept Recollected

There is a major distinction introduced into the dialectical structure of the concept in the final pages of our text, though it is possible to miss it because there are other things being discussed in these pages as well. Hegel specifies three dialectical moments in the process of knowing, of which the second is the concept in time and the third is the concept recollected. As for the first moment, Hegel suggests that there is a condition, a "knowing substance," antecedent to the "concept-form" *(Begriffsgestalt)* as such. Probably he uses the odd term "knowing substance" to suggest that this empty condition for possible knowledge is not yet a proper subject of experience, which could arise only together with the "concept form" in which it acquires content. This knowing substance "is the still undeveloped *in-itself,* or the ground and concept in its as yet unmoved simplicity, and therefore the *inwardness* or the self of the spirit that *is* not yet *there* [*das noch nicht* da ist]" (H 557; M 486; B 799). In order for there to be experience or knowledge there must be something capable of experiencing and knowing, and the "knowing substance" seems to signify this abstract receptivity. Calling it "inwardness" *(Innerlichkeit)* prepares us for the third moment in which what is experienced is interiorized or recollected *(er-innert).*

But in this first moment of empty inwardness spirit is not yet localized in time and place, "*is* not yet *there.*" In a surprising stroke a few pages later, Hegel correlates this "*self-less* substantiality" with the empty *Lichtwesen* (light-essence) with which natural religion begins. Light, the rising sun for instance, is the condition for the visual appearance of anything in the experienced world, yet the light itself has no content. Like abstract spatial extension, the still purer form of undifferentiated being, it corresponds to this substance without subjectivity that is the condition for all possible knowing, as the primordial unity of thought and being (H 559–60; M 488–89; B 802). Here thought and being unite in universal emptiness. Without this primal unity of thought and being there could be no concept, yet the spirit with its concept "*is* not yet *there*" in this original unity.

For the concept, like the spirit that animates it, has its necessary moment of concrete existence or "being-there." In this second moment in the process of knowing, the concept materializes in time: "*Time* is the *concept* itself that *is there,* and presents itself to consciousness as empty intuition" (H 558; M 487; B 800). The concept "is there" in the sights and sounds, the smells and tastes, the things, the living organisms, that we encounter in sensuous intuition *(Anschauung).* Our senses present us with a ceaseless flux, that is the primitive stuff of time. That this radically temporal world is the being-there of the concept does not imply that it is derivative, like a Neoplatonic diremption of a primal unity. The concept communicates no preestablished order to the world of experience. The concept has no a priori reality, imparts no prior meaning to the world. Its being-there "presents itself to consciousness as empty intuition," empty only in the sense that it has no predetermined meaning. The concept *is there* in this aimless fluid onrush that constantly transforms the landscape. It imparts no teleology to these successive transformations, but is simply the order of their succession, with no structural ordering immediately apparent to the experiencing consciousness. Its objects are always "poor" at first, without discernible significance, however rich they may be in sensuous vitality. Even the self-awareness of the "knowing substance" is "richer," for at least it is certain of itself. The "disclosure" of what is there in experience, on the contrary, "is in fact concealment" (H 557; M 486–87; B 799).

Hegel is perhaps recalling here the elusiveness that sense certainty proved to have in the opening chapter of our text. Its successive moments arise in the concept "earlier than the fulfilled whole the becoming of which is the movement of those moments" (H 558; M 487; B 800). So the concept is a whole after all, but this whole is the movement of those fluid moments in which the concept is there.

So we always begin in the confusion of this radical temporality of sensation. But that is not merely an unfortunate happenstance. Since "*time* is the *concept* itself that *is there*, . . . for this reason spirit necessarily appears in time, and it appears in time so long as it does not *grasp* its pure concept, that is, does not redeem time [*nicht die Zeit tilgt*]" (H 558; M 487; B 800). This little word "*tilgt*" has one of those double meanings Hegel loved. It means "obliterate" or "erase" or "destroy," but it also means "redeem" in the commercial sense, to pay off a debt or a mortgage. So when spirit grasps its "pure" concept it will have worked off or paid off its indenture to time. But both propositions in the quotation are important. Spirit is the child of time. If its ultimate task is to grasp its pure concept, to know itself, it cannot overleap the temporality of experience, since its concept "is there" necessarily in that endless flux, distributed fragmentarily over its great stream. Spirit itself is distributed, in a double sense. It is the experiencing subject, itself in a process of constant self-transformation, and it is the cascading material that presents itself in experience. The two sides are constantly joined in sensuous intuition, but also in representation, in which the stuff of experience is imaginatively shaped and formed. The ever-changing course of this conjunction has been selectively traced in the *Phenome-*

nology itself. Here spirit encounters its concept in its diaspora, in what Hegel now calls its "externalization [*Entaüsserung*]," in which its moments appear successively, disjunctively, "outwardly."

But now the other proposition: "Spirit necessarily appears in time," but only "so long as it does not *grasp* its pure concept, that is, does not obliterate/redeem time." This grasp of the pure concept is not temporal. With this possibility we have come to the third moment in Hegel's account of knowing in this final chapter. Time, he continues in the passage at hand,

> is the *outwardly* intuited pure self that is *not grasped* by the self, the merely intuited concept; when the latter grasps itself it transcends its time-form [*hebt er seine Zeitform auf*], conceives the intuiting [*begreift das Anschauen*], and is conceived and conceiving intuition. Time appears as the fate and necessity of spirit that is not completed within itself. (H 558; M 487; B 800)

Spirit's "completed" self-knowledge is no longer temporal, and no longer "outwardly intuited." The first moment, that of the "knowing substance," was self-enclosed, therefore empty of content and entirely inward. In this third moment, as Hegel goes on to suggest, what has been presented outwardly in the temporality of experience is inwardly comprehended. The inwardness is no longer empty but filled, in some sense "completed." In the final paragraph of the text, to which we shall turn presently, Hegel refers to this inward appropriation as "*Erinnerung*," as recollection, with a bow, of course, to Platonic *anemnesis*. But it also literally means "interiorizing."

In the suggestion that time is somehow transcended in this third moment, the passage before us parallels Hegel's introductory remarks to the chapter on Religion. The parallel is not surprising, since with religion we already make the transition from spirit in its temporal-historical diaspora to absolute spirit. "Religion" does not follow actual spirit as a new historical or posthistorical moment. Its essential categories are simply transhistorical. The chapter on Religion offers a categorially different way of grasping what has already been presented historically in the chapter on actual Spirit. That relation seems clear enough. But the relation of the final chapter to what comes before is not so clear. Here again Hegel distinguishes between a temporal being-there and an absolute moment that is no longer historical. But that distinction is sharpened by the distinction between outer and inner that was not employed in that earlier discussion introducing religion. Furthermore, Hegel now speaks of the interiorizing movement as in some sense a completion or fulfillment—*Vollendung*—of the external, temporal moment.

But exactly what sort of fulfillment is this, and how complete is this completion? An unresolved issue *seems* to arise, an ambiguity both sides of which are deeply rooted in Hegel's thinking. Is the passage from temporality to inner comprehension linear? Does the long pathway of the concept's external, temporal being-there really end in a single comprehensive interiorization, or does every interiorization of a course of experience give rise to new moments of externalized being-there? There are passages in the final chapter that can be read the first way, as if the curtain were being rung down on all possible "external" adventures of spirit. "The completed objective presentation" of its concept in time is simultaneously the moment in which the entire "substance" of the world becomes "self." In a passage already quoted Hegel declares: "Therefore, so long as spirit has not completed itself *in itself,* not as world spirit, it cannot attain its completion as *self-conscious* self."

This remark, to be sure, is conditional, leaving it an open question whether such a completion is achievable. Fully self-conscious spirit would have to recognize itself, not merely in the spirit of a people (Volksgeist) nor of an age (Zeitgeist), but in the all-inclusive Weltgeist, comprehending all nature and history. Hegel immediately contrasts this fulfillment with that of religion, which in its more limited way also comprehends the Weltgeist in its representation of the divine. There is not only a formal contrast (*Vorstellung* versus *Begriff*) but even, paradoxically, a historical succession: "The content of religion therefore declares what *spirit is* earlier in time than science does; but science is alone its true knowledge of itself" (H 559; M 488; B 802). Religious fulfillment is crude by comparison, since there is always something external, "alien," in its comprehension of spirit. It nourishes the "hope" of transcending what is alien *(das Fremdsein)* "in an external, alien manner." Only when spirit abandons this self-defeating hope can it turn "to itself, to its own world and present, because the alien manner transcended is the return into self-consciousness" (H 559; M 488; B 801–2). Here, indeed, Hegel goes on to suggest, all localized and temporalized being-there is transmuted into thought. In this unqualified sense, the history of spirit might itself bring forth a transcendence of history as such.

The passages in our text that lend themselves to such a reading do indirectly reflect a revolutionary impulse that we have often encountered in Hegel's life and work. The Preface to the *Phenomenology* registers his keen sense that he is living on the edge of a new age, that "our time is a time of birth and of passing over to a new period" (H 15; M 6; B 75). This conviction, as we have seen, inspired the intellectual struggles of Hegel's youth. It is logically strange to suppose that history itself might be aufgehoben in a new historical epoch, but Hegel never entirely abandoned this dream of his youth. It does seem to support a possible way of reading the conclusion of our text, though a closer reading cannot sustain it. Still this reading joins an important issue. In this case the phenomenological project reaches its culmination by transcending itself. There is, perhaps not quite or not yet, but in principle nothing still "alien" in experience. Recognizing itself in the Weltgeist, self-consciousness comprehends all things as aspects of itself. Again and again that possibility has arisen in the B-series, when self-consciousness was ascendant, but it has been presented critically, as a problem: that spirit comprehends itself at the expense of the alien vitality on which its experience depends.

We have seen this problem arise in different ways with Stoicism, skepticism, unhappy consciousness, with absolute freedom and terror, with the beautiful soul. If we read absolute knowing as a final consummation, not merely transhistorical but posthistorical, the problem arises again. Spirit knows itself as world spirit at the ironical cost of losing the world. If the phenomenological project falls to the ground the system becomes undialectical. It is simply an idealism, a myth of completed wisdom in an inwardness no longer in living dialectical communication with what is externally *there* in time and place. Spirit, furthermore, is no longer *there* in figurative, representational language, and the wise are presumably going to replace Christians and other colorful language-users some time soon. That Hegel believed in historical progress, even in the dawning of a new age, is undeniable. But that such a conviction led him to a dogmatic rather than a dialectical conclusion of the *Phenomenology* does not follow.

If Hegel was tempted by such a conclusion, which constitutes the "Hegelianism" of popular legend, he also recognized the difficulties with it; repeatedly in the closing pages of the *Phenomenology* he insisted on the *double* movement of the concept: every inner appropriation of the outer in self-consciousness engenders a new exteriorization in space and time, in nature and history. These closing pages are dense, and the double movement is contextualized differently in different passages. But it is always clear that the movement of the concept is not simply in one direction, from its *Dasein* in space and time to a single consummatory *Erinnerung*. Rather, *Dasein* and *Erinnerung* alternate in dialectical rhythm in the movement of the concept. Temporal *Dasein* is a permanent moment in the dialectical structure of the concept.

For instance, Hegel is explaining that "substance" becomes "subject": Against the "*self-less* substantiality" of the Oriental (and Spinozistic) unity of things external to all subjectivity, spirit recoils, asserts the self in its individuality. But only after spirit "exteriorizes" this individuality "in culture," where it gradually reduces all *Dasein* to a function of its own will, "to the thought of usefulness," does it "turn the thought of its innermost depth outward, and expresses the essence as I=I," the formula of absolute subject. "I=I," however, is no mere tautology. It is a dialectical identity in difference, dynamic, always an identity in the making.

> This I=I is the movement reflecting itself into itself; for since this identity as absolute negativity is the absolute difference, the self-identity of the I is juxtaposed against this pure difference, which as the pure difference and at the same time the difference objective to the self-knowing self must be expressed as *time,* so that just as previously the essence was expressed as the unity of thought and [spatial] extension it would now have to be grasped as the unity of thought and time. (H 560; M 489; B 802–3)

We will not try to chase down all the rabbits that are running through this dense thicket. What is clear is that the experienced world in space and time, far from dissolving into the pure inwardness of the self-conscious subject, is a necessity engendered within its own life. I=I entails difference as well as identity, and this difference, juxtaposed against the I in its simple identity, is as irreducibly temporal as it is spatial. I=I embraces the objectivity of the experienced world as well as the subjectivity of the subject; that is why it is the *absolute* subject. It is the essential totality, in the *movement* of which substance becomes subject: but "*this subject* is just as much *the substance*" (H 560; M 489; B 803). This substance/subject is the totality that necessarily exteriorizes itself. The being-there of its concept in time is neither a merely subjective construct nor an accidental eruption of an intractably "other" outside world. The externality of the experienced world is no mere appearance; it is a necessity in the dynamic life of that totality, both subject and substance, that Hegel calls "spirit." He goes on to say that its content is neither "cast into the empty abyss of the absolute" nor "snatched up externally from sense perception."

> But spirit has shown itself to us to be neither just the withdrawal of self-consciousness into its pure inwardness nor the mere sinking of self-consciousness into the substance and the non-being of its difference, but [spirit is] *this movement* of the self that externalizes [*entaüssert*] itself from itself and sinks itself into its substance, and likewise as subject has gone out of the substance into itself. (H 561; M 490; B 803–4)

Hegel reiterates this double movement in various terms, emphasizing that the concept in its externalization and interiorization are two moments in a continuous movement, neither finally or statically resolved into the other. The spiritual I "has neither to cling to itself in the *form* of *self-consciousness* against the form of substantiality and objectivity, as if it were afraid of its externalization," nor does it need, in the fashion of Schellingian *Indifferenz,* to plunge "the differences back into the abyss of the absolute," declaring "their identity therein." Avoiding both these types of idealistic reduction, Hegel asserts that "the power of the spirit is rather to remain identical with itself in its externalization" (H 561; M 490; B 804). Indeed, the externalization is necessary to the life of the spirit, without which it would be merely subjective.

Again, Hegel says that at the stage of knowing, spirit "has won the pure element of its being-there, the concept" (H 561–62; M 490; B 805). That is what differentiates knowing from other ways the self relates itself to its world. But it is not to say that this attainment of the concept concludes the concept's moment of externalization. "The content" of the concept "is according to the *freedom* of its *being* the self-externalizing self, or the *immediate* unity of self-knowledge. The pure movement of this externalization, considered with respect to content, constitutes its *necessity*" (H 562; M 490–91; B 805). To know is not the end of surprises. When the self recognizes itself in absolute spirit and its concept, it realizes that novelty, the adventure of externalization beyond what has yet appeared, is the very life of the concept. It is no happy or unhappy accident, but a necessity. It is impossible not to meet with surprises.

Hegel goes on to distinguish proper *Wissenschaft* from phenomenology. There is no longer the relentless differentiation in each of its moments between knowing and its truth, nor the Aufhebung of this difference that we have traced in the *Phenomenology*. "Since the moment has the form of the concept, it unites the objective form of truth and the knowing self in an immediate unity" (H 562; M 491; B 805). Be that as it may: but the truth with which the knower unites is the Bacchanalian revel! The world known is not the world tamed into an extension of the self. Quite the contrary: *Wissenschaft*, knowing in its most developed form, "contains within itself this necessity to externalize the form of the pure concept, and the passage of the concept into *consciousness*" (H 563; M 491; B 806). Externalization is a movement *out* of self-consciousness *into* the free play of objects as they present themselves to consciousness, and we are back to the self-forgetfulness of the sensuous consciousness with which the phenomenological journey began, a "release of itself from the form of its self" that is "the highest freedom and security of its knowledge of itself." The self-conscious self requires this moment of unself-conscious attention to the independent things of the world, without which it would lapse into a kind of solipsism in which the scientific foundation of knowledge would be lost.

But Hegel immediately adds, in the penultimate paragraph of our text, that even this moment of *Entaüsserung* in the scientifically informed knowing self does not exhaust its necessity: "Yet this externalization is still incomplete; it expresses the *relation* of self-certainty to the object, which just because it is in the relation has not won its complete freedom." The freedom in question is that of the external object, which is not complete until it has entirely broken free of the knowing self. This freedom of the object entails a further self-loss on the part of the subject—in order to achieve a deeper self-knowledge, linked to the environing reality of things. He who would find himself must lose himself. Self-conscious knowing, Hegel continues, in a passage already quoted, "knows not only itself, but also the negative of itself, or its limit. To know its limit means to know how to sacrifice itself. This sacrifice is the externalization in which spirit displays its process of becoming spirit in the form of *free accidental happening,* viewing its pure *self* as *time* outside it, and equally its *being* as space" (H 563; M 491–92; B 806–7).

This vital externalization of spirit in time and space, in history and nature, is never merely a superseded moment in its life. Every *Erinnerung* presupposes this *Entaüsserung,* and gives rise to it again. This rhythm, like the inhalation and exhalation of the breath, or the systole and diastole of blood to and from the heart, is the very life of the spirit.

iv. "The Recollection and the Golgotha of Absolute Spirit"

The sentence that ends Hegel's *Phenomenology* erupts in a stormy and stressful play of images, of which perhaps the most striking is the evocation of Golgotha, the place of the skull *(Schädelstätte)* on which, according to the gospel, the incarnate God was crucified. What can it mean to say that absolute spirit, too, has its Golgotha? We will end our study by addressing this question, and also, as a kind of coda to our theme, its implication for the interplay of dialectic and gospel in the development of Hegel's thinking. Golgotha is paired, oddly but suggestively, with recollection, which since Plato's *Meno* has been the metaphor par excellence for dialectic.

In order to contextualize this strange pairing of images we can resume where we left off in the preceding section: recollection or interiorization *(Erinnerung)* and externalization *(Entaüsserung)* are alternating phases in the life of spirit. That already suggests that Golgotha is an aspect of the externalizing phase. Now externalization, Hegel explains in the two final paragraphs of our text, is both spatial and temporal. In its physical extension in space, spirit appears as "nature" which, early and late, Hegel considered to be fundamentally cyclical. It is constantly changing, but constantly replenishing itself, comprising the "vital immediate becoming" of spirit: "But the other side of its becoming, *history,* is the *knowing,* self-*mediating* becoming—spirit externalized in time; but this externalization is equally the externalization of its own self; the negative is the negative of its own self" (H 563; M 492; B 807). Spirit materializes constantly in space, as natural process. This is its perduring physical reality. But in the concluding paragraph of the text, which begins with the above quotation, Hegel focuses primarily on the other mode of spirit's externalization, in historical time.

In its historical excursions spirit undergoes radical metamorphosis, as we saw in the chapter on actual Spirit. Human intentions, thoughts, passions, expressed in language and in action, often at cross-purposes, produce unpredictable consequences and unforeseen shapes of social life, which become new points of departure for still other transformations. Historical time is irreversible. Every new shape of conscious life marks a point of no return. Since spirit invests itself in this dynamic progression into novelty, its externalization in time is "self-*mediating*"; that is, it is constantly negating its own previous configuration and taking form anew. As the child of time, spirit is constantly reborn. Each rebirth is in one sense a new spirit, local and of its time, though "spirit" in the more capacious sense is its "becoming" through all its moments, transformed in each.

> This becoming presents a slow movement and succession of spirits, a gallery of images, each of which is endowed with the full richness of spirit, so that it moves so slowly because the self has to penetrate and to digest this entire richness of its substance. Since its fulfillment consists in perfectly *knowing* what *it is,* its substance, this knowledge is thus its *introversion* (insichgehen), in which it abandons its being-there and gives its shape over to recollection. (H 563; M 492; B 807)

Spirit's external existence, "its being-there" *(Dasein)* in historical reality, is entirely contingent. It simply happens and happens, and its happenings make up a succession in no predetermined order. There is no historical necessity in these happenings or in their succession. The only necessity is that spirit must appear in this purely contingent way. Only retrospectively can any sense be made of this succession, and discovering this sense is a slow process, usually lagging far behind the events themselves. This process is what Hegel means by "knowing," for which he here employs metaphors of digesting and recollecting.

Digesting is an organism's appropriation, as food, of something that had had an independent existence as a lobster or carrot. The chapter on Self-Consciousness begins with the food chain, a life process that sustains itself as a whole through the fact that every organism devours and digests those lower on the chain. That's "life." Here it also furnishes a metaphor for the interiorization of historical existence into knowledge, spirit cannibalizing and digesting its own external forms of being-there. This sublimated interior "life" of spirit is sustained through universal negation of its historical being-there.

The Platonic metaphor of recollection also expresses this interiorization of what has appeared outwardly in time and space. If, however, the Platonic *anemnesis* implies the recovery of antecedent prototypical forms in the temporal flux, Hegel's use of the metaphor is not entirely Platonic, at least in its application to historical realities. Spirit must construct the de-temporalized forms and categories into which it inter-nalizes its historically existing appearances. Still, as with Plato, the forms are intangible ideas.

Hegel had also employed the term *"Er-innerung"* in the rather poetic dénouement of the religion of art, where he spoke of the dissolution of classical pagan religions, and their purely aesthetic survival in works of art, as fruits broken from the tree that had produced them. The loss of the living culture in which the antique gods and goddesses had fruited, however, was more than compensated by their aesthetic preser-vation. For the spirit that "displays" these works to us is "more than" that living culture, being "the *Er-innerung* of the spirit that was still *veraüsserten* in that people." That passage anticipates the externaliza-tion/interiorization pattern of the text's conclusion, but there the modes of *Er-innerung* were works of classical literature, music, statuary, drama, and so forth: ideality expressed in sensuous media. Here, in the conclusion, everything that is either sensuous or temporal is negated as such. Yet the interior recollection does have a content, and some distil-late of historical *Dasein* does survive and is "preserved" in this purely conceptual mode; as was the case in the aesthetic recollection of a dead religion, Hegel insists that this recollection in which historical existence is "preserved . . . is the inner and in fact higher form of the substance" of this *Dasein* (H 564; M 492; B 807–8).

Each "previous" appearance in which spirit has been-there histori-cally is superseded, "aufgehoben," "but reborn out of knowledge—is the new being-there, a new world and a new shape of spirit" (H 564; M 492; B 807). There appear in fact to be two complementary ways in which the past is preserved: not only in knowledge or recollection, but in historical process itself. Although everything historical passes away, history continues, and the "new world" that arises from the ashes of the past begins "on a higher plateau" as a result of what had been accomplished earlier. Not that the cast of characters that populate the new world are necessarily aware of their debt to their predecessors. As we have seen in the chapter on actual Spirit, the protagonists of each new moment pursue their own quite novel projects and fall into their own follies in apparent forgetfulness of previous moments. In each new moment spirit seems to begin afresh and to unfold its new project "as if everything that went before were lost for it, and it had learned nothing from the experience of the earlier spirits" (H 564; M 452; B 807). Still, like scientists who pursue their new projects unaware of the history of science, or citizens ignorant of their nation's past, the new spirit, forgetful as it is, does nevertheless begin "on a higher plateau" built on the accomplishments and failures of its own earlier shapes of being-there.

These discrete historical shapes, each largely unconscious of its past, make up a progression that is the real substance of historical time. This progression is what Hegel calls a "gallery of images," like pictures at an exhibition—though a cinematic metaphor would be more apt, since the images succeed one another in time. He also speaks of it as a "kingdom of spirits" *(Geisterreich)*, though they are contemporaneous only to the spirit that recollects: "The kingdom of spirits that forms itself in this manner in its being-there constitutes a succession *(Aufein-anderfolge)*, in which one replaced the other and each took over the realm of the world from its predecessor" (H 564; M 492; B 808).

Presumably every culture, every Volksgeist, has its place in some more inclusive community of spirits. But here Hegel speaks of the Geisterreich in a more restrictive sense, comprising that succession of spirits that has undergone radical metamorphosis. If some cultures are too stable or isolated to join this exclusive club they are the lucky ones, spared the traumas of history. But this Geisterreich is historicized, in the long run progressively, at the fearful cost of traumatic negativity. Generations, richly developed ways of life, suffer torment and annihilation in their turn, of which Golgotha is emblematic. In this historical being-there of spirit they are preserved only in being the humus from which a new shape of spirit grows.

But there is also the other mode in which these spirits are preserved. To this *Entaüsserung* in history is juxtaposed the *Erinnerung* of knowledge, into which the succession of spirits is digested and sublimated. In this inward turn spirit is "absorbed into the night of its self-consciousness, but its vanished being-there is preserved in it" (H 563–64; M 492; B 807). Hegel had employed the image of an all-engulfing "pure night" in his conclusion to *Faith and Knowledge,* but there it signified the infinite metaphysical *Indifferenz* of the philosophy of identity in which all finite oppositions were engulfed (see Chapter 3). But in the Preface to the *Phenomenology*, as we have seen, he speaks disdainfully of that Schellingian "night" in which "all the cows are black." Here the night signifies the self-conscious inwardness in which spirit's outward excursions in historical time are preserved in their ideality in thought, as knowledge—and out of it is born a new historical world. So here we conclude, not with a metaphysical resolution of all time and becoming, but with that rhythm of temporal being-there and self-conscious recollection, outwardness and inwardness, that is the life of experience. It falls within the phenomenological project, continuing the alternation of A-series and B-series, consciousness and self-consciousness, that Hegel has traced through the entire text.

In fact this basic dyad is reproduced in the bewildering proliferation of terms and images that appear in the final paragraph of our text. They make up a series of antithetical pairs, each reproducing the dyad with particular emphasis to address a specific issue, and together furnishing a rich elaboration of the dyad. It may be worthwhile to list some of these pairs, together with some we have met before, signifying the dyad in our usual way, simply as A and B.

A	B
consciousness	self-consciousness
externalization	interiorization
being-there	knowing
substance	subject
spatial extension and time	depth
historical succession	phenomenological organization
experience	thought
Golgotha	recollection

It would be ironical if the *Phenomenology*, having discredited so many traditional dualisms, should itself end in dualism. Does it finally come to rest in these various expressions of the dyad? Is the juxtaposition A/B left unresolved, or is there at last a C, like the finale to a Beethoven symphony, that thunderously resolves all the tensions between A and B in their numerous inversions and variations? C might appropriately serve as abbreviation of the Concept, which certainly cannot be confined within either side of the dyad. It embraces both, as we have seen, in time and in recollection. We have also expressed the suspicion that the conflict between A and B resolved in the concept may be reproduced within the concept itself. Hegel would doubtless reply that the concept is no empty abstraction, but is dialectical, mediating between A and B. Nor is this mediation simply imposed by C, for neither A nor B can subsist in experience without the other. Each necessarily requires the other. Who says A *must* say B, and vice versa. C, furthermore, is the concept of self, or of spirit, which is unthinkable without *both* its materialization in A and its self-recognition in B. Those are the necessary conditions of its experience.

For instance, one of the expressions of A and B introduced in our final paragraph employs the metaphor of dimensions. A is expressed as the dimension of outward "extension" of spirit in space, and also its outward movement in time. Its other dimension is its inward "depth," in thought. These dimensions are inseparable and complementary. As we have seen, the "succession" of spirits outwardly in time constitutes the "kingdom of spirits": "Their goal is the revelation of the depth [of spirit], and this is *the absolute concept*" (H 564; M 492; B 808). But this "revelation" of the depth dimension of spirit in absolute *Begriff,* far from dissipating the spatiotemporal dimension, requires it as the medium of its revealing.

> This revelation is herewith the raising-up (Aufheben) of its depth or its *extension,* the negativity of this I withdrawn into itself, [a negativity] which is its externalization or substance—and [this revelation is] its *time,* that this externalization externalizes itself in its own self, and so in its extension just as in its depth is in the self. (H 564; M 493; B 808)

What Hegel is struggling to describe is a crucial instance of the principle of recognition. The inner depth of the self or spirit is disclosed in the outer extension and temporality of its existence in the world, even though this outer medium of its disclosure is quite other than the knowing subject as such, the negative of its inner depth. For this depth in its isolation, the "I withdrawn into itself" *(insichseienden Ich),* dwells in the darkness of "night," unknown both to others and to itself. It is revealed in the human activity in the spatiotemporal world in which it recognizes itself. The true self (spirit), contrary to traditional mysticism, is not the pure I withdrawn from the world of its experience. What is externalized there is precisely "its own self," which comprises both its depth and its extension.

So the self is dialectical through and through, recognizing itself, hence becoming a self, in the external world, in other spirits past and present, and in absolute spirit. "*The goal,* absolute knowing or the spirit knowing itself as spirit, has for its path the recollection of the spirits as they are in themselves [historically] and [as they] achieve the organization of their kingdom" (ibid.; this passage is continuous with the preceding and following quotations).

This self-recognitive knowledge of spirit entails the inner recollection of the spirits that have existed in the external world. In their temporal succession they comprise, as we have seen, a Geisterreich: a kingdom of spirits that is entirely of this world, by contrast to that kingdom of God that is "not of this world" (John 18:36, which actually refers to Jesus' kingship). On the other hand, the kingdom of God in the more primitive New Testament eschatology is also to appear in this world, when heaven itself descends to earth. That is a *Vorstellung* not entirely foreign to our text, since here the entire course of earthly history makes up a kingdom of spirits in its "organization." They are recollected both in their historical succession and in this "organization," of which we will hear more below.

The spirits, at any rate, are preserved both in an outward (A) and inward (B) fashion, as we have already seen. In the concluding sentence of our text, which is symphonic enough, this double preservation is stated in slightly different terms, but still follows the A/B pattern.

> Their preservation [*Aufbewahrung*], from the side of their freely appearing being-there in the form of contingency, is history, but from the side of their comprehended [*begriffnen*] organization is the [phenomenological] *science* of the *knowing of appearance;* both together, the comprehended history, form the recollection and the Golgotha of absolute spirit, the actuality, truth, and certainty of its throne, without which it would be a lifeless recluse [*leblose Einsame*]; only—
>> out of the chalice of this kingdom of spirits
>> foams forth for him his [own] infinitude.
> (H 564; M 493; B 808)

The frothy finale, adapted from Schiller's "Friendship," seems to call for a beer stein rather than a chalice, but it recalls truth's Bacchanalian revel. We note more dryly that there does seem to be a C here, a dialectical union of A and B. The spirits are preserved in the vital contingency or happenstance *(Zufälligkeit)* of history, and in the phenomenological dialectic exemplified in our entire text. The preservation of the spirits in history seems somewhat equivocal, certainly less vivid than their demise; and their preservation in the science of phenomenology employs the intangible medium of insightfully organized recollection. In neither case, separately, does their preservation seem robust. Separate the historical A and the philosophical B, and the first would be a play of active, passionate, lethal, but finally meaningless gestures; the second, the "lifeless recluse" of our finale, elsewhere called "the night" of spirit's self-consciousness and its "depth" without content, withdrawn into hollow profundity. Brought together, however, as dialectical moments in the life of a spirit absolute and finally one, history is seen to be purposeful in the long run. It even has a "goal": "spirit knowing itself as spirit" in the ultimate recognition scene; and science, for its part, finds in history its own incarnate existence, lively and companionable. The material world is itself an externalization of spirit, but history is that externalization in which spirit not only recognizes itself but is recognized in return, while science is spirit's recollection in organized thought of the disorganized, teeming life of the world. Absolute spirit, comprehended or conceptualized *(begriffne)* history, is the C that brings together and dialectically relates A and B.

More particularly, however, Hegel designates this C as "the recollection and the Golgotha of absolute spirit." That locution raises the same question we have entertained about the concept, whether the dyad, B and A, is after all reproduced in this C that is said to bring them together. Doubtless one should not read too much into Hegel's choice of words in this enthusiastic conclusion. Spirit's recollection and Golgotha are, after all, said to be "the actuality, truth, and certainty"—can this be another A, B, C?—"of its throne." This throne presumably signifies the surprising rule of absolute spirit over its seemingly unruly kingdom of spirits. But why are precisely its recollection and Golgotha so enthroned? *Erinnerung,* of course, has been a central and carefully thematized term in our text. But not the place of the skull, which makes a very strange and unexpected appearance on spirit's throne. Perhaps the image is employed as a metaphor for historical negativity, that each incarnation of spirit in history is annihilated in its turn, only to be "preserved" in its transfiguration into recollective knowledge. Hegel had concluded *Faith and Knowledge* with such an evocation of a speculative Good Friday and Easter. But here the word order does not support that pattern. "Golgotha and recollection" might have implied something of the sort, but the reverse order suggests no transfiguration of the first into the second, but quite a different relation: perhaps simply two forms of negativity, the dialectical and the historical. In the Preface, written a short time later, Hegel emphasizes in the strongest terms that "the tremendous power of the negative" is never surpassed in the life of the spirit (H 29; M 19; B 93).

Still "Golgotha" strikes a jarring note in the otherwise exuberant tones of this finale. Whatever Hegel may have intended by it, it casts a deadly pall for anyone who, like Hegel himself, has more than a passing acquaintance with the gospel story. The cross is a more conventional image; occupying a place of honor in most of the churches of Christendom (in many of them cast in gold and covered with jewels) it sometimes functions as a kind of logo, emblematic of the Christian religion generally. But no one has ever gilded the place of the skull, which is simply one of very many places set aside for torture and lingering death. Hegel was keenly aware, early and late, of the tragic side of human experience, with its trail of bloody sufferings. In the Introduction to his celebrated Lectures on the Philosophy of History in the 1820s he even likens human history to a butcher's "slaughterbench," an image no one has ever tried to sanctify. He refers to the *Phenomenology* itself, in the Introduction, as a pathway of doubt and despair, and this *via dolorosa* extends to the very conclusion of the text, ending, as it must, at Golgotha. It is, to be sure, the central paradox of the gospel that the event on Golgotha is the supreme sacrifice of God for the salvation of Adam's erring and suffering children. This paradox, in the idiom of what Hegel would regard as a religious *Vorstellung,* now furnishes an image of speculative truth. Not only the Christian God incarnate, but the absolute spirit suffers, suffers its Golgotha and dies. Absolute spirit dies in every death of any sort. Only "the tremendous power of the negative" is undying, but that too is absolute spirit. In the Preface, where he refers to this power, Hegel identifies it with death, without which there would be no life: For

> the life of the spirit is not the life that shrinks from death and protects itself from it, but the life that endures death and maintains itself in it. It wins its truth only when, in its utter laceration, it finds itself. (H 29–30; M19; B 93; cf. H 20; M 10; B 81)

Notes

1. Since most of the citations in this chapter will be from Hegel's *Phenomenology,* I propose to employ an abbreviation indicating the passage in the most widely used German text and in the two English translations. H refers to Hoffmeister, M to Miller, B to Baillie. So in the present case the full citation would read as follows: *Phänomenologie des Geistes,* 6th ed. nach dem Texte der Originalausgabe herausgegeben von Johannes Hoffmeister (Hamburg: Felix Meiner, philosophischen Bibliothek, bd. 114, 1952), 158–59; *Phenomenology of Spirit,* translated by A. V. Miller with analysis of the text and foreword by

J. N. Findlay (Oxford: Clarendon Press, 1977), 126; *The Phenomenology of Mind,* 2d ed., translated with an introduction and notes, by J. B. Baillie (London: Allen and Unwin; New York: Macmillan, 1955), 251. A newer edition of the German text has appeared as volume 9 in *Gesammelte Werke: Phänomenologie des Giestes,* ed. Wolfgang Bonsiepen und Reinhard Heede (Hamburg: Felix Meiner, 1980). Though I have made use of the valuable notes and apparatus to this edition, it seemed superfluous to cite yet another edition with every reference.

Translations of quoted material are, as always, my own, but I shall have had the benefit of consulting the renderings of these two courageous translators of this notoriously untranslatable work. I shall not always agree with either of them. But I shall simply translate quoted material as I think best. I am generally full of admiration for Mr. Miller's translation in particular. It is a considerable improvement over the Baillie translation, and we are fortunate to have the whole work this well rendered in English.

2. Jean Hyppolite, *Genesis and Structure of Hegel's Phenomenology of Spirit,* trans. Samuel Cherniak and John Heckman (Evanston: Northwestern University Press, 1974), 191, 198–99. Translated from the French original, *Genèse et Structure de la Phénoménologie de l'Esprit de Hegel* (Paris: Aubier, 1946).

3. Even so splendid a commentator as Hyppolite adopts such shortcuts. Of the three basic moments of unhappy consciousness, he says: "If we are to give historical examples, [must we?] the first stage corresponds to Judaism and the second to early forms of Christianity. The third stage leads from the European Middle Ages to the Renaissance and to modern reason" (*Genesis and Structure,* 196). Hyppolite acknowledges that "these are only historical examples" but in practice he constantly equates them, referring simply to "God," "Christ," "incarnation," "the Jewish people," and so forth. He even introduces (201) the language dubiously applied to the third part of Hegel's much later Lectures on the Philosophy of Religion, "the reign of the Father," "the reign of the Son," "the reign of the Spirit," as if Hegel were using that language in this section of the *Phenomenology* ("This Hegel calls the reign of the Father").

4. The monastic vows are only alluded to, not named, in our text (H 170; M 137; B 265–66). In Hegel's later writings, however, he regularly discussed the three vows as an epitome of medieval Christian piety, and he regularly pointed to their abrogation as the great Protestant achievement: The reformers and Protestant culture replaced celibacy with family life, poverty with the duty of gainful labor, unquestioning obedience with citizenship in a free state. Hegel laid such stress on these three developments because they corresponded neatly to the three moments of ethical life *(Sittlichkeit)* articulated in his *Philosophy of Right:* family, civil society, and the state. I have discussed this treatment of Protestantism in relation to the monastic vows in *In the Twilight of Christendom* (cited in Chapter 1, note 26), 51–55. See Hegel's "Rede bei der dritten Sakulärfeier der Übergabe der Augsburgischen Konfession," *Berliner Schriften,* 44–51; *Philosophie der Religion,* I-1, 305–8 and II-2, 202; *Philosophie der Weltgeschichte,* 4:828–29, 887–89; *Enzyklopädie,* Anmerkung to § 552. (All in the standard Felix Meiner editions.)

5. H. S. Harris suggests, in fact, that the "desire" referred to here is primarily sexual, linking the present passage with an important reference to the "natural" polarity of the sexes in the *Differenzschrift* (cited in Chapter 3, note 22) of 1800. "The extremely enigmatic dialectic of 'Leben und Begierde'" in the present section of the *Phenomenology* "begins to yield up its secrets when we read it as an account of *sexual* desire, an account of how the *genus* appears to the living consciousness that is not yet self-conscious, or as a phenomenology of *animal* awareness." Harris, "The Concept of Recognition in Hegel's Jena Manuscripts," in *Hegel in Jena: Die Entwicklung des Systems und die Zusammenarbeit mit Schelling,* ed. Henrich and Düsing, *Hegel-Studien,* supp. 20, (Bonn: Bouvier,

1980), 232. But this attractive suggestion will obscure as much as it clarifies if it is pushed to the point of simply identifying *Begierde* with sexuality. The "genus" *(Gattung)* referred to does not in this case necessarily imply sexuality, but is implicit in self-consciousness itself, which will recognize its generic (not genetic) being in itself.

6. Hyppolite *(Genesis and Structure,* 160) goes too far in arguing that self-consciousness is already the psychological telos of desire. He begins by stating, correctly, that "the end point of desire is not, as one might think superficially, the sensuous object—that is only a means—but the unity of the I with itself." But that end is already achieved in the immediate satisfaction of desire, which brings the I back to itself in the release of the tension of desire. But the I that achieves closure in this satisfaction is still abstract, as Hyppolite would agree. He means that the condition of concrete self-awareness is already implicit in desire: "Self-consciousness is desire, but what it desires, although it does not yet know this explicitly, is itself: it desires its own desire. And that is why it will be able to attain itself only through finding another desire, another self-consciousness. . . . Desire seeks itself in the other: man desires recognition from man." This attractive suggestion, which makes the psychological "desire" for recognition an unconscious feature of sensuous desire, trades on an ambiguity in the word "desire" that is not supported in Hegel's text. Nor is it contained in the German *Begierde,* that Hegel employs, which generally has a much more restricted meaning than Hyppolite implies. Hyppolite continues: "We have translated *Begierde* . . . as 'desire' [*désir*] rather than as 'appetite' [*appétit*], for this desire contains more than appears at first; although insofar as it bears on the various concrete objects of the world, it merges initially with sensuous appetite, it carries a much wider meaning. Fundamentally, self-consciousness seeks itself in this desire, and it seeks itself in the other." But in fact, as Gadamer points out, *Begierde* does not have the same broad range of meaning in German as *désir* in French (or as "desire" has in English). "Appetite" may be a bit too narrow, but the strongly sensuous connotation of *Begierde* does not permit us to make anything so psychically complex as recognition, in Hegel's sense, its object. Recognition represents a dialectical advance that transcends *Begierde,* rather than being dialectically contained within it. Hyppolite's usage follows that of Kojève in an otherwise brilliant passage on the need for recognition, which, however, cannot be described as "Desire directed toward another Desire." What Kojève intends by this phrase is a uniquely human possibility, as he points out, but in Hegel's view this human possibility transcends animal "life" precisely to the extent that mutual recognition is no longer conditioned by *Begierde.* Then the dialectic Kojève so splendidly expounds is for the first time in place. What makes this more than a merely verbal quibble is the fact that the two great French commentators, by playing on the possible ambiguity of "desire," import a kind of psychologistic reduction into the transition from raw desire to mutual recognition. See Alexandre Kojève, *Introduction to the Reading of Hegel,* ed. Allan Bloom, trans. James H. Nichols Jr. (New York: Basic Books, 1969), 4–7. Translated from *Introduction à la Lecture de Hegel,* 2d ed. (Paris: Gallimard, 1947). Cf. Hans-Georg Gadamer, "Hegels Dialektik des Selbstbewusstseins," *Materialien zu Hegels Phänomenologie des Geistes,* ed. Hans Friedrich Fulda and Dieter Henrich (Frankfurt am Main: Suhrkamp Taschenbuch, 1973), 241 n. 4.

7. *Grundlinien der Philosophie des Rechts,* ed. Johannes Hoffmeister, 4th ed. (Hamburg: Felix Meiner, 1955), 16 (Knox trans., 12).

8. *System der Sittlichkeit* (cited in Chapter 3, note 106), 32–34.

9. *Jenaer Systementwürfe I* (cited in Chapter 3, note 110), 307–326.

10. *Realphilosophie* (cited in Chapter 3, note 110), 202–217.

11. Ibid., 263.

12. *HtJ* (cited in Chapter 1, note 2), 377. See Chapter 2.

13. *Realphilosophie,* 202ff.

14. Hyppolite, who also wonders why love is not introduced at this point, suggests (*Genesis and Structure,* 164) that "love does not dwell sufficiently on the tragic nature of separation; it lacks 'the seriousness, the torment, the patience, and the labor of the negative.' For this reason the encounter between self-consciousnesses appears in the *Phenomenology* as a struggle between them for recognition." (The passage Hyppolite quotes is in the Preface, H 20; M 10; B 81.) The course Hegel follows is certainly the more tragic one, unless we consider the possibility that love may be the life-and-death struggle by another name. But if we accept the more unclouded view of love that both Hegel and Hyppolite seem to assume, it does not allow the free individuality of the partners to develop fully.

15. *Realphilosophie,* 209.

16. Ibid., 212.

17. *System der Sittlichkeit,* 33. "Herrschaft und Knechtschaft" is introduced on the next page.

18. *Enzyklopädie der philosophischen Wissenschaften* (1830), § 432 Zusatz. This paragraph of the *Enzyklopädie* appears in the skeletal treatment of the "Phänomenologie des Geistes" incorporated in the section on Subjective Spirit. Gadamer's suggestion appears in *Materialien zu Hegels Phänomenologie des Geistes,* 230.

19. *Die Vernunft in der Geschichte,* Introduction to the *Vorlesung über die Philosophie der Weltgeschichte,* delivered in the 1820s; 5th ed., ed. Johannes Hoffmeister (Hamburg: Felix Meiner, 1955), 92.

20. I do not mean to imply that Hegel gives anxiety the rich content Kierkegaard invests in it in *The Concept of Anxiety,* but then Kierkegaard devoted this entire ponderous work to the subject, inspiring equally ponderous treatments by Heidegger (in *Being and Time*) and Sartre (in *Being and Nothingness*) and other twentieth-century thinkers. Hegel introduces the concept in a few deft strokes in the present passage, but he does anticipate the existentialist treatments of it by recognizing this experience as a medium for the transcending sense of selfhood: in anxiety the slave discovers an inalienable freedom. Hegel does not distinguish terminologically between fear and anxiety, but uses *Angst* and *Furcht* interchangeably. However, the distinction the existentialists make by means of these terms is implicit in his treatment, since in this context he intends by both terms the quality later associated with *Angst,* that it has no particular, limited object. There is no external evidence that Kierkegaard had this passage in view in his treatment of the concept, but it seems to me likely that he did. *The Concept of Anxiety* is more laden than usual with anti-Hegelian polemics, but contrary to the standard, superficial view of Kierkegaard's relation to Hegel, the presence of anti-Hegelian polemics, far from being proof that Kierkegaard was free of Hegelian influence, is most pronounced in those works in which Hegelian motifs are most conspicuous. In this case the consonance is too strong to be laid entirely to coincidence, even acknowledging the undoubted originality Kierkegaard brings to the theme.

21. In a most unfortunate oversight, Miller has omitted this last clause, "for he has felt the fear of death, the absolute master," from his translation.

22. Kojève, *Reading of Hegel,* 20.

23. Marx, "Nationalökonomie und Philosophie," in *Die Frühschriften,* ed. Siegfried Landshut (Stuttgart: Kröner, 1953), 269. Easton and Guddat translate and edit this critique under the title, "Critique of Hegelian Dialectic and Philosophy in General," in a section entitled "Economic and Philosophic Manuscripts (1844)" in *Writings of the Young Marx on Philosophy and Society* (Garden City, N.Y.: Doubleday, 1967); the quoted passage appears on 321.

24. Kojève, *Reading of Hegel,* 44.

25. Ibid., 70.

26. Ibid., 44.

27. George Armstrong Kelly, "Notes on Hegel's 'Lordship and Bondage,'" in *Hegel: A Collection of Critical Essays,* ed. Alasdair MacIntyre (Garden City, N.Y.: Doubleday, Anchor Books, 1972), 195–96. This essay, first published in *Review of Metaphysics* 19, no. 4 (June 1966), has also been reprinted in German translation in Fulda and Henrich, *Materialien zu Hegels Phänomenologie des Geistes.*

28. See the Lecture Manuscript on Natural Law, in Rosenkranz, *Leben,* 136; *Dokumente,* 318, discussed above, 3:137–38. But Hegel discussed the Roman order in similar terms in all his courses of lectures during the 1820s.

29. Cf. Richard H. Popkin's *The History of Scepticism from Erasmus to Spinoza* (Berkeley and Los Angeles: University of California Press, 1979), a major theme of which is the association in the history of philosophy between the defense of religion, particularly of a fideistic sort, and a use of epistemological skepticism to undermine the sorts of rational or empirical grounds for attacking such beliefs. Of course Popkin also shows how skepticism was directed against religious claims as well.

30. Faust complains that two souls dwell in his breast, and "the one wants to separate itself from the other" (*Faust* 1, lines 1112–13), a theme that runs through his early monologues. Immediately thereafter, as if in answer to this complaint, Mephistopheles appears in the form of a poodle. From that point on Faust's two souls are represented in Mephistopheles, earthbound and cynical, and in himself, with his erotic "striving" for the boundless and sublime.

31. Mark C. Taylor, *Journeys to Selfhood: Hegel and Kierkegaard* (Berkeley and Los Angeles: University of California Press, 1980), handsomely compares these two thinkers in terms of the metaphor of journey, since for both of them the achievement of selfhood presupposes a psychic movement through many stations, with many ordeals along the way. Full selfhood is "spirit" for both, and the traveler must set out with the qualifications for becoming spirit already, but the experience of the journey is necessary for these qualifications to develop and fuse into a spiritual existence. Taylor brings out the parallels between Hegel and Kierkegaard in their conception of this "journey," but also shows how differently they conceived spirit, both as the goal of the journey and its pathway. Taylor devotes a good deal of analysis to the *Phenomenology* as the primary text in which Hegel's version of this journey is mapped, but he also rightly places great weight on the relation of identity and difference in the *Logic* as the point at which the Hegelian view of spirit stands or falls philosophically; see 141–62 for a fine exposition of this crucial point.

32. The quoted expressions are from Marx's famous statement about religion in *Zur Kritik der Hegelschen Rechtsphilosophie: Einleitung* (*Die Frühschriften,* 208; Easton and Guddat trans., 250).

33. See Chapter 1, "The Emergence of German Idealism," Chapter 2, "Folk Religion Versus Private Religion"; and Chapter 3, "Christianity Among the Religions."

34. According to the Anmerkung of the new Bonsiepen and Heede edition of *Phänomenologie des Geistes,* 486, Hegel has in mind his old bêtes noires, Reinhold and Bardili, as advocates of the universality of "Denken als Denken."

35. *Ethica* 5, prop. 33–36. Bonsiepen and Heede, *Phänomenologie des Geistes,* 487, suggest that Hegel may also have in mind a passage from Schiller, *Über Anmuth und Würde* (Leipzig, 1793), 109.

36. Mark Taylor, *Journeys to Selfhood,* 142.

37. It is the great strength of Hyppolite's commentary that he recognizes this centrality of unhappy consciousness in the problem of the entire work (e.g., *Genesis and Structure,*

190). In this orientation to the text Hyppolite was following the lead of Jean Wahl, *Le Malheur de la conscience dans la philosophie de Hegel* (Paris, 1929), an "existentialist" reading that inspired a good deal of interest in the earlier Hegel among French thinkers of the 1930s and 1940s.

38. Heading synoptic treatments of the *Phenomenology* are the three great French studies by Hyppolite, Kojève, and Wahl, to which we have already referred. But there are many other valuable commentaries and monographs to which I can refer only scantily or not at all, though I have profited greatly from some of them in composing this study. See the Bibliography of Selected Secondary Sources appended to this text for what I judge to be particularly useful twentieth-century studies of the early Hegel and/or the *Phenomenology*.

39. Friedrich Nicolin, "Zum Titelproblem der Phänomenologie des Geistes," *Hegel-Studien* (1967), 4:113–23. Also Pöggeler, *Hegels Idee einer Phänomenologie des Geistes,* 195–96, and the Editorischer Bericht to the Bonsiepen and Heede edition of the *Phänomenologie,* 469–71. Hoffmeister unfortunately published the suppressed original title after the Preface in his edition of the *Phänomenologie* (H 61).

40. Indeed, Hegel remarks that each of these four antecedent moments is itself "differentiated and divided into its own progression" of submoments, and uses Consciousness as an example of this further subdivision! (H 477; M 413; B 689.) Actually, in introducing the chapter on Spirit, Hegel already begins speaking of the previous moments as "consciousness, self-consciousness, and reason," in a central passage we will examine below (H 315; M 264; B 459).

41. *Briefe,* 1: 112f. (*Letters,* 110–11).

42. Editorischer Bericht in the Bonsiepen and Heede edition of the *Phänomenologie,* 459–63. I have made use of these valuable editorial notes for many of the details in this account of the composition of the work.

43. Quoted in Bonsiepen and Heede, *Phänomenologie,* 457, from *Catalogi scholarum in Academia Jenensi,* 172.

44. Rosenkranz, *Leben,* 202.

45. Unfortunately we know of this dispute only through a much later report by Hegel's son Karl, who gave an account of it in publishing an edition of Hegel's correspondence in 1887. Neither the original contract nor related correspondence with the publisher is extant, and there are no exact dates for the dispute. But since a new contract was drawn up when the portion of September 29, 1806, was published, the dispute must have occurred earlier that summer.

46. *Briefe,* 1:161f.

47. The story of Hegel's illegitimate son, rather hushed up in the literature, is recounted with relevant documentation in Walter Kaufmann's *Hegel,* 112–15. Frau Burkhardt had had two previous illegitimate children, and was a woman of the servant class. When Ludwig was four, Hegel placed him in a home for boys managed by the widowed sister of a friend, and in 1816, when Hegel and his wife moved to Heidelberg, they brought Ludwig to live with them.

48. Quoted in Bonsiepen and Heede, Editorischer Bericht, 457, from *Catalogi scholarum in Academia Jenensi,* 175. The German title, *Phänomenologie des Geistes,* was given in an announcement in the *Intelligenzblatt* of September 20, according to Hoffmeister (H XXXIII).

49. The announcement of the subsequent volume was included in a brief note in various literary journals announcing publication of the *Phenomenology*. This note, probably written by Hegel himself, is reprinted as a Beilage to the Bonsiepen and Heede

edition of the *Phänomenologie,* 446–47; cf. Editorischer Bericht, 471, and H XXXVII–XXXVIII.

50. Haering, "Die Entstehungsgeschichte der Phänomenologie des Geistes," *Verhand-lungen des 3. Hegelkongresses* (April 19–23, 1933), ed. B. Wigersma (Tübingen, 1934), 118–38. See also Hoffmeister's introduction to his edition of the *Phänomenologie,* which quotes from Haering's article at length and echoes his conclusions. But Hoffmeister argues that this change in the plan of the work did not result in any obvious break in the text, but that the new conception developed organically and necessarily out of the old (H XXVIII–XXXV). Hyppolite, *Genesis and Structure,* 52–53, maintains a similar position.

51. Pöggeler, *Hegels Idee,* 192–211.

52. There is this much to be said for this thesis of Haering's: that what was printed by the end of September 1806, did extend almost to the end of that chapter; and if that is what Hegel had completed in manuscript by February it might have seemed plausible to him that he could yet add the Logic to be included in the same volume and possibly to be completed by summer. Even with all allowance for authorial optimism, it is hard to credit that expectation on any other basis. Furthermore, the title assigned that chapter, "V. Certainty and Truth of Reason" does at least verbally seem to round off the dialectic of certainty and truth developed in the Introduction as the primary theme of the work.

53. *Briefe,* 1:136 (*Letters,* 119–20).

54. Haym remarks that the *Phenomenology* is "eine durch die Geschichte in Verwirrung und Unordnung gebrachte Psychology, und eine durch die Psychologie in Zerrüttung gebrachte Geschichte." *Hegel und seine Zeit,* 243.

55. *Briefe,* 1:161.

56. Haym, *Hegel und seine Zeit,* 238.

57. Pöggeler, *Hegels Idee,* 184–85.

58. Ibid., 193.

59. Ibid., 191–92. Pöggeler, a careful man, does not quite deny that one can understand the "idea" of the work without this explanation, but "one will . . . not wish to assert" that one can!

60. Ibid., 221–23.

61. Ibid., 164; cf. 164–66, 280–83.

62. Kenley Royce Dove, "Hegel's Phenomenological Method," *New Studies in Hegel's Philosophy,* ed. Warren E. Steinkraus (New York: Holt, Rinehart and Winston, 1971), 54–55. Where Dove cited passages from the text in parentheses I have placed small letters. The citations are as follows: (a). H 81; M 59–60; B 151. (b). H 85; M 63; B 156. (c). H 95; M 72; B 169–70. (d). H 103; M 79–80; B 180–81. (e). H 12; M 3; B 70.

63. Ibid., 55.

64. That is why, as Dove suggests (ibid., 54 n), Jacob Loewenberg's claim that the *Phenomenology* is a histrionic work, a dialogue in which "we" speak for consciousness, "histrionically impersonating" it and experiencing its "comic dénouement," is particularly apt with respect to the chapter on Consciousness. Loewenberg made this suggestion in his introduction to the Scribner edition of *Hegel Selections* (New York, 1929) and in two articles in *Mind* (October 1934; January 1935), then went on to write a lively commentary on the *Phenomenology* in dialogue form: *Hegel's Phenomenology: Dialogues on the Life of Mind* (LaSalle, Ill.: Open Court, 1965), which is especially successful in its rendering of the chapter on Consciousness. Not surprisingly, the dialogic form tends to grow more forced in treating subsequent chapters, except where the dialectic of Consciousness reappears.

65. Hoffmeister perpetuates an unfortunate misunderstanding in his edition of the work by introducing the chapter on Reason with a separate title page (H 173) bearing

the heading "[C. Vernunft]" that nowhere appears in the original edition. The original table of contents stands "(C) (AA) Vernunft," with double capitals for the subsequent chapters, "(BB) Der Geist," and so forth.

66. See also 328–29; M 276–77; B 479–80 for a passage showing how the elements of reason are fulfilled in the ethical world.

67. See, for instance, the conclusion of his last lecture in Jena, on September 18, 1806, quoted by Rosenkranz, *Leben,* 214–15. Schlomo Avineri quotes from these and similar remarks in discussing Hegel's optimistic expectations at this time, in *Hegel's Theory of the Modern State* (Cambridge: Cambridge University Press, 1972), 64; see also 71–74.

68. We have seen how in his early Jena years Hegel proposed to call this negative propaedeutic "Logic," not to be confused with the conception of a speculative logic that had already evolved when he wrote the *Phenomenology.* As Klaus Düsing points out, that early Logic did not proceed, like the *Phenomenology,* by a method of determinate negation with a positive result. Rather, Logic negated to clear the way for the Schellingian-Hegelian transcendental intuition, which simply postulated the positive identity. Düsing, "Idealistische Substanzmetaphysik," in *Hegel in Jena,* ed. Henrich and Düsing (1980), 33.

69. *Enzyklopädie der philosophischen Wissenschaften im Grundrisse* (Berlin, 1830), ed. Friedhelm Nicolin und Otto Pöggeler (Hamburg: Felix Meiner, 1959), §§ 413–439. The standard English version is the translation by William Wallace in three separate volumes, recently updated by A. V. Miller. The Introduction is included with the first volume, the so-called shorter *Logic.* §§ 413–39 are in the third volume, *Hegel's Philosophy of Mind,* Part 3 of *The Encyclopaedia of the Philosophical Sciences* (1830), trans. William Wallace, together with the Zusatze in Boumann's Text (1845), trans. A. V. Miller (Oxford: Oxford University Press, 1971). M. J. Petry has offered a new three-volume translation, with extended commentary, of the *Philosophy of Subjective Spirit* alone (Dordrecht: D. Reidel, 1978, 1979), from which he has selected paragraphs 413–39, with lecture notes by von Griesheim and von Kehler, German and English on facing pages, and has added his own excellent introduction and notes, in a separate volume that he has entitled *The Berlin Phenomenology* (Dordrecht: Reidel, 1981). Petry clearly considers this Berlin Phenomenology an improvement over the *Phenomenology* of 1807, which he calls the *Jena Phenomenology.*

70. For instance, in treating the Struggle for Recognition, Hegel now stresses the way this struggle has given rise to states, not yet as a matter of right but as a matter of sheer force (§433). In general, the treatment of Recognitive Self-Consciousness seems to describe a kind of prehistorical, pre-political stage in human development. The reason the demand for recognition involves a struggle is because we do not yet have the objective-ethical structure of family, civil society, and state, in which mutual recognition is secured without struggle (§ 431, Anmerkung, especially Petry ed., 78). Again, the reason that servitude is necessary in the development of the bondsman is so that he may earn the right to command by having first obeyed (§435, Petry ed., 88). The rich treatment of the terror of death and the transformation of nature through labor, as the modes of the bondsman's self-mastery, are largely suppressed.

71. Petry, *The Berlin Phenomenology,* xviii–xxv, outlines the "four distinct kinds of consciousness" worked out in these paragraphs, properly praising the analysis for its scientific coherence. But the "everyday consciousness," "to be regarded as differing in no essential respect from a planet's involvement in the solar system, or an element's involvement in a chemical compound etc.," is never allowed to speak for itself; and so its dialectical relation to spirit is not exhibited, either in its learning from experience or in its positive contribution to spirit's self-recognition. It is merely a "subject-matter."

72. *Wissenschaft der Logic,* ed. Lasson (Leipzig: Felix Meiner, 1934), 1:7; *Hegel's Science of Logic,* trans. A. V. Miller (London: Allen and Unwin; New York: Humanities Press, 1969), 28–29.

73. Petry exaggerates the extent to which Hegel distanced himself from the *Phenomenology,* in an otherwise interesting survey of immediate and later reactions to the work by others (*Berlin Phenomenology,* lxxviii–xci).

74. See Pöggeler's valuable hints about the difference between Hegel's earlier and later systematic conceptions in *Hegel's Idee,* 158ff.

75. See Chapter 3.

76. See Marx's comment in the Preface to *Capital,* which misconstrues the passage to good rhetorical effect: Avowing himself "the pupil of that mighty thinker," Marx says that with Hegel dialectic "is standing on its head. It must be turned *right side up again,* if you would discover the rational kernel within the mystical shell" (New York: Random House, Modern Library Edition), 25.

77. *Forord. Morskabslaesning for enkelte Staender efter Tid og Leilighed,* af Nicolaus Notabene (Copenhagen, 1844), 8:3; *Søren Kierkegaard Samlede Vaerker* (Gyldendal, 1963), 5: 246; *Prefaces,* trans. William McDonald (Tallahassee: Florida State University Press, 1989), 89.

78. See the comments on truth and falsehood a few paragraphs later in the preface (H 33–34; M 22–23; B 98–99).

79. The chief challenger is Pöggeler, *Hegels Idee einer Phänomenologie des Geistes,* 212–14, 261ff., who argues that this "point" is reached at "the beginning of real or objective spirit," that is, with the chapter on Spirit. This, he says, follows from Hegel's description of the concept of spirit in the chapter on Self-Consciousness, which is fulfilled in the chapter on Spirit, where the phenomenological presentation coincides with the final part of the (unwritten) System, the Science of Spirit. Pöggeler declares with some heat that those who place this "point" in the last chapter of the *Phenomenology* (e.g., Haering and Heidegger) seem unable to read the text! He mentions (262 n) Hans Friedrich Fulda and Jörg Splett among those who have followed his suggestion. Kenley Dove suggests that the "point" occurs with the transition to the chapter on Self-Consciousness ("Hegel's Phenomenological Method," in Steinkraus, *New Studies in Hegel's Philosophy,* 55–56). But if the "point" occurs in either of these chapters, it would seem to follow that the distinction between the "for itself" and the "in itself," or between the protagonist consciousness and "us," would thereafter dissolve. But, as Dove notes earlier (50), the "we" "nevertheless continues to appear," and, we may add, so does the for-itself, in distinction from the "we." Finally, however, it is difficult to believe that Hegel would devote almost the entire latter half of the *Phenomenology* to an analysis that corresponds directly to the Science of Spirit he intended to compose for the next volume! A comparison of the chapter on Spirit in the *Phenomenology* with the Philosophy of Spirit in the *Realphilosophie* already reveals quite a different structure and intention between a phenomenological and a systematic treatment. If anything, spirit's course through the chapter on Spirit is more tragic, more poignantly overtaken by doubt and despair, than anything that came before in the *Phenomenology.*

80. *Grundlinien der Philosophie des Rechts* (1821), § 299. See also §§ 185, 206.

81. Lauer, *A Reading of Hegel's Phenomenology of Spirit,* 200 n.

82. Bonsiepen and Heede, *Phänomenologie,* 512, cite specific passages, with illustrative quotations, from Holbach, *La christianisme dévoilé, ou examen des principes et des effets de la réligion chrétienne* (London, 1767).

83. This formulation is remarkably reminiscent of a remark that Hegel himself, under the influence of Fichte, had made five years earlier, in the opening paragraph of his treatise *The German Constitution:* "What can no longer be conceived *is* no more."

84. The view characterized and criticized in the early section on Force and Understanding (chapter 3, or the third section of the opening chapter on Consciousness, depending on how one counts the chapters) is clearly a version of Kant's theoretical philosophy, and the last two sections of the chapter on Reason, on Law-Giving Reason and Law-Testing Reason, plainly treat Kant's moral philosophy.

85. Bonsiepen and Heede, *Phänomenologie,* 517, point out that Hegel here virtually quotes from a saying by his old bête noir, Jacobi (*Werke,* 3:37f.). The Gospel passage is Mark 2:27. Hegel's account of conscience is closely modeled on that espoused by Jacobi and Fichte.

86. T. S. Eliot, *Murder in the Cathedral,* from Thomas's final speech in Part 1.

87. Bonsiepen and Heede, *Phänomenologie,* 518, especially emphasize the importance of Jacobi's treatment as the model for Hegel's analysis. As they point out, however, figures of this type were common in Romantic literature of the period. Novalis's *Heinrich von Ofterdingen,* published posthumously in 1802, would also furnish an example.

88. Hegel relates "faith" to the subterranean religion in a new and ingenious way in that introduction to the chapter on religion, through the "departed" spirit that is so central to the subterranean religion: The "faith" in the underworld and its powers of fate "becomes *faith* in *heaven,* because the departed self must unite with its universality," and so achieve a clarity about itself that it could not attain in the murk of the underworld (H 474; M 411; B 686).

89. In Hegel's later system, of course, as already in the *Realphilosophie,* religion is treated as a higher moment of absolute spirit than art. But Friedrich Theodor Vischer, the outstanding philosopher of art among the left-wing Hegelians, made a strong argument on Hegelian premises for reversing this order. See vol. 1, sec. 5, of the six large volumes of his major work, *Aesthetik oder Wissenschaft des Schönen* (Reutlingen, 1846–57; 2d ed., Munich, 1922–23), where he argues that religion is, in general, the "primitive . . . childhood form of the absolute spirit," where the subject is bound to a quasi-substantial object, whereas in art it is able to "find itself in the appearance of the world." See Hermann Glockner's study, *T. F. Vischers Ästhetik in ihrem Verhältnis zu Hegels Phänomenologie des Geistes* (Leipzig, 1920).

90. Walter Jaeschke, on the contrary, offers the surprising suggestion that the first form of Natural Religion, *Das Lichtwesen,* is an allusion to "the religion of Israel." As he mentions, most interpreters, at least among those who think the religion of light refers to some one tradition in particular, find an allusion to ancient Iranian religion in the passage (H 483–84; M 418–20; B 699–701 [Baillie identifies it as "parsee religion" in a footnote]). Jaeschke not only offers cogent arguments against that identification but points to some key phrases in Hegel's interpretation of Hebraic religion in the Berlin Lectures on the Philosophy of Religion (fifteen years and more later!) that seem to echo some of the language of this brief passage in the *Phenomenology.* My own view is that the language of that passage is too impressionistic to link it to any particular tradition with much assurance, but if it does refer to Hebraic religion its treatment of the subject is so thin as to be worse than no mention at all. See Jaeschke's *Reason in Religion,* trans. Stewart and Hodgson (cited in Chapter 1, note 75), 198–204.

In a translator's footnote to Jaeschke's book (204 n), Peter Hodgson calls attention to a frequent error in translating and discussing the section of the *Phenomenology* on "*Die offenbare Religion*" in English. It is commonly rendered "revealed religion," as if the German word were *geoffenbart,* which gives the term the connotation of something revealed in the past, in a "positive" sense. I confess that I translated it that way myself, until Hodgson called my attention to the error and convinced me that "revelatory religion" is both the more literal translation and the more suggestive of Hegel's presentation of a type of religion that is inherently revealing. Hodgson is also the editor and one of the translators of Hegel's *Lectures on the Philosophy of Religion* in three volumes (Berkeley and Los Angeles: University of California Press, 1984–87).

In those lectures of the 1820s, furthermore, an interesting change occurs in the position accorded the Jewish "Religion of Sublimity:" When Hegel gave the lectures in 1821 and 1824 its exposition precedes that of Greek Religion. But when he offered this course of lectures in 1827 he reversed that order, a significant change in his thinking given the plan of presenting forms of religion in an ascending scale. Hodgson's edition, following Jaeschke's German edition of the Lectures, carefully distinguishes among these versions presented in different years, the better to bring out just such changes.

91. Søren Kierkegaard, *Concluding Unscientific Postscript,* trans. Swenson and Lowrie (Princeton: Princeton University Press, 1944), 290–91. Immediately preceding the quoted passage, Kierkegaard declares that "to exist means first and foremost to be an individual, and that is why thought must look away from existence, for the individual does not let itself be thought, but only the universal. Faith's object is thus God's reality in existence, i.e., as an individual, i.e., that God has come to exist as an individual man."

Barth's critique of Hegel in his major historical work, *Die protestantische Theologie im 19 Jahrhundert,* is, to be sure, surprisingly respectful toward Hegel, and he himself could sound quite Hegelian in the latter volumes of the great *Dogmatik.* But on Christological issues, which for Barth were the heart of the matter, he always found Hegel beyond the pale. An interesting study is Michael Welker, "Barth und Hegel: Zur Erkenntnis eines methodischen Verfahrens bei Barth," *Evangelische Theologie* 43, no. 4 (July–August 1983): 307–28.

92. In suggesting that the death of the individual incarnation is a necessary condition for the incorporation of the spirit in the community, Hegel may have in mind the passage in the Gospel According to John (16:7–13) in which Jesus tells his disciples that unless he dies the Holy Spirit (who "will lead you into all truth") cannot come among them. But for Hegel this dual development is necessary for reasons that the fourth Evangelist surely did not have in mind!

In his later years, when Hegel was much given to quoting scripture in his lectures, the Fourth Gospel, with its many passages about the Holy Spirit that were easily adaptable to Hegelian interpretation, was his favorite source. The text from the present passage, "the spirit will lead you into all truth," was one of the four scriptural texts that Hegel most often quoted, according to Otto Kühler, who counted them. See Kühler, *Sinn, Bedeutung und Auslegung der heiligen Schrift in Hegels Philosophie* (Leipzig: S. Hirzel, 1939), 89.

93. Bonsiepen and Heede, *Phänomenologie,* 521, quote passages from Jakob Böhme's *Aurora, Oder Morgenröhte im Aufgang (Theosophie Revelata,* 1715, 1: 149, 178) that describe how the "glorious and beautiful king," now named Lucifer, was replaced after his fall "out of the light of God" by "another king out of the same godhead . . . named Jesus Christ."

94. Bonsiepen and Heede, *Phänomenologie,* 522, suggest that this reference to the wrath of God is another allusion to Böhme's *Theosophia Revelata* (1:98), which identifies it as the source of everlasting hellfire. Of course Saint Paul also refers to the wrath of God in Romans 1:18, the ὀργὴ θεοῦ that abandons rebellious human beings to their own wickedness. That use of the term seems closer to the intention of our text.

95. The previous reference to spiritual resurrection is presumably the passage quoted above, in which Hegel said that the death of the existing divine self "is thus its arising as spirit."

96. Again I refer the reader to my commentary on that conclusion to *Glauben und Wissen* (Chapter 3). But Hegel was by no means the first to refer to the death of God. The conclusion to *Glauben und Wissen* cites a reference to it by Pascal (see Chapter 3), and Bonsiepen and Heede, *Phänomenologie,* 520, quote a passage from the Weimar edition of Luther's *Werke* (50:589) in which Luther is drawing out the implications of the two natures in Christ: "As Christ is God and human being in one person / therefore what is said of him / as human being / that must one also say of God / namely / Christ has died / and Christ is God / therefore God has died." But Luther immediately adds, "not the separated God / but the God united with humanity / for of the separated God both statements are false"; that is, of God separated from humanity it is true neither that Christ is God nor that God has died. There is also a popular passion hymn well known to Hegel, dating from the seventeenth century, "O Traurigkeit, o Herzeleid," by Johann Rist, the second verse of which begins:

> O grosse Noht!
> Gott selbst ligt todt . . .

The terrible simplicity of these lines has caught the eye of more than one philosopher. That fact may have something to do with the revision of the second line, in the present *Evangelisches Kirchengesangbuch,* to read "Gotts Sohn liegt tot." Hegel continued to refer to the death of God (e.g., in *Philosophie der Religion,* vol. II-2 in the Lasson edition, 157–58), where he gives it a somewhat different interpretation than in the *Phenomenology.*

Bibliography of Selected Secondary Sources: Twentieth-Century Studies on the *Phenomenology of Spirit* and the Early Hegel

Althaus, Horst. *Hegel und die heroischen Jahre der Philosophie.* Munich: Carl Hanser, 1992.

Anderson, Deland S. *Hegel's Speculative Good Friday: The Death of God in Philosophical Perspective.* Atlanta, Ga.: Scholars Press, 1996.

Bloch, Ernst. *Subjekt-Objekt: Erlaüterungen zu Hegel.* Expanded ed. Frankfurt am Main: Suhrkamp, 1972.

Buchner, Hartmut. "Hegel im Übergang von Religion zu Philosophie." *Philosophische Jahrbuch* (1971): 82–97.

Dickey, Laurence. *Hegel: Religion, Economics, and the Politics of Spirit, 1770–1807.* Cambridge: Cambridge University Press, 1987.

Dilthey, Wilhelm. *Die Jugendgeschichte Hegels.* Berlin: Königlichen Akademie der Wissenschaften, 1905. Reissued in Dilthey's *Gesammelte Schriften,* Stuttgart: B. G. Teubner, 1962–65, vol. 4.

Dove, Kenley Royce. "Hegel's Phenomenological Method." In *New Studies in Hegel's Philosophy,* edited by Warren E. Steinkraus, 34–56. New York: Holt, Rinehart and Winston, 1971.

Düsing, Klaus. "Spekulation und Reflexion: Zur Zusammenarbeit Schellings und Hegels in Jena." *Hegel-Studien,* 5:95–128. Bonn: Bouvier, 1969.

Flay, Joseph C. *Hegel's Quest for Certainty.* Albany: State University of New York Press, 1984.

Fulda, Hans Friedrich, and Dieter Henrich, eds., *Materialien zu Hegels Phänomenologie des Geistes.* Frankfurt am Main: Suhrkamp Taschenbuch, 1973.

Gadamer, Hans Georg. *Hegel's Dialectic: Five Hermeneutical Studies.* Translated by Christopher Smith. New Haven: Yale University Press, 1976.

Garaudy, Roger. *Dieu est Mort: Etude sur Hegel.* Paris: Presses Universitaires de France, 1962.

Gray, J. Glenn. *Hegel's Hellenic Ideal.* New York: King's Crown Press, 1941. Reissued as *Hegel and Greek Thought,* New York: Harper and Row, 1968.

Haering, Theodor L. "Die Entstehungsgeschichte der *Phänomenologie des Geistes.*" *Verhandlungen des 3. Hegelkongresses,* 118–38. Tübingen: Auftrag des Internationalen Hegelbundes, 1934.

——. *Hegel: Sein Wollen und sein Werk.* Leipzig: B. G. Teubner, vol. 1, 1929; vol. 2, 1938.

Harris, H. S. *Hegel's Development: Night Thoughts (Jena, 1801–1806).* Oxford: Clarendon Press, 1983.

——. *Hegel's Development: Towards the Sunlight (1770–1801).* Oxford: Clarendon Press, 1972.

——. *Hegel's Ladder.* Vols. 1 and 2. Indianapolis, Ind.: Hackett, 1997.

Heidegger, Martin. *Hegels Phänomenologie des Geistes.* In *Heidegger Gesamtausgabe,* vol. 32. Frankfurt am Main: Vittorio Klostermann, 1980. Translated as *Hegel's Phenomenology of Spirit,* by Parvis Emad and Kenneth May. Bloomington: Indiana University Press, 1988.

Henrich, Dieter. *Hegel im Kontext.* Frankfurt am Main: Suhrkamp, 1967.

——. "Lautwein uber Hegel: Ein Dokument zu Hegels Biographie." *Hegel-Studien,* 3:39–77. Bonn: Bouvier, 1965.

Henrich, Dieter, and Klaus Düsing, eds. *Hegel in Jena: Die Entwicklung des Systems und die Zusammenarbeit mit Schelling. Hegel-Studien,* supp. 20. Bonn: Bouvier, 1980.

Hoffmeister, Johannes. *Hölderlin und Hegel.* Tübingen: J. C. B. Mohr, 1931.

Hyppolite, Jean. *Genèse et Structure de la Phénoménologie de l'Esprit de Hegel.* Paris: Aubier, Editions Montaigne, 1946. Translated as *Genesis and Structure of Hegel's Phenomenology of Spirit,* by Samuel Cherniak and John Heckman. Evanston, Ill.: Northwestern University Press, 1974.

Jaeschke, Walter. *Die Vernunft in der Religion: Studien zur Grundlegung der Religionsphilosophie Hegels.* Stuttgart: Friedrich Frommann, 1986. Translated as *Reason in Religion: The Foundations of Hegel's Philosophy of Religion,* by J. Michael Stewart and Peter C. Hodgson. Berkeley and Los Angeles: University of California Press, 1990.

Jamros, Daniel P., S.J. *The Human Shape of God: Religion in Hegel's Phenomenology of Spirit.* New York: Paragon House, 1994.

Kainz, Howard. *Hegel's Phenomenology, Part I: Analysis and Commentary.* Tuscaloosa: University of Alabama Press, 1976.

——. *Hegel's Phenomenology, Part II: The Evolution of Ethical and Religious Consciousness to the Dialectical Standpoint.* Athens: Ohio University Press, 1983.

Kaufmann, Walter. *Hegel: Reinterpretation, Texts, and Commentary.* Garden City, N.Y.: Doubleday, 1965.

Kelly, George Armstrong. *Hegel's Retreat from Eleusis: Studies in Political Thought.* Princeton: Princeton University Press, 1978.

———. *Idealism, Politics, and History: Sources of Hegelian Thought.* Cambridge: Cambridge University Press, 1969.

Kimmerle, Heinz. *Das Problem der Abgeschlossenheit des Denkens: Hegels "System der Philosophie" in den Jahren 1800–1804. Hegel-Studien,* supp. 8. Bonn: Bouvier, 1970.

———. "Zur Chronologie von Hegels Jenaer Schriften." *Hegel-Studien,* 4: 125–76. Bonn: Bouvier, 1967.

Kojève, Alexandre. *Introduction à la lecture de Hegel.* 2d ed. Paris: Gallimard, 1947. Translated as *Introduction to the Reading of Hegel,* by James H. Nichols, edited by Allan Bloom. New York: Basic Books, 1969.

Lauer, Quentin, S.J. *A Reading of Hegel's Phenomenology of Spirit.* New York: Fordham University Press, 1976, 1982.

Loewenberg, Jacob. *Hegel's Phenomenology: Dialogues on the Life of the Mind.* La Salle, Ill.: Open Court, 1965.

Lukács, Georg. *Der junge Hegel: Über die Beziehungen von Dialektik und Ökonomie.* Zurich: Europa, 1948; Berlin: Aufbau, 1954.

Pinkard, Terry. *Hegel's Phenomenology: The Sociality of Reason.* Cambridge: Cambridge University Press, 1994.

Pöggeler, Otto. "Hegel, der Verfasser des ältesten Systemprogramms des deutschen Idealismus." *Hegel-Studien,* supp. 4, pp. 17–32. Bonn: Bouvier, 1969.

———. *Hegels Idee einer Phänomenologie des Geistes.* Munich: Alber, 1973.

Rohrmoser, Günter. *Subjektivität und Verdinglichung: Theologie und Gesellschaft im Denken des jungen Hegel.* Gütersloh: Gütersloher Verlagshaus Gerd Mohn, 1961.

Rosen, Stanley. *G. W. F. Hegel: An Introduction to the Science of Wisdom.* New Haven: Yale University Press, 1974.

Taylor, Mark C. *Journeys to Selfhood: Hegel and Kierkegaard.* Berkeley and Los Angeles: University of California Press, 1980.

Trede, Heinrich. "Hegels frühe Logik (1801–1803/04): Versuch einer systematischen Rekonstruktion." *Hegel-Studien* 7: 123–68. Bonn: Bouvier, 1972.

Verene, Donald Phillip. *Hegel's Recollection: A Study of Images in the Phenomenology of Spirit.* Albany: State University of New York Press, 1985.

Wacker, Herbert. *Das Verhältnis des jungen Hegel zu Kant.* Berlin: Junker und Dünnhaupt, 1932.

Wahl, Jean. *Le Malheur de la conscience dans la philosophie de Hegel.* Paris: Rieder, 1929.

Westphal, Merold. *History and Truth in Hegel's Phenomenology.* Atlantic Highlands, N.J.: Humanities Press, 1979.

Williams, Robert R. *Recognition: Fichte and Hegel on the Other.* Albany: State University of New York Press, 1992.

Index